Mathematical Problems in Aerospace

Mathematical Problems in Aerospace

Editors

Yu Jiang
Haijun Peng
Hongwei Yang

Basel • Beijing • Wuhan • Barcelona • Belgrade • Novi Sad • Cluj • Manchester

Editors

Yu Jiang
Xi'an Satellite Control Center
Xi'an, China

Haijun Peng
Dalian University of Technology
Dalian, China

Hongwei Yang
Nanjing University of Aeronautics and Astronautics
Nanjing, China

Editorial Office
MDPI
St. Alban-Anlage 66
4052 Basel, Switzerland

This is a reprint of articles from the Special Issue published online in the open access journal *Mathematics* (ISSN 2227-7390) (available at: https://www.mdpi.com/journal/mathematics/special_issues/Mathematical_Problems_Aerospace).

For citation purposes, cite each article independently as indicated on the article page online and as indicated below:

Lastname, A.A.; Lastname, B.B. Article Title. *Journal Name* **Year**, *Volume Number*, Page Range.

ISBN 978-3-0365-9947-2 (Hbk)
ISBN 978-3-0365-9948-9 (PDF)
doi.org/10.3390/books978-3-0365-9948-9

Contents

 *mathematics* 

Review

Asteroids and Their Mathematical Methods

Yu Jiang [1,*], Yanshuo Ni [2], Hexi Baoyin [3], Junfeng Li [3] and Yongjie Liu [1]

[1] State Key Laboratory of Astronautic Dynamics, Xi'an Satellite Control Center, Xi'an 710043, China
[2] Beijing Institute of Spacecraft System Engineering, Beijing 100094, China
[3] School of Aerospace Engineering, Tsinghua University, Beijing 100084, China
* Correspondence: jiangyu_xian_china@163.com

Abstract: In this paper, the basic classification of asteroids and the history and current situation of asteroid exploration are introduced. Furthermore, some recent research progress on the orbital dynamics of asteroids, including models of the gravitational potential field, the dynamics near asteroids, hopping motion on the surface, and bifurcations under varying external parameters, is reviewed. In the meanwhile, the future research development such as the configuration and evolution of binary or triple asteroid systems and near-Earth asteroid defense is briefly discussed.

Keywords: mathematical physics; planetary science; applied mathematics; asteroids

MSC: 85-02

Citation: Jiang, Y.; Ni, Y.; Baoyin, H.; Li, J.; Liu, Y. Asteroids and Their Mathematical Methods. *Mathematics* **2022**, *10*, 2897. https://doi.org/10.3390/math10162897

Academic Editor: Rami Ahmad El-Nabulsi

Received: 12 July 2022
Accepted: 7 August 2022
Published: 12 August 2022

1. Introduction

Exploring, understanding, and trying to conquer one's own environment is the most fundamental driver of human progress. During this process, human beings have discovered new knowledge, created new technologies, and discovered the truth through practice. Cognition guides practice, and this new knowledge and these new technologies actively develop from perceptual knowledge to rational knowledge, thus actively guiding practice, which in turn guides human beings to transform the world and promotes the further expansion of human territory. From Alexander's expedition to the East to Zhang Qian's mission to the Western Regions, Zheng He's seven voyages to the West, and the space race in the middle of the 20th century, civilizations that have gained advantages in exploration have established scientific and technological advantages due to their exploration.

Although the exploration of travelers has been limited to land and sea due to technical reasons until modern times, the sages have never given up looking up at the stars. Moreover, the observation and understanding of the vast universe has constantly changed the human world view. Johannes Kepler derived Kepler's laws using the detailed observational data of Tycho Brahe, making Nicholas Copernicus's heliocentric theory recognized; Isaac Newton proposed the law of universal gravitation to explain the mathematical laws of celestial motion. In the three centuries after Newton and Kepler, the world's greatest mathematicians studied celestial mechanics very well. In the decades before the first launch event of the Soviet Union in 1957, celestial mechanics did not necessary appear in college courses. However, before human spaceflight missions, celestial mechanics for ancient mathematicians, mechanics, and astronomers was limited to predicting the orbits of naturally existing celestial bodies in the solar system. Only in recent decades has the problem of orbital design for visiting target planets under complex constraints appeared [1].

With the advancement in science and technology, the scope of the world recognized by mankind in the past 200 years has also reached an unprecedented level. William Herschel discovered Uranus with the help of a telescope in 1781. This is the first time that humans discovered a planet with a telescope. Before this, the six major planets have been known to humans since ancient times. Twenty years later, Giuseppe Piazzi discovered the first asteroid, (1) Ceres, on 1 January 1801. It was initially thought to be a new planet and is now within the orbit of Neptune under the current definition. Since Piazzi interrupted the observation on 11 February 1801 due to illness, people only lost the asteroid with the observation data of Ceres' orbit of about 3° in 41 days. Gauss used an orbit determination method he developed to determine Ceres' orbit nearly a year after its disappearance using short-term observational data. Thanks to the work of Gauss, Franz Xavier von Zach rediscovered Ceres. Gauss's calculation of Ceres clearly demonstrated that no assumptions were required and that the orbits of celestial bodies could be determined fairly accurately with just a few days of good observational data, followed by the discovery and orbit determination of (2) Pallas, (3) Juno, and (4) Vesta further verifies the efficiency of this method. This is also the first scientific progress made by humans based on small celestial bodies.

From the beginning of the 19th century to the middle of the 20th century, human beings gradually discovered more small objects in the solar system, but the related research was not given much attention because of their small masses. In the early 1950s, the development of intercontinental rockets allowed humans to use artificial spacecraft for spaceflight, and humans gradually began to plan space missions. Since the Soviet Union successfully launched Luna 1 in 1959, various major powers have made breakthroughs in near-Earth exploration and research on the Moon in the past 60 years of space exploration history. The main belt asteroids, the Jupiter system, the Saturn system, Pluto, the Kuiper Belt, and other solar system celestial bodies have been explored using various methods [2–11]. Especially since the 1970s, human beings have successively carried out many missions for small celestial bodies and have conducted in-depth and comprehensive research on small celestial bodies, both theoretically and practically. By studying the geological properties of celestial bodies and their space environment and exploring the formation and evolution history of the solar system, the chemical composition and internal structure of small celestial bodies have been preliminarily determined. The shapes of many small celestial bodies have been obtained through optical observations, radar observations, and photographs taken by fly-by missions. Among them, due to the irregular shape of small celestial bodies, the complexity of its nearby dynamic behavior, and its important research significance, the exploration of small celestial bodies has become an important part of deep space exploration, and countries have carried out space missions related to small celestial bodies. It has attracted a large number of scholars to study the dynamics of small celestial bodies [7,12–15]. It is widely accepted that small celestial bodies relatively completely retain the early information of the formation of the solar system [16–18]. Some small celestial bodies may also contain abundant rare metals and other resources needed by human beings, which have potential space mining value. The long-term effects of various perturbation forces in space and possible collisions between near-Earth celestial bodies may cause the small celestial bodies to change their original orbits and fall to the Earth, bringing devastating disasters to life. Some events are well-known—for example, the Tunguska explosion in 1909 and the meteorite impact in Chelyabinsk, Russia on 15 February 2013. Therefore, the observation and defense of near-Earth small objects is also a highly valued research subject [19,20]. In the past 50 years, the research on small celestial bodies in the solar system has already broken through the content of past astronomy, involving the development of nonlinear dynamics, including aerospace engineering, geology, biology, weapons research, and other fields.

For deep space explorations, it is inseparable from the content of close-range fly-by, imaging, landing, sampling, and returning. Compared with pure radar observations, these on-site explorations can provide more intuitive and richer details and evidence for scientific research on small celestial bodies and the defense of near-Earth small objects. The resource exploitation of small celestial bodies is even more inseparable from actual field detection. Some important missions that achieved sample returns from celestial bodies other than the Moon are Stardust, Hayabusa, Hayabusa 2, and OSIRIS-REx. One of the landmarks made by China to become one of the top aerospace powers around 2030 is to realize the sampling return of small celestial bodies.

In-depth research on the shape of small celestial bodies, nearby periodic orbital motions, and surface transition dynamics and quantitative analysis methods for quasi-periodic orbits is the scientific basis for completing the above tasks. In the process of close-range explorations, the orbits of probes near small celestial bodies are significantly different from those near large planets, and the internal mechanisms and laws have not been completely sorted out so far. What is certain is that the regularity of the geometric shape of the small celestial body largely determines the difference between the gravitational field near the small celestial body and the familiar spherical gravitational field near the large planet, which brings about a series of different dynamics and control problems. Therefore, exploring the indicators for scientifically describing the geometric shape of small celestial bodies has a great reference value for the preliminary analysis of the gravitational fields. In addition, considering that the mass of small celestial bodies is generally small, many space perturbations, including the Sun's gravity, may also have a relatively large influence on the motion of the probe. The richness of the orbital dynamics near small celestial bodies also provides a good soil for discovering and studying nonlinear dynamics in real systems and making them useful. The difficulties of the orbital dynamics and the limitations of the measurement methods make the data parameters obtained before approaching the target small celestial body still have a certain error with the real situation. These factors and the complex mechanical environment near the small celestial body jointly affect the exploration. The orbital design and control of orbiters near small bodies pose great challenges. Even for periodic orbits, considering various gravitational and perturbative effects, they may be perturbed into quasi-periodic orbits or produce chaotic motions. A thorough and accurate analysis of these orbits will aid in orbital design for exploration missions. Due to the strong irregular shape, complex topography, and fast rotation rate of small celestial bodies, the surface escape velocity of small celestial bodies is usually small. To truly realize the sampling return of small celestial bodies, it is necessary to select the soft-landing region and optimize the trajectory, which requires us to deeply study the dynamic laws of surface motions on small celestial bodies.

Although humans have now begun to explore the solar system, the small celestial bodies that account for the vast majority of solar system celestial bodies have only been visited by very few spacecraft. The continued exploration of the vast universe by mankind in the future is inseparable from the in-depth detection and research of small celestial bodies. By studying the shape regularity and nearby periodic orbits of small celestial bodies, the dynamic phenomena in the theory can be verified in the real system in science, enriching the scientific connotation of modern celestial mechanics and nonlinear dynamics [21,22].

2. Basic Classification and Exploration of Small Celestial Bodies

Since the 1980s, many deep space exploration missions related to small celestial bodies have been carried out. This section will introduce the general situation of small celestial bodies, deep space exploration missions, etc.

2.1. Overview of Small Celestial Bodies

Small celestial bodies usually refer to celestial bodies that exclude large planets and their satellites in the solar system, mainly including dwarf planets, asteroids, and comets [23,24]. Small celestial bodies orbit the Sun but are much smaller in size and mass than large planets. According to data from the IAU Minor Planet Center, as of 10 July 2021, a total of 1,091,258 small celestial bodies have been discovered in the solar system, of which there are 5 dwarf planets and 4603 comets, and the rest are asteroids [25]. Among these asteroids, 567,132 have been permanently numbered (orbits have been calculated) (more than 90% of them have been newly discovered in the past 20 years; see Figure 1) [26]. A total of 22,568 asteroids have been named [27].

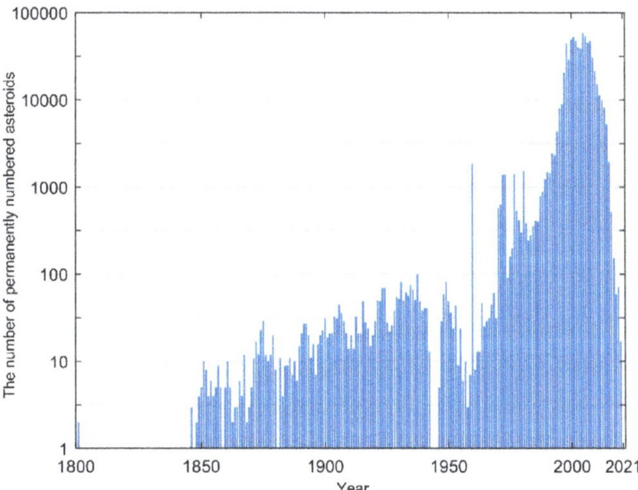

Figure 1. Statistics on the year of discovery of permanently numbered asteroids.

The semi-major axis of near-Earth asteroids is similar to that of Earth. There are currently 26,351 near-Earth asteroids, of which 940 are larger than 1 km in size. Scientists believe that the mass extinction 65 million years ago was caused by an asteroid about 10 km in size hitting the Earth [20]. The defense of near-Earth asteroids is also an important part of the field of deep space exploration. The orbital inclinations of near-Earth asteroids range from 0.02° to 154°, and the orbital eccentricity ranges from 0.062 to 0.999 [28,29]. According to its orbital semi-major axis a, perihelion distance q, and the relationship between the aphelion distance Q and the Earth, it can be divided into the Atira type, Aten type, Apollo type, and Amor type, as shown in Table 1.

Table 1. Classification of Near-Earth Asteroids.

Type	Semi-Major Axis a	Perihelion Distance q	Aphelion Distance Q
Atira	a < 1 AU	-	Q < 0.983 AU
Aten	a < 1 AU	-	Q > 0.983 AU
Apollo	a > 1 AU	q < 1.017 AU	-
Amor	a > 1 AU	1.017 AU < q < 1.3 AU	-

Atira-type and Amor-type asteroids are less dangerous to Earth because their orbits and Earth's orbits are inward and outward, respectively. Arten-type and Apollo-type asteroids are small celestial bodies with a greater potential danger to the Earth due to their inward and outward swept orbits and Earth's orbits, respectively.

Near-Mars asteroids are divided into Hungarian-type asteroids and Mars-orbiting asteroids. The semi-major axes of the Hungarian-type asteroids are between 1.78 and 2.00 AU, and they are located inside the Kirkwood gap, which is in a 1:4 resonance with Jupiter. Their orbital periods are about 2.5 years, roughly 3:2 resonant with Mars and 2:9 resonant with Jupiter. Their orbital eccentricities are less than 0.18, and their orbital inclinations are between 16° and 34°. The perihelion distance of the Mars orbit crossing the asteroid orbit is between the distance between the perihelion and the aphelion of Mars, that is, 1.381 AU < q < 1.666 AU. Asteroids with a perihelion distance q < 1.3 AU are classified as near-Earth asteroids. According to this classification standard, a total of 18,043 Mars-orbiting asteroids have been discovered so far.

Asteroids in the middle solar system are divided into main belt asteroids, Jupiter Trojan asteroids, and Hilda asteroids. The main-belt asteroids are located between the orbits of Mars and Jupiter, and the orbital semi-major axis a is between 2.1 and 3.3 AU. The orbital eccentricities of most main belt asteroids are less than 0.4, and the orbital inclination angles are less than 30°. The main belt is the area with the densest distribution of asteroids, and a total of 1,022,771 asteroids have been observed in the main belt. It is generally believed that the main-belt asteroids are the remnants of the original astrolabe that failed to form large planets due to the perturbation of Jupiter's huge gravitational force during the evolution of the solar system. According to the current definition, the three largest asteroids in the main belt are small celestial bodies: (4) Vesta, (2) Pallas, and (10) Hygiea. The Jupiter Trojan asteroids are located near the L4 and L5 points of the circular restricted three-body system. The L4 and L5 points are regarded as the stable equilibrium points of this system. The motion periods are basically the same as that of Jupiter, with a phase difference of about 60°. So far, 10,470 Jupiter Trojan-type asteroids have been observed. In addition to the Sun–Jupiter system, there are also four and six Trojan asteroids in the Sun–Mars and Sun–Neptune systems, respectively. So far, only one Trojan asteroid, 2010 TK7, has been discovered in the Sun–Earth system; this was done in 2010. It is located near the L4 point of the Sun–Earth system. A total of 4978 Hilda-type asteroids have been observed. Their semi-major axes are between 3.7 and 4.2 AU. Their orbital eccentricities are less than 0.3, and their orbital inclinations satisfy $i < 20°$. The Hilda-type asteroids are in a 2:3 resonance with the orbit of Jupiter and approach the L3, L5, and L4 points of the Sun–Jupiter system, in turn, in three orbital periods.

Asteroids in the outer solar system include Centaur and extra-Neptunian asteroids. Centaurs are small celestial bodies whose perihelions are outside the orbit of Jupiter and whose semi-major axes are smaller than Neptune's semi-major axis by 30 AU. Because the small celestial bodies here have the characteristics of asteroids and comets, they are mostly named after the centaur gods in Greek mythology. For example, (2060) Chiron and (60588) Echeclus have the comet numbers 95P/Chiron and 174P/Echeclus due to coma activity. Extra-Neptunian asteroids refer to the celestial bodies in the solar system whose semi-major axes are greater than 30 AU. Excluding the currently discovered (134340) Pluto, (136108) Haumea, (136472) Makemake, and (136199) Eris and four other dwarf planets, a total of 4,053 extra-Neptunian asteroids have been discovered so far. Most of these celestial bodies contain methane, ammonia, and water, which are volatile. The region outside Neptune between 30 and 50 AU from the Sun is called the Kuiper Belt. Similar to the main-belt asteroids, Kuiper Belt objects are also the original remnants that failed to form large planets. The interesting relations between Kuiper Belt objects and comets can be found in reference [30]. In addition, research on the orbital dynamics of Kuiper Belt objects plays an important role in the process of the human search for the ninth largest planet in the solar system. Based on the orbital eccentricity vector and angular momentum vector of six Kuiper Belt objects, Batygin [31] and Brown [32] inferred that there may be an unknown planet with a semi-major axis $a \approx 700$ AU and an eccentricity $e \approx 0.6$. This study has prompted scholars from various countries to conduct in-depth research and sky survey observations to find this potential ninth planet in the solar system [33].

According to the spectral characteristics, there are 17 types of asteroids: A, B, C, D, E, F, G, K, L, M, O, P, Q, R, S, T, V. Asteroids are mainly divided into three groups: C, S, and X [34–36], and a few other types are not included in these three groups. Group C asteroids contain a large amount of carbon, accounting for about 75% of the total number of asteroids in the solar system; group S asteroids contain a large number of silicates, accounting for about 17% of the total number; group M asteroids contain a large amount of iron and nickel and other metallic elements, which are considered to be the debris of the asteroid's impacted core and the source of iron meteorites [37]. The specific classification of asteroids according to their spectra can be found in Table 2. It should be noted that the diversity of the spectra of asteroids can be affected by space weathering [38,39].

Table 2. Spectral Classification of Asteroids.

Group	Type	Criterion	Representative
C	B	The general properties are the same as the C type, but the ultraviolet absorption below 0.5 μm is smaller, and the slight blueness is more obvious than the redness in the spectrum. The albedo also tends to be greater than the darker C-type.	(2) Pallas
	C	There is moderate absorption at UV wavelengths of 0.4–0.5 μm, and there are no obvious features but slight reddening at longer wavelengths. There is a mineral feature indicative of hydration known as water absorption around the wavelength of 3 μm.	(10) Hygiea
	F	Similar to B-type asteroids but lacks water absorption features indicative of hydrated minerals around wavelengths around 3 μm and differs from the B-type in the low-wavelength UV portion below 0.4 μm.	(704) Interamnia
	G	Similar to C-type asteroids but has strong absorption characteristics for ultraviolet wavelengths below 0.5 μm. There may also be absorption properties around 0.7 μm, implying the presence of layered silicate minerals such as clay and mica.	(1) Ceres
S	A	Significant olivine features at a 1 μm wavelength and strong reddening at wavelengths below 0.7 μm.	(446) Aeternitas
	K	There is moderate reddening at wavelengths below 0.75 μm and slight bluing at wavelengths above 0.75 μm.	(221) Eos
	L	There is strong reddening at wavelengths below 0.75 μm, and the spectrum is flat at wavelengths above 0.75 μm. Compared with the K type, the redness is more obvious in the visible band, and the spectrum in the infrared band is more gentle.	(83) Beatrix
	Q	There are prominent features of olivine and pyroxene in the 1 μm band, and their spectral changes indicate the possible presence of metallic substances. There is an absorption spectrum at 0.7 μm.	(1862) Apollo
	R	There are distinct olivine and pyroxene features at 1 μm and 2 μm. The spectrum is strongly reddened at wavelengths below 0.7 μm.	(349) Dembowska
	S	There is moderate spectral variation at wavelengths shorter than 0.7 μm and moderate spectral absorption at 1 μm and 2 μm wavelengths. There is also a shallow but broad spectral absorption around 0.63 μm.	(3) Juno
X	E	The albedo is greater than 0.3, the spectrum is flat and reddish, and there are no obvious features.	(44) Nysa
	M	The albedo is between 0.1 and 0.2, there are subtle spectral absorption lines in the bands above 0.75 μm and below 0.55 μm, and the overall spectrum is flat and slightly reddened, lacking obvious features.	(16) Psyche
	P	The albedo is less than 0.1, and the color is redder than that of the S-type asteroid, but it is not reflected in the spectral properties.	Sylvia
Not grouped	D	Very low albedo and featureless, light red electromagnetic spectrum.	(624) Hektor
	O	Strong spectral absorption in the band above 0.75 μm	(3628) Božněmcová
	T	The spectrum is moderately reddened, darker, and has moderate spectral absorption in the band below 0.85 μm.	(114) Kassandra
	V	There is strong spectral absorption in the bands above 0.75 μm and 1 μm and strong reddening in the bands below 0.7 μm.	(4) Vesta

Comets can be divided into the nucleus, coma, and tail. Comet nuclei are composed of loose water ice, rubble piles, solid carbon dioxide, methane, ammonia, etc. [40] Comets usually have long-period, highly eccentric orbits. Therefore, as the comet approaches the Sun, the water ice and volatile matter in the comet's nucleus will be heated and turned into gas, forming an observable atmosphere called a coma. The coma is affected by the solar wind and solar light pressure to produce a long tail facing away from the Sun, called a comet tail. Comets are perturbed by the gravitational force of Jupiter and other large planets during their operation, which may cause dramatic changes in their orbits or their own shapes or even disintegration: Comet Shoemaker-Levy 9 (Shoemaker-Levy 9) was destroyed by Jupiter in 1994. The gravity ripped apart into 21 pieces and crashed into Jupiter. Hsieh and Jewitt [41] inferred the existence of a population of comets originating in the main asteroid belt based on the optical data. In the past, people often used the presence of volatile gas as a criterion to distinguish asteroids and comets, but with the discovery of active centaurs, especially after the discovery that Ceres also has water vapor [42], the difference between asteroids and comets becomes less clear.

2.2. Exploration of Small Celestial Bodies

With the development of science and technology, the exploration of small celestial bodies has gradually developed from optical observation with telescopes in the 19th century to radar observation and visits through spacecraft. These three methods provide different kinds of information for the research and exploration of small celestial bodies.

Since Piazzi discovered Ceres, the vast majority of small objects have been discovered through optical observations. The introduction of astrophotography and scintillation comparators allowed optical observations to move away from relying on the naked eye to identify asteroids. Using advanced orbiting telescopes and observatories, it has been possible to obtain basic images of large-scale small celestial bodies through optical observation. The double asteroid system (45) Eugenia was discovered in this way [42]. Orbit information can also be used to calculate the size of small celestial bodies by observing the apparent magnitude. Moreover, the rotation period and spatial orientation of the rotation axis can be calculated from the light change information of small celestial bodies. The temperature and spectral information of asteroids can be determined through optical observations in visible light and infrared bands [39]. Different from the optical observation, radar observation is an active observation method, and radar observation can provide the orbit data of small celestial bodies with a higher relative accuracy and information such as small celestial body shape, rotation speed, and albedo. A higher-precision model of small celestial bodies (on the order of 10 m) can also be reconstructed through radar observations. Since the first high-precision shape model of (4769) Castalia was reconstructed in 1994, more and more small celestial body models have been obtained by this method. However, due to the attenuation of radar echoes, ideal radar observations require small celestial bodies to be close enough to Earth, so radar observations are mostly concentrated in near-Earth asteroids.

With the deepening of deep space exploration activities, the United States, the Soviet Union, and Europe have carried out space exploration activities for small celestial bodies since the 1980s. Japan and China have joined the deep space exploration team one after another. Table 3 lists the small object missions that have occurred and may be carried out in the future. Through these exploration missions, human beings have gained further understanding of the geological characteristics of small celestial bodies, the space environment, and the formation and evolution of the solar system.

The early exploration activities of small celestial bodies were mainly affected by the return of Halley's Comet (1P/Halley) in 1986, and the fly-by of the comet was the mainstay. The first exploration of small celestial bodies by humans was the International Cometary Explorer (ICE), jointly conducted by ESA and NASA in 1982. The predecessor of ICE was the first International Sun–Earth Explorer-3 (ISEE-3) located at the Sun–Earth L1 point. It was renamed as the International Comet Explorer to conduct comet exploration activities. After a low-altitude fly-by of the Moon on 22 December 1983 for gravity assistance, the International Comet Explorer passed through the tail of Comet 21P/Giacobini-Zinner at a distance of 7800 km from the nucleus in 1985, while the geomagnetic field downstream of the long tail blown by the solar wind was also detected during the Earth–Moon gravitational assistance and passed through the tail of Halley's Comet in 1986 [43–45]. From 1984 to 1985, when Halley's Comet returned, the Soviet Union launched Vega-1 and Vega-2 successively. In the process of exploring Venus, the two spacecraft were placed at distances of 10,000 km and 3000 km to conduct fly-bys of Halley's Comet. Japan also launched two probes, Sakigake and Suisei, to conduct fly-bys of Halley's Comet at distances of 7,000,000 km and 150,000 km. In 1985, ESA launched the Giotto probe to observe Halley's Comet. Giotto flew by Halley's Comet at a distance of 596 km in March 1986 and was the first probe to observe the comet at close range [46–48]. Giotto flew by Comet 26P/Grigg-Skjellerup at a distance of 200 km in 1992 after gravitational assistance in 1990. Vega 1, Vega 2, Pioneer, Comet, and Giotto are known as the "Halley Fleet" for their continuous exploration of Halley's Comet.

In 1989, NASA launched the Galileo probe on its way to Jupiter. It flew by (951) Gaspra and (243) Ida in 1991 and 1993, respectively, and discovered the moons (Dactyl) of Ida. This is the first time that humans have explored asteroids and double asteroid systems [49–52].

Table 3. Asteroid exploration missions.

Spacecraft	Agency	Start Date	Asteroid	Mission Type
International Comet Explorer	NASA ESA	1982	21P/Giacobini-Zinner	Fly-by
Vega 1/2	IKI	1984	1P/Halley	Fly-by
Pioneer/Comet	JAXA	1985	1P/Halley	Fly-by
Giotto	ESA	1985	1P/Halley 26P/Grigg–Skjellerup	Fly-by
Galileo	NASA	1989	(951) Gaspra (243) Ida	Fly-by
Near-Shoemaker	NASA	1996	(253) Mathilde (433) Eros	Fly-by/Orbiting/Landing
Cassini-Huygens	NASA	1997	(2685) Masursky	Fly-by
Deep Space 1	NASA	1998	(9969) Braille (19P/Borrelly)	Fly-by/Orbiting
Stardust	NASA	1999	(5535) Annefrank 81P/Wild 2 9P/Tempel 1	Fly-by
Comet Nucleus Tourer (Failed)	NASA	2002	2P/Encke 73P/Schwassmann-Wachmann 3 6P/d'Arrest	Fly-by
Hayabusa	JAXA	2003	(25143) Itokawa	Orbiting/Landing/Sample return
Rosetta	ESA	2004	(2867) Steins (21) Lutetia 67P/Churyumov-Gerasimenko	Orbiting/Landing/Sample return
Deep Impact/EPOXI	NASA	2005	9P/Tempel 1 103P/Hartley 2	Impact/ Fly-by
New Horizons	NASA	2006	132524 APL (134340) Pluto 2014 MU69	Fly-by
Dawn	NASA	2007	(4) Vesta (1) Ceres	Orbiting
Chang'e 2	CNSA	2010	(4179) Toutatis	Fly-by
Hayabusa 2	JAXA	2014	(162173) Ryugu	Orbiting/Landing/Sample return
OSIRIS-REx	NASA	2016	(101955) Bennu	Orbiting/Landing/Sample return
Don Quixote (in progress)	ESA	-	2003 SM84	Fly-by/Impact
Double Asteroid Redirection Test (DART)	NASA	2021	(65803) Didymos	Impact
Lucy	NASA	2021	15094 Polymele 21900 Orus	Fly-by
Psyche mission	NASA	2022	(16) Psyche	Orbiting
Tianwen 2 (in progress)	CNSA	2025	(469219) Kamo'oalewa (2016 HO3) 311P/PanSTARRS	Orbiting/Landing/Sample return Orbiting

In the 1990s, the exploration of small celestial bodies took various forms such as orbiting, impacting, landing, and sampling return. In 1996, NASA launched the Rendezvous–Shoemaker probe. Shoemaker was originally only planned for an orbital mission, but Dr. Bob Farquhar calculated that Shoemaker could successfully land in a saddle-shaped area on the southern surface of the small body (433) Eros without a soft-landing device. Shoemaker landed undamaged and continued to work for another 16 days, making it the first probe to soft-land an asteroid [53–57]. In 1997, NASA launched the Cassini-Huygens probe to probe Saturn. Cassini flew by (2685) Masursky on its way to Saturn in 2000, confirming that its diameter is between 15 and 20 km [58]. In 1998, the Deep Space 1 probe launched by NASA first flew by (9969) Braille in July 1999 and then rendezvoused with Comet Borrelly (19P/Borrelly) in September 2001 for observations [59–62]. In 1999, NASA launched the Stardust probe, which flew by (5535) Annefrank in 2002-11 and flew by 81P/Wild 2 in January 2004. The dust was sampled and returned. In February 2011, the probe visited 9P/Tempel 1 [63–71].

After entering the 21st century, in 2002, NASA launched the Comet Nucleus Tourer (CONTOUR), which plans to fly by Comet 2P/Encke, 73P/Schwassmann-Wachmann 3, and 6P/d'Arrest. Due to the failed launch, the mission has become the only small celestial object mission that has completely failed so far. In 2003, the Japan Aerospace Exploration Agency (JAXA) launched the Hayabusa probe to visit (25143) Itokawa. It landed on the asteroid in November 2005, collected some asteroid samples, and returned to the Earth. It is the first deep space exploration mission to sample and return asteroids [72–76]. In 2004, ESA launched the Rosetta comet probe to visit 67P/Churyumov-Gerasimenko, and on the way, it flew by (2867) Steins at a distance of 800 km in 2008 and flew over (21) Lutetia at a distance of 3160 km in 2010 [77]. On 12 November 2014, the lander Philae carried by the Rosetta probe landed in the pre-selected J region on the comet, becoming the first probe to land on the surface of a comet's nucleus [78–81]. In 2005, NASA launched the Deep Impact program to study the composition of the comet nucleus of Comet Tempel 1. In July of the same year, the impactor was released to complete the impact mission of Comet Tempel 1 and probe in deep space. For the first time in history, the material ejected from the surface of a comet had been measured [82–84]. The deep impact was then extended to the EPOXI mission, which conducted a fly-by of Comet 103P/Hartley 2 in November 2010 with the aid of Earth's gravity [85,86]. In 2006, NASA launched the New Horizon probe, which flew by 132,524 APL at a distance of 100,000 km in 2006 and approached the dwarf planet Pluto and its five moons in January 2015, becoming the first probe in history to visit a dwarf planet. It flew by Pluto at a distance of 12,500 km in July of the same year, after which NASA designated the fly-by of the Kuiper Belt small object 2014 MU69 as an extended mission of New Horizons [87]. In 2007, NASA launched the Dawn probe to visit (4) Vesta and the dwarf planet Ceres. Dawn arrived at the small celestial body (4) Vesta in July 2011. After the exploration, it flew to Ceres and arrived at Ceres in March 2015. This is the first probe in human history to orbit asteroids and dwarf planets in the main belt [88–91]. In 2010, the China National Space Administration (CNSA) launched Chang'e-2 probe to orbit the Moon. After that, the probe went to (4179) Toutatis in April 2012 and completed the mission of flying over (4179) Toutatis at a distance of 3.2 km in December 2012, which led to the obtention of a clear image of the surface of (4179) Toutatis for the first time [92–94]. Through this extended mission, China explored an asteroid for the first time, becoming the fourth country in the world to explore asteroids after the United States, Europe, and Japan. In 2014, after the Hayabusa mission, JAXA launched the Hayabusa-2 probe to detect (162173) Ryugu and used the blasting method to collect its deep samples and return. On 6 December 2020, the "Hyabusa 2" landed in the desert area of southern Australia and obtained 5.4 g of the sample, which aroused enthusiastic attention from all walks of life. In 2016, NASA launched the Pluto probe (OSIRIS-REx) to carry out a sampling return mission to (101955) Bennu. In December 2018, the probe reached the asteroid Bennu. After more than a year of short-range detection, a "touch and go" sampling was carried out to confirm that the sample was collected, and it is planned to arrive on Earth in September 2023.

In order to effectively deal with the potential collision threat of NEOs to Earth, scientists have been studying various means of NEO defense. For asteroid defense, the basic technical way is to use nuclear bombs for interception, use spacecraft for kinetic energy impact, or use laser ablation and other schemes. Other methods such as ion traction, gravitational drag, and mass drive are still in the argumentation stage. ESA launched a preliminary study of the Don Quijote project in 2006 and plans to test asteroid defense technology targeting 2003 SM84 or Destroyer (99942) Apophis in the future. NASA started the Double Asteroid Redirection Test (DART) in November 2021 to test the asteroid impact and defense against the binary asteroid system (65803) Didymos. According to the plan, the DART spacecraft will approach the target asteroid between the end of September and the beginning of October 2022 and finally hit the asteroid head-on at a speed of about

6.6 km/s. Such an impact would change the speed of the Moon in its orbit around the primary by one percent, and the period may be varied by a few minutes. China has been monitoring near-Earth asteroids since the 1950s. At the 7th International Academy of Astronautics Planetary Defense Conference, Yanhua Wu, Deputy Director of the Chinese Space Administration, mentioned that China will establish an organizational system and process to deal with the risk of asteroid impact.

In addition to planetary defense, research on the evolution of the solar system is also a focus related to small celestial bodies. NASA launched the Lucy probe in October 2021 and planned to fly by an asteroid in the inner main belt and five other Jupiter Trojan asteroids. NASA also plans to launch the Psyche spacecraft in 2022 to probe a series of questions related to the evolution of Psyche through its orbit.

The white paper "2016 China's Aerospace" proposes to deepen the demonstration and key technological breakthroughs in the main tasks of Mars sampling and return, asteroid exploration, Jupiter system and planetary transit detection, etc. In April 2019, the "Asteroid Exploration Mission Payload and Carrying Project Opportunities Announcement" issued by the National Space Administration confirmed that China's asteroid exploration mission will achieve a near-Earth asteroid sampling return and a main-belt comet orbit through one launch. In 2021, the first Mars exploration mission of China (Tianwen 1) has achieved great success. China plans to launch a small celestial body detector around 2025 and spend 10 years visiting two small celestial bodies: (2016) HO3 near-Earth asteroid and comet (133) P.

3. Research on Small Celestial Body Gravitational Field Environments and Orbital Mechanics

Deep space exploration missions related to small celestial bodies have stimulated a large number of studies on related issues, including analysis of the dynamic environment of small celestial body detectors, orbit design and control, the formation and evolution of celestial bodies, nonlinear dynamic characteristics, and other aspects. This section will introduce the research on the gravitational field model of small celestial bodies, the orbital dynamics, the surface transition dynamics, and the research on the gravitational field environment of small celestial bodies under the change of physical parameters, etc.

3.1. Research on the Gravitational Field Model of Small Celestial Bodies

The study of the periodic and quasi-periodic orbital dynamics around small irregular celestial bodies depends on the proper description of the dynamic model of the small celestial bodies. The work of Hamilton et al. [95] shows that the influence of the planetary gravitational perturbation is very small compared with the Sun's gravitational perturbation, and its influence can be ignored. Therefore, the dynamic equation of the particle moving near the small celestial body can be expressed as

$$\ddot{\mathbf{r}} = \mathbf{a} + \mathbf{a}_S \tag{1}$$

In the formula, $\mathbf{r}$ represents the position of the particle in the small celestial body coordinate system, $\mathbf{a}$ represents the acceleration obtained by the particle due to the gravitational force of the small celestial body, and $\mathbf{a}_S$ represents the acceleration obtained by the particle perturbed by the gravitational force of the Sun. Since the particle motion is considered, the influence of solar pressure perturbation can be ignored. For the distance range applicable to the dynamic model of small celestial bodies, generally consider the radius of the sphere affected by the gravitational force of the small celestial body relative to the gravitational force of the Sun:

$$\frac{R_1}{D} = \left(\frac{M_A}{M_S}\right)^{\frac{2}{5}} \tag{2}$$

In the formula, R_1 is the radius of the influence sphere, D is the revolving distance of the small celestial body around the Sun, M_A is the mass of the small celestial body, and M_S is the mass of the Sun. Within the range of the small celestial body's influence sphere radius

R_1, the gravitational force of the small celestial body can be regarded as the main force affecting the motion of the particle, and the Sun's gravitational force can be regarded as the perturbing force. For a more rigorous estimate, the radius at the point of gravitational neutralization for small bodies and the Sun can be considered:

$$\frac{R_2}{D} = \left(\frac{M_A}{M_S}\right)^{\frac{1}{2}} \tag{3}$$

In the formula, R_2 is the radius of the gravitational neutralization point. It is easy to see that $R_1 > R_2$. Yu [96] gave the gravitational radii of 23 small celestial bodies in his doctoral dissertation. Table 4 lists the radius range of the small celestial body's gravitational action, calculated according to Formulas (2) and (3). It is not difficult to see that the radius R_1 of the gravitational influence sphere is about two orders of magnitude larger than the radius R_2 at the gravitational neutralization point.

Table 4. Gravitational radius of asteroids.

Asteroids	MA/MS	D/AU	R_1/km	R_2/km
(216) Kleopatra	2.33×10^{-12}	[2.09, 3.49]	$[6.97 \times 10^3, 1.16 \times 10^4]$	$[4.78 \times 10^2, 7.99 \times 10^2]$
(243) Ida	2.11×10^{-14}	[2.74, 2.98]	$[1.39 \times 10^3, 1.51 \times 10^3]$	$[5.97 \times 10, 6.50 \times 10]$
(433) Eros	3.36×10^{-15}	[1.13, 1.78]	$[2.75 \times 10^2, 4.34 \times 10^2]$	$[9.83 \times 10^0, 1.55 \times 10]$
(1620) Geographos	1.30×10^{-17}	[0.83, 1.66]	$[2.19 \times 10, 4.38 \times 10]$	$[4.49 \times 10^{-1}, 8.98 \times 10^{-1}]$
(6489) Golevka	1.06×10^{-19}	[0.99, 4.02]	$[3.81 \times 10^0, 1.55 \times 10]$	$[4.83 \times 10^{-2}, 1.96 \times 10^{-1}]$

Small celestial bodies are irregular in shape, rotate faster than large planets, and have smaller masses. They are very different from the gravitational fields around large celestial bodies, showing the characteristics of asymmetry and irregularity. Therefore, in order to study the dynamics of small irregular celestial bodies, it is necessary to approximate their gravitational field with an appropriate model. Common approximate models of gravitational field are: the simple geometry model; the spherical harmonic and ellipsoidal harmonic function model; the particle group model; and the polyhedron model.

The simple geometry model has the characteristics of a simple structure, few shape parameters, and convenient calculation. It is easy to obtain analytical results and qualitative conclusions about shape parameters. The simple geometries commonly used for simulation in current research include the homogeneous thin straight rod model [97], the homogeneous ring model [98], the triaxial ellipsoid model [99], and the dipole model [100]. The early simple geometric models can only reflect the basic characteristics of small celestial bodies and cannot accurately simulate the surrounding gravitational field environment. With the continuous development of the study of simulating irregular gravitational fields with simple geometric models, the dipole model proposed by Zeng et al. [100] can better reflect the gravitational field near the equilibrium point of irregular small celestial bodies. Accuracy is also taken into account.

The main idea of the spherical harmonic model is to use infinite series to approximate the gravitational potential function of celestial bodies. It was first applied in the dynamics of near-Earth satellite orbits and then introduced into the study of gravitational field modeling of small celestial bodies to describe small celestial bodies. Using the spherical harmonic function method, the gravitational potential can be expanded as

$$U(\mathbf{r}) = \frac{GM_A}{r}\{1 + \sum_{l=1}^{\infty}\sum_{m=0}^{l}\left(\frac{r_e}{r}\right)^l P_{lm}(\sin(\phi))[C_{lm}\cos(m\lambda) + S_{lm}\sin(m\lambda)]\} \tag{4}$$

where G is the gravitational constant $G = 6.674\,28 \times 10^{-11}$ $m^3 \cdot kg^{-1} \cdot s^{-2}$; $\mathbf{r}$ is the position vector of the particle; r, ϕ, λ are the three components of the vector in spherical coordinates; M_A is the mass of the small celestial body; P_{lm} is the associative Legendre polynomial; r_e is the radius of the Brillouin sphere, reflecting the range of convergence of the series, that is, the applicable range of Formula (4); and C_{lm} and S_{lm} are spherical harmonic coefficients, reflecting the shape irregularity and inhomogeneity of internal mass distribution [101]. The advantage of this method is that the gravitational potential can be given analytically. It is convenient for obtaining theoretical solutions through analytical methods. In addition, once the spherical harmonic function coefficient is obtained, it can be directly substituted in the subsequent numerical calculation, which is convenient to use, especially for inversion calculation through flight data [102]. During the orbiting of Ceres by the Dawn probe, Takahashi et al. [103,104] used the spherical harmonic model to estimate the precise gravitational field of Ceres and iteratively iterated the known spherical harmonics to give the direction of its principal axis. The main limitations are that the model cannot be applied to the region located within the Brillouin sphere. The reason for this is that the series does not converge [105]. The truncation error in calculations may lead to large errors in the obtained gravitational field model in some cases [106].

Considering the convergence region of spherical harmonics, Hobson [107] uses Lamé polynomials to approximate the ellipsoidal harmonics model of the gravitational potential function. Pick [108] established the theory of ellipsoid harmonics on this basis. Using the ellipsoid harmonic method, the gravitational potential of a unit mass particle can be expanded as

$$U(\mathbf{r}) = GM_A \sum_{l=0}^{\infty} \sum_{m=1}^{2l+1} \alpha_{lm} \frac{F_{lm}(\lambda_1)}{F_{lm}(\lambda_e)} F_{lm}(\lambda_2) F_{lm}(\lambda_3) \tag{5}$$

In the formula, λ_1, λ_2, λ_3 are the ellipsoid coordinate components of the vector $\mathbf{r}$. λ_e is the parameter of the Brillouin ellipsoid, which reflects the range of convergence of the series, that is, the range of use of Formula (5). F_{lm} is the Lamé equation canonical solution, and α_{lm} is the ellipsoid harmonic coefficient [105]. A conversion method between spherical harmonics and ellipsoidal harmonics was proposed by Dechambre et al. [109] to simplify the solution process. The ellipsoid harmonic function model expands the convergence region of small celestial bodies while still retaining the characteristics of the spherical harmonic function model for easy calculation [110].

The convergence rate of the two models near the boundary of the convergence domain decreases rapidly as the distance from the particle to the small body decreases. In addition, the spherical harmonic function and ellipsoidal harmonic function models lack the information to judge whether the particle is located inside or outside the small irregular celestial body. Therefore, it cannot meet the calculation requirements of the global gravitational field in the application of studying the dynamics.

Particle swarm models are often used to model dynamic environments in asteroid evolution and near-Earth asteroid orbit collision avoidance problems. This model is a very intuitive method that discretizes the space where the small celestial body is located into a series of particles, calculating the gravitational force or gravitational potential of these particles separately and summing them up to obtain the overall gravitational force or gravitational potential of the small celestial body. Assuming that the small celestial body is divided into N voxels, the position coordinate of the i-th voxel is $\mathbf{r}_i$, and the mass is M_i. Then, the gravitational potential can be expressed as

$$U(\mathbf{r}) = \sum_{i=1}^{N} \frac{GM_i}{|\mathbf{r} - \mathbf{r}_i|} \tag{6}$$

The advantage of the method is that its algorithm is simple and easy to implement, and it can ensure the convergence. By increasing the number and distribution of divided voxels by appropriate rules, the accuracy of the gravitational field of small celestial bodies can be improved. Real-world problems such as distribution have good scalability [111,112].

However, this method also has some defects: the number of voxels increases rapidly with the accuracy requirements, which leads to a sharp increase in the amount of calculation and a great decrease in the calculation speed; it cannot provide a direct and effective judgment for whether the orbit of the particle intersects with the small irregular celestial body.

The polyhedron model is a numerical modeling method for the gravitational field of small irregular celestial bodies. Since the nineteenth century, in order to describe a rugged terrain in geology, scholars have studied the gravitational field of a simple polyhedron. MacMillan and Waldvogel [113,114] successively gave the analytical form of the gravitational potential energy of the cuboid and the general homogeneous polyhedron. The disadvantage is that the amount of calculation is large. In the 1990s, Werner [115,116] used a polyhedron in which every surface is a triangle to approximate the shape of a small irregular celestial body. Moreover, he used Gauss's theorem and Green's formula to simplify the triple integral. Werner also studied the orbital behavior around the regular tetrahedron, which was compared to the orbitals affected by the J_3 and J_{33} terms in the spherical harmonic model. Then, Werner et al. [117] sorted out the previous work, taking (4769) Castalia as an example, and introduced the modeling method of the polyhedral gravitational field in detail. Mirtich [118] also applied Gauss's theorem and Green's formula to replace the integral by summation and calculated the center of mass, the moment of inertia, the product of inertia, and other physical quantities of a homogeneous polyhedron.

The gravitational potential, gravitational force, and gravitational gradient tensors of the polyhedron at any point outside the homogeneous polyhedron can be expressed as [117,118]:

$$U(\mathbf{r})\frac{1}{2}G\sigma\sum_{e\in E}L_e(\mathbf{r}_e\cdot\mathbf{E}_e\cdot\mathbf{r}_e)-\frac{1}{2}G\sigma\sum_{f\in F}\theta_f(\mathbf{r}_f\cdot\mathbf{F}_f\cdot\mathbf{r}_f) \tag{7}$$

$$\nabla U(\mathbf{r})=G\sigma\sum_{e\in E}L_e(\mathbf{E}_e\cdot\mathbf{r}_e)-G\sigma\sum_{f\in F}\theta_f(\mathbf{F}_f\cdot\mathbf{r}_f) \tag{8}$$

$$\nabla^2 U(\mathbf{r})=G\sigma\sum_{e\in E}L_e\mathbf{E}_e-G\sigma\sum_{f\in F}\theta_f\mathbf{F}_f \tag{9}$$

In the formula, σ is the density of the homogeneous polyhedron P, E is the set of all edges on the surface f, F is the set of faces of the polyhedron P, $\mathbf{r}_e$ represents the vector from $\mathbf{r}$ to any point on edge e, $\mathbf{r}_f$ represents the vector from $\mathbf{r}$ to any point on the side f, L_e, E_e, F_f are the quantities related to the edge and the side, and θ_f is the solid angle formed by the points at the side f and r. Its specific calculation formula is

$$\theta_f=2\arctan\frac{\mathbf{r}_1\cdot(\mathbf{r}_2\times\mathbf{r}_3)}{r_1r_2r_3+r_3\mathbf{r}_1\cdot\mathbf{r}_2+r_1\mathbf{r}_2\cdot\mathbf{r}_3+r_2\mathbf{r}_1\cdot\mathbf{r}_3} \tag{10}$$

where $\mathbf{r}_1$ $\mathbf{r}_2$ $\mathbf{r}_3$ are the vector radii from the point at $\mathbf{r}$ to the three vertices on the side of the triangle. Denote

$$\Omega=\sum_{f\in F}\theta_f \tag{11}$$

when the point is inside the polyhedron P, $\Omega = 4\pi$; when the point is outside the polyhedron P, $\Omega = 0$. From this, the positional relationship between the point and the polyhedron can be determined.

The polyhedron model has no truncation error; the error only comes from the shape error and numerical calculation error between the model and the real celestial body. The calculation accuracy is high, and the polyhedron is not necessarily a convex polyhedron. Moreover, it can be well simulated near the surface and even inside the asteroid, and it can meet the requirements of global calculations. In the analysis of orbital dynamics, the polyhedron method also easily judges whether the particle is outside the asteroid. The main disadvantage of the polyhedron model is the large amount of calculation. Every time the gravity calculation needs to be performed on all edges and vertices, the calculation speed will be greatly reduced when the number of edges and vertices increases. (101955) Bennu's geometric shape based on the polyhedron model can be found in Figure 2.

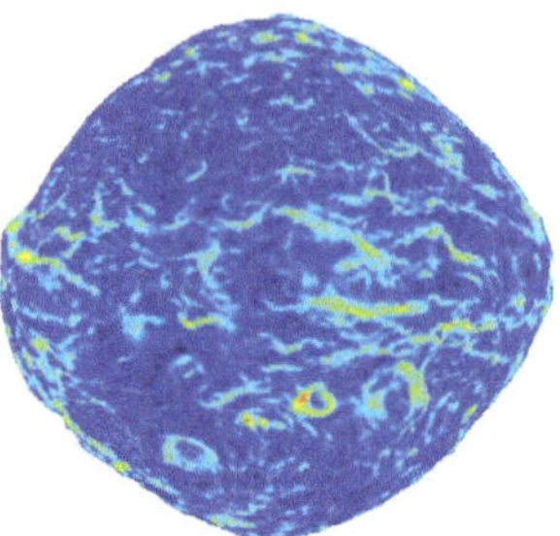

Figure 2. The geometric shape of (101955) Bennu based on the polyhedron model [119].

The above methods have their own advantages and disadvantages and need to be appropriately selected according to the characteristics of specific problems.

3.2. Research on Orbital Dynamics near Small Celestial Bodies

Based on the various dynamical models described in the previous section, the dynamic research on the vicinity of small irregular celestial bodies mainly includes the manifold structure and the local motion at the equilibrium point and its vicinity, large-scale periodic orbits and their bifurcations and resonances, quasi-periodic orbits, chaos, dynamic configuration, and the evolution of binary asteroids or multi-star systems. Dynamic equilibrium points, periodic orbits, and quasi-periodic orbits are important ways to study the phase space structure of complex dynamical systems.

The research related to equilibrium points started with the dynamic problem near small celestial bodies and has the most relevant research so far. Early research focused on the existence, quantity, and stability of equilibrium points near special geometries. Zhuravlev [120] first studied the stability of equilibrium points near the three-axis spheroid and calculated the stable and unstable regions.

Scheeres et al. [121,122] also used the spherical harmonic gravitational field model to calculate the position of the equilibrium point of (4769) Castalia and analyze its stability. Elipe et al. [123] found four equilibrium points in the gravitational field of a finite straight segment and analyzed their stability. Scheeres et al. [124] calculated the positions of the four equilibrium points of (25143) Itokawa. Mondelo et al. [125] calculated the positions of four equilibrium points of (4) Vesta and analyzed the stability. Liu et al. [126] analyzed the manifold structure near the equilibrium points in the gravitational field of a rotating homogeneous cube and the heteroclinic orbits between different equilibrium points. Yu et al. [127] calculated the coordinates of four equilibrium points in the gravitational field of (216) Kleopatra, linearized the eigenvalues of the matrix, and analyzed the stability based on this. Scheeres [128] calculated the equilibrium points of (1580) Betulia and 67P/Churyumov-Gerasimenko.

Jiang et al. [129] gave a linearized equation for motions near the equilibrium points, deduced a sufficient and necessary condition for the stability of the equilibrium point, and studied the characteristic root distribution, stability, and topological types of equilibrium points. According to the sub-manifold structure, the non-degenerate equilibrium points are divided into eight categories, which is a major advancement for scientists in correctly understanding the relevant characteristics of the equilibrium points of small celestial bodies. Wang et al. [130] used the polyhedron model to calculate the positions of the equilibrium points of 23 small celestial bodies and analyzed their stability. In particular, they found eight equilibrium points near the asteroid Bennu. This shows that the number and distribution of equilibrium points near small bodies are diverse and cannot be completely divided into two types determined by a simple geometric model.

Regarding the change in equilibrium points with the normalization parameters of the density and the rotational speed of small celestial bodies, Jiang et al. [131] found that equilibrium points always appear or annihilate in pairs, and the number of non-degenerate relative equilibrium points is odd. Wang et al. [132] took Bennu as an example to summarize the bifurcations of equilibrium points.

Since the 1990s, scientists have also conducted many studies on the periodic orbits in the gravitational field of small rotating irregular celestial bodies. The main focus is on the search for periodic orbits, orbit classification and stability analysis, and the dynamic bifurcation behavior due to changes in parameters such as the rotation speed of small celestial bodies and the energy integral of particle motion. Scheeres et al. [121,133] calculated the periodic orbits in the equatorial plane of (4) Vesta and (433) Eros using a three-axis ellipsoid model. Scheeres et al. [134] also used the second-order quadratic gravitational field model to calculate the frozen orbits and periodic orbits near Tutatis and analyzed the effects of the C_{20} and C_{30} terms on the frozen orbits. Antreasian et al. [135] and Scheeres et al. [136] successively used the second-order quadratic gravitational field model and the average method to analyze the motions near (433) Eros and found a family of retrograde periodic orbits, which were used for the Shoemaker mission. Shang et al. [137] investigated various periodic orbits near non-principal-axis rotation asteroids.

Scheeres et al. [138–142] also studied the influence of the C_{20} and C_{22} terms on the energy and angular momentum of the particle motion and numerically calculated the stable and unstable orbital regions in the parameter space. They further studied the orbital dynamics considering the non-spherical gravity of small celestial bodies, solar radiation pressure, and solar gravity and used the averaging method to find the frozen orbits near small celestial bodies. The property is closely related to the area-to-mass ratio of the spacecraft and the distance from the small celestial body to the Sun. Because the search for periodic orbits is very complicated, it is generally necessary to use symmetry for analysis and research, but the gravitational field of small irregular celestial bodies does not have this feature [128–143]. Yu et al. [144] proposed a global search method for 3D periodic orbit families in the vicinity of irregular small bodies by using the polyhedral model and the hierarchical grid method. The 29 periodic orbits are given by taking asteroid (216) Kleopatra as an example. The periodic orbits are classified into seven types according to the orbits of the four-dimensional symplectic manifold by calculating the eigenvalues of the monodromy matrix of periodic orbits [145]. Topological types, the bifurcation phenomenon, and the stability of periodic orbits with the continuation of energy are studied. Jiang et al. pointed out that periodic orbits move in a six-dimensional symplectic manifold and that its manifold structure is different from that of the four-dimensional case and re-classified the periodic orbits near small irregular celestial bodies into 13 topological types [132]. Applying this theory, Yu et al. [146] found periodic orbit families belonging to different topological types near (243) Ida and the bifurcation behavior in the continuation process in the periodical orbit search and continuation near (243) Ida. Jiang's theory provides a powerful tool for follow-up research to better understand the type and stability of periodic orbits near irregular small celestial bodies from the topological structure. Non-equatorial equilibrium points near an asteroid with gravitational orbit-attitude coupling perturbation were analyzed in reference [147]. Li et al. [148] calculated the geophysical environments and periodic orbits near 2016 HO3 by using different shape models.

With the development of orbital dynamics and calculation methods for spacecraft near asteroids, people's research on small celestial bodies has gradually expanded from single asteroids to binary asteroid systems and even systems comprised of multiple small bodies. Liang et al. [149] used the Poincare section and Jacobi constant to find the homoclinic and heteroclinic orbits connecting the equilibria near the contacting binary asteroids, which provided an important reference for designing low-energy transfer orbits between equilibria. Hou and Xin [150] constructed an explicit first-order solution to the rotations and the orbital motion in the planar two-body problem. Shi et al. [151] studied the equilibrium points and periodic orbits of the binary asteroid system (66391) 1999KW4 by the homotopy method based on the restricted full three-body problem. Wang and Fu [152] constructed a semi-analytical model for spacecraft near the primary of a binary asteroid system based on a perturbed two-body problem. For nonlinear dynamics of multiple body systems, the discrete element model is usually applied to simplify related calculations [153]. Jiang et al. [154] analyzed the dynamical configurations of the five triple-asteroid systems 45 Eugenia, 87 Sylvia, 93 Minerva, 216 Kleopatra, and 136617 1994CC and the six-body system 134340 Pluto. Figure 3 shows the dynamical configuration of binary asteroid system (66391) 1999 KW4. Valvano et al. [155] discussed the stability regions near the triple asteroid system 2001 SN 263 considering the effect of irregular shapes and the solar radiation pressure.

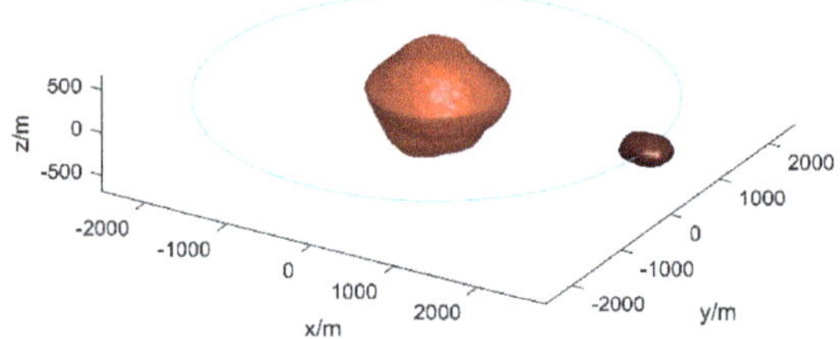

Figure 3. Dynamical configuration of binary asteroids 1999 KW4.

Due to the complex orbital shape near the small celestial body, the theoretically calculated periodic orbit may not be closed. Wang [156] expanded the definition of the resonant orbit from the orbital period satisfying the conventional relationship to the angular velocity of the particle moving around the small celestial body. In addition, some theoretical periodic orbits are affected by various perturbations, and the orbits will not be closed. Scheeres et al. [134] studied the quasi-periodic frozen orbit near (4179) Toutatis under the second-order quadratic gravitational field model. Chanut et al. used the polyhedron model to study the long-term motion of particles near the small celestial bodies (433) Eros and (216) Kleopatra [157,158].

Chaos phenomena are ubiquitous in the natural world and in engineering problems such as chemistry, mechanical systems, financial economics, and nanoscience [159–164]. The generation of chaotic phenomena in dynamics is usually closely related to bifurcation and resonance phenomena [165]. Studies on simple geometric models of gravitational fields have uncovered the chaotic behavior of particles. Elipe et al. [123] found the bifurcation caused by 1:1 resonance in the gravitational field of a finite straight segment and chaos due to parameter changes. Lindner et al. [166] discovered the chaotic phenomenon of particles moving around a line segment. Makarov et al. [167] found the chaotic phenomenon of the rotation of triaxial asteroids and minor planets. Since most of the small celestial bodies have strong irregular shapes, the resonance mechanism in the double asteroid or multi-asteroid system is more complicated, and the influence of the mutual coupling of orbit and attitude must be considered. Based on the sphere-ellipsoid model, Nadoushan et al. [168] found that aspheric factors and orbital eccentricity can significantly affect the size of the resonance region. After a certain critical value, the resonance regions intersect and lead to the appearance of chaos.

The YORP effect is a thermal-radiation torque acting on small asteroids and plays a crucial role in their physical and dynamical evolution. A detailed introduction can be found in Section 3.4. Cuk Nadoushan et al. [169] considered the solar gravitational perturbation, the orbital attitude dynamics, and the long-term evolution of the binary asteroid system under the YORP (Yarkovsky-O'Keefe-Radzievskii-Paddack) effect. They found the chaotic behavior of the attitude under the condition of small orbital eccentricity, even with the same rotation period. The widespread existence of chaotic phenomena makes it very important to distinguish between ordered and chaotic motions. Lyapunov Characteristic Exponents (LCE) [170] provide the distinction criterion from theoretical and numerical viewpoints and provide the chaotic intensity quantitative characterization. However, in practice, the numerical computation required to discover chaotic phenomena is time-consuming, especially for some chaotic motions that are very close to ordered motions. Froeschlé et al. [171,172] and Fouchard et al. [173] successively developed the Fast Lyapunov Indicator (FLI) and the Orthogonal Fast Lyapunov indicator (FLI) in response to the shortcomings of LCE. This provides an effective indicator for effectively distinguishing ordered and chaotic motions. Ni et al. [174] proposed to quantitatively analyze the indicators of quasi-periodic orbits from the perspective of frequency domain analysis and specifically analyzed the indicators of orbits in the gravitational field that neither escape nor collide with small celestial bodies. Among them, a complex orbit in the gravitational field of (6489) Golevka can be seen in Figure 4.

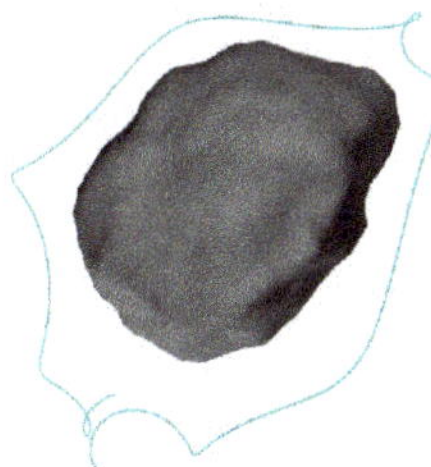

Figure 4. A complex orbit in the gravitational field of (6489) Golevka.

3.3. Research on Surface Motion Dynamics and the Capillary Phenomenon of Small Celestial Bodies

After exploring the special orbits near small bodies, people naturally pay attention to the selection of the soft-landing region and trajectory optimization, which are closely related to the transition dynamics on the surface of small celestial bodies. Generally speaking, the matter on the surface of irregular small celestial bodies may undergo transitions or even launch and escape behaviors. These motions are specifically classified into surface equilibria, motion confined on the surface, surface transition, and bouncing. For example, ESA's Rosetta probe's lander Philae clearly observed two bounces when it touched down on 67P/Churyumov–Gerasimenko, which means that Philae was observed to make three landings. It is noteworthy that the interval between the first landing and the final resting on the surface of the comet nucleus is 2 h. ESA did not fully consider the contact mechanics, collision, and bounce of the soft-landing process on the surface of irregular bodies. This led to the fact that the final soft-landing position of the lander was hundreds of meters away from the preset position.

A large number of previous studies have studied the physical and chemical properties of the surface particles of small celestial bodies, including the electrokinetic and rotational emission of dust particles in cometary cores [175] and the mineralogy and mineralogy of asteroid dust particles [176]. Moving particles and dust may be caused by a variety of reasons, including the YORP effect [177], the windmill effect on the surface of small celestial bodies [175], the collision and gravitational reconstruction of asteroid families and small moons [178], and the gravel disintegration of rubble-pile asteroids [179,180]. The disintegration of asteroid P/2013 R3 produced more than 10 distinct small bodies, numerous small grains, and a comet-like dust tail [180]. Most asteroids and comet nuclei have irregular shapes, and particles can move on the surface of small irregular bodies. To understand the dynamical behaviors of particles on the surfaces of irregular celestial bodies, we need to study the surface mechanical environment. In addition, the movement of the lander or the rover on the surface of the irregular small celestial body also needs to be studied. If the lander lands on the surface of an irregular small body, the collision and bounce of the lander on the irregular surface also exist [181].

Beginners choose simple shapes, including ellipsoids [182,183] and cubes [184], to help understand the surface motion. Guibout and Scheeres [182] discussed the existence and stability of surface equilibrium points for spheroids of revolution. Bellerose and Scheeres [183] used ellipsoids to simulate the shape and gravity of asteroids, studying hopping on flat surfaces. Belleros et al. [181] considered the motion and control of the surface exploration robot under the gravitational force of the uniformly rotating ellipsoid. Liu et al. [184] calculated the positions and eigenvalues of the surface equilibrium of a uniformly rotating cube. The non-degenerate equilibria in the gravitational field of general irregular celestial bodies can be divided into eight different types [129]. The motion confined on the surface of the irregular small celestial body is different from the motion in the gravitational field [185]. The former needs to consider the irregular gravitational force and the contact force, while the latter only considers the irregular gravitational force. Generally speaking, the transition or landing process of particles or landers on the surface of irregular celestial bodies includes orbital motion, collision, jumping motion, surface motion, and surface equilibria.

Considering a non-smooth surface with a constant coefficient of friction, the equilibria remain but are not as stable as the equilibria on a smooth surface [184]. Considering the precise gravity and irregular shape, Yu and Baoyin [186,187] numerically calculated the motion and particle migration of the rover on the asteroid surface and found that the most stable direction is the rotational pole direction, which can limit the rover's movement after landing. However, the friction phenomenon on the surface of irregular small celestial bodies has a stick-slip effect [188], and the surface transition particles may be charged [189]. The orbital motion, collision and jumping motion, surface motion, and surface equilibrium of particles released over three different regions (flat surface, concave region, convex region) relative to asteroid 6489 Golevka were investigated in [185]. The results showed that when the particles were released over a flat surface and concave region, the surface equilibrium can be reached in a short time.

In the research of water ice material in small celestial bodies, previous studies in several pieces of literature found that the water on Earth comes from asteroids [190,191]. Kanno et al. [192] analyzed the wavelengths of the infrared spectrum to confirm the presence of water and ice on class D asteroids. Asteroids may release meteoroids, which fall to Earth as meteor showers or meteors, bringing material to Earth [193–195]. Treiman et al. [193] studied the Eucrite from the asteroid (4) Vesta and found quartz in the meteorite, arguing that quartz originates from the deposition of liquid water and that water may originate from (4) Vesta. Campins et al. [196] reported the presence of water and ice on the surface of (24) Themis and the widespread distribution of this water and ice. Comets also tend to have water on them. Sunshine et al. [197] detected the presence of water and ice on Comet 9P/Tempel, indicating that the surface deposits of the comet nucleus are loose aggregates. Taylor [198] reported in detail the presence of water in Eucrite meteorites originating from the asteroid (4) Vesta. Zolensky et al. [199] discussed temperatures of alteration, water:rock ratios, and the oxygen isotopic composition of water by analyzing the record of low-temperature alteration in asteroids. Trigo-Rodríguez et al. [200] presented the action of water in asteroids by studying carbonaceous chondrite meteorites.

The research on capillary action on asteroid surfaces is closely related to the equilibrium points and surface motion of particles. The height of the water in the capillary tube on the surface of the asteroid depends on the irregular shape and the gravitational potential of the asteroid. Different surfaces produce different heights of water in the capillary tube, so the friction coefficients of different surfaces are different, resulting in the stability of the surface balance sex being different. It was found that the gravitational field and spin velocity of asteroids have a significant effect on the height of the liquid in the capillaries on the asteroid surface [201]. This research can be applied in the following four aspects: ① This research helps to further study the distribution of water and ice on the surface of asteroids, and the different distributions of water and ice are related to the different distributions of liquid lengths in the capillary [196]. ② On the scale of millions of years, water can corrode the surfaces of asteroids and the structure inside, and the surface material and shape of a large number of asteroids have changed through surface erosion, especially for rubble-pile asteroids. In other words, long-term erosion could cause asteroids to break up and disintegrate. Aqueous alteration processes in asteroids were investigated by Rotelli et al. [202] to better understand the increasing complexity towards prebiotic chemistry. ③ The different heights of the liquid in the capillary can affect the electrokinetic and rotational jets of gas and dust particles on the surface of small celestial bodies [189]. Under the action of sunlight pressure, the jet may form a mini fountain on the surface of small celestial bodies. The change in the length distribution of the liquid in the capillary causes the height of the fountain and the radius of the fountain envelope to change [189]. ④ The probe can carry some liquid to the surface of the asteroid, so the study of the height of the liquid in the capillary may also be applied to future asteroid missions.

3.4. *Dynamic Characteristics under Varying Parameters*

The rotational speed, density, shape, internal structure, and other physical parameters of small celestial bodies vary widely, resulting in very different dynamic behaviors in their gravitational fields. Taking the rotational speed as an example, there is only one equilibrium point in the gravity field of 1998KY26 when it is rapidly rotating. For (52760) 1998 ML14, comet 1P/Halley, and 9P/Tempel 1, the external equilibrium points are farther away from the small celestial body. Asteroid (216) Kleopatra has seven relative equilibrium points, which is different from the five relative equilibrium points of most asteroids [131]. The YORP effect of small celestial bodies is closely related to thermosphysical parameters. It is a phenomenon that the rotation axis and rotation speed of small celestial bodies vary slowly due to the photon moment generated by sunlight [203]. Studies have shown that the YORP effect can slowly change the rotation speed of small celestial bodies and even cause the rotational disintegration of small celestial bodies. For example, the YORP effect can make the rotation rate of the small celestial body 54509 (2000PH5) accelerate by $(2.0 \pm 0.2) \times 10^{-4}$ $(^\circ)/\mathrm{d}^2$ [204], and the rotation rate of the small celestial body (1620) Geographos can be accelerated by 1.15×10^{-8} $\mathrm{rad}/\mathrm{d}^2$ [205]. Numerical experiments show that the YORP effect can lead to the disintegration of rubble-like celestial bodies and the formation of small moons. The YORP effect may also indirectly affect the distribution and topological characteristics of the relative equilibrium points in the gravitational field. The shapes of asteroids may also be deformed as landslides and mass shedding occur. Similar to Comet Shoemaker-Levy 9, small rubble-like bodies can change their topography dramatically as they approach a planet, and some even disintegrate. Holsapple et al. [206,207] established the mechanical mechanism of tidal deformation caused by the influence of nearby larger celestial bodies. The variations in the shape, spin, and state during the slowly increasing angular momentum of rubble-pile, self-gravitating, homogeneous ellipsoidal bodies were investigated in reference [208,209]. Zhang et al. [210] found that three typical tidal response outcomes may appear on rubble piles, namely, deformation, scattering, and destruction. During the long-term evolution of small celestial bodies, their density, rotational speed, shape, and internal structure may change. The disintegration and gravitational aggregation of asteroids will also affect their internal structure, average density, and shape. These factors lead to changes in the parameters of small celestial bodies. If the parameters of the primary in binary asteroids with a large-scale ratio vary, it is bound to have an impact on the movement of the small moon. In addition, changes in parameters will also affect the movement of dust, particles, and gravel in the gravitational field of small celestial bodies.

Tanbakouei et al. [211] studied the mechanical properties of particles on the surface of asteroid 25143 Itokawa using the nanoindentation technique. They found that these particles of asteroid regolith can be more compacted than the minerals forming the particular LL chondrite associated with potentially hazardous asteroids. For the DART mission, the impact with the secondary of the Didymos system will cause a momentum transfer from the spacecraft to the binary asteroid. It is expected to change the orbit period of this system and force it to librate in the original orbit [212]. Furthermore, the primary may be reshaped due to landslides or internal deformation during this process. A detailed analysis can be seen in reference [213]. In 2024 October, the ESA Hera mission will be launched to obtain a detailed characterization of the physical properties of binary asteroids and of the crater caused by the DART mission [214]. For ringed asteroids, a change in the parameters may also lead to a variation in the parameters of the ring and even cause the formation or disappearance of the ring.

The influence of parameter changes on the dynamic behaviors in the gravitational field of small celestial bodies is very complex. Many scholars usually assume uniform mass distribution when modeling small celestial bodies. However, there may be mascons inside small celestial bodies, which make the mass distribution uneven. The density and distribution will inevitably have an impact on the gravitational field environment. Based on the polyhedron model, Chanut et al. [215] established a small celestial body model considering mascons. Aljbaae et al. [216] studied the gravitational field environment and the position of equilibrium points of the (21) Lutetia asteroid in the three cases: no mascons, three-layer mascons, or four-layer mascons. Chanut et al. [217] studied the orbital stability in the equatorial plane of the asteroid (101955) Bennu under the conditions of uniform mass and non-uniform mass distribution and found that, for Bennu, it is more appropriate to divide the mascon structure into 10 layers. Jiang [218] considered the position and topology transitions of the equilibrium points in the gravitational field of (2867) Steins with single-layer similarity, single-layer spherical, multi-layer similarity, and multi-layer spherical mascons. Jiang et al. [219] studied the bifurcation types corresponding to the collision and annihilation of equilibrium points during increasing the spin rate of (216) Kleopatra. It was found that the number of non-degenerate equilibrium points is changed from seven to five, then to three, and, finally, to 1. Moreover, they found a conserved quantity about the equilibrium points and deduced that the number of non-degenerate equilibrium points in the gravitational field of small celestial bodies can only be an odd number. Considering the shape effect on the environment of the gravitational field, the homotopy analysis method was used to generate continuous shape variation from small celestial bodies to simple symmetric geometric bodies (such as spheres, ellipsoids, and cubes), and the bifurcation phenomena of equilibrium points in the gravitational field are studied in [220].

4. Summary and Future Development

This paper introduces the general situation of small celestial bodies, summarizes the history and status of international missions, and sorts out the research progress of the orbital mechanics of spacecraft, such as modeling the gravitational field, orbital dynamics, surface motion dynamics, and dynamic properties under varying parameters. First, building an accurate gravitational model of small bodies lays the foundation for research on orbital dynamics. Taking into account the resource constraints of the onboard computer, how to balance computational efficiency and computational accuracy is still a key issue in modeling the gravitational field of asteroids. Second, considering the needs and constraints of real missions, the design of low-energy transfer orbits and corresponding control schemes deserves more attention. It is an important way to make full use of the orbital dynamics near asteroid systems, such as invariant manifolds and heteroclinic orbits. Moreover, studying the evolution of multiple asteroid systems is of great significance for understanding the origin of the solar system. Finally, the impact monitoring of near-Earth objects and estimating the impact probability with the Earth is the first step towards planetary defense. Furthermore, investigations on the means of deflecting a potentially hazardous object and the evaluation of the defense effectiveness also need the jointed efforts of international communities.

China achieved the first fly-by exploration of small celestial bodies in 2012 and plans to implement the mission of orbiting, landing on, and obtaining sampling returns from small celestial bodies in 2025. At present, the exploration mission of small bodies has entered the engineering development stage. The core technology needed to realize the orbiting of and landing on small celestial bodies lies in the orbital dynamics and control of spacecraft. The strong irregular shape of small celestial bodies causes their gravitational fields to be very different. This brings great challenges to the design and control of the orbit. Therefore, it is necessary to conduct a more comprehensive and in-depth study on related orbital mechanics.

Author Contributions: Conceptualization, Y.J. and Y.N.; methodology, Y.N.; validation, J.L., H.B. and Y.L.; formal analysis, Y.N.; investigation, Y.J. and Y.N.; resources, Y.J.; data curation, Y.N.; writing—original draft preparation, Y.J. and Y.N.; writing—review and editing, Y.L.; visualization, Y.N.; supervision, J.L. and H.B.; project administration, J.L. and H.B.; funding acquisition, Y.J. All authors have read and agreed to the published version of the manuscript.

Funding: This research was funded by the National Natural Science Foundation of China, grant number U21B2050.

Institutional Review Board Statement: Not applicable.

Informed Consent Statement: Not applicable.

Data Availability Statement: Not applicable.

Conflicts of Interest: The authors declare no conflict of interest.

References

1. Battin, R.H. *An Introduction to the Mathematics and Methods of Astrodynamics*, revised ed.; AIAA: Reston, VA, USA, 1999.
2. Breakwell, J.V.; Gillespie, R.W.; Ross, S. Researches in interplanetary transfer. *ARS J.* **1961**, *31*, 201–208. [CrossRef]
3. Clarke, V.C., Jr. Design of lunar and interplanetary ascent trajectories. *AIAA J.* **1963**, *1*, 1559–1567. [CrossRef]
4. Clarke, V.C., Jr.; Bollman, W.E.; Roth, R.Y.; Scholey, W.J.; Hamilton, T.W. *Design Parameters for Ballistic Inter Planetary Trajectories, Part I. One-Way Transfers to Mars and Venus*; JPL Technical Report No. 32–77; The Jet Propulsion Laboratory: La Cañada Flintridge, CA, USA, 1963.
5. Mickelwait, A.B.; Tompkins, E.H.; Park, R.A. Three-dimensional interplanetary trajectories. *IRE Trans. Mil. Electron.* **1959**, *MIL-3*, 149–159. [CrossRef]
6. Vasile, M.; Zazzera, F.B. Optimizing low-thrust and gravity assist maneuvers to design interplanetary trajectories. *J. Astronaut. Sci.* **2003**, *51*, 13–35. [CrossRef]
7. Vasile, M. A systematic-heuristic approach for space trajectory design. *Ann. N. Y. Acad. Sci.* **2004**, *1017*, 234–254. [CrossRef] [PubMed]
8. Kubota, T.; Kuroda, Y.; Kunii, Y.; Natakani, I. Small, light-Weight Rover "Micro5" for Lunar Exploration. *Acta Astronaut.* **2003**, *52*, 447–453. [CrossRef]
9. Zheng, Y.; Ouyang, Z.; Li, C.; Liu, J.; Zou, Y. China's Lunar Exploration Program: Present and future. *Planet. Space Sci.* **2008**, *56*, 881–886. [CrossRef]
10. Li, C.; Wang, C.; Wei, Y.; Lin, Y. China's present and future lunar exploration program. *Science* **2019**, *365*, 238–239. [CrossRef] [PubMed]
11. Rayman, M.D.; Varghese, P.; Lehman, D.H.; Livesay, L.L. Results from the Deep Space 1 Technology Validation Mission. *Acta Astronaut.* **2000**, *47*, 475–487. [CrossRef]
12. Jean, I.; Misra, A.; Ng, A.; Dutta, S. Orbital Dynamics of a Spacecraft in the Vicinity of a Binary Asteroid System: Impact of Solar Radiation Pressure on Orbital Motion. In Proceedings of the 2018 Space Flight Mechanics Meeting, Kissimmee, FL, USA, 8–12 January 2018.
13. Takahashi, Y. Gravity Field Characterization around Small Bodies. Ph.D. Thesis, University of Colorado at Boulder, Boulder, CO, USA, 2013.
14. Martin, R.G.; Livio, M. On the formation and evolution of asteroid belts and their potential significance for life. *Mon. Not. R. Astron. Soc. Lett.* **2013**, *428*, L11–L15. [CrossRef]
15. Lange, C.; Ho, T.M.; Grimm, C.D.; Grundman, J.T.; Ziach, C.; Lichtenheldt, R. Exploring Small Bodies: Nano- and micro lander options derived from the Mobile Asteroid Surface Scout. *Adv. Space Res.* **2018**, *62*, 2055–2083. [CrossRef]
16. Taylor, S.R. *Solar System Evolution: A New Perspective*; Cambridge University Press: Cambridge, UK, 2001; p. 460.
17. McSween, H., Jr.; Huss, G. *Cosmochemistry*; Cambridge University Press: Cambridge, UK, 2010.
18. Weidenschilling, S.J. Formation of Planetesimals and Accretion of the Terrestrial Planets. *Space Sci. Rev.* **2000**, *92*, 295–310. [CrossRef]
19. Chapman, C.R.; Morrison, D. Impacts on the Earth by asteroids and comets: Assessing the hazard. *Nature* **1994**, *367*, 33–40. [CrossRef]
20. Trigo-Rodríguez, J.M. *Asteroid Impact Risk: Impact Hazard from Asteroids and Comets*; Springer: Cham, Switzerland, 2022.
21. Morbidelli, A. *Modern Celestial Mechanics: Aspects of Solar System Dynamics*; Springer: La Turbie, France, 2002.

22. Shilnikov, L.P.; Shilnikov, A.L.; Turaev, D.V.; Chua, L.O. *Methods of Qualitative Theory in Nonlinear Dynamics*; World Scientific: Hackensack, NJ, USA, 2001.
23. Arnold, J.R. The Origin of Meteorites as Small Bodies. II. The Model. *Astrophys. J.* **1965**, *141*, 1536–1547. [CrossRef]
24. Wilson, L.; Keil, K.; Love, S.J. The Internal Structures and Densities of Asteroid. *Meteorit. Planet. Sci.* **1999**, *34*, 479–483. [CrossRef]
25. IAU Minor Planet Center. Latest Published Data [EB/OL]. Available online: https://minorplanetcenter.net/mpc/summary (accessed on 10 July 2021).
26. IAU Minor Planet Center. Discovery Circumstances: Numbered Minor Planets [EB/OL]. Available online: http://www.minorplanetcenter.net/iau/lists/NumberedMPs.html (accessed on 10 July 2021).
27. IAU Minor Planet Center. Minor Planet Names: Alphabetical List [EB/OL]. Available online: http://www.minorplanetcenter.net/iau/lists/MPNames.html (accessed on 10 July 2021).
28. Morbidelli, A.; Bottke, W.F., Jr.; Froeschl, C.; Michel, P. Origin and evolution of Near-earth Objects. In *Asteroids III*; Bottke, W.F., Cellino, A., Paolicchi, P., Binzel, R.P., Eds.; University of Arizona Press: Tucson, AZ, USA, 2002; pp. 409–422.
29. Ma, P.; Baoyin, H. Research on the Threat and Defense of Near-Earth Asteroid. *J. Deep Space Explor.* **2016**, *3*, 10–17. (In Chinese)
30. Jewitt, D. Kuiper Belt and Comets: An observational perspective. In *Trans-Neptunian Objects and Comets, Swiss Society for Astrophysics and Astronomy*; Springer: Berlin/Heidelberg, Germany, 2008.
31. Batygin, K.; Brown, M.E. Evidence for a Distant Giant Planet in the Solar System. *Astron. J.* **2016**, *151*, 22. [CrossRef]
32. Brown, M.E.; Batygin, K. Observational Constraints on the Orbit and Location of Planet Nine in the Outer Solar System. *Astrophys. J. Lett.* **2016**, *824*, L23. [CrossRef]
33. Beust, H. Orbital clustering of distant Kuiper Belt Objects by Hypothetical Planet 9. Secular or Resonant? *Astron. Astrophys.* **2016**, *590*, L2. [CrossRef]
34. Johnson, T.V.; Fanale, F.P. Optical properties of carbonaceous chondrites and their relationship to asteroids. *J. Geophys. Res.* **1973**, *78*, 8507–8518. [CrossRef]
35. Bus, S.J.; Binzel, R.P. Phase II of the Small Main-Belt Asteroid Spectroscopic Survey: A Feature-Based Taxonomy. *Icarus* **2002**, *158*, 146–177. [CrossRef]
36. Pieters, C.M.; McFadden, L.A. Meteorite and asteroid reflectance spectroscopy: Clues to early solar system processes. *Annu. Rev. Earth Planet. Sci.* **1994**, *22*, 457–497. [CrossRef]
37. Christou, A.A.; Wiegert, P. A Population of Main Belt Asteroids Co-Orbiting with Ceres and Vesta. *Icarus* **2012**, *217*, 27–42. [CrossRef]
38. Nesvorný, D.; Jedicke, R.; Whiteley, R.J.; Ivezi, E. Evidence for asteroid space weathering from the Sloan Digital Sky Survey. *Icarus* **2005**, *173*, 132–152. [CrossRef]
39. Vernazza, P.; Binzel, R.P.; Rossi, A.; Fulchignoni, M.; Birlan, M. Solar wind as the origin of rapid reddening of asteroid surfaces. *Nature* **2009**, *458*, 993–995. [CrossRef]
40. Umbach, R.; Jockers, K.; Geyer, E.H. Spatial Distribution of Neutral and Ionic Constituents in Comet P/Halley. *Astron. Astrophys. Suppl. Ser.* **1998**, *127*, 479–499I. [CrossRef]
41. Hsieh, H.H.; Jewitt, D. A population of comets in the Main Asteroid Belt. *Science* **2006**, *312*, 561–563. [CrossRef] [PubMed]
42. Küppers, M.; O'Rourke, L.; Bockelée-Morvan, D.; Zakharov, V.; Lee, S.; von Allmen, P.; Carry, B.; Teyssier, D.; Marston, A.; Muller, T.; et al. Localized sources of Water Vapour on the Dwarf Planet (1) Ceres. *Nature* **2014**, *505*, 525–527. [CrossRef] [PubMed]
43. Ogilvie, K.W.; Coplan, M.A.; Bochsler, P.; Geiss, J. Ion Composition Results During the International Cometary Explorer Encounter with Giacobini-Zinner. *Science* **1986**, *232*, 374–377. [CrossRef]
44. Smith, E.J.; Tsurutani, B.T.; Slavin, J.A.; Jones, D.E.; Siscoe, G.L.; Mendis, D.A. International Cometary Explorer Encounter with Giacobini-Zinner: Magnetic Field Observations. *Science* **1986**, *232*, 382–389. [CrossRef]
45. Von Rosenvinge, T.T.; Brandt, J.C.; Farquhar, R.W. The International Cometary Explorer Mission to Comet Giacobini-Zinner. *Science* **1986**, *232*, 353–356. [CrossRef]
46. Kissel, J.; Brownlee, D.E.; Büchler, K.; Clark, B.; Fechtig, H.; Grun, E.; Hornung, K.; Igenbergs, E.; Jessberger, E.; Krueger, F.; et al. Composition of Comet Halley Dust Particles from Giotto Observations. *Nature* **1986**, *321*, 336–337. [CrossRef]
47. Levasseur-Regourd, A.C.; Bertaux, J.L.; Dumont, R.; Festou, M.; Giese, R.; Giovane, F.; Lamy, P.; Blanc, J.M.; Liebaria, A.; Weinberg, J.L. Optical Probing of Comet Halley from the Giotto Spacecraft. *Nature* **1986**, *321*, 341–344. [CrossRef]
48. McDonnell, J.; Alexander, W.M.; Burton, W.M.; Bussoletti, E.; Clark, D.H.; Grard, R.; Grun, E.; Hanner, M.; Hughes, D.; Igenbergs, E.; et al. Dust Density and Mass Distribution near Comet Halley from Giotto Observations. *Nature* **1986**, *321*, 338–341. [CrossRef]
49. Belton, M.J.S.; Veverka, J.; Thomas, P.; Helfenstein, P.; Simonelli, D.; Chapman, C.; Davies, M.E.; Greeley, R.; Greenberg, R.; Head, J.; et al. Galileo encounter with 951 Gaspra: First pictures of an asteroid. *Science* **1992**, *257*, 1647–1652. [CrossRef]
50. Belton, M.J.S.; Chapman, C.R.; Thomas, P.C.; Davies, M.E.; Greenberg, R.; Klaasen, K.; Byrnes, D.; D'Amario, L.; Synnott, S.; Johnson, T.V.; et al. Bulk-Density of Asteroid 243-Ida from the Orbit of Its Satellite Dactyl. *Nature* **1995**, *374*, 785–788. [CrossRef]
51. Chapman, C.R.; Veverka, J.; Thomas, P.C.; Klaasen, K.; Belton, M.J.; Harch, A.; McEwen, A.; Johnson, T.V.; Helfenstein, P.; Davies, M.E.; et al. Discovery and Physical-Properties of Dactyl, a Satellite of Asteroid 243-IDA. *Nature* **1995**, *374*, 783–789. [CrossRef]
52. Veverka, J.; Belton, M.; Klaasen, K.; Chapman, C. Galileo's Encounter with 951 Gaspra: Overview. *Icarus* **1994**, *107*, 2–17. [CrossRef]
53. Veverka, J.; Thomas, P.; Harch, A.; Clark, B.; Bell, J.F., III; Carcich, B.; Cheng, A.; Joseph, J.; Chapman, C.; Malin, M.; et al. NEAR's Flyby of 253 Mathilde: Images of a C asteroid. *Science* **1997**, *278*, 2109–2114. [CrossRef]

54. Veverka, J.; Thomas, P.; Harch, A.; Clark, B.; Bell, J.F., III; Joseph, J.; Chapman, C.; Miller, J.K.; Cheng, A.; Carcich, B.; et al. NEAR at Eros: Imaging and Spectral Results. *Science* **2000**, *289*, 2088–2097. [CrossRef] [PubMed]
55. Yeomans, D.K.; Barriot, J.P.; Dunham, D.W.; Farquhar, R.W.; Giorgini, J.D.; Helfrich, C.E.; Konopliv, A.S.; McAdams, J.; Miller, J.K.; Owen, W.M.; et al. Estimating the Mass of Asteroid 253 Mathilde from tracking Data During the NEAR Flyby. *Science* **1997**, *278*, 2106–2109. [CrossRef]
56. Yeomans, D.K.; Antreasian, P.G.; Barriot, J.P.; Chesley, S.R.; Dunham, D.W.; Farquhar, R.W.; Giorgini, J.D.; Helfrich, C.E.; Konopliv, A.S.; McAdams, J.V.; et al. Radio Science Results During the NEAR-Shoemaker Spacecraft Rendezvous with Eros. *Science* **2000**, *289*, 2085–2088. [CrossRef]
57. Zuber, M.T.; Smith, D.E.; Cheng, A.F.; Garvin, J.B.; Aharonson, O.; Cole, T.D.; Dunn, P.J.; Guo, Y.; Lemoine, F.G.; Neumann, G.A.; et al. The Shape of 433 Eros from the NEAR-Shoemaker Laser Rangefinder. *Science* **2000**, *289*, 2097–2101. [CrossRef]
58. Burton, M.E.; Buratti, B.; Matson, D.L.; Lebreton, J.P. The Cassini/Huygens Venus and Earth flybys: An Overview of Operations and Results. *J. Geophys. Res. Space Phys.* **2001**, *106*, 30099–30107. [CrossRef]
59. Farnham, T.L.; Cochran, A.L. A McDonald Observatory Study of Comet 19P/Borrelly: Placing the Deep Space 1 Observations into a Broader Context. *Icarus* **2002**, *160*, 398–418. [CrossRef]
60. Kerr, R.A. Deep Space 1 Traces Braille Back to Vesta. *Science* **1999**, *285*, 993–994. [CrossRef]
61. Soderblom, L.A.; Boice, D.C.; Britt, D.; Brown, R.H.; Buratti, B.J.; Hicks, J.; Hillier, J.; Lee, R.; Meler, R.; Nelson, J.; et al. Deep Space 1 MICAS Observations of 9969 Braille. *Bull. Am. Astron. Soc.* **1999**, *31*, 1127.
62. Soderblom, L.A.; Becker, T.L.; Bennett, G.; Boice, D.C.; Britt, D.T.; Brown, R.H.; Buratti, B.J.; Isbell, C.; Giese, B.; Hare, T.; et al. Observations of Comet 19P/Borrelly by the Miniature Integrated Camera and Spectrometer Aboard Deep Space 1. *Science* **2002**, *296*, 1087–1091. [CrossRef]
63. Belton, M.J.; Meech, K.J.; Chesley, S.; Pittchova, J.; Carcich, B.; Drahus, M.; Harris, A.; Gillam, S.; Veverka, J.; Mastrodemos, N.; et al. Stardust-NExT, Deep Impact, and the Accelerating Spin of 9P/Tempel 1. *Icarus* **2011**, *213*, 345–368. [CrossRef]
64. Brownlee, D.E.; Horz, F.; Newburn, R.L.; Zolensky, M.; Duxbury, T.C.; Sandford, S.; Sekanina, Z.; Tsou, P.; Hanner, M.S.; Clark, B.C.; et al. Surface of Young Jupiter Family Comet 81P/Wild 2: View from the Stardust Spacecraft. *Science* **2004**, *304*, 1765–1769. [CrossRef]
65. Duxbury, T.C. *The Exploration of Asteroid Annefrank by STARDUST*; Asteroids Comets Meteors: Berlin, Germany, 2002.
66. Duxbury, T.C. *The Flyby of Asteroid Annefrank by STARDUST for Wild2 Testing*; Asteroids Comets Meteors: Berlin, Germany, 2002.
67. Farquhar, R.; Kawaguchi, J.I.; Russell, C.; Schwehm, G.; Veverka, J.; Yeomans, D. Spacecraft Exploration of Asteroids: The 2001 Perspective. In *Asteroids III*; University of Arizona Press: Tucson, AZ, USA, 2002; pp. 367–376.
68. Ishiguro, M.; Kwon, S.M.; Sarugaku, Y.; Hasegawa, S.; Usui, F.; Nishiura, S.; Nakada, Y.; Yano, H. Discovery of the Dust Trail of the Stardust Comet Sample Return Mission Target: 81P/Wild 2. *Astrophys. J. Lett.* **2003**, *589*, L101. [CrossRef]
69. Ishii, H.A.; Bradley, J.P.; Dai, Z.R.; Chi, M.; Kearsley, A.T.; Burchell, M.J.; Browning, N.D. Comparison of Comet 81P/Wild 2 Dust with Interplanetary Dust from Comets. *Science* **2008**, *319*, 447–450. [CrossRef]
70. Kissel, J.; Krueger, F.R.; Silén, J.; Clark, B.C. The Cometary and Interstellar Dust Analyzer at Comet 81P/Wild 2. *Science* **2004**, *304*, 1775–1776. [CrossRef]
71. Sekanina, Z.; Brownlee, D.E.; Economou, T.E.; Tuzzolino, A.J.; Green, S.F. Modeling the Nucleus and Jets of Comet 81P/Wild 2 Based on the Stardust Encounter Data. *Science* **2004**, *304*, 1769–1774. [CrossRef]
72. Abe, S.; Mukai, T.; Hirata, N.; Barnouin-Jha, O.S.; Cheng, A.F.; Demura, H.; Gaskell, R.W.; Hashimoto, T.; Hiraoka, K.; Honda, T. Mass and local Topography Measurements of Itokawa by Hayabusa. *Science* **2006**, *312*, 1345–1347. [CrossRef]
73. Fujiwara, A.; Kawaguchi, J.; Yeomans, D.K.; Abel, M.; Mukai, T.; Okada, T.; Saito, J.; Yano, H.; Yoshikawa, M.; Scheeres, D.J. The rubble-Pile Asteroid Itokawa as Observed by Hayabusa. *Science* **2006**, *312*, 1330–1334. [CrossRef]
74. Kaasalainen, M.; Kwiatkowski, T.; Abe, M.; Piironen, J.; Nakamura, T.; Ohba, Y.; Dermawan, B.; Farnham, T.; Colas, F.; Lowry, S. CCD Photometry and Model of MUSES-C Target (25143) 1998 SF36. *Astron. Astrophys.* **2003**, *405*, L29–L32. [CrossRef]
75. Saito, J.; Miyamoto, H.; Nakamura, R.; Ishiguro, M.; Michikami, T.; Nakamura, A.M.; Demrua, H.; Sasaki, S.; Hirata, N.; Honda, C.; et al. Detailed Images of Asteroid 25143 Itokawa from Hayabusa. *Science* **2006**, *312*, 1341–1344. [CrossRef]
76. Yano, H.; Kubota, T.; Miyamoto, H.; Okada, T.; Scheeres, D.J.; Takagi, Y.; Yoshida, K.; Abe, M.; Abe, S.; Barnouin-Jha, O.; et al. Touchdown of the Hayabusa Spacecraft at the Muses Sea on Itokawa. *Science* **2006**, *312*, 1350–1353. [CrossRef]
77. Barucci, M.A.; Fulchignoni, M.; Rossi, A. Rosetta Asteroid Targets: 2867 Steins and 21 Lutetia. *Space Sci. Rev.* **2007**, *128*, 67–78. [CrossRef]
78. Barucci, M.A.; Fulchignoni, M.; Fornasier, S.; Dotto, E.; Vernazza, P.; Birlan, M.; Binzel, R.; Carvano, J.; Merlin, F.; Barbieri, C.; et al. Asteroid Target Selection for the New Rosetta Mission Baseline: 21 Lutetia and 2867 Steins. *Astron. Astrophys.* **2005**, *430*, 313–317. [CrossRef]
79. Glassmeier, K.H.; Boehnhardt, H.; Koschny, D.; Kuhrt, E.; Richter, I. The Rosetta Mission: Flying Towards the Origin of the Solar System. *Space Sci. Rev.* **2007**, *128*, 1–21. [CrossRef]
80. Scheeres, D.J.; Marzari, F.; Tomasella, L.; Vanzani, V. ROSETTA Mission: Satellite Orbits Around a Cometary Nucleus. *Planet. Space Sci.* **1998**, *46*, 649–671. [CrossRef]
81. Ulamec, S.; Espinasse, S.; Feuerbacher, B.; Hilchenhach, M.; Moura, D.; Rosenbauer, H.; Scheuerle, H.; Willnecker, R. Rosetta Lander—Philae: Implications of an Alternative Mission. *Acta Astronaut.* **2006**, *58*, 435–441. [CrossRef]

82. A'Hearn, M.F.; Belton, M.J.S.; Delamere, W.A.; Kissel, J.; Klaasen, K.; McFadden, L.; Meech, K.; Melosh, H.; Schultz, P.; Sunshine, J.; et al. Deep Impact: Excavating Comet Tempel 1. *Science* **2005**, *310*, 258–264. [CrossRef] [PubMed]
83. Harker, D.E.; Woodward, C.E.; Wooden, D.H. The Dust Grains from 9P/Tempel 1 Before and After The Encounter with Deep Impact. *Science* **2005**, *310*, 278–280. [CrossRef]
84. Lisse, C.M.; Van Cleve, J.; Adams, A.C.; Ahearn, M.F.; Ferhandez, Y.R.; Farham, T.L.; Armus, L.; Grillmarir, C.J.; Ingalls, J.; Sunshine, J.M. Spitzer Spectral Observations of the Deep Impact Ejecta. *Science* **2006**, *313*, 635–640. [CrossRef]
85. A'Hearn, M.F.; Belton, M.J.; Delamere, W.A.; Feaga, L.M.; Hampton, D.; Kissel, J.; Klaasen, K.P.; McFadden, L.A.; Meech, K.J.; Melosh, H.J.; et al. EPOXI at Comet Hartley 2. *Science* **2011**, *332*, 1396–1400. [CrossRef]
86. Meech, K.J.; A'Hearn, M.F.; Adams, J.A.; Bacci, P.; Bai, J.; Barrera, L.; Battelino, M.; Bauer, J.M.; Becklin, E.; Bhatt, B.; et al. EPOXI: Comet 103P/Hartley 2 Observations from a Worldwide Campaign. *Astrophys. J. Lett.* **2011**, *734*, L1. [CrossRef]
87. Stern, S.A. The New Horizons Pluto Kuiper belt mission: An overview with historical context. In *New Horizons*; Springer: Los Angeles, CA, USA, 2009.
88. Rayman, M.D.; Fraschetti, T.C.; Raymond, C.A.; Russell, C. Dawn: A Mission in Development for Exploration of Main Belt Asteroids Vesta and Ceres. *Acta Astronaut.* **2006**, *58*, 605–616. [CrossRef]
89. Reddy, V.; Nathues, A.; Le Corre, L.; Sierks, H.; Li, J.; Gaskell, R.; McCoy, T.; Beck, A.W.; Schroder, S.E.; Pieters, C.M.; et al. Color and Albedo Heterogeneity of Vesta from Dawn. *Science* **2012**, *336*, 700–704. [CrossRef] [PubMed]
90. Russell, C.T.; Capaccioni, F.; Coradini, A.; Sanctis, M.C.; Feldman, W.C.; Jaumann, R.; Keller, H.U.; McCord, T.B.; McFadden, L.A.; Mottola, S.; et al. Dawn Mission to Vesta and Ceres. *Earth Moon Planets* **2007**, *101*, 65–91. [CrossRef]
91. Russell, C.T.; Raymond, C.A.; Coradini, A.; McSween, H.Y.; Zuber, M.T.; Nathues, A.; Sanctis, M.C.D.; Jaumann, R.; Konopliv, A.S.; Preusker, F. Dawn at Vesta: Testing the Protoplanetary Paradigm. *Science* **2012**, *336*, 685–686. [CrossRef] [PubMed]
92. Huang, J.; Ji, J.; Ye, P.; Wang, X.; Yan, J.; Meng, L.; Wang, S.; Li, C.; Li, Y.; Qiao, D.; et al. The Ginger-Shaped Asteroid 4179 Toutatis: New Observations from a Successful Flyby of Chang'e-2. *Sci. Rep.* **2013**, *3*, 3411. [CrossRef]
93. Zhao, Y.; Wang, S.; Hu, S.; Ji, J. A Research on the Imaging Strategy and Imaging Simulation of Toutatis in the Chang'e-2 Flyby Mission. *Chin. Astron. Astrophys.* **2014**, *38*, 163–171.
94. Zou, X.; Li, C.; Liu, J.; Wang, W.; Li, H.; Ping, J. The Preliminary Analysis of the 4179 Toutatis Snapshots of the Chang'E-2 Flyby. *Icarus* **2014**, *229*, 348–354. [CrossRef]
95. Hamilton, D.P.; Burns, J.A. Orbital Stability Zones About Asteroids: II. The Destabilizing Effects of Eccentric Orbits and of Solar Radiation. *Icarus* **1992**, *96*, 43–64. [CrossRef]
96. Yu, Y. Research on Orbital Dynamics in Gravitational Field of Small Celestial Bodies. Ph.D. Thesis, Tsinghua University, Beijing, China, 2014.
97. Riaguas, A.; Elipe, A.; López-Moratalla, T. Non-Linear Stability of the Equilibria in the Gravity Field of a Finite Straight Segment. *Celest. Mech. Dyn. Astron.* **2001**, *81*, 235–248. [CrossRef]
98. Broucke, R.; Elipe, A. The Dynamics of Orbits in a Potential Field of a Solid Circular Ring. *Regul. Chaotic Dyn.* **2005**, *10*, 129–143. [CrossRef]
99. Romanov, V.A.; Doedel, E.J. Periodic Orbits Associated with the Libration Points of the Homogeneous Rotating Gravitating Triaxial Ellipsoid. *Int. J. Bifurc. Chaos* **2012**, *22*, 1230035. [CrossRef]
100. Zeng, X.; Jiang, F.; Li, J.; Baoyin, H. Study on the Connection Between the Rotating Mass Dipole and Natural Elongated Bodies. *Astrophys. Space Sci.* **2015**, *356*, 29–42. [CrossRef]
101. Liu, L. *Spacecraft Orbit Theory*; National Defense Industry Press: Beijing, China, 2000. (In Chinese)
102. Miller, J.K.; Konopliv, A.S.; Antreasian, P.G.; Bordi, J.J.; Chesley, S.; Helfrich, C.E.; Scheeres, D.J.; Owen, W.M.; Wang, T.C.; Williams, B.G.; et al. Determination of Shape, Gravity, and Rotational State of Asteroid 433 Eros. *Icarus* **2002**, *155*, 3–17. [CrossRef]
103. Takahashi, Y.; Grebow, D.; Kennedy, B.; Rambaux, N.; Castillo-Rogez, J. Forward Modeling of Ceres' Gravity Field for Planetary Protection Assessment. In Proceedings of the AIAA/AAS Astrodynamics Specialist Conference, Long Beach, CA, USA, 13–16 September 2016; AIAA: Reston, VA, USA, 2016; p. 5262.
104. Takahashi, Y.; Bradley, N.; Kennedy, B. Determination of Celestial Body Principal Axes via Gravity Field Estimation. *J. Guid. Control Dyn.* **2017**, *40*, 3050–3060. [CrossRef]
105. Romain, G.; Jean-Pierre, B. Ellipsoidal Harmonic Expansions of the Gravitational Potential: Theory and Application. *Celest. Mech. Dyn. Astron.* **2001**, *79*, 235–275. [CrossRef]
106. Rossi, A.; Marzari, F.; Farinella, P. Orbital Evolution Around Irregular Bodies. *Earth Planets Space* **1999**, *51*, 1173–1180. [CrossRef]
107. Hobson, E.W. *The Theory of Spherical and Ellipsoidal Harmonics*; Cambridge University Press: Cambridge, UK, 1931.
108. Pick, M.; Picha, J.; Vyskocil, V. *Theory of the Earth's Gravity Field*; Elsevier Scientific Pub Co.: Amsterdam, The Netherlands, 1973.
109. Dechambre, D.; Scheeres, D.J. Transformation of Spherical Harmonic Coefficients to Ellipsoidal Harmonic Coefficients. *Astron. Astrophys.* **2002**, *387*, 1114–1122. [CrossRef]
110. Garmier, R.; Barriot, J.P.; Konopliv, A.S.; Yeomans, D.K. Modeling of the Eros gravity Field as an Ellipsoidal Harmonic Expansion from the NEAR Doppler Tracking Data. *Geophys. Res. Lett.* **2002**, *29*, 721–723. [CrossRef]
111. Britt, D.T.; Yeomans, D.; Housen, K.; Consolmagno, G. Asteroid Density, Porosity, and Structure. In *Asteroids III*; University of Arizona Press: Tucson, AZ, USA, 2002; pp. 485–500.
112. Geissler, P.; Petit, J.M.; Durda, D.D.; Greenberg, R.; Bottke, W.; Nolan, M.; Moore, J. Erosion and Ejecta Reaccretion on 243 Ida and Its Moon. *Icarus* **1996**, *120*, 140–157. [CrossRef]

113. MacMillan, W.D. *The Theory of the Potential*; McGraw-Hill: New York, NY, USA, 1930.
114. Waldvogel, J. The Newtonian Potential of Homogeneous Polyhedra. *Z. Angew. Math. Phys. ZAMP* **1979**, *30*, 388–398. [CrossRef]
115. Werner, R.A. The Gravitational Potential of a Homogeneous Polyhedron or Don't Cut Corners. *Celest. Mech. Dyn. Astron.* **1994**, *59*, 253–278. [CrossRef]
116. Werner, R.A. *On the Gravity Field of Irregularly Shaped Celestial Bodies*; The University of Texas at Austin: Austin, TX, USA, 1996.
117. Werner, R.A.; Scheeres, D.J. Exterior Gravitation of a Polyhedron Derived and Compared with Harmonic and Mascon Gravitation Representations of Asteroid 4769 Castalia. *Celest. Mech. Dyn. Astron.* **1996**, *65*, 313–344. [CrossRef]
118. Mirtich, B. Fast and Accurate Computation of Polyhedral Mass Properties. *J. Graph. Tools* **1996**, *1*, 31–50. [CrossRef]
119. Nolan, M.C.; Magri, C.; Howell, E.S.; Benner, L.A.; Giorgini, J.D.; Hergenrother, C.W.; Scheeres, D.J.; Hudson, R.S.; Ostro, S.J.; Lauretta, D.S.; et al. Shape model and surface properties of the OSIRIS-REx target Asteroid (101955) Bennu from radar and lightcurve observations. *Icarus* **2013**, *226*, 629–640. [CrossRef]
120. Zhuravlev, S.G. About the Stability of the Libration Points of a Rotating Triaxial Ellipsoid in a Degenerate Case. *Celest. Mech.* **1973**, *8*, 75–84. [CrossRef]
121. Scheeres, D.J. Dynamics about Uniformly Rotating Triaxial Ellipsoids: Applications to Asteroids. *Icarus* **1994**, *110*, 225–238. [CrossRef]
122. Scheeres, D.J.; Ostro, S.J.; Hudson, R.S.; Werner, R.A. Orbits Close to Asteroid 4769 Castalia. *Icarus* **1996**, *121*, 67–87. [CrossRef]
123. Elipe, A.; Lara, M. A Simple Model for the Chaotic Motion Around (433) Eros. *J. Astronaut. Sci.* **2003**, *51*, 391–404. [CrossRef]
124. Scheeres, D.; Broschart, S.; Ostro, S.; Benner, L. The Dynamical Environment About Asteroid 25143 Itokawa, Target of the Hayabusa Mission. In Proceedings of the AIAA/AAS Astrodynamics Specialist Conference and Exhibit, Providence, RI, USA, 16–19 August 2004; AIAA: Reston, VA, USA, 2004; p. 4864.
125. Mondelo, J.M.; Broschart, S.; Villac, B. Dynamical Analysis of 1:1 Resonances Near Asteroids-Application to Vesta. In Proceedings of the AIAA/AAS Astrodynamics Specialist Conference, Toronto, ON, Canada, 2–5 August 2010; AIAA: Reston, VA, USA, 2010; p. 8373.
126. Liu, X.; Baoyin, H.; Ma, X. Equilibria, Periodic Orbits Around Equilibria, and Heteroclinic Connections in the Gravity Field of a Rotating Homogeneous Cube. *Astrophys. Space Sci.* **2011**, 333, 409–418. [CrossRef]
127. Yu, Y.; Baoyin, H. Orbital Dynamics in the Vicinity of Asteroid 216 Kleopatra. *Astron. J.* **2012**, *143*, 62. [CrossRef]
128. Scheeres, D.J. Orbit Mechanics About Asteroids and Comets. *J. Guid. Control Dyn.* **2012**, *35*, 987. [CrossRef]
129. Jiang, Y.; Baoyin, H.; Li, J.; Li, H. Orbits and Manifolds near the Equilibrium Points Around a Rotating Asteroid. *Astrophys. Space Sci.* **2014**, *349*, 83–106. [CrossRef]
130. Wang, X.; Jiang, Y.; Gong, S. Analysis of the Potential Field and Equilibrium Points of Irregular-shaped Minor Celestial Bodies. *Astrophys. Space Sci.* **2014**, *353*, 105–121. [CrossRef]
131. Jiang, Y.; Yu, Y.; Baoyin, H. Topological Classifications and Bifurcations of Periodic Orbits in the Potential Field of Highly Irregular-Shaped Celestial Bodies. *Nonlinear Dyn.* **2015**, *81*, 119–140. [CrossRef]
132. Wang, X.; Li, J.; Gong, S. Bifurcation of Equilibrium Points in the Potential Field of Asteroid 101955 Bennu. *Mon. Not. R. Astron. Soc.* **2016**, *455*, 3725–3734. [CrossRef]
133. Scheeres, D.J. Analysis of Orbital Motion Around 433 Eros. *J. Astronaut. Sci.* **1995**, *43*, 427–452.
134. Scheeres, D.J.; Ostro, S.J.; Hudson, R.S.; Dejong, E.M.; Suzuki, S. Dynamics of Orbits Close to Asteroid 4179 Toutatis. *Icarus* **1998**, *132*, 53–79. [CrossRef]
135. Antreasian, P.; Helfrich, C.; Miller, J.; Owen, W.; Williams, B.; Yeomans, D.; Giorgini, J.; Dunham, D.; Farquhar, R.; McAdams, J. Preliminary Considerations for NEAR's Low-Altitude Passes and Landing Operations at 433 Eros. In Proceedings of the AIAA/AAS Astrodynamics Specialist Conference and Exhibit, Boston, MA, USA, 10–12 August 1998; AIAA: Reston, VA, USA, 1998; p. 4397.
136. Scheeres, D.J.; Williams, B.G.; Miller, J.K. Evaluation of the Dynamic Environment of an Asteroid: Applications to 433 Eros. *J. Guid. Control Dyn.* **2000**, *23*, 466–479. [CrossRef]
137. Shang, H.; Wu, X.; Qin, X.; Qiao, D. Periodic motion near non-principal-axis rotation asteroids. *Mon. Not. R. Astron. Soc.* **2017**, *471*, 3234–3244. [CrossRef]
138. Scheeres, D.J.; Hu, W. Secular Motion in a 2nd Degree and Order-Gravity Field with No Rotation. *Celest. Mech. Dyn. Astron.* **2001**, *79*, 183–200. [CrossRef]
139. Hu, W.; Scheeres, D.J. Spacecraft Motion About Slowly Rotating Asteroids. *J. Guid. Control Dyn.* **2002**, *25*, 765–779. [CrossRef]
140. Hu, W.; Scheeres, D.J. Numerical Determination of Stability Regions for Orbital Motion in Uniformly Rotating Second Degree and Order Gravity Fields. *Planet. Space Sci.* **2004**, *52*, 685–692. [CrossRef]
141. Hu, W.D.; Scheeres, D.J. Periodic Orbits in Rotating Second Degree and Order Gravity Fields. *Chin. J. Astron. Astrophys.* **2008**, *8*, 108. [CrossRef]
142. Hu, W.D.; Scheeres, D.J. Averaging Analyses for Spacecraft Orbital Motions Around Asteroids. *Acta Mech. Sin.* **2014**, *30*, 295–300. [CrossRef]
143. Scheeres, D.J. Orbital Mechanics About Small Bodies. *Acta Astronaut.* **2012**, *72*, 1–14. [CrossRef]
144. Yu, Y.; Baoyin, H. Generating Families of 3D Periodic Orbits About Asteroids. *Mon. Not. R. Astron. Soc.* **2012**, *427*, 872–881. [CrossRef]
145. Marsden, J.E.; Ratiu, T.S. *Introduction to Mechanics and Symmetry*; Springer: New York, NY, USA, 1999.

146. Yu, Y.; Baoyin, H.; Jiang, Y. Constructing the Natural Families of Periodic Orbits near Irregular Bodies. *Mon. Not. R. Astron. Soc.* **2015**, *453*, 3269–3277. [CrossRef]
147. Wang, Y.; Xu, S. Non-equatorial equilibrium points around an asteroid with gravitational orbit-attitude coupling perturbation. *Astrodynamics* **2020**, *4*, 1–16. [CrossRef]
148. Li, X.; Scheeres, D.J.; Qiao, D.; Liu, Z. Geophysical and orbital environments of asteroid 469219 2016 HO_3. *Astrodynamics* **2022**, *2*, 1–21. [CrossRef]
149. Liang, Y.; Xu, M.; Xu, S. Homoclinic/Heteroclinic Connections of Equilibria and Periodic Orbits of Contact Binary Asteroids. *J. Guid. Control Dyn.* **2017**, *40*, 2042–2061. [CrossRef]
150. Hou, X.; Xin, X. A note on the full two-body problem and related restricted full three body problem. *Astrodynamics* **2018**, *2*, 39–52. [CrossRef]
151. Shi, Y.; Wang, Y.; Xu, S. Equilibrium Points and Associated Periodic Orbits in the Gravity of Binary Asteroid Systems: (66391) 1999 KW4 as an Example. *Celest. Mech. Dyn. Astron.* **2018**, *130*, 32. [CrossRef]
152. Wang, Y.; Fu, T. Semi-analytical orbital dynamics around the primary of a binary asteroid system. *Mon. Not. R. Astron. Soc.* **2020**, *495*, 3307–3322. [CrossRef]
153. Richardson, D.C.; Leinhardt, Z.M.; Melosh, H.J.; Bottke, W.F. Gravitational aggregates: Evidence and evolution. *Asteroids III* **2002**, *1*, 501–515.
154. Jiang, Y.; Zhang, Y.; Baoyin, H.; Li, J. Dynamical configurations of celestial systems comprised of multiple irregular bodies. *Astrophys. Space Sci.* **2016**, *361*, 306. [CrossRef]
155. Valvano, G.; Winter, O.C.; Sfair, R.; Oliverira, R.M.; Borderes-Motta, G. 2001 SN_{263}—the contribution of their irregular shapes on the neighbourhood dynamics. *Mon. Not. R. Astron. Soc.* **2022**, *515*, 606–616. [CrossRef]
156. Wang, X. Research on Dynamics near the Equilibrium Points of Irregular Small Celestial Bodies. Ph.D. Thesis, Tsinghua University, Beijing, China, 2017.
157. Chanut, T.G.G.; Winter, O.C.; Tsuchida, M. 3D Stability Orbits Close to 433 Eros Using an Effective Polyhedral Model Method. *Mon. Not. R. Astron. Soc.* **2014**, *438*, 2672–2682. [CrossRef]
158. Chanut, T.G.G.; Winter, O.C.; Amarante, A.; Araujo, N.C. 3D Plausible Orbital Stability Close to Asteroid (216) Kleopatra. *Mon. Not. R. Astron. Soc.* **2015**, *452*, 1316–1327. [CrossRef]
159. Zhao, Z.; Chen, L. Chemical Chaos in Enzyme Kinetics. *Nonlinear Dyn.* **2009**, *57*, 135–142. [CrossRef]
160. Farshidianfar, A.; Saghafi, A. Global Bifurcation and Chaos Analysis in Nonlinear Vibration of Spur Gear Systems. *Nonlinear Dyn.* **2014**, *75*, 783–806. [CrossRef]
161. Nordstrøm Jensen, C.; True, H. On a New Route to Chaos in Railway Dynamics. *Nonlinear Dyn.* **1997**, *13*, 117–129. [CrossRef]
162. Gao, Q.; Ma, J. Chaos and Hopf Bifurcation of a Finance System. *Nonlinear Dyn.* **2009**, *58*, 209–216. [CrossRef]
163. Hu, W.; Deng, Z.; Wang, B.; Ouyang, H. Chaos in an Embedded Single-Walled Carbon Nanotube. *Nonlinear Dyn.* **2013**, *72*, 389–398. [CrossRef]
164. Todorović, N.; Wu, D.; Rosengren, A.J. The Arches of Chaos in the Solar System. *Sci. Adv.* **2020**, *48*, 1313. [CrossRef]
165. Chirikov, B.V. A Universal Instability of Many–Dimensional Oscillator Systems. *Phys. Rep.* **1979**, *52*, 263–379. [CrossRef]
166. Lindner, J.F.; Lynn, J.; King, F.W.; Logue, A. Order and Chaos in the Rotation and Revolution of a Line Segment and a Point Mass. *Phys. Rev. E* **2010**, *81*, 036208. [CrossRef]
167. Makarov, V.V.; Goldin, A.; Tkachenko, A.V.; Veras, D.; Noyelles, B. Chaos over order: Mapping 3D rotation of triaxial asteroids and minor planets. *Mon. Not. R. Astron. Soc.* **2022**, *513*, 2076–2087. [CrossRef]
168. Jafari Nadoushan, M.; Assadian, N. Widespread Chaos in Rotation of the Secondary Asteroid in a Binary System. *Nonlinear Dyn.* **2015**, *81*, 2031–2042. [CrossRef]
169. Ćuk, M.; Nesvorný, D. Orbital Evolution of Small Binary Asteroids. *Icarus* **2010**, *207*, 732–743. [CrossRef]
170. Benettin, G.; Galgani, L.; Giorgilli, A.; Strelcyn, J.M. Lyapunov Characteristic Exponents for Smooth Dynamical Systems and for Hamiltonian Systems; a Method for Computing All of Them. Part 1: Theory. *Meccanica* **1980**, *15*, 9–30. [CrossRef]
171. Froeschlé, C.; Lega, E.; Gonczi, R. Fast Lyapunov Indicators. Application to Asteroidal Motion. *Celest. Mech. Dyn. Astron.* **1997**, *67*, 41–62. [CrossRef]
172. Froeschlé, C.; Lega, E. On the Structure of symplectic Mappings. The fast Lyapunov Indicator: A Very Sensitive Tool. In *New Developments in the Dynamics of Planetary Systems*; Springer: Dordrecht, The Netherlands, 2001; pp. 167–199.
173. Fouchard, M.; Lega, E.; Froeschlé, C.; Froeschlé, C. On the Relationship between fast Lyapunov Indicator and Periodic Orbits for Continuous Flows. *Celest. Mech. Dyn. Astron.* **2002**, *83*, 205–222. [CrossRef]
174. Ni, Y.; Turitsyn, K.; Baoyin, H.; Li, J. Entropy Method of Measuring and Evaluating Periodicity of Quasi-Periodic Trajectories. *Sci. China Phys. Mech. Astron.* **2018**, *61*, 064511. [CrossRef]
175. Levasseur-Regourd, A.C.; Rotundi, A.; Bentley, M.S.; Corte, V.D.; Renard, J.B. Physical properties of dust particles in cometary comae: From clues to evidence with the Rosetta mission. *Science* **2006**, *314*, 1716–1719.
176. Ishiguro, M.; Hanayama, H.; Hasegawa, S.; Sarugaku, Y.; Nakamura, A.M. Interpretation of (596) Scheila's Triple Dust Tails. *Astrophys. J. Lett.* **2011**, *741*, L24–L28. [CrossRef]
177. Golubov, O.; Scheeres, D.J.; Krugly, Y.N. A 3-dimensional model of tangential yorp. *Astrophys. J.* **2014**, *794*, 1–9. [CrossRef]
178. Michel, P.; Benz, W.; Tanga, P. Collisions and Gravitational Reaccumulation: Forming Asteroid Families and Satellites. *Science* **2001**, *294*, 1696–1700. [CrossRef]

179. Asphaug, E.; Ostro, S.J.; Hudson, R.S.; Scheeres, D.; Benz, W. Disruption of Kilometre-Sized Asteroids by Energetic Collisions. *Nature* **1998**, *393*, 437–440. [CrossRef]
180. Jewitt, D.; Agarwal, J.; Li, J.; Weaver, H.; Mutcher, M.; Larson, S. Disintegrating Asteroid P/2013 R3. *Astrophys. J. Lett.* **2014**, *784*, L8. [CrossRef]
181. Bellerose, J.; Girard, A.; Scheeres, D.J. Dynamics and Control of Surface Exploration Robots on Asteroids. *Lect. Notes Control Inf. Sci.* **2009**, *381*, 135–150.
182. Guibout, V.; Scheeres, D.J. Stability of Surface Motion on Rotating Ellipsoids. *Celest. Mech. Dyn. Astron.* **2003**, *87*, 263–290. [CrossRef]
183. Bellerose, J.; Scheeres, D. Dynamics and Control for Surface Exploration of Small Bodies. In Proceedings of the AIAA/AAS Astrodynamics Specialist Conference and Exhibit, Honolulu, HI, USA, 18–21 August 2008; AIAA: Reston, VA, USA, 2008.
184. Liu, X.; Baoyin, H.; Ma, X. Dynamics of Surface Motion on a Rotating Massive Homogeneous Body. *Sci. China Phys. Mech. Astron.* **2013**, *56*, 818–829. [CrossRef]
185. Jiang, Y.; Zhang, Y.; Baoyin, H. Surface Motion Relative to the Irregular Celestial Bodies. *Planet. Space Sci.* **2016**, *127*, 33–43. [CrossRef]
186. Yu, Y.; Baoyin, H. Modeling of Migrating Grains on Asteroid's Surface. *Astrophys. Space Sci.* **2014**, *355*, 43–56. [CrossRef]
187. Yu, Y.; Baoyin, H.X. Routing the Asteroid Surface Vehicle with Detailed Mechanics. *Acta Mech. Sin.* **2014**, *30*, 301–309. [CrossRef]
188. Fahnestock, E.G.; Scheeres, D.J. Binary Asteroid Orbit Expansion due to Continued YORP Spin-up of the Primary and Primary Surface Particle Motion. *Icarus* **2009**, *201*, 135–152. [CrossRef]
189. Oberc, P. Electrostatic and Rotational Ejection of Dust Particles from a Disintegrating Cometary Aggregate. *Planet. Space Sci.* **1997**, *45*, 221–228. [CrossRef]
190. Morbidelli, A.; Chambers, J.; Lunine, J.I.; Petti, J.M.; Robert, F.; Valsecchi, G.B. Source Regions and Timescales for the Delivery of Water to the Earth. *Meteorit. Planet. Sci.* **2000**, *35*, 1309–1320. [CrossRef]
191. Mottl, M.J.; Glazer, B.T.; Kaiser, R.I.; Meech, K. Water and Astrobiology. *Geochemistry* **2007**, *67*, 253–282. [CrossRef]
192. Kanno, A. The First Detection of Water Absorption on a D Type Asteroid. *Geophys. Res. Lett.* **2003**, *30*, 1909. [CrossRef]
193. Treiman, A.H.; Lanzirotti, A.; Xirouchakis, D. Ancient Water on Asteroid 4 Vesta: Evidence from a Quartz Veinlet in the Serra de Magé Eucrite Meteorite. *Earth Planet. Sci. Lett.* **2004**, *219*, 189–199. [CrossRef]
194. Ray, D.; Misra, S. Contrasting Aerodynamic Morphology and Geochemistry of Impact Spherules from Lonar Crater, India: Some Insights into Their Cooling History. *Earth Moon Planets* **2014**, *114*, 59–86. [CrossRef]
195. Patil, A.; Malhotra, A.; Patra, A.K.; Prasad, T.R.; Mathews, J.D. Evidence of Meteoroid Fragmentation in Specular Trail Echoes Observed Using Gadanki MST Radar. *Earth Moon Planets* **2015**, *114*, 89–99. [CrossRef]
196. Campins, H.; Hargrove, K.; Pinilla-Alonso, N.; Howell, E.S.; Kelley, M.S.; Licandro, J.; Mothe-Diniz, T.; Fernandez, Y.; Ziffer, J. Water Ice and Organics on the Surface of the Asteroid 24 Themis. *Nature* **2010**, *464*, 1320–1321. [CrossRef]
197. Feaga, L.M.; A'Hearn, M.F.; Sunshine, J.M.; Groussin, O. Asymmetry of Gaseous CO_2 and H_2O in the Inner Coma of Comet Tempel 1. In Proceedings of the 37th Annual Lunar and Planetary Science Conference, League City, TX, USA, 13–17 March 2006.
198. Taylor, G.J. The Complicated Geologic History of Asteroid 4 Vesta. *Planet. Res. Discov. Rep.* **2009**, *135*, 1–7.
199. Zolensky, M.E.; Krot, A.N.; Benedix, G. Record of low-temperature alteration in asteroids. *Rev. Mineral. Geochem.* **2008**, *68*, 429–462. [CrossRef]
200. Trigo-Rodríguez, J.M.; Rimola, A.; Tanbakouei, S.; Soto, V.C.; Lee, M. Accretion of water in carbonaceous chondrites: Current evidence and implications for the delivery of water to early Earth. *Space Sci. Rev.* **2019**, *215*, 18–27. [CrossRef]
201. Jiang, Y.; Baoyin, H. Capillary action in a crack on the surface of asteroids with an application to 433 Eros. *New Astron.* **2016**, *47*, 91–96. [CrossRef]
202. Rotelli, L.; Trigo-Rodríguez, J.M.; Moyano-Cambero, C.E.; Carota, E.; Botta, L.; Di Mauro, E.; Saladino, R. The key role of meteorites in the formation of relevant prebiotic molecules in a formamide/water environment. *Nature* **2016**, *6*, 38888. [CrossRef] [PubMed]
203. Bottke, W.F.; Vokrouhlicky, D.; Rubincam, D.P.; Broz, M. The effect of Yarkovsky thermal forces on the dynamical evolution of asteroids and meteoroids. In *Asteroids III*; Bottke, W.F., Ed.; University of Arizona Press: Tucson, AZ, USA, 2002.
204. Taylor, P.A.; Margot, J.L.; Vokrouhlicky, D.; Scheeres, D.J.; Pravec, P.; Lowry, S.C.; Fitzsimmons, A.; Nolan, M.C.; Ostro, S.J.; Benner, L.A.; et al. Spin Rate of Asteroid (54509) 2000 PH5 Increasing due to the YORP Effect. *Science* **2007**, *316*, 274–277. [CrossRef]
205. Durech, J.; Vokrouchlicky, D.; Higgins, D.; Krugly, Y.N.; Gaftonyuk, N.M.; Shevchenko, V.G.; Hamanowa, H.; Reddy, V.; Dyvig, R.R. Detection of the YORP Effect on Asteroid (1620) Geographos. *Astron. Astrophys.* **2008**, *489*, L25–L28. [CrossRef]
206. Holsapple, K.A.; Michel, P. Tidal Disruptions: A Continuum Theory for Solid Bodies. *Icarus* **2006**, *183*, 331–348. [CrossRef]
207. Holsapple, K.A.; Michel, P. Tidal disruptions. II. A Continuum Theory for Solid Bodies with Strength, with Applications to the Solar System. *Icarus* **2008**, *193*, 283–301. [CrossRef]
208. Holsapple, K.H. Equilibrium figures of spinning bodies with self-gravity. *Icarus* **2004**, *172*, 272–303. [CrossRef]
209. Holsapple, K.H. On YORP-induced spin deformations of asteroids. *Icarus* **2010**, *205*, 430–442. [CrossRef]
210. Zhang, Y.; Michel, P. Tidal Distortion and Disruption of Rubble-Pile Bodies Revisited. Soft-Sphere Discrete Element Analyses. *Astron. Astrophys.* **2020**, *640*, A102. [CrossRef]
211. Tanbakouei, S.; Trigo-Rodríguez, J.M.; Sort, J.; Michel, P.; Blum, J.; Nakamura, T.; Williams, I. Mechanical properties of particles from the surface of asteroid 25143 Itokawa. *Astron. Astrophys.* **2019**, *669*, A119. [CrossRef]

212. Meyer, A.J.; Gkolias, I.; Gaitanas, M.; Agrusa, H.F.; Scheeres, D.J.; Tsiganis, K.; Pravec, P.; Benner, L.A.; Ferrari, F.; Michel, P. Libration-induced Orbit Period Variations Following the DART Impact. *Planet. Sci. J.* **2021**, *242*, 13–26. [CrossRef]
213. Hirabayashi, M.; Schwartz, S.R.; Yu, Y.; Davis, A.B.; Chesley, S.R.; Fahnestock, E.G.; Michel, P.; Richardson, D.C.; Naidu, S.P.; Scheeres, D.J.; et al. Constraints on the perturbed mutual motion in Didymos due to impact-induced deformation of its primary after the DART impact. *Mon. Not. R. Astron. Soc.* **2017**, *472*, 1641–1648.
214. Michel, P.; Küppers, M.; Bagatin, A.C.; Carry, B.; Charnoz, S.; De Leon, J.; Carnelli, I.; Gordo, P.; Green, S.F.; Juzi, M.; et al. The ESA Hera Mission: Detailed Characterization of the DART Impact Outcome and of the Binary Asteroid (65803) Didymos. *Planet. Sci. J.* **2022**, *3*, 160. [CrossRef]
215. Chanut, T.G.G.; Aljbaae, S.; Carruba, V. Mascon Gravitation Model Using a shaped Polyhedral Source. *Mon. Not. R. Astron. Soc.* **2015**, *450*, 3742–3749. [CrossRef]
216. Aljbaae, S.; Chanut, T.; Carruba, V.; Souchay, J.; Prado, A.; Amarante, A. The Dynamical Environment of Asteroid 21 Lutetia According to Different Internal Models. *Mon. Not. R. Astron. Soc.* **2017**, *464*, 3552–3560. [CrossRef]
217. Chanut, T.; Aljbaae, S.; Prado, A.; Carruba, V. Dynamics in the Vicinity of (101955) Bennu: Solar Radiation Pressure Effects in Equatorial Orbits. *Mon. Not. R. Astron. Soc.* **2017**, *470*, 2687–2701. [CrossRef]
218. Jiang, Y.; Baoyin, H.; Li, H. Collision and Annihilation of Relative Equilibrium Points Around Asteroids with a Changing Parameter. *Mon. Not. R. Astron. Soc.* **2015**, *452*, 3924–3931. [CrossRef]
219. Jiang, Y.; Baoyin, H. Annihilation of Relative Equilibria in the Gravitational Field of Irregular-Shaped Minor Celestial Bodies. *Planet. Space Sci.* **2018**, *161*, 107–136. [CrossRef]
220. Liu, Y.; Jiang, Y.; Li, H. Bifurcations of Relative Equilibrium Points During Homotopy Deformation of Asteroids. *Celest. Mech. Dyn. Astron.* **2021**, *133*, 42–66. [CrossRef]

Article

Polynomial Chaos Expansion-Based Enhanced Gaussian Process Regression for Wind Velocity Field Estimation from Aircraft-Derived Data

Marius Marinescu [1], Alberto Olivares [1], Ernesto Staffetti [1,*] and Junzi Sun [2]

[1] School of Telecommunication Engineering, Universidad Rey Juan Carlos, Fuenlabrada, 28942 Madrid, Spain
[2] Faculty of Aerospace Engineering, Delft University of Technology, 2629 HS Delft, The Netherlands
* Correspondence: ernesto.staffetti@urjc.es

Abstract: This paper addresses the problem of spatiotemporal wind velocity field estimation for air traffic management applications. Using data obtained from aircraft, the eastward and northward components of the wind velocity field inside a specific air space are calculated as functions of time. Both short-term wind velocity field forecasting and wind velocity field reconstruction are performed. Wind velocity data are indirectly obtained from the states of the aircraft flying in the relevant airspace, which are broadcast by the ADS-B and Mode-S aircraft surveillance systems. The wind velocity field is estimated by combining two data-driven techniques: the polynomial chaos expansion and the Gaussian process regression. The former approximates the global behavior of the wind velocity field, whereas the latter approximates the local behavior. The eastward and northward wind components of the wind velocity field must be estimated, which causes the problem to be a multiple-output problem. This method enables the estimation of the wind velocity field at any spatiotemporal location using wind velocity observations from any spatiotemporal location, eliminating the need for spatial and temporal grids. Moreover, since the method proposed in this article allows for the probability distributions of the estimates to be computed, it causes the computation of the confidence intervals to be possible. Furthermore, since the method presented in this paper allows for data assimilation, it can be used online to continuously update the wind velocity field estimation. The method is tested on different wind scenarios and different training-test data configurations, by means of which the consistency between the results of the wind velocity field forecasting and the wind velocity field reconstruction is checked. Finally, the ERA5 meteorological reanalysis data of the European Centre for Medium-Range Weather Forecasts are used to validate the proposed technique. The results show that the method is able to reliably estimate the wind velocity field from aircraft-derived data.

Keywords: polynomial chaos expansion; Gaussian process regression; air traffic management; wind velocity field estimation; ADS-B; Mode S

MSC: 62M20

Citation: Marinescu, M.; Olivares, A.; Staffetti, E.; Sun, J. Polynomial Chaos Expansion-Based Enhanced Gaussian Process Regression for Wind Velocity Field Estimation from Aircraft-Derived Data. *Mathematics* **2023**, *11*, 1018. https://doi.org/10.3390/math11041018

Academic Editors: Yu Jiang, Haijun Peng and Hongwei Yang

Received: 22 December 2022
Revised: 3 February 2023
Accepted: 9 February 2023
Published: 16 February 2023

1. Introduction

1.1. Motivation

Uncertainty is pervasive in the Air Traffic Management (ATM) system, and weather is one of the most significant sources of uncertainty. Four-Dimensional (4D) trajectories will be central elements in the future ATM paradigm; it relies on Trajectory-Based Operations (TBO) because aircraft will be allowed to fly 4D trajectories based on the preferences of the airlines, with the obligation to precisely follow them for traffic synchronization. This means that aircraft trajectories must be predicted with great precision based on reliable meteorological forecasts. Therefore, precise wind information is required to increase trajectory predictability, i.e., the correspondence between planned and actual trajectories [1,2].

Currently, most wind predictions used in aircraft trajectory planning come from Numerical Weather Prediction (NWP) models. NWP meteorological forecasts have a low update rate, typically once every 6 h, and have a coarse spatial resolution. Moreover, observations are mainly gathered from radiosondes, which are launched at specific times, no more than four times per day. All these factors cause using NWP to be inadequate for TBO [3,4]. Therefore, using aircraft-derived data could improve the spatial and temporal resolution of wind forecasts [5].

This paper studies the problem of the spatiotemporal estimation of the wind velocity field within a given air space, in which the eastward and northward components of the wind velocity field are estimated as functions of time using aircraft-derived data. Both short-term wind velocity field forecasting and wind velocity field reconstruction are carried out within a specific air space, in this case, the Terminal Maneuvering Area of the Adolfo Suarez Madrid-Barajas (LEMD) airport, which is located at an altitude of 610 m above sea level. More precisely, the considered airspace is a cuboidal region with a base size of 500×500 km centered at the LEMD airport, with heights ranging from 0.61 km to 14 km. In particular, Mode-S and ADS-B surveillance systems [6,7] will be used in this article to derive the wind velocity, which is indirectly obtained using the relation among the following vectors: the ground speed, the air speed, and the wind velocity itself. A detailed description of the ADS-B and Mode-S technologies can be found in [7].

Several atmospheric data assimilation techniques, which are intended to combine different information sources to estimate the state of the atmosphere, were developed [8]. However, most methods for assimilating these non-conventional aircraft-derived meteorological data are designed to assimilate them into NWP models [9–11].

In this article, a different approach to the problem of estimating the state of the atmosphere using aircraft-derived meteorological data is followed. Specifically, the problem of wind velocity field estimation using aircraft-derived wind observations is solved based on a combination of the Polynomial Chaos Expansion (PCE) and the Gaussian Process Regression (GPR) methods, which will be referred to as PCE-GPR. The wind is modeled as a random field with the spatiotemporal position as the input and the wind velocity as the output. The combination of these two techniques is suitable for representing random fields since the PCE models the mean function of the random field and approximates the global behavior of the wind velocity field, whereas the GPR represents the auto-covariance function and approximates the local behavior of such a wind velocity field.

1.2. State of the Art

In [12], a Kalman Filter (KF) was used to estimate the wind speed profile along descent paths using aircraft-derived data. The KF was adapted to account for the uncertainty due to the distance at which observations are collected. This uncertainty was added to the measurement covariance matrix of the KF as a function of the horizontal distance between the observation and estimation locations.

In [13], a novel algorithm for inferring the wind velocity vector from ADS-B data, capable of working in both small and large turning angle situations, is studied. A circle fitting problem is considered, and a sequential least squares optimization algorithm is used.

In [14], the Kriging technique was employed to estimate the wind velocity and temperature fields in the airspace surrounding an airport using aircraft-derived data. Moreover, the same technique was used to predict wind velocity and temperature profiles along descending paths.

In [15], a novel technique that combines particle filtering and Lagrangian transportation was used to partially reconstruct the wind velocity and temperature fields in those regions of the airspace surrounding an airport where a sufficient amount of aircraft-derived data are available. In [16], the technique was further studied, where meteo-particle parameters were optimized and an extrapolation method, based on Delaunay triangulation, to construct a complete wind velocity field was presented.

In [2], the B-splines method was employed to estimate the wind speed profile along descent paths using aircraft-derived data to update the optimal descent trajectory in real-time.

In [17], two approaches to improve the wind velocity data to support TBO are explored: by providing interpolated inter-forecast wind velocity and temperature data and by using aircraft-derived atmospheric observations, such as wind velocity and temperature, to update the forecasted conditions.

In [18], a comparison between several techniques based on the KF and the GPR for wind speed profile estimation from aircraft-derived data in the vertical direction of a given geographical location was conducted, showing that the technique based on the GPR outperforms the methods based on the KF.

In [19], the techniques based on the KF and the GPR for wind speed profile estimation from aircraft-derived data presented in [18] were generalized to wind velocity profile estimation in the vertical direction of a given geographical location, showing that the technique based on the GPR outperforms the methods based on the KF in this case as well.

Finally, in [20], the GPR technique presented in [19] for wind velocity profile estimation in the vertical direction of a given geographical location was extended to the reconstruction and the short-term prediction of the wind velocity field within a given air space. The results showed that the reconstruction has a performance comparable to that of the method proposed in [15] with the advantage of providing an estimate of the entire wind velocity field within a given air space.

In this paper, the PCE is used to enhance the GPR technique. In [21], Wiener first introduced the term PCE for representing the Gaussian distributions using Hermite polynomials.

In [22], the Wiener PCE was extended to other canonical distributions. In [23], the PCE was further extended to arbitrary distributions, which can be specified either analytically, numerically as histograms, or as raw data sets with the introduction of the arbitrary Polynomial Chaos Expansion (aPCE). The aPCE only requires the existence of a finite number of statistical moments and does not rely on the complete knowledge or even on the existence of a probability density function. The aPCE is especially suitable for data-driven applications where no other information is known about the probability distribution of the data, as it eliminates the need to assign parametric probability distributions not sufficiently supported by the available data.

The main contribution of this paper is an innovative method, the PCE-GPR technique, for the reconstruction and short-term prediction of the wind velocity field. The method is iterative and fast, ensuring real-time assimilation of aircraft-derived data is possible. Additionally, the PCE-GPR approach, which previously only allowed for the estimation of scalar output variables, is extended in this study to estimate two output variables: the wind velocity components.

In this paper, the GPR technique employed in [20] is combined with PCE to solve the same problem, generalizing and improving the previous methodology. The PCE-GPR technique was recently introduced in [24] for uncertainty quantification and in [25] for rare event estimation. In both articles, it is referred to as Polynomial Chaos Kriging (PCK). To the best of the authors' knowledge, the PCE-GPR method has not yet been used for wind velocity field reconstruction and wind velocity field short-term forecasting using aircraft-derived data.

Notice that the terms Kriging and GPR are used interchangeably in the literature. Indeed, GPR and Kriging are essentially the same method, with differences in notation, conceptualization, and in the computation of the confidence intervals of the estimations [26].

The capability of the PCE-GPR method to reconstruct the wind velocity field and to provide short-term predictions within a certain air space was tested using historical aircraft-derived data. Wind velocity observations from two different days characterized by different wind behaviors were chosen. In particular, on the first day, the wind was weaker with a higher degree of directional dispersion, whereas, on the second day, it was stronger with a lower degree of directional dispersion. The data sets were split into training and test sets in two different ways, namely by randomly selecting sets of individual observations and by randomly selecting sets of flights. Moreover, the wind velocity field estimates obtained through the PCE-GPR method were validated using the meteorological reanalysis data retrieved from the ERA5 repository of the European Centre for Medium-Range Weather Forecasts (ECMWF). The results of the validation show that the estimates are consistent with the reanalysis data, demonstrating the capability of the method presented in this article to estimate the wind velocity even in those regions of the air space in which a reduced number of observations are available.

The paper is structured as follows. The procedure for obtaining the aircraft-derived data and the results of the exploratory analysis of the obtained data sets are described in Section 2.1. The GPR technique is introduced in Section 2.2, and the mathematical development of the PCE method is described in Section 2.3. The combination of both methods is explained in Section 2.4, and the extension of the PCE-GPR method to multi-output processes is presented in Section 2.5. The results of the numerical experiments are described in Section 3 and discussed in Section 4. Finally, Section 5 contains the conclusions.

2. Methods

2.1. Data Derivation and Exploratory Analysis

This section presents the procedure through which the wind velocity information is derived from the ADS-B and Mode S data. In addition, the main results of the exploratory analysis of these aircraft-derived data are also summarized.

2.1.1. Data Source

The data employed in this work were supplied by the Spanish Air Navigation Service Provider (ENAIRE). Specifically, the data were extracted from the All-Purpose Structured EUROCONTROL Surveillance Information Exchange (ASTERIX) database, which contains a great amount of flight information, as described in the technical reports of EUROCONTROL [27], from which the ADS-B [28] and Mode-S [29] data were obtained. More precisely, two data sets were extracted from this database. The observations of the first data set, which contains data with lower wind speeds and higher dispersion in the wind direction, correspond to 23 February 2020. It will be referred to as the Day 1 data set. The observations of the second data set, which contains data with higher wind speeds and lower dispersion in the wind direction, correspond to 21 December 2019. It will be referred to as the Day 2 data set. The observations in both data sets were obtained from 08:00 to 14:00 UTC, which corresponds to the time period with the maximum level of traffic at the LEMD airport.

2.1.2. ADS-B and Mode S Systems

The ADS-B system automatically transmits the position and ground speed of the aircraft approximately every 0.5 s. Mode S is a selective interrogation system used to transmit additional flight information. Aircraft are interrogated by surveillance radars and reply through a transponder by means of the so-called Mode S Enhanced Surveillance communication protocol. In fact, the Mode S extended squitter transponder is the most common implementation of ADS-B. In particular, as described in [29], binary data store registers 50 and 60 contain the information necessary for deriving the wind velocity, as it will be explained in Section 2.1.3. For further details on surveillance technologies, the reader is referred to [7].

2.1.3. Wind Velocity Derivation from ADS-B and Mode S Data

The vector that represents the wind velocity can be obtained as the difference between the vectors that represent the ground speed and the actual airspeed using the true airspeed, the ground speed, and the heading and track angles. The relationship between the ground speed, true airspeed, and wind velocity vectors, denoted as V_{gs}, V_{tas}, and V_w, respectively, is shown in Figure 1, where χ_g, χ_a, and χ_w represent the track angle, the heading angle, and the wind direction angle, respectively. Thus, the wind velocity data sets employed in this work were built from the wind velocity observations derived from different aircraft states, which were obtained through the ADS-B and Mode-S surveillance technologies.

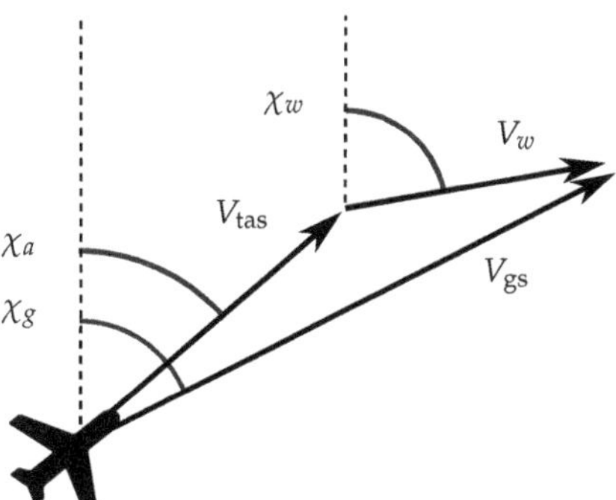

Figure 1. Relationship among the true airspeed, ground speed, and wind velocity vectors.

2.1.4. Exploratory Data Analysis

Table 1 shows the main statistics of the wind velocity of the Day 1 and Day 2 data sets. Circular statistics were used to compute the mean and dispersion of angles [30]. It can be seen that the average wind speed in the Day 2 data set is around 3 times larger than in the Day 1 data set, whereas the dispersion of the wind direction is about 10 times lower. The dispersion of the wind direction, in circular statistics, is measured by a percentage. A 100% dispersion means that the direction of the wind velocity observations is uniformly distributed in all directions, whereas a 0% dispersion means that all the wind velocity observations have the same direction.

Table 1. Main statistics of the wind velocity.

	Wind Speed (m/s)		**Wind Direction (Deg)**	
	Day 1	Day 2	Day 1	Day 2
Min.	0	0.013	0.01	163.79
Max.	56.04	100.75	359.99	351.55
Mean	17.80	60.56	307.16	166.66
Dispersion	11.30	16.67	19.40 (%)	2.11 (%)

The spatial configuration of the Day 1 data set is represented in Figure 2, in which the coverage region over the Iberian Peninsula, together with the flight routes, can be observed. Using this kind of data set to estimate wind velocity fields is a challenging task, since they are non-uniformly distributed in the air space.

For a detailed exploratory analysis of these two data sets, the reader is referred to [20].

2.2. Gaussian Process Regression

Gaussian Processes (GP) are stochastic processes that allow for a wide variety of properties to be modeled, including linearity, continuity, smoothness, differentiability, symmetry, and periodicity. GP can be completely determined by their mean and covariance functions. The deterministic trends of the GP are represented by the mean functions, whereas their stochastic properties are described by the covariance functions, which are usually referred to as kernel functions.

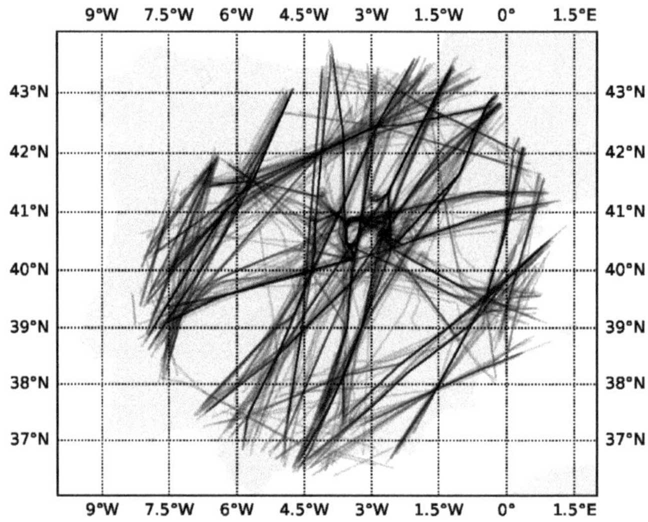

Figure 2. Aircraft flight routes for the Day 1 data set.

GPR may be thought of as a general regression model, which can be employed in many research areas, such as machine learning [31] or functional data analysis [32]. Given some predictor variables $\mathbf{x} = (x_1, x_2, \ldots, x_d)$, a GPR model provides a prediction $\mathcal{M}(\mathbf{x})$ of the value of a scalar output variable y, assuming the mapping $y = \mathcal{M}(\mathbf{x})$ to be a realization of a Gaussian random process, and generalizing the linear regression model

$$y = \mathbf{x}^T \boldsymbol{\beta} + \varepsilon, \tag{1}$$

in which $\varepsilon \sim N(0, \sigma^2)$, $\boldsymbol{\beta} = (\beta_1, \beta_2, \ldots, \beta_d)$ represent the parameters of the regression model, and σ^2 denotes the error variance.

GPR introduces a new term $f(\mathbf{x})$ in the linear model (1), which is assumed to be a Gaussian process, i.e., it is assumed that, jointly, the random variables $\{f(\mathbf{x}_1), f(\mathbf{x}_2), f(\mathbf{x}_3), \ldots, f(\mathbf{x}_n)\}$ have zero-mean Gaussian distribution with covariance function $K(\mathbf{x}, \mathbf{x}')$, for any collection of observations $\{\mathbf{x}_1, \mathbf{x}_2, ..., \mathbf{x}_n\}$. Additionally, the linear term in (1) is replaced by a basis function $h(\cdot)$, which projects the predictor variable $\mathbf{x}$ into a p-dimensional feature space. Thus, the GPR model can be formulated as:

$$y = \mathcal{M}(\mathbf{x}) = h(\mathbf{x})^T_{1\times p} \boldsymbol{\beta}_{p\times 1} + f(\mathbf{x}) + \varepsilon. \tag{2}$$

Given a set of observations $(\boldsymbol{\mathcal{X}}, \mathcal{Y}) = \{(\mathbf{x}^j, y^j), j = 1, 2, \ldots, n\}$ that relate the input variables $\mathbf{x}$ with the output variable y through the GPR model (2), it can be shown that $\hat{y}$, the predicted output variable at point $\hat{\mathbf{x}}$, is also Gaussian distributed [31]. As a consequence, GPR is able to provide both an estimation of the output variable and its associated probability distribution.

2.3. Polynomial Chaos Expansion

Following [33], this section presents the PCE method, which allows for the computation of an analytical model that maps an input random vector onto an output random variable under certain hypotheses.

Let $(\Omega, \mathcal{F}, \mathcal{P})$ be a probability space, with Ω the space of events, $\mathcal{F}$ a σ-algebra, and $\mathcal{P}$ a probability measure. Assume that there exists an unknown deterministic mapping $\mathcal{M}$ from a d-dimensional input parameter space to a one-dimensional output space, namely $\mathcal{M} : \mathbb{R}^d \to \mathbb{R}$, such that $y = \mathcal{M}(\mathbf{x})$, with $\mathbf{x} = (x_1, x_2, \ldots, x_d)$.

If the input vector $\mathbf{x}$ is assumed to be affected by uncertainties, it can be represented by a random vector $\mathbf{X} = (X_1, X_2, \ldots, X_d)$ with a joint Probability Density Function (PDF) $f_{\mathbf{X}} = (f_{X_1}, f_{X_2}, \ldots, f_{X_d})$, and then $Y = \mathcal{M}(\mathbf{X})$ is an output random variable, which is obtained by propagating the input vector uncertainties through the mapping $\mathcal{M}$.

PCE is a spectral decomposition method that provides a computationally efficient way to calculate an analytical representation that maps the input random vector $\mathbf{X}$ onto the output random variable Y, under two hypotheses. The output random variable Y is assumed to be a second-order variable, namely:

$$E[Y^2] = \int_{\mathbb{R}^d} \mathcal{M}^2(\mathbf{x}) f_{\mathbf{X}}(\mathbf{x}) d\mathbf{x} < +\infty.$$

Additionally, each component $X_i, i = 1, 2, \ldots, d$, of the input random vector $\mathbf{X}$ is assumed to have finite moments of all orders.

Provided that these two assumptions are fulfilled, the output random variable Y can be represented by the following PCE

$$Y(\mathbf{X}) = \mathcal{M}(\mathbf{X}) = \sum_{\boldsymbol{\alpha} \in \mathbb{N}^d} c_{\boldsymbol{\alpha}} \Psi_{\boldsymbol{\alpha}}(\mathbf{X}), \tag{3}$$

where $\{c_{\boldsymbol{\alpha}}, \boldsymbol{\alpha} \in \mathbb{N}^d\}$ are the coefficients of the expansion and $\{\Psi_{\boldsymbol{\alpha}}(\cdot),\ \boldsymbol{\alpha} \in \mathbb{N}^d\}$ is a basis of polynomials orthonormal with respect to the probability measure $\mathcal{P}$ represented by the joint PDF $f_{\mathbf{X}}$, namely

$$\int_{\mathbb{R}^d} \Psi_{\boldsymbol{\alpha}}(\mathbf{x}) \Psi_{\boldsymbol{\beta}}(\mathbf{x}) f_{\mathbf{X}}(\mathbf{x})\, d\mathbf{x} = \delta_{\boldsymbol{\alpha}\boldsymbol{\beta}}, \tag{4}$$

with $\delta_{\boldsymbol{\alpha}\boldsymbol{\beta}}$ denoting the Kronecker delta and $\boldsymbol{\alpha}, \boldsymbol{\beta} \in \mathbb{N}^d$ representing multi-indexes.

Assuming that the input random vector $\mathbf{X}$ has statistically independent components, each multivariate polynomial $\Psi_{\boldsymbol{\alpha}}$ of the PCE basis $\{\Psi_{\boldsymbol{\alpha}}(\cdot),\ \boldsymbol{\alpha} \in \mathbb{N}^d\}$ can be computed as the tensor product of d univariate orthogonal polynomials as follows

$$\Psi_{\boldsymbol{\alpha}}(\mathbf{x}) = \prod_{i=1}^{d} \psi_{\alpha_i}^{(i)}(x_i), \tag{5}$$

where each univariate polynomial $\psi_{\alpha_i}^{(i)}(\cdot), i = 1, 2, \ldots, d$, is the component of degree α_i of a basis of univariate polynomials orthonormal with respect to the marginal PDF f_{X_i} of $\mathbf{X}$, namely the PDF of the random variable X_i. The component α_i of the multi-index $\boldsymbol{\alpha} = (\alpha_1, \alpha_2 \ldots, \alpha_d) \in \mathbb{N}^d$ designates the degree of the multivariate polynomial $\Psi_{\boldsymbol{\alpha}}$ in the i-variable, for $i = 1, 2, ..., d$. The total degree of $\Psi_{\boldsymbol{\alpha}}$ is calculated as $|\boldsymbol{\alpha}| = \sum_{i=1}^{d} \alpha_i$.

In practice, the infinite terms of the PCE (3) must be truncated to a finite sum. There are different ways to choose a truncation scheme, in which a set of multi-indexes is selected. The most commonly used truncation scheme consists of setting an upper bound p on the total degree $|\boldsymbol{\alpha}|$ of the multivariate polynomials $\Psi_{\boldsymbol{\alpha}}$, namely the set of multi-indexes:

$$\mathcal{A}^{d,p} = \{\boldsymbol{\alpha} \in \mathbb{N}^d : |\boldsymbol{\alpha}| \leq p\}. \tag{6}$$

Thus, the truncated PCE that approximates the infinite series (3) can be formulated as

$$Y_{PC}(\mathbf{X}) = \mathcal{M}_{PC}(\mathbf{X}) = \sum_{k=1}^{|\mathcal{A}^{d,p}|} c_k \Psi_k(\mathbf{X}), \tag{7}$$

where

$$|\mathcal{A}^{d,p}| = \frac{(d+p)!}{d!p!}.$$

There are different ways to construct the basis of orthonormal polynomials $\{\Psi_{\boldsymbol{\alpha}}(\cdot),\ \boldsymbol{\alpha} \in \mathbb{N}^d\}$. In general, the computation of each $\Psi_{\boldsymbol{\alpha}}$ requires the availability of the marginal distributions of $X_i, i = 1, 2, \ldots, d$, which are employed in the tensor product (5). However, a wide variety of univariate distributions is associated with a specific family of orthonormal polynomials [22]. In this case, it is straightforward to compute the basis of orthonormal polynomials. For instance, the Hermite polynomials are associated with the Gaussian distribution.

When the distributions of the input random variables $X_i, i = 1, 2, \ldots, d$, have no family of orthonormal polynomials associated, a common approach consists of directly constructing the basis of orthonormal polynomials using Stiltjes or Gram–Schmidt orthogonalization [34].

As mentioned in the Introduction, a more general approach is the aPCE [23], which consists of constructing the basis of orthonormal polynomials from the statistical moments of the input random variables $X_i, i = 1, 2, \ldots, d$. Thus, this approach does not require the availability or even the existence of a functional representation of the marginal PDFs $f_{X_i}, i = 1, 2, \ldots, d$. However, in the aPCE approach a large number of input samples is necessary for an accurate estimation of higher order moments [35].

In this paper, the Kernel Density Estimation (KDE) [36] was employed to estimate the marginal PDFs $f_{X_i}, i = 1, 2, \ldots, d$, and then the Stiltjes orthogonalization was used to build the corresponding basis of the orthonormal polynomials. More specifically, given a set $\mathcal{X}_i = \{x_i^1, x_i^2, \ldots, x_i^n\}$ of n observations of the input random variable X_i, the kernel density estimate of the marginal PDF f_{X_i} was calculated as

$$\hat{f}_{X_i}(x) = \frac{1}{n\eta} \sum_{j=1}^{n} K\left(\frac{x - x_i^j}{\eta}\right), \tag{8}$$

where $K(\cdot)$ represents the kernel function and η denotes an appropriate kernel bandwidth. In particular, a Gaussian kernel was used, and the corresponding kernel bandwidth was learned from the set of observations $\mathcal{X}_i$ by means of the Silverman's rule [37].

Once the truncation scheme (6) was selected, the coefficients c_k, $k = 1, 2, \ldots, |\mathcal{A}^{d,p}|$, of the truncated expansion (7) can be calculated using different approaches, such as Galerkin projection, collocation, numerical integration, or regression [22].

In this paper, given a set of observations of the input random vector and the corresponding output random variable, namely $(\boldsymbol{\mathcal{X}}, \mathcal{Y}) = \{(\mathbf{x}^j, y^j), j = 1, 2, \ldots, n\}$ the expansion coefficients have been estimated using regression. More specifically, the vector of expansion coefficients $\mathbf{c} = (c_1, c_2, \ldots, c_{|\mathcal{A}^{d,p}|})$ was estimated by solving the least squares minimization problem:

$$\hat{\mathbf{c}} = \arg\min_{\mathbf{c} \in \mathbb{R}^{|\mathcal{A}^{d,p}|}} \sum_{j=1}^{n} \left(y^j - Y_{PC}(\mathbf{x}^j)\right)^2 = \arg\min_{\mathbf{c} \in \mathbb{R}^{|\mathcal{A}^{d,p}|}} \sum_{j=1}^{n} \left(y^j - \sum_{k=1}^{|\mathcal{A}^{d,p}|} c_k \Psi_k(\mathbf{x}^j)\right)^2. \tag{9}$$

In particular, the vector of expansion coefficients $\hat{\mathbf{c}}$ estimated in (9) was calculated as

$$\hat{\mathbf{c}} = (\mathbf{A}^T\mathbf{A})^{-1}\mathbf{A}^T \begin{pmatrix} y^1 \\ y^2 \\ \vdots \\ y^n \end{pmatrix},$$

where $a_{jk} = \Psi_k(\mathbf{x}^j), j = 1, 2, \ldots, n,\ k = 1, 2, \ldots, |\mathcal{A}^{d,p}|$, are the entries of matrix $\mathbf{A}$.

2.4. Polynomial Chaos Expansion-Based Enhanced Gaussian Process Regression

As explained in Section 2.2, the GPR model (2) interpolates local variations of the output variable y as a function of experimental observations of the predictor variables $\mathbf{x}$, whereas the PCE model (3) approximates the global behavior of the mapping $y = \mathcal{M}(\mathbf{x})$ by means of a set of orthonormal polynomials, as described in Section 2.3. Therefore, as pointed out in [24], the aim of combining PCE and GPR is to capture at the same time both the global behavior and the local variability of the mapping that relates the output variable y to the predictor variables $\mathbf{x}$. To this end, the trend of the GPR model (2), represented by the term $h(\mathbf{x})^T_{1\times p}\boldsymbol{\beta}_{p\times 1}$, is replaced by the truncated PCE (7), so that the PCE-GPR model can be formulated as follows:

$$y = \mathcal{M}(\mathbf{x}) = \sum_{k=1}^{|\mathcal{A}^{d,p}|} c_k \Psi_k(\mathbf{x}) + f(\mathbf{x}) + \varepsilon. \quad (10)$$

The ability of capturing local and global properties through the PCE-GPR model (10) is analyzed in [24] through several benchmark analytical functions, such as the Rastrigin function [38], which is a two-dimensional function that combines a quadratic term and a high-frequency trigonometric term. The contour plot of the Rastrigin function is illustrated in Figure 3a–d to show the approximations of the Rastrigin function by the GPR, PCE, and PCE-GPR models, which were generated using 128 sample points from a standard normal bivariate distribution, respectively.

It can be seen in Figure 3b that the GPR model properly approximates the local extrema of the Rastrigin function, whereas the global feature of the function is barely learned by this model. Conversely, Figure 3b shows how the PCE model reproduces the global behaviour of the Rastrigin function while missing out on the local extrema. Finally, the capability of the PCE-GPR model to combine both characteristics of the Rastrigin function is illustrated in Figure 3d.

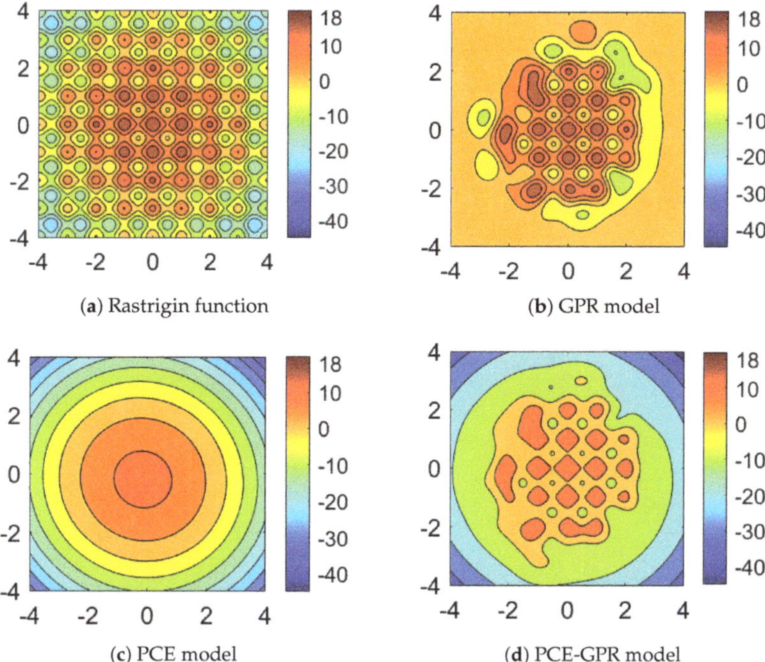

(**a**) Rastrigin function (**b**) GPR model

(**c**) PCE model (**d**) PCE-GPR model

Figure 3. The Rastrigin function and its approximation by the GPR, PCE, and PCE-GPR models.

2.5. *Adaptation of PCE-GPR to the Wind Velocity Output*

As mentioned before, this paper addresses the problem of spatiotemporal wind velocity field estimation. More specifically, the eastward and northward components of the wind velocity, which will be referred to as u and v components, respectively, are inferred at different altitudes as functions of time from aircraft-derived data. Therefore, the single output PCE-GPR model described in Section 2.4 must be extended to this multiple-output setting.

The GPR method cannot be directly generalized to multi-output processes in a unique and effective way. The ability of the GPR model to estimate multiple-outputs, seeking to take advantage of the knowledge about the relation between them, is still a field of active research. Usually, a covariance function describing both the auto-correlation of the output variables as well as the correlation among them is included in the formulation of the model [39]. However, the formulation of a covariance function for multiple correlated output variables is a difficult task. Besides, the estimation efficiency of a GPR model can be significantly reduced if the covariance structure among outputs is mis-specified [40]. Therefore, the common approach in practice is to address these estimation problems by means of independent single-output GPR models.

In this paper, the following approach was followed to adapt the PCE-GPR method to the wind velocity output. First, the wind speed and wind direction were predicted using three outputs, namely $(y_1, y_2, y_3) = (r, \cos\gamma, \sin\gamma)$, with r being the wind speed and γ the wind velocity direction. Then, the u and v components were retrieved as $(u, v) = (r\cos\gamma, r\sin\gamma)$.

The motivation behind this approach is threefold. The estimation of the wind velocity using independent single-output GPR models has already been proven to be effective in [20]. Moreover, since they are two different physical magnitudes, the separation between the wind speed and the wind direction predictions benefits the training process of the PCE-GPR model. Finally, because each of the three output variables (y_1, y_2, y_3) are trained independently, parallel computing can be used.

3. Results

3.1. Model Set Up

In this section, the PCE-GPR model layout is presented, namely the selection of the model parameters, which include the total degree of the truncated PCE expansion, the hyperparameter vector of the kernel function, and the error standard deviation.

The total degree p of the truncated PCE expansion included in (10) was selected between 1 and 10. More specifically, the value of p that provides the least leave-one-out error, ϵ_{LOO}, was chosen, where

$$\epsilon_{LOO} = \frac{1}{n}\sum_{j=1}^{n}\left(\frac{y^j - Y_{PC}(\mathbf{x}^j)}{1-\nu_j}\right)^2,$$

with $\nu_j, j = 1, 2, \ldots, n$, being the jth diagonal term of the matrix $\mathbf{A}(\mathbf{A}^T\mathbf{A})^{-1}\mathbf{A}^T$ [24].

The covariance function in (10) was computed using the squared exponential kernel [31], namely

$$K(\mathbf{x}, \mathbf{x}'|\boldsymbol{\theta}) = \sigma_f^2 e^{-R^2}, \tag{11}$$

with

$$R = \sqrt{\sum_{i=1}^{d}\frac{(x_i - x_i')^2}{\sigma_i^2}},$$

where $\boldsymbol{\theta} = (\sigma_f, \sigma_1, \sigma_2, \sigma_3, \sigma_4)$ is the hyperparameter vector and $d = 4$, since the components of the input vector $\mathbf{x}$ are the coordinates of the spatiotemporal position of the aircraft. The kernel function (11) produces continuous and smooth GP samples, thus providing a smooth regression capable of uniformly approximating any continuous function on a compact subset contained in the input space [41].

Moreover, the correlation between two spatiotemporal input points decreases as a function of the weighted Euclidean distance. Since, in the wind velocity estimation the input variables have different length scales, each input variable $x_i, i = 1, 2, 3, 4$, in the kernel function (11) was scaled by a factor σ_i^2. The hyperparameter σ_f, referred to as the signal standard deviation, allows the auto-covariance to be adapted to the output scale. To achieve a fast and accurate estimation of the hyperparameter vector $\boldsymbol{\theta}$, the subset of the data method [31], together with the block coordinate descent approximation [42], were used during the training phase of the model.

Finally, according to [12], the standard deviation σ of the model error ε in (10) was set to 3 m/s, which is the typical wind instrumental error.

3.2. Wind Velocity Field Reconstruction

The capability of the PCE-GPR method to reconstruct the wind velocity fields within a particular air space using historical aircraft-derived data is studied in this section. More specifically, the wind velocity field was reconstructed around the LEMD airport employing the wind velocity data sets introduced in Section 2.1.1 using data collected over a one-hour period. In particular, a cuboidal region centered at the LEMD airport with base size 500 × 500 km and altitude ranging between 0.6 km and 14 km was used. Moreover, both aircraft-derived data sets were split into training and test sets using two different approaches:

- By randomly choosing sets of individual observations, which will be referred to as data set randomly split by observation.
- By randomly selecting sets of flights, employing the individual observations gathered from them, which will be referred to as a data set randomly split by flight.

Specifically, in both cases, 20% of the data were kept for testing to assess the accuracy of the wind velocity field reconstruction. Thus, four different PCE-GPR models were trained. The computational time of the training phase for each of these models was less than 5 min.

Three different measurements of the estimation error were computed for each of the four models, namely the Root Mean Square Error (RMSE), the Mean Absolute Error (MAE), and the Median Absolute Deviation (MAD), which are reported in Table 2.

Table 2. Wind velocity field reconstruction: Estimation errors for the u and v components of the wind velocity.

		Data Set Split by Observation		**Data Set Split by Flight**	
Measure of Error	**Component**	**Day 1**	**Day 2**	**Day 1**	**Day 2**
RMSE (m/s)	u	2.26 (18%)	1.50 (21%)	5.84 (1%)	6.06 (−4%)
	v	1.46 (44%)	1.45 (22%)	4.79 (14%)	4.84 (1%)
MAE (m/s)	u	1.17 (22%)	0.99 (22%)	4.46 (−1%)	4.37 (−2%)
	v	0.83 (43%)	1.05 (19%)	3.45 (13%)	3.59 (3%)
MAD (m/s)	u	0.53 (23%)	0.64 (22%)	3.60 (−6%)	3.03 (−2%)
	v	0.49 (31%)	0.80 (15%)	2.44 (9%)	2.70 (5%)

It can be seen that the values of the estimation errors of the wind velocity components for both the Day 1 and Day 2 data sets are similar. Conversely, the values of the estimation errors significantly differ depending on the data splitting procedure chosen. This is due to the fact that the spatiotemporal distance between the training and test observations is higher when the data sets are randomly split by flight, which causes the estimation to be more challenging.

Table 2 also reports, between parentheses, the relative improvement obtained in comparison with the values of the estimation errors reported in [20], in which the wind velocity field reconstruction was carried out using the GPR method without the enhancement provided by the PCE. It can be seen that the PCE-GPR method considerably outperforms the GPR method when the data sets are randomly split by observation, whereas the incorporation of the PCE into the GPR model does not statistically improve the estimation errors already achieved when the data sets are randomly split by flight.

Figure 4 shows the rose diagrams of the wind velocity estimation errors for each of the four models, which can be thought of as circular histograms. The values in the inner circumferences represent percentages of the total data set, whereas the quantities in the outer circumference denote angles representing the wind velocity direction errors that are expressed in degrees. Moreover, a color scale is used to indicate the wind speed. It can be seen that the estimation errors of the wind velocity direction are symmetrically distributed around 0 degrees, showing a low dispersion. Moreover, the dispersion is particularly low when the data sets are randomly split by observation. Likewise, the estimation errors of the wind speed adopt low values, ranging between 0 and 5 m/s.

The wind velocity fields reconstructed using the PCE-GPR method from the Day 1 data set, at a given instant in time and for different altitudes ranging from 2 to 12 km, are shown in Figure 5, together with the value of the associated mean wind speed $\bar{s}_w$. A selection of members of the corresponding training and test data sets are also depicted. It can be observed that the reconstructed wind velocity fields properly fit the data and behave smoothly.

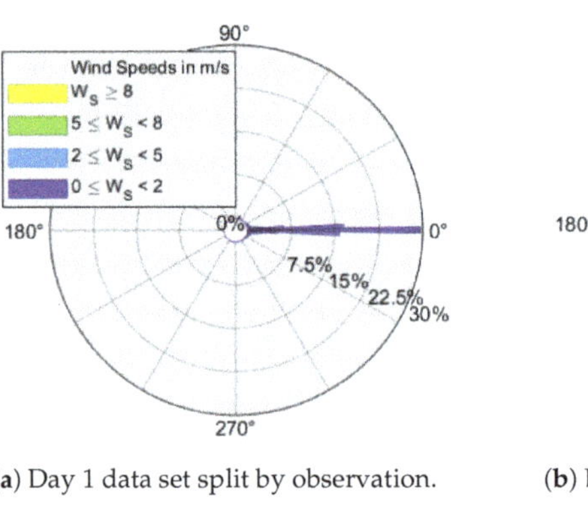

(**a**) Day 1 data set split by observation.

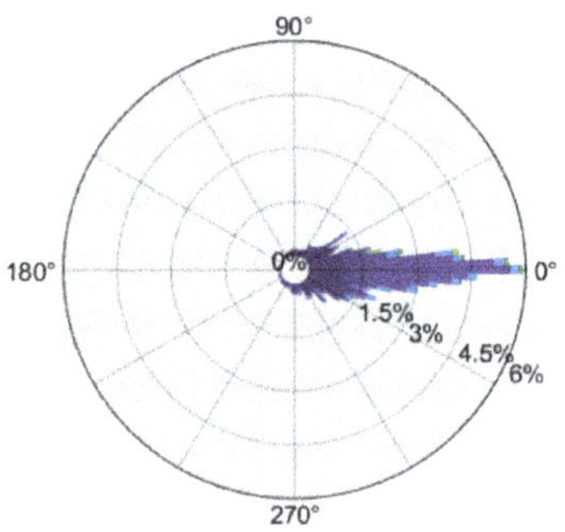

(**b**) Day 1 data set split by flight.

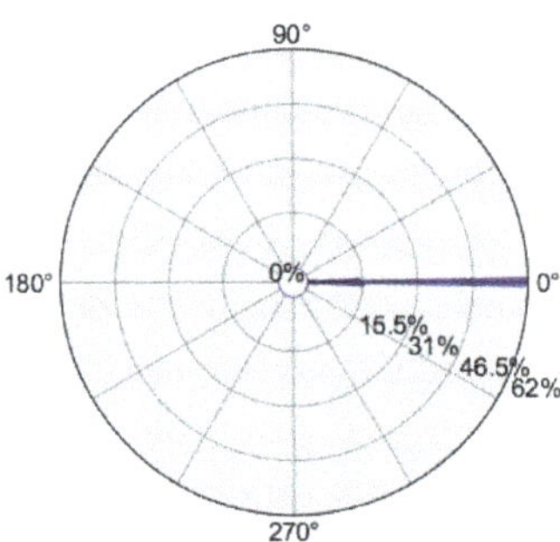

(**c**) Day 2 data set split by observation.

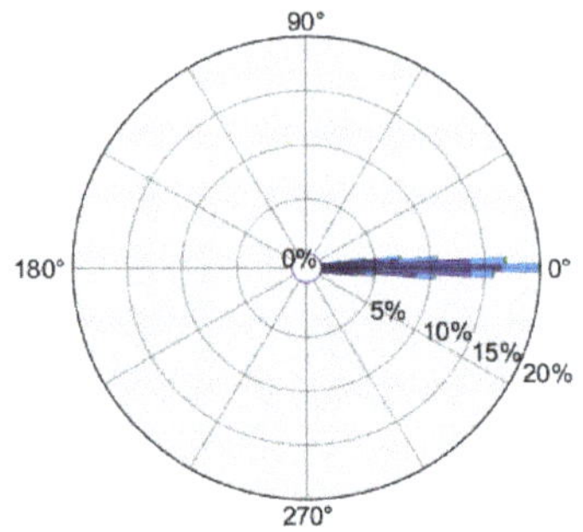

(**d**) Day 2 data set split by flight.

Figure 4. Rose diagrams of the wind velocity estimation errors.

In addition, to complement Figure 5, the rose diagrams that represent the wind velocity estimation errors segmented by height are shown in Figure 6. It can be seen that, at altitudes below 10 km, the wind speed is low, ranging from 0 km/h to 36 km/h, and the wind direction variability is high. This effect can be observed in the first three rose diagrams.

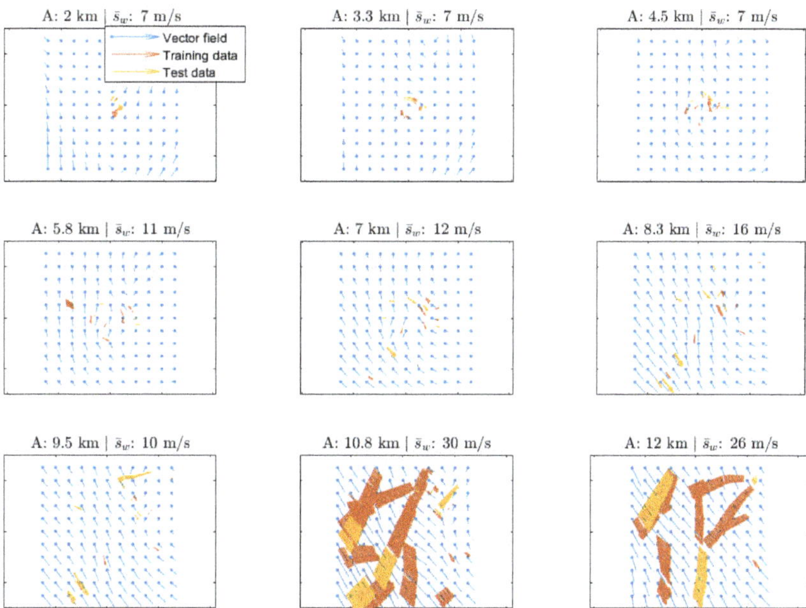

Figure 5. Wind velocity field reconstruction: Reconstructed wind velocity field obtained using the Day 1 data set and the PCE-GPR method for different altitudes (A). A selection of members of the training and test data sets, along with the mean wind speed ($\bar{s}_w$), are also included.

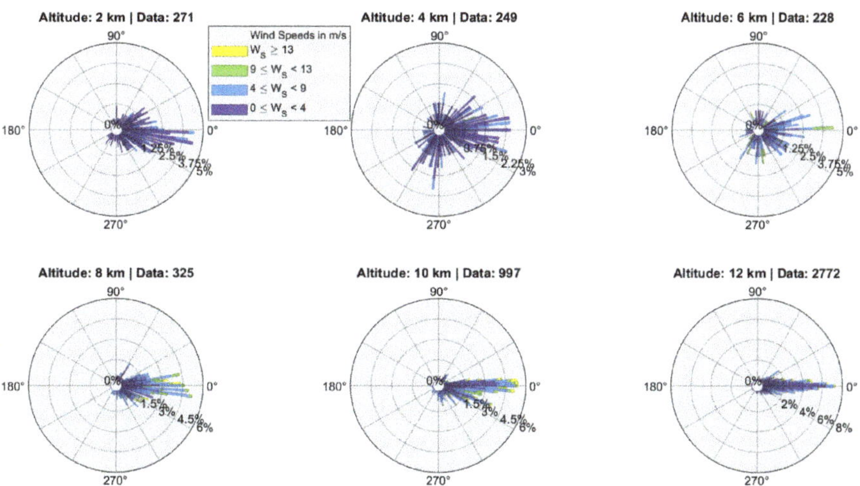

Figure 6. Rose diagrams of the wind velocity estimation errors, segmented by altitude, for the Day 1 data set split by flight.

The reconstruction of the wind speed dynamics from 14:10 to 15:00 UTC at cruise altitude (10.3 km) for the Day 2 data set is illustrated in Figure 7 by means of an isotach map. It can be seen how the contour bars gradually change over the considered space and time period.

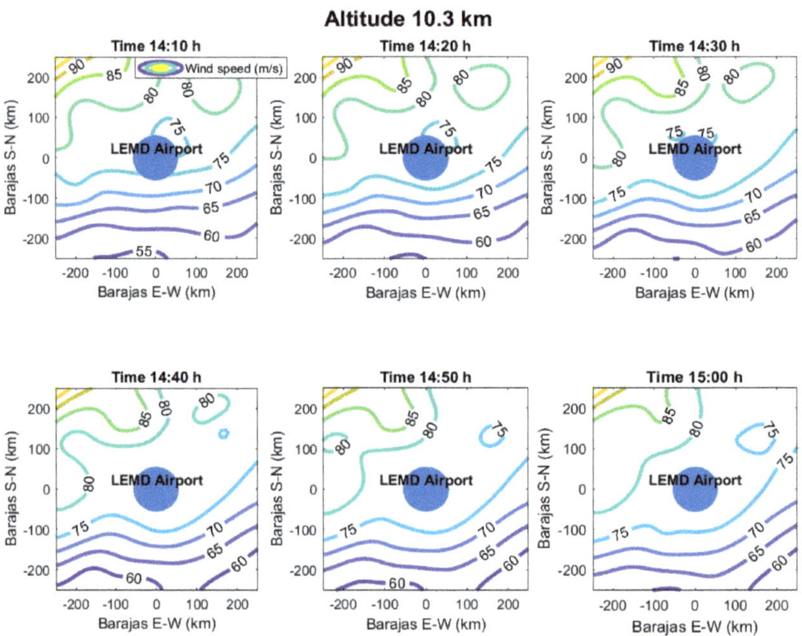

Figure 7. Wind speed reconstruction from 14:10 to 15:00 UTC at cruise altitude for the Day 2 data set.

3.3. Wind Velocity Field Short-Term Prediction

The capability of the PCE-GPR method to provide the short-term wind velocity field predictions is studied in this section. In particular, several wind velocity fields were predicted around the LEMD airport using the two data sets introduced in Section 2.1.1. Each of these short time horizon predictions consists of a 15 min ahead forecast, in which the PCE-GPR model was trained using data from the previous hour and the corresponding prediction was compared to the test data available at this short time horizon. The estimation errors of these predictions were collected and aggregated. More specifically, the RMSE, the MAE, and the MAD were computed and are summarized in Table 3.

Table 3. Wind velocity field prediction: Estimation errors for the u and v components of the wind velocity field.

Measure of Error	Component	Day 1	Day 2
RMSE (m/s)	u	5.28 (6%)	6.37 (13%)
	v	5.16 (6%)	5.80 (8%)
MAE (m/s)	u	4.00 (12%)	4.19 (29%)
	v	3.93 (12%)	4.40 (15%)
MAD (m/s)	u	3.00 (4%)	3.25 (12%)
	v	3.07 (3%)	3.52 (4%)

It can be observed that the magnitude of the estimation errors shown in Table 3 for the wind velocity field prediction is similar to the magnitude of the estimation errors reported in Table 2 for the wind velocity field reconstruction using the data sets randomly split by flight. This higher value of the estimation uncertainty with respect to the wind velocity field reconstruction using the data sets randomly split by observation is due to the fact that, unlike the PCE-GPR reconstruction model, the PCE-GPR prediction model solely relies on past observations of the wind velocity.

Table 3 also reports, between parentheses, the relative improvement obtained in comparison with the values of the estimation errors reported in [20], in which the wind velocity field prediction was carried out using the GPR method without the improvement provided by the PCE. It can be seen that, for all error measures, the PCE-GPR method outperforms the GPR method. Therefore, the PCE-GPR model yields better short-term forecasts than those provided by the GPR model, which already provided short-term predictions with reasonable estimation errors.

Figure 8 presents the wind velocity field prediction at cruise altitude obtained using the Day 2 data set and the PCE-GPR method for different instants in time. In addition, some of the members of the test data sets along with the mean wind speed at each instant in time are also shown. It can be seen that the predicted wind velocity fields largely agree with the observations.

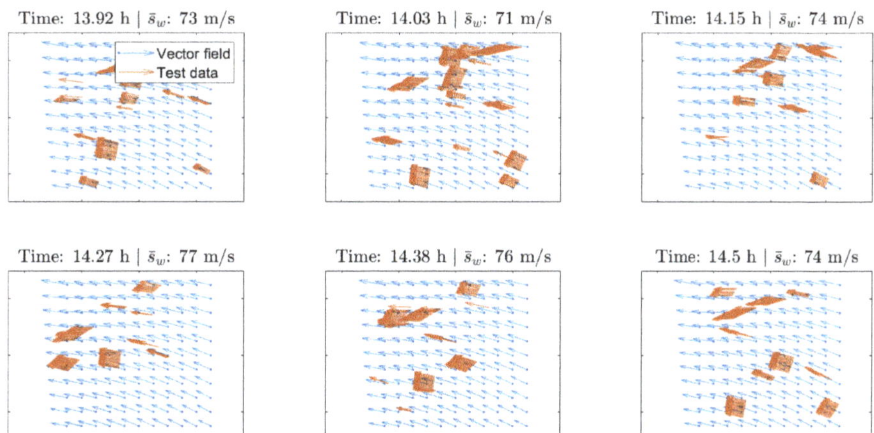

Figure 8. Wind velocity field prediction: Predicted wind velocity field at cruise altitude obtained using the Day 2 data set and the PCE-GPR method for different instants in time. A selection of members of the test data sets, along with the mean wind speed ($\bar{s}_w$), are also included.

3.4. Validation of the PCE-GPR Model

This section presents the validation of the PCE-GPR model. More specifically, the obtained estimates are compared with the observations available in the ECMWF ERA5 reanalysis database, which contains global atmospheric reanalysis data for each altitude level with a resolution of 0.25 degrees in the latitude and longitude.

In order to assess whether the aircraft-derived data agree with the reanalysis data, a comparison between the aircraft-derived data and the ECMWF ERA5 data was carried out in [20]. The differences between the aircraft-derived data and the reanalysis data were calculated for each hour ranging between 09:00 and 15:00 UTC, with a time gap of 15 min and an altitude difference of 1000 ft. Since the ECMWF ERA5 data are provided at the grid points, a linear interpolation was used to compute the reanalysis observations corresponding to the locations at which aircraft-derived observations were available. It can be seen in ([20], Table 4) that, for both the Day 1 and Day 2 data sets, the wind speed bias is less than 3 m/s, whereas the wind direction bias is less than 4 degrees. Moreover, the MAE of the wind speed is similar for both data sets, whereas the dispersion in the wind direction is significantly higher for the Day 1 data set. However, despite the difference, it is expected that the estimates provided by the PCE-GPR model agree on average with the reanalysis data.

The following steps were performed to compare the estimates of the PCE-GPR method with the ECMWF ERA5 reanalysis data. First, the reanalysis data corresponding to the Day 1 and Day 2 data sets were extracted from the ECMWF ERA5 database. Various instants in time and altitudes were considered for each data set. More precisely, the ECMWF ERA5 reanalysis data for altitudes of 5.6, 9.3, 10.5, 11.2, 12, and 12.9 km, corresponding to times 09:00, 12:00, and 15:00 UTC were considered. A cuboidal space centered at the LEMD airport with base size 500 $\times$ 500 km was used to represent the relevant airspace. Then, the PCE-GPR model was trained on the aircraft-derived data observed in the relevant airspace and an estimation was performed at every grid point of the ECMWF ERA5 data set. The obtained estimates were compared with the ECMWF ERA5 reanalysis observations. Finally, several measures of error were calculated.

The comparison between the estimates of the wind speed and the wind direction computed using the PCE-GPR technique and the ECMWF ERA5 observations, for both the Day 1 and Day 2 data sets, are shown in Table 4. It can be seen that all the measures are even smaller than those reported in ([20], Table 4), except for the MAE of the wind speed for the Day 2 data set, which is almost the same. This is because the wind velocity field estimates provided by using the PCE-GPR method are smoother than the aircraft-derived data, which contain noise. Since the measurement noise ε is incorporated into the model (2), the PCE-GPR acts as a noise filter.

Table 4. Validation of the PCE-GPR model: Comparison between the estimates obtained using the PCE-GPR method and the ECMWF ERA5 reanalysis data.

Measure	Variable	Day 1	Day 2
Bias (m/s)	Wind speed	−2.75	−0.24
MAE (m/s)	Wind speed	4.5	5.79
Bias (deg)	Wind direction	2.06	−1.36
Dispersion (%)	Wind direction	8.5	0.33

Notice that most of the aircraft-derived observations are located at cruise altitudes close to the LEMD airport. Nevertheless, the estimates provided by using the PCE-GPR model are also similar to the reanalysis data when the aircraft-derived observations near the ECMWF ERA5 grid points are not available, which shows the ability of the PCE-GPR method to yield reasonable wind velocity field estimations.

4. Discussion

Aircraft-derived wind velocity data employed in this article were supplied by ENAIRE. Specifically, they were extracted from the ASTERIX database. The wind velocity was indirectly obtained from the state of the aircraft. An exploratory analysis of the data can be found in [20], where it was observed that the noise in the wind speed increases in the data collected during aircraft turning maneuvers. The data availability and quality are expected to increase after the deployment of the European System-Wide Information Management (SWIM), an ongoing European project [43,44], which consists of a unified infrastructure to exchange the flight information, including the wind velocity directly measured by the aircraft.

The method proposed in this article was tested in different wind scenarios and different training-test data configurations. Specifically, two sets of data collected on two different days with different wind intensities and directions were selected. Each data set was randomly split in two different ways, namely by observation and by flight.

The method was tested first in the wind vector field reconstruction using both data sets. The performance of the method in terms of errors is similar. In particular, as expected, the data set configuration obtained by randomly splitting the data set by flight led to the worst wind vector field reconstruction errors in comparison to the data set configuration obtained by randomly splitting the data set by observation because, in the first case, the observations are less evenly distributed in space. However, in all training-test data configurations, these errors are unbiased and have little dispersion. Therefore, it can be concluded that the method is not affected by the wind scenario in wind vector field reconstruction.

The proposed method has also been tested in wind vector field short-term prediction using both data sets. The performance of the method, in terms of errors, is again similar. The prediction errors are higher than the reconstruction errors using the data set configuration obtained by randomly splitting the data set by observation but are similar to the reconstruction errors using the data set configuration obtained by randomly splitting the data set by flight. Therefore, it can be concluded that the errors in the short-term wind velocity field prediction are reasonably small, given that wind velocity information is only based on the past observations and therefore carries a higher level of uncertainty compared to wind velocity field reconstruction.

The performance in terms of the estimation errors of the method proposed in this paper was compared with that of the Gaussian process regression method presented by the same authors in [20]. The results demonstrate that the good performance of the previous method was further improved. Moreover, the obtained estimates were validated using an external data set, namely the ECMWF ERA5 reanalysis data, which are a reliable collection of historical atmospheric data. This comparison has shown that there is consistency between the obtained estimates and the ECMWF ERA5 reanalysis data, including the regions in which the aircraft-derived data broadcasting is low or nonexistent.

5. Conclusions

In this paper, a technique for short-term wind velocity field forecasting and wind velocity field reconstruction using aircraft-derived wind velocity data was presented. The wind velocity data were obtained in an indirect way from the states of the aircraft transmitted by the ADS-B and Mode-S aircraft surveillance systems. The amount of wind velocity data derived from aircraft states continuously transmitted airborne is large, causing these aircraft surveillance systems to be a suitable source for data assimilation algorithms. The proposed technique combines the Gaussian process regression method with the arbitrary polynomial chaos expansion, which causes the Gaussian process regression to be more precise since it models the mean spatiotemporal behavior of the wind through polynomial functions rather than linear functions.

The main advantages of the method are that it does not rely on spatial and temporal grids and that new observations can be assimilated in less than 5 min, causing it to be suitable for short-term forecasting. The ultimate goal of the method presented in this article is to increase aircraft trajectory predictability in TBO, which is an operational concept that is expected to be implemented soon [45].

Future research will concentrate on showing the advantages of the improved wind velocity information obtained through the method described in this paper on the predictability of aircraft trajectories in the TBO framework. These advantages have already been demonstrated in some articles, such as [2], where the optimal descent trajectory is updated in real-time using wind velocity profiles, and [12], where KF-based wind velocity profiles are used for reducing the temporal spacing error between aircraft.

Author Contributions: The authors equally contributed to the paper. All authors have read and agreed to the published version of the manuscript.

Funding: This research was partially supported by the grants number RTI2018-098471-B-C33 and PID2021-122323OB-C31 of the Spanish Government.

Data Availability Statement: The data used in this paper are property of ENAIRE, the Spanish National Air Navigation Service Provider, and are covered by a confidentiality agreement. Interested researchers can contact ENAIRE (informacion@enaire.es) for details on obtaining access.

Acknowledgments: The authors would like to thank Enrique Gismera Gómez, Ruth Otero Fraguas, and Iciar Sánchez Zorzano from ENAIRE for providing the data.

Conflicts of Interest: The authors declare no conflict of interest.

References

1. Hernández-Romero, E.; Valenzuela, A.; Rivas, D. Probabilistic multi-aircraft conflict detection and resolution considering wind forecast uncertainty. *Aerosp. Sci. Technol.* **2020**, *105*, 105973. [CrossRef]
2. Dalmau, R.; Prats, X.; Baxley, B. Using broadcast wind observations to update the optimal descent trajectory in real-time. *J. Air Transp.* **2020**, *28*, 82–92. [CrossRef]
3. Reynolds, T.G.; McPartland, M. Establishing wind information needs for four dimensional trajectory-based operations. In Proceedings of the 1st International Conference on Interdisciplinary Science for Innovative Air Traffic Management, Daytona Beach, FL, USA, 25–27 June 2012.
4. Reynolds, T.G.; McPartland, M.; Teller, T.; Troxel, S. Exploring wind information requirements for four dimensional trajectory-based operations. In Proceedings of the 11th USA/Europe Air Traffic Management Research and Development Seminar, Lisbon, Portugal, 23–26 June 2015.
5. de Haan, S. High-resolution wind and temperature observations from aircraft tracked by Mode-S air traffic control radar. *J. Geophys. Res. Atmos.* **2011**, *116*, D10111. [CrossRef]
6. Sun, J.; Vû, H.; Ellerbroek, J.; Hoekstra, J.M. pyModeS: Decoding Mode-S surveillance data for open air transportation research. *IEEE Trans. Intell. Transp. Syst.* **2020**, *21*, 2777–2786. [CrossRef]
7. Sun, J. *The 1090 Megahertz Riddle: A Guide to Decoding Mode S and ADS-B Signals*; TU Delft OPEN Publishing: Delft, The Netherlands, 2021.
8. Guzzi, R. *Data Assimilation: Mathematical Concepts and Instructive Examples*; Springer: Cham, Switzerland, 2016.
9. de Haan, S.; Stoffelen, A. Assimilation of high-resolution Mode-S wind and temperature observations in a regional NWP model for nowcasting applications. *Weather Forecast.* **2012**, *27*, 918–937. [CrossRef]
10. Cardinali, C.; Isaksen, L.; Andersson, E. Use and impact of automated aircraft data in a global 4DVAR data assimilation system. *Mon. Weather Rev.* **2003**, *131*, 1865–1877. [CrossRef]
11. Talagrand, O. Assimilation of observations, an introduction. *J. Meteorol. Soc. Jpn.* **1997**, *75*, 191–209. [CrossRef]
12. de Jong, P.M.A.; van der Laan, J.J.; in 't Veld, A.C.; van Paassen, M.M.; Mulder, M. Wind-profile estimation using airborne sensors. *J. Aircr.* **2014**, *51*, 1852–1863. [CrossRef]
13. Liu, T.; Xiong, T.; Thomas, L.; Liang, Y. ADS-B based wind speed vector inversion algorithm. *IEEE Access* **2020**, *8*, 150186–150198. [CrossRef]
14. Dalmau, R.; Pérez-Batlle, M.; Prats, X. Estimation and prediction of weather variables from surveillance data using spatio-temporal Kriging. In Proceedings of the 2017 IEEE/AIAA 36th Digital Avionics Systems Conference, St. Petersburg, FL, USA, 17–21 September 2017.
15. Sun, J.; Vû, H.; Ellerbroek, J.; Hoekstra, J.M. Weather field reconstruction using aircraft surveillance data and a novel meteo-particle model. *PLoS ONE* **2018**, *13*, e0205029. [CrossRef]
16. Zhu, J.; Wang, H.; Li, J.; Xu, Z. Research and optimization of meteo-particle model for wind retrieval. *Atmosphere* **2021**, *12*, 1114. [CrossRef]
17. Enea, G.; McPartland, M. Wind enhancements for trajectory based operations automation. In Proceedings of the AIAA Aviation 2022 Forum, Chicago, IL, USA, 27 June–1 July 2022.
18. Marinescu, M.; Olivares, A.; Staffetti, E.; Sun, J. Wind profile estimation from aircraft derived data using Kalman filters and Gaussian process regression. In Proceedings of the 14th USA/Europe ATM Research and Development Seminar, Virtual Event, 20–23 September 2021.
19. Marinescu, M.; Olivares, A.; Staffetti, E.; Sun, J. On the estimation of vector wind profiles using aircraft-derived data and Gaussian process regression. *Aerospace* **2022**, *9*, 377. [CrossRef]
20. Marinescu, M.; Olivares, A.; Staffetti, E.; Sun, J. Wind field estimation from aircraft derived data using Gaussian process regression. *PLoS ONE* **2022**, *17*, e0276185. [CrossRef] [PubMed]
21. Wiener, N. The homogeneous chaos. *Am. J. Math.* **1938**, *60*, 897–936. [CrossRef]
22. Xiu, D.; Karniadakis, G.E. The Wiener-Askey polynomial chaos for stochastic differential equations. *SIAM J. Sci. Comput.* **2002**, *24*, 619–644. [CrossRef]
23. Oladyshkin, S.; Nowak, W. Data-driven uncertainty quantification using the arbitrary polynomial chaos expansion. *Reliab. Eng. Syst. Saf.* **2012**, *106*, 179–190. [CrossRef]
24. Schöbi, R.; Sudret, B.; Wiart, J. Polynomial-chaos-based Kriging. *Int. J. Uncertain. Quantif.* **2015**, *5*, 171–193. [CrossRef]
25. Schöbi, R.; Sudret, B.; Marelli, S. Rare event estimation using polynomial-chaos Kriging. *ASCE-ASME J. Risk Uncertain. Eng. Syst. Part A Civ. Eng.* **2017**, *3*, D4016002. [CrossRef]
26. Martino, L.; Read, J. A joint introduction to Gaussian processes and relevance vector machines with connections to Kalman filtering and other kernel smoothers. *Inf. Fusion* **2021**, *74*, 17–38. [CrossRef]
27. ASTERIX Official Web Page. Available online: https://www.eurocontrol.int/asterix (accessed on 15 November 2022).
28. EUROCONTROL Technical Document Part12-CAT021. Available online: https://www.eurocontrol.int/publication/cat021-eurocontrol-specification-surveillance-data-exchange-asterix-part-12-category-21 (accessed on 15 November 2022).
29. EUROCONTROL Technical Document Part04-CAT048. Available online: https://www.eurocontrol.int/publication/cat048-eurocontrol-specification-surveillance-data-exchange-asterix-part4 (accessed on 15 November 2022).
30. Jammalamadaka, S.R.; Sengupta, A. *Topics in Circular Statistics*; World Scientific Publishing: Singapore, 2001.

31. Rasmussen, C.E.; Williams, C. *Gaussian Processes for Machine Learning*; MIT Press: Cambridge, MA, USA, 2006.
32. Shi, J.Q.; Choi, T. *Gaussian Process Regression Analysis for Functional Data*; Chapman and Hall: London, UK, 2011.
33. Torre, E.; Marelli, S.; Embrechts, P.; Sudret, B. Data-driven polynomial chaos expansion for machine learning regression. *J. Comput. Phys.* **2019**, *388*, 601–623. [CrossRef]
34. Wan, X.; Karniadakis, G.E. Beyond Wiener-Askey expansions: Handling arbitrary PDFs. *J. Sci. Comput.* **2006**, *27*, 455–464. [CrossRef]
35. Oladyshkin, S.; Nowak, W. Incomplete statistical information limits the utility of high-order polynomial chaos expansions. *Reliab. Eng. Syst. Saf.* **2018**, *169*, 137–148. [CrossRef]
36. Gramacki, A. *Nonparametric Kernel Density Estimation and Its Computational Aspects*; Springer: Cham, Switzerland, 2018.
37. Silverman, B.W. *Density Estimation for Statistics and Data Analysis*; Chapman and Hall: London, UK, 1986.
38. The Modified Rastrigin Function. Available online: https://uqworld.org/t/modified-rastrigin-function/126 (accessed on 15 November 2022).
39. Wang, B.; Chen, T. Gaussian process regression with multiple response variables. *Chemom. Intell. Lab. Syst.* **2015**, *142*, 159–165. [CrossRef]
40. Stein, M.L. The loss of efficiency in Kriging prediction caused by misspecifications of the covariance structure. *Geostatistics* **1989**, *4*, 273–282.
41. Micchelli, C.A.; Xu, Y.; Zhang, H. Universal kernels. *J. Mach. Learn. Res.* **2006**, *7*, 2651–2667.
42. Bo, L.; Sminchisescu, C. Greedy block coordinate descent for large scale Gaussian process regression. In Proceedings of the Proceedings of the Twenty-Fourth Conference on Uncertainty in Artificial Intelligence, Helsinki, Finland, 9–12 July 2008.
43. Masutti, A. Single European sky—A possible regulatory framework for System Wide Information Management (SWIM). *Air Space Law* **2011**, *36*, 275–292. [CrossRef]
44. SWIM Project. Available online: https://www.eurocontrol.int/concept/system-wide-information-management (accessed on 15 November 2022).
45. AIRBUS: 4D-TBO. Available online: https://www.airbus.com/en/newsroom/stories/2020-12-4d-tbo-a-new-approach-to-aircraft-trajectory-prediction (accessed on 15 November 2022).

 *mathematics*

Article

The Shape Entropy of Small Bodies

Yanshuo Ni [1,*], He Zhang [1], Junfeng Li [2], Hexi Baoyin [2] and Jiaye Hu [3]

1. Beijing Institute of Spacecraft System Engineering, Beijing 100094, China
2. School of Aerospace Engineering, Tsinghua University, Beijing 100084, China
3. Aerospace Engineering Consulting (Beijing) Co., Ltd., China Aerospace Academy of Systems Science and Engineering, Beijing 100048, China

* Correspondence: niyanshuo007@163.com

Abstract: The irregular shapes of small bodies usually lead to non-uniform distributions of mass, which makes dynamic behaviors in the vicinities of small bodies different to that of planets. This study proposes shape entropy (SE) as an index that compares the shapes of small bodies and spheres to describe the shape of a small body. The results of derivation and calculation of SE in two-dimensional and three-dimensional cases show that: SE is independent of the size of geometric figures but depends on the shape of the figures; the SE difference between a geometric figure and a circle or a sphere, which is the limit of SE value, reflects the difference between this figure and a circle or a sphere. Therefore, the description of shapes of small bodies, such as near-spherical, ellipsoid, and elongated, can be quantitatively described via a continuous index. Combining SE and the original inertia index, describing the shape of small bodies, can define the shapes of small bodies and provide a reasonably simple metric to describe a complex shape that is applicable to generalized discussion and analysis rather than highly detailed work on a specific, unique, polyhedral model.

Keywords: entropy; applied mathematics; mathematical physics; small body

MSC: 70F15; 37M25

Citation: Ni, Y.; Zhang, H.; Li, J.; Baoyin, H.; Hu, J. The Shape Entropy of Small Bodies. *Mathematics* **2023**, *11*, 878. https://doi.org/10.3390/math11040878

Academic Editors: Gabriel Eduard Vilcu and Jean-Charles Pinoli

Received: 17 December 2022
Revised: 4 February 2023
Accepted: 7 February 2023
Published: 9 February 2023

1. Introduction

Small Solar System Bodies (hereafter called small bodies) offer unique opportunities to study the mechanical structures, different processes, and responses that are related to the origin, evolution, and current architecture of the Solar System [1]. Small bodies are all other objects orbiting the Sun that are neither planets, dwarf planets, nor satellites, according to International Astronomical Union (IAU) resolutions five and six (Resolution_GA26-5-6) [2,3]. Therefore, a small body lacks sufficient mass for its self-gravity to overcome rigid body forces and assume hydrostatic equilibrium in a nearly round shape [2], which leads to irregular shapes of small bodies.

The shapes of small bodies span from spherical to ellipsoidal and elongated [4]. It is the irregular distribution of mass in space, caused by irregular shapes, that makes the dynamic characteristics of small bodies, such as equilibrium points [5–7] and periodic orbits [8–13], different from that of planets, provides rich research contents for celestial mechanics and nonlinear dynamics, and brings challenges to the orbit design and control of spacecraft in the vicinity of small bodies. Besides, fly-by, impacting, and rendezvous missions to small bodies demand that the shape of small bodies is accurately known to select the best-suited image processing technique for optical navigation, such as the center of brightness, intensity weighted centroiding, correlation with Lambertian spheres, and center finding by correlation [14,15]. However, this information may not always be available from ground-based observation for interplanetary missions. Spacecraft should be able to return good navigation results with the proper technique according to the shape, though small bodies can assume a wide variety of shapes.

Although the shape regularity of a small body significantly impacts the dynamical characteristics of its gravitational field and the robustness of the image processing for optical navigation, there is a lack of sufficient description, research, and quantitative analysis on the regularity of a small body, simulated by a polyhedral model with a single parameter, for further understanding on the dynamic behavior related to shapes of small bodies. Hu and Scheeres [16] defined an index describing the shape of a small body according to its principal moments of inertia, which is developed from Scheeres et al. [17]

$$\rho = \frac{I_y - I_x}{I_z - I_x}, \tag{1}$$

where the z-axis is the principal axis with maximum inertia, and the x-axis is with minimum inertia, i.e., $I_x \leq I_y \leq I_z$. According to Equation (1), the index is $\rho \in [0, 1]$. When $\rho = 0$, the shape of the small body is symmetric about the z-axis; when $\rho = 1$, the shape is symmetric about the x-axis. This shape index can describe the mass distribution characteristics of small bodies and reflect the shape of small bodies to a certain extent. However, when the shape of a small body is close to a sphere, that is, the three-axis inertias are very close, this index cannot accurately describe the shape characteristics of a small body, especially the approximation between the small body and the sphere.

Although it is possible to describe the regularity of the shape of a small body by spherical harmonic coefficients, the similarity between the shape of the small body and the sphere can only be accurately described by the multi-dimensional array composed of many spherical harmonic coefficients, which is not conducive to directly judging the shape similarity of different small bodies through a few indicators. If we investigate the coefficients C_{20}, C_{22}, and S_{22} [18], we can find that these three coefficients still reflect the relationship between the inertia of small bodies.

Approximating a small body to a triaxial ellipsoid [19,20] is also possible to describe the regularity of the shape of a small body; however, the gravitational field in the vicinity of a triaxial ellipsoid is different from that of the small body, and the dynamical characteristics in the triaxial ellipsoid case [20] is thus distinct from the polyhedron case [21], which is more accurate.

Jiang et al. [22] reviewed the common approximate models of gravitational fields, such as the simple geometry models [23–27], the spherical harmonic and ellipsoidal harmonic function model [28–33], the particle group model [34], and the polyhedral model [35–38]. In the studies of dynamic characteristics, the accuracy of the description of the gravitational field near irregular small bodies and the collision test is much more of a concern. Therefore, it is more reasonable to select the polyhedral model as the gravitational field model of the particle motion near an irregular small body [39–42].

Buonagura et al. [43] developed a shape-cube method to describe the shapes of small bodies from regular to irregular. Fifteen small bodies were placed into three layers according to whether they were near-spherical bodies, approximated to ellipsoids, or elongated and irregular bodies. In this shape-cube method, shapes of small bodies can be described as linear combinations of the starting ones. However, there is still a lack of a continuous index to quantitatively describe which small bodies should be recognized as near-spherical bodies, approximated to ellipsoids, or elongated bodies. Since Buonagura et al. used this method to assess the image processing robustness of small-body shapes and to compare the best technique, it would be better to have an index to define layers.

In this research, with the concept of entropy in statistical physics, a characteristic shape index, called shape entropy, is proposed to compare the shape difference between small bodies and uniform spheres. Entropy mainly describes the degree of data concentration, which differs from the variance as entropy has more tremendous advantages in describing the degree of data concentration with a multimodal distribution. When the data set distributes near several peaks, the variance will reflect that the data is not centralized enough, while the entropy can still reflect the data set with obvious peaks. Ni et al. have given a detailed description and derivation [44].

In order to illustrate the applicability of shape entropy, firstly, in Section 2, the shape differences among regular polygons, rectangles, ellipses, and circles with different aspect ratios are compared by using shape entropy using the 2D continuous case. Secondly, in Section 3, the shape differences among three kinds of regular polyhedrons, cuboids, triaxial ellipsoids with different axial length ratios, and spheres are compared by using shape entropy using the 3D continuous case. Finally, in Section 4, combined with the characteristics of the polyhedral models, the shape entropies are used to describe the shape differences between the small bodies and the homogeneous spheres of equal volume in the cases of three-dimensional discretization, and the results are compared with that of Equation (1).

2. Shape Entropy in the 2D Continuous Cases

2.1. Definition

A plane geometric figure is compared with a circle. According to the polar coordinates defined in Figure 1, we have a normalized quantity

$$p_s(\theta) = \frac{r_s(\theta)^2/2}{\int_0^{2\pi} (r_s(\theta)^2/2)\mathrm{d}\theta}, \tag{2}$$

where $r_s(\theta)$ is a single-valued function, and the denominator part depicts the area of the plane geometry, making

$$\int_0^{2\pi} p_s \mathrm{d}\theta = 1. \tag{3}$$

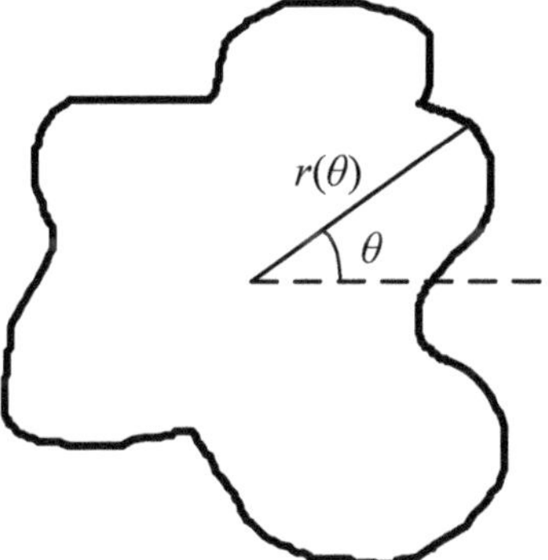

Figure 1. An illustration of arbitrary planar geometry.

The shape entropy in the 2D continuous case is defined as

$$S = -\int_0^{2\pi} p_s \log(p_s)\mathrm{d}\theta. \tag{4}$$

For a circle with radius a, we have $r_s(\theta) \equiv a$, thus

$$p_s(\theta) = \frac{r_s(\theta)^2/2}{\int_0^{2\pi} (r_s(\theta)^2/2)\mathrm{d}\theta} = \frac{a^2/2}{\pi a^2} = \frac{1}{2\pi}, \tag{5}$$

$$S = -\int_0^{2\pi} p_s \log(p_s)\mathrm{d}\theta = \log(2\pi) = 1.83788\ldots \tag{6}$$

2.2. Regular Polygons

The shape entropies of regular polygons are calculated and compared with the result of Equation (6). The calculation diagram is illustrated in Figure 2.

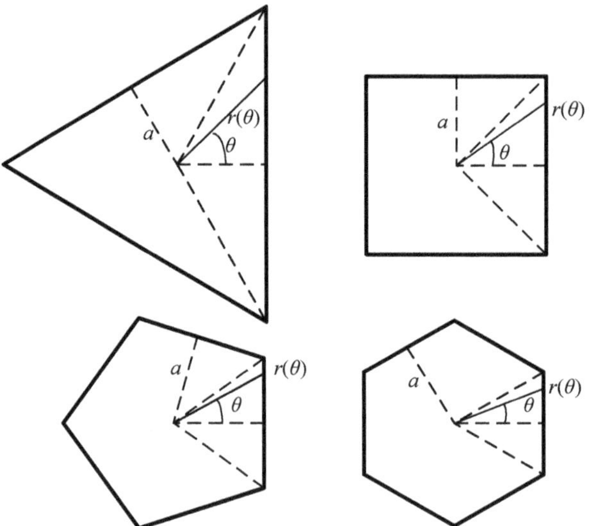

Figure 2. An illustration of regular polygon shape entropy calculations.

For a regular triangle with an inscribed circle radius a, we have

$$r_s(\theta) = \frac{a}{\cos\theta}, \theta \in \left[-\frac{\pi}{3}, \frac{\pi}{3}\right], \tag{7}$$

$$p_s(\theta) = \frac{r_s(\theta)^2/2}{3\int_{-\frac{\pi}{3}}^{\frac{\pi}{3}} (r_s(\theta)^2/2)\mathrm{d}\theta} = \frac{\frac{a^2}{2\cos^2\theta}}{6\sqrt{3}a^2} = \frac{1}{12\sqrt{3}\cos^2\theta}, \tag{8}$$

$$S = -3\int_{-\frac{\pi}{3}}^{\frac{\pi}{3}} p_s \log(p_s)\mathrm{d}\theta = 1.74557\ldots \tag{9}$$

The derivation of their entropies can be referred to as Appendix A for the square, regular pentagon, and regular hexagon cases. The results are summarized in Table 1.

Table 1. The shape entropies of regular polygons.

Number of Sides of Regular Polygons	Shape Entropy S
3	1.74557 ...
4	1.81549 ...
5	1.82964 ...
6	1.83412 ...
...	...
∞	$\log(2\pi) = 1.83788\ldots$

It is not difficult to see that the shape entropy is independent of the size of the geometry, a, and only related to the shape. With the increase of the regular n-sided shape, n, the value of S tends to be closer to the circular case $\log(2\pi) = 1.83788\ldots$ In fact, it can be obtained through calculation

$$\begin{aligned}
&\lim_{n\to+\infty} -n\int_{-\frac{\pi}{n}}^{\frac{\pi}{n}} \frac{\frac{a^2}{2\cos^2\theta}}{n\int_{-\frac{\pi}{n}}^{\frac{\pi}{n}}\left[\frac{a^2}{2\cos^2\theta}\right]\mathrm{d}\theta} \log\left\{\frac{\frac{a^2}{2\cos^2\theta}}{n\int_{-\frac{\pi}{n}}^{\frac{\pi}{n}}\left[\frac{a^2}{2\cos^2\theta}\right]\mathrm{d}\theta}\right\}\mathrm{d}\theta \\
&= \lim_{n\to+\infty} -n\int_{-\frac{\pi}{n}}^{\frac{\pi}{n}} \left\{\frac{\sec^2\theta}{n\int_{-\frac{\pi}{n}}^{\frac{\pi}{n}}\sec^2\theta\mathrm{d}\theta}\log\left[\frac{\sec^2\theta}{n\int_{-\frac{\pi}{n}}^{\frac{\pi}{n}}\sec^2\theta\mathrm{d}\theta}\right]\right\}\mathrm{d}\theta = \log(2\pi),
\end{aligned} \tag{10}$$

so that the series of shape entropy of the regular n-sided shape $\{S_n\}$ tends to the shape entropy of a circle $\log(2\pi) = 1.83788\ldots$ when n tends to $+\infty$. Note that entropy in statistical physics describes the concentration of states, and the value of entropy is the largest when the probabilities of all states are equal. Thus, when r_s are equal, corresponding to the most regular case, the shape entropy in 2D cases is the largest.

2.3. Rectangles and Ellipses

For a rectangle with a long side $2a$ and a short side $2b$, Equations (2)–(4) are transformed as

$$r_s(\theta) = \begin{cases} \frac{a}{\cos\theta}, \theta \in [0, \arctan(b/a)] \\ \frac{b}{\sin\theta}, \theta \in \left[\arctan(b/a), \frac{\pi}{2}\right] \end{cases}, \tag{11}$$

$$p_s(\theta) = \frac{r_s(\theta)^2/2}{4\int_0^{\frac{\pi}{2}}(r_s(\theta)^2/2)\mathrm{d}\theta} = \begin{cases} \frac{a}{8b\cos^2\theta}, \theta \in [0, \arctan(b/a)] \\ \frac{b}{8a\sin^2\theta}, \theta \in \left[\arctan(b/a), \frac{\pi}{2}\right] \end{cases}, \tag{12}$$

$$S = -4\int_0^{\frac{\pi}{2}} p_s \log(p_s)\mathrm{d}\theta. \tag{13}$$

The shape entropy of any rectangle can be calculated via Equations (11)–(13).

For an ellipse with a major axis $2a$ and a minor axis $2b$, Equations (2)–(4) are transformed as

$$r_s(\theta) = \frac{ab}{\sqrt{b^2\cos^2\theta + a^2\sin^2\theta}}, \tag{14}$$

$$p_s(\theta) = \frac{r_s(\theta)^2/2}{\int_0^{\pi}(r_s(\theta)^2/2)\mathrm{d}\theta} = \frac{ab}{2\pi\left[b^2\cos^2\theta + a^2\sin^2\theta\right]}, \tag{15}$$

$$S = -\int_0^{2\pi} p_s \log(p_s)\mathrm{d}\theta. \tag{16}$$

It should be noted that Equation (14) is not the parametric equation of an ellipse.

The shape entropy of any ellipse can be calculated via Equations (14)–(16).

For different shapes of rectangles and ellipses represented by a:b, their shape entropies are calculated and summarized as Table 2.

For rectangles, when a:b tends to 1:1, S tends to the shape entropy of the square 1.81549... and when a:b = 1:1, Equations (11)–(13) degenerate to the square case Equations (A1)–(A3). The shape entropy of a rectangle is independent of the size of the rectangle and only depends on its shape, which is consistent with the general understanding.

For ellipses, when a:b tends to 1:1, S tends to the shape entropy of the circle 1.83788 ... and when a:b = 1:1, Equations (14)–(16) degenerate to the circle case Equations (5) and (6). Similarly, as in the rectangles cases, the shape entropy of an ellipse is independent of the size and only depends on its shape, which is also consistent with the general understanding.

Comparing the results of Table 2, it can also be found that when a rectangle and an ellipse with the same length ratio are compared, the shape of the ellipse is closer to the circle, which is also consistent with general cognition.

Table 2. The shape entropies of rectangles and ellipses.

a:*b*	Rectangle	Ellipse
3:1	1.49387 ...	1.55019 ...
2:1	1.68228 ...	1.72009 ...
1.5:1	1.76905 ...	1.79706 ...
1:1	1.81549...	log(2π) = 1.83788 ...

For non-convex shapes described in Figure 3, Equations (11) and (12) are transformed as

$$r_s(\theta) = \begin{cases} \frac{a}{\cos\theta}, & \theta \in [0, \arctan(b/a)] \\ \sqrt{x^2(\theta) + y^2(\theta)}, \theta \in \left[\arctan(b/a), \frac{\pi}{2}\right] \\ \text{where } x(\theta) = \frac{ac}{c-b+a\tan\theta}, y(\theta) = x(\theta)\tan\theta \end{cases}, \quad (17)$$

$$p_s(\theta) = \frac{r_s(\theta)^2/2}{4\int_0^{\frac{\pi}{2}} (r_s(\theta)^2/2) d\theta} = \begin{cases} \frac{a^2}{2\cos^2\theta[4ab-2a(b-c)]}, \theta \in [0, \arctan(b/a)] \\ \frac{x^2(\theta)+y^2(\theta)}{2[4ab-2a(b-c)]}, \theta \in \left[\arctan(b/a), \frac{\pi}{2}\right] \end{cases}. \quad (18)$$

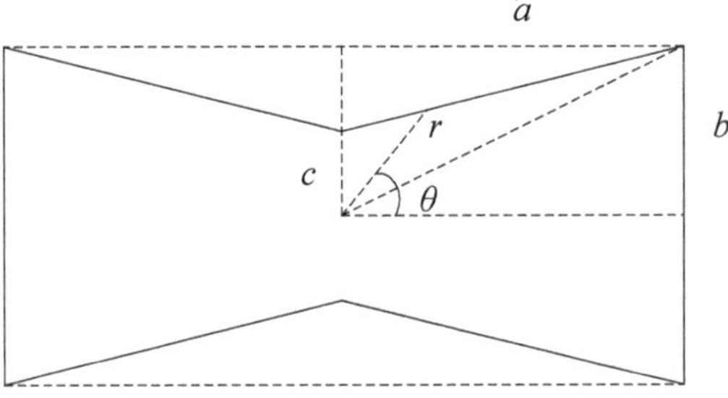

Figure 3. An illustration of the non-convex shapes transformed from a rectangle.

The shape entropies of non-convex shapes from Figure 3 are calculated as Equations (13), (17) and (18). Setting b = 1, c varying from 0.1 to 1 and a = 1, 1.5, $\sqrt{3}$, and 2, the shape entropies are shown in Figure 4. The results show that non-convex shapes are more irregular as c decreases, which is intuitive. Therefore, it is reasonable to compare the difference between the two-dimensional shape and the circle with the shape entropy defined by Equations (2)–(4).

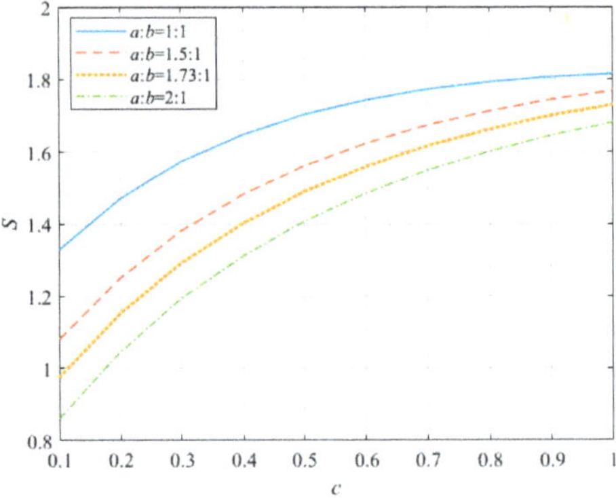

Figure 4. The shape entropies of non-convex shapes are shown in Figure 3, provided that b = 1, a = 1, 1.5, $\sqrt{3}$, 2, and $c \in [0.1, 1]$.

3. Shape Entropy in the 3D Continuous Cases

3.1. Definition

In this section, the description of the shape entropy is extended from 2D to 3D to compare the difference between spatial geometry and a sphere. According to the spherical coordinates defined in Figure 5, we can write a similar normalized quantity as in Section 2.

$$p_s(\theta,\phi) = \frac{\sin\phi \; r_s(\theta,\phi)^3/3}{\int_0^{2\pi}\int_0^{\pi}\left(r_s(\theta,\phi)^3/3\right)\sin\phi \mathrm{d}\phi \mathrm{d}\theta}, \tag{19}$$

where r_s (θ, ϕ) is a single-valued function, and the denominator part depicts the volume of the spatial geometry, making

$$\int_0^{2\pi}\int_0^{\pi} p_s(\theta,\phi)\mathrm{d}\phi \mathrm{d}\theta = 1. \tag{20}$$

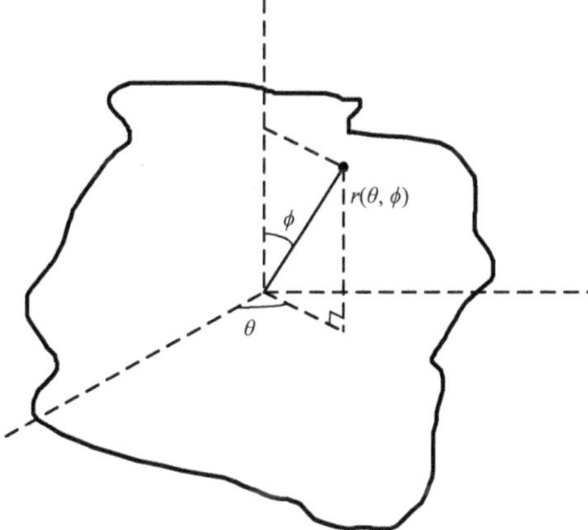

Figure 5. An illustration of arbitrary spatial geometry.

The shape entropy in the 3D continuous case is defined as

$$S = -\int_0^{2\pi}\int_0^{\pi} p_s(\theta,\phi)\log[p_s(\theta,\phi)]\mathrm{d}\phi \mathrm{d}\theta. \tag{21}$$

For a sphere with r_s $(\theta, \varphi) \equiv a$, Equation (19) is transformed as

$$p_s(\theta,\phi) = \frac{\sin\phi \; r_s(\theta,\phi)^3/3}{\int_0^{2\pi}\int_0^{\pi}\left(r_s(\theta,\phi)^3/3\right)\sin\phi \mathrm{d}\phi \mathrm{d}\theta} = \frac{\sin\phi \; a^3/3}{4\pi a^3/3} = \frac{\sin\phi}{4\pi}, \tag{22}$$

and the shape entropy calculated via Equation (21) is

$$S = -\int_0^{2\pi}\int_0^{\pi} p_s(\theta,\phi)\log[p_s(\theta,\phi)]\mathrm{d}\phi \mathrm{d}\theta = \log(2\pi) + 1 = 2.83788\ldots \tag{23}$$

3.2. Regular Polyhedrons

In this subsection, the shape entropies of a regular tetrahedron, hexahedron, and octahedron are derived and summarized in Table 3. For a regular tetrahedron, 1/24 of it is taken according to symmetry, as shown in Figure 6, and it can be deduced that:

$$r_s(\theta,\phi) = \frac{a}{\cos\phi}, \theta \in \left[0, \frac{\pi}{3}\right], \phi \in \left[0, \arctan\left(\frac{\sqrt{2}}{\cos\theta}\right)\right], \tag{24}$$

$$\begin{aligned} p_s(\theta,\phi) &= \frac{\sin\phi r_s(\theta,\phi)^3/3}{24\int_0^{\frac{\pi}{3}}\int_0^{\arctan[\frac{\sqrt{2}}{\cos\theta}]}\left(r_s(\theta,\phi)^3/3\right)\sin\phi d\phi d\theta} \\ &= \frac{\sin\phi a^3/3/\cos^3\phi}{8\sqrt{3}a^3} = \frac{\sin\phi}{24\sqrt{3}\cos^3\phi}, \end{aligned} \tag{25}$$

$$S = -24\int_0^{\frac{\pi}{3}}\int_0^{\arctan[\frac{\sqrt{2}}{\cos\theta}]} p_s(\theta,\phi)\log[p_s(\theta,\phi)]d\phi d\theta = 2.60889\ldots \tag{26}$$

Table 3. The shape entropies of regular polyhedrons.

Number of Faces of Regular Polyhedrons	Shape Entropy S
4	2.60889 ...
6	2.73379 ...
8	2.82407...
Spherical case	log(2π) + 1 = 2.83788...

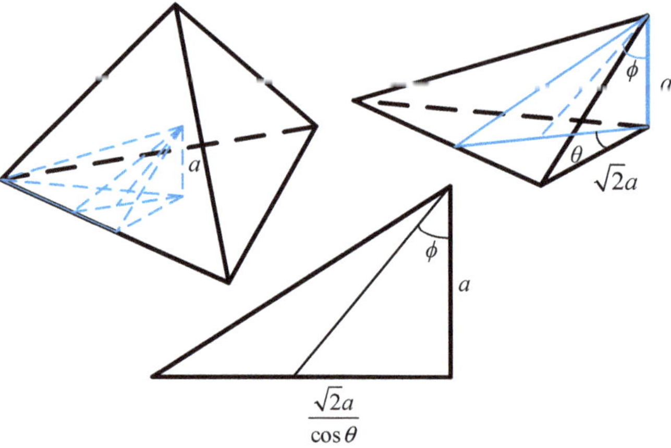

Figure 6. An illustration of a regular tetrahedron and the calculation of its shape entropy.

For a regular hexahedron with an edge length of $2a$, as shown in Figure 7, one-eighth of the hexahedron is taken according to symmetry. In this part, the distance from the point on the surface to the centroid of the regular hexahedron can be determined according to θ and φ into four parts:

$$r_s(\theta,\phi) = \begin{cases} \frac{a}{\cos\phi}, & \theta \in \left[0, \frac{\pi}{4}\right], \phi \in [0, \arctan(\cos\theta)] \\ \frac{a}{\cos\theta\sin\phi}, & \theta \in \left[0, \frac{\pi}{4}\right], \phi \in \left[\arctan(\cos\theta), \frac{\pi}{2}\right] \\ \frac{a}{\cos\phi}, & \theta \in \left[\frac{\pi}{4}, \frac{\pi}{2}\right], \phi \in [0, \arctan(\sin\theta)] \\ \frac{a}{\sin\theta\sin\phi}, & \theta \in \left[\frac{\pi}{4}, \frac{\pi}{2}\right], \phi \in \left[\arctan(\sin\theta), \frac{\pi}{2}\right] \end{cases}, \tag{27}$$

then we have

$$p_s(\theta,\phi) = \frac{{r_s}^3(\theta,\phi)\sin\phi}{24a^3}, \tag{28}$$

$$S = -8\int_0^{\frac{\pi}{2}}\int_0^{\frac{\pi}{2}} p_s(\theta,\phi)\log[p_s(\theta,\phi)]\mathrm{d}\phi\mathrm{d}\theta = 2.73379\ldots \tag{29}$$

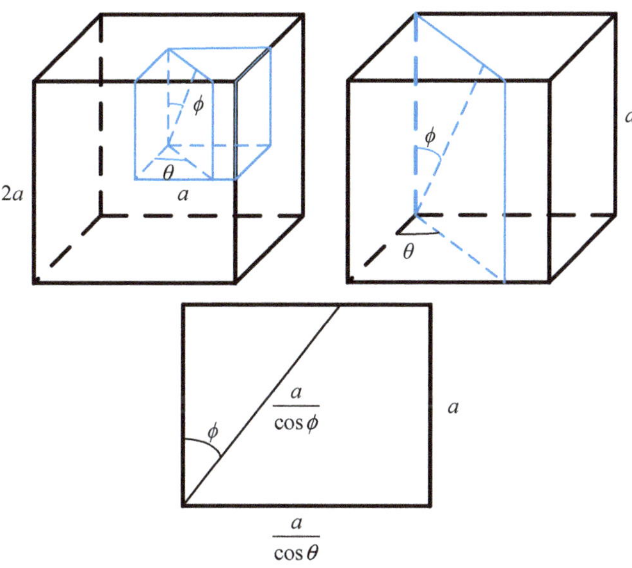

Figure 7. An illustration of a regular hexahedron and the calculation of its shape entropy.

For a regular octahedron with an edge length of $2a$, as shown in Figure 8, one-eighth of the octahedron is taken according to symmetry. In this part, using the sine theorem and cosine theorem, the distance from the point on the surface of the original regular octahedron to the centroid can be expressed as:

$$r_s(\theta,\phi) = \frac{\sqrt{2}a}{\cos\phi + \sqrt{2}\cos\theta\sin\phi}, \theta \in \left[-\frac{\pi}{4},\frac{\pi}{4}\right], \phi \in \left[0,\frac{\pi}{2}\right], \tag{30}$$

Equation (19) is transformed as

$$\begin{aligned} p_s(\theta,\phi) &= \frac{\sin\phi\, r_s(\theta,\phi)^3/3}{8\int_{-\frac{\pi}{4}}^{\frac{\pi}{4}}\int_0^{\frac{\pi}{2}}\left(r_s(\theta,\phi)^3/3\right)\sin\phi\mathrm{d}\phi\mathrm{d}\theta} \\ &= \frac{\sin\phi\, r_s(\theta,\phi)^3/3}{8\sqrt{3}a^3/3} = \frac{\sin\phi\, r_s(\theta,\phi)^3}{8\sqrt{3}a^3}, \end{aligned} \tag{31}$$

so, the shape entropy of a regular octahedron is

$$S = -8\int_{-\frac{\pi}{4}}^{\frac{\pi}{4}}\int_0^{\frac{\pi}{2}} p_s(\theta,\phi)\log[p_s(\theta,\phi)]\mathrm{d}\phi\mathrm{d}\theta = 2.82407\ldots \tag{32}$$

It is not difficult to see that the shape entropy of 3D continuous cases, defined in Section 3.1, is independent of the size of the geometry, a, and is only related to the shape. With the face increasing of regular polyhedrons, the value of S is closer to the spherical case $\log(2\pi) + 1 = 2.83788\ldots$

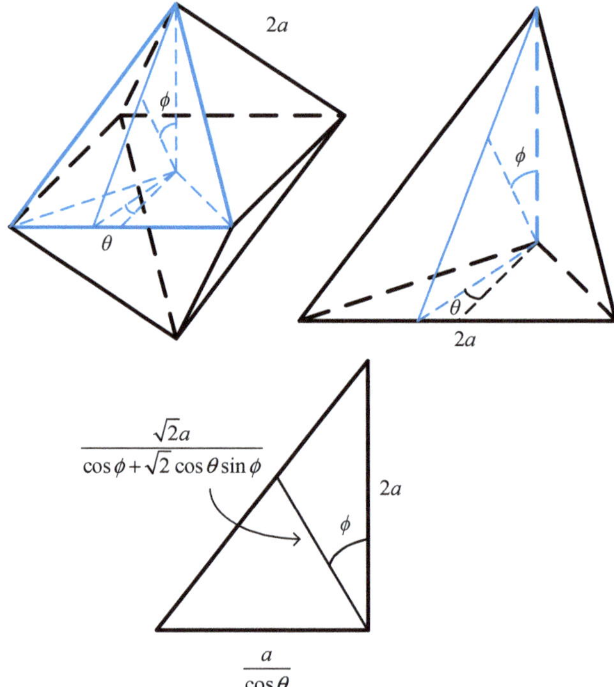

Figure 8. An illustration of a regular octahedron and the calculation of its shape entropy.

3.3. Cuboids and Triaxial Ellipsoids

For a cuboid with edge lengths $2a$, $2b$ and $2c$ respectively ($a > b > c$), it can be deduced that

$$r_s(\theta,\phi) = \begin{cases} \frac{c}{\cos\phi}, & \theta \in \left[0, \arctan\left(\frac{a}{b}\right)\right], \phi \in \left[0, \arctan\left(\frac{c}{b}\cos\theta\right)\right] \\ \frac{b}{\cos\theta\sin\phi}, & \theta \in \left[0, \arctan\left(\frac{a}{b}\right)\right], \phi \in \left[\arctan\left(\frac{c}{b}\cos\theta\right), \frac{\pi}{2}\right] \\ \frac{c}{\cos\phi}, & \theta \in \left[\arctan\left(\frac{a}{b}\right), \frac{\pi}{2}\right], \phi \in \left[0, \arctan\left(\frac{c}{a}\sin\theta\right)\right] \\ \frac{a}{\sin\theta\sin\phi}, & \theta \in \left[\arctan\left(\frac{a}{b}\right), \frac{\pi}{2}\right], \phi \in \left[\arctan\left(\frac{c}{a}\sin\theta\right), \frac{\pi}{2}\right] \end{cases}, \quad (33)$$

Equation (19) is transformed as

$$\begin{aligned} p_s(\theta,\phi) &= \frac{r_s{}^3(\theta,\phi)\sin\phi}{24abc} \\ &= \begin{cases} \frac{c^2\sin\phi}{24ab\cos^3\phi}, & \theta \in \left[0, \arctan\left(\frac{a}{b}\right)\right], \phi \in \left[0, \arctan\left(\frac{c}{b}\cos\theta\right)\right] \\ \frac{b^2}{24ac\cos^3\theta\sin^2\phi}, & \theta \in \left[0, \arctan\left(\frac{a}{b}\right)\right], \phi \in \left[\arctan\left(\frac{c}{b}\cos\theta\right), \frac{\pi}{2}\right] \\ \frac{c^2\sin\phi}{24ab\cos^3\phi}, & \theta \in \left[\arctan\left(\frac{a}{b}\right), \frac{\pi}{2}\right], \phi \in \left[0, \arctan\left(\frac{c}{a}\sin\theta\right)\right] \\ \frac{a^2}{24bc\sin^3\theta\sin^2\phi}, & \theta \in \left[\arctan\left(\frac{a}{b}\right), \frac{\pi}{2}\right], \phi \in \left[\arctan\left(\frac{c}{a}\sin\theta\right), \frac{\pi}{2}\right] \end{cases}, \end{aligned} \quad (34)$$

and the shape entropy of the cuboid is

$$S = -8\int_0^{\frac{\pi}{2}}\int_0^{\frac{\pi}{2}} p_s(\theta,\phi)\log[p_s(\theta,\phi)]\mathrm{d}\phi\mathrm{d}\theta. \quad (35)$$

The shape entropy of an arbitrary cuboid can be calculated by Equations (33)–(35). Shape entropies of cuboids with different combinations of a and b, provided that $c = 1$, are calculated, and the results are shown in Figure 9. When $a{:}b{:}c = 1{:}1{:}1$, Equation (33) degenerates to Equation (27), and the shape entropy equals the hexahedron case 2.73379....

It is shown again that the shape entropy of a cuboid is independent of the size, and only depends on the shape of the cuboid.

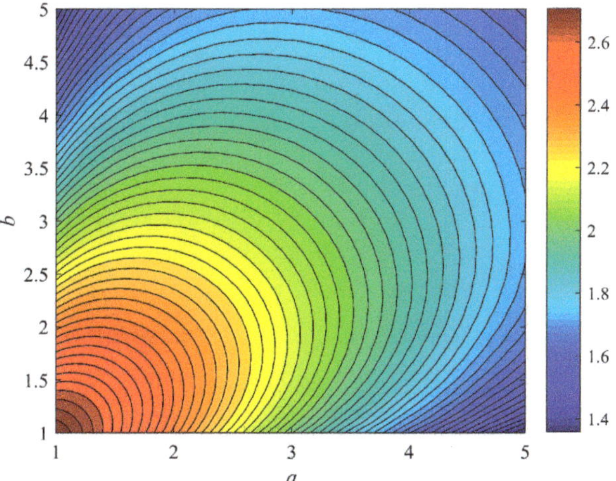

Figure 9. The shape entropies of cuboids with different edge length ratios of a and b, provided that $c = 1$. The blue area suggests a more irregular shape. The lower left corner corresponds to the regular hexahedron.

For an ellipsoid with triaxial lengths $2a$, $2b$ and $2c$ respectively ($a > b > c$), it can be deduced that

$$r_s(\theta,\phi) = \frac{abc}{\sqrt{b^2c^2cos^2\phi\sin^2\theta + a^2c^2\sin^2\phi\sin^2\theta + a^2b^2\cos^2\phi}}, \tag{36}$$

$$\begin{aligned} p_s(\theta,\phi) &= \frac{\sin\phi\ r_s(\theta,\phi)^3/3}{\int_0^{2\pi}\int_0^{\pi}\left(r_s(\theta,\phi)^3/3\right)\sin\phi\mathrm{d}\phi\mathrm{d}\theta} \\ &= \frac{\sin\phi\ r_s(\theta,\phi)^3/3}{4\pi abc/3} = \frac{\sin\phi\ r_s(\theta,\phi)^3}{4\pi abc}, \end{aligned} \tag{37}$$

$$S = -\int_0^{2\pi}\int_0^{\pi} p_s\log(p_s)\mathrm{d}\phi\mathrm{d}\theta. \tag{38}$$

It should also be noted that Equation (36) is not the parametric equation of an ellipsoid.

The shape entropy of an arbitrary ellipsoid can be calculated by Equations (36)–(38). Shape entropies of ellipsoids with different combinations of a and b, provided that $c = 1$, are calculated, and results are shown in Figure 10. When a:b:c = 1:1:1, Equation (36) degenerates to the sphere case, and the shape entropy equals the sphere case. It is shown again that the shape entropy of an ellipsoid is independent of the size, and only depends on the shape of the ellipsoid.

By comparing the results of a few values of a and b, summarized in Table 4, it can also be deduced that the shape of the ellipsoid is closer to the sphere when a cuboid and an ellipsoid with the same axial/edge length ratio are compared. When $c = 1$, the difference between the shape entropy of the ellipsoid and the cuboid calculated by different combinations of a and b is shown in Figure 11. It can be seen that when the shape is close to slender, the difference between the shape of the ellipsoid and the cuboid is more significant; when the shape is nearly flat, the difference between the ellipsoid and the cuboid is relatively small; when the axial/edge length ratio is 1:1:1, the shape difference between the two is minimal.

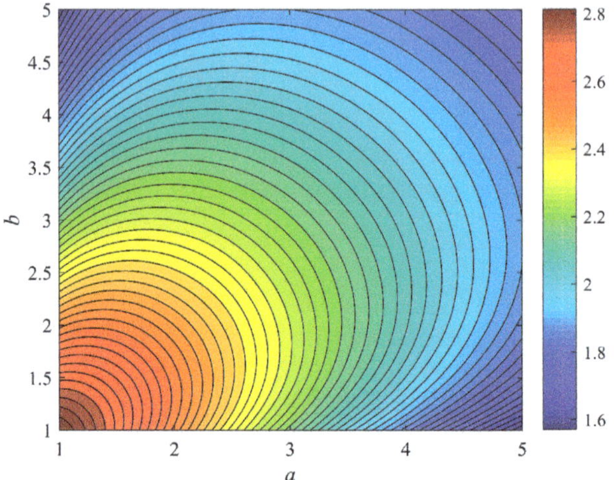

Figure 10. The shape entropies of ellipsoids with different axial length ratios of *a* and *b*, provided that $c = 1$. The blue area suggests a more irregular shape. The lower left corner corresponds to the sphere.

Table 4. The shape entropies of cuboids and ellipsoids.

a:*b*:*c*	Cuboid	Ellipsoid
3:2:1	2.15642 . . .	2.29111 . . .
2:2:1	2.37094 . . .	2.48964 . . .
2:1.5:1	2.43230 . . .	2.55064 . . .
1:1:1	2.73379....	$\log(2\pi) + 1 = 2.83788\ldots$

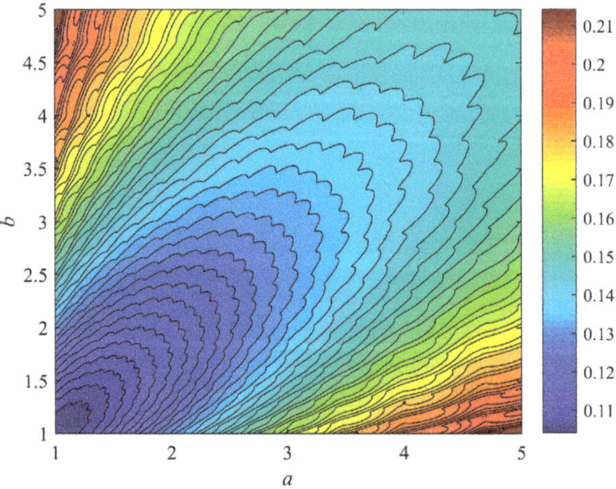

Figure 11. The differences in shape entropies of ellipsoids and cuboids with different axial length ratios. The blue area suggests less difference. Since it is assumed that $c = 1$ for all shapes shown, diagonal line $a = b$ corresponds to flat shapes, and axis *a* or *b* corresponds to slender shapes.

4. Shape Entropy Applied to Polyhedral Models of Small Bodies

4.1. Definition

Since the polyhedral models of small bodies are discrete vertex-face models, we transform Equation (19) as

$$p_S^n = \frac{r_S^n}{\sum\limits_{n=1}^{N} r_S^n}, \tag{39}$$

where r_S^n denotes the distance between the nth vertex and the centroid, and N denotes the number of vertices. Equation (39) is a normalized quantity whose denominator part is the sum of the distances from all vertices to the centroid, making

$$\sum_{n=1}^{N} p_S^n = 1. \tag{40}$$

The shape entropy of the polyhedral model of a small body is defined as

$$S = -\sum_{n=1}^{N} p_S^n \log(p_S^n) - \log(N). \tag{41}$$

At the last term of Equation (41), log(N) is subtracted to eliminate the influence caused by the different number of vertices of polyhedral models. When the object is a sphere, each point is the same distance from the centroid, and the shape entropy is

$$S = -\sum_{n=1}^{N} \frac{1}{N} \log\left(\frac{1}{N}\right) - \log(N) = log(N) - \log(N) = 0. \tag{42}$$

By comparing the shape entropy S, as defined by Equations (39)–(41), we can compare the shape of the polyhedral model with that of the homogeneous sphere with equal volume.

4.2. Results

The shape entropies, S, of some polyhedral models [45] of small bodies are calculated according to Equations (39)–(41) and are listed in Table 5 in the order of S from large to small, listed together with the values of ρ from Equation (1). It can be seen that although the shape entropies of the first four small bodies are the same, the range of ρ is extensive. It can be seen more clearly from Figure 12 that the four near-spherical small bodies, corresponding to points 1–4, are on the most right in the figure, and their shapes are close to spheres (Figure 13). Although the four small bodies approximated to ellipsoids (Figure 14), corresponding to points 5–8, have specific differences in shape and spheres, they are obviously different from the shape of elongated small bodies, corresponding to points 9–12 (Figure 15), on the left of the figure.

Only ρ calculated by Equation (1) cannot describe the shape well. When the principal moments of inertia of the small body are relatively close, the ρ values differ significantly. However, the appearances of small bodies are similar, such as the four small bodies numbered 1–4. The appearance and shape of small bodies with similar ρ values may also differ significantly, such as small bodies 6 and 8, and 9–12. The shape of the polyhedral model can be compared with that of the homogeneous sphere of the same volume sphere with the help of Equation (42), and the shape of the small body can be better described together with Equation (1).

According to the results in Table 5 and Figure 12, the shapes of small bodies from near-spherical to elongated can be described with shape entropy from large to small. The new description is quantitative rather than terms without accurate definitions, although the exact demarcation for near-spherical, ellipsoids, and elongated can be further discussed. In this work, we suggest that so-called near-spherical bodies have shape entropies larger than -0.004, small bodies approximated to ellipsoids corresponding to those whose entropies lie between −0.02 and −0.004, and small bodies with shape entropies less than −0.02 can be labeled as elongated. It would also be more applicable in a further discussion on characteristics related to shapes.

Table 5. The shape entropies of polyhedral models of small bodies.

Name of Small Bodies	Shape Entropy S	Vertices	Faces	ρ from Equation (1)	No. in Figure 12
52760 (1998 ML_{14})	−0.001118600	8162	16,320	0.877608	1
101955 Bennu	−0.001171272	1348	2692	0.320574	2
1998 KY_{26}	−0.001469927	2048	4092	0.823293	3
4 Vesta	−0.003386096	2522	5040	0.165797	4
9P/Tempel	−0.008419353	16,022	32,040	0.779807	5
6489 Golevka	−0.011491285	2048	4092	0.964472	6
3103 Eger	−0.013905315	997	1990	0.648360	7
951 Gaspra	−0.019957635	2522	5040	0.914083	8
4769 Castalia	−0.028763986	2048	4092	0.896695	/
2063 Bacchus	−0.034839183	2048	4092	0.986248	/
25143 Itokawa	−0.039069503	25,350	49,152	0.932418	/
1P/Halley	−0.039881773	2522	5040	0.934006	/
1620 Geographos	−0.042576975	8192	16,380	0.942497	/
4486 Mithra	−0.049464462	3000	5996	0.860466	/
1996 HW_1	−0.057551792	1392	2780	0.973871	/
433 Eros	−0.060992619	99,846	196,608	0.978736	9
216 Kleopatra	−0.074191101	2048	4092	0.990365	10
243 Ida	−0.085757437	2522	5040	0.883693	11
103P/Hartley	−0.098676873	16,022	32,040	0.975002	12

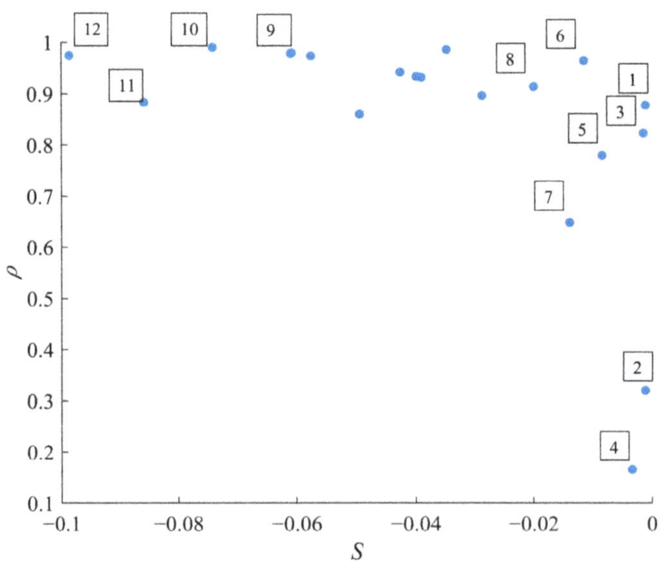

Figure 12. The distribution of shape entropies (S) and ρ from Equation (1) of different small bodies. No. 1–12 can be referred in Table 5, and their shapes are shown in Figures 13–15.

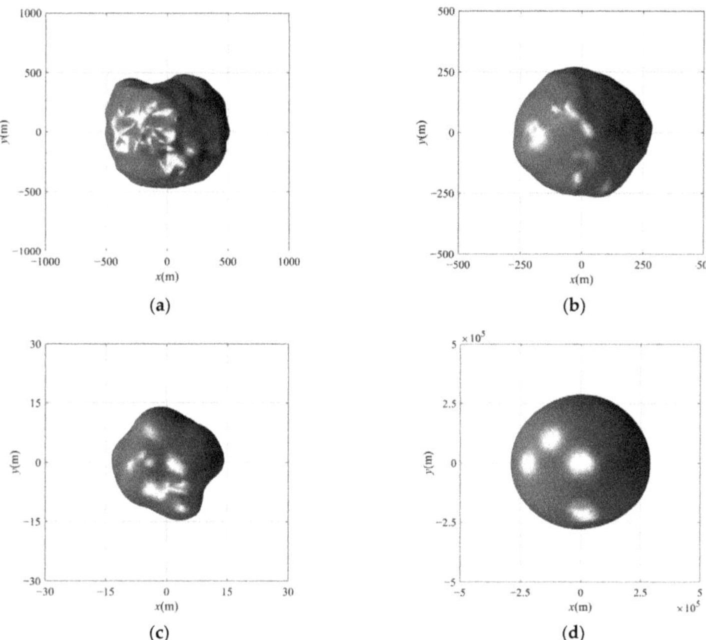

Figure 13. Polyhedral models corresponding to points 1–4 in Figure 12. (**a**) 52,760 (1998 ML_{14}). (**b**) 101,955 Bennu. (**c**) 1998 KY_{26}. (**d**) 4 Vesta.

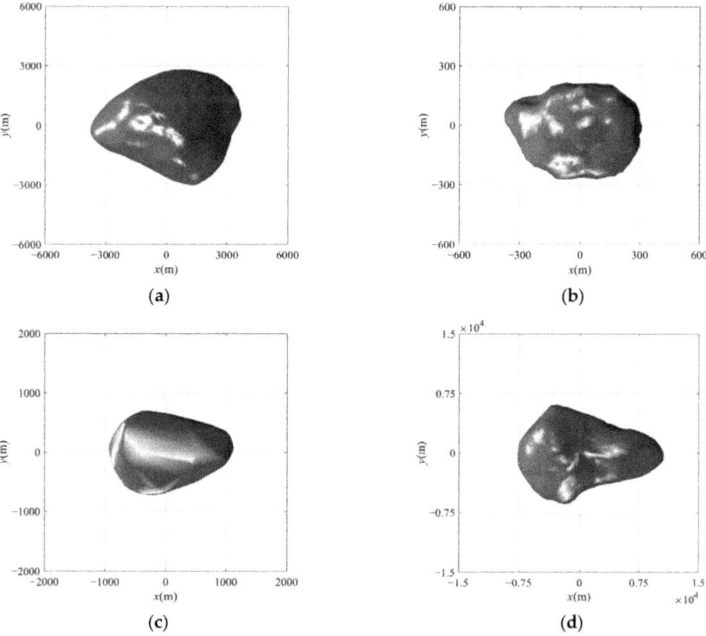

Figure 14. Polyhedral models corresponding to points 5–8 in Figure 12. (**a**) 9P/Tempel. (**b**) 6489 Golevka. (**c**) 3103 Eger. (**d**) 951 Gaspra.

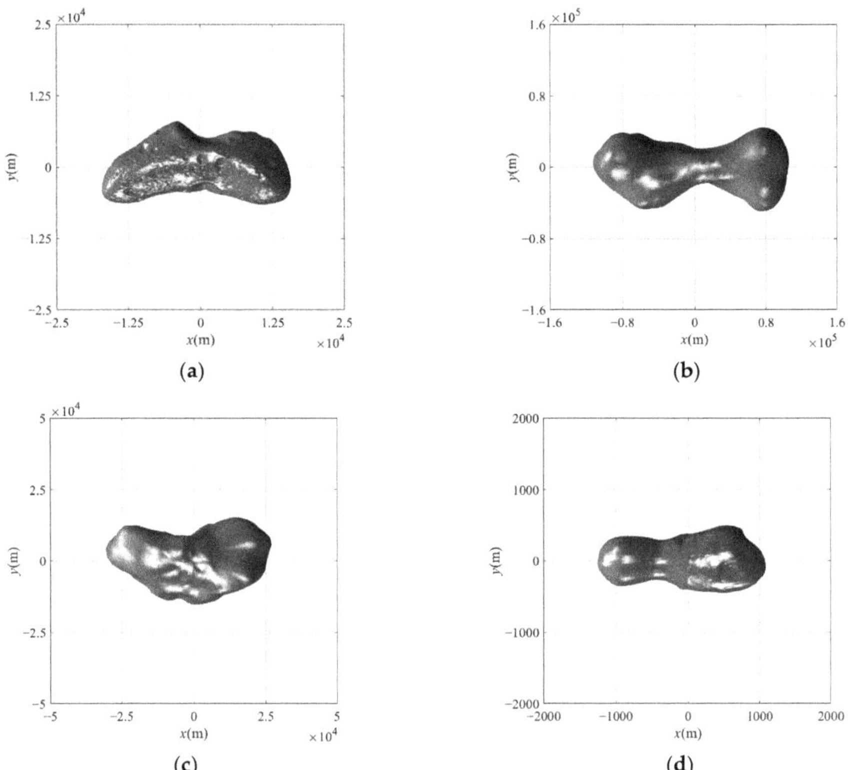

Figure 15. Polyhedral models corresponding to points 9–12 in Figure 12. (**a**) 433 Eros. (**b**) 216 Kleopatra. (**c**) 243 Ida. (**d**) 103P/Hartley.

5. Conclusions

This study proposes shape entropy as an index to compare the shape differences between small bodies and homogeneous spheres of equal volume. First, the methods of comparing plane geometry with circle and space geometry with sphere by using the shape entropy in continuous cases are given, and then the shape entropy applied to discrete cases is derived for polyhedral models. The shape entropy is independent of the size of the geometry and only depends on the shape.

In comparing plane geometric figures with circles, the shape entropies of circles and regular polygons are derived and calculated. It is proved that when n tends to infinity, the shape entropy of the regular n-sided shape tends to that of the circle. The shape entropies of rectangles and ellipses are derived and calculated, respectively. The shape entropy is used to compare the rectangle and ellipse with the same edge/axis length ratio. The shape entropies of dumbbell-like non-convex shapes transformed from rectangles are also calculated, and results show that such shapes are more irregular as their necks are more narrow, which is intuitive. Derivation and calculation prove that comparing plane geometries with circles by shape entropies is reasonable.

In comparing space geometric figures with spheres, due to the limited number of regular polyhedrons, the shape entropies of spheres, regular tetrahedrons, regular hexahedrons, and regular octahedrons are derived and calculated. It is found that the shape entropy of regular polyhedrons approaches the shape entropy of spheres with the increase in the number of faces. The shape entropies of cuboids and ellipsoids are derived and calculated, respectively. The rationality is verified by comparing different edge/axial length ratios until they degenerate to cube and sphere, respectively. The shape differences between cuboids and ellipsoids with the same edge/axial length ratio are compared by using shape entropy. The difference between an ellipsoid and a cuboid is more significant when the shape is close to slender. The difference between an ellipsoid and a cuboid is relatively small when the shape is nearly flat. When the axial/edge length ratio is 1:1:1, the shape difference between the ellipsoid and the cuboid is the smallest. Derivation and calculation prove that comparing space geometries with spheres with shape entropies is reasonable.

Sections 2 and 3 show that shape entropy is suitable for comparing 2D and 3D geometric figures with circles and spheres under continuous conditions, and the entropies of circles and spheres are the limit values in 2D and 3D cases, respectively. The difference between the shape entropy of each geometric figure and the limit value reflects the difference between this figure and the circle or sphere in shape.

A discrete form of the shape entropy is defined for small bodies simulated by polyhedral models. The shape entropies of 19 small bodies with polyhedral models are calculated, which describes the comparison results between small bodies and homogeneous spheres of equal volume. The shape comparison results between different small bodies are compared using both the shape entropy, S, and the inertia index, ρ, proposed by Hu and Scheeres [16]. For small bodies with shape entropies larger than −0.004, the inertia indices vary in the whole range of [0, 1] due to the three-axis inertia being very close; thus can not describe so-called near-spherical small bodies well. The shape entropy of a sphere body is zero, and the shape entropy of a small body decreases as the shape varies from near-spherical to elongated. The former so-called near-spherical small bodies, small bodies approximated to ellipsoids, and elongated small bodies, in Buonagura et al. [43], can be referred to as shape entropies larger than −0.004, between −0.02 and −0.004, and smaller than −0.02, respectively.

Therefore, shape entropy is a continuous index and provides a reasonably simple metric to quantitatively describe a complex shape (such as the shape of small bodies) in a generalized discussion and analysis, including further research on the shape effect of dynamic behaviors in the vicinity of small bodies (which is related to both shape/mass distribution and rotation rate and, therefore, is limited to reflect behaviors independently) and on-board optical navigations during interplanetary missions, as mentioned in the introduction, rather than highly detailed work on a specific, unique, polyhedral model.

Author Contributions: Conceptualization, Y.N. and J.L.; methodology, Y.N.; validation, H.Z., H.B. and J.L.; formal analysis, Y.N.; investigation, J.H.; data curation, Y.N.; writing—original draft preparation, Y.N. and J.H.; writing—review and editing, H.Z., J.L. and H.B.; visualization, J.H. and Y.N.; supervision, J.L. and H.B.; project administration, J.L. and H.B.; funding acquisition, H.Z. All authors have read and agreed to the published version of the manuscript.

Funding: This research is funded by the National Key R&D Program of China (grant No. 2020YFE0202100).

Institutional Review Board Statement: Not applicable.

Informed Consent Statement: Not applicable.

Data Availability Statement: All data generated or analyzed during this study are included in this published article as equations, figures, and tables.

Conflicts of Interest: The authors declare no conflict of interest.

Appendix A

For a square with an inscribed circle radius a, we have

$$r_s(\theta) = \frac{a}{\cos\theta}, \theta \in \left[-\frac{\pi}{4}, \frac{\pi}{4}\right], \tag{A1}$$

$$p_s(\theta) = \frac{r_s(\theta)^2/2}{4\int_{-\frac{\pi}{4}}^{\frac{\pi}{4}} (r_s(\theta)^2/2)\mathrm{d}\theta} = \frac{\frac{a^2}{2\cos^2\theta}}{4a^2} = \frac{1}{8\cos^2\theta}, \tag{A2}$$

$$S = -4\int_{-\frac{\pi}{4}}^{\frac{\pi}{4}} p_s \log(p_s) \mathrm{d}\theta = 1.81549\ldots \tag{A3}$$

For a regular pentagon with an inscribed circle radius a, we have

$$r_s(\theta) = \frac{a}{\cos\theta}, \theta \in \left[-\frac{\pi}{5}, \frac{\pi}{5}\right], \tag{A4}$$

$$p_s(\theta) = \frac{r_s(\theta)^2/2}{5\int_{-\frac{\pi}{5}}^{\frac{\pi}{5}} (r_s(\theta)^2/2) \mathrm{d}\theta} = \frac{\frac{a^2}{2\cos^2\theta}}{5 \times 2\sqrt{5 - 2\sqrt{5}}a^2}, \tag{A5}$$

$$S = -5\int_{-\frac{\pi}{5}}^{\frac{\pi}{5}} p_s \log(p_s) \mathrm{d}\theta = 1.82964\ldots \tag{A6}$$

For a regular hexagon with an inscribed circle radius a, we have

$$r_s(\theta) = \frac{a}{\cos\theta}, \theta \in \left[-\frac{\pi}{6}, \frac{\pi}{6}\right], \tag{A7}$$

$$p_s(\theta) = \frac{r_s(\theta)^2/2}{6\int_{-\frac{\pi}{6}}^{\frac{\pi}{6}} (r_s(\theta)^2/2) \mathrm{d}\theta} = \frac{\frac{a^2}{2\cos^2\theta}}{4\sqrt{3}a^2} = \frac{1}{8\sqrt{3}\cos^2\theta}, \tag{A8}$$

$$S = -6\int_{-\frac{\pi}{6}}^{\frac{\pi}{6}} p_s \log(p_s) \mathrm{d}\theta = 1.83412\ldots \tag{A9}$$

References

1. Zhang, Y.; Michel, P. Shapes, structures, and evolution of small bodies. *Astrodyn* **2021**, *5*, 293–329. [CrossRef]
2. IAU2006 General Assembly. Resolution B5: Definition of a Planet in the Solar System. Available online: https://www.iau.org/static/resolutions/Resolution_GA26-5-6.pdf (accessed on 9 December 2022).
3. Spohn, T. Small Solar System Body. In *Encyclopedia of Astrobiology*; Gargaud, M., Irvine, W.M., Amils, R., James, H., Pinti, D.L., Quintanilla, J.C., Rouan, D., Spohn, T., Tirard, S., Viso, M., Eds.; Springer: Berlin/Heidelberg, Germany, 2011; pp. 1516–1517. [CrossRef]
4. Sugiura, K.; Kobayashi, H.; Inutsuka, S. Toward understanding the origin of asteroid geometries-variety in shapes produced by equal-mass impacts. *Astron. Astrophys.* **2018**, *620*, A167. [CrossRef]
5. Yu, Y.; Baoyin, H. Orbital dynamics in the vicinity of asteroid 216 Kleopatra. *Astron. J.* **2012**, *143*, 62. [CrossRef]
6. Jiang, Y.; Baoyin, H.; Wang, X.; Yu, Y.; Li, H.; Peng, C.; Zhang, Z. Order and chaos near equilibrium points in the potential of rotating highly irregular-shaped celestial bodies. *Nonlinear Dyn.* **2016**, *83*, 231–252. [CrossRef]
7. Wang, X.; Jiang, Y.; Gong, S. Analysis of the Potential Field and Equilibrium Points of Irregular-shaped Minor Celestial Bodies. *Astrophys. Space Sci.* **2014**, *353*, 105–121. [CrossRef]
8. Yu, Y.; Baoyin, H. Generating families of 3D periodic orbits about asteroids. *Mon. Not. R. Astron. Soc.* **2012**, *427*, 872–881. [CrossRef]
9. Yu, Y.; Baoyin, H.; Jiang, Y. Constructing the natural families of periodic orbits near irregular bodies. *Mon. Not. R. Astron. Soc.* **2015**, *453*, 3269–3277. [CrossRef]
10. Jiang, Y.; Yu, Y.; Baoyin, H. Topological classifications and bifurcations of periodic orbits in the potential field of highly irregular-shaped celestial bodies. *Nonlinear Dyn.* **2015**, *81*, 119–140. [CrossRef]
11. Jiang, Y.; Baoyin, H.; Li, H. Periodic motion near the surface of asteroids. *Astrophys. Space Sci.* **2015**, *360*, 63. [CrossRef]
12. Ni, Y.; Jiang, Y.; Baoyin, H. Multiple bifurcations in the periodic orbit around Eros. *Astrophys. Space Sci.* **2016**, *361*, 170. [CrossRef]
13. Lan, L.; Ni, Y.; Jiang, Y.; Li, J. Motion of the moonlet in the binary system 243 Ida. *Acta Mech. Sin.* **2018**, *34*, 214–224. [CrossRef]
14. Gil-Fernandez, J.; Ortega-Hernando, G. Autonomous vision-based navigation for proximity operations around binary asteroids. *CEAS Space J.* **2018**, *10*, 287–294. [CrossRef]
15. Pellacani, A.; Cabral, F.; Alcalde, A.; Kicman, P.; Lisowski, J.; Gerth, I.; Burmann, B. Semi-autonomous attitude guidance using relative navigation based on line of sight measurements: Aim scenario. *Acta Astronaut.* **2018**, *152*, 496–508. [CrossRef]
16. Hu, W.; Scheeres, D.J. Numerical determination of stability regions for orbital motion in uniformly rotating second degree and order gravity fields. *Planet. Space Sci.* **2004**, *52*, 685–692. [CrossRef]
17. Scheeres, D.J.; Ostro, S.J.; Hudson, R.S.; Werner, R.A. Orbits close to asteroid 4769 Castalia. *Icarus* **1996**, *121*, 67–87. [CrossRef]
18. de Pater, I.; Lissauer, J.J. *Planetary Sciences*, 2nd ed.; Cambridge University Press: Cambridge, UK, 2015; pp. 247–248. [CrossRef]
19. Zhuravlev, S.G. Stability of the libration points of a rotating triaxial ellipsoid. *Celest. Mech.* **1972**, *6*, 255–267. [CrossRef]

20. Scheeres, D.J. Dynamics about uniformly rotating triaxial ellipsoids: Applications to asteroids. *Icarus* **1994**, *110*, 225–238. [CrossRef]
21. Jiang, Y. Equilibrium points and periodic orbits in the vicinity of asteroids with an application to 216 Kleopatra. *Earth Moon Planets* **2015**, *115*, 31–44. [CrossRef]
22. Jiang, Y.; Ni, Y.; Baoyin, H.; Li, J.; Liu, Y. Asteroids and Their Mathematical Methods. *Mathematics* **2022**, *10*, 2897. [CrossRef]
23. Riaguas, A.; Elipe, A.; López-Moratalla, T. Non-Linear Stability of the Equilibria in the Gravity Field of a Finite Straight Segment. *Celest. Mech. Dyn. Astron.* **2001**, *81*, 235–248. [CrossRef]
24. Broucke, R.; Elipe, A. The Dynamics of Orbits in a Potential Field of a Solid Circular Ring. *Regul. Chaotic Dyn.* **2005**, *10*, 129–143. [CrossRef]
25. Romanov, V.A.; Doedel, E.J. Periodic Orbits Associated with the Libration Points of the Homogeneous Rotating Gravitating Triaxial Ellipsoid. *Int. J. Bifurc. Chaos* **2012**, *22*, 1230035. [CrossRef]
26. Zeng, X.; Jiang, F.; Li, J.; Baoyin, H. Study on the Connection between the Rotating Mass Dipole and Natural Elongated Bodies. *Astrophys. Space Sci.* **2015**, *356*, 29–42. [CrossRef]
27. Zhang, Y.; Qian, Y.; Li, X.; Yang, X. Resonant orbit search and stability analysis for elongated asteroids. *Astrodynamics* **2023**, *7*, 51–67. [CrossRef]
28. Miller, J.K.; Konopliv, A.S.; Antreasian, P.G.; Bordi, J.J.; Chesley, S.; Helfrich, C.E.; Scheeres, D.J.; Owen, W.M.; Wang, T.C.; Williams, B.G.; et al. Determination of Shape, Gravity, and Rotational State of Asteroid 433 Eros. *Icarus* **2002**, *155*, 3–17. [CrossRef]
29. Takahashi, Y.; Bradley, N.; Kennedy, B. Determination of Celestial Body Principal Axes via Gravity Field Estimation. *J. Guid. Control Dyn.* **2017**, *40*, 3050–3060. [CrossRef]
30. Romain, G.; Jean-Pierre, B. Ellipsoidal Harmonic Expansions of the Gravitational Potential: Theory and Application. *Celest. Mech. Dyn. Astron.* **2001**, *79*, 235–275. [CrossRef]
31. Rossi, A.; Marzari, F.; Farinella, P. Orbital Evolution around Irregular Bodies. *Earth Planets Space* **1999**, *51*, 1173–1180. [CrossRef]
32. Dechambre, D.; Scheeres, D.J. Transformation of Spherical Harmonic Coefficients to Ellipsoidal Harmonic Coefficients. *Astron. Astrophys.* **2002**, *387*, 1114–1122. [CrossRef]
33. Garmier, R.; Barriot, J.P.; Konopliv, A.S.; Yeomans, D.K. Modeling of the Eros gravity Field as an Ellipsoidal Harmonic Expansion from the NEAR Doppler Tracking Data. *Geophys. Res. Lett.* **2002**, *29*, 721–723. [CrossRef]
34. Geissler, P.; Petit, J.M.; Durda, D.D.; Greenberg, R.; Bottke, W.; Nolan, M.; Moore, J. Erosion and Ejecta Reaccretion on 243 Ida and Its Moon. *Icarus* **1996**, *120*, 140–157. [CrossRef]
35. Werner, R.A. The Gravitational Potential of a Homogeneous Polyhedron or Don't Cut Corners. *Celest. Mech. Dyn. Astron.* **1994**, *59*, 253–278. [CrossRef]
36. Werner, R.A. *On the Gravity Field of Irregularly Shaped Celestial Bodies*; The University of Texas at Austin: Austin, TX, USA, 1996.
37. Werner, R.A.; Scheeres, D.J. Exterior Gravitation of a Polyhedron Derived and Compared with Harmonic and Mascon Gravitation Representations of Asteroid 4769 Castalia. *Celest. Mech. Dyn. Astron.* **1996**, *65*, 313–344. [CrossRef]
38. Mirtich, B. Fast and Accurate Computation of Polyhedral Mass Properties. *J. Graph. Tools* **1996**, *1*, 31–50. [CrossRef]
39. Zhang, Y.; Yu, Y.; Baoyin, H. Dynamical behavior of flexible net spacecraft for landing on asteroid. *Astrodynamics* **2021**, *5*, 249–261. [CrossRef]
40. Zhao, Y.; Yang, H.; Hu, J. The Fast Generation of the Reachable Domain for Collision-Free Asteroid Landing. *Mathematics* **2022**, *10*, 3763. [CrossRef]
41. Li, X.; Scheeres, D.J.; Qiao, D.; Liu, Z. Geophysical and orbital environments of asteroid 469219 2016 HO3. *Astrodyn.* **2023**, *7*, 31–50. [CrossRef]
42. Oki, Y.; Yoshikawa, K.; Takeuchi, H.; Kikuchi, S.; Ikeda, H.; Scheeres, D.J.; McMahon, J.W.; Kawaguchi, J.; Takei, Y.; Mimasu, Y.; et al. Orbit insertion strategy of Hayabusa2's rover with large release uncertainty around the asteroid Ryugu. *Astrodyn* **2020**, *4*, 309–329. [CrossRef]
43. Buonagura, C.; Pugliatti, M.; Topputo, F. Image Processing Robustness Assessment of Small-Body Shapes. *J. Astronaut. Sci.* **2022**, *69*, 1744–1765. [CrossRef]
44. Ni, Y.; Turitsyn, K.; Baoyin, H.; Li, J. Entropy Method of Measuring and Evaluating Periodicity of Quasi-periodic Trajectories. *Sci. China Phys. Mech. Astron.* **2018**, *61*, 064511. [CrossRef]
45. Neese, C.E. Small Body Radar Shape Models V2.0. EAR-A-5-DDRRADARSHAPE-MODELS-V2.0, NASA Planetary Data System. 2004. Available online: https://data.nasa.gov/Earth-Science/SMALL-BODY-RADAR-SHAPE-MODELS-V2-0/qckk-73zc (accessed on 9 December 2022).

Article

Non-Cooperative Target Attitude Estimation Method Based on Deep Learning of Ground and Space Access Scene Radar Images

Chongyuan Hou [1,*], Rongzhi Zhang [1], Kaizhong Yang [1], Xiaoyong Li [2], Yang Yang [1], Xin Ma [1], Gang Guo [1], Yuan Yang [1], Lei Liu [2] and Feng Zhou [2]

1 School of Automation Science and Engineering, Faculty of Electronic and Information Engineering, Xi'an Jiaotong University, Xi'an 710049, China
2 Key Laboratory of Electronic Information Countermeasure and Simulation Technology of Ministry of Education, Xidian University, Xi'an 710071, China
* Correspondence: houzenan@163.com

Abstract: Determining the attitude of a non-cooperative target in space is an important frontier issue in the aerospace field, and has important application value in the fields of malfunctioning satellite state assessment and non-cooperative target detection in space. This paper proposes a non-cooperative target attitude estimation method based on the deep learning of ground and space access (GSA) scene radar images to solve this problem. In GSA scenes, the observed target satellite can be imaged not only by inverse synthetic-aperture radar (ISAR), but also by space-based optical satellites, with space-based optical images providing more accurate attitude estimates for the target. The spatial orientation of the intersection of the orbital planes of the target and observation satellites can be changed by fine tuning the orbit of the observation satellite. The intersection of the orbital planes is controlled to ensure that it is collinear with the position vector of the target satellite when it is accessible to the radar. Thus, a series of GSA scenes are generated. In these GSA scenes, the high-precision attitude values of the target satellite can be estimated from the space-based optical images obtained by the observation satellite. Thus, the corresponding relationship between a series of ISAR images and the attitude estimation of the target at this moment can be obtained. Because the target attitude can be accurately estimated from the GSA scenes obtained by a space-based optical telescope, these attitude estimation values can be used as training datasets of ISAR images, and deep learning training can be performed on ISAR images of GSA scenes. This paper proposes an instantaneous attitude estimation method based on a deep network, which can achieve robust attitude estimation under different signal-to-noise ratio conditions. First, ISAR observation and imaging models were created, and the theoretical projection relationship from the three-dimensional point cloud to the ISAR imaging plane was constructed based on the radar line of sight. Under the premise that the ISAR imaging plane was fixed, the ISAR imaging results, theoretical projection map, and target attitude were in a one-to-one correspondence, which meant that the mapping relationship could be learned using a deep network. Specifically, in order to suppress noise interference, a UNet++ network with strong feature extraction ability was used to learn the mapping relationship between the ISAR imaging results and the theoretical projection map to achieve ISAR image enhancement. The shifted window (swin) transformer was then used to learn the mapping relationship between the enhanced ISAR images and target attitude to achieve instantaneous attitude estimation. Finally, the effectiveness of the proposed method was verified using electromagnetic simulation data, and it was found that the average attitude estimation error of the proposed method was less than 1°.

Keywords: deep learning; radar image; attitude estimation; non-collaborate target

MSC: 68T07

Citation: Hou, C.; Zhang, R.; Yang, K.; Li, X.; Yang, Y.; Ma, X.; Guo, G.; Yang, Y.; Liu, L.; Zhou, F. Non-Cooperative Target Attitude Estimation Method Based on Deep Learning of Ground and Space Access Scene Radar Images. *Mathematics* **2023**, *11*, 745. https://doi.org/10.3390/math11030745

Academic Editors: Yu Jiang, Haijun Peng and Hongwei Yang

Received: 28 December 2022
Revised: 29 January 2023
Accepted: 30 January 2023
Published: 2 February 2023

1. Introduction

Determining the attitude of a non-cooperative target in space has important application value in the aerospace field. Potential applications include assessing the flight state of a malfunctioning satellite, preparing target information for space debris-related missions [1,2], and estimating the point on the ground where a remote sensing satellite's lens is pointing by estimating its attitude [3].

Inverse synthetic-aperture radar (ISAR) is a type of ground-based radar used for space targets. It can be used to acquire target images under all weather conditions and at all times.

Because the ISAR imaging detection of space targets can obtain information about a target's attitude over a long distance, it is an important means of estimating the attitudes of non-cooperative targets in space.

In terms of ISAR image attitude determination, because a single ISAR image of a single station is not sufficient for three-dimensional space attitude estimation, multi-station ground-based radar co-vision has been used in many studies for ISAR image attitude determination [4,5]. For attitude estimation based on sparse image data, informatics methods are used, such as multi-feature fusion [6], compressed sensing [7], a hidden Markov model [8], accommodation parameters [9], and a Gaussian window [10]. In recent years, with the development of artificial intelligence neural network technology, the application of a deep learning network to attitude estimation using ISAR images has obtained better simulation data [3,11,12]. Although various methods are used, ISAR-based image attitude estimation is still less accurate than optical-image attitude estimation.

In terms of optical-image attitude determination, in recent years, convolutional neural network (CNN) technology has realized highly accurate reconstruction and attitude estimation based on optical images. In fields such as human-organ image reconstruction [13–15], multi-view image reconstruction [16,17], wave modeling [18], face modeling [19], architectural modeling [20], and human pose analysis, a CNN can achieve three-dimensional reconstruction and attitude estimation [21,22].

In space-based optical image attitude determination, CNNs are mainly used in fields such as space target imaging [23–26] and autonomous rendezvous and docking [27,28]. Its attitude determination method is often combined with the three-dimensional modeling and recognition of the target [29,30]. In recent years, artificial neural networks have achieved good application results in the fields of the three-dimensional reconstruction and the attitude estimation of targets in space [31–34].

This paper is structured as follows. Section 2 presents a method of non-cooperative target attitude estimation. This is a non-cooperative target attitude estimation method based on the machine learning of GSA scene radar images. Section 3 presents the construction method for the GSA scenes. Section 4 gives the framework used for the machine learning. Section 5 shows how the effectiveness of the attitude estimation method proposed in this paper was verified using a test bed with high-fidelity simulation data. Section 6 summarizes the full text.

2. Non-Cooperative Target Attitude Estimation Method Based on Machine Learning of Radar Images in GSA Scenes

A direct way to use radar images to determine attitude is to use a deep learning neural network to learn radar images. After training, the network can output the attitude.

However, this is based on the premise that the training dataset shows a one-to-one correspondence between the radar images and attitude values.

This requires the training data to meet two necessary conditions.

(1) There is a one-to-one correspondence between the radar images and attitude values.

First, the observation coordinate system shown in Figure 1 needs to be defined.

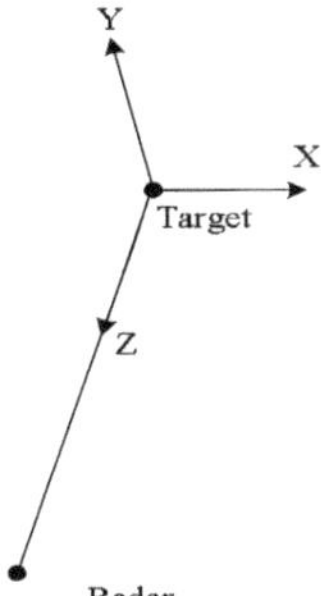

Figure 1. Schematic diagram of the observation coordinate system.

The vector direction of the target pointing to the radar is taken as the Z axis, and the direction of the cross product between the relative velocity direction and the Z axis is taken as the Y axis. The right-hand rule is used with Z and Y to determine the X axis, and the origin of the coordinate system is located at the centroid of the target.

The attitude angle in the following observation coordinate system then needs to be defined.

The Euler angle that rotates from the target body coordinate system, Body, to the observation coordinate system, Obs, is the attitude angle in the observation system.

Finally, the following lemma needs to be given.

Lemma 1. *The attitude angles of a space target in the observation coordinate system have a one-to-one correspondence with the ISAR images.*

Only when the attitudes are defined in the observation coordinate system can the target radar images have a one-to-one correspondence with the attitude values. In other words, if two radar images are identical, they must have the same attitude values in the observation coordinate system. This is because when the attitude angle of the observation system is determined, the angles between the direction of the radar waves irradiating the target and the X, Y, and Z axes of the target body coordinate system are uniquely determined.

(2) The data should come from GSA scenes.

When the radar images the target, in order to obtain an accurate value for the target's attitude, a space-based satellite should be used to simultaneously image the target and estimate the attitude, as shown in Figure 2 below.

As stated in the literature review, methods have been developed to determine the attitude based on optical images, and determining the attitude of a target based on space-based optical images is also an engineering problem that has been solved. Therefore, this is not the research content of this paper. The only problem that needs to be solved is the simultaneous use of a satellite in space to optically image the target at the moment of radar imaging. This concerns the construction of GSA scenes, as discussed in the next section.

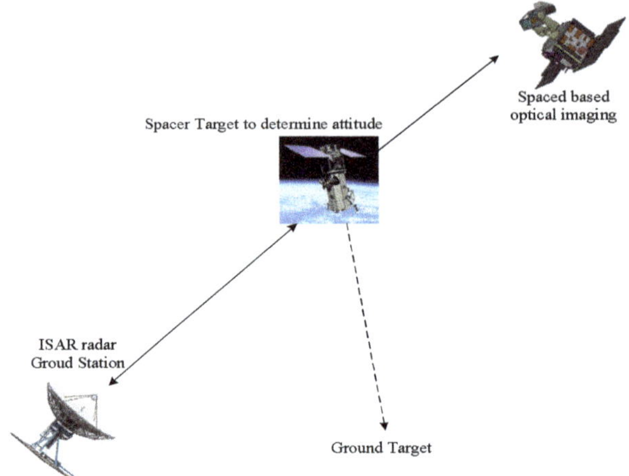

Figure 2. GSA scene.

3. Building of GSA Scene with Co-Vision from Space and Earth

3.1. Methods and Ideas

Here, the ground station is designated as GS. The target satellite to be observed by the GSA is *Sat_Target*, and the shooting satellite is *Sat_Obs*. The basic idea of building GSA scenes is to slightly change the orbital parameters of *Sat_Obs*, Ha (apogee height) and Hp (perigee height), so that *Sat_Obs* is close to *Sat_Target* while *Sat_Target* can be observed by the ISAR of GS, thus generating GSA scenes.

3.2. Method for Solving Orbital Maneuver

3.2.1. Step 1: Alignment Maneuver of the Track Surface Intersection

The intersection vector of the *Sat_Obs* orbital plane and *Sat_Target* orbital plane is set as $\overline{OC}$, which can be expressed as follows:

$$\begin{cases} Sat\_Target_{orbit\_normal\_vector} = [\sin(i_1)\cdot\cos(\theta_1), \sin(i_1)\cdot\sin(\theta_1), \cos(i_1)] \\ Sat\_Obs_{orbit\_normal\_vector} = [\sin(i_2)\cdot\cos(\theta_2), \sin(i_2)\cdot\sin(\theta_2), \cos(i_2)] \\ \overline{OC} = Sat\_Target_{orbit\_normal\_vector} \times Sat\_Obs_{orbit\_normal\_vector} \end{cases}, \quad (1)$$

When *Sat_Target* and GS have access, the geocentric vector of *Sat_Target* is $\overline{OT}$, as shown in Figure 3.

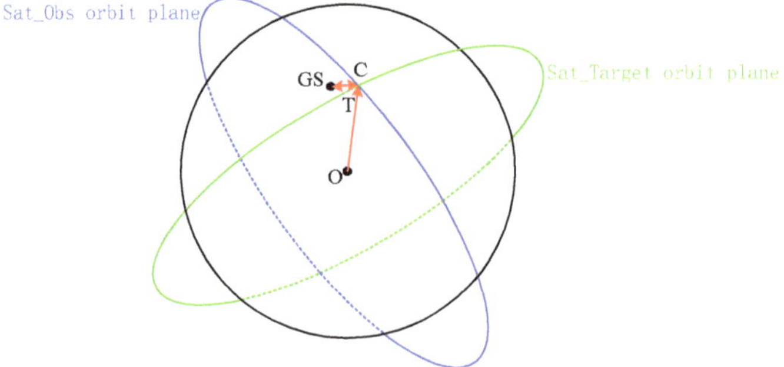

Figure 3. GSA scene building principle.

As shown in Figure 3, as long as $\overline{OC}$ and $\overline{OT}$ coincide, GSA can be generated.

$$\begin{cases} X = \cos(i_2)\cdot\sin(i_1)\cdot\sin(\theta_1) - \cos(i_1)\cdot\sin(i_2)\cdot\sin(\theta_2) \\ Y = \cos(i_1)\cdot\sin(i_2)\cdot\cos(\theta_2) - \sin(i_1)\cdot\cos(i_2)\cdot\cos(\theta_1) \\ Z = \sin(i_1)\cdot\sin(i_2)\cdot\sin(\theta_2 - \theta_1) \\ \overline{OC}_x = \frac{X}{\sqrt{X^2+Y^2+Z^2}} \\ \overline{OC}_y = \frac{Y}{\sqrt{X^2+Y^2+Z^2}} \\ \overline{OC}_z = \frac{Z}{\sqrt{X^2+Y^2+Z^2}} \end{cases}, \quad (2)$$

where θ_1 and θ_2 are defined as follows:

$$\begin{cases} \theta_1 = \left(\Omega_1 - \frac{\pi}{2}\right) + \dot{\Omega}_1\cdot\Delta t \\ \dot{\Omega}_1 = -\frac{3\cdot n_1\cdot J_2\cdot R_e^2}{2\cdot a_1^2\left(1-e_1^2\right)^2}\cdot\cos(i_1) \\ \theta_2 = \left(\Omega_2 - \frac{\pi}{2}\right) + \dot{\Omega}_2\cdot\Delta t \\ \dot{\Omega}_2 = -\frac{3\cdot n_2\cdot J_2\cdot R_e^2}{2\cdot a_2^2\left(1-e_2^2\right)^2}\cdot\cos(i_2) \end{cases}, \quad (3)$$

where Ω, n, i, a, and e are the right ascension, horizontal velocity, inclination, semi-major axis, and eccentricity of the ascending node of satellite *Sat_Target* and satellite *Sat_Obs*, respectively. Re is the Earth's radius, and J2 is the J2-perturbed parameter.

The required orbital adjustment can be obtained using the following algorithm. This algorithm mainly realizes the alignment of the two orbital plane intersections by using the change in the orbital plane intersection caused by the orbital plane precession of the J2 gravitational term.

Algorithm 1. Step A: Calculate all the access of *Sat_Target* to GS, and get the sequence of [*T_access*, *XYZ_access*], where *T_access* is the sequence of all the access moments, and *XYZ_access* is the XYZ position coordinates in the J2000 coordinate system corresponding to these access moments.

Step B: Search for a suitable *T_access* within the acceptable range of a and e changes, so as to satisfy the following:

$$\overline{OC} = XYZ\_access, \quad (4)$$

As long as the above equation is satisfied, intersection point C of the orbital planes of the two satellites can be made accessible to GS, thereby completing the alignment of the intersecting orbital planes.

3.2.2. Step 2: In-Plane Pursuit Orbital Maneuver

Only the orbital plane conditions are produced in the last step, and it is necessary to carry out orbit control of *Sat_Obs* in the orbital plane one or two orbital periods before reaching the intersection point, as well as mild control of a, e, and ω (argument of perigee), so that *Sat_Obs* can chase after *Sat_Target* in the orbital plane and reach *XYZ_access* at time *T_access*. This problem can be solved as a Lambert problem. This kind of in-plane catching-up problem has been well solved in academia, so no further description is given here.

3.3. Calculation Example

The initial conditions are listed in Table 1. The latitude and longitude of GS are 31.1 N 121.3 E.

Table 1. Initial calculation conditions.

	Sat_Target	*Sat_Obs*
Epoch (UTC)	27 November 2022 16:00:00.000	27 November 2022 16:00:00.000
Ha (km)	700	700
Hp (km)	600	350
i (°)	43	99
Ω (°)	290	10
ω (°)	100	0
M (°)	200	316.5

ω is Augment of Perigee and M is Mean Anomaly.

Based on *Sat_Target* and GS, the [*T_access*, *XYZ_access*] sequence is calculated first, and then shooting changes Ha and Hp to minimize the difference between $\left[\overline{OC}_x, \overline{OC}_y, \overline{OC}_z\right]$ and *XYZ_access*.

This example shows that when the apogee altitude of *Sat_Obs* increases by 19 km and the perigee altitude increases by 29.3 km, $\left[\overline{OC}_x, \overline{OC}_y, \overline{OC}_z\right]$ can almost coincide with *XYZ_access* when *T_access* is 2022-12-4 11:28:29, and the difference is equivalent to a distance between them of only 6 km, as shown in Figure 4. This distance is sufficient for *Sat_Obs* to perform high-definition imaging and high-precision attitude determination of *Sat_Target* using an optical telescope.

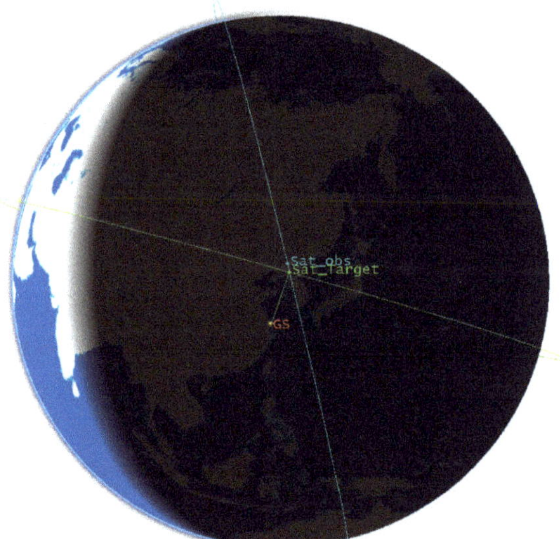

Figure 4. Calculation example scene.

4. Attitude Estimation Based on Deep Network

4.1. Brief Introduction

Space target state estimation aims to obtain state parameters such as the target's on-orbit attitude movement and geometric structure. It is a key technology for completing tasks such as target action intention analysis, troubleshooting potential failure threats, and predicting on-orbit situations. This study had the goal of providing a method for determining the real attitude of a target using an optical telescope and learning the mapping relationship between ISAR images and the real attitudes using a deep network so as to efficiently realize instantaneous attitude estimation based on single-frame ISAR images.

4.2. Attitude Estimation Modeling

In the orbital coordinate system, the on-orbit attitude of a three-axis stable space target remains unchanged. ISAR is used to observe the target for a long time. The movement of the target along its orbit makes the target rotate relative to the radar line of sight and produce Doppler modulation on the echo. A sequence of high-resolution ISAR images of the target can be obtained by the sub-aperture division and imaging processing of the echo data.

An ISAR observation and imaging model of a three-axis stable space target is shown in Figure 5, in which O-XYZ represents the orbital coordinate system. In the long-term continuous observation process, the radar line of sight at each observation moment forms a green curved surface in Figure 5. Among these, the direction vector of the radar line of sight at time t_m is determined by pitch angle α_{t_m} and azimuth angle β_{t_m}. Specifically, α_{t_m} is the angle between the radar line of sight and its projection vector $\boldsymbol{l}_{t_m}$ on the XOY plane, and β_{t_m} is the rotation angle of $\boldsymbol{l}_{t_m}$ and the X axis in the counterclockwise direction, with $\alpha(t_m) \in [-\pi/2, \pi/2]$ and $\beta(t_m) \in [0, 2\pi]$. The radar line-of-sight direction vector at time t_m can be expressed as follows:

$$\boldsymbol{r}_{t_m} = (\cos\alpha_{t_m}\cos\beta_{t_m}, \cos\alpha_{t_m}\sin\beta_{t_m}, \sin\alpha_{t_m})^T, \tag{5}$$

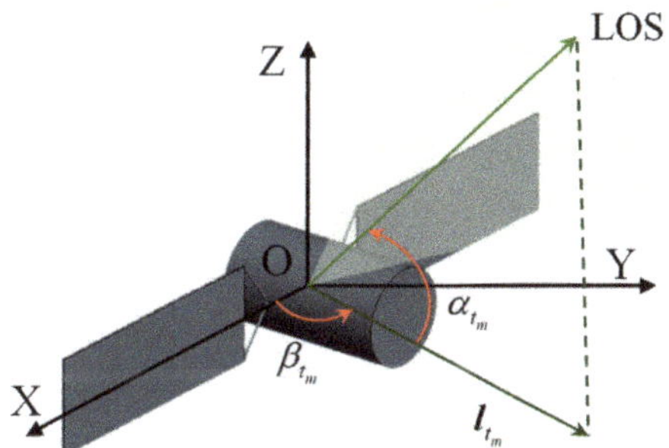

Figure 5. ISAR observation and imaging model.

For the kth scattering center, P_k, on the target, its coordinates are recorded as $(x_k, y_k, z_k)^T$. The projection of the scattering center in the distance direction of the ISAR imaging plane is shown as follows:

$$r_k(t_m) = \boldsymbol{r}_{t_m}^T \cdot (x_k, y_k, z_k)^T, \tag{6}$$

The velocity of the scattering center along the distance direction is calculated as follows:

$$v_k(t_m) = \boldsymbol{d}_{t_m}^T \cdot (x_k, y_k, z_k)^T, \tag{7}$$

where

$$\begin{aligned} \boldsymbol{d}_{t_m} &= \dot{\boldsymbol{r}}_{t_m} \\ &= \Big(-\sin\alpha_{t_m}\cos\beta_{t_m}\dot{\alpha}_{t_m} - \cos\alpha_{t_m}\sin\beta_{t_m}\dot{\beta}_{t_m}, \\ &\quad -\sin\alpha_{t_m}\sin\beta_{t_m}\dot{\alpha}_{t_m} + \cos\alpha_{t_m}\cos\beta_{t_m}\dot{\beta}_{t_m}, \cos\alpha_{t_m}\dot{\alpha}_{t_m}\Big)^T \end{aligned}, \tag{8}$$

and $\dot{\alpha}_{t_m}$ and $\dot{\beta}_{t_m}$ represent the change rates of the pitch angle and azimuth angle at time t_m, respectively. Then, the Doppler of scattering center P_k at time t_m can be obtained:

$$d_k(t_m) = -\frac{2v_k(t_m)}{\lambda}, \tag{9}$$

where λ is the wavelength of the signal emitted by the radar. Therefore, at time t_m, the projection position of scattering center P_k on the imaging plane satisfies the following equation:

$$\begin{pmatrix} r_k(t_m) \\ d_k(t_m) \end{pmatrix} = \begin{pmatrix} \boldsymbol{r}_{t_m}^T \\ \boldsymbol{d}_{t_m}^T \end{pmatrix} \cdot \begin{pmatrix} x_k \\ y_k \\ z_k \end{pmatrix}, \tag{10}$$

where $(r_k(t_m), d_k(t_m))^T$ is the projection coordinates of the scattering center, and $\mathbf{A}_{t_m} = (\boldsymbol{r}_{t_m}, \boldsymbol{d}_{t_m})^T$ is the imaging projection matrix.

The on-orbit attitude of the target is defined by the Euler angle, and α, β, and γ represent the azimuth, pitch, and yaw of the attitude angle, respectively. Compared to the target body coordinate system, the target attitude in the orbit coordinate system is determined by the three-dimensional rotation matrix, $\mathbf{R}$, as follows:

$$\mathbf{R} = \mathbf{R}_\alpha \cdot \mathbf{R}_\beta \cdot \mathbf{R}_\gamma, \tag{11}$$

where $\mathbf{R}_\alpha$, $\mathbf{R}_\beta$, and $\mathbf{R}_\gamma$ represent the rotation matrices corresponding to the Euler angles. Assuming that the coordinates of scattering center P_k are $(x_k^r, y_k^r, z_k^r)^T$ in the target body coordinate system, the following equation is obtained:

$$\begin{pmatrix} x_k \\ y_k \\ z_k \end{pmatrix} = \mathbf{R} \cdot \begin{pmatrix} x_k^r \\ y_k^r \\ z_k^r \end{pmatrix}, \tag{12}$$

Then, considering the attitude of the target in the orbital coordinates, the projection relation of the ISAR imaging of the scattering center at time t_m can be completely expressed as follows:

$$\begin{pmatrix} r_k(t_m) \\ d_k(t_m) \end{pmatrix} = \begin{pmatrix} \boldsymbol{r}_{t_m}^T \\ \boldsymbol{d}_{t_m}^T \end{pmatrix} \cdot \left(\mathbf{R} \cdot \begin{pmatrix} x_k^r \\ y_k^r \\ z_k^r \end{pmatrix} \right). \tag{13}$$

4.3. Attitude Estimation Based on Deep Network

In order to realize the instantaneous attitude estimation of the space target, this section proposes instantaneous attitude estimation methods based on a deep network, namely ISAR image enhancement based on UNet++ [35] and instantaneous attitude estimation based on the shifted window (swin) transformer [36]. Finally, the training steps of the proposed methods are given.

4.3.1. ISAR Image Enhancement Based on UNet++

ISAR observes and receives the echoes from non-cooperative targets, compensates the translation components, which are not beneficial to imaging, and then transforms them into turntable models for imaging. However, because of the occlusion effect, the key components of the target can be missing in the imaging results, and the quality of the imaging results can be poor under noisy conditions. These problems can lead to a low-accuracy attitude estimation based on a deep network. To enhance the ISAR imaging results, UNet++, which has strong feature extraction ability, is used to learn the mapping relationship between the ISAR imaging results and theoretical binary projection images, and to provide high-quality imaging results for subsequent attitude estimation.

A flow chart of the ISAR image enhancement based on UNet++ is shown in Figure 6. The network input is the ISAR imaging result, and the deep features of the ISAR image are extracted through a series of convolution and down-sampling operations. The image is then restored by up-sampling, and more high-resolution information is obtained by using a dense jump connection. Thus, the details of the input image can be more completely restored, and the restoration accuracy can be improved. In order to make full use of the structural advantages of UNet++ and to apply it to ISAR image enhancement, a convolution layer with one channel is added after $\mathbf{X}^{0,1}$, $\mathbf{X}^{0,2}$, $\mathbf{X}^{0,3}$, and $\mathbf{X}^{0,4}$, and its output is averaged to obtain the final ISAR image enhancement result.

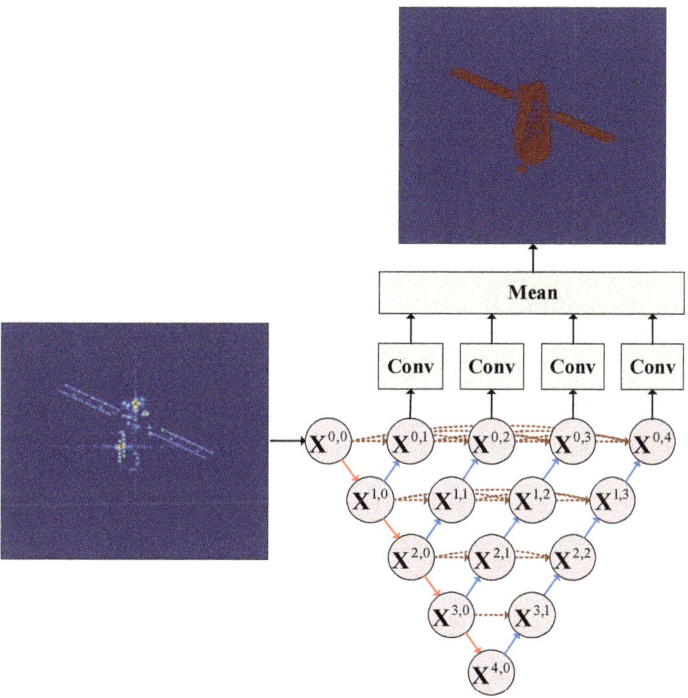

Figure 6. Flow chart of ISAR image enhancement based on UNet++.

Let $o^{i,j}$ represent the output of node $\mathbf{X}^{i,j}$, where i represents the down-sampling layer number of the encoder, and j represents the convolution layer number of the dense hopping connection. The output of each node can then be expressed as follows:

$$o^{i,j} = \begin{cases} \mathcal{H}\left(\mathcal{D}\left(o^{i-1,j}\right)\right), & j = 0 \\ \mathcal{H}\left(\left[\left[o^{i,k}\right]_{k=0}^{j}, \mathcal{U}\left(o^{i+1,j-1}\right)\right]\right), & j > 0' \end{cases} \tag{14}$$

where $\mathcal{H}(\cdot)$ represents two convolution layers with linear rectification activation functions. The convolution kernel size is 3×3, and the number of convolution kernels is shown in Table 2. As shown by the red downward arrow in Figure 6, $\mathcal{D}(\cdot)$ represents the down-sampling operation, which is realized by a pool layer with 2×2 kernels, as shown by the blue upward arrow in Figure 6. $\mathcal{U}(\cdot)$ represents the up-sampling operation, which is realized by a deconvolution layer with 2×2 kernels and a step size of 2. In addition, $[\cdot]$ indicates a splicing operation, and the brown arrow indicates a dense jump connection.

Table 2. Number of convolution kernels.

Node	$\mathbf{X}^{0,0-4}$	$\mathbf{X}^{1,0-3}$	$\mathbf{X}^{2,0-2}$	$\mathbf{X}^{3,0-1}$	$\mathbf{X}^{4,0}$
Number of convolution kernels	32	64	128	256	512

To achieve better ISAR image enhancement results, the proposed method uses theoretical binary projection images as labels for end-to-end training, and the loss function is defined as the normalized mean square error between network output X^{output} and label X^{label},

$$L_1\left(X^{output}, X^{label}\right) = \frac{\|X^{output} - X^{label}\|_F}{\|X^{label}\|_F}, \tag{15}$$

where $\|\cdot\|_F$ represents the Frobenius norm.

4.3.2. Instantaneous Attitude Estimation Based on Swin Transformer

When the radar line of sight is fixed, the attitude angle has a one-to-one correspondence to the enhanced ISAR image. Therefore, this study used the swin transformer to learn the mapping relationship.

A flow chart of the instantaneous attitude estimation based on the swin transformer is shown in Figure 7. First, an enhanced ISAR imaging result with a size of $\mathrm{H} \times \mathrm{W} \times 1$ is inputted into the network. It is then divided into non-overlapping patch sets by patch partition, based on a patch of 4×4 adjacent pixels, and each patch is flattened in the channel direction to obtain a feature map of $\frac{\mathrm{H}}{4} \times \frac{\mathrm{W}}{4} \times 16$. Four stages are then stacked to build feature maps of different sizes for attention calculation. The first stage changes the feature dimension from 16 to C using linear embedding, and the other three stages are down-sampled by patch merging. Thus, the height and width of the feature maps are halved, and the depth is doubled. The feature map sizes are $\frac{\mathrm{H}}{8} \times \frac{\mathrm{W}}{8} \times 2\mathrm{C}$, $\frac{\mathrm{H}}{16} \times \frac{\mathrm{W}}{16} \times 4\mathrm{C}$, and $\frac{\mathrm{H}}{32} \times \frac{\mathrm{W}}{32} \times 8\mathrm{C}$. After changing the dimension of the feature maps, the swin transformer modules are repeatedly stacked, with the swin transformer modules in subsequent stages stacked 2, 2, 6, and 2 times. A single swin transformer module is shown in the dashed box on the right side of Figure 7. It is connected using layer normalization (LN) with a windows multi-head self-attention (W-MSA) module, or a shifted windows multi-head self-attention (SW-MSA) module, in which the LN layer is used to normalize different channels of the same sample to ensure the stability of the data feature distribution. Among them, the self-attention mechanism [37] is the key module of the transformer, and its calculation method is as follows:

$$\mathrm{A} = \mathrm{Attention}(Q, K, V) = \mathrm{SoftMax}\left(QK^T/\sqrt{d}\right)V, \tag{16}$$

where Q is the query, K is the key, V is the value, and d is the query dimension.

Multi-head self-attention is used to process the original input sequence into self-attention groups, splice the results, and perform a linear transformation to obtain the final output result:

$$\begin{array}{c} \mathrm{MultiHead}(Q, K, V) = \mathrm{Concat}(\mathrm{head}_1, \ldots, \mathrm{head}_h)W^O \\ \text{where } \mathrm{head}_i = \mathrm{Attention}\left(QW_i^Q, KW_i^K, VW_i^V\right) \end{array}, \tag{17}$$

where each self-attention module defines $d_k = d_v = d_{\mathrm{model}}/h$, and the weight matrix satisfies the following:

$$W_i^Q \in \mathbb{R}^{d_{\mathrm{model}} \times d_k}, W_i^K \in \mathbb{R}^{d_{\mathrm{model}} \times d_k}, W_i^V \in \mathbb{R}^{d_{\mathrm{model}} \times d_k}, W_i^O \in \mathbb{R}^{hd_v \times d_{\mathrm{model}}}, \tag{18}$$

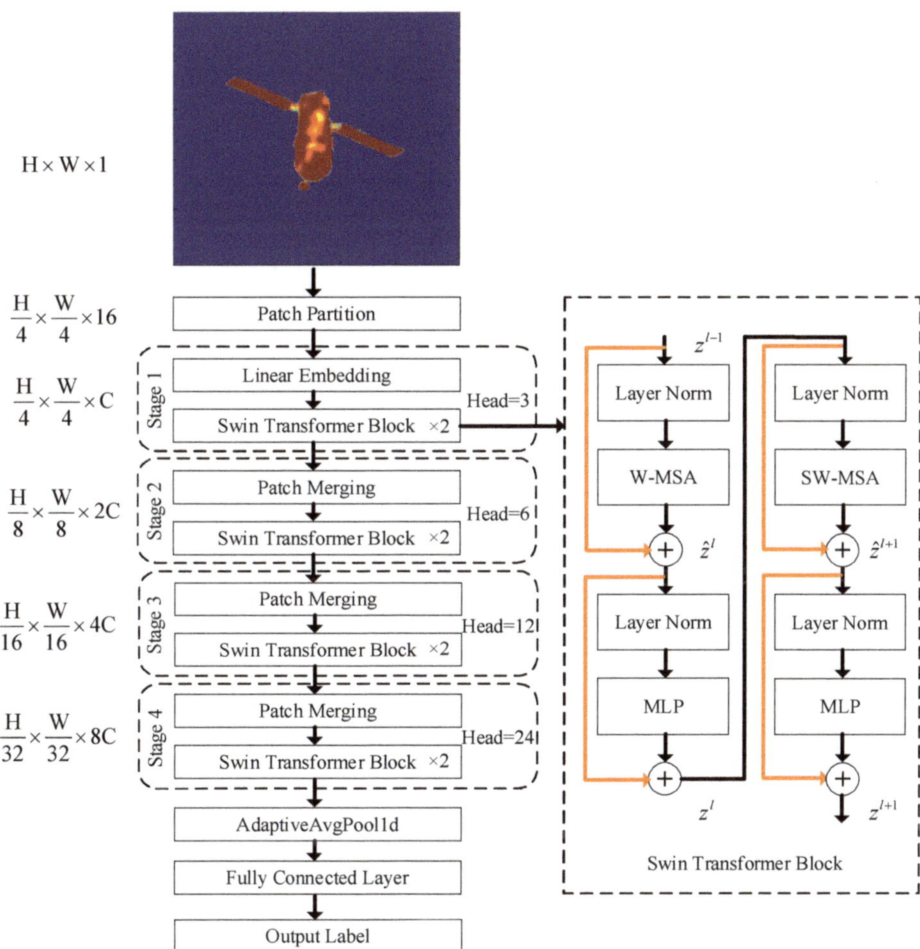

Figure 7. Flow chart of attitude estimation based on swin transformer.

W-MSA in the swin transformer module further divides the image block into non-overlapping areas and calculates the multi-head self-attention in the areas. In W-MSA, only the self-attention calculation is performed in each window. Thus, the information cannot be transmitted between windows. Therefore, the SW-MSA module is introduced. After the non-overlapping windows are divided in the Lth layer, the windows are re-divided in the L^{th+1} layer with an offset of half the window distance, which allows the information of some windows in different layers to interact. Next, another LN layer is inputted to connect the multilayer perceptron (MLP). The MLP is a feedforward network that uses the GeLU function as an activation function, with the goal of completing the non-linear transformation and improving the fitting ability of the algorithm. In addition, subsequent stages have 3, 6, 12, and 24 heads. The residual connection added to each swin transformer module is shown in the yellow line in Figure 7. This module has two different structures and needs to be used in pairs: the first structure uses W-MSA, and the second structure connects with SW-MSA. During the process of passing through this module, the output of each part is shown in Equations (19)–(22):

$$\hat{z}^{l} = \text{W\_MSA}\left(\text{LN}\left(z^{l-1}\right)\right) + z^{l-1}, \tag{19}$$

$$\mathrm{z}^{l} = \mathrm{MLP}\left(\mathrm{LN}\left(\hat{\mathrm{z}}^{l}\right)\right) + \hat{\mathrm{z}}^{l} \tag{20}$$

$$\hat{\mathrm{z}}^{l+1} = \mathrm{SW\_MSA}\left(\mathrm{LN}\left(\mathrm{z}^{l}\right)\right) + \mathrm{z}^{l} \tag{21}$$

$$\mathrm{z}^{l+1} = \mathrm{MLP}\left(\mathrm{LN}\left(\hat{\mathrm{z}}^{l+1}\right)\right) + \hat{\mathrm{z}}^{l+1} \tag{22}$$

The dimension of the last stage output feature is $\frac{\mathrm{H}}{32} \times \frac{\mathrm{W}}{32} \times 8\mathrm{C}$. A feature vector with a length of 8C can be obtained by a one-dimensional AdaptiveAvgPool1d with an output dimension of 1, and the Euler angle estimation can be obtained by a fully connected layer with a dimension of 3.

The network loss function is defined as the mean square error between output Euler angle y^{output} and label Euler angle y^{label}:

$$L_2\left(y^{output}, y^{label}\right) = \frac{1}{N}\sum_{i=1}^{N}\left(y_i^{output} - y_i^{label}\right)^2, \tag{23}$$

where three Euler angles are represented as $N = 3$.

The swin transformer has the hierarchy, locality, and translation invariance characteristics. The hierarchy is reflected in the feature extraction stage, which uses a hierarchical construction method similar to a CNN. The input image is down-sampled 4 times, 8 times, and 16 times to obtain a multi-scale feature map. The locality is mainly reflected in the process of the self-attention calculation, in which the calculation is constrained in a divided local non-overlapping window. The calculation complexity of W-MSA and traditional MSA is as follows:

$$\begin{aligned} \Omega(\mathrm{MSA}) &= 4hwC^2 + 2(hw)^2C \\ \Omega(\mathrm{W\text{-}MSA}) &= 4hwC^2 + 2M^2hwC \end{aligned}, \tag{24}$$

where M is the window size for the self-attention calculation. It can be seen that the complexity of the algorithm has changed from a square relationship with the image size to a linear relationship, which greatly reduces the amount of calculation and improves the efficiency of the algorithm. In SW-MSA, the division of non-overlapping windows is offset by half a window compared with W-MSA, which allows the information of the upper and lower windows to effectively interact. Compared with the common sliding window design in a CNN, it retains the translation invariability without reducing the accuracy.

4.3.3. Network Training

The proposed method consists of two deep networks, the UNet++ for ISAR image enhancement and the swin transformer for attitude estimation. During network training, the epoch is set to 100, the batch size is set to 32, and the initial learning rate is set to $2e-4$. With an increase in the epoch, exponential attenuation is then performed with an attenuation rate of 0.98. Finally, the network parameters are optimized using the Adam optimizer. For each epoch, the network training steps can be summarized as follows:

(1) Randomly obtain an ISAR imaging result for the batch size from a training dataset;

(2) Input the ISAR imaging results into UNet++, output the enhanced ISAR imaging results, and calculate the loss function according to Equation (15);

(3) Input the enhanced ISAR imaging results into the swin transformer, output the Euler angle estimation values, and calculate the loss function according to Equation (22);

(4) Update the swin transformer network parameters;

(5) Update the UNet++ network parameters;

(6) Repeat steps 1–5 until all the training data are taken.

After the network is trained, any ISAR imaging result can be inputted into the network to simultaneously realize ISAR image enhancement and instantaneous attitude estimation.

5. Data Simulation Verification Results

5.1. Basic Settings

This section shows how Tiangong was chosen as the observation target. Its three-dimensional model is shown in Figure 8. After obtaining a three-dimensional model, an attitude estimation simulation experiment was carried out to verify the effectiveness of the proposed method. First, an echo was simulated by FEKO electromagnetic calculation software using the simulation parameters listed in Table 3.

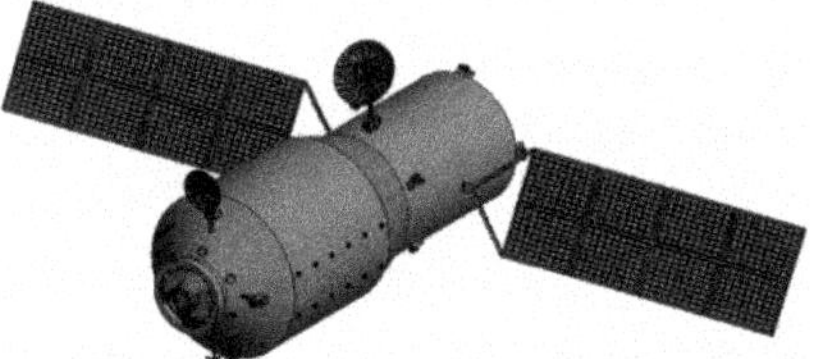

Figure 8. Three-dimensional model of Tiangong.

Table 3. Radar simulation parameters.

Carrier frequency	15 GHz
Bandwidth	1.6 GHz
Pitch angle	0°
Accumulation angle	5.1°
Distance points	256
Azimuth points	256

5.2. Data Generation and Processing

(1) Data set generation: As can be seen from Table 3, the radar line of sight was fixed, the pitch angle was 0°, the azimuth angle varied from −2.55 to +2.55, and the angular interval was 0.02°. At this time, the ISAR imaging results showed a one-to-one correspondence to its attitude angle (namely the Euler angle). Therefore, in order to obtain the training dataset, a total of 5000 ISAR imaging results with randomly varying attitude angles were generated by simulation, and a theoretical binary projection diagram was generated by Equation (10). The ISAR imaging results, theoretical binary projection diagram, and attitude angles were used for training. Three Euler angles were randomly distributed between −45° and +45°, with 4000 ISAR imaging results used for training sets and 1000 used for testing sets.

(2) ISAR image enhancement: First, ISAR imaging results were taken as network inputs, and UNet++ was trained with theoretical binary projection as the label. After training UNet++, ISAR imaging results were randomly used for testing. An imaging result is shown in Figure 9. It can be seen that the network output and theoretical binary projection results were similar after the ISAR imaging results were enhanced by the proposed method, which proved the effectiveness of the proposed method.

(3) Instantaneous attitude estimation: In order to realize instantaneous attitude estimation, the original ISAR images and image enhancement results were used as inputs, and the true value of the Euler angle was used as a label to train the swin transformer. Table 4 lists the average Euler angle estimation error on 1000 test datasets after training. It can be seen that the attitude estimation error with image enhancement was smaller than that without image enhancement, which proved the effectiveness of the proposed method. Random ISAR imaging results were taken for testing. Test data 1 is shown in Figures 10 and 11, and the attitude estimation results are listed in Tables 5 and 6. It can be seen that the data enhancement results were clear enough to show the structural components of the target, and the attitude estimation result was more accurate with less error, which proved the effectiveness of the proposed method.

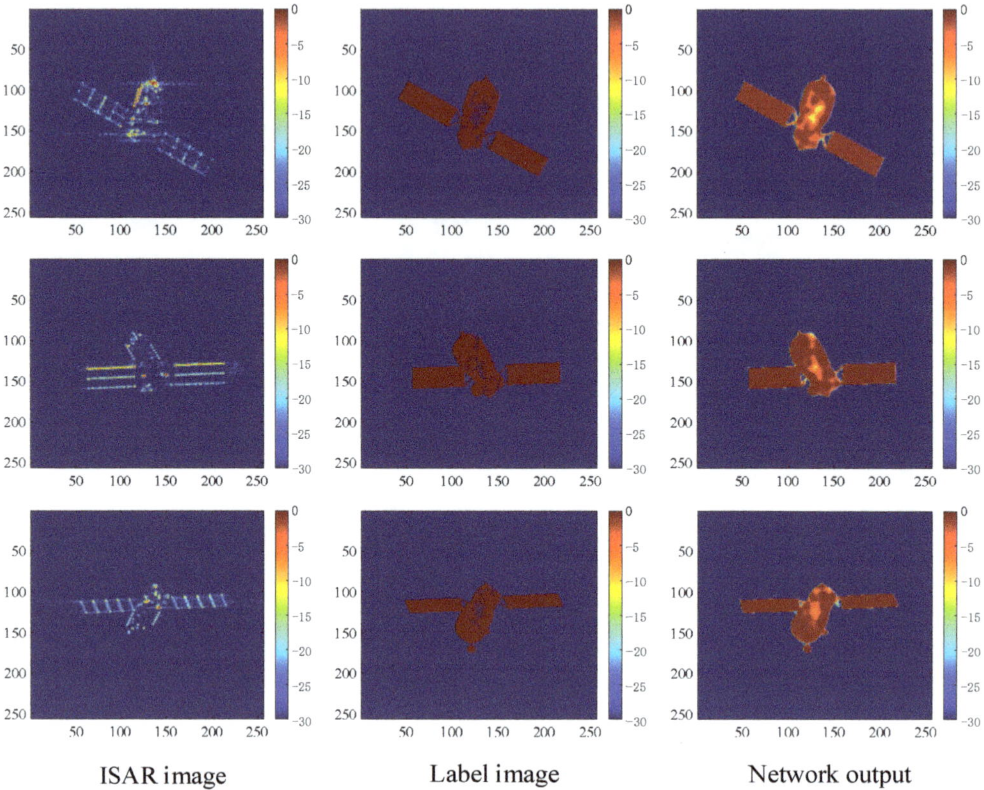

Figure 9. ISAR image enhancement results based on UNet++.

Table 4. Euler angle estimation error based on swin transformer.

	z/°	y/°	x/°
Without image enhancement	1.3867	1.2231	1.7971
With image enhancement	0.7302	0.7050	0.9579

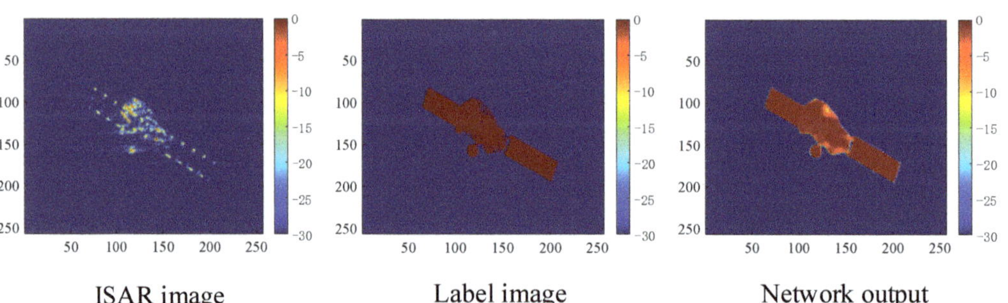

Figure 10. The imaging results of test data 1.

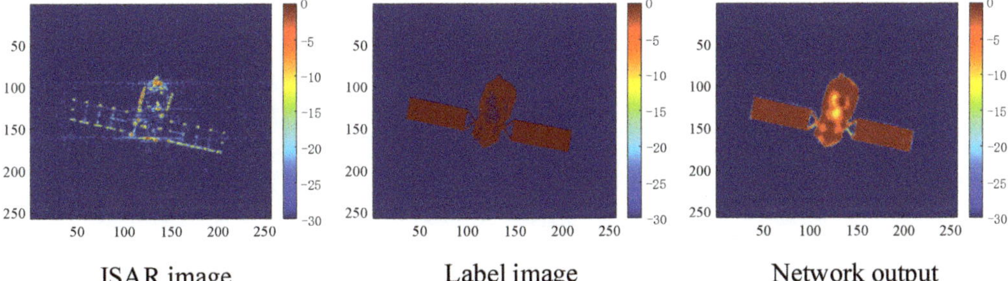

Figure 11. The imaging results of test data 2.

Table 5. The attitude estimation results of test data 1.

		z/°	y/°	x/°
Label		−27.0569	−20.4094	20.2146
Without image enhancement	Estimated value	−27.9102	−21.9417	19.6320
	Error	0.8533	1.5322	0.5827
With image enhancement	Estimated value	−27.1155	−19.9481	19.5822
	Error	0.0587	−0.4613	0.6325

Table 6. The attitude estimation results of test data 2.

		z/°	y/°	x/°
Label		−13.5862	−35.0809	−14.4134
Without image enhancement	Estimated value	−14.7988	−36.1443	−15.7292
	Error	1.2125	1.0634	1.3158
With image enhancement	Estimated value	−13.5347	−35.6672	−14.7969
	Error	−0.0515	0.5863	0.3835

5.3. Noise Robustness Analysis

To analyze the robustness of the proposed method to noise, the signal-to-noise ratio (SNR) of the training dataset was set to randomly change within a range of −3 dB to +15 dB, and the test SNR was set to 0, 5, and 10 dB. Table 7 shows the average Euler angle estimation error of 1000 test samples after the network training. It can be seen that the proposed method had the smallest estimation error under the different SNR conditions, and the fluctuation was small, which proved that the proposed method is robust to noise.

Table 7. Average Euler angle estimation error values of test set under different SNR conditions.

	SNR	z/°	y/°	x/°
Without image enhancement	0 dB	1.4405	1.4354	1.9950
	5 dB	1.3620	1.3414	1.8249
	10 dB	1.3100	1.3210	1.7834
With image enhancement	0 dB	0.6179	0.8326	0.8755
	5 dB	0.6193	0.8047	0.8147
	10 dB	0.6163	0.8052	0.8047

At the same time, two random test images were selected for visual analysis. The imaging results are shown in Figures 12 and 13, and the Euler angle estimation results are listed in Tables 8 and 9.

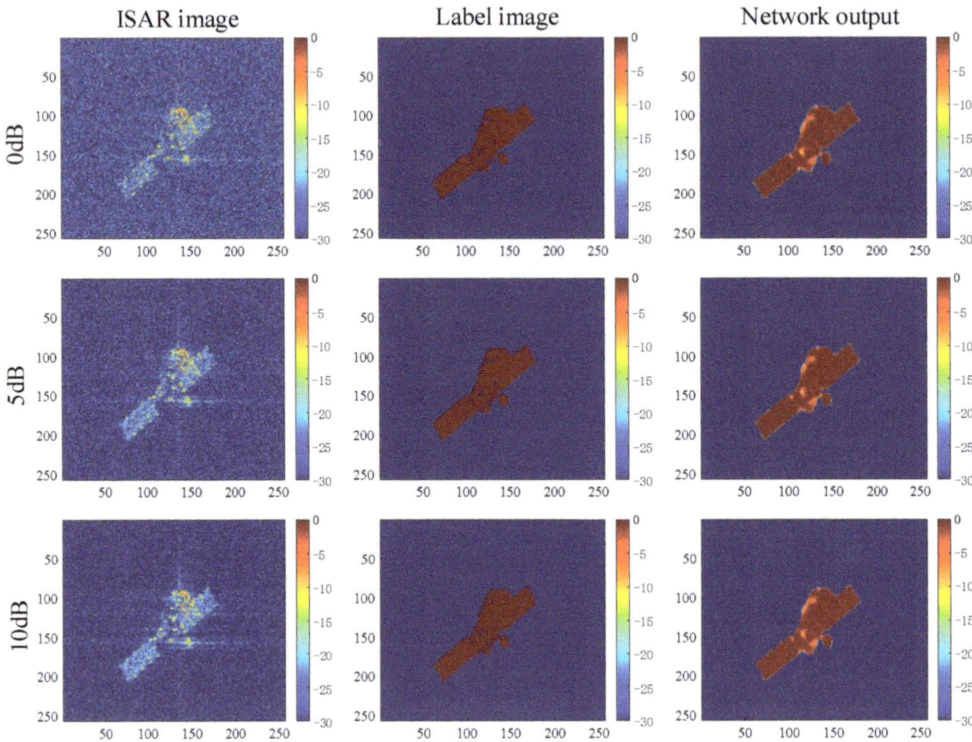

Figure 12. The imaging results of test data 3 under different SNRs.

Table 8. The Euler angle estimation results of test data 3.

	SNR		**z/°**	**y/°**	**x/°**
		Label	36.9615	−36.9176	−21.4118
Without image enhancement	0 dB	Estimated value	37.9141	−37.9030	−18.1337
		Error	−0.9525	0.9853	−3.2781
	5 dB	Estimated value	37.4324	−37.2864	−19.9296
		Error	−0.4708	0.3687	−1.4822
	10 dB	Estimated value	37.6068	−36.9699	−19.4128
		Error	−0.6452	0.0522	−1.9990
With image enhancement	0 dB	Estimated value	37.0437	−37.0494	−21.7160
		Error	−0.0821	0.1318	0.3042
	5 dB	Estimated value	36.8439	−37.1574	−21.9101
		Error	0.1177	0.2398	0.4983
	10 dB	Estimated value	36.9237	−36.8922	−21.3185
		Error	0.0379	−0.0254	−0.0933

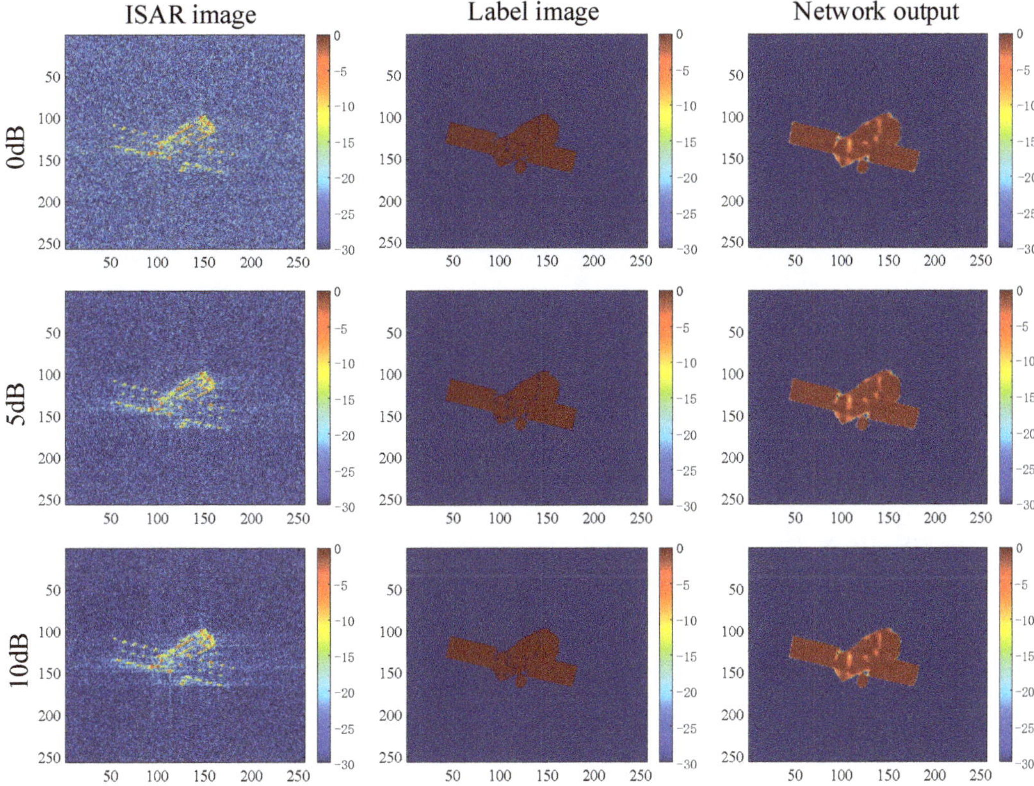

Figure 13. The imaging results of test data 4 under different SNRs.

Table 9. The Euler angle estimation results of test data 4.

	SNR		z/°	y/°	x/°
		Label	−10.3241	−17.8594	−41.7762
Without image enhancement	0 dB	Estimated value	−9.9148	−18.7568	−42.4823
		Error	−0.4093	0.8973	0.7061
	5 dB	Estimated value	−11.0111	−20.0738	−42.1863
		Error	0.6869	2.2144	0.4101
	10 dB	Estimated value	−11.3889	−19.4947	−41.9493
		Error	1.0647	1.6352	0.1731
With image enhancement	0 dB	Estimated value	−10.9262	−17.8358	−41.8396
		Error	0.6021	−0.0236	0.0634
	5 dB	Estimated value	−10.7412	−17.5429	−42.0876
		Error	0.4171	−0.3165	0.3114
	10 dB	Estimated value	−10.9565	−17.6848	−41.9112
		Error	0.6323	−0.1746	0.1350

6. Conclusions

This paper presented an effective method for estimating the attitude of a non-cooperative target in space using deep learning based on radar images of GSA scenes. This method generates many GSA scenes through orbital maneuvers. Taking advantage of the fact that the attitude of the target in the GSA scenes can be estimated more accurately by space-based optical telescopes, these attitude estimates are used as a training dataset of ISAR images. Deep learning training is then carried out on the ISAR images of the GSA scenes. An experimental verification under simulation conditions showed that the attitude estimation accuracy of the method for non-cooperative targets could reach a level of within 1°. The high estimation accuracy of this method would allow it to be widely used in fields such as malfunctioning satellite state analysis and space target detection.

Author Contributions: Methodology, C.H., R.Z., K.Y. and X.L.; project administration, Y.Y. (Yang Yang), X.M. and G.G.; software, Y.Y. (Yuan Yang); validation, F.Z. and L.L. All authors have read and agreed to the published version of the manuscript.

Funding: This work is supported by the National Key Research and Development Program of China [Grant number 2016YFB0501301]; the National Key Research and Development Program of China [Grant number 2017YFC1500904]; and the National 973 Program of China [Grant number 613237201506].

Data Availability Statement: There was no data created, and the conditions for data generation have been described in the article.

Acknowledgments: Thanks to author Yi Lu for his great contributions to the idea for and the writing of the article.

Conflicts of Interest: The authors declare that they have no conflict of interest.

References

1. Huo, C.Y.; Yin, H.C.; Wei, X.; Xing, X.Y.; Liang, M. Attitude estimation method of space targets by 3D reconstruction of principal axis from ISAR image. *Procedia Comput. Sci.* **2019**, *147*, 158–164. [CrossRef]
2. Du, R.; Liu, L.; Bai, X.; Zhou, Z.; Zhou, F. Instantaneous attitude estimation of spacecraft utilizing joint optical-and-ISAR observation. *IEEE Trans. Geosci. Remote Sens.* **2022**, *60*, 5112114. [CrossRef]
3. Wang, J.; Du, L.; Li, Y.; Lyu, G.; Chen, B. Attitude and size estimation of satellite targets based on ISAR image interpretation. *IEEE Trans. Geosci. Remote Sens.* **2021**, *60*, 5109015. [CrossRef]
4. Zhou, Y.; Zhang, L.; Cao, Y. Attitude estimation for space targets by exploiting the quadratic phase coefficients of inverse synthetic aperture radar imagery. *IEEE Trans. Geosci. Remote Sens.* **2019**, *57*, 3858–3872. [CrossRef]
5. Zhou, Y.; Zhang, L.; Cao, Y. Dynamic estimation of spin spacecraft based on multiple-station ISAR images. *IEEE Trans. Geosci. Remote Sens.* **2020**, *58*, 2977–2989. [CrossRef]
6. Wang, J.; Li, Y.; Song, M.; Xing, M. Joint estimation of absolute attitude and size for satellite targets based on multi-feature fusion of single ISAR image. *IEEE Trans. Geosci. Remote Sens.* **2022**, *60*, 5111720. [CrossRef]
7. Wang, F.; Eibert, T.F.; Jin, Y.Q. Simulation of ISAR imaging for a space target and reconstruction under sparse sampling via compressed sensing. *IEEE Trans. Geosci. Remote Sens.* **2015**, *53*, 3432–3441. [CrossRef]
8. Zhou, Y.; Wei, S.; Zhang, L.; Zhang, W.; Ma, Y. Dynamic estimation of spin satellite from the single-station ISAR image sequence with the hidden Markov model. *IEEE Trans. Aerosp. Electron. Syst.* **2022**, *58*, 4626–4638. [CrossRef]
9. Kou, P.; Liu, Y.; Zhong, W.; Tian, B.; Wu, W.; Zhang, C. Axial attitude estimation of spacecraft in orbit based on ISAR image sequence. *IEEE J. Sel. Top. Appl. Earth Obs. Remote Sens.* **2021**, *14*, 7246–7258. [CrossRef]
10. Wang, Y.; Cao, R.; Huang, X. ISAR imaging of maneuvering target based on the estimation of time varying amplitude with Gaussian window. *IEEE Sens. J.* **2019**, *19*, 11180–11191. [CrossRef]
11. Xue, R.; Bai, X.; Zhou, F. SAISAR-Net: A robust sequential adjustment ISAR image classification network. *IEEE Trans. Geosci. Remote Sens.* **2021**, *60*, 5214715. [CrossRef]
12. Xie, P.; Zhang, L.; Ma, Y.; Zhou, Y.; Wang, X. Attitude estimation and geometry inversion of satellite based on oriented object fetection. *IEEE Geosci. Remote Sens. Lett.* **2022**, *19*, 4023505. [CrossRef]
13. Tang, S.; Yang, X.; Shajudeen, P.; Sears, C.; Taraballi, F.; Weiner, B.; Tasciotti, E.; Dollahon, D.; Park, H.; Righetti, R. A CNN-based method to reconstruct 3-D spine surfaces from US images in vivo. *Med. Image Anal.* **2021**, *74*, 102221. [CrossRef] [PubMed]
14. Kim, H.; Lee, K.; Lee, D.; Baek, N. 3D Reconstruction of Leg Bones from X-Ray Images Using CNN-Based Feature Analysis. In Proceedings of the 2019 International Conference on Information and Communication Technology Convergence (ICTC), Jeju, Republic of Korea, 16–18 October 2019; pp. 669–672. [CrossRef]
15. Joseph, S.S.; Dennisan, A. Optimised CNN based brain tumour detection and 3D reconstruction. *Comput. Methods Biomech. Biomed. Eng. Imaging Vis.* **2022**, 1–16. [CrossRef]
16. Ge, Y.; Zhang, Q.; Shen, Y.; Sun, Y.; Huang, C. A 3D reconstruction method based on multi-views of contours segmented with CNN-transformer for long bones. *Int. J. Comput. Assist. Radiol. Surg.* **2022**, *17*, 1891–1902. [CrossRef] [PubMed]
17. Murez, Z.; Van As, T.; Bartolozzi, J.; Sinha, A.; Badrinarayanan, V.; Rabinovich, A. Atlas: End-to-End 3D Scene Reconstruction from Posed Images. In Proceedings of the European Conference on Computer Vision 2020, Glasgow, UK, 23–28 August 2020; pp. 414–431. [CrossRef]
18. Pistellato, M.; Bergamasco, F.; Torsello, A.; Barbariol, F.; Yoo, J.; Jeong, J.Y.; Benetazzo, A. A physics-driven CNN model for real-time sea waves 3D reconstruction. *Remote Sens.* **2021**, *13*, 3780. [CrossRef]

19. Winarno, E.; Al Amin, I.H.; Hartati, S.; Adi, P.W. Face recognition based on CNN 2D-3D reconstruction using shape and texture vectors combining. *Indones. J. Electr. Eng. Inform.* **2020**, *8*, 378–384. [CrossRef]
20. Tong, Z.; Gao, J.; Zhang, H. Recognition, location, measurement, and 3D reconstruction of concealed cracks using convolutional neural networks. *Constr. Build. Mater.* **2017**, *146*, 775–787. [CrossRef]
21. Radenović, F.; Tolias, G.; Chum, O. Fine-tuning CNN image retrieval with no human annotation. *IEEE Trans. Pattern Anal. Mach. Intell.* **2019**, *41*, 1655–1668. [CrossRef]
22. Afifi, A.J.; Magnusson, J.; Soomro, T.A.; Hellwich, O. Pixel2Point: 3D object reconstruction from a single image using CNN and initial sphere. *IEEE Access* **2020**, *9*, 110–121. [CrossRef]
23. Space Based Space Surveillance SBSS. Available online: http://www.globalsecurity.org/space/systems/sbss.htm (accessed on 26 December 2022).
24. Sharma, J. Space-based visible space surveillance performance. *J. Guid. Control Dyn.* **2000**, *23*, 153–158. [CrossRef]
25. Ogawa, N.; Terui, F.; Mimasu, Y.; Yoshikawa, K.; Ono, G.; Yasuda, S.; Matsushima, K.; Masuda, T.; Hihara, H.; Sano, J.; et al. Image-based autonomous navigation of Hayabusa2 using artificial landmarks: The design and brief in-flight results of the first landing on asteroid Ryugu. *Astrodynamics* **2020**, *4*, 89–103. [CrossRef]
26. Anzai, Y.; Yairi, T.; Takeishi, N.; Tsuda, Y.; Ogawa, N. Visual localization for asteroid touchdown operation based on local image features. *Astrodynamics* **2020**, *4*, 149–161. [CrossRef]
27. Kelsey, J.M.; Byrne, J.; Cosgrove, M.; Seereeram, S.; Mehra, R.K. Vision-Based Relative Pose Estimation for Autonomous Rendezvous and Docking. In Proceedings of the 2006 IEEE Aerospace Conference, Big Sky, MT, USA, 4–11 March 2006; p. 20. [CrossRef]
28. Cinelli, M.; Ortore, E.; Laneve, G.; Circi, C. Geometrical approach for an optimal inter-satellite visibility. *Astrodynamics* **2021**, *5*, 237–248. [CrossRef]
29. Wang, H.; Zhang, W. Infrared characteristics of on-orbit targets based on space-based optical observation. *Opt. Commun.* **2013**, *290*, 69–75. [CrossRef]
30. Zhang, H.; Jiang, Z.; Elgammal, A. Satellite recognition and pose estimation using homeomorphic manifold analysis. *IEEE Trans. Aerosp. Electron. Syst.* **2015**, *51*, 785–792. [CrossRef]
31. Yang, X.; Wu, T.; Wang, N.; Huang, Y.; Song, B.; Gao, X. HCNN-PSI: A hybrid CNN with partial semantic information for space target recognition. *Pattern Recognit.* **2020**, *108*, 107531. [CrossRef]
32. Guthrie, B.; Kim, M.; Urrutxua, H.; Hare, J. Image-based attitude determination of co-orbiting satellites using deep learning technologies. *Aerosp. Sci. Technol.* **2022**, *120*, 107232. [CrossRef]
33. Shi, J.; Zhang, R.; Guo, S.; Yang, Y.; Xu, R.; Niu, W.; Li, J. Space targets adaptive optics images blind restoration by convolutional neural network. *Opt. Eng.* **2019**, *58*, 093102. [CrossRef]
34. De Vittori, A.; Cipollone, R.; Di Lizia, P.; Massari, M. Real-time space object tracklet extraction from telescope survey images with machine learning. *Astrodynamics* **2022**, *6*, 205–218. [CrossRef]
35. Zhou, Z.; Siddiquee, M.M.; Tajbakhsh, N.; Liang, J. Unet++: Redesigning skip connections to exploit multiscale features in image segmentation. *IEEE Trans. Med. Imaging* **2020**, *39*, 1856–1867. [CrossRef] [PubMed]
36. Liu, Z.; Lin, Y.; Cao, Y.; Hu, H.; Wei, Y.; Zhang, Z.; Lin, S.; Guo, B. Swin transformer: Hierarchical vision transformer using shifted Windows. *arXiv* **2021**, arXiv:2103.14030.
37. Vaswani, A.; Shazeer, N.; Parmar, N.; Uszkoreit, J.; Jones, L.; Gomez, A.N.; Kaiser, Ł.; Polosukhin, I. Attention is All You Need. In Proceedings of the 31st Conference on Neural Information Processing Systems (NIPS 2017), Long Beach, CA, USA, 4–9 December 2017.

Article

Approximations for Secular Variation Maxima of Classical Orbital Elements under Low Thrust

Zhaowei Wang [1], Lin Cheng [2] and Fanghua Jiang [1,*]

1 School of Aerospace Engineering, Tsinghua University, Beijing 100084, China
2 School of Astronautics, Beihang University, Beijing 100083, China
* Correspondence: jiangfh@tsinghua.edu.cn; Tel.: +86-010-6279-4365

Abstract: The reachability assessment of low-thrust spacecraft is of great significance for orbital transfer, because it can give a priori criteria for the challenging low-thrust trajectory design and optimization. This paper proposes an approximation method to obtain the variation maximum of each orbital element. Specifically, two steps organize the contribution of this study. First, combined with functional approximations, a set of analytical expressions for the variation maxima of orbital elements over one orbital revolution are derived. Second, the secular approximations for the variation maxima of the inclination and the right ascension of the ascending node are derived and expressed explicitly. An iterative algorithm is given to obtain the secular variation maxima of the other orbital elements the orbital elements other than the inclination and right ascension of the ascending node. Numerical simulations for approximating the variation maxima and a preliminary application in estimation of the velocity increment are given to demonstrate the efficiency and accuracy of the proposed method. Compared with the indirect method used alone for low-thrust trajectory optimization, the computation burden of the proposed method is reduced by over five orders of magnitude, and the computational accuracy is still high.

Keywords: low-thrust orbital transfer; trajectory optimization; variations of orbital elements; reachability assessment; estimation of velocity increment

MSC: 70M20

Citation: Wang, Z.; Cheng, L.; Jiang, F. Approximations for Secular Variation Maxima of Classical Orbital Elements under Low Thrust. *Mathematics* **2023**, *11*, 744. https://doi.org/10.3390/math11030744

Academic Editors: Yu Jiang and Haijun Peng

Received: 1 January 2023
Revised: 24 January 2023
Accepted: 26 January 2023
Published: 2 February 2023

1. Introduction

Interplanetary space missions propelled by solar electric propulsion, such as the Deep Space 1 [1] and BepiColombo [2], have demonstrated that low-thrust propulsion can be an alternative propulsion other than the traditional chemical propulsion for space exploration missions. Benefiting from its high propellant efficiency, this low-thrust electric propulsion system is drawing increasing attention from researchers. Space missions propelled by the low-thrust propulsion system are increasing rapidly [3,4]. Assessment of the state reachability of the low-thrust spacecraft provides meaningful reference for the preliminary design of space missions, such as multitarget missions [3,5], multiple debris removal missions [6], and collision avoidance missions [7–9]. It enables us to develop a smarter autonomous spacecraft [10]. Existing studies mainly focus on the reachability of impulsive spacecraft, while there are few studies on the reachability of low-thrust spacecraft. Therefore, this paper aims to develop a methodology that assesses the reachability of low-thrust orbital transfers. It should be able to benefit the global trajectory optimization for multitarget missions.

Numerous researchers focus on the reachability of spacecraft propelled with impulsive thrust [11–17]. For example, the upper bound [12] for the reachable domain was determined for spacecraft with a single fixed-magnitude impulse. Vinh et al. [15] analyzed the reachable surface of an interceptor at a given time. Otherwise, the reachability was also analyzed for spacecraft with a given impulse in a definite direction, such as a tangent impulse [16] and a norm impulse [17]. These studies have given wide analyses of the reachability of spacecraft with different impulses.

The reachability assessment of the low-thrust spacecraft can be obtained by solving for the variation ranges of orbital elements. The variation extrema of orbital elements can be modeled as optimal control problems [18]. The indirect methods and direct methods [19], specifically, such as the primer vector theory [20,21] and the convex optimization [22], are usually applied to solving the optimal control problems. However, the initial guesses of the shooting unknowns and multiple shooting strategies are usually needed by the indirect and direct methods. Moreover, the equations of the motion of the spacecraft propelled by the low thrust is generally non-integrable. Thus, numerical propagation of the low-thrust trajectories is fundamental but time-consuming when used to solve the trajectory optimization problems [19,23–25]. To improve the solution efficiency, two major ways have been developed. The first way is to simplify the motion equation. For example, the Fourier series expansions were applied to approximate the thrust profiles [26–28] and the equations of motion [29–31]. However, a nonlinear programming solver was needed to generate an approximate optimal trajectory by optimizing the coefficients of the Fourier series. The second way is to predict the evolution of the orbital elements [32] of low-thrust spacecraft, specifically, such as the semi-analytical theory [33], the orbital averaging method [34], and the asymptotic solution for the orbital motion subjected to constant thrust [35,36]. With the short-periodic terms ignored, Gao et al. [34] have made significant efforts to find an analytical solution for the evolutions of the orbital elements considering the J2 perturbation and the Earth shadow. Recently, innovative artificial intelligence methods such as machine learning have been applied in orbital guidance and control [37–39]. However, the machine learning methods are now still suffering from unknown black-box optimization models. To some extent, these two ways, simplifying the equations of motion and predicting the orbital evolution, can improve the computational efficiency and convergence rate when used to solve the optimal control problems. However, these methods are still time-consuming because they still rely heavily on numerical methods.

In order to assess the reachability of a low-thrust transfer, an effective approximation is necessary to obtain the variation ranges of the classical orbital elements of low-thrust spacecraft propelled over a long period of time. The variation maximum of each orbital element will be investigated analytically in this paper, and their variation minima can be obtained in the same way, but is omitted here for the sake of conciseness. The contribution of this paper is accomplished in two steps. Firstly, combined with functional approximations, the variation maxima of classical orbital elements over one orbital revolution are derived analytically by applying the local optimal control profile. Secondly, a set of explicit expressions are derived and an iteration algorithm is established to obtain the approximation for the secular maximum of each orbital element. The simulation results will demonstrate the efficiency and accuracy of the proposed method over the indirect method.

The rest of this paper is organized as follows. In Section 2, Gauss's variational equations for classical orbital elements are listed, and several simplifying assumptions are stated. In Section 3, the analytical approximation to the secular variation maximum of each classical orbital element is proposed. The model for the indirect method used to solve the variation maxima of the orbital elements is expressed first in Section 4, and then the simulations for the approximations of the variation maxima and the estimation of the velocity increment are described. Finally, the conclusion is drawn in Section 6.

2. Gauss's Variational Equations and Simplifying Assumptions

Gauss's variational equations will be listed, where the thrust acceleration vector is projected onto the tangential-normal coordinate frame. Then, three assumptions will be stated, based on which Gauss's variational equations are simplified so that the secular variation maxima of the classical orbital elements can be investigated analytically.

2.1. Gauss's Variational Equations for Classical Orbital Elements

The Gauss's variational equations with respect to time t in tangential-normal coordinates are expressed in the forms [11]

$$\frac{\mathrm{d}a}{\mathrm{d}t} = \frac{2a^2 v}{\mu} a_t \tag{1}$$

$$\frac{\mathrm{d}e}{\mathrm{d}t} = \frac{1}{v}\left[2(e+\cos f)a_t - \frac{r}{a}\sin f a_n\right] \tag{2}$$

$$\frac{\mathrm{d}i}{\mathrm{d}t} = \frac{r\cos\theta}{h} a_h \tag{3}$$

$$\frac{\mathrm{d}\Omega}{\mathrm{d}t} = \frac{r\sin\theta}{h\sin i} a_h \tag{4}$$

$$\frac{\mathrm{d}\omega}{\mathrm{d}t} = \frac{1}{ev}\left[2\sin f a_t + \left(2e + \frac{r}{a}\cos f\right)a_n\right] - \frac{r\sin\theta\cos i}{h\sin i} a_h \tag{5}$$

$$\frac{\mathrm{d}f}{\mathrm{d}t} = \frac{h}{r^2} - \frac{1}{ev}\left[2\sin f a_t + \left(2e + \frac{r}{a}\cos f\right)a_n\right] \tag{6}$$

where $\theta = \omega + f$ denotes the argument of latitude, $r = \frac{h^2}{\mu(1+e\cos f)}$ represents the orbital radius, and $v = \frac{\mu}{h}\sqrt{e^2+1+2e\cos f}$ represents the orbital velocity. The vector $\boldsymbol{a} = [a_t, a_n, a_h]$ denotes the propulsive acceleration vector projected onto the tangential-normal coordinate frame, which is shown in Figure 1. The unit vector $\boldsymbol{e_t}$ lies in the plane of the osculating orbit along the velocity vector, $\boldsymbol{e_h}$ is along the specific angular momentum vector, and $\boldsymbol{e_n}$ is towards the central body and forms the right-handed coordinate system with the other two components.

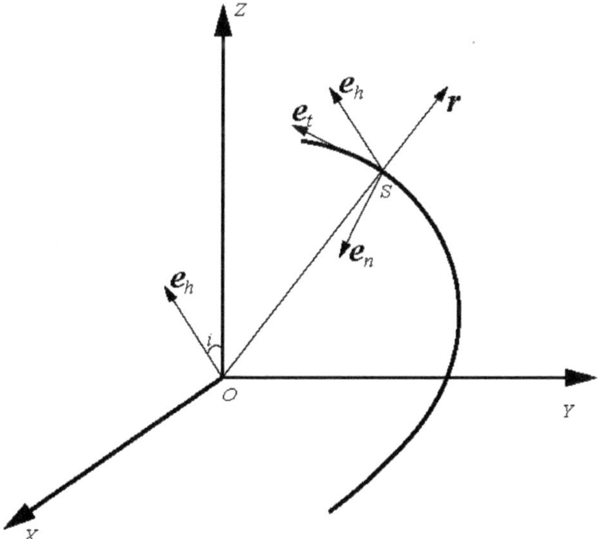

Figure 1. Tangential-normal coordinate frame.

2.2. Simplifying Assumptions

To approximate the secular variations of the classical orbital elements, some assumptions are needed to simplify the variational Equations (1)–(6). They are as follows

1. The fuel consumption is small and ignored due to the low magnitude of the thrust compared to the total mass of the spacecraft. Consequently, the magnitude of the propulsive acceleration $a_{\max}$ becomes constant because of the constant low-thrust magnitude $T_{\max}$. Thus, the following equation holds

$$\|\boldsymbol{a}\| = \frac{T_{\max}}{m} = a_{\max} = \text{const} \tag{7}$$

The thrust magnitude $T_{\max}$ is modeled as a function of the maximum thruster input power $P_{\max}$ and specific impulse I_{sp} as [40]

$$T_{\max} = \frac{2\eta P_{\max}}{I_{\text{sp}} g_0} \tag{8}$$

where η denotes the thruster efficiency, whose value together with $P_{\max}$ are selected from [40]. They are assumed to be constant in this paper to obtain a constant low-thrust magnitude. Meanwhile, $g_0 = 9.80665\,\text{m/s}^2$ is the standard gravitational acceleration.

2. The variation of the true anomaly caused by the three components of $\boldsymbol{a}$ can be ignored because its maximum $a_{\max}$ is much smaller than the central gravitational acceleration [34].

$$\frac{\mathrm{d}f}{\mathrm{d}t} \approx \frac{h}{r^2} \tag{9}$$

In Equation (9), the approximation of the Equation (6) can be derived when the effect on $\mathrm{d}f/\mathrm{d}t$ caused by the low thrust is small enough compared to the term h/r^2 (a similar approximation can also obtained in [36,41]).
Divided by Equation (9), Gauss's variational equations of classical orbital elements are transformed into the following differential equations in terms of the true anomaly

$$\frac{\mathrm{d}a}{\mathrm{d}f} = \frac{2a^2r^2v}{\mu h} a_t \tag{10}$$

$$\frac{\mathrm{d}e}{\mathrm{d}f} = \frac{r^2}{hv}\left[2(e+\cos f)a_t - \frac{r}{a}\sin f a_n\right] \tag{11}$$

$$\frac{\mathrm{d}i}{\mathrm{d}f} = \frac{r^3\cos\theta}{h^2} a_h \tag{12}$$

$$\frac{\mathrm{d}\Omega}{\mathrm{d}f} = \frac{r^3\sin\theta}{h^2\sin i} a_h \tag{13}$$

$$\frac{\mathrm{d}\omega}{\mathrm{d}f} = \frac{r^2}{hev}\left[2\sin f a_t + \left(2e + \frac{r}{a}\cos f\right)a_n\right] - \frac{r^3\sin\theta\cos i}{h^2\sin i} a_h \tag{14}$$

3. Owing to their very small variations within one revolution, the orbital elements are assumed to be unchanged within every orbital revolution when the related right sides of Equations (10)–(14) are used to estimate the variations of orbital elements immediately after the revolution.

3. Secular Variation Maximum of Single Classical Orbital Element

Based on the previous assumptions, the approximations for the secular variation maxima of the classical orbital elements are derived and expressed as some semi-analytical formulas in this section. First, we try to derive the approximation for the variation maximum of each orbital element over one orbital revolution analytically. Second, we focus only on the variations of the orbital elements immediately after integer revolutions but ignore the short-term variations within one orbital revolution.

The procedure for approximating the secular variation maxima of the classical orbital elements is shown in Figure 2.

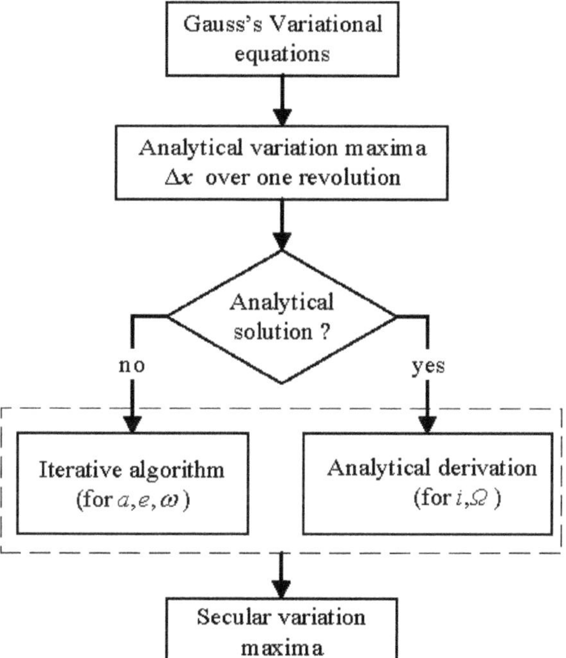

Figure 2. Procedure for approximating the secular variation maxima.

As shown in Figure 2, the secular variation maximum of each orbital element is obtained through two steps. The variation maximum over one orbital revolution, Δx, is solved at first. Then, the approximations for the secular variation maxima of the orbital elements are divided into two groups. For the three orbital elements a, e, and ω, an iterative algorithm is used to obtain their secular variation maxima. Meanwhile, two analytical solutions are derived to obtain those for i and Ω.

3.1. Secular Variation Maximum of Semi-Major Axis

Replacing the orbital velocity in Equation (10) with its well-known expression with respect to the COE results in the semi-major axis with respect to the true anomaly:

$$\frac{\mathrm{d}a}{\mathrm{d}f} = \frac{2a_t a^3(1-e^2)}{\mu} \frac{\sqrt{1+e^2+2e\cos f}}{(1+e\cos f)^2} \tag{15}$$

which demonstrates that the well-known way to maximize the variation of the semi-major axis is to apply the acceleration along the tangent direction.

When the orbital elements remain unchanged within one revolution, as assumed in Section 2.2, the variation maximum of the semi-major axis over one revolution, denoted by Δa_N, is derived

$$\Delta a_N = \frac{2a_{N-1}^3(1-e_{N-1}^2)a_t}{\mu} C_{I,N-1} \tag{16}$$

where the parameter $C_{I,N-1}$ expressed by the definite integral (17) remains unchanged, as the eccentricity e_{N-1} remains unchanged within the $(N-1)$-th orbital revolution.

$$\begin{aligned} C_{I,N-1} &= \int_0^{2\pi} \frac{\sqrt{1+e_{N-1}^2+2e_{N-1}\cos f}}{(1+e_{N-1}\cos f)^2} \mathrm{d}f \\ &= \frac{4\mathrm{EllipticE}(e_{N-1})}{1-e_{N-1}^2} \end{aligned} \tag{17}$$

where $\mathrm{EllipticE}(e_{N-1})$ denotes the complete elliptic integral with the form [42]

$$\mathrm{EllipticE}(e_{N-1}) = \int_0^1 \frac{\sqrt{-e_{N-1}^2 t^2+1}}{\sqrt{-t^2+1}} \mathrm{d}t \tag{18}$$

When the thrust acceleration is applied along the tangent direction, the variation of the eccentricity is derived, as follows

$$\begin{aligned} e_N &= e_{N-1} + \Delta e_N \\ \Delta e_N &= \frac{2a_t a_{N-1}^2 (1-e_{N-1}^2)^2}{\mu} \\ &\int_0^{2\pi} \frac{e_{N-1}+\cos f}{(1+e_{N-1}\cos f)^2\sqrt{1+e_{N-1}^2+2e_{N-1}\cos f}} \mathrm{d}f \end{aligned} \tag{19}$$

The closed-form solution for Equation (19) can be expressed as

$$\begin{aligned} &\int \frac{e+\cos f}{(1+e\cos f)^2\sqrt{1+e^2+2e\cos f}} \mathrm{d}f \\ &= \frac{1}{-1+e^2}\Bigg(-\frac{1}{e}\mathrm{i}\sqrt{(1+e)^2}\mathrm{EllipticE}\Big(\mathrm{i}\sinh^{-1}(\tan(\frac{f}{2}))|\frac{(e-1)^2}{(e+1)^2}\Big) \\ &+ 4\mathrm{i}\frac{1}{\sqrt{(1+e)^2}}\mathrm{EllipticPi}\Big(\frac{1-e}{1+e};\mathrm{i}\sinh^{-1}(\tan(\frac{f}{2}))|\frac{(e-1)^2}{(e+1)^2}\Big) \\ &+ \frac{(e-1)\tan\left(\frac{f}{2}\right)\left(e^2+2e\cos(f)+1\right)}{e(e\cos(f)+1)}\Bigg) \end{aligned} \tag{20}$$

where $\mathrm{EllipticE}(\phi|m)$ and $\mathrm{EllipticPi}(n;\phi|m)$ are the complete elliptic integrals of the second kind and the third kind, respectively, which can be obtained in [42].

By combining Equation (16) with Equation (19), we can design an iterative algorithm, as shown in Algorithm 1, to obtain the approximations of the secular variation maxima of the semi-major axis and the consequent variation of the eccentricity.

Algorithm 1: Iterative algorithm.

Input:
Initial orbital elements a_0, e_0, i_0, Ω_0, and ω_0
For each loop iteration of each subsection:
1. Calculate the variation maxima $\Delta \boldsymbol{x}_N$ over one orbital revolution
2. Add the variations of the orbital elements $\boldsymbol{x}_N = \Delta \boldsymbol{x}_N + \boldsymbol{x}_{N-1}$

Stopping conditions:
The time of flight reaches the given value.
Output:
Approximations for the variation of the orbital elements $\boldsymbol{x}_N$

3.2. Secular Variation Maximum of Eccentricity

Two spherical angles α and β are introduced to represent the propulsive acceleration vector, as shown in Equation (21). The out-of-plane (yaw) steering angle β is measured from the orbit plane to the thrust vector. The in-plane thrust-steering angle α is measured from the velocity vector to the projection of the thrust vector onto the orbit plane [43]. Therefore, the three components of the propulsive acceleration vector are expressed by

$$\begin{aligned} a_t &= a_{\max} \cos\beta \cos\alpha \\ a_n &= a_{\max} \cos\beta \sin\alpha \\ a_h &= a_{\max} \sin\beta \end{aligned} \tag{21}$$

Some researchers have derived the optimal thrust angle that maximizes the rate of the change of the orbital elements [43–45]. By applying the optimal control theory, one can deduce the optimal thrust angles that maximize the change rate of each orbital element. Specifically, they satisfy $\partial\dot{x}/\partial\alpha^* = 0$ and $\partial\dot{x}/\partial\beta^* = 0$. Then, the optimal control profile to maximize the eccentricity is obtained as $\beta^* = 0$. Meanwhile, the optimal thrust angle α^* satisfies

$$\begin{aligned} \sin\alpha^* &= \frac{B_e}{\sqrt{A_e^2 + B_e^2}} \\ \cos\alpha^* &= \frac{A_e}{\sqrt{A_e^2 + B_e^2}} \end{aligned} \tag{22}$$

where the parameters A_e and B_e hold the forms

$$\begin{aligned} A_e &= 2(e + \cos f) \\ B_e &= -\frac{r}{a}\sin f \end{aligned} \tag{23}$$

Furthermore, combining the optimal control profile in Equation (22) with Equations (11) and (21), the variation maximum of the eccentricity over the N-th orbital revolution is obtained as

$$\Delta e_N = \frac{a_{\max} a_{N-1}^2 (1 - e_{N-1}^2)^2}{\mu} \int_0^{2\pi} \frac{\sqrt{A_{e,N-1}^2 + B_{e,N-1}^2}}{\rho_{N-1}^2 \sqrt{1 + e_{N-1}^2 + 2e_{N-1}\cos f}} \mathrm{d}f \tag{24}$$

In Equation (24), $A_{e,N-1}$ and $B_{e,N-1}$ represent the values of the parameters A_e and B_e corresponding to the revolution number $N-1$, respectively. Meanwhile, the parameter ρ_{N-1} is defined as $1 + e_{N-1}\cos f$. Then, substituting the optimal control profile in Equation (22) into Equation (10) yields the variation of the semi-major axis over one revolution

$$\Delta a_N = \frac{2a_{\max} a_{N-1}^3 (1 - e_{N-1}^2)}{\mu} \int_0^{2\pi} \frac{A_{e,N-1}\sqrt{1 + e_{N-1}^2 + 2e_{N-1}\cos f}}{\sqrt{A_{e,N-1}^2 + B_{e,N-1}^2}\rho_{N-1}^2} \mathrm{d}f \tag{25}$$

The optimal control Equation (22) that maximizes the variation of the eccentricity leads to the variation equation of the argument of periapsis in the following form

$$\begin{aligned} \frac{\mathrm{d}\omega}{\mathrm{d}f} = & \frac{a_{\max} a^2 (1 - e^2)^2}{\mu e (1 + e\cos f)^2 \sqrt{1 + e^2 + 2e\cos f}} \\ & \left(\frac{2\sin f A_e}{\sqrt{A_e^2 + B_e^2}} + (2e + \frac{1 - e^2}{1 + e\cos f}) \frac{B_e}{\sqrt{A_e^2 + B_e^2}} \right) \end{aligned} \tag{26}$$

As the above equation with respect to the true anomaly is an odd function, thus the variation of the argument of periapsis in each orbital revolution is equal to zero. Then, it satisfied that $\Delta\omega = 0$, and $\omega_N = \omega_0$.

The two integral parts in Equations (24) and (25), respectively, have no analytical primitive functions; however, they can be expanded in a power series in the eccentricity. Thus, the polynomial approximations $P_e(e) = \sum_{k=0}^{4} p_{e,k}e^k$ and $P_a(e) = \sum_{k=0}^{4} p_{a,k}e^k$ are employed to represent the two integrals. The analytical expressions of the variations of the eccentricity and the semi-major axis are expressed as:

$$\begin{aligned} \Delta e_N &= \frac{a_{\max} a_{N-1}^2}{\mu} P_e(e_N) \\ \Delta a_N &= \frac{2a_{\max} a_{N-1}^3}{\mu} P_a(e_N) \end{aligned} \tag{27}$$

Using the Equation (27), one can obtain the secular approximation of the upper bound for the eccentricity Δe_N by applying the iterative algorithm in Algorithm 1. The consequent variation of the semi-major axis can be obtained as well.

3.3. Secular Variation Maximum of Inclination

It can be inferred from Equation (12) that the variation of orbital inclination only depends on the normal acceleration a_h. Therefore, the other two components of the propulsive acceleration vector are set to zero. Accordingly, the semi-major axis and the eccentricity are invariant, i.e., $a = a_0$ and $e = e_0$, and the differential equation of the inclination becomes

$$\frac{\mathrm{d}i}{\mathrm{d}f} = \frac{a_h p_0^2}{\mu} \frac{\cos\theta}{(1 + e_0 \cos f)^3} \tag{28}$$

The optimal control profile a_h to maximize the inclination variation has two parts: the direction and the magnitude. The magnitude is always equal to $a_{\max}$. Since the value of $\cos\theta$ changes periodically, the sign of a_h within one revolution will be switched according to the instantaneous value of $\cos\theta$. Therefore, the optimal control profile to maximize the variation of the inclination is founded by

$$\begin{aligned} &|a_h| = a_{\max} \\ &\mathrm{sgn}(a_h) = \begin{cases} 1 & \theta \in [2k\pi - \frac{\pi}{2}, 2k\pi + \frac{\pi}{2}] \\ -1 & \theta \in [2k\pi + \frac{\pi}{2}, 2k\pi + \frac{3\pi}{2}] \end{cases} \end{aligned} \tag{29}$$

where the parameter $k \in \mathrm{Z}$ represents an arbitrary integer. The variation maximum of the inclination over one revolution can be integrated directly.

$$\begin{aligned} \Delta i = &\frac{a_{\max} \cos\omega p_0^2}{\mu} \int_0^{2\pi} \frac{\mathrm{sgn}(a_h) \cos f}{(1 + e_0 \cos f)^3} \mathrm{d}f \\ &- \frac{a_{\max} \sin\omega p_0^2}{\mu} \int_0^{2\pi} \frac{\mathrm{sgn}(a_h) \sin f}{(1 + e_0 \cos f)^3} \mathrm{d}f \end{aligned} \tag{30}$$

These two integrals in Equation (30) have general analytical primitive functions, which are expressed in terms of the eccentric anomaly E [46]

$$\begin{aligned} H &= \int_{f_0}^{f} \frac{\cos f}{(1 + e\cos f)^3} \mathrm{d}f \\ &= -\left(1 - e^2\right)^{-\frac{5}{2}} \times \left[\frac{3eE}{2} - \left(1 + e^2\right)\sin E + \frac{e}{4}\sin 2E - \left(\frac{3eE_0}{2} - \left(1 + e^2\right)\sin E_0 + \frac{e}{4}\sin 2E_0\right)\right] \\ G &= \int_{f_0}^{f} \frac{\sin f}{(1 + e\cos f)^3} \mathrm{d}f \\ &= (1 - e^2)^{-2}\left(-\cos E + \frac{e}{4}\cos 2E + \cos E_0 - \frac{e}{4}\cos 2E_0\right) \end{aligned} \tag{31}$$

Here, we use the H_i and G_i to denote the primitive functions of the two integrals in Equation (30). The variation maximum of the inclination over one revolution can be written as

$$\Delta i = \frac{a_{\max} \cos \omega p_0^2}{\mu} H_i - \frac{a_{\max} \sin \omega p_0^2}{\mu} G_i \tag{32}$$

Meanwhile, the variational equations of the right ascension of the ascending node and the argument of periapsis under the optimal control profile (29) are expressed as

$$\begin{aligned} \frac{\mathrm{d}\Omega}{\mathrm{d}f} &= \frac{a_h p_0^2}{\mu \sin i} \frac{\sin(\omega + f)}{(1 + e \cos f)^3} \\ \frac{\mathrm{d}\omega}{\mathrm{d}f} &= -\cos i \frac{\mathrm{d}\Omega}{\mathrm{d}f} \end{aligned} \tag{33}$$

As the variation maximum of the inclination is obtained analytically, we will propose two strategies with different computational efficiency and accuracy to solve for the secular variation maximum of the inclination.

3.3.1. Strategy 1

The variation of the argument of the periapsis is small when investigating the variation maximum of the inclination. Therefore, it can be ignored to obtain an explicit analytical solution. When the argument of periapsis remains unchanged, the variation maximum of the inclination and the variation of Ω and ω are represented as

$$\begin{aligned} \Delta i &= \frac{a_{\max} \cos \omega_0 p_0^2}{\mu} H_i - \frac{a_{\max} \sin \omega_0 p_0^2}{\mu} G_i = \text{const} \\ \Delta \Omega &= \frac{a_h p_0^2 \sin \omega_0}{\mu \sin i} H_i + \frac{a_h p_0^2 \cos \omega_0}{\mu \sin i} G_i = \text{const} \\ \Delta \omega &= 0 \end{aligned} \tag{34}$$

Similarly, the differential equations for the variation maxima of the inclination and the right ascension of the ascending node, with respect to the number of orbital revolutions, are given as

$$\begin{aligned} \frac{\mathrm{d}i}{\mathrm{d}N} &= C_i \\ \frac{\mathrm{d}\Omega}{\mathrm{d}N} &= \frac{C_\Omega}{\sin(i)} \end{aligned} \tag{35}$$

where $C_i = \Delta i$ and C_Ω are both constant. Meanwhile, C_Ω holds the form

$$C_\Omega = \frac{a_h p_0^2 \sin \omega_0 H_\Omega}{\mu} + \frac{a_h p_0^2 \cos \omega_0 G_\Omega}{\mu} \tag{36}$$

We can solve the differential equations (35) for the variation maximum of inclination and the consequent variations of the right ascension of the ascending node. They are of the forms

$$\begin{aligned} i_N &= i_0 + C_i N \\ \Omega_N &= \Omega_0 + \frac{C_\Omega}{C_i} [\ln(\tan \frac{i_0 + C_i N}{2}) - \ln(\tan \frac{i_0}{2})] \end{aligned} \tag{37}$$

This shows that the maximum of the inclination increases linearly under the normal propulsive acceleration.

3.3.2. Strategy 2

For a higher accuracy, we take the small variation of the argument of periapsis into account. The variations of i, Ω and ω over one revolution are expressed as

$$\begin{aligned} \Delta i_N &= \frac{a_{\max} \cos \omega_{N-1} p_0^2}{\mu} H_i - \frac{a_{\max} \sin \omega_{N-1} p_0^2}{\mu} G_i \\ \Delta \Omega_N &= \frac{a_h p_0^2 \sin \omega_{N-1}}{\mu \sin i_{N-1}} H_i + \frac{a_h p_0^2 \cos \omega_{N-1}}{\mu \sin i_{N-1}} G_i \\ \Delta \omega_N &= -\cos i_{N-1} \Delta \Omega_N \end{aligned} \tag{38}$$

The variations of i, Ω, and ω over one revolution are obtained analytically by Equation (38). The secular variation maximum of the inclination and the variations of the right ascension of the ascending node and the argument of periapsis can be obtained through the iterative algorithm given in Algorithm 1.

3.4. Secular Variation Maximum of Right Ascension of the Ascending Node

Similar to the approximation of the inclination, the variation of the right ascension of the ascending node depends only on the normal acceleration a_h. Meanwhile, $a = a_0$ and $e = e_0$ are still satisfied. The variational Equation (13) is rewritten as

$$\frac{\mathrm{d}\Omega}{\mathrm{d}f} = \frac{a_h p_0^2}{\mu \sin i} \frac{\sin(\omega_0 + f)}{(1 + e \cos f)^3} \tag{39}$$

To maximize the variation of the right ascension of the ascending node over one orbital revolution, the magnitude of the acceleration in the norm direction should achieve its maximum $a_{\max}$. When the inclination angle is equal to 0 or π, the variational equations will be singular. Therefore, the inclination range, $(0, \pi)$, is considered to avoid the singularities. Then, the sign of a_h depends on the value of the sine function $\sin(\omega_0 + f)$. Consequently, the optimal control profile to maximize the variation of Ω is derived as

$$\begin{aligned} |a_h| &= a_{\max} \\ \mathrm{sgn}(a_h) &= \begin{cases} 1 & \theta \in [2k\pi, 2k\pi + \pi] \\ -1 & \theta \in [2k\pi + \pi, 2(k+1)\pi] \end{cases} \end{aligned} \tag{40}$$

Substituting the optimal control profile (40) into the differential Equation (39), results in the variation maximum of the right ascension of the ascending node $\Delta\Omega$ over one revolution. The method to maximize the right ascension of the ascending node is same as the one to maximize the inclination. The only difference is that the optimal control profiles (40) and (29) are applied, respectively. Therefore, the secular maximum of the right ascension of the ascending node can be obtained by Equations (37) and (38) from the two strategies proposed in Section 3.3. Meanwhile, the consequent variations of the inclination and the argument of periapsis are obtained as well.

The approximation of the right ascension of the ascending node in the previous part of this subsection is obtained, assuming no other orbital perturbation acceleration is considered except the low-thrust acceleration. In the low-Earth orbit, the variations of Ω and ω caused by the second order zonal harmonic of the Earth's gravitational potential, J_2, are not small enough. In the next part of this subsection, the variation maximum of the right ascension of the ascending node is conducted by considering the J_2 perturbation and the low-thrust acceleration.

The variational equations for the orbit elements, $\boldsymbol{x} = [a, e, i, \Omega, \omega]$, considering the low thrust acceleration and the J_2 perturbation, can be expressed as $\mathrm{d}\boldsymbol{x}/\mathrm{d}t = \mathrm{d}\boldsymbol{x}_{LT}/\mathrm{d}t + \mathrm{d}\boldsymbol{x}_{J_2}/\mathrm{d}t$, where $\mathrm{d}\boldsymbol{x}_{LT}/\mathrm{d}t$ and $\mathrm{d}\boldsymbol{x}_{J_2}/\mathrm{d}t$ represent the components of the variational equations under the low-thrust acceleration and the J_2 perturbation, respectively, and $\mathrm{d}\boldsymbol{x}_{LT}/\mathrm{d}t$ holds the form in Equations (1)–(6). Neglecting the short-term effect of the J_2 perturbation, one can obtain the variational equations $\mathrm{d}\boldsymbol{x}_{J_2}/\mathrm{d}t$ [47].

$$\begin{aligned}
\frac{\mathrm{d}a_{J_2}}{\mathrm{d}t} &= \frac{\mathrm{d}e_{J_2}}{\mathrm{d}t} = \frac{\mathrm{d}i_{J_2}}{\mathrm{d}t} = 0 \\
\frac{\mathrm{d}\Omega_{J_2}}{\mathrm{d}t} &= -\frac{3}{2}J_2\sqrt{\mu}(\frac{R_E}{1-e^2})^2 a^{-\frac{7}{2}}\cos i \\
\frac{\mathrm{d}\omega_{J_2}}{\mathrm{d}t} &= \frac{3}{2}J_2\sqrt{\mu}(\frac{R_E}{1-e^2})^2 a^{-\frac{7}{2}}(2-\frac{5}{2}\sin^2 i)
\end{aligned} \tag{41}$$

where $J_2 = 1.08262668 \times 10^{-3}$ is the coefficient of the flattening perturbation and $R_E = 6{,}378{,}137$ m. The average changes of the orbital elements $a, e,$ and i caused by the J_2 perturbation per orbit are null.

The variation maximum of Ω and the consequent variations of i and ω over one orbital revolution, considering the effect of the low-thrust acceleration and the J_2 perturbation, hold the form

$$\begin{aligned}
\Delta\Omega_N &= \Delta\Omega_{LT,N} + \Delta\Omega_{J_2,N} \\
\Delta i_N &= \Delta i_{LT,N} + \Delta i_{J_2,N} \\
\Delta\omega_N &= \Delta\omega_{LT,N} + \Delta\omega_{J_2,N}
\end{aligned} \tag{42}$$

where $\Delta\Omega_{LT,N}, \Delta i_{LT,N}$, and $\Delta\omega_{LT,N}$ donate the variations over one revolution caused by the given optimal control low thrust expressed in Equation (40). $\Delta\Omega_{LT,N}, \Delta i_{LT,N}$, and $\Delta\omega_{LT,N}$ donate the variations caused by the J_2 perturbation over one revolution, and they can be derived as

$$\begin{aligned}
\Delta\Omega_{J_2,N} &= -3\pi J_2(\frac{R_E}{a_0(1-e_0^2)})^2\cos i_{N-1} \\
\Delta i_{J_2,N} &= 0 \\
\Delta\omega_{J_2,N} &= 3\pi J_2(\frac{R_E}{a_0(1-e_0^2)})^2(2-\frac{5}{2}\sin^2 i_{N-1})
\end{aligned} \tag{43}$$

We can obtain the secular variation maximum of the right ascension of the ascending node, as well as the consequent variation of the inclination and the argument of periapsis, by combining the Equation (42) and the iterative algorithm given in Algorithm 1.

3.5. Secular Variation Maximum of Argument of Periapsis

The variation of the argument of periapsis depends on all the three components of the propulsive acceleration vector. Thus, Equations (21) are used to represent the acceleration vector. By substituting Equation (21) into Equation (14), we can derive the parameterized differential equation of the argument of periapsis.

$$\frac{\mathrm{d}\omega}{\mathrm{d}f} = \frac{a_{\max}p^2}{h(1+e\cos f)^2}(A\cos\beta\cos\alpha + B\cos\beta\sin\alpha + C\cos\beta)) \tag{44}$$

where

$$\begin{aligned}
A &= \frac{1}{ev}2\sin f \\
B &= \frac{1}{ev}\left(2e + \frac{r}{a}\cos f\right) \\
C &= -\frac{r\sin\theta\cos i}{h\sin i}
\end{aligned} \tag{45}$$

As the term $\frac{r^2}{h}$ in Equation (44) is always positive, one can deduce the optimal thrust angles by applying the optimal control theory.

$$\begin{aligned} \cos\alpha^* &= \frac{A}{\sqrt{A^2+B^2}} \\ \sin\alpha^* &= \frac{B}{\sqrt{A^2+B^2}} \\ \cos\beta^* &= \frac{\sqrt{A^2+B^2}}{\sqrt{A^2+B^2+C^2}} \\ \sin\beta^* &= \frac{C}{\sqrt{A^2+B^2+C^2}} \end{aligned} \tag{46}$$

Substituting the optimal control profile (46) into Equation (44), we can obtain the variation maximum of the argument of periapsis over one revolution.

$$\Delta\omega_{LT,N} = \int_0^{2\pi} \frac{a_{\max} p_{N-1}^2}{h_{N-1}} \frac{\sqrt{A_{N-1}^2 + B_{N-1}^2 + C_{N-1}^2}}{(1+e_{N-1}\cos f)^2} \mathrm{d}f \tag{47}$$

The consequent variations of the other orbital elements over one revolution can also be obtained by applying the control profile (46). Then, by using the designed iterative algorithm in Algorithm 1, we can obtain the secular variation maximum of the argument of periapsis and the consequent variations of the other elements.

Two primary additional analysis can also be performed. First, a correction for the variation of the argument of periapsis over one revolution is conducted. The variation with the time of the argument of latitude is [11]

$$\frac{\mathrm{d}\omega}{\mathrm{d}t} + \frac{\mathrm{d}f^{\mathrm{real}}}{\mathrm{d}t} = \frac{h}{r^2} - \frac{r\sin(\omega+f)\cos i}{h\sin i} \approx \frac{h}{r^2} \tag{48}$$

where the f^{real} denotes the exact value of the true anomaly. The approximation in Equation (48) is based on the assumption that the normal acceleration is small enough to produce a negligible effect. By dividing Equation (48) by the assumption in Equation (9), the following expression can be derived.

$$\frac{\mathrm{d}f^{\mathrm{real}}}{\mathrm{d}f} \approx 1 - \frac{\mathrm{d}\omega}{\mathrm{d}f} \tag{49}$$

The following expression can be obtained by integrating the Equation (49).

$$\Delta f^{\mathrm{real}} = 2\pi - \Delta\omega_{LT,N} \tag{50}$$

The variation maximum of the argument of periapsis over one revolution with a correction, denoted by $\Delta\omega_N^{\mathrm{cor}}$, can be obtained by the linear interpolation as

$$\Delta\omega_{LT,N}^{\mathrm{cor}} = \frac{2\pi}{2\pi - \Delta\omega_N}\Delta\omega_{LT,N} \tag{51}$$

Second, parameter $K = \frac{\max(A^2+B^2)}{\max(C^2)}$ is used to evaluate the magnitude ratio of A^2+B^2 to C^2. The parameter K can be expanded in the power series in the eccentricity. The approximation of K can be expressed as $K \approx 4/(e^2\cot^2 i)$. Its values for different eccentricity and inclination are shown in Figure 3. It can be inferred that the smaller the eccentricity and the closer the inclination to $\pi/2$, the bigger the value of K. To some extent, the parameter K indicates the effect of the acceleration component a_h on the variation maximum of the argument of periapsis. Combining the Equation (21) and the optimal thrust angle in Equation (46), the bigger the value of K is, the closer the applied acceleration a_h is to zero.

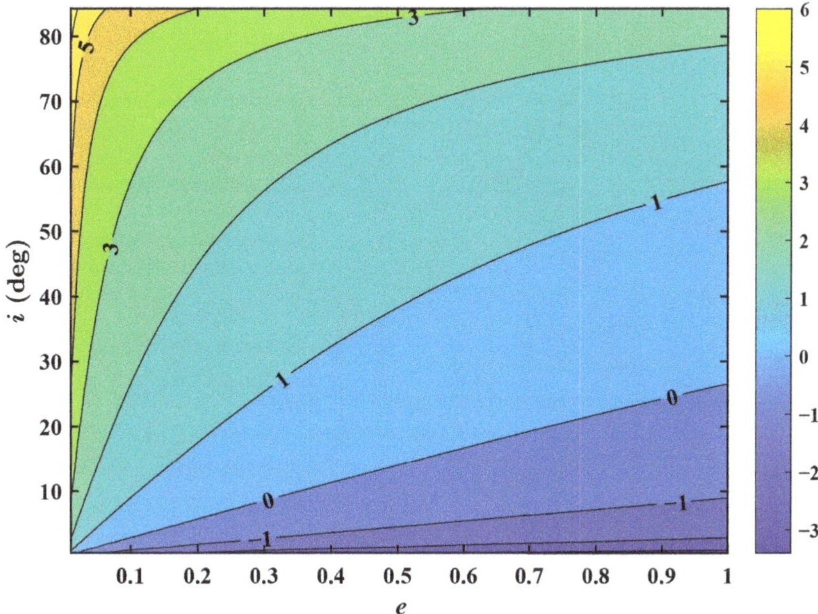

Figure 3. Value of parameter $\log_{10} K$ for different inclination and eccentricity.

When the value of K is large, $A^2 + B^2 + C^2 \approx A^2 + B^2$, and the acceleration component a_h is small and ignored. Then, the optimal control profile is transferred as

$$\begin{aligned} a_t^* &= a_{\max} \frac{A}{\sqrt{A^2 + B^2}} \\ a_n^* &= a_{\max} \frac{B}{\sqrt{A^2 + B^2}} \\ a_h^* &= 0 \end{aligned} \tag{52}$$

Substituting the simplified optimal control profile into Equations (10)–(14), we can find that the variational equations of the semi-major axis and the eccentricity are odd functions. Thus, their variations over one revolution are zero. Meanwhile, the variation of the inclination and the right ascension of the ascending node are small and ignored. Therefore, $a = a_0, e = e_0, i = i_0, \Omega = \Omega_0$, and the variation of the argument of periapsis over one revolution is simplified as

$$\Delta\omega_{LT,N} = \int_0^{2\pi} \frac{a_{\max} p_0^2}{h_0} \frac{\sqrt{A_0^2 + B_0^2}}{(1 + e_0 \cos f)^2} \mathrm{d}f = \text{const} \tag{53}$$

It means that the variation maximum of the argument of periapsis caused by the low-thrust acceleration is constant over each revolution when the parameter K is large.

From the former parts of this subsection, we can obtained the variation maximum of the argument of periapsis caused by the low-thrust acceleration. Meanwhile, the variation caused by the J_2 perturbation has been derived in Equation (43). By using the formulas in Equation (42) and the iterative algorithm given in Algorithm 1, we can now obtain the secular variation maximum of the argument of periapsis, considering both the low-thrust acceleration and the J_2 perturbation.

4. Numerical Simulations

In the first part of this section, the optimization model of the indirect method is established. To validate the optimality of the indirect method, we conducted several simulations to compare the solutions to those obtained by GPOPS version 1.0 [48], which is a MATLAB software for solving multiple-phase optimal control problems using the Gauss pseudospectral method. Meanwhile, simulations for the variation maxima of the orbital elements over a fixed flight time are conducted to demonstrate the efficiency and accuracy of the proposed method compared with the indirect method. Then, a preliminary application of the proposed method is conducted to estimate the velocity increments of orbital transfers. All the simulations are coded in C++ and performed on a personal desktop with an Intel Core i7-7700 CPU of 3.6 GHz and 16.00 GB of RAM.

4.1. Simulations for Variation Maximum of Each Orbital Element

In this study, the approximation solutions obtained by the proposed method are compared with those by an indirect method. The optimization model is established first by considering the mass consumption. The nonlinear optimal control model that maximizes the variation maximum of the semi-major axis over a fixed flight time is taken as an example and given as follows.

Minimize:

$$J = -a(tf) \tag{54}$$

Subject to

$$\begin{aligned} \dot{\boldsymbol{X}}(t) &= \boldsymbol{f}(\boldsymbol{X}, \boldsymbol{u}, m, t) \\ \dot{m}(t) &= -\frac{T_{\max} u}{I_{\rm sp} g_0} \\ \boldsymbol{X}(t_0) &= \boldsymbol{X}_0, m(t_0) = m_0 \end{aligned} \tag{55}$$

where $\boldsymbol{u}$ denotes the control vector, $\boldsymbol{u} = \frac{T_{\max} u}{m}\boldsymbol{\alpha}$. $\boldsymbol{\alpha}$ is an unit vector and denotes the direction of the control vector. The engine thrust ratio is $u \in [0,1]$. The state $\boldsymbol{X}$ represents $\boldsymbol{X} = [a, e, i, \Omega, \omega, f]^{\rm T}$. The right-hand side of the first equation in Equation (55) represents Gauss's variational equations in Equations (1)–(6), and it holds the form as $\boldsymbol{f}(\boldsymbol{X}, \boldsymbol{u}, m, t) = \boldsymbol{M}\boldsymbol{u}$. The final conditions are expressed as

$$\begin{aligned} &\boldsymbol{X}(t_f) = [a(t_f), e(t_f), i(t_f), \Omega(t_f), \omega(t_f), f(t_f)]^{\rm T} = \text{free} \\ &m(t_f) = \text{free} \\ &\text{ToF} = t_f - t_0 \end{aligned} \tag{56}$$

First, by introducing the costate vector $\boldsymbol{\lambda} = [\boldsymbol{\lambda}_X, \lambda_m]$, which is known as the functional Lagrange multiplier, the Hamiltonian is built as [49]

$$H = \boldsymbol{\lambda}_{\boldsymbol{X}}^{\rm T} \boldsymbol{M}\boldsymbol{u} - \lambda_m \frac{T_{\max}}{I_{\rm sp} g_0} u \tag{57}$$

The costate differential equations that are termed as Euler-Lagrange equations are given as $\dot{\boldsymbol{\lambda}}_{\boldsymbol{X}} = -\partial H / \partial \boldsymbol{X}$ and $\dot{\lambda}_m = -\partial H / \partial m$. By applying the optimal control theory [50], we can obtain the final costate $\boldsymbol{\lambda}(tf) = \frac{\partial(-a(t_f))}{\partial \boldsymbol{X}(t_f)} = [-1, 0, 0, 0, 0, 0]^{\rm T}$, and the final mass costate $\lambda_m(tf) = \frac{\partial(-a(t_f))}{\partial m(tf)} = 0$.

The optimal thrust direction and magnitude, which minimize the Hamiltonian, are determined by [49]

$$\begin{aligned} u &= 1 \\ \boldsymbol{\alpha} &= -\frac{\boldsymbol{M}^{\rm T} \boldsymbol{\lambda}_{\boldsymbol{X}}}{||\boldsymbol{M}^{\rm T} \boldsymbol{\lambda}_{\boldsymbol{X}}||} \end{aligned} \tag{58}$$

Given the initial costates $\boldsymbol{\lambda}(t_0)$ and the initial state in Equation (55), we can obtain the final states and costates by integrating the differential equations of the states and costates. Meanwhile, the final states are free and the final costates should satisfy their final values. Therefore, the optimal control problem yields a two-point boundary value problem consisting of a set of equations of the form:

$$\boldsymbol{\Phi} = [\boldsymbol{\lambda}_{\mathbf{X}}(t_f), \lambda_m(t_f)]^{\mathrm{T}} - [-1,0,0,0,0,0,0]^{\mathrm{T}} = \mathbf{0} \tag{59}$$

where Equation (59) is called the shooting function. MinPack-1 [51], a package of FORTRAN subprograms for the numerical solution of the systems of nonlinear equations and nonlinear least-squares problems is used here to solve the shooting functions in the indirect method. Then, we can obtain the variation maximum over a finite flight time of the semi-major axis. Meanwhile, the solution of the indirect method in solving the variation maxima of the other elements can be also obtained in this way, but is omitted here for the sake of conciseness.

Four numerical simulation cases including three geocentric orbital transfers and one heliocentric orbital transfer are given to substantiate the proposed method. In each case, the simulation of approximating the secular variation maximum of each orbital element is carried out individually. The spacecraft parameters are selected as $P_{\max} = 2.86\,\mathrm{kW}$, $\eta = 0.6$, and $I_{\mathrm{sp}} = 3500$ s from a NEXT engine [40], and the initial mass is $m_0 = 1000\,\mathrm{kg}$. Thus, the constant acceleration magnitude is $a_{\max} = 10^{-4}\,\mathrm{m/s^2}$, corresponding to the mass-flow rate 2.91×10^{-6} kg/s. The fixed flight times are set to 50 days and 400 days for cases 1–3 and case 4, respectively. The mean equatorial radius of the Earth, R_E, is used to normalize the values of the semi-major axis in cases 1–3. The astronomical unit, AU, is used in case 4. The simulation parameters with a wide range of initial orbital elements are listed in Table 1. The eccentricity is near singularity in case 1 and the thrust-to-gravity ratio is large in case 4. The variation maxima of the argument of periapsis are very huge over a short flight time, being much lower than 50 days in both of these two cases. Therefore, the simulations for argument of periapsis in case 1 and case 4 are omitted.

Table 1. Parameters for initial orbital elements.

Case	a_0	e_0	i_0, **deg**	Ω_0, **deg**	ω_0, **deg**	f_0, **deg**
1	1.1759, R_E	0.001	10	30	10	0
2	3.9196, R_E	0.5	55	150	130	0
3	5.8011, R_E	0.3	100	270	250	0
4	1.0, AU	0.0167	5	30	50	0

As shown in Table 2, the solutions produced by the indirect method for case 3 are compared with those of GPOPS. The percentage errors are on the order of one-thousandth. It indicates that when solving the secular variations of orbital elements, the performance of the indirect method is comparable to that of GPOPS in terms of the optimality. Although GPOPS is a powerful MATLAB software for solving multiple-phase optimal control problems, good initial guesses of the state and control are also needed to guarantee the convergence and to obtain a good local optimal solution. In this paper, the solutions of the indirect method are used as references to compare with those of the proposed method.

Table 2. Comparison of the solutions solved by GPOPS and the indirect method for Case 3.

Case 3	a_f, R_E	e_f	i_f, **deg**	Ω_f, **deg**	ω_f, **deg**
Indirect method	7.6628	0.4875	104.9775	275.8517	291.4525
GPOPS	7.6775	0.4837	105.0753	275.8700	290.1070
Percentage error	1.9×10^{-3}	7.8×10^{-3}	9.3×10^{-4}	6.6×10^{-5}	4.6×10^{-3}

The computational times spent by the proposed method and the indirect method are listed in Table 3. The numbers after S1 and S2 are the computational times of the strategy 1 and 2 proposed in Section 3.3. The subscripted symbols represent the computational times. For example, t_a represents the computational time in solving the variation maximum of the semi-major axis. It shows that the propose method spends tens of microseconds to obtain a variation maximum of one orbital element and the indirect method spends several seconds in general. Due to the limited number of orbital revolutions in case 4, both of the two methods require less computational time than they do in the other cases. Compared with the numerical indirect method, the proposed method greatly saves the computational time. In general, the computational time for approximating the secular variation maximum of each orbital element could be reduced by over five orders of magnitude. The computational times for solving the variational maxima by the proposed strategy 1 are reduced by over seven orders of magnitude.

Table 3. Computational times.

	Proposed Method					**Indirect Method**				
Case	$t_a, \times 10^{-5}$ s	$t_e, \times 10^{-5}$ s	$t_i, \times 10^{-5}$ s	$t_\Omega, \times 10^{-5}$ s	$t_\omega, \times 10^{-5}$ s	t_a, s	t_e, s	t_i, s	t_Ω, s	t_ω, s
1	6.2	7.3	S1: 0.08 S2: 20	S1: 0.04 S2: 19	/	25.64	4.58	150.73	6.91	/
2	1.1	1.2	S1: 0.05 S2: 3.3	S1: 0.06 S2: 3.2	10	10.19	71.48	1.51	5.84	16.07
3	1.0	0.7	S1: 0.09 S2: 1.9	S1: 0.08 S2: 1.9	20	1.44	15.65	1.15	9.02	27.67
4	0.093	0.016	0.011	0.083	/	0.036	0.032	0.082	0.367	/

The variation maxima of orbital elements over a fixed flight time are listed in Table 4. The results obtained by the proposed method are slightly less than those by the indirect method. The indirect method provides better solutions of the variation maxima with longer computational times. Compared with the indirect method, the percentage errors of the solutions obtained by the proposed method are on the order of the one-thousandth for cases 1–3. From the approximations for the secular variations of the inclination and the right ascension of the ascending node in cases 1–3, we can find that the accuracies of the two strategies conducted in Section 3.3 are similar, but their computational times are quite different. The approximations for the secular variation maxima of the right ascension of the ascending node considering the J_2 perturbation and low thrust by the proposed method are also consistent with the accuracy solutions of the indirect method. In case 2, when the J_2 perturbation is taken into account, the variation maximum of the right ascension of the ascending node decreases, while the variation maximum of the periapsis argument grows. These simulation results are consistent with the results of the analysis of Equation (41). In case 2, the signs of the differentials of the right ascension of the ascending node and the argument of periapsis under the J_2 perturbation are negative and positive, respectively. On the contrary, in case 3, the J_2 perturbation decreases the right ascension of the ascending node and increases the argument of periapsis. Meanwhile, for case 4, which has a higher thrust-to-gravity ratio, the percentage error increases to the order of one percent.

Table 4. Variation maxima of the orbital elements over a fixed flight time.

	x_f	Proposed	Indirect Method	Percentage Error
Case 1	a_f, R_E	1.3287	1.3297	8.2×10^{-4}
	e_f	0.0923	0.0928	6.3×10^{-3}
	i_f, deg	S1: 12.1615 S2: 12.1615	12.1647	2.6×10^{-4} 2.6×10^{-4}
	Ω_f, deg	S1: 42.4473 S2: 42.4287	42.6318	4.3×10^{-3} 4.7×10^{-3}
Case 2	a_f, R_E	4.8558	4.8658	2.1×10^{-3}
	e_f	0.6369	0.6376	1.1×10^{-3}
	i_f, deg	S1: 59.9658 S2: 59.9955	60.1101	2.4×10^{-3} 1.9×10^{-3}
	Ω_f, deg	S1: 156.6328 S2: 156.8552	156.9221	1.8×10^{-3} 1.6×10^{-3}
	$\Omega_f(J_2)$, deg	152.2657	152.8683	3.9×10^{-3}
	ω_f, deg	147.5200	147.9650	3.0×10^{-3}
	$\omega_f(J_2)$, deg	147.5433	147.9809	2.9×10^{-3}
Case 3	a_f, R_E	7.6366	7.6628	3.4×10^{-3}
	e_f	0.4863	0.4875	2.4×10^{-4}
	i_f, deg	S1: 104.9113 S2: 104.9107	104.9775	6.3×10^{-4} 6.4×10^{-4}
	Ω_f, deg	S1: 275.6966 S2: 275.6077	275.8517	5.6×10^{-4} 8.8×10^{-4}
	$\Omega_f(J_2)$, deg	275.8296	276.0224	6.9×10^{-4}
	ω_f, deg	287.4059	291.4525	13×10^{-3}
	$\omega_f(J_2)$, deg	287.3791	290.9265	12×10^{-3}
Case 4	a_f, AU	1.2387	1.2684	2.6×10^{-2}
	e_f	0.1952	0.2081	6.2×10^{-2}
	i_f, deg	9.2333	9.5141	2.9×10^{-3}
	Ω_f, deg	78.5656	84.9038	7.5×10^{-2}

4.2. Estimation of the Velocity Increment

As the variation maxima of the COE of low-thrust spacecraft have been obtained effectively, one application for the proposed method is to estimate the velocity increment of the orbital transfer. Simulations of two minimum-time orbital transfer examples, whose COE are listed in Table 5, are designed to estimate the ΔV. The spacecraft is launched into a middle Earth orbit, and the initial semi-major axis is 27,906 km and the initial inclination is 40 deg. For the example 1, we aim to increase the inclination only. The initial inclination is 40 degrees. The final orbital inclinations range from 42 degrees to 56 degrees. In example 2, we test the orbital transfers from initial orbits with different eccentricities to the targets. The initial eccentricities range from 0.0106 to 0.4106. The increments of the semi-major axis and the inclination between the target orbit and the initial orbit are 3000 km and 5 degrees, respectively.

Table 5. Orbit elements of the initial orbit and the target.

	Example 1		Example 2	
Orbit Elements	**Initial Orbit**	**Target**	**Initial Orbit**	**Target**
Semi-major axis, km	27,906	27,906	27,906	30,906
Eccentricity	0.0106	0.0106	0.0106–0.4106	free
Inclination, deg	40	42–56	40	45

The indirect method is used to solve for the accurate velocity increments for the time optimal orbital transfer problem of the simulation examples. The time optimal problem of the indirect method is modeled for the orbital transfer problem.

Minimize:

$$J = \int_{t_0}^{t_0+\mathrm{ToF}} 1\mathrm{d}t \tag{60}$$

Subject to

$$\begin{aligned}
&\dot{\boldsymbol{X}}(t) = \boldsymbol{f}(\boldsymbol{X}, \boldsymbol{u}, m, t) \\
&\dot{m}(t) = -\frac{T_{\max} u}{I_{\mathrm{sp}} g_0} \\
&\boldsymbol{X}(t_0) = \boldsymbol{X}_0, m(t_0) = m_0
\end{aligned} \tag{61}$$

The final conditions are expressed as

$$\begin{aligned}
&\text{Example 1}: \begin{cases} [a(t_f), e(t_f), i(t_f)]^{\mathrm{T}} = [a_0, e_0, i_f]^{\mathrm{T}} \\ [\Omega(t_f), \omega(t_f), f(t_f), m(t_f)]^{\mathrm{T}} = \text{free} \\ \mathrm{ToF} = \text{free} \end{cases} \\
&\text{Example 2}: \begin{cases} [a(t_f), i(t_f)]^{\mathrm{T}} = [a_f, i_f]^{\mathrm{T}} \\ [e(t_f), \Omega(t_f), \omega(t_f), f(t_f), m(t_f)]^{\mathrm{T}} = \text{free} \\ \mathrm{ToF} = \text{free} \end{cases}
\end{aligned} \tag{62}$$

By solving the time optimal transfer problem, we can obtain the minimum transfer time ToF_I. Then, the velocity increments are calculated by integrating the immediate propulsive acceleration from t_0 to $t_0 + \mathrm{ToF}_I$ as $\Delta V_I = \int_{t_0}^{t_0+\mathrm{ToF}_I} ||\boldsymbol{u}||\mathrm{d}t$. The percentage error is calculated by $\frac{|\Delta V_P - \Delta V_I|}{\Delta V_I}$. $\Delta V_P = a_{\max}\mathrm{ToF}_P$ represents the velocity increment solved by the proposed method. The ToF_P is obtained by adding up the transfer time until the desired final orbital elements are reached.

For the inclination increment problem of example 1, the velocity increments estimated by the proposed method and the indirect method are shown in Figure 4. The ΔV increases with the increase in the inclination. In general, the percentage error grows with the increase in the inclination of the target.

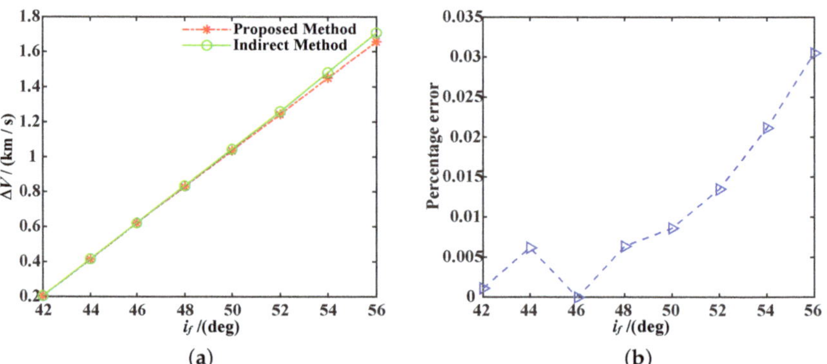

Figure 4. Comparison of ΔV, for example 1. (**a**) ΔV solved by the two methods. (**b**) Percentage error of the estimation of ΔV.

In example 2, the velocity increment estimated by the proposed method is obtained by taking the vector addition of the tangential component $\Delta V_{P,t}$ and the normal component $\Delta V_{P,h}$. First, using the proposed method in Section 3.1, we can increase the semi-major axis to its target by applying the tangent acceleration. The time of flight is calculated as

$\text{ToF}_P = \sum_1^N \text{ToF}_{P,k}$. The semi-major axis of the target is the stopping condition, then the flight time can be obtained by the linear interpolation as $a_{N-1} \leq a_f < a_N$

$$\text{ToF}_{P,t} = \sum_{k=1}^{N-1} \text{ToF}_{P,k} + \frac{a_f - a_{N-1}}{a_N - a_{N-1}} \text{ToF}_{P,N} \tag{63}$$

where the $\text{ToF}_{P,k}$ denotes the flight time of the k-th orbital revolution. The velocity increment $\Delta V_{P,t}$ can be calculated as $\Delta V_{P,t} = a_{\max} \text{ToF}_{P,t}$.

Then, using the proposed method in Section 3.3, we can obtain the flight time $\Delta V_{P,h}$, by linear interpolation, as $i_{N-1} \leq i_f < i_N$

$$\text{ToF}_{P,h} = \sum_{k=1}^{N-1} \text{ToF}_{P,k} + \frac{i_f - i_{N-1}}{i_N - i_{N-1}} \text{ToF}_{P,N} \tag{64}$$

The velocity increment $\Delta V_{P,h}$ can be calculated as $\Delta V_{P,h} = a_{\max} \text{ToF}_{P,h}$. Thus, the total velocity increment is calculated as $\Delta V_P = \sqrt{\Delta V_{P,t}^2 + \Delta V_{P,h}^2}$.

In example 2, the velocity increments estimated by the two methods are shown in Figure 5a, and the percentage error of the proposed method in estimating the ΔV is shown in Figure 5b. Though, the differences of the semi-major axis and of the inclination between the target and initial orbits are equal, respectively, it shows that the velocity increment decreases with the increase in initial eccentricity. Meanwhile, when the eccentricity is smaller, the percentage error of the velocity increment estimated by the proposed method is small.

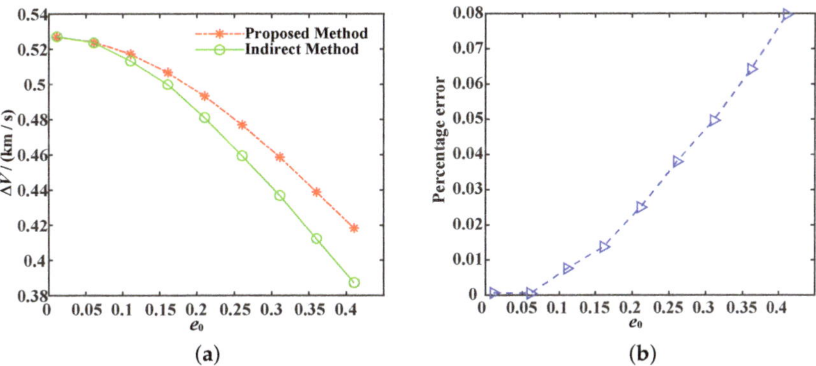

Figure 5. Comparison of ΔV for example 2. (**a**) ΔV solved by the two methods. (**b**) Percentage error of the estimation of ΔV.

Finally, the computational time of the proposed method in estimating the velocity increment of the orbital transfer is compared with the indirect method. For both of the examples, we estimate the velocity increments of eight transfers from the initial orbits to the targets. The average computational times are calculated and listed in Table 6. The proposed method takes 0.43 ms on average and 0.061 ms on average to estimate the velocity increments for a single transfer in examples 1 and 2, respectively. However, the indirect method spends tens of seconds and several seconds on average. Compared with the indirect method, the computational time of the proposed method could be reduced by over five orders of magnitude. It indicates that the proposed method has a great advantage in computational time saving in estimating the velocity increment of the orbital transfer.

Table 6. Computational times of two methods.

Average Computational Time	Example 1	Example 2
Proposed method, s	4.3×10^{-4}	6.1×10^{-5}
Indirect method, s	82	8.8

5. Discussion

The assessment of the state reachability of the low-thrust spacecraft provides a meaningful reference for the preliminary design of space missions. We conduct an efficient method for approximating the variation maxima to assess the reachability. The direct method solver, GPOPS, is used as a comparison to validate the optimality of the indirect method. It indicates that the performance of the indirect method is comparable to that of GPOPS in terms of the optimality. By solving the time-consuming numerical shooting functions, the indirect method works out the solution. Compared with the solution of the indirect method, the approximations for the secular variation maxima obtained by the proposed method are of high efficiency and accuracy. Though the indirect method gives a better solution, the proposed method reduces the computational time by over five orders of magnitude, and the percentage error is on the order of one-thousandth in general. Compared with strategy 2, strategy 1 gives a similar solution, but its computational time is reduced a lot. The accuracy and efficiency are still guaranteed, considering the J_2 perturbation and low-thrust acceleration. Meanwhile, the simulation results of cases 1–3 in Table 4 are consistent with the analysis of the analytical expressions. The estimation of the velocity increment for two kinds of orbital transfers is conducted and demonstrates the usefulness of the proposed method.

However, there are some limitations to this paper. We applied some simplified assumptions of the variational equations to obtain the analytical solution, such as the neglects of the mass consumption and the variation of the true anomaly caused by the low thrust. Though these assumptions are applied, the accuracy is still guaranteed. Meanwhile, the application of the proposed method in estimating the velocity increment of the orbital transfer is conducted in several special cases, such as the increment of the inclination and the semi-major axis. A further application in estimating the velocity increment for a general orbital transfer is of great significance.

6. Conclusions

In this paper, an approximation method is established to obtain the secular variation maxima of the classical orbital elements of low-thrust spacecraft over a finite flight time. First, the variation maxima of each orbital element over one revolution are derived analytically by applying the optimal control profile. The power series in the eccentricity are employed to expand the integrals, which have no analytical primitive functions. Then, an iterative algorithm is established to obtain the secular variation maxima of the semi-major axis, the eccentricity, and the argument of periapsis. Meanwhile, two strategies with a number of explicit expressions are conducted to approximate the secular variation maxima of the inclination and the right ascension of the ascending node. Particularly, the variation maxima of the right ascension of the ascending node and the argument of the periapsis take into account the effects of the low-thrust acceleration and of the J_2 perturbation of the Earth.

Two kinds of simulations are given to compare the solutions of the proposed method with the indirect method. The simulations of the variation maximum of each orbital element are conducted and demonstrate the efficiency and accuracy of the proposed method. In general, the percentage errors in approximating the variational maxima are on the order of one thousandth. Meanwhile, a preliminary application of the approximation of the secular variation maxima is given to estimate the velocity increments of low-thrust orbital transfers. The simulation demonstrates that the proposed method has a high estimating accuracy compared with the indirect method. The percentage error is on the order of one percent. In particular, both kinds of simulations indicate that the computational times of the proposed method are reduced by over five orders of magnitude, as compared with the indirect method.

7. Future Work

In this paper, we have demonstrated an efficient method with analytical derivations to approximate the secular maxima of the classical orbital elements and the preliminary application of the proposed method. It is foreseeable that the fast and accurate estimate of the variation maxima of the orbital elements can provide a priori information for the low-thrust trajectory design and optimization. Thus, the proposed method can bring benefits to the sequence search of multi-target low-thrust missions. Meanwhile, given the limitations of this paper, it will be important that future research investigates the variation maxima of the orbital elements, considering the mass consumption. Additionally, a significant topic for future research might be the estimation of the velocity increment for a general orbital transfer, taking into account the combination of various orbital elements.

Author Contributions: Z.W. and L.C. completed the preliminary research and provided the numerical part; Z.W. and F.J. conceived and wrote the paper; F.J. supervised the overall work and reviewed the paper. All authors have read and agreed to the published version of the manuscript.

Funding: This work was supported by the National Natural Science Foundation of China (No. 12022214).

Institutional Review Board Statement: Not applicable.

Informed Consent Statement: Not applicable.

Data Availability Statement: The data presented in this study are available on request from the corresponding author.

Conflicts of Interest: The authors declare no conflict of interest.

Nomenclature

Symbols	
a	Semi-major axis
e	Eccentricity
i	Inclination
Ω	Right ascension of ascending node
ω	Argument of periapsis
f	True anomaly
h	Magnitude of specific angular momentum
μ	Gravitational constant
$\boldsymbol{a}$	Propulsive acceleration vector
$\Delta \boldsymbol{x}$	Variation group of the classical orbital elements over one orbital revolution
$\boldsymbol{x}_N$	Values of the orbital elements after N orbital revolutions
$T_{\max}$	Thrust magnitude
R_E	Mean equatorial radius of the Earth
J_2	Second order zonal harmonic of the Earth's gravitational potential
ΔV	Velocity increment
$\boldsymbol{X}$	Group of the orbital elements
$\boldsymbol{u}$	Thrust vector
u	Engine thrust ratio
$\boldsymbol{\alpha}$	Unit vector of thrust direction
ToF	Time of flight
$\boldsymbol{\lambda}$	Lagrange multiplier associated with state, i.e., costate
H	Hamiltonian
AU	Astronomical unit
$\boldsymbol{\Phi}$	Combination of shooting functions
m	Instantaneous mass of spacecraft
β	Out-of-plane (yaw) steering angle
α	In-plane thrust-steering angle

Subscripts	
LT	Low thrust
J_2	J_2 perturbation
P	Proposed method
I	Indirect method
N	N-th orbital revolution
0	Initial time
f	Final time

References

1. Rayman, M.D.; Williams, S.N. Design of the first interplanetary solar electric propulsion mission. *J. Spacecr. Rocket.* **2002**, *39*, 589–595. [CrossRef]
2. Benkhoff, J.; Van Casteren, J.; Hayakawa, H.; Fujimoto, M.; Laakso, H.; Novara, M.; Ferri, P.; Middleton, H.R.; Ziethe, R. BepiColombo—Comprehensive exploration of Mercury: Mission overview and science goals. *Planet. Space Sci.* **2010**, *58*, 2–20. [CrossRef]
3. Alemany, K.; Braun, R. Survey of Global Optimization Methods for Low-Thrust, Multiple Asteroid Tour Missions. In Proceedings of the AAS/AIAA Space Flight Mechanics Meeting, Sedona, AZ, USA, 28 January–1 February 2007.
4. Morante, D.; Sanjurjo Rivo, M.; Soler, M. A Survey on Low-Thrust Trajectory Optimization Approaches. *Aerospace* **2021**, *8*, 88. [CrossRef]
5. Chen, Y.; Baoyin, H.; Li, J. Accessibility of main-belt asteroids via gravity assists. *J. Guid. Control Dyn.* **2014**, *37*, 623–632. [CrossRef]
6. Liu, E.; Yan, Y.; Yang, Y. Analysis and determination of capture area for space debris removal based on reachable domain. *Adv. Space Res.* **2021**, *68*, 1613–1626. [CrossRef]
7. Dahl, J.; de Campos, G.R.; Olsson, C.; Fredriksson, J. Collision avoidance: A literature review on threat-assessment techniques. *IEEE Trans. Intell. Veh.* **2018**, *4*, 101–113. [CrossRef]
8. Holzinger, M.; Scheeres, D. Applied reachability for space situational awareness and safety in spacecraft proximity operations. In Proceedings of the AIAA Guidance, Navigation, and Control Conference, Chicago, IL, USA, 10–13 August 2009; p. 6096.
9. Xu, Z.; Chen, X.; Huang, Y.; Bai, Y.; Chen, Q. Collision prediction and avoidance for satellite ultra-close relative motion with zonotope-based reachable sets. *Proc. Inst. Mech. Eng. Part G J. Aerosp. Eng.* **2019**, *233*, 3920–3937. [CrossRef]
10. Lee, S.; Hwang, I. Reachable set computation for spacecraft relative motion with energy-limited low-thrust. *Aerosp. Sci. Technol.* **2018**, *77*, 180–188. [CrossRef]
11. Battin, R.H. *An Introduction to the Mathematics and Methods of Astrodynamics*, Revised Edition; American Institute of Aeronautics and Astronautics: Reston, VA, USA, 1999.
12. Xue, D.; Li, J.; Baoyin, H.; Jiang, F. Reachable Domain for Spacecraft with a Single Impulse. *J. Guid. Control Dyn.* **2010**, *33*, 934–942. [CrossRef]
13. Li, X.H.; He, X.S.; Zhong, Q.F. Investigation on Reachable Domain of Satellite with a Single Impulse. *Adv. Mater. Res.* **2012**, *433–440*, 5759–5766. [CrossRef]
14. Wen, C.; Peng, C.; Gao, Y. Reachable domain for spacecraft with ellipsoidal Delta-V distribution. *Astrodynamics* **2018**, *2*, 265–288. [CrossRef]
15. Vinh, N.X.; Gilbert, E.G.; Howe, R.M.; Sheu, D.; Lu, P. Reachable domain for interception at hyperbolic speeds. *Acta Astronaut.* **1995**, *35*, 1–8. [CrossRef]
16. Zhang, G.; Cao, X.; Ma, G. Reachable domain of spacecraft with a single tangent impulse considering trajectory safety. *Acta Astronaut.* **2013**, *91*, 228–236. [CrossRef]
17. Zhang, J.; Yuan, J.; Wang, W.; Wang, J. Reachable domain of spacecraft with a single normal impulse. *Aircr. Eng. Aerosp. Technol.* **2019**, *91*, 977–986. [CrossRef]
18. Li, X.; He, X.; Zhong, Q.; Song, M. Reachable domain for satellite with two kinds of thrust. *Acta Astronaut.* **2011**, *68*, 1860–1864. [CrossRef]
19. Betts, J.T. Survey of Numerical Methods for Trajectory Optimization. *J. Guid. Control Dyn.* **1998**, *21*, 193–207. [CrossRef]
20. Russell, R.P. Primer vector theory applied to global low-thrust trade studies. *J. Guid. Control Dyn.* **2007**, *30*, 460–472. [CrossRef]
21. Li, X.; Qiao, D.; Chen, H. Interplanetary transfer optimization using cost function with variable coefficients. *Astrodynamics* **2019**, *3*, 173–188. [CrossRef]
22. Liu, X.; Lu, P.; Pan, B. Survey of convex optimization for aerospace applications. *Astrodynamics* **2017**, *1*, 23–40. [CrossRef]
23. Vasile, M.; Minisci, E.; Locatelli, M. Analysis of some global optimization algorithms for space trajectory design. *J. Spacecr. Rocket.* **2010**, *47*, 334–344. [CrossRef]
24. Topputo, F.; Zhang, C. Survey of Direct Transcription for Low-Thrust Space Trajectory Optimization with Applications. *Abstr. Appl. Anal.* **2014**, *2014*, 1–15. [CrossRef]
25. Tang, G.; Jiang, F.; Li, J. Low-thrust trajectory optimization of asteroid sample return mission with multiple revolutions and moon gravity assists. *Sci. China Phys. Mech. Astron.* **2015**, *58*, 114501. [CrossRef]

26. Hudson, J.S.; Scheeres, D.J. Orbital targeting using reduced eccentric anomaly low-thrust coefficients. *J. Guid. Control Dyn.* **2011**, *34*, 820–831. [CrossRef]
27. Ko, H.C.; Scheeres, D.J. Essential thrust-Fourier-coefficient set of averaged Gauss equations for orbital mechanics. *J. Guid. Control Dyn.* **2014**, *37*, 1236–1249. [CrossRef]
28. Caruso, A.; Bassetto, M.; Mengali, G.; Quarta, A.A. Optimal solar sail trajectory approximation with finite Fourier series. *Adv. Space Res.* **2021**, *67*, 2834–2843. [CrossRef]
29. Taheri, E.; Abdelkhalik, O. Initial three-dimensional low-thrust trajectory design. *Adv. Space Res.* **2016**, *57*, 889–903. [CrossRef]
30. Huo, M.; Zhang, G.; Qi, N.; Liu, Y.; Shi, X. Initial trajectory design of electric solar wind sail based on finite Fourier series shape-based method. *IEEE Trans. Aerosp. Electron. Syst.* **2019**, *55*, 3674–3683. [CrossRef]
31. Zhang, T.; Wu, D.; Jiang, F.; Zhou, H. A New 3D Shaping Method for Low-Thrust Trajectories between Non-Intersect Orbits. *Aerospace* **2021**, *8*, 315. [CrossRef]
32. Nie, T.; Gurfil, P. Long-term evolution of orbital inclination due to third-body inclination. *Celest. Mech. Dyn. Astron.* **2021**, *133*, 1–33. [CrossRef]
33. Colombo, C.; Vasile, M.; Radice, G. Semi-Analytical Solution for the Optimal Low-Thrust Deflection of Near-Earth Objects. *J. Guid. Control Dyn.* **2009**, *32*, 796–809. [CrossRef]
34. Gao, Y.; Kluever, C. Analytic orbital averaging technique for computing tangential-thrust trajectories. *J. Guid. Control Dyn.* **2005**, *28*, 1320–1323. [CrossRef]
35. Gonzalo, J.L.; Bombardelli, C. Multiple scales asymptotic solution for the constant radial thrust problem. *Celest. Mech. Dyn. Astron.* **2019**, *131*, 37. [CrossRef]
36. Carlo, M.D.; da Graça Marto, S.; Vasile, M. Extended analytical formulae for the perturbed Keplerian motion under low-thrust acceleration and orbital perturbations. *Celest. Mech. Dyn. Astron.* **2021**, *133*, 13. [CrossRef]
37. Izzo, D.; Märtens, M.; Pan, B. A survey on artificial intelligence trends in spacecraft guidance dynamics and control. *Astrodynamics* **2019**, *3*, 287–299. [CrossRef]
38. Tsukamoto, H.; Chung, S.J.; Slotine, J.J. Learning-based Adaptive Control via Contraction Theory. *arXiv* **2021**, arXiv:2103.02987.
39. Gaudet, B.; Linares, R.; Furfaro, R. Deep reinforcement learning for six degree-of-freedom planetary landing. *Adv. Space Res.* **2020**, *65*, 1723–1741. [CrossRef]
40. Gao, Y.; Kluever, C. Engine-switching strategies for interplanetary solar-electric-propulsion spacecraft. *J. Spacecr. Rocket.* **2005**, *42*, 765–767. [CrossRef]
41. Henninger, H.C.; Biggs, J.D. Near time-minimal Earth to L1 transfers for low-thrust spacecraft. *J. Guid. Control Dyn.* **2017**, *40*, 2999–3004. [CrossRef]
42. Abramowitz, M.; Stegun, I.A. *Handbook of Mathematical Functions with Formulas, Graphs, and Mathematical Tables*; US Government Printing Office: Washington, DC, USA, 1964; Volume 55.
43. Kluever, C.A. Simple guidance scheme for low-thrust orbit transfers. *J. Guid. Control Dyn.* **1998**, *21*, 1015–1017. [CrossRef]
44. Petropoulos, A.E. *Simple Control Laws for Low-Thrust Orbit Transfers*; Jet Propulsion Laboratory, National Aeronautics and Space Administration: Pasadena, CA, USA, 2003.
45. Bassetto, M.; Quarta, A.A.; Mengali, G. Locally-optimal electric sail transfer. *Proc. Inst. Mech. Eng. Part G J. Aerosp. Eng.* **2019**, *233*, 166–179. [CrossRef]
46. Vallado, D.A. *Fundamentals of Astrodynamics and Applications*; Springer Science & Business Media: Berlin/Heidelberg, Germany, 2001; Volume 12.
47. Sidi, M.J. *Spacecraft Dynamics and Control: A Practical Engineering Approach*; Cambridge University Press: Cambridge, UK, 1997; Volume 7.
48. Rao, A.V.; Benson, D.A.; Darby, C.; Patterson, M.A.; Francolin, C.; Sanders, I.; Huntington, G.T. Algorithm 902: Gpops, a matlab software for solving multiple-phase optimal control problems using the gauss pseudospectral method. *ACM Trans. Math. Softw. (TOMS)* **2010**, *37*, 1–39. [CrossRef]
49. Jiang, F.; Baoyin, H.; Li, J. Practical Techniques for Low-Thrust Trajectory Optimization with Homotopic Approach. *J. Guid. Control Dyn.* **2012**, *35*, 245–258. [CrossRef]
50. Hull, D.G. *Optimal Control Theory for Applications*; Springer Science & Business Media: Berlin/Heidelberg, Germany, 2013.
51. Moré, J.J.; Garbow, B.S.; Hillstrom, K.E. *User Guide for MINPACK-1*; Argonne National Laboratory: Argonne, IL, USA, 1980; ANL-80-74.

 mathematics

Article

Deep Neural Network-Based Footprint Prediction and Attack Intention Inference of Hypersonic Glide Vehicles

Jingjing Xu, Changhong Dong and Lin Cheng *

School of Astronautics, Beihang University, Beijing 100191, China
* Correspondence: chenglin5580@buaa.edu.cn

Abstract: In response to the increasing threat of hypersonic weapons, it is of great importance for the defensive side to achieve fast prediction of their feasible attack domain and online inference of their most probable targets. In this study, an online footprint prediction and attack intention inference algorithm for hypersonic glide vehicles (HGVs) is proposed by leveraging the utilization of deep neural networks (DNNs). Specifically, this study focuses on the following three contributions. First, a baseline multi-constrained entry guidance algorithm is developed based on a compound bank angle corridor, and then a dataset containing enough trajectories for the following DNN learning is generated offline by traversing different initial states and control commands. Second, DNNs are developed to learn the functional relationship between the flight state/command and the corresponding ranges; on this basis, an online footprint prediction algorithm is developed by traversing the maximum/minimum ranges and different heading angles. Due to the substitution of DNNs for multiple times of trajectory integration, the computational efficiency for footprint prediction is significantly improved to the millisecond level. Third, combined with the predicted footprint and the hidden information in historical flight data, the attack intention and most probable targets can be further inferred. Simulations are conducted through comparing with the state-of-the-art algorithms, and results demonstrate that the proposed algorithm can achieve accurate prediction for flight footprint and attack intention while possessing significant real-time advantage.

Keywords: reentry guidance; footprint prediction; attack intention inference; deep neural network

MSC: 85; 97R40

Citation: Xu, J.; Dong, C.; Cheng, L. Deep Neural Network-Based Footprint Prediction and Attack Intention Inference of Hypersonic Glide Vehicles. *Mathematics* **2023**, *11*, 185. https://doi.org/10.3390/math11010185

Academic Editor: Daniel-Ioan Curiac

Received: 18 November 2022
Revised: 23 December 2022
Accepted: 23 December 2022
Published: 29 December 2022

1. Introduction

Hypersonic glide vehicles have attracted much attention in recent decades due to their dominant advantages on fast speed, wide attack range, and strong maneuverability. The whole flight time from the beginning entry to the final attack can be shortened to within one hour, which results in a daunting challenge for the interception system of the defensive side. Acquiring the feasible footprint and possible intention of an attacking HGV as early as possible and getting more time for the interception system is crucial for a successful defense. However, most of the existing methods/algorithms suffer the drawbacks of insufficient prediction accuracy and poor real-time performance. In this study, we focus on an online footprint prediction and attack intent inference algorithm for HGVs by leveraging the utilization of deep neural networks, and we achieve performance improvement for both prediction accuracy and computational speed.

The footprint is the set of terminals of all possible trajectories. Traditionally, the footprint is generated by traversing the maximum/minimum ranges and different heading angles using a baseline trajectory planner. The method difference for footprint generation is mainly reflected in the method difference for the planner design. The methods for footprint generation can be roughly divided into three categories. (1) Trajectory optimization methods, such as the Legendre pseudospectral method [1,2], the Gauss pseudospectral method [3], the hp-adaptive Radau pseudospectral method, and convex optimization [4–6] are utilized to generate the landing footprint. (2) The quasi-equilibrium glide condition (QEGC) [7] simplifies footprint generation. In [8], footprint generation is simplified to find the solutions to closest approaches to a moving virtual target. On the basis of [8], a selection scheme of a virtual target is proposed to increase the applicability of this method [9]. In [10], based on the simplified dynamics model, the convex optimization is utilized to generate the maximum crossrange trajectory. Footprint generation under the failure of the control components was solved by QEGC in [11]. (3) Based on the Evolved Acceleration Guidance Logic for Entry (EAGLE), drag acceleration-energy profiles can be designed for footprint generation [12]. On the basis of EAGLE, footprint generation algorithms follow drag acceleration–energy profiles tracking scheme satisfying the no-fly zone constraint in [13]. However, the existing footprint generation methods inevitably require numerical integration, and the time-consuming integration calculation and algorithm iteration cannot meet the real-time requirements for online footprint generation.

At the same time, few published studies pay attention to the discussion about attack intention for an attacking HGV, which specifically refers to information mining from past flight data and assists the defensive side to deploy interceptor systems for the most possible attack targets. Representative work is reviewed here. On the basis of the traditional state extrapolation prediction ideas in [14,15], a Bayesian trajectory prediction method based on intention inference is proposed. Aiming at the uncertainty of HGVs maneuvering, it is one of the effective ways to improve the accuracy of long-term trajectory prediction to reasonably infer the flight intention based on the characteristics of target motion. The trajectory prediction accuracy of this method is high in the short term, but the long-term prediction accuracy is low. The intention analysis only provides a reference for the long-term trajectory prediction, and cannot analyze the final attack target. In [16], a dynamic Bayesian network is used to infer the relationship between HGVs and attack targets to achieve attack intention prediction. However, this method can only determine the final attack target in the middle and later stages of the flight and cannot provide guidance for early warning and defense. DNN-based maneuver pattern recognition, such as penetration, attack, transportation, civil aviation flight, reconnaissance, etc., is designed in [17]. In summary, there are few studies to discuss the online attack intention for a flying HGV, and the main reasons are summarized as follows. (1) The real-time requirement for online footprint generation cannot be met. (2) The control strategy is unknown. Due to the aerodynamic force, HGVs perform non-inertial maneuver driven by the control command, and it is very difficult to exactly identify their control strategies. (3) HGVs are highly maneuverable. HGVs can theoretically attack every target within a large footprint through maneuvering changes. Due to the restrictions of the no-fly zone and the need for maneuver penetration, it is unavoidable that the control variable may change sharply. Compared with ballistic missiles, the intention analysis for HGVs is more difficult due to HGVs' strong maneuverability.

In recent years, DNNs have been widely used in the aerospace field [18]. Multi-layer feedforward neural networks are utilized to approximate the mapping relationship between the real-time flight states of high lifting vehicles and guidance commands in [19]. In [20,21], a neural network predictor assists in calculating guidance parameters. In our previous study [22], DNN is developed to replace the trajectory integrator to help achieve real-time numerical predictor–corrector guidance (NPCG). In this study, we focus on the online prediction of feasible footprint and attack intention for HGVs, and DNN and data mining technologies help achieve the combined advantages on real-time performance and prediction accuracy. Specifically, the following three contributions are emphasized. (1) A baseline multi-constrained entry guidance algorithm is developed based on a compound bank angle corridor, and then a dataset containing enough trajectories for the following DNN learning is generated offline by traversing different initial states and control commands. (2) DNNs are developed to learn the functional relationship between the flight state/command and the corresponding ranges; on this basis, an online footprint prediction algorithm is developed by traversing the maximum/minimum ranges and different heading angles. Due to the substitution of DNN for trajectory integration, the computational efficiency for footprint prediction is significantly improved to the millisecond level. (3) Combined with the predicted footprint and the hidden information in historical flight data, the attack intention and most probable targets can be further inferred. A forgetting mechanism helps the proposed attack intention inference algorithm to still be effective when the HGVs change their attack target during the flight. Simulations are given to estimate the effectiveness of the proposed techniques.

This study is organized as follows: The problem formulation of reentry is described in Section 2. In Section 3, a DNN is developed to approximate the ranges, following which an intelligent DNN-based footprint algorithm is proposed. In Section 4, an intent inference algorithm is proposed. Simulations are given in Section 5 to evaluate the performance of the proposed algorithm. Section 6 summarizes this study.

2. Problem Formulation

The purpose of this study is to achieve online footprint generation and attack intention inference of an enemy HGV. In this section, reentry dynamics, constraints, and control parameterization are provided and analyzed.

2.1. Reentry Dynamics

In order to achieve the footprint prediction of a flying HGV, it is necessary to describe its reentry dynamical motion. Without considering the influence of the Earth's rotation, the three-degree-of-freedom motion model is given as [23]:

$$\begin{aligned}
&\dot{r} = v\sin\theta \\
&\dot{\lambda} = v\cos\theta\sin\psi/(r\cos\phi) \\
&\dot{\phi} = v\cos\theta\cos\psi/r \\
&\dot{v} = -D/m_0 - g\sin\theta \\
&\dot{\theta} = (1/v)\left[L\cos\sigma/m_0 + \left(v^2/r - g\right)\cos\theta\right] \\
&\dot{\psi} = (1/v)\left[L\sin\sigma/(m_0\cos\theta) + v^2/r\cos\theta\sin\psi\tan\phi\right] \\
&\dot{S}_e = v\cos\theta/r
\end{aligned} \tag{1}$$

where r represents the geocentric distance of the vehicle, λ and ϕ represent the longitude and latitude, v is the speed of the vehicle relative to the Earth, θ represents the trajectory inclination angle, ψ represents the heading angle. S_e is the cumulative range angle of the vehicle; m_0 is the mass of the vehicle, which remains constant during reentry, σ denotes the bank angle, and g is the acceleration of gravity, which is calculated by a simple inverse square model [22]:

$$g = \frac{R_0^2}{(R_0 + h)^2} g_0, \tag{2}$$

where $g_0 = 9.8\ \mathrm{m/s^2}$ is the gravitational acceleration at sea level, and $R_0 = 6378$ km is the average radius of the Earth.

The atmospheric density ρ is expressed as [24,25]:

$$\rho = \rho_0 e^{-h/\beta}, \tag{3}$$

where $\rho_0 = 1.225\ \mathrm{kg/m^3}$ represents the atmospheric density at sea level, and $\beta = 7200$ m.

The variables L and D represent the lift and drag of the vehicle, and the expressions are [23]:

$$L = 0.5\rho v^2 C_L S_{ref}, \tag{4}$$

$$D = 0.5\rho v^2 C_D S_{ref}, \tag{5}$$

where S_{ref} represents the aerodynamic reference area of the vehicle, and C_L and C_D represent the lift and drag coefficients of the vehicle, which are related to the speed of the vehicle and the angle of attack α. During reentry, α takes the form of a three-section profile related to flight speed v [22]:

$$\alpha = \begin{cases} \alpha_{\max} & v > v_1 \\ (\alpha_{\max} - \alpha_{\min})(v - v_2)/(v_1 - v_2) & v_2 < v < v_1 \\ \alpha_{\min} & v < v_2 \end{cases} \tag{6}$$

where $\alpha_{\max} = 20°$ is the maximum allowable angle of attack, $\alpha_{\min} = 8.5°$ is the angle of attack at the maximum lift-to-drag ratio, and $v_1 = 4700$ m/s, $v_2 = 3100$ m/s are velocity nodes.

As a result, the bank angle σ is the only control variable for reentry; $\mathbf{x}_{state} = [h, \theta, \phi, v, \gamma, \psi]^T$ represents the current state of the vehicle.

2.2. Reentry Constraints

In order to ensure the safety and meet the mission requirements of the vehicles, the HGVs need to meet the path constraints and terminal constraints during reentry. Path constraints include heating rate constraint, overload constraint, dynamic pressure constraint, and equilibrium glide condition. These expressions are as follows [23]:

$$\dot{Q}(t) = \frac{C_1}{\sqrt{R_d}} \left(\frac{\rho}{\rho_0}\right)^{0.5} \left(\frac{v}{V_C}\right)^{3.15} \leq \dot{Q}_{\max}, \tag{7}$$

$$n(t) = \sqrt{\left[\frac{L}{m_0 g_0}\right]^2 + \left[\frac{D}{m_0 g_0}\right]^2} = q(t)\sqrt{C_L^2 + C_D^2}\frac{S_{ref}}{m_0 g_0} \leq n_{\max}, \tag{8}$$

$$q(t) = \frac{1}{2}\rho v^2 \leq q_{\max}, \tag{9}$$

$$L \cos \sigma_{QEGC}/m_0 + \left(v^2/r - g\right) = 0, \tag{10}$$

where $\dot{Q}(t)$ represents the heating rate at the stagnation point, $\dot{Q}_{\max}$ is the upper limit of the allowable heating rate, C_1 and R_d are the overall design parameters of the vehicle, V_c represents the first cosmic velocity, $n(t)$ represents the actual total overload, n_{max} is the upper limit of allowable overload, $q(t)$ represents the actual dynamic pressure, q_{max} is the upper limit of allowable dynamic pressure, and σ_{QEGC} is the equilibrium glide angle.

To ensure a successful transition to the terminal area energy management (TAEM), the final reentry segment must meet specific position and velocity requirements. Terminal constraints include [23]:

$$h\left(t_f\right) = h_f,\ v\left(t_f\right) = v_f,\ \lambda\left(t_f\right) = \lambda_f,\ \phi\left(t_f\right) = \phi_f, \tag{11}$$

where h_f, v_f, λ_f, ϕ_f are the altitude, speed, longitude, and latitude of the end of the reentry flight.

Terminal latitude and longitude constraints are usually transformed into the range constraint $S_e(t_f) = S_{go}$; S_{go} is defined as the spherical distance from the vehicle to the target [22]:

$$S_{go} = \arccos\left[\sin \lambda \sin \lambda_f + \cos \lambda \cos \lambda_f \cos\left(\phi - \phi_f\right)\right]. \tag{12}$$

2.3. Control Parameterization

In this subsection, the noted reentry constraints in Section 2.2 are transformed into the upper and lower boundaries for the bank angle. Then, by weighting the upper and lower boundaries, the bank angle profile can be determined, which corresponds to trajectories of different ranges. By traversing different initial reentry conditions and different weighting coefficients, a dataset composed of trajectories can be generated offline and used to train DNNs for range prediction.

2.3.1. Bank Angle Corridor

HGVs need to satisfy path constraints, terminal constraints, and control constraints. Constraining trajectories within reasonably constructed corridors is a way to deal with multiple constraints. Common corridors include height–velocity corridors, bank angle corridors, drag acceleration corridors, etc. In this study, a compound bank angle corridor is employed [22]. We substitute the atmospheric density Equation (3) and aerodynamic Equations (4) and (5) into the heating rate, overload, and dynamic pressure constraint Equations (7)–(9). Denoting $H_{\dot{Q}_{\max}}$, $H_{n_{\max}}$, $H_{q_{\max}}$ as the height boundary of the maximum heating rate, overload, and dynamic pressure according to the speed v, as shown in Figure 1, the height constraint according to v can be obtained as

$$H > \frac{2}{\beta}\ln\left[\frac{C_1}{\dot{Q}_{\max}\sqrt{R_d}}\left(\frac{V}{V_C}\right)^{3.15}\right] = H_{\dot{Q}_{\max}}(V), \tag{13}$$

$$H > \frac{1}{\beta}\ln\left[\frac{\rho_0 V^2 S\sqrt{C_D^2 + C_L^2}}{2n_{\max} m_0 g_0}\right] = H_{n_{\max}}(V), \tag{14}$$

$$H > \frac{1}{\beta}\ln\left(\frac{\rho_0 V^2}{2q_{\max}}\right) = H_{q_{\max}}(V), \tag{15}$$

$$H(V) > H_{\text{down}}(V) = \max\left(H_{\dot{Q}_{\max}}, H_{n_{\max}}, H_{q_{\max}}\right). \tag{16}$$

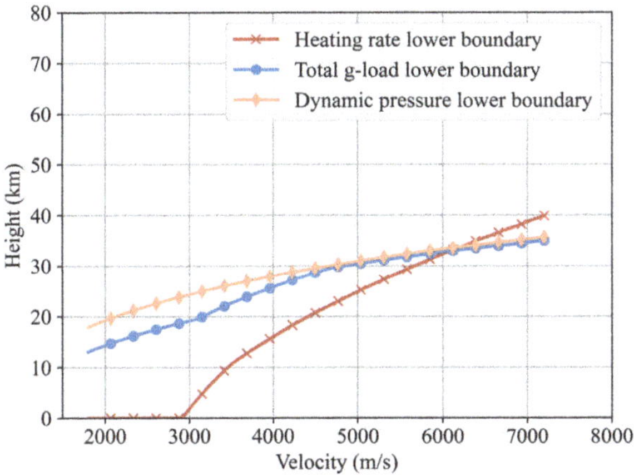

Figure 1. Lower boundary of the height–velocity corridor.

According to the QEGC, with known height and speed, the equilibrium glide angle σ_{QEGC} can be determined as

$$\sigma_{QEGC} = \cos^{-1}\frac{m_0(g - V^2/r)}{L}. \tag{17}$$

The $H_{down}(V)$ is a function of speed, and the $\sigma_{QEGC_{up}}$ corresponding to $H_{down}(V)$ can be obtained by Equation (17). The definition of QEGC determines

$$\sigma_{QEGC_{down}}(V) = 0. \tag{18}$$

Therefore, the bank angle needs to be less than $\sigma_{QEGC_{up}}(V)$ and greater than $\sigma_{QEGC_{down}}(V)$:

$$\sigma_{QEGC_{down}}(V) \leq \sigma(V) \leq \sigma_{QEGC_{up}}(V). \tag{19}$$

So far, we have obtained the upper and lower bounds of the bank angle corridor for the incoming HGVs to satisfy the path constraints. In the initial glide segment, due to the high flight altitude, the flight aerodynamic force is insufficient. In order to prevent the vehicle from falling too fast to generate a large amount of aerodynamic heat, the bank angle keeps a small constant value in the initial glide segment. In this paper, σ_{Imax} represents the maximum allowable bank angle amplitude during the initial glide segment. It is determined so that the heating rate in the initial glide segment is exactly equal to $\dot{Q}_{\max}$, that is, $\max(\dot{Q}(\sigma_{I\max})) = \dot{Q}_{\max}$. The velocity at the end of the initial glide segment is expressed as the velocity corresponding to the maximum heating rate, denoted as v_{If}.

In order to ensure the smooth handover of the reentry flight and the TAEM, the terminal of the reentry flight must satisfy both the range constraints and the terminal constraints. Combined with the QEGC, the terminal equilibrium glide angle σ_{TAEM} can be obtained by bringing the terminal states h_f, v_f into Equation (10).

Based on the above analysis, a bank angle corridor must comprehensively consider path constraints and terminal constraints. In the initial glide segment, the constant bank angle needs to be less than $\sigma_{I\max}$, and in the equilibrium glide segment, the bank angle profile is restricted between $\sigma_{E\max}$ and $\sigma_{E\min}$. In addition, in order to ensure the terminal altitude h_f and speed v_f constraints, the bank angle at the end of reentry is set as σ_{TAEM}. Considering the analysis results of the three sections, the bank angle corridor of the entire reentry flight can finally be obtained, where the upper bound is composed of $\sigma_{I\max}$, $\sigma_{E\max}$, and σ_{TAEM}, and the lower bound is composed of $\sigma_{E\min}$ and σ_{TAEM}. The final compound bank angle corridor is shown in Figure 2, with the upper bound denoted as $\sigma_{\max}(v)$ and the lower bound denoted as $\sigma_{\min}(v)$. In the process of trajectory planning, as long as the bank angle is limited within the corridor, the path constraints and the terminal height and speed constraints are satisfied to a certain extent.

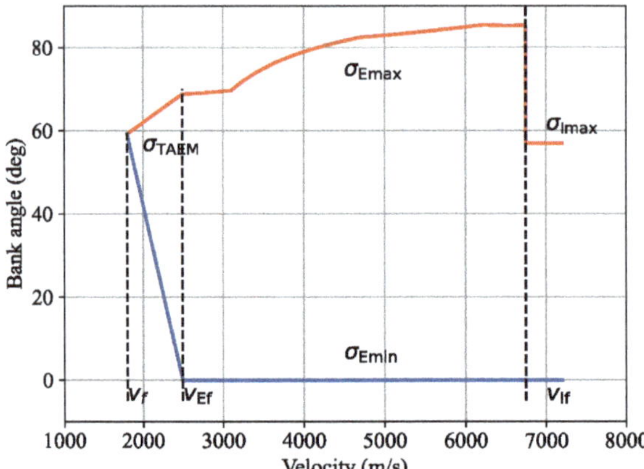

Figure 2. Compound bank angle corridor.

2.3.2. Control Parameterization

According to Equation (1), it is easy to obtain the derivative relationship between range and speed as

$$\left|\frac{dS_e}{dv}\right| = \left|\frac{v\cos\theta/r}{-D/m_0 - g\sin\theta}\right|. \tag{20}$$

It can be known from QEGC that $r \approx R_0$, $\theta \approx 0$. Bringing Equation (5) into Equation (20), the derivative relationship between range and speed becomes

$$\left|\frac{dS_e}{dv}\right| = \left|\frac{m_0}{-1/2\rho v C_D S_{ref} R_0}\right|. \tag{21}$$

Here, $|dS_e/dv|$ decreases exponentially with an increase in height h. Combined with QEGC, h is inversely proportional to σ_{TAEM}. Finally, it can be concluded that the smaller the bank angle, the smaller the $|dS_e/dv|$, and the stronger the gliding capability of the vehicle. Therefore, the bank angle profile $\sigma_{design}(v)$ is weighted by the upper and lower bounds of the compound corridor, and its expression is

$$\sigma_{design}(v) = \omega \cdot \sigma_{\min}(v) + (1 - \omega) \cdot \sigma_{\max}(v), \tag{22}$$

where ω is the weighting coefficient, which can adjust the height of the entire bank angle profile to obtain different downrange, and the downrange increases monotonically with ω.

Traditionally, given the initial states $\mathbf{x}_{state0}$ and weighting coefficient ω, a complete trajectory is obtained by integrating dynamic differential equations:

$$\mathbf{x}_{state} = \mathbf{x}_{state0} + \int_{t_0}^{t_f} \dot{\mathbf{x}}_{state} \mathrm{d}t. \tag{23}$$

where $\dot{\mathbf{x}}_{state}$ is calculated by Equation (1). Generally, the fourth-order Runge–Kutta is selected as the trajectory integrator.

Different weighting coefficients ω can integrate different feasible trajectories. As shown in Figure 3, when ω traverses $[0, 1]$, all possible trajectories at the current state of the HGV can be generated, and the corresponding terminal points compose the footprint. The generation of a trajectory is inseparable from the long-term integration, and the long flight time of the HGVs and the large number of trajectories required to form the footprint lead to the exponential increase for computational burden, which makes it difficult to meet the real-time requirements of online footprint generation. Therefore, in the next section, we try to use DNNs to replace the traditional integrator to solve the problem in which the traditional footprint generation methods cannot meet the real-time performance.

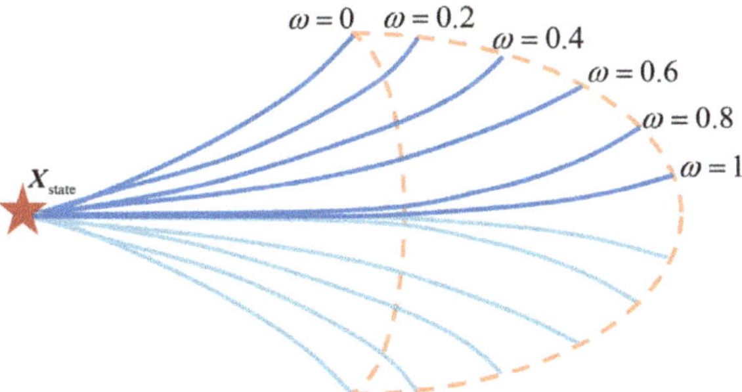

Figure 3. The footprint formed by trajectories with different weighting coefficients.

As such, the reentry problem is formulated, and a baseline predictor–corrector reentry guidance is developed based on a compound bank angle corridor, which can be used to generate feasible reentry trajectories. In the remainder of this study, we will focus on the following two study purposes: online footprint prediction and online attack intention inference. The details are given in the following two sections.

3. DNN-Based Footprint Prediction

This section focuses on the first purpose of this study, that is, online footprint prediction. Specifically, first, a DNN is trained to approximate the nonlinear functional relationship between flight states and ranges. Second, the trained DNN is leveraged to achieve the real-time performance and accuracy for range prediction. Third, on the basis of the trained DNN, an online footprint prediction algorithm is developed.

3.1. DNN Development for Range Prediction

This subsection focuses on the generation of the dataset and the construction of the DNN. First, based on Section 2.3.2, reentry trajectories of different ranges can be obtained offline. The downrange and crossrange of the reentry flight is uniquely determined by the three flight states h, v, θ, and the weighting coefficient ω of the compound bank corridor. Different initial states and weighting coefficients are randomly selected to generate 10,000 trajectories, and 100 sample points are randomly selected from each trajectory. Specifically, the selection rules are shown in Table 1. Finally, a total of 1 million data samples are obtained, as shown in Figure 4, where the input are the flight states h, v, θ, and the weighting coefficients ω, and the output is the downrange and crossrange. The dataset is further divided into three sub-datasets, namely the training set, validation set, and test set, according to the ratio of 0.8:0.1:0.1. On this basis, Scikit-learn further normalizes the input and output of the dataset.

Table 1. Initial state space.

State	Values	Distribution
$h(t_0)$	100 ± 20 km	Uniform
$v(t_0)$	7200 ± 200 m/s	Uniform
$\theta(t_0)$	-1 ± 1 deg	Uniform
ω	$[0, 1]$	Uniform

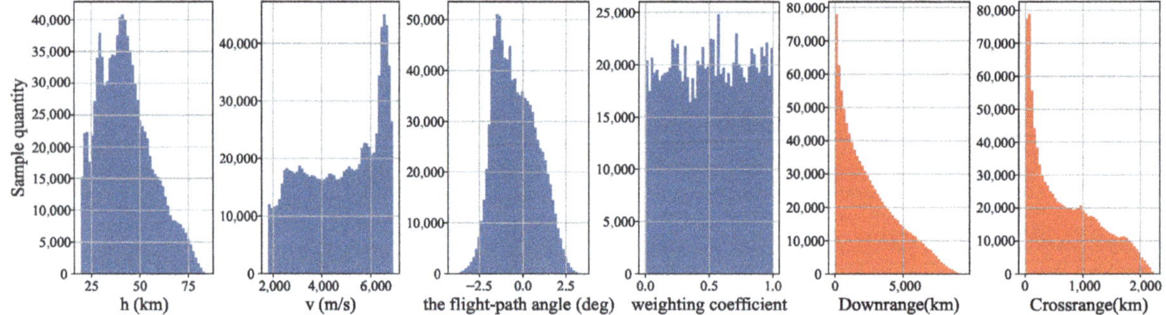

Figure 4. Distribution histograph of input and output of the dataset.

Second, a fully connected feedforward neural network is utilized to approximate the ranges. The input of the network is $\mathbf{x} = [h,\ v,\ \theta]$ and ω, and the prediction results of the network is the downrange Net_{dpre} and the crossrange Net_{cpre}. The design of the network refers to the optimized network design in [20,22,26]. The network is set up with 6 hidden layers and 128 neural units per layer. The activation functions of the hidden layers adopt Tanh $[-1, 1]$; the activation function of the output layer adopts ReLU $[0, +\infty]$. The Adam algorithm is used to adjust the network weights to minimize the mean square error. The initial learning rate is 0.001, and the exponential decay coefficient is 10^{-6}.

3.2. Accuracy and Rapidity Analysis

In this subsection, learning results and figures are used to illustrate the real-time performance and accuracy of the DNN approximation for ranges. We use the Pearson product–moment correlation coefficient to quantitatively evaluate the learning effect of the DNN. Table 2 gives the statistical results of the approximation error. At the same time, Figure 5 shows the error distribution histogram. Considering the very large range of the reentry, this error is reasonable and acceptable.

Table 2. Error statistics of the DNN-based range prediction.

	Net_{dpre}	Net_{cpre}
Mean error	0.508 km	0.196 km
Mean square error	0.458 km	0.152 km
Maximum error	17.01 km	9.642 km
Correlation coefficient	0.9999906	0.9999728

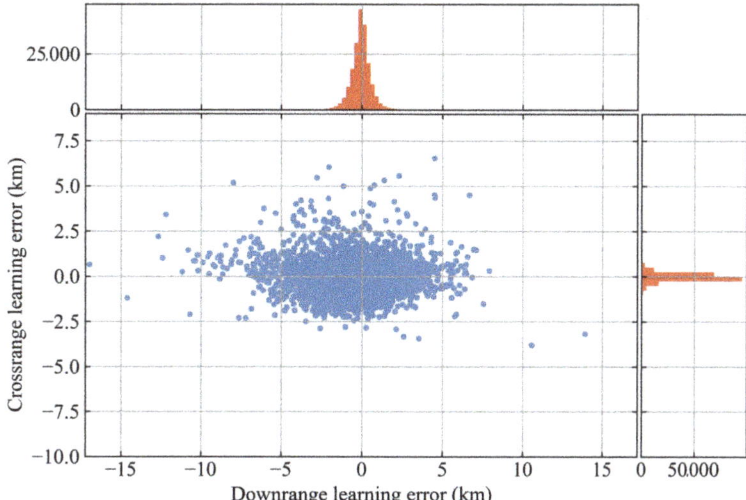

Figure 5. Error histogram of the DNN-based range prediction.

Table 3 gives the computational time it takes to predict ranges for different times by DNN and integrator. We can see that a single prediction by integrator takes 50 times as long as a single prediction by DNN. As the number of predictions grows, the rapidity of DNN becomes more and more significant, and the average time spent on a prediction by DNN becomes less and less. DNN not only has good real-time performance for a single prediction, but also is more suitable for multiple predictions. As footprint generation and intent inference require multiple range predictions, DNN is a good way to meet real-time requirements.

Table 3. The time consumption of range prediction by trajectory integrator and DNN.

Method	**DNN**			**Integrator**	
The Number of Times of Range Prediction	**1**	**10**	**10,000**	**1**	**10**
Total Time Consumption	0.041 s	0.054 s	0.29 s	1.86 s	13.07 s
Average Time Consumption	0.041 s	5.43 ms	0.029 ms	1.86 s	1.31 s

In summary, we can conclude that the trained DNN can meet the real-time requirement and has a good fitting accuracy on the ranges. Based on the above conclusions, DNN can be utilized for online footprint prediction and intent inference.

3.3. Real-Time Footprint Prediction

In this subsection, an online footprint prediction algorithm is developed on the basis of the trained DNN. Traditionally, the footprint is generated by traversing the ranges using a baseline trajectory planner. However, the traditional planner cannot meet the real-time requirements due to the long integration time. As discussed in Section 3.2, DNN can replace the integrator to predict the ranges according to the flight states and the weighting coefficient meeting the real-time requirement and ensuring a good fitting accuracy. Therefore, in this study, DNN is utilized to generate the footprint by traversing the ranges.

Knowing state $\mathbf{x}_{in} = [h_{in}, v_{in}, \theta_{in}]$, when $\omega_i \subseteq [0,1]$, the corresponding downrange $Net_{dpre}\big|_{\omega=\omega_i}$ and crossrange $Net_{cpre}|_{\omega=\omega_i}$ are obtained. Here, $Net_{cpre}|_{\omega=\omega_i}$ only represents the maximum lateral maneuverability and does not mean that the value of the crossrange must be $Net_{cpre}|_{\omega=\omega_i}$. By the bank angle reversals, the actual crossrange can be any number between $[-Net_{cpre}|_{\omega=\omega_i}, Net_{cpre}|_{\omega=\omega_i}]$.

As shown in Figure 6, the boundaries of the footprint consist of the following four sides:

- Lower boundary: The downrange is $Net_{dpre}\big|_{\omega=0}$, and the crossrange traverses $[-Net_{cpre}|_{\omega=0}, Net_{cpre}|_{\omega=0}]$. The downrange of this edge is the minimum downrange;
- Upper boundary: The downrange is $Net_{dpre}\big|_{\omega=1}$, and the crossrange traverses $[-Net_{cpre}|_{\omega=1}, Net_{cpre}|_{\omega=1}]$. The downrange of this edge is the maximum downrange;
- Right boundary: When $\omega_i \subseteq (0,1)$, the downrange is $Net_{dpre}\big|_{\omega=\omega_i}$, and the crossrange is $Net_{cpre}|_{\omega=\omega_i}$ (Based on the heading direction of the enemy vehicle at the current moment, the lateral range of the left deviation is negative, and the right deviation is positive);
- Left boundary: When $\omega_i \subseteq (0,1)$, the downrange is $Net_{dpre}\big|_{\omega=\omega_i}$, and the crossrange is $-Net_{cpre}|_{\omega=\omega_i}$.

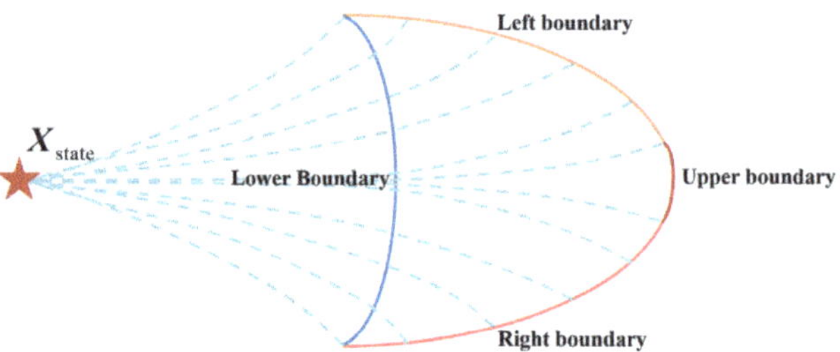

Figure 6. A footprint diagram.

Now we know the current longitude λ_{in} , latitude ϕ_{in}, heading angle ψ_{in} of the flying HGV, and the predicted range sequence of the boundary of the footprint. It is also necessary to convert the downrange sequence $Net_{dpre}\big|_{\omega=\omega_i}$ and the crossrange sequence $Net_{cpre}|_{\omega=\omega_i}$ into the longitude sequence λ_f and latitude sequence ϕ_f of the boundary of the footprint.

$$A_d = \frac{Net_{dpre}\big|_{\omega=\omega_i}}{R_0} \tag{24}$$

$$A_c = \frac{Net_{cpre}|_{\omega=\omega_i}}{R_0} \tag{25}$$

$$\psi_f = \arcsin\frac{A_c}{A_d} + \psi_{in} \tag{26}$$

$$\phi_f = \pi/2 - \arccos(\sin(\phi_{in})\cos(A_d) + \cos(\phi_{in})\sin(A_d)\cos(\psi_f)) \tag{27}$$

$$\lambda_f = \lambda_{in} + \arcsin(\sin(\psi_f)\sin(A_d)/\cos(\phi_f)) \tag{28}$$

So far, as long as the current states $\mathbf{x}_{in} = [h_{in}, \lambda_{in}, \phi_{in}, v_{in}, \theta_{in}, \psi_{in}]$ are known, the latitude and longitude of the footprint can be calculated. After the footprint is known, it can be determined which targets are within the attack zone at the current moment. One simple way of finding whether a target is inside or outside the footprint is a ray casting algorithm [27]. As shown in Figure 7, one can draw a ray from this target and count the number of points at which the ray intersects the footprint. If the number is odd, the target is inside the footprint; otherwise, it is outside the footprint.

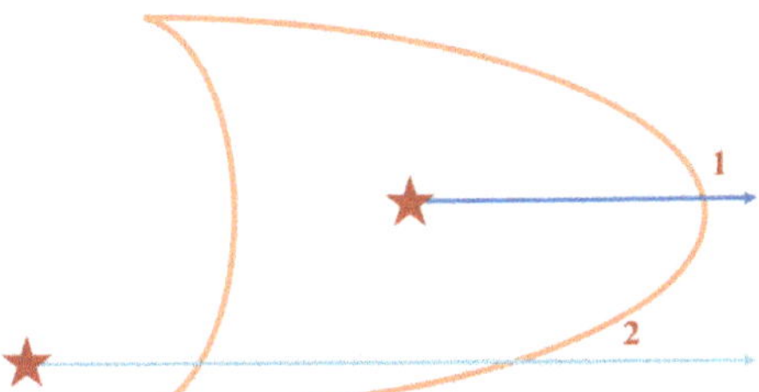

Figure 7. Ray casting algorithm.

This section focuses on the problem of HGVs footprint prediction. Fast and accurate prediction of the footprint can maximize the effectiveness of pre-deployed interceptor forces. First, we generate a large number of HGV trajectories offline and use DNN to learn the range accurately. Results show that DNN approximation for ranges has real-time performance and accuracy. Then, based on it, the footprint can be generated rapidly by predicting a series of ranges, and targets can be judged as to whether they are within the footprint. However, there are many targets in the footprint. In the following section, an online attack intention inference algorithm that calculates the target probability to be attacked in the footprint is proposed.

4. Attack Intention Inference

This section focuses on the second purpose of this study, that is, online attack intention inference. This section contains three parts. The first part introduces the criteria of intention inference. Target reachability and the historical data, including the orientation and the control strategy of the HGVs, are taken into consideration. A forgetting mechanism is proposed in the second part in case the enemy changes the target during flight. The third part describes the attack intention inference system and potential performance.

4.1. Intention Inference Criteria

Although landmarks outside the footprint can be excluded according to Section 3.3, there are many landmarks remaining in the footprint and we cannot judge which one is the attack target. During the flight of HGVs, as long as the landmarks still stay in the footprint, they can be attacked by proactive maneuvers of the vehicle. Using only the flight state at the current moment, the attack intention cannot be inferred. How to combine the current footprint prediction with the historical flight data is the key point of this section.

Through in-depth mining of the internal information hidden in the trajectories, three evaluation criteria are set. First, the control strategy of HGVs will not change sharply when the HGV aims at one specific target. Second, in order to achieve precise strikes, the HGVs' heading angle should be maintained around the target direction. Third, landmarks with higher importance are more likely to be attacked.

4.1.1. Change Detection of the Control Strategy

Due to the high speed of HGVs, a slight change in the control command will lead to a obvious change in the trajectory, and it is very likely to lead to an increase in miss distance and lose stability. Therefore, in the actual flight process, frequent and sharp changes of the control command are avoided. The bank angle shows piecewise linear characteristics when the guidance strategy is reference trajectory-based guidance (RTG) [28,29]. The bank angle is constantly corrected in small amplitudes according to the remaining downrange when the guidance strategy is NPCG [22,30].

As shown by the red line in Figure 8, if the landmark is the attack target, the weighting coefficient ω inferred from the detected historical flight state to attack this landmark is almost unchanged. As shown by the blue line in Figure 8, if the landmark is not the target, the distance between the vehicle and the landmark is not always decreasing. The weighting coefficient ω inferred from the detected historical flight state to attack this landmark changes sharply.

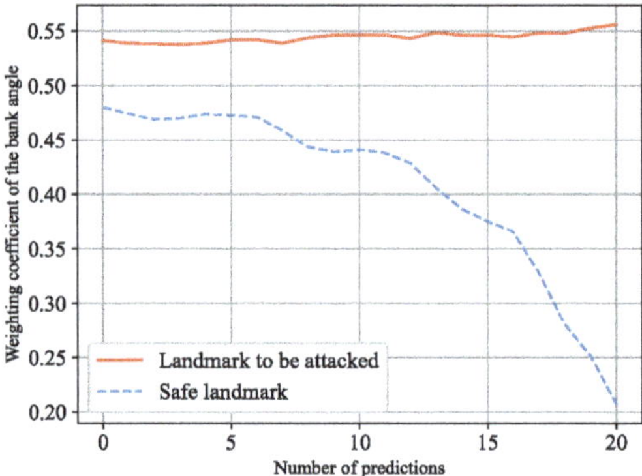

Figure 8. Change tendency of inferred ω.

When the defender does not know the enemy's attack intention and can only detect the flight states, how to infer the weighting coefficient ω when an HGV is going to attack one specific landmark will be explained below. Suppose there are m landmarks, and we need to infer whether they are likely to be attacked and which landmark is most likely to be attacked. The state $\mathbf{x}_k = [h_k, \lambda_k, \phi_k, v_k, \theta_k, \psi_k]$ of the HGV at the current time t_k and the latitude ϕ_j and longitude λ_j of the jth landmark are known. The steps of estimating the weighting coefficient $\omega_j(t_k)$ if a HGV is going to attack the jth landmark at the current moment t_k by the gradient descent method are as follows. The flowchart is shown in Figure 9.

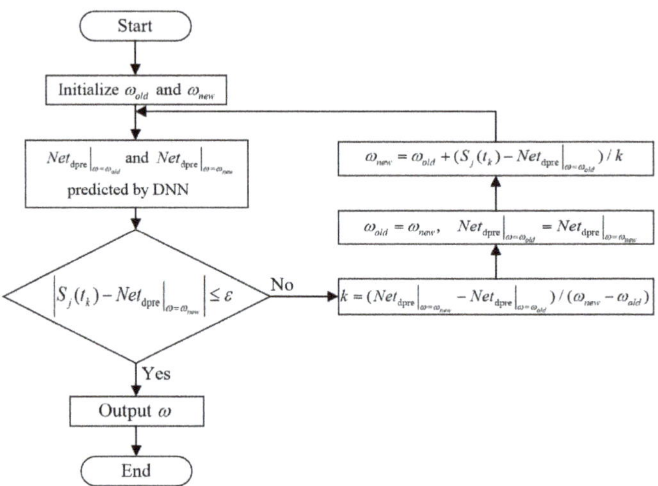

Figure 9. Flowchart for estimating ω using gradient descent.

- Step1: Set $\omega_{old} = 0.5$, $\omega_{new} = 0.6$. According to $\mathbf{x}_k = [h_k, v_k, \theta_k]$, ω_{old} and ω_{new}, $Net_{dpre}\big|_{\omega=\omega_{old}}$ and $Net_{dpre}\big|_{\omega=\omega_{new}}$ can be predicted by DNN. Then, calculate the distance $S_j(t_k)$ between the current latitude ϕ_k and longitude λ_k of the HGV and the latitude ϕ_j and longitude λ_j of the jth landmark.
- Step2: Calculate $k = (\, Net_{dpre}\big|_{\omega=\omega_{new}} - Net_{dpre}\big|_{\omega=\omega_{old}})/(\omega_{new} - \omega_{old})$. Then, set $\omega_{old} = \omega_{new}$, $Net_{dpre}\big|_{\omega=\omega_{old}} = Net_{dpre}\big|_{\omega=\omega_{new}}$.
- Step3: Calculate $\omega_{new} = \omega_{old} + (S_j(t_k) - Net_{dpre}\big|_{\omega=\omega_{old}})/k$. The new downrange $Net_{dpre}\big|_{\omega=\omega_{new}}$ is obtained by DNN.
- Step4: If $\left|S_j(t_k) - Net_{dpre}\big|_{\omega=\omega_{new}}\right| \leq \varepsilon$ (ε is the allowable deviation of the downrange), output $\omega_j(t_k) = \omega_{new}$. If $\left|S_j(t_k) - Net_{dpre}\big|_{\omega=\omega_{new}}\right| > \varepsilon$, return to Step2.

So far, we have obtained $\omega_j(t_k)$ if the enemy HGV intends to attack the jth landmark at t_k. Similarly, we can calculate the weighting coefficient $\omega_j(t_k)(j = 1, 2, \ldots, m)$ if the vehicle intends to attack each remaining landmark at t_k. Not only that, given the current states and historical states $\mathbf{x}_i = [h_i, \lambda_i, \phi_i, v_i, \theta_i, \psi_i](i = 1, 2, \ldots, k)$ of the vehicle, we can get the sequence of weighting coefficients to attack each landmark corresponding to time $\omega_j(t_i(i = 1, 2, \ldots, k))(j = 1, 2, \ldots, m)$.

For each landmark j, there is a sequence of weighting coefficients $\omega_j(t_i(i = 1, 2, \ldots, k))$ with respect to time $t_i(i = 0, 1, \ldots, k)$. Use variance $\mathrm{var}(\omega_j(t_i(i = 1, 2, \ldots, k)))$ to characterize the change detection of the control strategy of the jth landmark. Normalize $\mathrm{var}(\omega_j(t_i(i = 1, 2, \ldots, k)))(j = 1, 2, \ldots, m)$ of each landmark to $[0, 1]$ and sort it. The smaller the variance $\mathrm{var}(\omega_j(t_i(i = 1, 2, \ldots, k)))$ is, the more likely the jth landmark is to be attacked. By continuously detecting new states of the vehicle in a new moment, the variance sequence can be updated and sorted to predict which landmark is the most likely to be attacked.

4.1.2. The Cumulative Deviation of ψ and the LOS

In order to strike one specific target, the heading angle ψ of the HGV is maintained around the target direction, and the deviation between the ψ and the line of sight (LOS) is not very large. As shown by the red line in Figure 10, if the landmark is the attack target, due to the bank angle reversals, ψ will swing left and right around the LOS. As shown by the blue line in Figure 10, if the landmark is not the target, the deviation between ψ and the LOS of the landmark is relatively large. As the flight time becomes longer, the deviation becomes larger and larger, and ψ is likely to be on one side of the LOS and will no longer swing left and right around the LOS.

When the defender does not know the enemy's attack intention and can only detect the flight states, how to characterize and rank the deviation between the ψ and LOS will be explained below. The expression $\psi(t_k)$ is the heading angle of the vehicle at the current moment t_k; $\mathrm{LOS}_j(t_k)$ is the LOS between the vehicle and the jth landmark at t_k; $\psi(t_k) - \mathrm{LOS}_j(t_k)$ represents the deviation of the heading angle of the vehicle and the LOS of the jth landmark. Given $\psi(t_i)(i = 1, 2, \ldots, k)$ and $\mathrm{LOS}_j(t_i)(i = 1, 2, \ldots, k)$ at $t_i(i = 0, 1, \ldots, k)$, the mean of the cumulative deviation $|\mathrm{mean}(\psi(t_i) - \mathrm{LOS}_j(t_i)(i = 1, 2, \ldots, k))|$ between the heading angle of the vehicle and the LOS of the jth landmark at all times can be calculated. For each landmark, the mean sequence $|\mathrm{mean}(\psi(t_i) - \mathrm{LOS}_j(t_i)(i = 1, 2, \ldots, k))|$ $(j = 1, 2, \ldots, m)$ can be calculated, normalized to $[0, 1]$, and sorted. The smaller the mean $|\mathrm{mean}(\psi(t_i) - \mathrm{LOS}_j(t_i)(i = 1, 2, \ldots, k))|$, the more likely the jth landmark is to be attacked. Continuously detecting the states of the vehicle in a new moment can update and sort the mean sequence of the deviation of the ψ and the LOS.

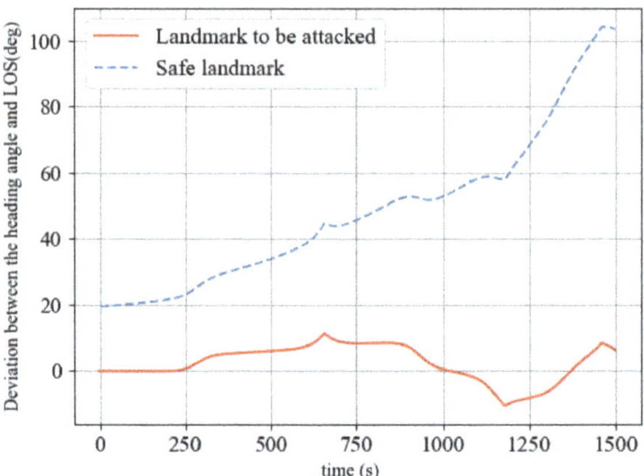

Figure 10. Deviation of the heading angle and the LOS.

4.1.3. The Importance of Landmarks

Among the multitudinous input landmarks, it is impossible that all the landmarks have the same degree of importance. In actual wars, attackers are more inclined to attack large cities, economically developed areas, and areas with high population density. Therefore, the importance of the landmarks needs to be scored on a $[0,1]$ scale. The smaller the importance degree weight I_j, the more important the jth landmark is. Because some of the less important landmarks are close to the important landmarks, $\mathrm{var}(\omega(t_i(i=1,2,\ldots,k)))$ and $|\mathrm{mean}(\psi_i - LOS_i)(i=1,2,\ldots,k)|$ of the less important landmarks are numerically close to those of the important landmarks, which may lead the system to judge that less important landmarks are also likely to be attacked. The importance weights I solve the problem of less important landmarks interfering with the attack intention inference system.

4.2. Forgetting Mechanism

With the development of reentry guidance, the maneuvering form of HGVs has become more and more complex. In actual flight, in order to bypass the no-fly zone and avoid being detected by radar, HGVs may conduct proactive maneuvers or change the attack target during flight. In order to instantly identify an HGV's changing target and re-predict its new target, this subsection proposes a forgetting mechanism.

Exponentially weighted moving average (EWMA) is a variable-weight mean calculation method, which has been widely used in machine learning and technical analysis of financial data [31]. EWMA is designed as such that older data are given lower weights. The weights fall exponentially as the data get older. EWMA is used because recent input data have a greater impact on the average value, and it can better reflect the recent data information.

Let $x_i(i=1,2,\ldots,t)$ be the dynamic input data, then the average μ_t at time t can be expressed as

$$\mu_t = \beta\mu_{t-1} + (1-\beta)x_t = (1-\beta)(x_t + \beta x_{t-1} + \beta^2 x_{t-2} + \ldots + \beta^{t-1}x_1), \quad (29)$$

where β is the decay rate, and the value is between $[0,1]$. The smaller the β, the more the mean is affected by the recent input data. However, μ_t is very different from the mean value due to too little input data at the beginning. Therefore, the deviation correction is performed on Equation (29):

$$\mu_t = (1-\beta)/(1-\beta^t)(x_t + \beta x_{t-1} + \beta^2 x_{t-2} + \ldots + \beta^{t-1}x_1). \quad (30)$$

So far, we have obtained the average value μ_t of the dynamic input data represented by EWMA. In [31], exponentially weighted moving variance (EWMV) is proposed to describe the variance of variable weights. The formula of EWMV is expressed as

$$\sigma_t^2 = \beta\sigma_{t-1}^2 + \beta(1-\beta)(x_t - \mu_{t-1})^2. \tag{31}$$

Similarly, EWMV is designed to be more affected by the recent input data, so the variance of the older data is given lower weights that fall exponentially as the data get older. On the basis of Equations (30) and (31), EWMV is improved. We replace the mean μ_t in the variance Equation (31) with the latest data x_t from the dynamic input data. The improved EWMV is expressed as

$$\sigma_t{}^2 = (1-\beta)/(1-\beta^t)[(x_t - x_t)^2 + \beta(x_{t-1} - x_t)^2 + \ldots + \beta^{t-1}(x_1 - x_t)^2]. \tag{32}$$

In summary, we design the mean and variance with forgetting properties. We substitute EWMV for the variance in Section 4.1.1 and EWMA for the mean in Section 4.1.2. In this way, the change detection of the control strategy and the cumulative deviation between the ψ and the LOS is more affected by the recent flight states. This is conducive to predicting the enemy's attack intention at every moment without knowing whether and when to change the attack target during flight.

4.3. Attack Intention Inference System and Algorithm

This section will briefly describe the algorithm of the attack intention inference system and its potential performance. Referring to the pseudocode below, we will describe the Algorithm 1 of the attack intention inference system in detail.

Algorithm 1 Attack Intention Inference Algorithm

Data: new flight states of the enemy HGV $\mathbf{x}_k = [h_k, \lambda_k, \phi_k, v_k, \theta_k, \psi_k]$ at time t_k, landmarks, importance of landmarks I
Result: ranked P_k
while *detect the new states* $\mathbf{x}_k$ *at* t_k **do**
  predict $footprint(t_k)$ by DNN ;
  for *each landmark j in landmarks* **do**
    if *landmark j within* $footprint(t_k)$ **then**
      Calculate $\omega_j(t_k)$ by DNN $\rightarrow \omega_j[k]$;
      Calculate $\psi(t_k) - \text{LOS}_j(t_k) \rightarrow \Delta\psi_j[k]$;
      $\text{Var}(\omega_j) \leftarrow \text{EWMV}(\omega_j)$;
      $\text{Mean}(\Delta\psi_j) \leftarrow \text{EWMA}(\Delta\psi_j)$;
      $P(t_k)[j] = \alpha_1\text{Var}(\omega_j) + \alpha_2|\text{Mean}(\Delta\psi_j)| + \alpha_3 I_j$;
  rank $P(t_k)$;
  return ranked $P(t_k)$;

First, we predict the current footprint by DNN approximation for ranges and determine whether the input landmarks are within the footprint according to Section 3.3. If the landmark is within the footprint, the probability of it being attacked will be estimated. Combined with the forgetting mechanism in Section 4.2, the normalized $\text{var}(\omega(t_i)$ $(i = 1, 2, \ldots, k))$ and$|\text{mean}(\psi(t_i) - \text{LOS}(t_i)(i = 1, 2, \ldots, k))|$ of each landmark can be calculated according to Sections 4.1.1 and 4.1.2. Weighting them with landmark importance weights I yields the probability of each landmark of being attacked,

$$P = \alpha_1\text{var}(\omega(t)) + \alpha_2|\text{mean}(\psi(t) - \text{LOS}_j(t))| + \alpha_3 I, \tag{33}$$

where $\alpha_1, \alpha_2, \alpha_3$ are the weights of intention inference criteria, satisfying $\alpha_1 + \alpha_2 + \alpha_3 = 1$; $\alpha_1, \alpha_2, \alpha_3$ can be set and adjusted according to actual operational needs and the importance of each criteria. Then, we calculate and sort P of each landmark. The smaller the P, the greater the probability of the landmark to be attacked. The defending side continuously detects the current states of the flying HGV, updates and sorts in real-time P to infer the intention of the HGV. As time progresses, the accuracy of the intention inference system greatly improves.

This proposed algorithm has the following potential advantages.

1. Ability to quickly and accurately predict the footprint: Since the DNN replaces the traditional integrator to approximate the ranges, the footprint prediction meets the real-time requirements while ensuring high accuracy;
2. Ability to infer the intention of enemy HGVs: The underlying logic of the attack intention inference system in this study is that the defender infers from the perspective of the attacker. First, the control strategy of HGVs will not change sharply when the HGV aims at one specific target. Second, in order to achieve precise strikes, the HGVs' heading angle should be maintained around the target direction. Third, attackers are more willing to attack important landmarks. It is precisely because these criteria are condensed from the rules discovered from the trajectory planning of the attacker side that the defending side can use these criteria to infer the enemy's intention;
3. Ability to identify enemy HGVs changing attack intention online and re-predict new targets: Mean and variance with forgetting properties makes the system more affected by the recent flight states. Therefore, the forgetting mechanism can gradually forget the early intention and predict new target based on the data of the recent period;
4. Good real-time performance: Both the footprint prediction and the change detection of the control strategy avoid long-term trajectory integration, and DNN greatly improves the computational efficiency.

The next section uses simulation examples to verify the aforementioned performance of the algorithm.

5. Simulations and Results

This section focuses on the performance verification of the proposed algorithm. Specifically, three experiments are conducted. The first experiment is to verify the accuracy of the footprint prediction algorithm. The second experiment verifies the effectiveness of the intention inference system. The third experiment verifies that the system is suitable for inferring the intention of the enemy to change the target during the flight. The forth subsection discusses the advantages and disadvantages of the algorithm. The common areo vehicle (CAV) designed by Boeing Company in 1998 has two configurations. In this study, the vehicle for simulation is the CAV-L with lower lift-to-drag ratio, and its aerodynamic data and overall design parameters are shown in [32].

5.1. Evaluation of Footprint Prediction

First, the accuracy and real-time performance of the DNN-based footprint predictions are evaluated by comparing it with the traditional integrator. Given the flight states of an enemy CAV, the results of footprint prediction using DNN and traditional integrator are shown in Figure 11. It can be seen that the footprint predicted by the two methods almost overlap. Table 4 shows the comparison of the coordinates of the following five typical points calculated by DNN and integrator. Point A has the largest downrange and crossrange of 0; B has the largest downrange and the corresponding maximum lateral maneuverability; C has the largest crossrange; D has the minimum downrange and the corresponding maximum lateral maneuverability; and E has the minimum downrange and crossrange of 0. It can be seen that the deviation between the coordinates predicted by the two methods is very small. The time consumption of one footprint prediction by DNN is 0.85 s, and at the same time, the time consumption of one footprint prediction by integrator is 52.71 s. Consequently, DNN-based footprint prediction is accurate and greatly improves real-time performance.

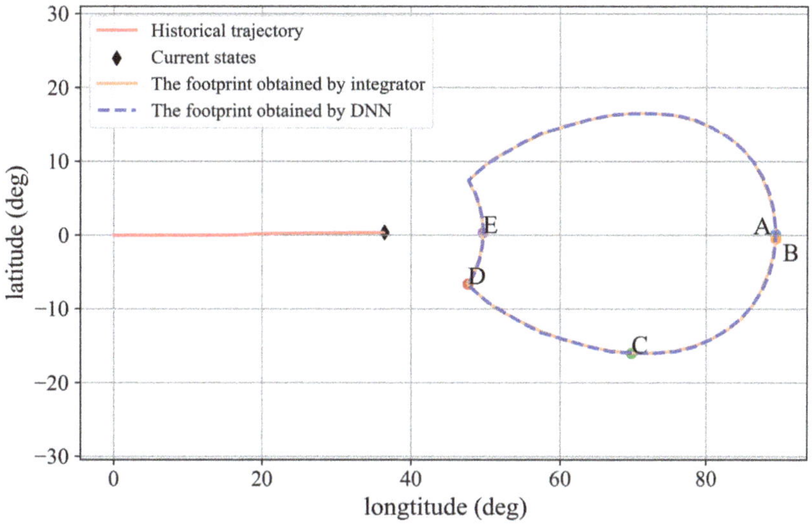

Figure 11. Comparison of footprint predicted by integrator and DNN.

Table 4. Comparison of the footprint prediction by integrator and DNN.

	Integrator	DNN	Deviation
Coordinates of A (deg)	$(89.397, 0.160)$	$(89.381, 0.160)$	$(1.6 \times 10^{-2}, -9.2 \times 10^{-5})$
Coordinates of B (deg)	$(89.391, -0.459)$	$(89.376, -0.358)$	$(1.5 \times 10^{-2}, -0.101)$
Coordinates of C (deg)	$(69.712, -16.017)$	$(69.849, -15.973)$	$(-0.137, -4.4 \times 10^{-2})$
Coordinates of D (deg)	$(47.587, -6.653)$	$(47.632, -6.772)$	$(-4.5 \times 10^{-2}, 0.119)$
Coordinates of E (deg)	$(49.592, 0.330)$	$(49.693, 0.330)$	$(-0.101, 2.6 \times 10^{-4})$

5.2. Typical Intention Inference Simulation

In this section, we turn our attention to demonstrating the effectiveness of the typical intention inference. Part of the information of the flying CAV is shown in Table 5. Of course, this information is unknown to the defender, and the defender can only detect the states of the CAV during the flight. Twenty-five landmarks B$\sim$Z with longitude between [90° W, 140° W], latitude between [20° S, 60° S], and the importance weights I between $[0, 1]$ are generated by random numbers. We set a landmark A with longitude of 100° W, latitude of 40° S, and importance I of 0. We set the weight of each intention inference criterion to $\alpha_1 = 0.8$, $\alpha_2 = 0.1$, $\alpha_3 = 0.1$, respectively. The probability of attacking these 26 landmarks is predicted and ranked in real time. The first jump of CAV was detected at 282 s. Due to the complex dynamic characteristics of the initial descent phase of HGV, intention inference was not performed in the initial glide segment. The first prediction is at 285 s. The prediction interval is 5 s.

Table 5. The information of the incoming CAV (unknown to the defender).

Initial Longitude	Initial Latitude	Longitude of the Target	Latitude of the Target	Guidance Law
180°	0°	100° W	40° S	NPCG

The result is shown in the Figure 12, which contains the following information.

- Historical trajectory of the CAV;
- Footprint at the current state;
- Landmarks that may be attacked within the footprint;
- Temporarily safe landmarks outside the footprint;
- Landmarks within the footprint are ranked by probability of being attacked.

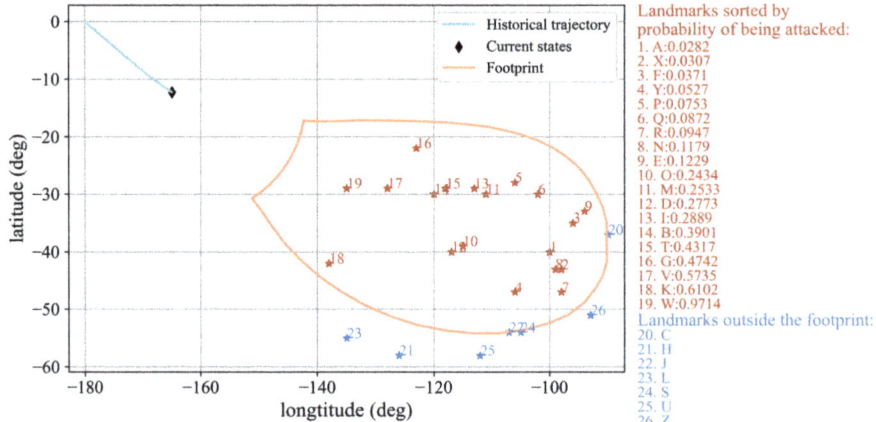

Figure 12. Footprint and intention inference at 305 s.

After five predictions (at 305 s), it is predicted that the target of the incoming CAV is A, as shown in Figure 12. The reason for needing five predictions is that the change detection of the control strategy and the cumulative deviation between the ψ and the LOS are characterized by the variance and mean in the intention inference system, requiring >2 sample data to calculate variance and mean. Predicting the correct attack intention within 25 s shows that the system has good foresight.

The prediction at 800 s is shown in Figure 13. It can be seen that the footprint becomes smaller and the number of landmarks that may be attacked decreases. The landmark that is most likely to be attacked is still A, which shows the intention inference system has good stability. As shown in Figure 14, the footprint is shrunk to the range containing only A at 1195 s. Consequently, the DNN-based intention inference system has good performance of effectiveness, perspective, and stability.

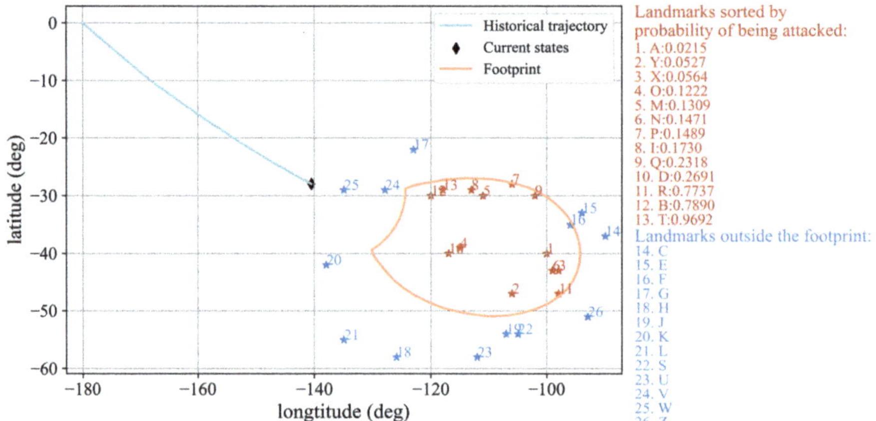

Figure 13. Footprint and intention inference at 800 s.

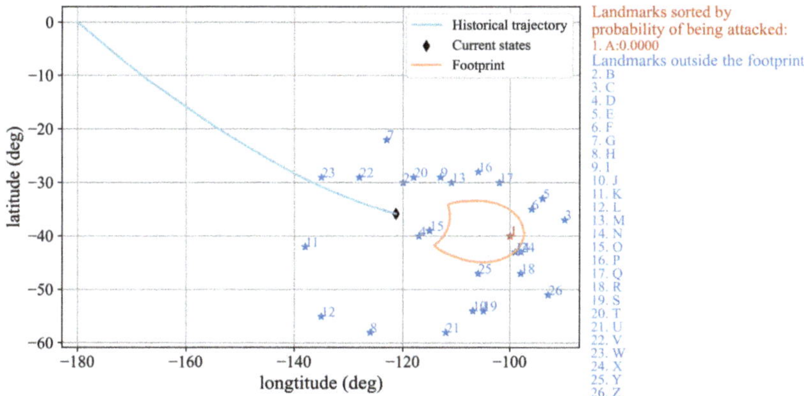

Figure 14. Footprint and intention inference at 1195 s.

5.3. Evaluation of Forgetting Mechanism

This section verifies the effectiveness of the forgetting mechanism by predicting the intention of a CAV that changes its attack target during the flight. Part of the information of the flying CAV is shown in Table 6. The vehicle originally intended to attack Landmark A at 100° W, 40° S, but changed its attack intention at 500 s to attack Landmark B at 120° W, 30° S. Of course, the above information and whether and when to change the attack target is unknown to the defender. Twenty-four landmarks C∼Z with longitude between [90° W, 140° W], latitude between [20° S, 60° S], and the importance weights I between $[0, 1]$ are generated by random numbers. We set a landmark A with longitude of 100° W, latitude of 40° S, and importance I of 0, and set a landmark B with longitude of 120° W, latitude of 30° S, and importance I of 0. We set the weight of each intention inference criterion to $\alpha_1 = 0.85$, $\alpha_2 = 0.05$, $\alpha_3 = 0.1$, respectively. The decay rate of forgetting mechanism is set to 0.7. The probability of attacking these 26 landmarks is predicted and ranked in real time. The first prediction is at 290 s. The prediction interval is 10 s.

Table 6. The flying CAV information (unknown to the defender).

Initial Coordinates of the CAV	Coordinates of the Original Target	Time When the Target Is Changed	Coordinates of the Changed Target	Guidance Law
(180°, 0°)	(100° W, 40° S)	500 s	(20° W, 30° S)	RTG

For ease of observation, the light blue dotted line in the graph represents the original trajectory if the CAV has not changed its attack target during the flight.

After four predictions (at 320 s), it is predicted that the target of the CAV is A, as shown in Figure 15. During 320∼500 s, results show that the CAV intended to attack A.

As shown in Figure 16, the prediction results begin to change at 510 s, which means the system quickly recognizes that the enemy is maneuvering to change its attack target. The probability P_B of B became smaller, and the rank moved forward; P_A of A increased, and the rank went backward. This shows that the system gradually reduces the impact of the initial trajectory on the predicted results through the forgetting mechanism and gradually forgets that the CAV is going to attack landmark A at the beginning. At 520 s, it is predicted that the CAV changes to attack landmark B, which means that the forgetting mechanism of this system is responsive, forward-looking, and accurate. The prediction results fluctuate with small amplitude between 560 s and ∼580 s and stabilize after 590 s, showing that B is most likely to be attacked, as shown in Figure 17. Consequently, the forgetting mechanism can quickly identify that the enemy has changed its intention and quickly re-predict the new attack target correctly. The prediction results are accurate and stable, and fewer predictions are required to re-predict the new target after maneuvering.

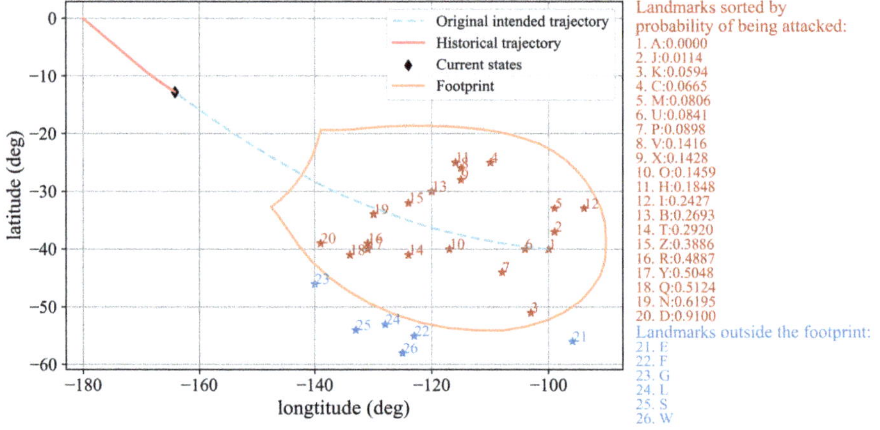

Figure 15. Footprint and intention inference at 320 s.

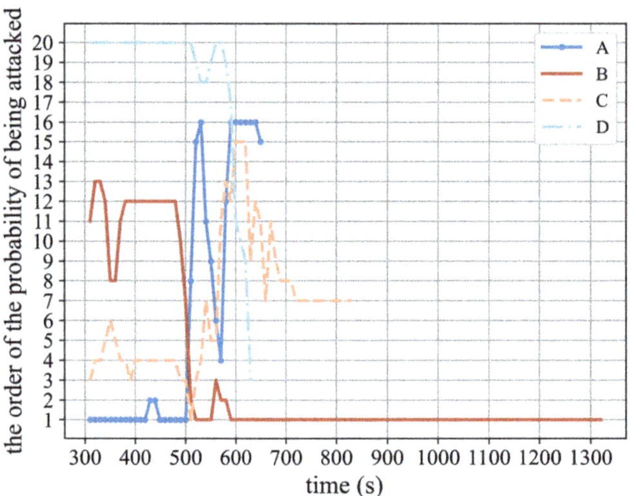

Figure 16. Ranking of probability of being attacked over time.

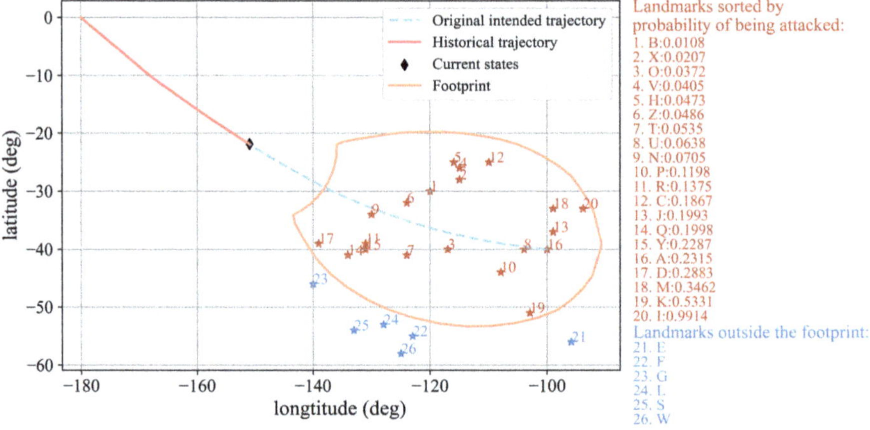

Figure 17. Footprint and intention inference at 590 s.

5.4. Advantages and Disadvantages

Combined with the above three typical simulations, the advantages of footprint prediction and intention inference system are summarized below.

1. The system has good real-time performance.
   A maximum of 4.74 s is required for one footprint prediction and intention inference (predictions are made for 26 landmarks) due to the substitution of DNN for trajectory integration. Therefore, as long as each prediction period is more than 5 s, it can reconcile the requirements for real-time performance. Table 7 exhibits the comparison of the time consumption by trajectory integrator and DNN. We can see from the Table 7 that a high-precision trajectory integration is time-consuming due to the long flight time. For this reason, it is difficult to meet the demand of real-time performance for footprint prediction and intention inference. In contrast, the DNN shows obvious improvement of the real-time performance while ensuring an acceptable prediction accuracy.
2. This system can infer the intention of HGVs that change attack target during flight.
   This system adopts EWMA and improves EWMV. Mean and variance with forgetting properties makes the system more affected by the recent flight states. Therefore, the forgetting mechanism can infer in a timely manner that the flying HGV has maneuvered and predict its new attack target.
3. The system is forward-looking.
   The first few predictions after the initial descent segment can basically determine which landmark is most likely to be attacked. The flight time of a reentry is about 30 min, and the flight time of the initial descent segment is about five minutes. Forty seconds after the initial descent segment, the most likely landmark to be attacked can be predicted, leaving as much time as possible for the defender to intercept the enemy. In addition, when the HGV changes its attack target during its reentry, the system can also analyze that the HGV has changed its attack intention and predict the new target within 20 s.
4. The DNN-based footprint prediction can not only provide decision-making reference for the defender, but also be utilized for the attacker to generate the current footprint of the own HGV.
   The current literature on footprint generation of HGVs is only from the perspective of the attacker. The footprint of HGVs provides critical information for trajectory planning, such as providing guidance for entering into the TAEM. It takes an average time of 13.42 s to generate a footprint in [13]. Compared with the footprint generation based on the Gaussian pseudospectral method, the calculation speed of [13] has been greatly improved, but it still has room for improvement. If the DNN is utilized to replace the traditional integrator to generate the footprint from the perspective of the attacker, the calculation time of each generation can be less than 1 s, which greatly improves the real-time performance of battlefield mission planning. In addition, since the model, aerodynamic parameters, guidance law, and constraints are completely known, the accuracy of generating the footprint of the friendly HGV will be greatly improved compared with the accuracy of predicting the footprint of the enemy in this study.

Table 7. The comparison of the time consumption by trajectory integrator and DNN.

	One Range Prediction		One Footprint Prediction		One Intention Inference	
	Integrator	**DNN**	**Integrator**	**DNN**	**Integrator**	**DNN**
Time consumption	1.53 s	0.6 ms	52.71 s	0.85 s	189.95 s	3.66 s

The system still has the following shortcomings that need to be improved:

1. This system can only infer the probability of attacking the set landmarks. If the set landmarks do not include the enemy's real attack target, the system may only speculate that a set landmark close to the real target is most likely to be attacked.
2. Because the research object of the intention inference in this study is non-cooperative vehicles, the overall design parameters and aerodynamic parameters of them are not completely known, and many of them are estimated based on reverse engineering estimation methods [33]. Therefore, the ranges approximated by DNN in this study are not accurate when the enemy model deviates greatly from the hypothetical model in this study, and the predicted footprint will also not be so accurate. In particular, landmarks near the boundary of the footprint are also likely to be attacked.
   In the future work, we will introduce parameter identification into the footprint prediction and intention inference system to improve the inaccuracy of range prediction and footprint prediction. One solution is to identify lift, drag, aircraft mass, reference area, and bank angle through aerodynamic parameter identification, as suggested in [15]. Another solution is to refer to the idea in [34], that is, to identify the disturbance of the standard aerodynamic data through Kalman filtering. In future work, the aerodynamic parameters will be identified according to the trajectory information of the flying HGVs in real time, and the aerodynamic model fitted by the existing public information or public literature will be continuously corrected. Using the revised aerodynamic model, DNNs can predict more accurate ranges, footprint, and intention in real time.

6. Conclusions

In this paper, a DNN-based footprint prediction and intention inference of HGVs is proposed. First, a baseline multi-constrained entry guidance algorithm is developed based on a compound bank angle corridor, and then a dataset containing enough trajectories for the following DNN learning is generated offline by traversing different initial states and control commands. Second, DNNs replace traditional integrator to approximate the relationship between the flight state/command and the ranges. On this basis, an online footprint prediction algorithm is developed by traversing the ranges meeting the real-time requirements and ensuring high accuracy. Third, the intention inference system performs online intelligent prediction of the target probability to be attacked. Target reachability, importance, and historical data including the orientation and the control strategy of the HGVs are taken into consideration. A forgetting mechanism is proposed to help the intention inference algorithm to be effective when the HGVs change their attack target during the flight. On these bases, DNN-based footprint prediction and intention inference of HGVs is proposed.

Simulations are given to substantiate the effectiveness and the real-time capability of the proposed techniques. The results show that the calculation time of each footprint generation and intention inference is about 4.51 s, reconciling the requirements for real-time performance while ensuring high accuracy. The system can infer the final attack target correctly in the early stage of reentry flight and can instantly identify the enemy's change of attack intention and re-predict the new attack target.

Author Contributions: Conceptualization, L.C., C.D. and J.X.; methodology, L.C. and J.X.; software, J.X.; validation, C.D.; investigation, L.C. and J.X.; resources, C.D. and L.C.; data curation, C.D. and L.C.; writing—original draft preparation, L.C. and J.X.; writing—review and editing, L.C. and J.X.; supervision, C.D. and L.C.; project administration, C.D. and L.C. All authors have read and agreed to the published version of the manuscript.

Funding: This research is supported by the National Natural Science Foundation of China (No. 11902174).

Institutional Review Board Statement: Not applicable.

Informed Consent Statement: Not applicable.

Data Availability Statement: The data presented in this study are available in Sections 2.1, 3.1 and 5.

Conflicts of Interest: The authors declare no conflict of interest.

References

1. Fahroo, F.; Doman, D.B.; Ngo, A.D. Footprint generation for reusable launch vehicles using a direct pseudospectral method. In Proceedings of the IEEE 2003 American Control Conference, Denver, CO, USA, 4–6 June 2003; Volume 3, pp. 2163–2168.
2. Fahroo, F.; Doman, D. A direct method for approach and landing trajectory reshaping with failure effect estimation. In Proceedings of the AIAA Guidance, Navigation, and Control Conference and Exhibit, Providence, RI, USA, 16–19 August 2004; p. 4772.
3. Tian, B.; Fan, W.; Su, R.; Zong, Q. Real-time trajectory and attitude coordination control for reusable launch vehicle in reentry phase. *IEEE Trans. Ind. Electron.* **2014**, *62*, 1639–1650. [CrossRef]
4. Benedikter, B.; Zavoli, A.; Colasurdo, G.; Pizzurro, S.; Cavallini, E. Convex optimization of launch vehicle ascent trajectory with heat-flux and splash-down constraints. *J. Spacecr. Rocket.* **2022**, *59*, 900–915. [CrossRef]
5. Benedikter, B.; Zavoli, A.; Colasurdo, G.; Pizzurro, S.; Cavallini, E. Autonomous Upper Stage Guidance Using Convex Optimization and Model Predictive Control. In Proceedings of the AIAA ASCEND Forum, Online, 16–18 November 2020; p. 4268. [CrossRef]
6. Benedikter, B.; Zavoli, A.; Colasurdo, G.; Pizzurro, S.; Cavallini, E. Autonomous Upper Stage Guidance with Robust Splash-Down Constraint. *arXiv* **2022**, arXiv:2212.06518.
7. Lu, P. Asymptotic analysis of quasi-equilibrium glide in lifting entry flight. *J. Guid. Control Dyn.* **2006**, *29*, 662–670. [CrossRef]
8. Lu, P.; Xue, S. Rapid generation of accurate entry landing footprints. *J. Guid. Control Dyn.* **2010**, *33*, 756–767. [CrossRef]
9. Li, H.; Zhang, R.; Zhaoying, L.; Zhang, R. Footprint problem with angle of attack optimization for high lifting reentry vehicle. *Chin. J. Aeronaut.* **2012**, *25*, 243–251. (In Chinese) [CrossRef]
10. Liu, X.; Shen, Z.; Lu, P. Solving the maximum-crossrange problem via successive second-order cone programming with a line search. *Aerosp. Sci. Technol.* **2015**, *47*, 10–20. [CrossRef]
11. Ngo, A.; Doman, D. Footprint determination for reusable launch vehicles experiencing control effector failures. In Proceedings of the AIAA Guidance, Navigation, and Control Conference and Exhibit, Monterey, CA, USA, 5–8 August 2002; p. 4775.
12. Saraf, A.; Leavitt, J.; Ferch, M.; Mease, K. Landing footprint computation for entry vehicles. In Proceedings of the AIAA Guidance, Navigation, and Control Conference and Exhibit, Providence, RI, USA, 16–19 August 2004; p. 4774.
13. Fu, S.; Lu, T.; Yin, J.; Xia, Q. Rapid algorithm for generating entry landing footprints satisfying the no-fly zone constraint. *Int. J. Aerosp. Eng.* **2021**, *2021*, 8827377. [CrossRef]
14. Zhang, K.; Xiong, J.; Li, F.; Fu, T. Bayesian Trajectory Prediction for a Hypersonic Gliding Reentry Vehicle Based on Intent Inference. *J. Astronaut.* **2018**, *39*, 1258–1265. (In Chinese)
15. Hu, Y.; Gao, C.; Li, J.; Jing, W.; Li, Z. Novel trajectory prediction algorithms for hypersonic gliding vehicles based on maneuver mode on-line identification and intent inference. *Meas. Sci. Technol.* **2021**, *32*, 115012. [CrossRef]
16. Luo, Y.; Tan, X.; Wang, H.; Qu, Z. Method for predicting the attack intention of hypersonic vehicles. *J. Xidian Univ.* **2019**, *46*, 113–119. (In Chinese)
17. Zhou, W.; Yao, P.Y.; Zhang, J.; Wang, X.; Wei, S. Combat Intention Recognition for Aerial Targets Based on Deep Neural Network. *Acta Aeronaut. Et Astronaut. Sin.* **2018**, *39*, 322468–322476.
18. Izzo, D.; Märtens, M.; Pan, B. A survey on artificial intelligence trends in spacecraft guidance dynamics and control. *Astrodynamics* **2019**, *3*, 287–299. [CrossRef]
19. Li, Z.; Sun, X.; Hu, C.; Liu, G.; He, B. Neural network based online predictive guidance for high lifting vehicles. *Aerosp. Sci. Technol.* **2018**, *82*, 149–160. [CrossRef]
20. Horn, J.F.; Schmidt, E.M.; Geiger, B.R.; DeAngelo, M.P. Neural network-based trajectory optimization for unmanned aerial vehicles. *J. Guid. Control Dyn.* **2012**, *35*, 548–562. [CrossRef]
21. Schierman, J.; Hull, J.; Ward, D. Adaptive guidance with trajectory reshaping for reusable launch vehicles. In Proceedings of the AIAA Guidance, Navigation, and Control Conference and Exhibit, Monterey, CA, USA, 5–8 August 2002; p. 4458.
22. Cheng, L.; Jiang, F.; Wang, Z.; Li, J. Multiconstrained real-time entry guidance using deep neural networks. *IEEE Trans. Aerosp. Electron. Syst.* **2020**, *57*, 325–340. [CrossRef]
23. Lu, P. Entry guidance: A unified method. *J. Guid. Control Dyn.* **2014**, *37*, 713–728. [CrossRef]
24. Wen, T.; Zeng, X.; Circi, C.; Gao, Y. Hop reachable domain on irregularly shaped asteroids. *J. Guid. Control. Dyn.* **2020**, *43*, 1269–1283. [CrossRef]
25. Yang, H.; Li, S.; Bai, X. Fast homotopy method for asteroid landing trajectory optimization using approximate initial costates. *J. Guid. Control. Dyn.* **2019**, *42*, 585–597. [CrossRef]
26. Cheng, L.; Wang, Z.; Song, Y.; Jiang, F. Real-time optimal control for irregular asteroid landings using deep neural networks. *Acta Astronaut.* **2020**, *170*, 66–79. [CrossRef]
27. Shimrat, M. Algorithm 112: Position of point relative to polygon. *Commun. ACM* **1962**, *5*, 434. [CrossRef]
28. Wang, X.; Guo, J.; Tang, S.; Qi, S.; Wang, Z. Entry trajectory planning with terminal full states constraints and multiple geographic constraints. *Aerosp. Sci. Technol.* **2019**, *84*, 620–631. [CrossRef]

29. Zhang, D.; Liu, L.; Wang, Y. On-line reentry guidance algorithm with both path and no-fly zone constraints. *Acta Astronaut.* **2015**, *117*, 243–253. [CrossRef]
30. Li, Z.; Yang, X.; Sun, X.; Liu, G.; Hu, C. Improved artificial potential field based lateral entry guidance for waypoints passage and no-fly zones avoidance. *Aerosp. Sci. Technol.* **2019**, *86*, 119–131. [CrossRef]
31. Finch, T. Incremental calculation of weighted mean and variance. *Univ. Camb.* **2009**, *4*, 41–42.
32. Phillips, T.H. A common aero vehicle (CAV) model, description, and employment guide. *Schafer Corp. AFRL AFSPC* **2003**, *27*, 1–12.
33. LI, H.; Jin, X.; LIN, P. Modeling and Analyzing of Common Aero Vehicle with Parametric Configuration. *J. Astronantics* **2011**, *32*, 2305–2311.
34. Cui, N.; Lu, B.; Fu, Y.; Zhang, X. Aerodynamic Parameter Identification of a Reentry Vehicle Based on Kalman Filter Method. *J. Chin. Inert. Technol.* **2014**, *6*, 755–758. (In Chinese)

Article

Design of Ganymede-Synchronous Frozen Orbit around Europa

Xuxing Huang [1], Bin Yang [1], Shuang Li [1,*], Jinglang Feng [2] and Josep J. Masdemont [3]

1 College of Astronautics, Nanjing University of Aeronautics and Astronautics, Nanjing 210016, China
2 Department of Mechanical and Aerospace Engineering, University of Strathclyde, Glasgow G1 1XQ, UK
3 IEEC & Universitat Politècnica de Catalunya, 08028 Barcelona, Spain
* Correspondence: lishuang@nuaa.edu.cn

Abstract: A Ganymede-synchronous frozen orbit around Europa provides a stable spatial geometry between a Europa probe and a Ganymede lander, which facilitates the observation of Ganymede and data transmission between probes. However, the third-body gravitation perturbation of Ganymede continues to accumulate and affect the long-term evolution of the Europa probe. In this paper, the relative orbit of Ganymede with respect to Europa is considered to accurately capture the perturbation potential. The orbital evolution behaviors of the Europa probe under the non-spherical gravitation of Europa and the third-body gravitation of Jupiter and Ganymede are studied based on a double-averaging framework. Then, the initial orbital conditions of the Ganymede-synchronous frozen orbit are developed. A station-keeping maneuver was performed to maintain the orbital elements to achieve the Ganymede-synchronous and frozen behaviors. A numerical simulation showed that the consumption for orbital maintenance is acceptable.

Keywords: Jovian system; Ganymede-synchronous orbit; frozen orbit; Europa probe

MSC: 85-10; 70F15

Citation: Huang, X.; Yang, B.; Li, S.; Feng, J.; Masdemont, J.J. Design of Ganymede-Synchronous Frozen Orbit around Europa. *Mathematics* **2023**, *11*, 41. https://doi.org/10.3390/math11010041

Academic Editor: Junseok Kim

Received: 23 November 2022
Revised: 18 December 2022
Accepted: 19 December 2022
Published: 22 December 2022

1. Introduction

One of the scientific objectives for a practical Jovian system mission is exploring the Galilean moons such as Europa and Ganymede. NASA is carrying out the Europa Clipper mission to tour the Galilean moons by multiple fly-bys [1]. The Europa Clipper probe requires a wide-breadth imaging system to achieve global coverage with about 50 fly-bys, which constricts the imaging resolutions. The original design of the Europa Clipper mission includes a surface lander to improve the exploration efficiency [1]. However, this lander was canceled later due to budget issues. The ESA's Jupiter Icy Moons Explorer (JUICE) will employ a high inclination that orbits around one of the Galilean moons to achieve global observing capacity [2,3]. Meanwhile, the imaging resolution of JUICE is improved with frequent revisits compared to that of the Europa Clipper mission. Theoretically, the exploration efficiency can be further enhanced if the JUICE probe carries a surface lander to investigate the surface of another Galilean moon, such as Ganymede. However, a probe orbiting around a Galilean moon suffers from multiple perturbations, resulting in a complicated evolution of the orbit. Meanwhile, to manage the data relay, the geometry of the Europa probe and the Ganymede lander should keep a stable transmission condition, which is also determined by the long-term orbital behavior of the Europa probe.

In order to study the long-term evolution behavior of the Galilean moon probe, researchers applied the mean element theory to eliminate the short-period variations in the orbital elements [4,5]. It was first employed to construct the secular evolution model with respect to classic orbital elements under the non-spherical gravitation perturbation of the central body such as the zonal terms J2 and J3 [6], the harmonic term C22 [7], and irregular celestial body shapes [8,9]. Later, the third-body gravitation perturbation of the planet was taken into account, and the secular evolution behavior was studied in the planetary system exploration mission [5,10–12]. Scheeres et al. [11] and Broucke [13] derived the secular Lagrange equations of a Europa probe under Europa's non-spherical gravitation and Jovian third-body gravitation perturbations. They both employed a double-averaging method to eliminate the periodic terms of the motions of the probe around Europa and of Europa around Jupiter. The orbits around Europa are summarized as the stable orbits with low inclinations and the unstable orbits with high inclinations. More recently, further studies were performed to search for frozen orbits around Europa by considering more complex dynamic models [14–17]. The studies focus on the behaviors of the frozen orbits in aspect of the eccentricity, inclination, and argument of periapsis, which denote the motion with respect to the central moon. The evolution of the longitude of the ascending node, which represents the orbital behavior with respect to another Galilean moon, is always neglected. However, in order to achieve a stable condition for transmission, for instance, a moon-synchronous behavior, the evolution of the longitude of the ascending node should also be taken into account.

In previous studies, the methods of designing a series of synchronous orbits were proposed, such as the sun-synchronous orbit in the Sun–Earth system [18,19], around a comet [20], and the lunar synchronous orbit in the Earth–Moon system [21]. These synchronous orbits are generated by drifting the longitude of the ascending node in specific periods considering non-spherical gravitation perturbation [18] and solar radiation pressure [20]. A Galilean-moon-synchronous orbit, taking the Ganymede-synchronous orbit around Europa as an example, experiences a periodic behavior with respect to Ganymede. When Europa and Ganymede are synodic, the angle between the Europa–Ganymede vector and the normal vector of the orbital plane is a constant. Consequently, the orbit possesses a fixed spatial geometry with respect to Ganymede, which provides a periodic observing chance of Ganymede and a constant data transmission configuration between the Europa probe and the Ganymede lander. However, although the perturbation on the Europa probe from Ganymede gravity is small [22–24], this perturbation continues to accumulate due to the fixed space geometry. This brings about a long-term effect on the orbital evolution of the Europa probe. However, the corresponding evolution behavior has not been analyzed yet. Meanwhile, due to the fact that the orbital conditions of the synchronous are strict, an orbital maneuver is employed to loosen the constraint of the orbital condition and to generate the artificial synchronous orbits. Macdonald et al. generated an artificial sun-synchronous orbit by maintaining the right ascension of the ascending node [18]. This orbit can be of arbitrary inclination and semi-major axis. Wang et al. developed control strategies to eliminate the drift of the argument of periapsis and generated artificial sun-synchronous frozen orbits [25]. Wu et al. proposed a design method for an artificial sun-synchronous frozen orbit around Mars [26]. These research examples illustrate that an orbital maneuver can be executed to maintain the orbital elements to satisfy specific orbital constraints and generate artificial orbits.

This paper addresses the problem of the orbit evolution behavior of a Europa probe under Ganymede's gravitation perturbation and generates a Ganymede-synchronous frozen orbit around Europa. The main contributions are summarized as follows: (1) Long-term Lagrange planetary equations for a Europa probe considering multiple gravitation perturbations are derived. Due to a transient impact on the probe when Ganymede is close to Europa, Ganymede's gravitation is considered using an averaging method and a numerically double averaging framework [27]. Then, the Lagrange equations of the Europa probe in terms of classical orbital elements are obtained. (2) The long-term evolution behavior for a high-inclination near-circular orbit is analyzed. Since the perturbation of Ganymede's gravitation accumulates, the analysis was conducted by numerical simulations to estimate the major influence on the orbit. The orbital conditions of the Ganymede-synchronous frozen orbit are summarized on the basis of these behaviors. (3) A design method for a Ganymede-synchronous frozen orbit is developed. In order to maintain a fixed perturbing effect of Ganymede's gravitation, the design method is searching for an orbit with a synchronous behavior with respect to the longitude of the ascending node, and frozen behavior with respect to the inclination and argument of periapsis. Inspired by [28], the impulsive consumption of orbit maintenance is evaluated. The rest of the paper is organized as follows: In Section 2, a dynamic model of a Europa probe considering Jovian and Europa's non-spherical gravitations is introduced. Long-term perturbation potential and corresponding Lagrange's equations are derived based on the double-averaging method in Section 3. Then, the analyses of the orbital behaviors are performed in Section 4. Finally, the conclusion of the paper is presented in Section 5.

2. Dynamic Model

For the Jupiter–Europa–Ganymede–probe system where Europa and Ganymede are orbiting around Jupiter and the probe is orbiting around Europa, the coordinate systems and the equations of motion are established in this section. Then, a Legendre expansion is performed to simplify the perturbing potential.

2.1. Dynamical Model of Europa Probe

When Ganymede's gravitation is considered, the perturbation effects on a Europa probe include Europa's non-spherical gravitation and Jovian and Ganymede's third-body gravitations. In this case, the perturbing potential from Europa's non-spherical gravitation is calculated in the Europa-centric coordinate system, while the perturbing potentials from Jovian and Ganymede's gravities and their positions are generally obtained in the Jovian-centric coordinate system. These coordinate systems and corresponding parameters are shown in Figure 1. In this figure, the Jovian-centric Jovian equator inertial (JCI) coordinate system $[X_J, Y_J, Z_J]$ and Jovian equator are shown in black. The X_J-axis points to the Jupiter equinox, the Z_J-axis is aligned with the Jupiter rotation axis, and the Y_J-axis completes the right-handed frame. The Europa-centric inertial (ECI) coordinate system $[X_E, Y_E, Z_E]$ and Ganymede-centric inertial coordinate system $[X_G, Y_G, Z_G]$, which also represent the revolutions of Europa and Ganymede around Jupiter, are illustrated in red and blue, respectively. The X_E-axis is in the intersection line between the Jovian equator and Europa's revolution plane, the Z_E-axis is normal to Europa's revolution plane, and the Y_E-axis satisfies the positively oriented frame. In this case, the angle between X_J and X_E is defined as the longitude of the ascending node Ω_E of Europa's revolution orbit with respect to Jupiter, and the angle between the fundamental planes of these two systems is the inclination i_E of Europa's revolution orbit. It should be noted that Europa's equator and Europa's revolution plane around Jupiter are assumed as coplanar since the axial tilt between these two planes around Jupiter is 0.0965°. Similarly, the X_G-axis coincides with the intersection between the Jovian equator and Ganymede's revolution plane, the Z_G-axis is normal to Ganymede's revolution plane, and the Y_G-axis completes the right-hand frame. The angle between X_J and X_G defines the longitude of the ascending node Ω_G of Ganymede's revolution orbit around Jupiter. Additionally, the angle between the fundamental planes of these two systems is the inclination i_G of Ganymede's revolution plane.

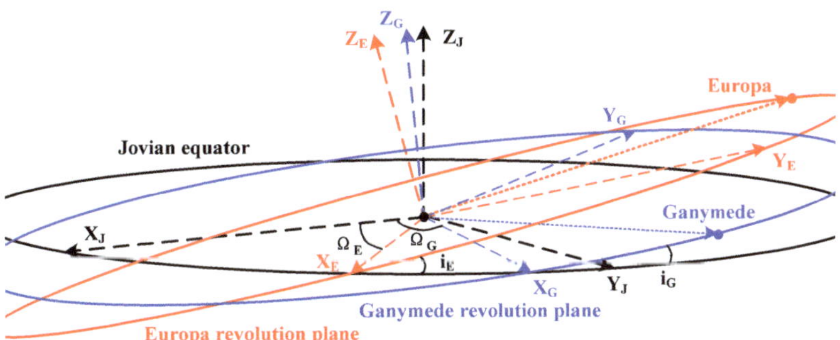

Figure 1. The definition of coordinate systems for a Europa probe.

Depending on the definition of the Europa probe, the motion of the probe is described in the Europa-centric inertial coordinate system and suffers from the perturbations from Europa's non-spherical gravitation, Jovian third-body gravitation, and Ganymede's third-body gravitation. According to the research of Cinelli [17], as the mass of the probe is much smaller than those of Europa, Jupiter, and Ganymede, the equation of motion of the Europa probe can be expressed as:

$$\frac{d^2\boldsymbol{r}}{dt^2} = -\mu_{\mathrm{E}}\frac{\boldsymbol{r}}{r^3} - \mu_{\mathrm{J}}\left(\frac{\boldsymbol{r}_{\mathrm{JP}}}{r_{\mathrm{JP}}^3} + \frac{\boldsymbol{r}_{\mathrm{EJ}}}{r_{\mathrm{EJ}}^3}\right) - \mu_G\left(\frac{\boldsymbol{r}_{\mathrm{GP}}}{r_{\mathrm{GP}}^3} + \frac{\boldsymbol{r}_{\mathrm{EG}}}{r_{\mathrm{EG}}^3}\right) \tag{1}$$

where $\ddot{\boldsymbol{r}}$ represents the acceleration vector of the probe; μ_E, μ_J, μ_G are the gravitational parameters of Europa, Jupiter, and Ganymede, respectively; $\boldsymbol{r}$ represents the position vector of the probe in an Europa-centric inertial coordinate system, $r = ||\boldsymbol{r}||$; $\boldsymbol{r}_{\mathrm{JP}}$ and $\boldsymbol{r}_{\mathrm{EJ}}$ are the vectors from Jupiter to the probe and from Europa to Jupiter, $r_{\mathrm{JP}} = ||\boldsymbol{r}_{\mathrm{JP}}||$, $r_{\mathrm{EJ}} = ||\boldsymbol{r}_{\mathrm{EJ}}||$, respectively; $\boldsymbol{r}_{\mathrm{GP}}$ and $\boldsymbol{r}_{\mathrm{EG}}$ are the vectors from Ganymede to the probe and from Europa to Ganymede, $r_{\mathrm{GP}} = ||\boldsymbol{r}_{\mathrm{GP}}||$, $r_{\mathrm{EG}} = ||\boldsymbol{r}_{\mathrm{EG}}||$, respectively.

Based on the above equation of motion, the perturbing potential on the probe due to Europa's non-spherical gravitation is given by [17]

$$\mathrm{R_E} = \frac{\mu_{\mathrm{E}}}{r}\left[1 - \frac{J_2 R_{\mathrm{E}}^2}{2r^2}\left(3\sin^2\varphi - 1\right)\right] \tag{2}$$

where J_2 represents the coefficient of Europa's $\mathrm{J_2}$ non-spherical gravitation; R_{E} represents Europa's radius; φ is the latitude of the probe regarding to the Europa.

Moreover, the perturbing potential on the probe due to Jovian gravitation is given as follows [17]:

$$\mathrm{R_J} = \frac{\mu_J}{r_{\mathrm{JP}}} - \frac{\mu_{\mathrm{J}}}{r_{\mathrm{EJ}}^3}\boldsymbol{r}\cdot\boldsymbol{r}_{\mathrm{EJ}} \tag{3}$$

The perturbing potential on the probe due to Ganymede's gravity is given as follows:

$$\mathrm{R_G} = \frac{\mu_{\mathrm{G}}}{r_{\mathrm{GP}}} - \frac{\mu_{\mathrm{G}}}{r_{\mathrm{EG}}^3}\boldsymbol{r}\cdot\boldsymbol{r}_{\mathrm{EJ}} \tag{4}$$

Moreover, the relative positions between Jupiter, Europa, Ganymede, and the probe are illustrated in Figure 2. The angle α is the angle between the distances r (the distance between the probe and Europa) and r_{EG} (the distance between Europa and Ganymede). Meanwhile, angle β defines the angle between the distances r_{EJ} (the distance between Europa and Jupiter) and r_{JG} (the distance between Jupiter and Ganymede). Consequently, distance r_{GP}, from Ganymede to the probe, is determined by distances r, r_{JE}, and r_{JG}, as well as the angles α and β, which can be calculated in a simple trigonometric way as follows:

$$r_{\mathrm{GP}} = \sqrt{r^2 + r_{\mathrm{EG}}^2 - 2rr_{\mathrm{EG}}\cos\alpha} \tag{5}$$

$$r_{\mathrm{EG}} = \sqrt{r_{\mathrm{JG}}^2 + r_{\mathrm{EJ}}^2 - 2r_{\mathrm{JG}}r_{\mathrm{EJ}}\cos\beta} \tag{6}$$

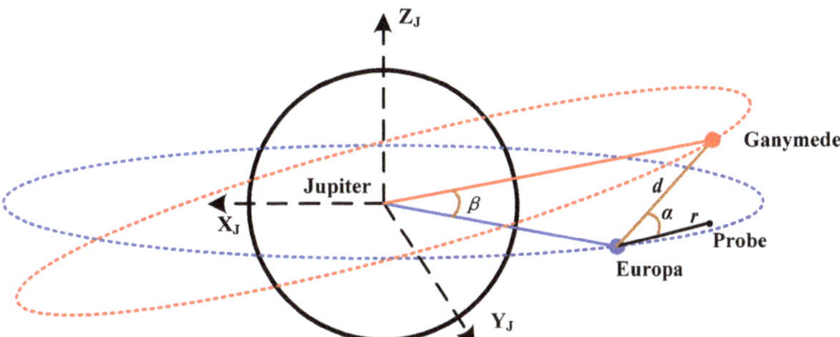

Figure 2. Positions of the planet, moons, and the probe.

The intersection angles α and β can be calculated as follows:

$$\cos\alpha = \frac{1}{r_{\mathrm{EG}}}(K_1 \cos u + K_2 \sin u) \tag{7}$$

$$\begin{aligned} \cos\beta &= \cos\Delta\Omega_{\mathrm{III}} \cos u_{\mathrm{E}} \cos u_{\mathrm{G}} + \sin\Delta\Omega_{\mathrm{III}} \cos i_{\mathrm{G}} \cos u_{\mathrm{E}} \sin u_{\mathrm{G}} \\ &- \sin\Delta\Omega_{\mathrm{III}} \cos i_{\mathrm{E}} \sin u_{\mathrm{E}} \cos u_{\mathrm{G}} \\ &+ (\cos\Delta\Omega_{\mathrm{III}} \cos i_{\mathrm{E}} \cos i_{\mathrm{G}} + \sin i_{\mathrm{E}} \sin i_{\mathrm{G}}) \sin u_{\mathrm{E}} \sin u_{\mathrm{G}} \end{aligned} \tag{8}$$

where a, e, I, Ω, ω, and f are semi-major axis, eccentricity, inclination, longitude of the ascending node, argument of periapsis, and true anomaly, respectively, which constitutes the set of orbital elements oe, oe = $[a, e, i, \Omega, \omega, f]$. The symbol u is defined as the argument of latitude, $u = \omega + f$. Particularly, the orbital elements without subscript denote the orbit of the probe in the ECI coordinate system. The subscripts "E" and "G" represents the orbital elements of Europa and Ganymede in the JCI coordinate system. $\Delta\Omega_{\mathrm{III}}$ is the difference of longitude of the ascending node between Ganymede's and Europa's revolution orbits, $\Delta\Omega_{\mathrm{III}} = \Omega_{\mathrm{E}} - \Omega_{\mathrm{G}}$. The detailed expressions of variables K_1 and K_2 are given in Equations (35)–(39) of Appendix A.

Meanwhile, because Europa's and Ganymede's revolution orbits around Jupiter are near-circular, this study also considered the simplified conditions that the eccentricities of Europa's and Ganymede's revolution orbits are 0, and the inclinations of both Galilean moons are 0°. In these situations, both longitudes of the ascending nodes and arguments of periapsis of these two moons are 0°, respectively. These conditions are summarized as follows

$$\begin{cases} e_{\mathrm{E}} = 0,\ i_{\mathrm{E}} = 0,\ \Omega_{\mathrm{E}} = 0,\ \omega_{\mathrm{E}} = 0 \\ e_{\mathrm{G}} = 0,\ i_{\mathrm{G}} = 0,\ \Omega_{\mathrm{G}} = 0,\ \omega_{\mathrm{G}} = 0 \end{cases} \tag{9}$$

Therefore, the distance between Europa and Ganymede is simplified as below:

$$r'_{\mathrm{EG}} = \sqrt{a_{\mathrm{G}}^2 + a_{\mathrm{E}}^2 - 2a_{\mathrm{G}}a_{\mathrm{E}} \cos\beta} \tag{10}$$

and angle β in Equation (10) is given as $\beta = f_{\mathrm{G}} - f_{\mathrm{E}}$. The position vectors in Equations (5)–(8) are derived as follows:

$$\begin{cases} X_{\mathrm{EG}} = a_{\mathrm{G}} \cos f_{\mathrm{G}} - a_{\mathrm{E}} \cos f_{\mathrm{E}} \\ Y_{\mathrm{EG}} = a_{\mathrm{G}} \sin f_{\mathrm{G}} - a_{\mathrm{E}} \sin f_{\mathrm{E}} \\ Z_{\mathrm{EG}} = 0 \end{cases} \tag{11}$$

It should be emphasized that since Europa and Ganymede are Galilean moons orbiting around Jupiter, the Europa–Ganymede distance r_{EG} oscillates significantly, which makes the mean relative motion of Ganymede around Europa significantly different from that in other cases due to the apparent motion of Jupiter around Europa. The long-term orbit evolution behaviors of the Europa probe under the proposed accurate model and simplified model are investigated in the next section.

2.2. Legendre Expansion

Since previous studies have already discussed the long-term effect of Europa's non-spherical gravitation perturbation and Jovian gravitation perturbation, the influence of Ganymede's third-body gravitation perturbation is the main focus here. In order to simplify the derivation, the perturbing potential in Equation (4) is split into individual terms as follows:

$$\begin{cases} R_{G,a} = \frac{\mu_G}{r_{GP}} \\ R_{G,b} = -\frac{\mu_G r \cos\alpha}{r_{EG}^2} \end{cases} \quad (12)$$

According to Equations (5), (6), and (12), the perturbing effect from Ganymede's gravitation on the probe depends on the relative motion between Ganymede and Europa, especially the relative distance r_{EG} in Equation (6).

Based on the classic Legendre expansion method in Appendix A, the perturbing potential $R_{G,a}$ is given in Equation (16). Considering the magnitudes of distances r and r_{EG}, the expansion is truncated to zero order, first order, and second order, respectively.

$$\begin{cases} R_{G,a,0} = \frac{\mu_G}{r_{EG}} \\ R_{G,a,1} = \frac{\mu_G r}{r_{EG}^2} \cos\alpha \\ R_{G,a,2} = \mu_G \frac{r^2}{2r_{EG}^3}\left(3\cos^2\alpha - 1\right) \end{cases} \quad (13)$$

From Equation (13), the zero-order term of the Ganymede gravitation potential is irrelevant to the orbital elements of the probe. Therefore, this term is neglected in the following analysis. Furthermore, the first-order term compensates the potential $R_{G,b}$ in Equation (12). Therefore, the potential term $R_{G,a,2}$ dominates the Ganymede gravitation perturbation on the long-term evolution of Europa probe.

Furthermore, according to Equation (12), the variable that denotes the relative motion of Ganymede to Europa is the Europa–Ganymede distance r_{EG}. From the definition in Equation (6), the distance r_{EG} is determined by the motions of Europa and Ganymede, whose orbits are not exactly circular and coplanar. In this situation, it is difficult to analytically expand the distance r_{EG} to high order. Consequently, only the mean motion of the Europa probe is considered rather than the accurate model. Then, applying the simplified model in Equations (10) and (11), both the mean motion of the Europa probe and the mean relative motion of Ganymede around Europa are considered. The Legendre expansion is employed again towards the Europa–Ganymede distance r_{EG}. Since the magnitudes of Europa's and Ganymede's semi-major axes are approximated, the expression of the distance r_{EG} is truncated up to the fifth order (about 0.1 of order of magnitude) to guarantee the accuracy.

3. Long-Term Evolution and Analysis

In order to develop a Ganymede-synchronous frozen orbit around Europa, this section first derives the mean motion of the Europa probe. Then, the control strategy for generating a Ganymede-synchronous frozen orbit is provided.

3.1. Double-Averaging Method

In the Europa probe case, the magnitude of the orbital period for 1RE-3RE of semi-major axis is 10^4, while the revolution periods of Jovian and Ganymede's apparent motions around Europa are about 3×10^5 s and 6×10^5 s, respectively. Therefore, the motion of the probe can be considered as a fast variable. Consequently, the secular effect of Ganymede gravitation can be obtained by eliminating the short-period term oscillations with a double-averaging method. The first averaging is performed regarding the mean motion of the probe to obtain the mean variations of the orbital elements in one orbital period:

$$\langle R \rangle = \frac{1}{T}\int_0^T R(t)dt = \frac{1}{2\pi}\int_0^{2\pi} \frac{R(f)\eta^3}{(1+e\cos f)^2}df \quad (14)$$

where $T = 2\pi/n$ represents the orbital period of the probe and $n = \sqrt{\mu/a^3}$ is its related mean motion, while $\eta = \sqrt{1-e^2}$.

Then, the second averaging is performed with respect to Ganymede's apparent motion around Europa to obtain the mean variations in one revolution period. This second averaging is given as follows:

$$\langle\langle \mathrm{R} \rangle\rangle = \frac{1}{T_{\mathrm{A,G}}}\int_0^{T_{A,G}} \langle \mathrm{R} \rangle dt = \frac{1}{2\pi}\int_0^{2\pi} \frac{\eta_{\mathrm{E}}^3 \langle \mathrm{R} \rangle}{(1+e_{\mathrm{E}}\cos f_{\mathrm{E}})^2} df_{\mathrm{E}} \tag{15}$$

where T_{A} represents the periods of Jovian and Ganymede's apparent motions around Europa. The Jovian apparent motion period T_{A} equals the revolution period of Europa around Jupiter. The period of Ganymede's apparent motion $T_{\mathrm{A,G}}$ is the synodic period of the relative motion of Ganymede to Europa as shown in Equation (15), where $n_{\mathrm{E}} = \sqrt{\mu_{\mathrm{J}}/a_{\mathrm{E}}^3}$ and $n_{\mathrm{G}} = \sqrt{\mu_{\mathrm{J}}/a_{\mathrm{G}}^3}$. It should be noted that the orbit of Ganymede's apparent motion around Europa is not a conic curve, and hence the right part of Equation (15) is invalid for Ganymede's mean motion.

$$T_{\mathrm{A,G}} = \frac{2\pi}{n_{\mathrm{E}} - n_{\mathrm{G}}} \tag{16}$$

Using the double-averaging method, the mean motion of the probe under Europa's non-spherical gravitation, Jovian third-body gravitation and Ganymede's third-body gravitation is obtained.

3.2. Mean Motion of the Probe around Europa

Based on the perturbing potential $R_{\mathrm{G,a,2}}$, an accurate Europa–Ganymede distance r_{EG} is first derived with the averaging method in Equation (14). The average potential of the probe under Ganymede's gravitation in one orbit period is given as follows:

$$\begin{aligned}\langle \mathrm{R}_{\mathrm{G,a,2}} \rangle &= \tfrac{\mu_{\mathrm{G}} a^2}{2r_{\mathrm{EG}}^5}\left[\tfrac{3}{2}K_1^2(5e^2\cos^2\omega - e^2 + 1) + \tfrac{3}{2}K_2^2(5e^2\sin^2\omega - e^2 + 1)\right. \\ &\left. +9K_1K_2e^2\sin\omega\cos\omega - \tfrac{3}{2}e^2 + 1\right]\end{aligned} \tag{17}$$

where the definitions of K_1 and K_2 are provided in Appendix A.

Since Ganymede's apparent motion around Europa is non-elliptical, the Europa–Ganymede distance r_{EG} is time-varying significantly, which makes it difficult to derive Ganymede's mean apparent motion analytically using the double-averaging method in Equation (18). In this situation, the average potential for the Europa probe under Europa's non-spherical gravitation and Jovian and Ganymede's third-body gravitation is given as:

$$\langle \mathrm{R}_{\mathrm{A}} \rangle = \langle \mathrm{R}_{\mathrm{G,a,2}} \rangle + \langle\langle \mathrm{R}_{\mathrm{E}} \rangle\rangle + \langle\langle \mathrm{R}_{\mathrm{J}} \rangle\rangle \tag{18}$$

$$\langle\langle \mathrm{R}_{\mathrm{E}} \rangle\rangle = \frac{\mu_{\mathrm{E}} J_{2,\mathrm{E}}}{4a^3\eta^3}\left(2 - 3\sin^2 i\right) \tag{19}$$

$$\langle\langle \mathrm{R}_{\mathrm{J}} \rangle\rangle = \frac{\mu_{\mathrm{J}} a^2}{4a_{\mathrm{E}}^3}\left[\left(1 - \frac{3}{2}\sin^2 i\right)\left(1 + \frac{3}{2}e^2\right) + \frac{15}{4}e^2\cos 2\omega \sin^2 i\right] \tag{20}$$

It should be emphasized that since the orbit of the probe and that of Jovian apparent motion around Europa are both near-circular, the double-averaging method is employed to eliminate the short-period terms of the probe and Jovian motions in research [11].

By substituting the potential term with the accurate average potential in the Lagrange planetary equations (seeing Appendix B), the equations of motion of the orbital elements are obtained analytically. The long-term evolution model for the Europa probe is given as follows:

$$\frac{da}{dt} = 0 \tag{21}$$

$$\frac{de}{dt}=\frac{3\mu_G\eta e}{4nr_{EG}^5}\left[5\left(K_1^2-K_2^2\right)\sin 2\omega-6K_1K_2\cos 2\omega\right]+\frac{15\mu_J\eta e}{8a_E^3 n}\sin^2 i\sin 2\omega \tag{22}$$

$$\begin{aligned}\frac{di}{dt}= & -\frac{3\mu_G}{4n\sin i r_{EG}^5}\left[\cos i e^2\left(5K_1^2\cos 2\omega-5K_2^2\cos 2\omega-6K_1K_2\cos 2\omega\right)\right.\\ & +2K_1K_{1,\Omega}\left(5e^2\cos 2\omega-e^2+1\right)+2K_2K_{2,\Omega}\left(5e^2\sin 2\omega-e^2+1\right)\\ & \left.+3e^2\left(K_{1,\Omega}K_2+K_1K_{2,\Omega}\right)\sin 2\omega\right]-\frac{15\mu_J e^2}{16a_E^3 n\eta}\sin 2i\sin 2\omega\end{aligned} \tag{23}$$

$$\begin{aligned}\frac{d\Omega}{dt}= & \frac{3\mu_G}{4\sin i r_{EG}^5}\left[2K_2K_{2,i}\left(5e^2\sin^2\omega-e^2+1\right)+3e^2K_1K_{2,i}\sin 2\omega\right]\\ & \frac{3\mu_J\cos i}{8a_E^3 n\eta}\left(5e^2\cos 2\omega-3e^2-2\right)-\frac{3J_2nR_E^2}{2a^2\eta^4}\cos i\end{aligned} \tag{24}$$

$$\begin{aligned}\frac{d\omega}{dt}= & \frac{3\mu_G\eta}{2nr_{EG}^5}\left[K_1^2\left(5\cos^2\omega-1\right)+K_2^2\left(5\sin^2\omega-1\right)+3K_1K_2\sin 2\omega-1\right]\\ & +\frac{3\mu_J}{8a_E^3 n\eta}\left[5\cos^2 i-1+5\sin^2 i\cos 2\omega+e^2(1-5\cos 2\omega)\right]+\frac{3J_2nR_E^2}{4a^2\eta^4}\left(5\cos^2 i-1\right)\end{aligned} \tag{25}$$

It can be seen from the Lagrange equations that the semi-major axis keeps constant during the evolution, which means that Ganymede's gravitation has no secular influence on the orbital energy of the probe. The variables in these Lagrange equations are provided in Equation (6) and in Equations (32)–(36) of Appendix A. Furthermore, although the analytical form of the mean potential of Ganymede's gravity is difficult to obtain, the long-term evolution behavior of the probe can be studied following the accurate and simplified model using numerical propagation. Based on the double-averaging method in Equation (15), the average Lagrange equations of the probe's orbital elements are computed as follows:

$$\left\langle\left\langle\frac{d\varphi}{dt}\right\rangle\right\rangle=\frac{1}{T_{A,G}}\int_0^{T_{A,G}}\left\langle\frac{d\varphi}{dt}\right\rangle dt \tag{26}$$

where φ represents the orbital element of the probe.

To validate the long-term evolution behavior based on the double-averaging method, a large-eccentricity, high-inclination orbit is taken as an example to simulate the orbital behavior under the accurate average model. The adopted values of the gravitational parameters of Jupiter, Europa, and Ganymede are given in Table 1. The initial orbital conditions of the probe are set to for $a = 1.2\,R_E$, $i = 93°$, $\Omega = 0°$, and $\omega = 0°$, unless otherwise specified in the following simulations. Eccentricity $e = 0.1$ is selected, and the evolution duration is set as 150 days. The orbital evolutions of the eccentricity, inclination, longitude of the ascending node and argument of periapsis are given in Figure 3. Blue and red curves represent the oscillating and mean orbits, respectively. Note that the semi-major axis remains constant and is not propagated.

Table 1. Dynamical parameters of the Jovian system [23,24].

Parameter	Value
μ_J	126,686,534.9218 km^3/s^2
μ_E	3202.74 km^3/s^2
μ_G	9887.83 km^3/s^2
$J_{2,E}$	0.0004355
R_E	1560.8 km
a_E	671,100 km
e_E	0.0094
i_E	0.465°
a_G	1,070,587.5 km
e_G	0.00195
i_G	0.135°

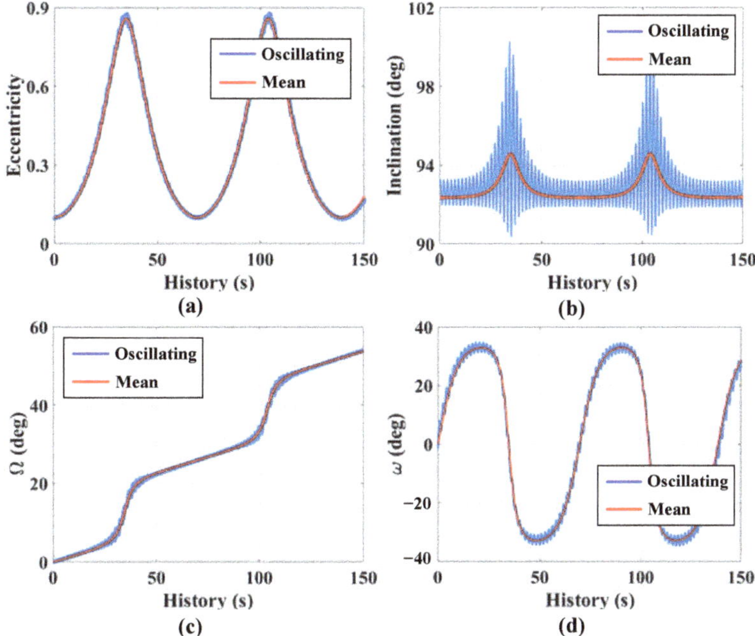

Figure 3. Evolution behavior of a probe around Europa, for a = 1.2 R_E, e = 0.1, i = 93°, Ω = 0°, and ω = 0°. Subplots (**a–d**) are the behaviors of the eccentricity, inclination, longitude of the ascending node and argument of periapsis, respectively.

As shown in Figure 3, the long-term evolution tendencies of the mean orbital elements and the oscillating orbital elements are consistent with each other. By removing the short-period oscillation, the evolution of the mean elements are smoother than that of the oscillating elements, which makes the mean orbit more applicable for the analysis of long-term evolution. Moreover, the orbital elements also suffer from long-period oscillations, which is similar to the research by Scheeres et al. [11]. This behavior suggests that Europa's non-spherical gravitation and Jovian third-body gravitation are the major perturbations, while Ganymede's gravitation is the weak perturbation. In the next section, the perturbing effect of Ganymede's gravitation on the secular motion of the Europa probe is further analyzed, and a Ganymede-synchronous frozen orbit is generated.

3.3. Sensitivity Analysis

Based on the long-term models in Equations (21)–(25), the effects of Ganymede's gravitation on the orbital elements with respect to the initial phase angle are studied. This initial phase angle is the difference between the initial longitude of the ascending node and the argument of latitude of Europa, i.e., $\Omega - u_E$. The average rates of change of the eccentricity and inclination are shown in Figure 4. The initial conditions of a near-circular orbit are considered by setting e = 0.001, ω = 35°. The average rates of change are propagated using the numerical integration method. From Figure 4a, it can be seen that the oscillation amplitude was four orders of magnitude smaller than the value of the rate of change, which suggests that Ganymede's gravitation perturbation on the eccentricity is weaker compared to those of Europa's non-spherical gravitation and Jovian gravitation. According to the literature [11,13], the eccentricity evolution mainly depends on the inclination and argument of periapsis.

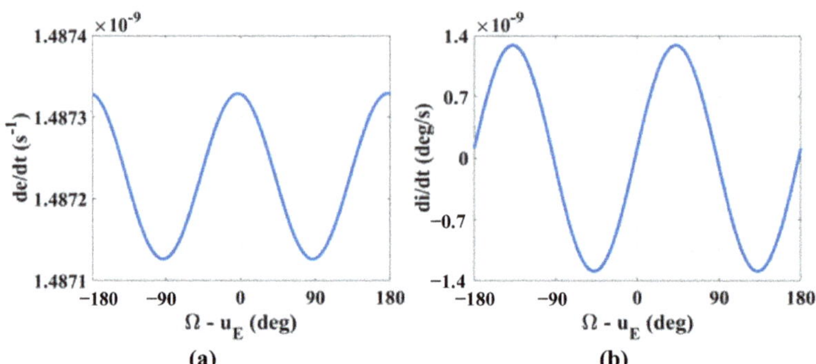

Figure 4. Rates of change of the eccentricity (**a**) and inclination (**b**), for $a = 1.2\ R_E$, $e = 0.001$, $i = 93°$, and $\omega = 35°$.

According to the average rate of change of the inclination in Figure 4b, the rate of change of the inclination oscillates significantly, which is different from that of the eccentricity. This suggests that for a near-circular orbit, the perturbing effects due to Europa's non-spherical gravitation and Jovian gravitation are small, while Ganymede's gravitation dominates the evolution of the inclination. Moreover, the initial phase angle $\Omega - u_E$ determinates the value of the average rate of change. For a Ganymede-synchronous orbit, the initial phase angle is fixed with respect to both Europa and Ganymede for each Ganymede-apparent revolution period. In this situation, the average rate of change of the inclination is constant, which drifts the inclination continuously. Four zero-rate change conditions are obtained when the initial phase angle $\Omega - u_E$ approximates $-92.5°$, $-3°$, $87.5°$, and $177°$. These conditions keep the inclination constant under Ganymede's gravitation with a Ganymede-synchronous orbit.

Moreover, the average rates of change of the longitude of the ascending node and argument of periapsis with respect to the initial phase angle $\Omega - u_E$ are studied. The initial orbital conditions of the probe are $e = 0.001$ and $\omega = 35°$. The calculation results are shown in Figure 5. Similarly, the average rates of change are propagated using the numerical integral method. According to Figure 5a, for the average rate of change of the longitude of the ascending node, the oscillation amplitude is eight orders of magnitude smaller than the value of the average rate of change. This means that Ganymede's gravitation has little effect on the longitude of the ascending node. Meanwhile, the literature [11,13] shows that the semi-major axis and inclination determine the rate of change of the longitude of the ascending node when considering Europa's non-spherical gravitation and Jovian gravitation perturbations. Therefore, to generate the Ganymede-synchronous frozen orbit, it can be assumed that the evolution of the longitude of the ascending node is decoupled with the initial phase angle $\Omega - u_E$ to simplify the design of the initial orbital conditions.

Furthermore, from Figure 5b it can be seen that the oscillation amplitude of the argument of periapsis is four orders of magnitude smaller than the value of the average rate of change. Therefore, Ganymede's gravitation perturbation on the argument of periapsis is a small disturbance. In order to generate a Ganymede-synchronous frozen orbit whose argument of periapsis is fixed, a station-keeping (SK) maneuver is employed to cancel out the slight drift caused by Ganymede's gravity.

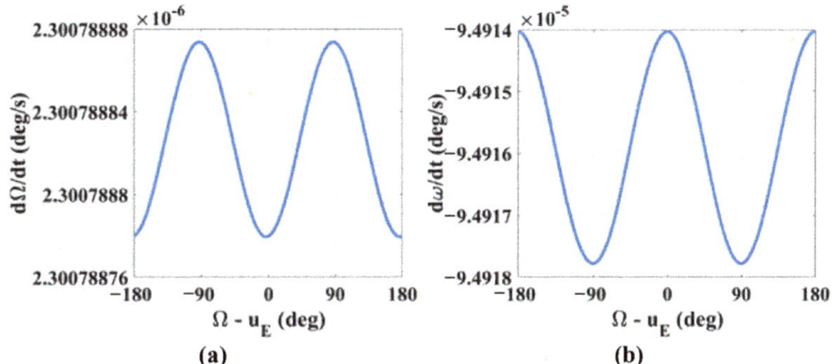

Figure 5. Rates of change of the longitude of the ascending node (**a**) and the argument of periapsis (**b**), for a = 1.2 R_E, e = 0.001, i = 93°, and ω = 35°.

Next, the rate of change of the inclination with respect to the eccentricity and inclination are studied. The results are shown in Figure 6 for i = 93° (a) and e = 0.001 (b). Note that the distributions of the rate of change in other conditions are similar and not given here. The rate of change of the inclination with respect to the eccentricity is provided in Figure 6a. According to the distribution of the rate of change of the inclination di/dt, the orbits are divided into an elliptic case (for an elliptic orbit with eccentricity larger than 0.1) and a near-circular case (with eccentricity smaller than 0.1). For an elliptic orbit, the eccentricity has an influence on the rate of change of the inclination. However, for a near-circular orbit, the rate of change of the inclination is nearly constant with respect to the eccentricity. Therefore, small eccentricity is considered for the initial condition of the Ganymede-synchronous frozen orbit. Nevertheless, the effect of the eccentricity on the rate of change of the inclination is neglected.

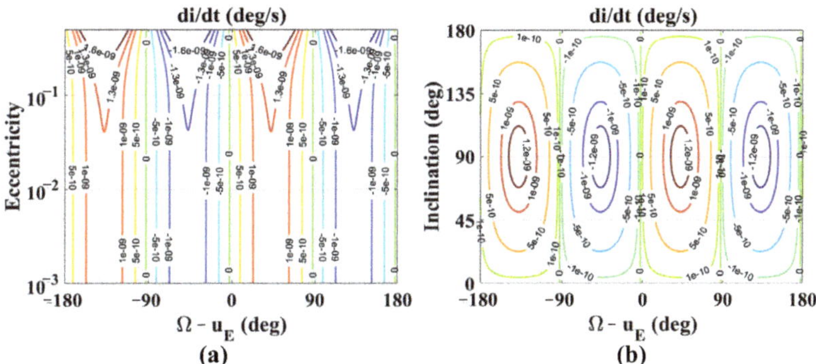

Figure 6. Rates of change of the inclination with respect to the eccentricity in subplot (**a**) and inclination (**b**) in subplot (**a**), for a = 1.2 R_E.

Then, the rate of change with respect to the inclination is shown in Figure 6b. According to Figure 6b, the rate of change of the inclination is divided into positive regions where the initial phase angle $\Omega - u_E$ is (−180°, −90°) and (0°, 90°) and negative regions where the initial phase angle $\Omega - u_E$ is (−90°, 0°) and (90°, 180°). Between these regions, the contour line of di/dt = 0 deg/sec is obtained (define this line as DIZL). Due to the fact that for the synchronous frozen orbit the initial phase angle $\Omega - u_E$ and inclination keep constant, the rate of change of the inclination is fixed. Therefore, the initial condition should locate on the DIZL to achieve the frozen behavior.

Finally, the rate of change of the inclination with respect to the argument of periapsis is analyzed. A series of eccentricities 0.1, 0.05, 0.01, and 0.001 are taken as examples to study the evolution of di/dt. The results are contoured in Figure 7 for e = 0.1 (a), e = 0.05 (b),

$e = 0.01$ (c), and $e = 0.001$ (d). According to Figure 7a for eccentricity $e = 0.1$, the argument of periapsis dominates the rate of change of the inclination for an elliptic orbit. The DIZLs are discovered when the argument of periapsis is about $-180°$, $-90°$, $0°$, and $90°$. Figure 7b,c show the transition of di/dt between the elliptic orbit and the near-circular orbit. With the eccentricity descending, the effect of the argument of periapsis decreases. Furthermore, for a near-circular orbit in Figure 7d, this rate of change mainly depends on the initial phase angle $\Omega - u_E$. The initial phase angles $\Omega - u_E$ of the DIZL are about $-91°$, $-1°$, $89°$, and $179°$. Therefore, when a near-circular Ganymede-synchronous orbit is considered, the initial argument of periapsis can be chosen arbitrarily.

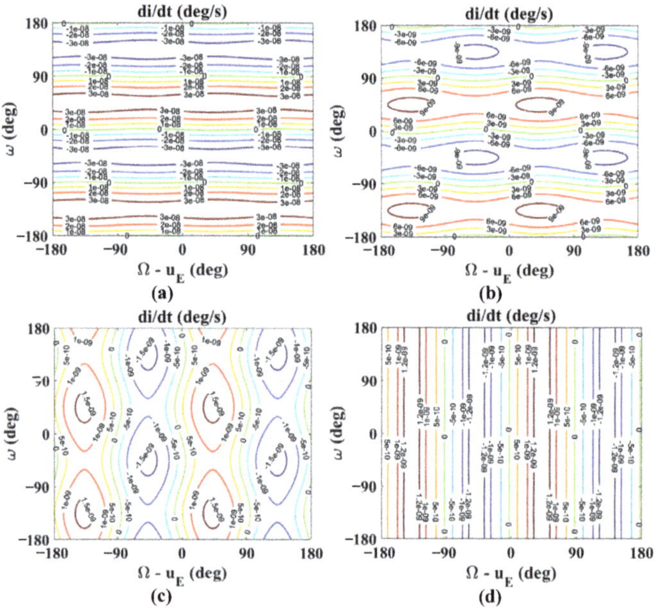

Figure 7. Rates of change of the inclination with respect to the argument of periapsis for $e = 0.1$ (**a**), $e = 0.05$ (**b**), $e = 0.01$ (**c**), and $e = 0.001$ (**d**).

4. Design of a Ganymede-Synchronous Frozen Orbit

4.1. Conditions of Synchronous Frozen Orbit

A Ganymede-synchronous frozen orbit around Europa constitutes synchronous behavior with respect to Ganymede and frozen behavior in terms of the orbital elements. For Ganymede-synchronous behavior, when the Europa–Ganymede distance r_{EG} approaches the minimum, the intersection angle of the orbital plane and the Europa–Ganymede vector should be a constant. Consequently, the geometry between the orbit and Ganymede is fixed. This Ganymede-synchronous condition can be described as in Equation (27). The rate of change of the longitude of the ascending node should be equal to the drift rate of the elongation in the inertial coordinate system to achieve Ganymede-synchronous behavior.

$$\left\langle\left\langle\frac{d\Omega}{dt}\right\rangle\right\rangle = \frac{du}{dt} \tag{27}$$

According to the synodic motion between Europa and Ganymede, the drift rate of the elongation is given as follows:

$$\frac{du}{dt} = 2n_G - n_E \tag{28}$$

In addition, the literature [17] shows that a large velocity increment (ΔV) is needed to freeze the eccentricity because of the drift of the argument of periapsis. A more cost-efficient way is to freeze the inclination and argument of periapsis. Meanwhile, the value of the argument of periapsis should be in the regions of (−90°, 0°) and (90°, 180°), where the eccentricity continuously decreases. In this situation, the orbit keeps circularizing and achieves a long lifetime. These frozen conditions are summarized as follows:

$$\left\langle\left\langle \frac{di}{dt} \right\rangle\right\rangle = 0 \tag{29}$$

$$\left\langle\left\langle \frac{d\omega}{dt} \right\rangle\right\rangle = 0 \tag{30}$$

4.2. Preliminary Design of a Ganymede-Synchronous Frozen Orbit

Based on the dynamical evolution of the orbital elements and the conditions of the synchronous frozen orbit, the design method for a Ganymede-synchronous frozen orbit was developed. Since the accurate model is time-varying, it is difficult to analytically design a Ganymede-synchronous frozen orbit. Therefore, a preliminary design method based on the simplified model was developed and is given in Algorithm 1.

Algorithm 1 Design Method for a Ganymede-Synchronous Frozen Orbit

Input: Semi-major axis a, eccentricity e;
Output: Inclination i, initial phase angle $\Omega - u_E$, argument of periapsis
1: Assign $oe_0 = [a, e]$ as the initial conditions;
2: Assign $\frac{d\Omega}{dt} = \frac{du}{dt}$ as the expected rate of change of the longitude of ascending node;
3. Main
4: Inclination $i \leftarrow \frac{d\Omega}{dt}$;
5: DIZL and DWZL $\left(\frac{di}{dt}, \frac{d\omega}{dt}\right) \leftarrow (a, e, i)$;
6: Initial phase angle and argument of periapsis $(\Omega - u_E, \omega) \leftarrow \left(\frac{di}{dt}, \frac{d\omega}{dt}\right)$;
7: end

Firstly, a semi-major axis is chosen according to the mission requirement. In this study, the initial eccentricity is set as e = 0.001. Then, according to literatures [11,14], the rate of change of the longitude of the ascending node is determined by the inclination. The inclination of the orbit is solved based on the synchronous condition in Equation (30). The rate of change of the longitude of the ascending node and the corresponding Ganymede-synchronous condition are shown in Figure 8. The purple dotted line represents the synchronous condition with respect to Ganymede. From Figure 8, because the drift rate of the elongation is negative, the inclination of the Ganymede-synchronous orbit ranges from 78.8° to 81.8° which is equivalent to about 98.96% and 98.98% of global coverage. For the semi-major axis a = 1.2 R_E, the obtained inclination is given as i = 78.842°.

After obtaining the inclination, the longitude of the ascending node and argument of periapsis are designed. The contour lines of the inclination di/dt = 0 deg/sec (denoted as DIZL) and argument of periapsis dω/dt = 0 deg/sec (denoted as DWZL) with respect to the eccentricity are calculated. For the inclination i = 78.842°, the intersection of DIZL and DWZL is shown in Figure 9. Blue and red points represent DIZL and DWZL, respectively. From Figure 9, it is seen that the argument of periapsis of the intersection of the DIZL and DWZL was about –133.1°, −46.9°, 46.9°, and 133.1°. In order to keep the eccentricity decreasing, the argument of periapsis ω = 133.1° was chosen as the initial condition. The intersection line with respect to eccentricity is given in Figure 10, in which the initial phase angle $\Omega - u_E$ is nearly constant when the eccentricity is small. In this situation, initial phase angle $\Omega - u_E$ = 87.46° was chosen in the preliminary design phase. This orbit was considered as an expected orbit. The method of maintaining this orbit with the accurate model is discussed in the following section.

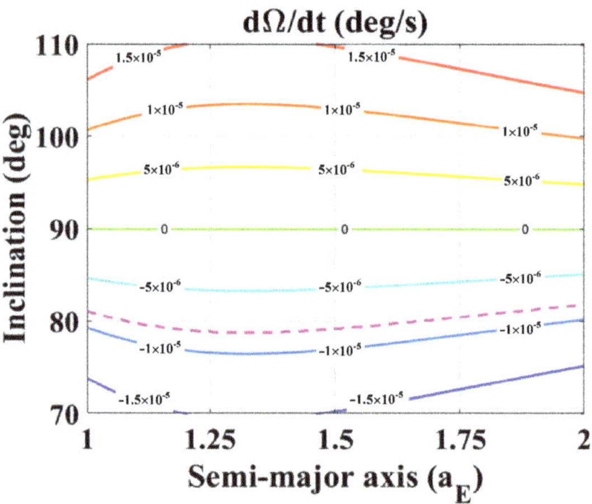

Figure 8. Rate of change of the longitude of the ascending node for $a = 1.2\ R_E$ and $e = 0.001$.

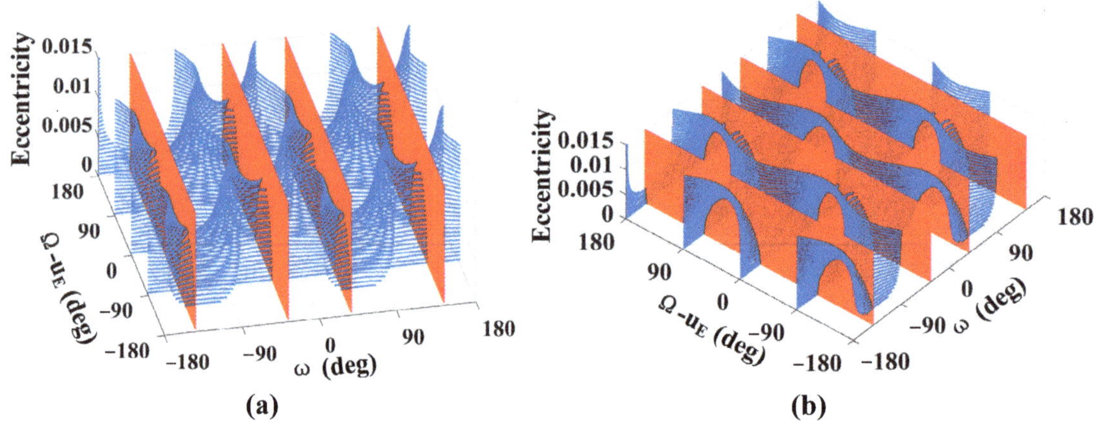

Figure 9. Distributions of DIZL and DWZL. Subplots (**a**) and (**b**) are two different viewpoints.

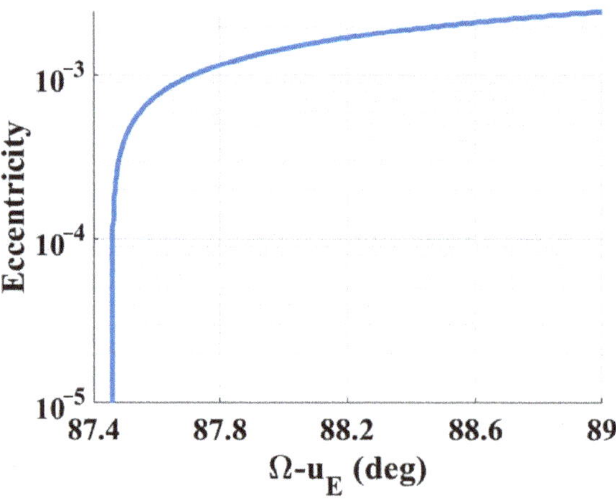

Figure 10. Distribution of DIZL.

4.3. Orbit Maintenance with Accurate Model

Since the expected orbit was designed based on the simplified model in the preliminary phase, the actual orbit under an accurate dynamical model naturally drifts and deviates from the expected orbit. Therefore, in this section, the SK maneuver is designed to maintain the inclination, longitude of the ascending node, and argument of periapsis at their expected values. The ΔV consumptions for the inclination, longitude of the ascending node, and argument of periapsis are evaluated by taking the impulse propulsion as follows:

$$\begin{cases} \Delta V_i = \sqrt{\frac{\mu_E}{a\eta^2}}(1 + e\cos\omega)\Delta i \\ \Delta V_\Omega = \sqrt{\frac{\mu_E}{a\eta^2}}(1 + e\sin\omega)\sin i\Delta\Omega \\ \Delta V_\omega = \sqrt{\frac{\mu_E}{a\eta^2}}\Delta\omega \end{cases} \tag{31}$$

Using this SK strategy, the Ganymede-synchronous frozen orbit was validated by a numerical simulation. Except the perturbations of Europa's J2 non-spherical gravitation, Jovian and Ganymede's third body gravitations, the perturbations of Jovian J2 non-spherical gravitation and solar gravitation were both considered to guarantee the accuracy. The initial conditions were a = 1.2 R_E, e = 0.001, i = 78.842°, Ω = 120.7575°, and ω = 133.07°. In order to achieve a collinear behavior of $u_E - e_G = 0°$, the initial date MJD was selected as MJD = 62504.384619. The SK period was set as one synodic period of the Europa–Ganymede revolution $T_{A,G}$. Fifteen numbers of SK maneuvers were performed to evaluate ΔV consumption. The evolution of the orbit is shown in Figure 11, and ΔV consumptions of the inclination (blue line), longitude of the ascending node (black line), and argument of periapsis (red line) are given in Figure 12.

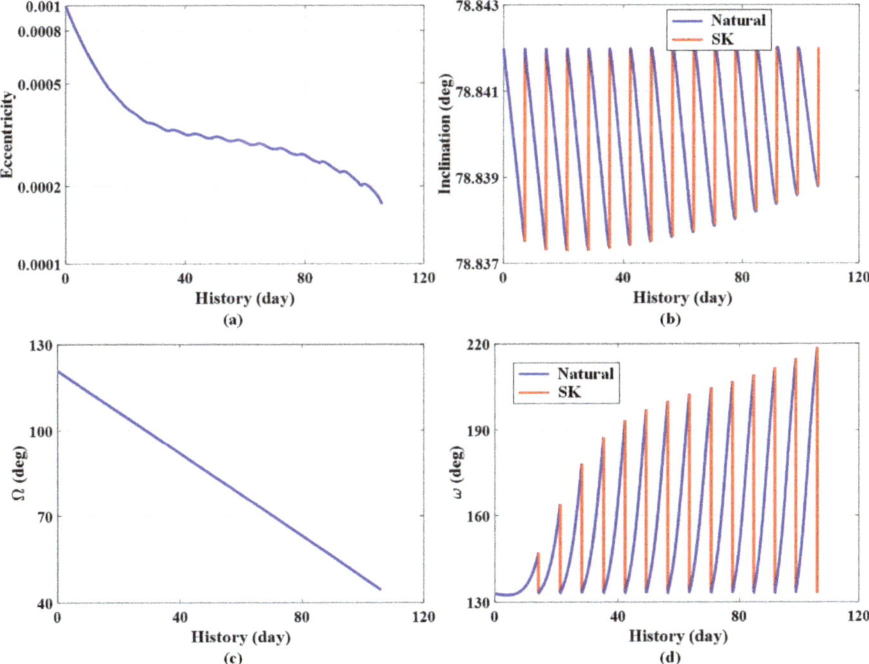

Figure 11. Evolutions of orbital elements, for a = 1.2 R_E, e = 0.001, i = 78.842°, Ω = 120.7575°, and ω = 133.07°. Subplots (**a–d**) show the evolutions of the eccentricity, inclination, longitude of the ascending node and argument of periapsis, respectively.

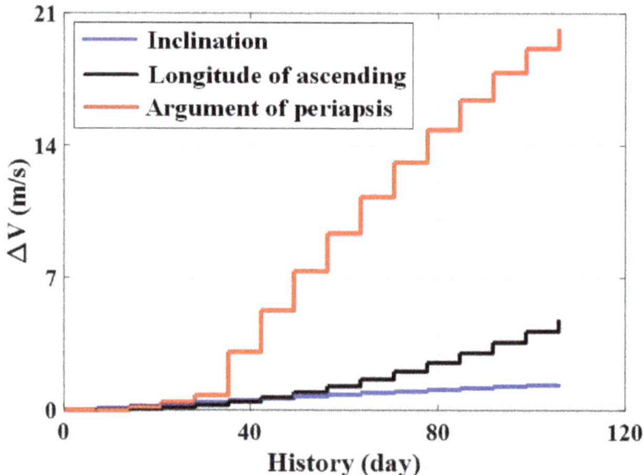

Figure 12. Consumption of the Ganymede-synchronous frozen orbit.

In Figure 11, the blue and red curves represent the evolution of natural drift and SK maneuver, respectively. According to Figure 11, the eccentricity kept decreasing, which circularized the orbit. Due to the difference between the simplified dynamical model and accurate model, the inclination oscillated in a small amplitude, while the argument of periapsis oscillated heavily. The SK maneuver was employed to directly maintain these two elements at the expected values. Meanwhile, the longitude of the ascending node kept decreasing. According to the numerical calculation, the evolution period of the longitude was about 500 days, which equaled the synodic period of Europa and Ganymede. In this situation, the orbit demonstrated Ganymede-synchronous behavior.

Furthermore, according to Figure 12, for about 105 days of evolution, the maintaining ΔV for the inclination, longitude of the ascending node, and argument of periapsis were 1.36 m/s, 4.8 m/s, and 20 m/s. The total ΔV consumption was about 26.16 m/s, which was 0.25 m/s per day. This is an acceptable ΔV for a practical mission. Most of the ΔV is consumed to maintain the argument of periapsis, while maintaining the inclination cost the least ΔV. This suggests that the effect of an accurate dynamic model has little influence on the evolution of the inclination.

5. Conclusions

This paper focuses on the long-term evolution behavior of a probe around Europa. The non-spherical gravitation perturbation of Europa and the third-body gravitation perturbations of Ganymede and Jupiter were considered to derive the Lagrange equation based on the double-averaging framework. Then, a design method of a Ganymede-synchronous frozen orbit was proposed using the simplified model. The angle between the normal vector of this orbit and the Europa–Ganymede vector is constant when Europa and Ganymede come synodic. In this situation, the Europa probe has the stable capacity to observe Ganymede and to transmit data with the Ganymede lander.

The numerical simulation showed that Ganymede's gravity has a small but continuously accumulated effect on the inclination. The rate of change of the inclination mainly depends on the argument of periapsis for an elliptic orbit, while it is determined by the phase angle between the longitude of the ascending node and the Europa–Ganymede vector. Moreover, due to the difference between the accurate model and the simplified model, the obtained orbit drifts slightly. A station-keeping maneuver was employed to maintain the longitude of the ascending node and argument of periapsis. With the proposed maintenance method, the eccentricity of the Ganymede-synchronous frozen orbit kept decreasing, while the inclination and argument of periapsis maintained the expected values. The evolution period of the longitude of the ascending node was 500 days, which achieved Ganymede-synchronous behavior. The total maintenance ΔV consumption was 26.16 m/s for 105 days of evolution, or 0.25 m/s per day, which is acceptable for practical mission application.

Author Contributions: Conceptualization, X.H. and B.Y.; methodology, X.H.; software, B.Y.; validation, X.H. and B.Y.; formal analysis, X.H.; investigation, B.Y.; resources, X.H.; data curation, X.H. and J.F.; writing—original draft preparation, B.Y. and J.F.; writing—review and editing, J.F. and J.J.M.; visualization, X.H.; supervision, S.L. and J.J.M.; project administration, S.L. and J.J.M.; funding acquisition, S.L. and J.J.M. All authors have read and agreed to the published version of the manuscript.

Funding: This research received no external funding.

Institutional Review Board Statement: Not applicable.

Informed Consent Statement: Not applicable.

Acknowledgments: The work described in this paper was supported by the Postgraduate Research & Practice Innovation Program of Jiangsu Province (Grant No. KYCX20_0220) and the Chinese Scholarship Council (Grant No. 202006830124), funded by the Science and Technology on Space Intelligent Control Laboratory (Grant No. HTKJ2020KL502019, 6142208200203 and 2021–JCJQ–LB–010–04). The authors fully appreciate their financial support.

Conflicts of Interest: The authors declare no conflict of interest.

Appendix A

In this paper, Jovian and Ganymede's apparent motions orbiting around Europa are considered. The distance from the Europa-to-Ganymede intersection is determined by the angle α. Angle α is expressed using Equation (7), whose variables are given as follows:

$$\begin{cases} K_1 = X_{EG}\cos\Omega + Y_{EG}\sin\Omega \\ K_{1,\Omega} = -X_{EG}\sin\Omega + Y_{EG}\cos\Omega \end{cases} \tag{A1}$$

$$\begin{cases} K_2 = -X_{EG}\sin\Omega\cos i + Y_{EG}\cos\Omega\cos i + Z_{EG}\sin i \\ K_{2,i} = X_{EG}\sin\Omega\sin i - Y_{EG}\cos\Omega\sin i + Z_{EG}\cos i \\ K_{2,\Omega} = -X_{EG}\cos\Omega\cos i - Y_{EG}\sin\Omega\cos i \end{cases} \tag{A2}$$

$$X_{EG} = \frac{a_G\eta_G^2}{1+e_G\cos f_G}(\cos\Delta\Omega\cos u_G - \cos i_G\sin\Delta\Omega\sin u_G) - \frac{a_G\eta_E^2}{1+e_E\cos f_E}\cos u_E \tag{A3}$$

$$\begin{aligned} Y_{EG} &= \tfrac{a_G\eta_G^2}{1+e_G\cos f_G}[\cos i_E(\sin\Delta\Omega\cos u_G + \cos i_G\cos\Delta\Omega\sin u_G) + \sin i_E\sin i_G\sin u_G] \\ &-\tfrac{a_E\eta_E^2}{1+e_E\cos f_E}\sin u_E \end{aligned} \tag{A4}$$

$$\begin{aligned} Z_{EG} &= \tfrac{a_G\eta_G^2}{1+e_G\cos f_G}(\sin\Delta\Omega\cos u_G + \cos i_G\cos\Delta\Omega\sin u_G) \\ &+\tfrac{a_E\eta_E^2}{1+e_E\cos f_E}\cos i_E\sin i_G\sin u_G \end{aligned} \tag{A5}$$

where $\Delta\Omega_{III} = \Omega_E - \Omega_G$.

The classical Legendre polynomial expansion is applied to express the perturbing potential in Equation (12) into individual terms. This expansion is shown as follows:

$$\frac{1}{\|\mathbf{r} - \mathbf{r}\prime\|} = \frac{1}{\sqrt{r^2 + r'^2 - 2rr'\cos\gamma}} = \frac{1}{r}\sum_{n=0}^{\infty}\left(\frac{r'}{r}\right)^n P_n(\cos\gamma) \tag{A6}$$

$$\cos\gamma = \frac{\boldsymbol{r}\cdot\boldsymbol{r}\prime}{rr'} \tag{A7}$$

$$P_n(x) = \frac{1}{2^n n!}\frac{d^n}{dx^n}\left(x^2-1\right)^n \tag{A8}$$

Appendix B

In order to study the long-term evolution of orbital elements, the Lagrange planetary equations which derive the effect of perturbing potential on the orbital elements are given as follows:

$$\begin{cases} \frac{da}{dt} = \frac{2}{na}\frac{\partial R}{\partial M} \\ \frac{de}{dt} = \frac{1}{na^2e}\left(\eta^2\frac{\partial R}{\partial M} - \eta\frac{\partial R}{\partial \omega}\right) \\ \frac{di}{dt} = \frac{1}{na^2\eta\sin i}\left(\cos i\frac{\partial R}{\partial \omega} - \frac{\partial R}{\partial \Omega}\right) \\ \frac{d\Omega}{dt} = \frac{1}{na^2\eta\sin i}\frac{\partial R}{\partial i} \\ \frac{d\omega}{dt} = \frac{\eta}{na^2e}\frac{\partial R}{\partial e} - \frac{\cos i}{na^2\eta\sin i}\frac{\partial R}{\partial i} \end{cases} \tag{A9}$$

Then, the long-term evolution of Europa probe's orbital elements can be obtained.

References

1. Campagnola, S.; Buffington, B.B.; Lam, T.; Petropoulos, A.E.; Pellegrini, E. Tour design techniques for the Europa Clipper mission. *J. Guid. Control. Dyn.* **2019**, *42*, 2615–2626. [CrossRef]
2. Bayer, T.; Bittner, M.; Buffington, B.; Castet, J.F.; Dubos, G.; Jackson, M.; Lee, G.; Lewis, K.; Kastner, J.; Schimmels, K.; et al. Europa clipper mission update: Preliminary design with selected instruments. In Proceedings of the 2018 IEEE Aerospace Conference, Big Sky, MT, USA, 3–10 March 2018; pp. 1–19. [CrossRef]
3. Dougherty, M.K.; Grasset, O.; Bunce, E.; Coustenis, A.; Titov, D.V.; Erd, C.; Blanc, M.; Coates, A.J.; Coradini, A.; Drossart, P.; et al. JUICE (JUpiter ICy moon Explorer): A European-led mission to the Jupiter system. *EPSC-DPS Jt. Meet.* **2011**, *2011*, 1343.
4. Kozai, Y. The motion of a close earth satellite. *Astron. J.* **1959**, *64*, 367. [CrossRef]
5. Ely, T.A. Mean element propagations using numerical averaging. *J. Astronaut. Sci.* **2014**, *61*, 275–304. [CrossRef]
6. Scheeres, D.J.; Hu, W. Secular motion in a 2nd degree and order-gravity field with no rotation. *Celest. Mech. Dyn. Astron.* **2001**, *79*, 183–200. [CrossRef]
7. de Almeida Prado, A.F.B. Third-body perturbation in orbits around natural satellites. *J. Guid. Control Dyn.* **2003**, *26*, 33–40. [CrossRef]
8. Baresi, N.; Scheeres, D.J.; Schaub, H. Bounded relative orbits about asteroids for formation flying and applications. *Acta Astronaut.* **2016**, *123*, 364–375. [CrossRef]
9. Fu, T.; Wang, Y. Orbital Stability Around the Primary of a Binary Asteroid System. *J. Guid. Control Dyn.* **2021**, *44*, 1607–1620. [CrossRef]
10. Anderson, J.D.; Schubert, G.; Jacobson, R.A.; Lau, E.L.; Moore, W.B.; Sjogren, W.L. Europa's differentiated internal structure: Inferences from four Galileo encounters. *Science* **1998**, *281*, 2019–2022. [CrossRef]
11. Scheeres, D.J.; Guman, M.D.; Villac, B.F. Stability analysis of planetary satellite orbiters: Application to the Europa orbiter. *J. Guid. Control Dyn.* **2001**, *24*, 778–787. [CrossRef]
12. Low, S.Y.W.; Moon, Y.; Tao, L.W.; Tan, C.W. Designing a reference trajectory for frozen repeat near-equatorial low earth orbits. *J. Spacecr. Rocket.* **2022**, *59*, 84–93. [CrossRef]
13. Broucke, R.A. Long-term third-body effects via double averaging. *J. Guid. Control Dyn.* **2003**, *26*, 27–32. [CrossRef]
14. Lara, M. Simplified equations for computing science orbits around planetary satellites. *J. Guid. Control Dyn.* **2008**, *31*, 172–181. [CrossRef]
15. Hesar, S.G.; Scheeres, D.J.; McMahon, J.W. Sensitivity analysis of the OSIRIS-REx terminator orbits to maneuver errors. *J. Guid. Control Dyn.* **2017**, *40*, 81–95. [CrossRef]
16. Abouelmagd, E.I. Periodic solution of the two–body problem by KB averaging method within frame of the modified newtonian potential. *J. Astronaut. Sci.* **2018**, *65*, 291–306. [CrossRef]
17. Cinelli, M.; Ortore, E.; Circi, C. Long lifetime orbits for the observation of Europa. *J. Guid. Control Dyn.* **2019**, *42*, 123–135. [CrossRef]
18. Macdonald, M.; McKay, R.; Vasile, M.; Frescheville, F.B.D. Extension of the sun-synchronous orbit. *J. Guid. Control Dyn.* **2010**, *33*, 1935–1940. [CrossRef]
19. Byram, S.M.; Scheeres, D.J. Stability of sun-synchronous orbits in the vicinity of a comet. *J. Guid. Control Dyn.* **2009**, *32*, 1550–1559. [CrossRef]
20. Ugai, S.; Ichikawa, A. Lunar Synchronous Orbits in the Earth-Moon Circular-Restricted Three-Body Problem. *J. Guid. Control Dyn.* **2010**, *33*, 995–1000. [CrossRef]
21. Jaworski, S.; Kindracki, J. Feasibility of Synchronized CubeSat Missions from Low Earth Orbit to Near-Earth Asteroids. *J. Spacecr. Rocket.* **2020**, *57*, 1232–1245. [CrossRef]
22. Anderson, J.D.; Jacobson, R.A.; Lau, E.L.; Moore, W.B.; Schubert, G. Io's gravity field and interior structure. *J. Geophys. Res. Planets* **2001**, *106*, 32963–32969. [CrossRef]
23. Anderson, J.D.; Jacobson, R.A.; Lau, E.L.; Moore, W.B.; Olsen, O.; Schubert, G.; Thomas, P.C. Shape, mean radius, gravity field and interior structure of Ganymede. *AAS/Div. Planet. Sci. Meet. Abstr.* **2001**, *33*, 35–39.

24. Anderson, J.D.; Jacobson, R.A.; McElrath, T.P.; Moore, W.B.; Schubert, G.; Thomas, P.C. Shape, mean radius, gravity field, and interior structure of Callisto. *Icarus* **2001**, *153*, 157–161. [CrossRef]
25. Wang, G.B.; Meng, Y.H.; Zheng, W.; Tang, G.J. Artificial Sun synchronous frozen orbit control scheme design based on J 2 perturbation. *Acta Mech. Sin.* **2011**, *27*, 809–816. [CrossRef]
26. Wu, Z.; Jiang, F.; Li, J. Artificial Martian frozen orbits and Sun-Synchronous orbits using continuous low-thrust control. *Astrophys. Space Sci.* **2014**, *352*, 503–514. [CrossRef]
27. Ho, K.; Wang, H.; DeTrempe, P.A.; du Jonchay, T.S.; Tomita, K. Semi-Analytical Model for Design and Analysis of On-Orbit Servicing Architecture. *J. Spacecr. Rocket.* **2020**, *57*, 1129–1138. [CrossRef]
28. Chujo, T.; Takao, Y. Synodic Resonant Halo Orbits of Solar Sails in Restricted Four-Body Problem. *J. Spacecr. Rocket.* **2022**, *56*, 2129–2147. [CrossRef]

Article

Associated Fault Diagnosis of Power Supply Systems Based on Graph Matching: A Knowledge and Data Fusion Approach

Laifa Tao [1,2,3], Haifei Liu [1,2,3], Jiqing Zhang [4], Xuanyuan Su [1,2,3], Shangyu Li [1,2,3], Jie Hao [5], Chen Lu [1,2,3], Mingliang Suo [1,2,3] and Chao Wang [1,2,3,*]

1 Institute of Reliability Engineering, Beihang University, Beijing 100191, China
2 Science & Technology on Reliability & Environmental Engineering Laboratory, Beijing 100191, China
3 School of Reliability and Systems Engineering, Beihang University, Beijing 100191, China
4 China International Engineering Consulting Corporation, Beijing 100048, China
5 AVIC Xi'an Flight Automatic Control Research Institute, Xi'an 710076, China
* Correspondence: wangchaowork@buaa.edu.cn

Abstract: With the rapid development of more-electric and all-electric aircraft, the role of power supply systems in aircraft is becoming increasingly prominent. However, due to the complex coupling within the power supply system, a fault in one component often leads to parameter abnormalities in multiple components within the system, which are termed associated faults. Compared with conventional faults, the diagnosis of associated faults is difficult because the fault source is hard to trace and the fault mode is difficult to identify accurately. To this end, this paper proposes a graph-matching approach for the associated fault diagnosis of power supply systems based on a deep residual shrinkage network. The core of the proposed approach involves supplementing the incomplete prior fault knowledge with monitoring data to obtain a complete cluster of associated fault graphs. The association graph model of the power supply system is first constructed based on a topology with characteristic signal propagation and the associated measurements of typical components. Furthermore, fault propagation paths are backtracked based on the Warshall algorithm, and abnormal components are set to update and enhance the association relationship, establishing a complete cluster of typical associated fault mode graphs and realizing the organic combination and structured storage of knowledge and data. Finally, a deep residual shrinkage network is used to diagnose the associated faults via graph matching between the current state graph and the historical graph cluster. The comparative experiments conducted on the simulation model of an aircraft power supply system demonstrate that the proposed method can achieve high-precision associated fault diagnosis, even under circumstances where there are an insufficient number of samples and missing parameters.

Keywords: deep residual shrinkage network; association graph model; knowledge and data fusion; Warshall algorithm; power supply system

MSC: 94C12

Citation: Tao, L.; Liu, H.; Zhang, J.; Su, X.; Li, S.; Hao, J.; Lu, C.; Suo, M.; Wang, C. Associated Fault Diagnosis of Power Supply Systems Based on Graph Matching: A Knowledge and Data Fusion Approach. *Mathematics* **2022**, *10*, 4306. https://doi.org/10.3390/math10224306

Academic Editor: Yolanda Vidal

Received: 2 October 2022
Accepted: 14 November 2022
Published: 17 November 2022

1. Introduction

Decades ago, the ideas of more-electric aircraft (MEA) and all-electric aircraft (AEA) came into being [1]. In AEA, not only would all replaceable systems be replaced by electrical systems, but the propulsion power would also use electrochemical energy (e.g., batteries and fuel cells). At the same time, electrification has increased the supply of electric energy. With the continuous development of aircraft electrification, the requirements for the quality of aircraft power supply are increasing. Meanwhile, the complexity of aircraft power systems is also gradually increasing, which leads to higher requirements for the safety, maintainability, reliability, and testability of aircraft power supply systems [2,3].

Fault diagnosis is one of the important links in fault prediction and health management technologies [4,5]. Its purpose is to identify whether the system's working state is normal and whether it has deteriorated using intelligent algorithms in a certain working environment by combining the system's historical status information, fault information, working condition information, and other multi-source information, as well as historical parameter data. Then, fault isolation and location according to data characteristics can be realized [6,7]. Due to the complexity of the technical conditions of modern industrial processes, the influence of internal interaction loops is becoming increasingly prominent. When one monitoring variable is abnormal, it can easily cause changes in other monitoring variables through the relationships between faults, thus leading to related faults [8]. As a result, it is important to be able to analyze the fault source and locate the fault based on the numerous alarm data and their relationships. Power supply systems have such characteristics in real life. Therefore, the problem we aim to solve in this paper is how to correlate fault diagnosis and fault location through the node characteristics of the power supply system and their correlations.

There are mainly four kinds of fault diagnosis methods for power supply systems: knowledge-based [9,10], model-based [11,12], data-driven, and fault detection and diagnosis methods based on external equipment [13–15]. The model-based fault diagnosis method can mathematically express the research object and reveal the fault generation mechanism through the mathematical model. However, it is difficult to account for the coupling between components and their interactions with the environment during the modeling process. This results in models with limited ability to represent real faults and a high level of model complexity [16–18].

The data-driven fault diagnosis algorithm needs many historical data samples to support the model construction and training process. However, power supply systems have problems, such as difficulty obtaining fault samples, sample imbalance, etc. In addition, many data-driven algorithms lack certain physical meaning and interpretability, which makes it difficult to further apply and popularize the algorithm model. Data driven models, such as deep learning models, involve a large amount of computation and complex super parameters. How to further deploy them is also a problem to be considered [19–23]. The fault diagnosis of power supply systems based on external equipment is mainly carried out by actively applying different signals, via the system performance under different states, or through fault diagnosis rules. The authors of [24] proposed a development and implementation method for a permanent magnet synchronous motor controller for safety-critical applications. The authors of [25] proposed a method of fault diagnosis for aircraft secondary power distribution systems based on multi-valued logic and added cable fault detection and location functions to a traditional solid-state power controller.

The knowledge-based fault diagnosis method mainly uses knowledge to establish a diagnosis model. It performs fault inference analysis using object mechanisms, structure–function relationships, qualitative parameter analyses, and historical fault diagnosis experiences. Fault diagnosis expert systems and qualitative model-based methods are widely used [26–28]. However, in recent years, knowledge is used to remedy the problem of insufficient fault information in the data-driven model, to improve the adaptability and diagnostic ability of the model, and to make the model more targeted. The knowledge is supplemented in a data-driven way to improve the efficiency of model construction. At present, knowledge and data fusion is still in the exploration stage, and there are few related research achievements. Its main methods can be roughly divided into two categories: knowledge and data fusion model based on graph theory and knowledge and data fusion method based on the evidential reasoning model.

In association fault diagnosis, existing methods tend to focus on the correlation between parameters, the temporal relationship of fault propagation, and the probabilistic correlation of fault occurrence [29–34]. For special objects such as power supply systems, the parameter forms are often voltage, current, impedance, etc. The signal characteristics are relatively simple. It is difficult to analyze the association relationship only through parameters, and the propagation speed of current signals is fast. It is difficult to directly analyze the association between faults through time series, and the confidence of the probability association between faults is low when the data are incomplete. Therefore, we can summarize the urgent problem in the field of fault diagnosis as how to combine the advantages of data-driven and knowledge-driven models to quickly diagnose and locate faults through the correlations of components in different fault modes and their association patterns [35].

To solve the above problem, this paper proposes a high-level construction method of typical associated fault patterns of power supply systems based on a graph model. Based on anomaly monitoring and fault path tracking, the proposed method supplements the incomplete prior fault knowledge with monitoring data to obtain a complete cluster of associated fault graphs and realizes the fusion of knowledge and data. The main innovation points and contributions of this study can be summarized as follows:

(1) A knowledge and data fusion approach is proposed to diagnose the associated faults of power supply systems. The anomaly monitoring and fault path tracking based on the Warshall algorithm utilize historical data to supplement the incomplete prior fault knowledge, which establishes the complete cluster of typical associated fault mode graphs and realizes the organic combination and structured storage of knowledge and data.

(2) The proposed graph-matching strategy based on a deep residual contraction network achieves high precision with regard to fault diagnosis, even under the circumstances of an insufficient number of samples and missing parameters. The comparative experiments verify the depth feature extraction ability of the proposed method, as well as its high accuracy, noise resistance, and robust diagnostic capability.

(3) The proposed method preliminarily realizes deep association diagnosis and path backtracking under the condition of insufficient traditional FMEA knowledge and incomplete association information and provides an effective technical approach to solve accurate online fault diagnosis under strong coupling in the power supply system.

The remainder of this paper starts with a preliminary overview in Section 2. Then, Section 3 describes the two main methods of this study, including the association graph model based on knowledge and data fusion and the enhancement of component-associated knowledge based on the Warshall algorithm. The case studies in Section 4 show the process of the diagnosis of associated faults in power supply systems. The results indicate the priority of the methods in terms of accuracy under normal and missing-parameter situations. The paper closes with the main conclusions in Section 5.

2. Preliminary Overview

2.1. Warshall Algorithm

Definition 1. *Set digraph* $G = \langle V, E \rangle$, *set vertex* $V = \{v_1, v_2, \ldots, v_n\}$, *set edge* $E = \{e_1, e_2, \ldots, e_n\}$, *and define the adjacency matrix of digraph G as:*

$$A = (a_{ij})_{n \times n'} \tag{1}$$

where, a_{ij} *is the number of edges adjacent* v_i *to the vertex* v_j, $i = 1, 2, \ldots, n, j = 1, 2, \ldots, n$.

The Warshall algorithm is an algorithm for finding the transitive closure of adjacency [36]. In order to solve the problem of the large computation of the reachable matrix, the algorithm starts from the adjacency matrix A to obtain the matrix sequence $A, A_1, A_2, \ldots, A_n$. In order to judge the reachable path of each node in the matrix, the intermediate elements are fixed. Through the traversal of the intermediate elements, the path between two points is found to meet the requirement that only the nodes in the middle pass through $\{v_1, v_2, \ldots, v_k\}$ so that the algorithm only needs to perform sub addition n^3

times and sub multiplication n^3 times without matrix iteration. As a result, the number of calculations is reduced effectively. The algorithm steps are as follows [37]:

Step 1: Set matrix $F = A$, where A represents the adjacency matrix, 1 represents that there are edges between nodes, and 0 represents that there are no edges between nodes;

Step 2: Set $i = 1$;

Step 3: For any j, if $F[j,i] = 1$, then $F[j,k] = F[j,k] + F[j,i]$, where $k = 1, 2, \ldots, n$;

Step 4: i plus 1;

Step 5: If $i < n$, go to Step 2;

Step 6: The algorithm ends.

The final matrix F is the reachable matrix, which can determine whether there is a path in the two nodes. If there is a path, it is represented by 1, and if not, it is represented by 0.

The Warshall algorithm will be used in Section 3.2 to achieve associated knowledge enhancement and updates on component associations based on abnormality monitoring and fault path retrieval so that the organic integration and structured storage of knowledge and data are realized.

2.2. Frechet Distance

The Frechet distance is a curve similarity measure algorithm. It considers not only the similarity of curves but also the distance between the data points of curves. It can evaluate the correlation between curves comprehensively, with the advantages of high diagnostic accuracy, speed, and adaptability [38,39]. Its calculation is described below.

The Frechet distance starts by calculating the values of the metric functions of different data points of a curve to the points on another curve. Then, the maximum values of the different metric functions are used as the set of Frechet distances to be determined. The final Frechet distance is the value of the lower bound of the Frechet distance to be determined. To calculate the Frechet distance, first set the binary group (S, d) as a metric space, where d is a metric function of S. Thus, the strict mathematical definition of the Frechet distance is as follows [40]:

Definition 2. *Set the binary group (S, d) as a metric space, where d is a metric function of S. To define the Frechet distance, the following conditions must be met:*

(1) *The mapping γ of F on the unit interval $[0,1]$ is continuous.*

(2) *The vector ξ is mapped from the unit interval to itself, i.e., $\xi : [0,1] \to [0,1]$, and the mapping relation has the following conditions: the mapping function is continuous non-degenerate and ξ is full projective, at which point the function ξ is said to be a reparametrized function of the unit curve $[0,1]$.*

(3) *Let A and B be two continuous curves on S; that is, $A : [0,1] \to S$, $B : [0,1] \to S$. $d(x)$ is the metric function of S. Then, let α and β be two reparametrized functions of the unit interval. Then, the Frechet distance $F(A, B)$ of the curves A and B is defined as:*

$$F(A,B) = \inf_{\alpha,\beta,t \in [0,1]} \max\{d(A(\alpha(t)), B(\beta(t))\}, \tag{2}$$

The Frechet distance is sometimes referred to as "leash distance". As is shown in Figure 1, the dog walks along its own set trajectory between the owner and the dog, the owner's trajectory is A, the dog's trajectory is B. There is a rope between the owner and the dog to constrain the longest distance between them. During the travel, the Frechet distance is the minimum value of the rope that can ensure both can move along the trajectory.

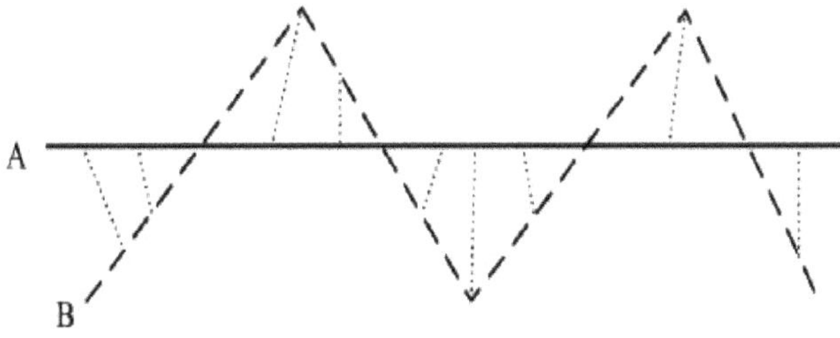

Figure 1. Typical structure diagram of convolutional neural network.

In this study, the optimal correlation analysis method needs to be selected to have the best correlation fuzzy metric effect, which can differentiate different modes. In a normal state, the correlation between the input signal and output signal of a component should be kept within a certain range, and when a fault occurs, the distance will change. Thus, the identification of different fault modes can be achieved based on the change in correlation.

The Frechet distance is used in the following correlation metric-based component fault diagnosis method. Typically, a distance metric is applied to the range of values and curve similarity between the operating parameters and the normal parameters. Then, we determine the extent to which the parameter deviates from the normal operating conditions combined with a distance threshold. When the distance value deviates from the threshold value, the component can be identified as abnormal.

2.3. Deep Residual Shrinkage Network

2.3.1. Convolutional Neural Networks (CNN)

Convolutional neural network is a classical deep learning model, which adds convolution to the traditional network to extract features. With development, it is now utilized in not only image processing but natural language and time series handling. Some widely used CNN models are LeNet-5, AlexNet, VGGNet, ResNet and so on [41,42].

A typical CNN contains three major layers, namely, a convolutional layer, pooling layer and fully connected layer. The network uses gradient descent to minimize the loss function for the purpose of adjusting the weight parameters in the network layer by layer, and the accuracy of the network is improved through iterative back-propagation training. LeNet-5 does not have an input layer. There are 7 layers in total, including 5 hidden layers (excluding pooling layers), that is, the number of layers that can train parameters is 5. VGGNet is mainly proposed to solve the problem that Lenet's recognition of large size pictures is not satisfactory. Compared with LeNet, AlexNet has a deeper network structure, with a total of eight hidden layers, including five convolutional layers and three full connection layers. However, although AlexNet has a good effect, it does not give the design direction of deep neural network, that is, how to make the network deeper. VGGNet strictly uses 3×3 small-scale convolution and pooling layer to construct depth of CNN, achieving good results. Small convolution can reduce parameters and facilitate stacking convolution layers to increase depth, that is, deepen the network and reduce convolution. At the same time, there is another network, ResNet, which uses the residual connection structure to make the network deeper from the perspective of avoiding gradient disappearance or explosion. There are five versions in total, of which ResNet-18 is the 18-layer version.

2.3.2. Deep Residual Network

In traditional CNNs, due to the complexity of the input parameters, it is often necessary to increase the depth of the model in order to improve the feature extraction capability and classification ability of the model. When too many hidden layer structures are added to the network structure, it may lead to a problem of gradient disappearance and step explosion. During the construction of the model, the parameters of each iteration of the model need to be back-propagated. The important operation during back propagation is the derivation of the gradient from the model error. The gradients will be accumulated and piled up in the network. As the number of hidden layers increases, the gradient will grow or decay exponentially with the number of layers, which is the phenomenon of gradient explosion and gradient disappearance. This will affect the running speed of the model and the classification effect.

As a new deep learning method, the core contribution of a deep residual network (ResNet) is to introduce the idea of identity mapping to the traditional network structure [43]. The core idea is to transfer the features of shallow data to the deep network through identity mapping so that the deep network contains the feature information of the shallow mesh structure, which greatly reduces the probability of gradient disappearance and gradient explosion, thus enhancing the feature extraction ability of the network model [44]. The specific structure is shown in Figure 2. When data are input, on the one hand, the data will pass through the residual path and a residual network is built on the residual path. After the input data pass through the path, a residual item $F(x)$ will be obtained, and the data x will also be output through the identity mapping model. Currently, the learned feature is $x + F(x)$. The goal of the residual network is to fit the residual term $F(x)$.

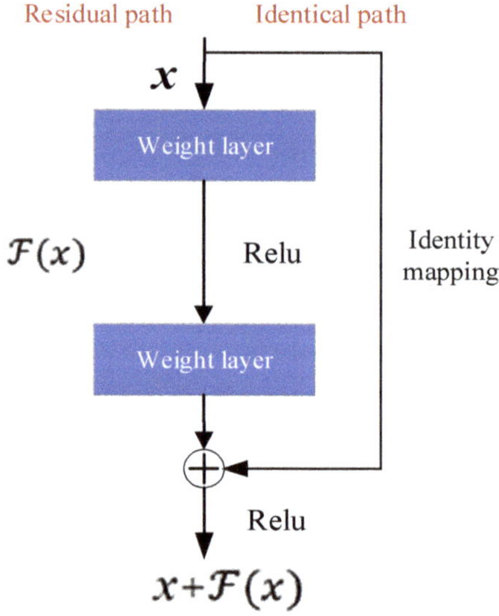

Figure 2. Schematic graph of residual unit.

By increasing the residual units, the training difficulty of the network parameters in the model is greatly reduced through the same path, the feature extraction ability of the original CNN is enhanced, the gradient disappearance and gradient explosion problems in the model are greatly reduced, and a model with stronger classification ability is trained to better adapt to complex data conditions.

2.3.3. Deep Residual Shrinkage Network

In general, the collected data often contain noisy information and redundant parameters unrelated to the target problem due to the limitations of the data collection methods or the influence of the working environment. It will affect the output accuracy of the model on the one hand and the operation efficiency of the model on the other. To solve this problem, the deep residual reduction network improves the original residual module based on the above-mentioned deep residual network. Additionally, the influence of target-independent features on the results is minimized by adding a soft thresholding operation. That is, features with absolute values less than the threshold are assigned to 0 by a nonlinear transformation in the soft thresholding operation, which "shrinks" the redundant features in the direction of 0, thus enabling feature selection [45]. Referring to the related article [46,47], the basic structure of the deep residual reduction network is as follows (Figure 3):

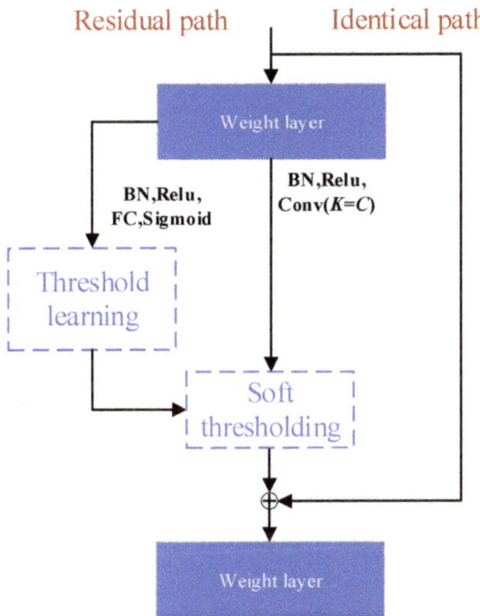

Figure 3. Basic structure of deep residual shrinkage network.

The principle of the soft threshold function is as follows:

$$y = \begin{cases} x - thr & x > thr \\ 0 & -thr \le x \le thr, \\ x + thr & x < -thr \end{cases} \tag{3}$$

where x represents the input feature, y represents the output feature, and thr represents the threshold value.

In the neural network model, a gradient operation is required for the features of each layer; that is, the derivation of the above formula. The results are as follows:

$$\frac{\partial y}{\partial x} = \begin{cases} 1 & x > thr \\ 0 & -thr \le x \le thr, \\ 1 & x < -thr \end{cases} \tag{4}$$

It can be seen that soft thresholding can limit the gradient to 0 and 1, thus preventing the problem of gradient disappearance and gradient explosion. Additionally, it can be seen that the key problem of soft thresholding is the acquisition of a threshold, and the self-learning of a threshold for different features can reduce sample noise and redundant feature interference, which is an advantage of deep residual shrinkage networks.

The threshold value in the residual shrinkage network is obtained by using the absolute operation and the GAP layer (global average pooling layer) to simplify the feature and convert it into a one-dimensional vector. The feature is marked as $A = \{a_{jic}\}$, where i, j, c represent the length, width, and number of channels of the input feature map, respectively. On the other hand, features are propagated to the two-layer full connection layer network (FC layer). Finally, the output of the FC network is scaled to the range of (0,1) via the following formula:

$$\alpha = \frac{1}{1 + e^{-z}}, \tag{5}$$

where α represents the scaling coefficient and z represents the characteristics of neurons. Thus, the expression of the threshold value can be obtained as follows:

$$\tau = \alpha \cdot \text{average}\left|a_{i,j,c}\right|, \tag{6}$$

where τ represents the calculated threshold value. In the deep residual shrinkage network, the threshold value τ must be positive and cannot be greater than the maximum absolute value of the feature map. Otherwise, according to the formula, the final output will be 0. Through this soft thresholding method, the threshold value can be kept within a small positive range. Due to the special structure of the depth residual shrinkage network, each sample can form a set of thresholds according to its own characteristic graph so that noise and redundant features can be reduced for specific samples.

The deep residual shrinkage network and the other neural networks mentioned are used in this work to conduct the mining and classification of features for the cluster of associated fault modes and to diagnose the current operating conditions in the power supply system. The comparison of different networks is shown by case studies in Section 4.

3. Proposed Method

There are two core steps of the proposed method. First, the initial graph models for different fault modes are established by extracting features sensitive to fault information and combining them with a priori knowledge of the power supply systems. Secondly, through data-driven correlation metrics and path tracking, model enhancement for correlated faults is achieved, which complements the absence of priori knowledge about associated faults and provides the main innovation of the proposed method.

3.1. Association Graph Model Based on Knowledge and Data Fusion

Since most of the currents generated in the power supply system are AC signals with high frequency and high fluctuation characteristics, the processing methods using time domain signals are often prone to loss of information. Thus, the pre-processing of the signal is required to extract the required fault state characteristic information from the complex signal. Commonly used signal analysis methods include time domain analysis, frequency domain analysis, and time-frequency domain analysis. This paper utilizes the Hilbert–Huang (HHT) transform-based time-frequency domain signal feature extraction method to analyze the signals and extract the features more adequately. At the same time, this paper also performs signal feature extraction via RMS, which is an important parameter to characterize the energy and stability of AC signals in circuit analysis.

The HHT transform can decompose high-frequency signals and obtain the instantaneous frequency and instantaneous amplitude of the signals. The RMS feature, as a common parameter in circuit analysis, can reflect the trend of circuit energy changes over time. Therefore, the feature extraction method in this study can obtain the feature information of data from three aspects: frequency, amplitude, and trend, which can achieve the retention or even enhancement of the fault characteristics.

Next, we build the association graph model based on knowledge and data fusion. There is a wide range of associations between components in the power supply system, and the associations are often distinguished in different operating states. Therefore, graph models can be established to describe the component associations in different operating states. There are two objectives, which are to realize the backtracking of abnormal component propagation paths under different associated fault states and to realize fault diagnosis based on the associated characteristics of components under different fault states. Specifically, there are many components in the power supply system, and there are natural physical connections between the components. In order to describe the association relationships of components in the power supply system, the components in the power supply system are regarded as nodes, while the association metrics between components are regarded as edge weights in the graph model to ultimately obtain an undirected weighted graph (defined as follows).

Definition 3. *Undirected weighted graph means that the edges in the graph model are undirected and weighted. The so-called undirected refers to any point pair* (i, j) *and* (j, i)*corresponding to the same edge, and vertex i and vertex j are also called the two endpoints of the undirected edge. The adjacency matrix of the undirected weighted graph G is:*

$$A = (a_{ij})_{n \times n'} \tag{7}$$

where a_{ij} *is the weight of the edge* v_j *adjacent to the vertex* v_i*,* $i = 1, 2, \ldots, n, j = 1, 2, \ldots, n$*.*

By analyzing the association between components in different fault modes, we obtain the association diagram model of the power supply system in different states. Meanwhile, the actions of various power controllers inside the power supply system can affect or block the propagation of fault signals, so the association of components in fault states may occur outside the physical structure. Therefore, it is necessary to combine the associated fault states together.

Since the electrical energy of the power supply system is generated by the primary power supply and then transmitted to the supply load through the secondary power supply, it can be assumed that the fault signal of the component is also propagated along the direction of electrical energy transmission. Therefore, the propagation direction of the electrical signal can be added to the original undirected weighted graph to create a directed weighted graph. The directed weighted graph gives directions to the edges based on the undirected weighted graph, which can further characterize the bidirectional propagation relationship between nodes. Therefore, the association graph model of the power supply system is constructed by combining the knowledge of the functional structure and the current transmission direction, as is shown in Figure 4. In the constructed association graph model, the transmission direction of the electrical signal is specified by the direction of the arrow and represented by the association degree results of the components. The system topology is simplified by the physical connection associations of the components. In the figure below, the yellow part indicates the components of the main power supply equipment of each channel, including the auxiliary exciter, rectifier bridge, main exciter, rotary rectifier, and main motor; light green indicates the next layer of signal transmission, including the AC load and each transformer rectifier; brown indicates the rectification part of each transformer rectifier; dark green indicates each transformer rectifier; red indicates each bus; and blue indicates each DC load. The hierarchical representation of the association graph allows the transmission level and direction to be clearly seen, providing support for further analysis.

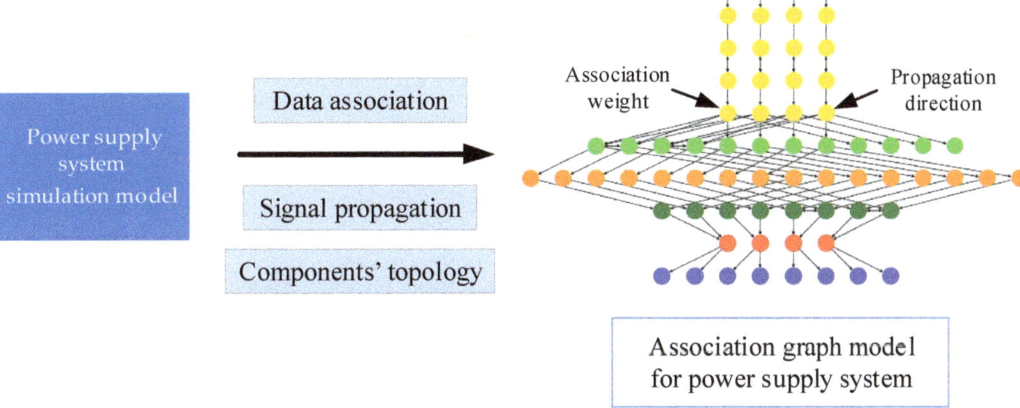

Figure 4. Reconstruction and reduction of the power supply system association graph model.

The graph model visually represents and structures the associations between components through nodes and edges so that the graph model can be used as an identification criterion for different fault modes. Thus, the identification of associated fault modes can be realized in Section 4.

3.2. Enhancement of Component Associated Knowledge Based on the Warshall Algorithm

The associated faults in the power supply system are often caused by the transmission of fault signals from the fault source to the associated components, resulting in a drift in the monitoring signals of the components. Additionally, this causes association alarms, making it difficult to identify the fault source and diagnose the fault mode. However, the topology of the power supply system is already determined. When the data are incomplete, it is difficult to fully explore the associations between the components due to the influence of monitoring noise and the uncertainty of the operating mode present in the data. The situation gets worse when the knowledge is incomplete as well. Although the association graph model of the power supply system developed in 3.1 can locate the fault source to a certain extent, the presence of the power controller still often affects or hinders the propagation of the fault signals due to the complexity of the associated faults. In the association fault model, there will always be components associated with the power supply system outside of its physical structure. Therefore, it is necessary to enhance the association knowledge based on component anomaly detection.

Definition 4. *Set digraph* $G = \langle V, E \rangle$*, set vertext* $V = \{v_1, v_2, \ldots, v_n\}$*, set edge* $E = \{e_1, e_2, \ldots, e_n\}$*, and define the adjacency matrix of digraph G as:*

$$A = (a_{ij})_{n\times n}, \tag{8}$$

where a_{ij} *is the number of edges adjacent* v_i *to the vertex* v_j*,* $i = 1,2,\ldots,n, j = 1,2,\ldots,n$*.*

In the directed graph, if a node can reach the target node through other nodes in the graph, it is considered that there is a reachable path between the node and the target node. Then, the existing alarm component set can be analyzed through the directed graph, the fault propagation path can be inferred with, and the fault source can be found. In this paper, the accessibility matrix is used to trace the source of typical associated fault modes, and thus the knowledge of the association graph model can be enhanced.

The accessibility matrix of digraph G is:

$$P = (P_{ij})_{n\times n}, \tag{9}$$

where $p_{ij} = 1$ if and only if the vertex v_i can reach the vertex v_j, otherwise $p_{ij} = 0$, $i = 1,2,\ldots,n$, $j = 1,2,\ldots,n$.

In this paper, Warshall's method is used to calculate the accessibility matrix and to further enhance the knowledge of the association graph model. The algorithm flow is as follows (Figure 5):

Firstly, the graph model is structured and stored according to the power supply system association graph model through the adjacency matrix. Secondly, the accessibility matrix is calculated through the Warshall algorithm to analyze the accessibility path of the association graph model. Then, according to the actual detection parameters of the power supply system, component fault detection based on association measurement is carried out, and a set of associated fault alarm components is obtained. According to the hierarchical structure of the association graph model, the accessibility path traversal of the alarm component set is performed in reverse (i.e., from the load level to the main power level). When the path cannot be traced forward, the last backtracking point is considered as the fault source under a certain path.

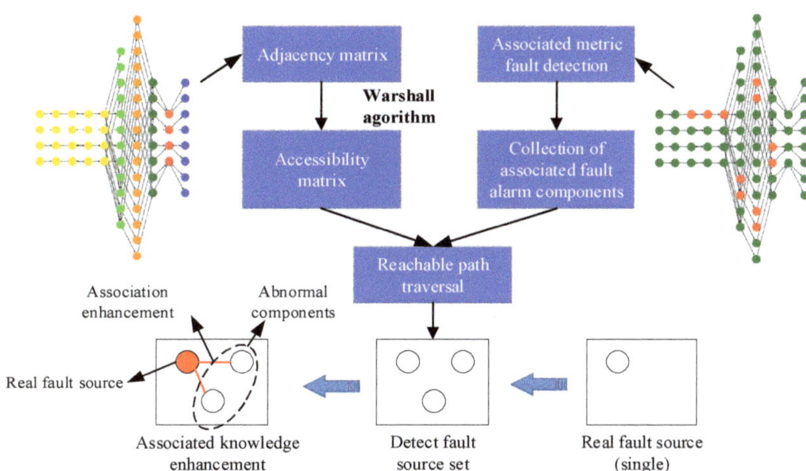

Figure 5. Knowledge enhancement process of power supply system association graph model.

In addition, with the association measurement algorithm based on Frechet distance proposed in this paper, the associations between different components can be obtained and applied to fault feature classification and fault diagnosis. Therefore, in the association graph model of the power supply system, the associations between components, i.e., weights, can be replaced by the association measurement results, thus organically combining data and knowledge. In addition, the graph structure can be stored in matrix form via adjacency matrices. Each adjacency matrix can be considered a graph. Multiple data under each associated fault mode can be considered a cluster of graphs. Multiple data under multiple associated fault modes can form a typical cluster of associated fault mode graphs. Component associations and signaling under different associated fault modes are stored to form a knowledge base to provide a basis for fault diagnosis. The associated fault mode clusters are defined as follows:

$$Graph = \left[g_{ij}\right]_{f\times n'} \quad (10)$$

$$g = [Frechet(a,b)]_{m\times m'} \quad (11)$$

where g_{ij} represents the j-th graph under the mode of the i-th associated fault mode; $Frechet(a,b)$ represents the Frechet-associated metric between component a and component b, f represents the number of fault modes in the clusters, n represents the number of fault samples, and m represents the number of power supply system components included in the clusters.

4. Case Studies

4.1. Construction of the Simulation Model

The data in this paper come from an aviation AC main power supply simulation model. This paper combines research data and experimental verification to construct a simulation model of a typical aircraft four-channel power supply system based on the Simulink tool in MATLAB. Moreover, this paper also combines the real parameter data of the power supply system provided for model modification and improvement. In this model, four three-phase alternators are used to supply power, which constitute a constant-speed and constant-frequency AC power supply system, and its four AC channels are not connected in parallel. The secondary power supply uses variable voltage rectifiers for a 270 V variable voltage rectifier and a 28 V variable voltage rectifier, and each is connected to one 270 V variable voltage rectifier and one 28 V variable voltage rectifier (high voltage and low voltage), respectively. At the same time, the first and second channels' DC power supply comes through the convergence bar for power integration, and the third and fourth channels' DC power supply comes through the convergence bar for power integration. The DC power supplies are connected to two hydraulic pump loads (high voltage loads, working in parallel) and two resistors (low voltage loads, working in parallel). There are also four AC loads in the system, represented by two three-phase resistors, which are connected to four generators. The simulation model graph of the power supply system is as follows (Figure 6):

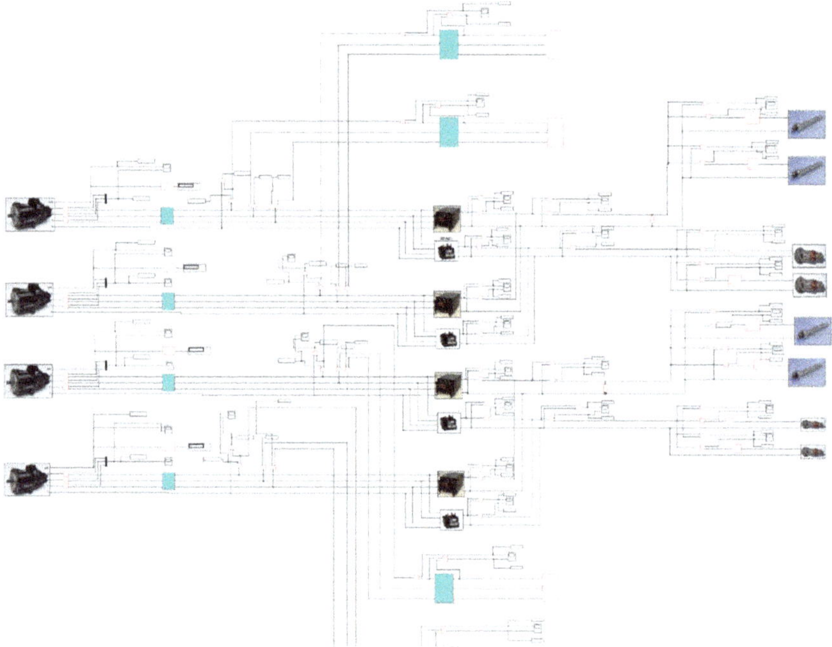

Figure 6. Power supply system simulation model.

In the power supply system structure used in this paper, the four channels of AC power are independently powered and connected to the AC load, while the DC power is sinked and distributed through the DC sink bar. In order to analyze the power supply modes in different channels and to obtain the complete data characteristics, the circuit switching logic in the fault state is not considered in this study.

In order to realize the fault characterization and parameter change analysis of the power supply system under different fault modes, it is necessary to collect and analyze the parameters of each component at each level. Therefore, a total of 218 measurement points including the power supply system level, equipment level, and component level are added to this model in order to monitor the status of 4 levels, 12 pieces of equipment, and 60 components in the power supply system.

4.2. Establishment of the Associated Fault Diagnosis Model

This paper uses the deep residual contraction network model to carry out fault diagnosis based on the power supply system's associated fault mode graph. The model construction process is shown in Figure 7.

First, construct a cluster of associated fault modes based on the topological knowledge and historical parameter information. Second, construct a deep residual shrinkage network model based on the residual shrinkage network units. Third, complete the training of the fault diagnosis model library based on the cluster of associated fault modes. Then, generate an association graph based on the actual measured parameters. The process uses the association metric analysis technique of actual monitoring parameters and the association graph model. Finally, input the association graph into the trained deep residual shrinkage network model for diagnosis and obtain the diagnosis results.

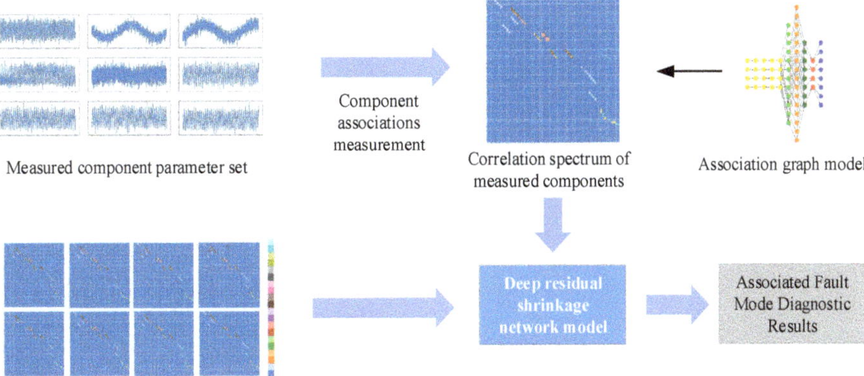

Figure 7. Schematic graph of power supply system associated fault diagnosis model.

To start with, we proceed with the associated fault detection based on the Frechet distance metric. The purpose is to obtain the set of abnormalities in each fault mode and to visually display the associated graph model. The associated fault detection results of a typical power supply system under the first channel are shown in Figure 8. The green nodes in the figure represent components with normal parameters and the red nodes represent components with abnormal parameters. From the results, it can be seen that when the associated faults occur, the fault source and the associated components will have abnormal parameters to some extent.

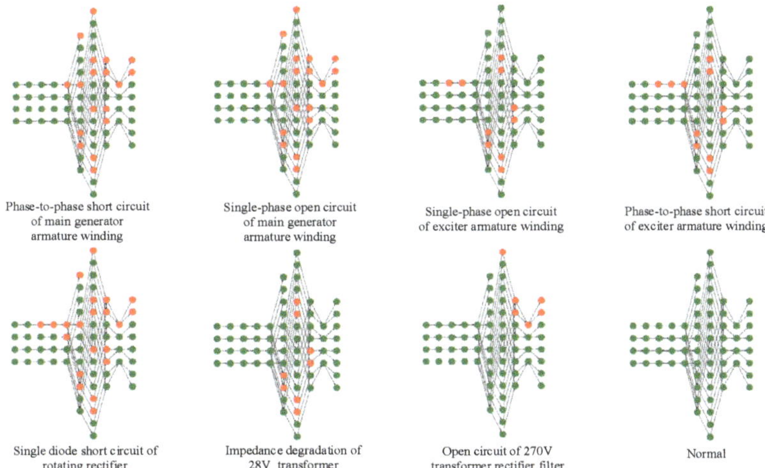

Figure 8. Detection results of associated faults of typical power supply systems.

The following conclusions can be drawn from the analysis of the associated fault detection results:

(1) Under different associated fault modes, the sets of abnormal components caused by different associations are different due to the complexity of the power supply system connection structure, functional composition, and transmission mode. It is difficult to comprehensively analyze the component associations under different associated faults using only a simple power supply system structure.

(2) In the power supply system, the association direction of the fault-related components caused by the fault source is not only related to the power supply system structure. Due to the incomplete selection of the electrical energy control and component acquisition parameters of the generator controller in the power supply system, associations outside the power supply system structure often occur. For example, a phase-to-phase short-circuit fault in the armature winding of the main generator, No. 1, causes a fault not only in low-voltage transformer No. 1 but also in low-voltage transformer No. 2. This is because the low-voltage DC bus of the power supply system is converged by transformers No. 1 and No. 2. Therefore, it is necessary to strengthen the associations of the association graph model of the power supply system according to the fault detection results in different fault modes.

(3) In typical associated faults of the power supply system, the propagation direction of the fault signal is not necessarily unidirectional. For example, the open-circuit fault of a single diode of the rotating rectifier can also cause a parameter shift for the exciter. Therefore, when constructing the association graph model, it is also necessary to consider the associations of the bi-directional connected components.

(4) The associations of each component of the power supply system need to further rely on component anomaly detection analysis and fault path back analysis. This is to analyze and strengthen the association features such as transmission direction of fault signals and component association outside the physical structure in the power supply system so as to improve the feature extraction capability and fault diagnosis capability of the model.

Further, the enhancement of component-associated knowledge is performed based on knowledge and data fusion. Take the phase-to-phase short-circuit fault in the armature winding of the exciter of the power supply system as an example. Figure 9 shows the backtracking path and fault source detection after the accessible path traversal of the fault alarm set. As can be seen from the fault alarm component set, the fault in the exciter armature winding is transmitted to the 28 V transformer rectifier through the rotating rectifier and the main motor, causing a series of associated fault representations. The red path is the fault tracing path consistent with the true fault source, while the yellow path can only be traced back to LV transformer #2. In fact, there are two sources of faults, the main exciter #1 and the LV transformer #2. This indicates that, due to the generator controller, the fault signal from the rectification of transformer #1 28 V may affect the rectification of transformer #2 28 V in order to ensure that the current and voltage of the circuit meet the target requirements, thus causing a deviation in the parameters of transformer #2 LV. Therefore, the associations under the fault path should be considered in the association graph model. The research content of this paper assumes that the fault source of the associated fault mode in the power supply system is a single fault source or a double fault source of the same component. Therefore, the associations of the original association graph model are enhanced by the blue path, thus further improving the ability of the model to represent the overall state of the power supply system.

The association graph model of the power supply system constructed in this paper is further updated with knowledge through the fault path retrieval and association enhancement under each typical associated fault mode. Further, the model is more capable of representing the associations of components under different fault states, thus further enhancing the fault diagnosis capability. The improved association graph model of the power supply system is shown in Figure 10. In the updated association model, the clusters of the components are not changed. However, the fault path retrieval based on the Warshall algorithm enhances the association knowledge of the components. On the one hand, the association direction of the components is supplemented with the original edges; on the other hand, the association outside the physical structure shown by the components, i.e., the edges in the graph, is enhanced in the associated fault mode.

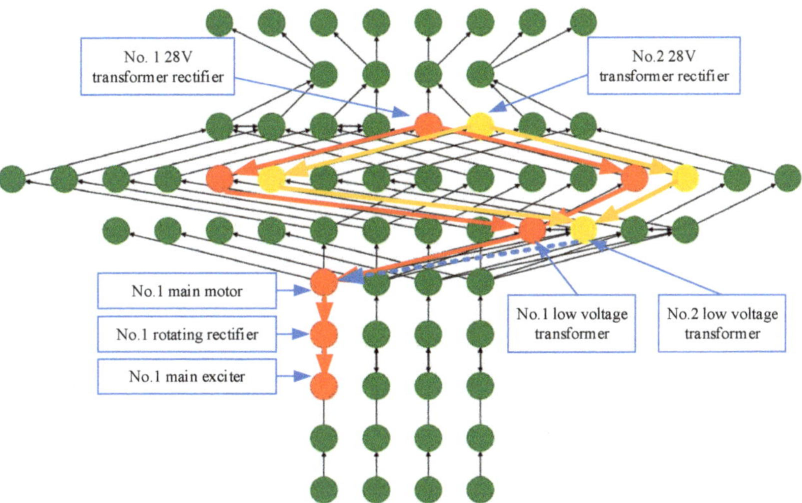

Figure 9. Example graph of phase-to-phase short-circuit fault backtracking of exciter armature winding.

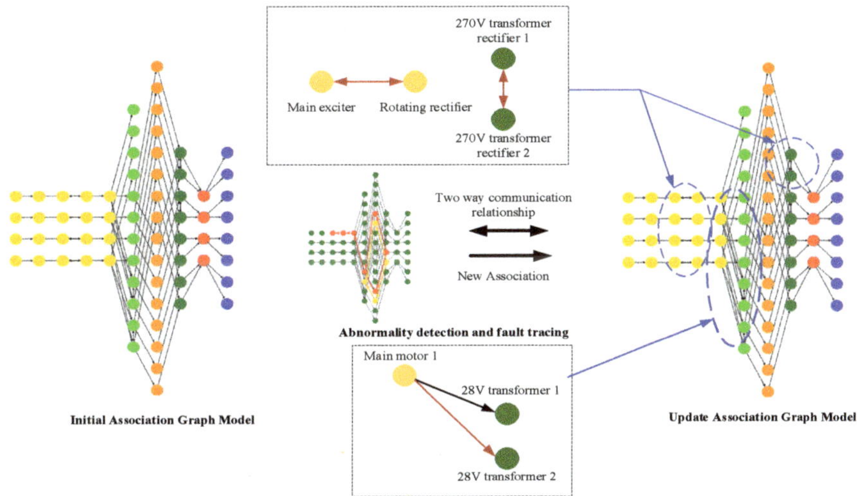

Figure 10. The power supply system's association graph model.

Then, we obtain the results of a cluster of associated fault modes based on the Frechet distance and the Warshall algorithm.

In the graphs, the horizontal and vertical coordinates represent the serial numbers of the components, respectively, and the weight corresponding to the coordinates (a, b) is the weight of the associated measurement between component a and component b, as shown in Table 1.

In Figure 11, different colors represent the weights of each aspect, which means that the differences in association measurements between components can be shown. As can be seen from the figure, both the basic structure of the cluster of association modes and the connection topology between components remain unchanged, which is mainly because the structure of the association graph model does not change. Nevertheless, the associations between components change under different fault modes, and the weights of the edges change accordingly. Figure 12 shows a comparison of the associated fault graphs under normal conditions and under the phase-to-phase short-circuit of the excitation armature winding.

Table 1. Associated mode cluster component serial number name comparison table.

No.	Components	No.	Components	No.	Components	No.	Components
0	Pilot exciter 1	17	Main motor 2	34	High variable filter 13	51	270 V regulating 4
1	Pilot exciter 2	18	Main motor 3	35	High variable filter 14	52	28 V regulating 1
2	Pilot exciter 3	19	Main motor 4	36	Low variation filter 11	53	28 V regulating 2
3	Pilot exciter 4	20	AC load 1	37	Low variation filter 12	54	28 V regulating 3
4	Rectifier bridge 1	21	AC load 2	38	Low variation filter 13	55	28 V regulating 4
5	Rectifier bridge 2	22	AC load 3	39	Low variation filter 14	56	High voltage busbar 1
6	Rectifier bridge 3	23	AC load 4	40	High variable filter 21	57	High voltage busbar 2
7	Rectifier bridge 4	24	High voltage transformer 1	41	High variable filter 22	58	Low voltage busbar 1
8	Main exciter 1	25	High voltage transformer 2	42	High variable filter 23	59	Low voltage busbar 2
9	Main exciter 2	26	High voltage transformer 3	43	High variable filter 24	60	Fuel pump 1
10	Main exciter 3	27	High voltage transformer 4	44	Low variation filter 21	61	Fuel pump 2
11	Main exciter 4	28	Low voltage transformer 1	45	Low variation filter 22	62	Fuel pump 3
12	Rotating rectifier 1	29	Low voltage transformer 2	46	Low variation filter 23	63	Fuel pump 4
13	Rotating rectifier 2	30	Low voltage transformer 3	47	Low variation filter 24	64	Heater 1
14	Rotating rectifier 3	31	Low voltage transformer 4	48	270 V regulating 1	65	Heater 2
15	Rotating rectifier 4	32	High variable filter 11	49	270 V regulating 2	66	Heater 3
16	Main motor 1	33	High variable filter 12	50	270 V regulating 3	67	Heater 4

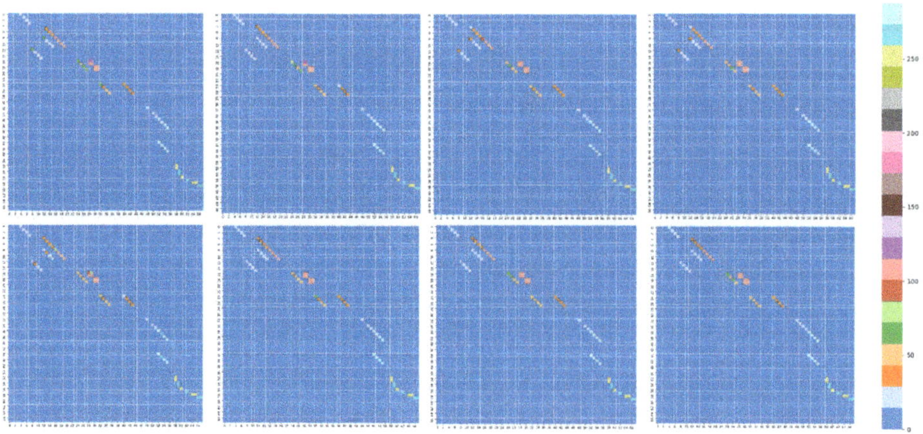

Figure 11. Schematic graph of a cluster of associated fault mode results.

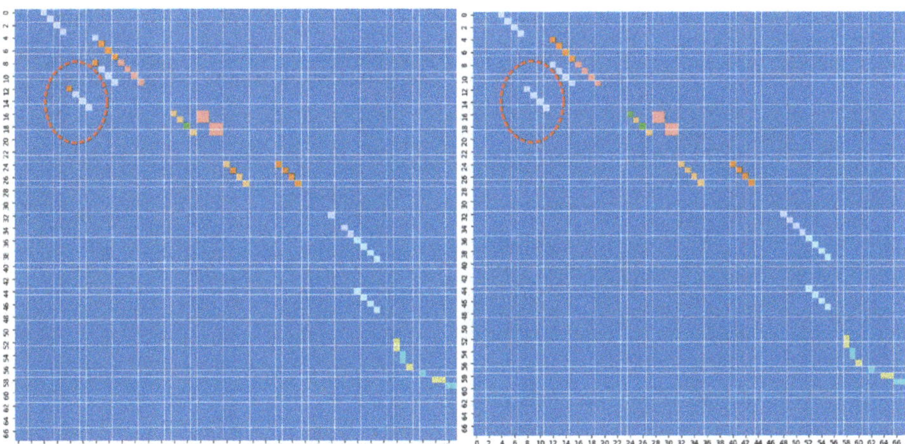

Figure 12. Comparison of associated fault graph.

As is shown in Figure 12, the associations of the components highlighted in the two graphs have changed, and the coordinates are (8, 12) and (12, 8), respectively. In the graphs, 4 represents No. 1 main exciter and 12 represents No. 1 rotating rectifier. The change also verified that the armature winding of the exciter has a phase-to-phase short-circuit fault and further verified the rationality and interpretability of the construction of the graphs.

Based on this, this study constructs a cluster of typical associated fault modes of the power supply system, organically integrates the structural knowledge of the power supply system, signal propagation direction, and parameter characteristics, and realizes the enhancement of data-based associations. Finally, structured storage is carried out. On the one hand, the associations and signal propagation relationship of each component of the power supply system can be obtained through the graphs, and on the other hand, the characteristics of the components are deeply extracted. The graphs can directly reflect the changes in component associations caused by the change of parameter characteristics under different fault conditions, thus saving storage space and providing a basis for improving the efficiency of the diagnosis model.

4.3. Diagnosis Results and Analysis

4.3.1. Data Introduction

In this part, the relevant fault diagnosis models of the power supply system are validated using simulation modeling of a typical aircraft power supply system and data sets created in fault injections. The data set includes seven typical fault injections: phase-to-phase short-circuit in the main generator armature winding, single phase open-circuit in the main generator armature winding, single phase open-circuit in the exciter armature winding, phase-to-phase short-circuit in the exciter armature winding, single diode short-circuit in the rotary rectifier, impedance attenuation in the 28 V transformer rectifier, and open-circuit and normal in the 270 V transformer rectifier filter inductor. Together with the fault data of single-fault point injections and double-fault point injections, there are 42 fault modes. By adding Gaussian noise with a signal-to-noise ratio of 5, 50 sets of samples are generated for each fault mode, and 43 sets of associated fault mode hierarchies for different fault types are generated by the above method of constructing the associated mode hierarchies for power supply systems. Each group has 50 graphs as training and testing data for the deep residual shrinkage network.

4.3.2. Operating Environment

In this section, the deep residual systolic network model is built by PyTorch, and the model is trained and validated. Compared with other deep learning frameworks, the PyTorch framework has the advantages of simple design and high operational efficiency. The fault diagnosis model related to power supply systems based on a deep residual systolic network proposed in this study is built with PyTorch 1.9.0.

4.3.3. Diagnosis Results

In this section, a network model based on deep residual shrinkage is constructed for a power supply system-associated fault diagnosis. Forty sets of samples are used as the training and validation sets, and the last 10 sets of samples are used as the test set for model testing and validation. The model is trained for 300 iterations, and the convolution kernel parameter is set to 3. The training loss and final confusion matrix during model training are shown in Figures 13 and 14.

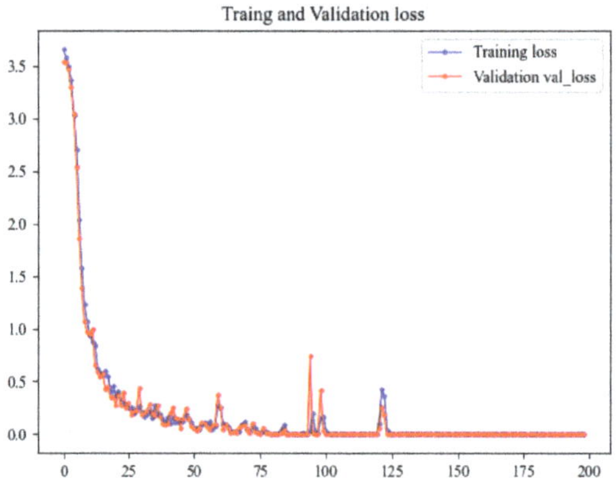

Figure 13. Training loss in the process of associated fault diagnosis.

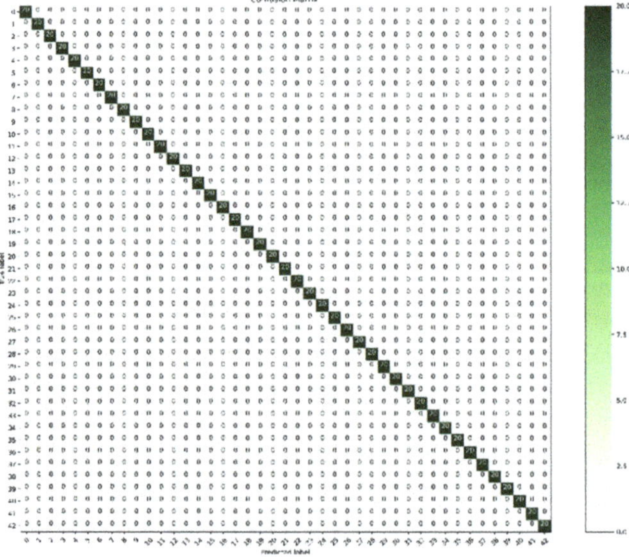

Figure 14. Confusion matrix in the process of associated fault diagnosis.

From the above fault diagnosis results, it is apparent that, on the one hand, the deep residual shrinkage network model constructed in this paper can realize the feature mining and classification of the association fault pattern graphs. Moreover, due to the soft threshold and identity mapping in the deep residual unit, the model converges faster and can effectively reduce the redundant information and noise interference in the graph model, and the accuracy rate of association fault diagnosis reaches 100%. On the other hand, it can be seen from the loss function that the trend of the loss function of the training set is basically consistent with that of the validation set. This indicates that the associated fault mode mapping of the power supply system in this paper can still construct data features with strong consistency under the condition of noise, which means it can be used for fault diagnosis.

4.3.4. Validation and Comparison

To further verify that the correlation metric based on the Frechet distance in this paper is optimal, the effects of several common correlation metrics are compared. Here, the correlation metric is calculated and the results are analyzed using the parameters under different fault modes, such as exciter output voltage and rotating rectifier input voltage, selected from normal conditions, exciter armature winding phase short circuit, exciter armature winding open circuit, main generator armature winding single phase open circuit, rotating rectifier single diode open circuit, and 28 V varactor impedance degradation. The different algorithms are evaluated using three parameters: intra-cluster sum of squares, contour coefficients, and CH metrics. The mathematical definitions of the several methods are as follows:

(1) Cluster sum of square

$$CSS = \sum_{j=0}^{m}\sum_{i=1}^{n}(x_i - \mu_i)^2, \tag{12}$$

n represents the number of data points in each class, m represents the number of clusters, x_i represents the data points, and μ_i represents the mean value of each class.

(2) Contour coefficient

$$S(i) = \frac{b(i) - a(i)}{\max(a(i), b(i))}, \tag{13}$$

where $a(i)$ denotes the average distance from each point i to other points in the cluster and $b(i)$ denotes the average distance from each point to all other points in the cluster.

(3) Calinski–Harabaz index (CH)

$$\mathrm{CH}(k) = \frac{\mathrm{BGSS}}{K-1} / \frac{\mathrm{WGSS}}{n-K} \tag{14}$$

$$\mathrm{WGSS} = \frac{1}{2}\left[(n_1 - 1)\overline{d}_1^2 + \cdots + (n_K - 1)\overline{d}_K^2\right] \tag{15}$$

$$\mathrm{BGSS} = \frac{1}{2}\left[(K-1)\overline{d}^2 + (n-K)A_K\right] \tag{16}$$

$$A_K = \frac{1}{n-K}\sum_{i=1}^{n}(n_i - 1)\left(\overline{d}^2 - \overline{d}_i^2\right) \tag{17}$$

where n is the number of samples in the data set, K is the number of categories, $\overline{d}_j^2$ is the average distance between samples in the j-th category, $j = 1, 2, \cdots, k$, and $\overline{d}^2$ is the average distance between all samples. A larger CH indicator indicates that the clustering result is more concentrated within clusters and more dispersed between clusters, i.e., there is a better clustering effect.

In this paper, the correlation analysis method is used to achieve the correlation measure of components in different states from the parameter level. Common correlation analysis methods are as follows:

(1) Pearson's correlation coefficient

Pearson correlation coefficient is a common analysis index in vector similarity analysis [48–51] that is mainly used to portray the linear correlation between two vectors. A coefficient output result of 0 means that there is no correlation between two vectors, a positive result means a positive correlation, and a negative result means a negative correlation. Its calculation formula is as follows:

$$\begin{aligned} \rho_{X,Y} &= \frac{\mathrm{cov}(X,Y)}{\sigma_X\sigma_Y} = \frac{E((X-\mu_X)(Y-\mu_Y))}{\sigma_X\sigma_Y} \\ &= \frac{E(XY)-E(X)E(Y)}{\sqrt{E(X^2)-E^2(X)}\sqrt{E(Y^2)-E^2(Y)}} \end{aligned}, \tag{18}$$

(2) Parametric analysis based on the gray correlation analysis model

The basic idea of gray correlation analysis is to reflect the correlation between parameters through the degree of similarity of the curve geometry between the data of each parameter [52–55]. It is mainly applied to the description and analysis of the developmental changes between parameters within the system [56]. Let the reference series be $X_o(t)$ and the comparison series be $X_i(t)$, then the gray correlation degree is calculated as.

$$\eta_i(t) = \frac{m+\rho M}{\Delta_i(t)+M},\ \rho \in [0,1], \tag{19}$$

where $\Delta_i(t) = |x_0(t) - x_i(t)|$, $i = 1,2,\cdots m$, $t = 1,2,\cdots,n$, $M = \max(\Delta_i(t))$, $m = \min(\Delta_i(t))$.

(3) Mahalanobis distance

The Mahalanobis distance is a method of measuring the similarity between two sample sets starting from the perspective of the distribution characteristics of the sample set [57–60], and its main feature involves considering the connection between different features to be able to be independent of the measurement scale. It is often used to measure the distance between multidimensional time series parameters, and the Mahalanobis distance between the data vectors x and y is:

$$D_{\mathrm{M}}(x,y) = \sqrt{(x-y)^{\mathrm{T}}\sum\nolimits^{-1}(x-y)}, \tag{20}$$

where $\sum^{-1}$ is the covariance matrix of the multidimensional random variables.

(4) Cosine similarity

The cosine similarity measures the cosine of the angle between the vectors by converting the parameters into vectors to determine the consistency of the direction between the two vectors, which further determines the correlation of the parameters [61–64]. Therefore, this method is commonly used to determine the consistency of the variation between two parameters. The range of values is between −1 and 1, with −1 indicating that the two vectors are the exact opposite and 1 indicating that they are exactly the same. The cosine similarity between sequence X and sequence Y is:

$$\mathrm{sim}(X,Y) = \cos\theta = \frac{\sum\limits_{i=1}^{n}(X_i \times Y_i)}{\sqrt{\sum\limits_{i=1}^{n} X_i^2 \times \sqrt{\sum\limits_{i=1}^{n} Y_i^2}}}, \tag{21}$$

(5) DTW (dynamic time warping algorithm)

The DTW (dynamic time warping) algorithm, commonly used for speech similarity recognition, has the main advantage of being able to measure the similarity of two time series data, especially two data of different lengths, through a dynamic planning algorithm [65–68]. The basic algorithm of dynamic time regularization is as follows. Assuming that two time series are X and Y, set their lengths as n and m, respectively, where:

$$\begin{aligned} X &= x_1, x_2, \ldots, x_i, \ldots, x_n \\ Y &= y_1, y_2, \ldots, y_j, \ldots, y_m \end{aligned} \tag{22}$$

To calculate the shortest path between the two, first construct a $n \times m$ path matrix W where each element in the matrix corresponds to the Euclidean distance between the two points, i.e.,:

$$w = d\left(x^{th}, y^{th}\right), \tag{23}$$

$$d(x_i, y_j) = \sqrt{(x_i - y_j)^2}, \tag{24}$$

When the path matrix is constructed, the minimum cumulative distance between the two sequences, i.e., the DTW distance, is calculated as follows:

$$DTW(X,Y) = \min\left\{ \sqrt{\sum_{K=1}^{K} w_k / K}, \right. \tag{25}$$

where K is the number of alignment points and w_k is an element of the path matrix representing the distance between x and y in the k-th group of points.

A comparative situation analysis for each distance metric algorithm with different metric parameters is shown in Table 2:

Table 2. Associated mode clusters' component serial number name comparison table.

Metric Algorithm	CSS	Contour Factor	CH
Pearson correlation coefficient	3.4692	0.0536	199.5176
Grey correlation analysis	11.6526	−0.1574	21.9299
Mahalanobis distance	5.0645	0.6025	116.6640
Cosine similarity	0.5429	0.1715	2694.7450
Dynamic Time Warping	0.0080	0.7599	343,059.7323
Frechet distance	0.0001	0.9425	15,413,927.6165

From the comparison of the indicators, it can be seen that the clustering concentration of the Frechet distance is much higher than that of other algorithms, which proves that for the characteristic parameters of the power supply system in this paper, the Frechet distance can sharply identify the changes to the data in terms of curve trends and numerical distances so as to achieve more accurate fault diagnosis.

In more detail, firstly, the Pearson correlation coefficient and gray correlation analysis methods are used to measure the correlation between the change trends of two series. In this study, however, the data are characterized as stable variation data that maintain certain fluctuation characteristics, and it is difficult to analyze their correlation by variation trends, so it is difficult to distinguish different failure modes. Secondly, the Marxian distance and cosine distance can measure the similarity between two stable sample data; however, both have the disadvantage of not being sensitive to the absolute value of the specific value of the sample, i.e., the size of the data value has little effect on the results. However, through the aforementioned analysis, the current and voltage tend to change only numerically in certain fault modes and do not change in frequency, so it is difficult for both to achieve excellent results in certain fault modes. Both the dynamic time regularization algorithm and the Frechet distance analyze the correlation between parameters from the dimension of path similarity of time series, while it can be seen from the results that the Frechet distance has a better clustering effect.

To further verify the improvement in diagnostic capability brought by the deep residual shrinkage network proposed in this paper, two neural networks are tested additionally, including ResNet18 and basic CNN. These methods are commonly used after research [69–73]. The diagnostic accuracy and confusion matrix of each model is shown in Figures 15 and 16.

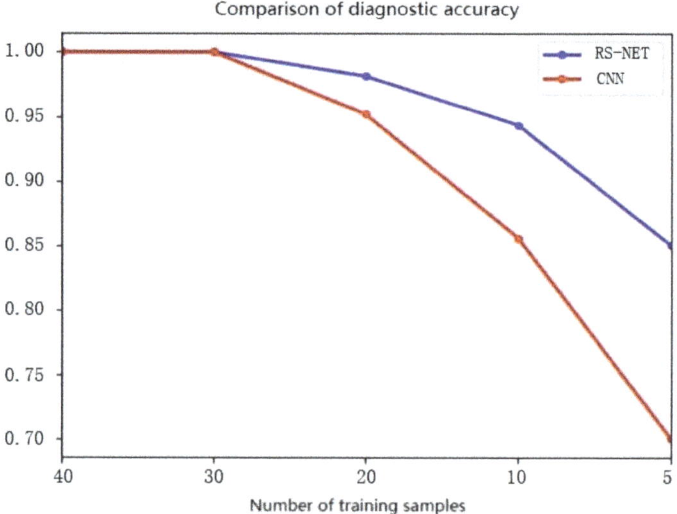

Figure 15. Comparison chart of fault diagnosis accuracy of two methods by number of samples.

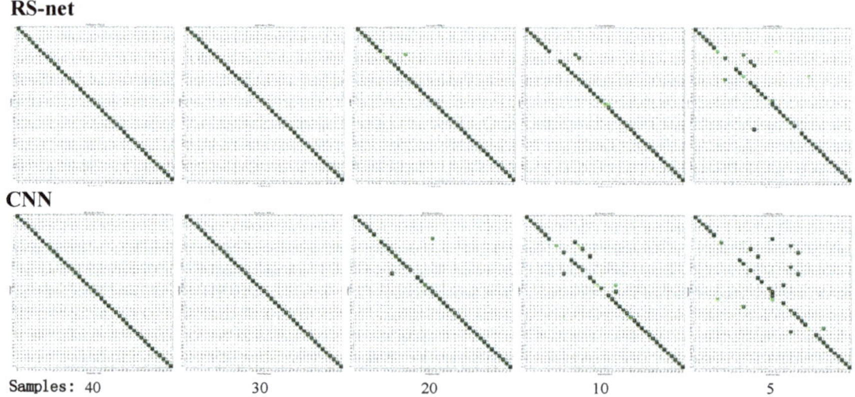

Figure 16. Comparison of confusion matrix of two methods with different numbers of training samples.

At the same time, we have adopted AutoGluon 0.5.2, which uses automatic super parameter adjustment, model selection or integration, architecture search and data processing to rapidly prototype the original data for deep learning and classical machine learning solutions. We applied some other nsetworks trained by AutoGluon, and obtained the accuracy results, whose values are all distributed between 0.7386 and 0.7727, far from 0.9907 of the deep neural shrinkage network proposed in this paper (Table 3).

Table 3. Accuracy results for several networks trained by AutoGluon.

No.	Model	Accuracy
1	WeightedEnsemble_L2	0.7727
2	RandomForestGini	0.7386
3	LightGBMXT	0.7636
4	CatBoost	0.7636
5	XGBoost	0.7705
6	LightGBMLarge	0.7568
7	NeuralNetTorch	0.7523
8	NeuralNetFastAI	0.7545
9	LightGBM	0.7409
10	KNeighborsUnif	0.7409
11	The proposed model	0.9907

The superiority of neural networks can be clearly seen from the results. From the comparison of the above diagnosis results, it can be seen that the associated fault diagnosis model based on the deep residual shrinkage network model proposed in this paper is significantly less affected by the size of the fault samples than the traditional CNN model. This is mainly because the residual shrinkage unit in the model reduces the interference of the model with redundant data and noise and can better achieve the feature extraction and classification of the associated fault mode graphs. Through the cross-sectional comparison of test results, the fault diagnosis accuracy of both can be maintained above 70% when the amount of data is only five groups. This can prove that the construction method of clusters of associated fault modes proposed in this paper can achieve robust fault feature extraction and structured storage of noisy parameter data and has excellent performance in terms of fault diagnosis. It can alleviate the problem of insufficient data samples under actual operating conditions.

To further verify the superiority of the association graph model, we apply the feature extraction results directly in three networks for training. Several classical machine learning models trained with AutoGluon including WeightedEnsemble_L2, RandomForestGini, KNeighborsUnif, SVM and XGBoost. The comparison of the diagnostic accuracy with and without the association graph model is shown below. We obtained the accuracy results of training samples of 5, 10, 20, 30 and 40, respectively, and averaged them (Table 4).

Table 4. Comparison of the diagnostic accuracy with and without the association graph model.

No.	Model	Accuracy with Graph Model	Accuracy without Graph Model
1	WeightedEnsemble_L2	0.7727	0.7341
2	RandomForestGini	0.7386	0.7341
3	KNeighborsUnif	0.7409	0.7386
4	SVM	0.7334	0.7080
5	XGBoost	0.7705	0.7293

It can be seen from the table that the association graph model has brought about improvement for all models, with 5.65% at most and 0.31% at least. This is because the association graph model integrates knowledge and data and has more information than the unstructured stored feature extraction results.

To further validate the feature extraction capability of the associated fault mode graphs of the power supply system proposed in this paper, specific fault points are removed in this paper. This is carried out to verify the robustness and accuracy of the feature extraction and fault diagnosis of the model in the absence of parameters. In the experiment, the data points of No. 1 main motor, No. 1 rectifier, No. 1 auxiliary exciter, No. 1 main exciter, and No. 1 rotary rectifier in the associated fault graph of the power supply system are set to zero to simulate the actual monitoring environment in which the monitoring parameters of No. 1 main power supply are missing in order to verify the fault diagnosis effect of the model under the condition of missing fault parameters. Figure 17 shows the graphs of the normal state before and after the missing parameters. From the figure, it can be seen that due to the missing parameters of the main power supply components, the points of the related fault mode graph are also missing.

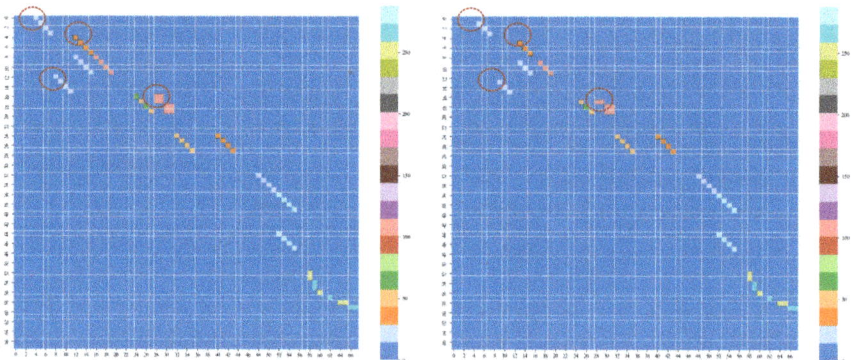

Figure 17. Comparison graph of normal state-associated fault mode graph before and after missing parameters.

In this paper, the training set and the test set are processed for parameter loss at the same time. With 40 groups of samples as the training set and 10 groups of samples as the test set, the deep residual shrinkage network model and CNN model are constructed and trained. The results of the confusion matrix are shown in Figure 18.

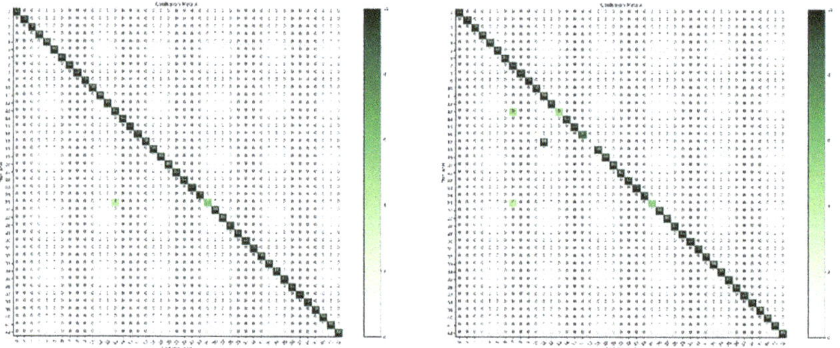

Figure 18. Comparison of the two confusion matrices in the case of missing parameters.

The test results show that the deep residual shrinkage network model constructed in this paper can achieve the diagnosis of typical associated fault modes with 99.07% accuracy, even when the main power parameters of the first channel are completely missing. In addition, the diagnosis accuracy by CNN reaches 95.35%, which reflects the robustness of the model for feature extraction in this paper. Due to the structural expression of component and parameter associations in the cluster, the graph model has the ability of feature extraction against parameter loss, thus adapting to the actual usage environment.

Further analysis reveals that in the confusion matrix of the deep residual shrinkage network, the misclassification of the model is mainly fault 13 and fault 25, which correspond to the phase-to-phase short-circuit in the first channel of the armature winding and the impedance drop fault in the first channel of the 28 V transformer rectifier, respectively. Since they are closely related to the main power supply parameters, some feature information is lost, leading to a decrease in the diagnostic accuracy of the model. The misclassification of the CNN is mainly for faults 7, 13, 11, 17, and 25, corresponding to the faults single-phase open-circuit of the excitation armature winding of the first channel, phase-to-phase short-circuit of the excitation armature winding of the first channel, impedance drop of the 28 V transformer rectifier of the first channel, phase-to-phase short-circuit of the excitation armature winding (first and second channels), and single-phase open-circuit of the excitation armature winding (first and second channels), respectively.

The experiment proves that the graph model-based component analysis and associated fault diagnosis model can solve the problems of information structured storage and complex feature extraction for power supply systems based on knowledge and data fusion. Additionally, it can realize accurate fault diagnosis of typical associated fault modes and achieve high accuracy diagnosis under the circumstances of insufficient samples and missing parameters. In short, the model has good robustness and adaptability.

5. Conclusions

This paper proposes a knowledge and data fusion approach for the associated fault diagnosis of power supply systems. Based on the graph model, the proposed approach organically combines the hierarchical structure, signal transmission direction, and data association relationship of the power supply system to construct the initial cluster of typical associated fault mode graphs, solving the problem of assigning data information to the power supply system structure and associating knowledge and parameters. Then, the accessibility matrix of the association graph model is calculated according to the Warshall algorithm, and the fault path set is obtained by backtracking the component fault detection results based on the association measurement. By comparison with the real fault source, the association relationship is updated and the incomplete prior fault knowledge is supplemented, establishing the final cluster of typical associated fault mode graphs. Finally, a deep residual reduction network model is constructed for graph matching, realizing the diagnosis of associated faults. Compared with other models, the proposed model can achieve more high-precision associated fault diagnosis, even under difficult situations such as insufficient sample size or missing parameters, demonstrating its robustness and adaptability.

Author Contributions: Data curation, J.Z.; Formal analysis, J.Z. and X.S.; Funding acquisition, C.L. and C.W.; Methodology, L.T. and H.L.; Writing—original draft, J.H. and C.W.; Validation, S.L. and M.S.; Investigation, X.S.; Supervision, C.W. All authors have read and agreed to the published version of the manuscript.

Funding: This study was supported by the National Natural Science Foundation of China (Grant Nos. 61973011 and 61903015), the Fundamental Research Funds for the Central Universities (Grant No. KG21003001), National key Laboratory of Science and Technology on Reliability and Environmental Engineering (Grant No. WDZC2019601A304), as well as the Capital Science & Technology Leading Talent Program (Grant No. Z191100006119029).

Conflicts of Interest: The authors declare no conflict of interest.

References

1. Weimer, J.A. Electrical power technology for the more electric aircraft. In Proceedings of the [1993 Proceedings] AIAA/IEEE Digital Avionics Systems Conference, Fort Worth, TX, USA, 25–28 October 1993.
2. Barzkar, A.; Ghassemi, M. Electric Power Systems in More and All Electric Aircraft: A Review. *IEEE Access* **2020**, *8*, 169314–169332. [CrossRef]
3. Thapa, N.; Ram, S.; Kumar, S.; Mehta, J. All electric aircraft: A reality on its way. *Mater. Today Proc.* **2021**, *43*, 175–182. [CrossRef]
4. Park, J.Y.; Lim, I.S.; Choi, E.J.; Kim, M.S. Fault diagnosis of thermal management system in a polymer electrolyte membrane fuel cell. *Energy* **2021**, *214*, 119062. [CrossRef]
5. Saeed, U.; Jan, S.U.; Lee, Y.D.; Koo, I. Fault diagnosis based on extremely randomized trees in wireless sensor networks. *Reliab. Eng. Syst. Saf.* **2020**, *205*, 107284. [CrossRef]
6. Wu, X.; Zhang, Y.; Cheng, C.; Peng, Z. A hybrid classification autoencoder for semi-supervised fault diagnosis in rotating machinery. *Mech. Syst. Signal Process.* **2021**, *149*, 107327. [CrossRef]

7. Vogl, G.W.; Weiss, B.A.; Helu, M. A review of diagnostic and prognostic capabilities and best practices for manu-facturing. *J. Intell. Manuf.* **2019**, *30*, 79–95. [CrossRef]
8. Jiang, Y.; Yin, S.; Kaynak, O. Optimized Design of Parity Relation Based Residual Generator for Fault Detection: Data-Driven Approaches. *IEEE Trans. Ind. Inform.* **2020**, *17*, 1449–1458. [CrossRef]
9. Lawhorn, D.; Rallabandi, V.; Dan, M.I. A Network Graph Technique for the Design of Electric Aircraft Power Systems. In Proceedings of the IEEE Transportation Electrification Conference and Expo, Chicago, IL, USA, 22–26 June 2020.
10. Meng, F.; Yang, S.; Wang, J.; Xia, L.; Liu, H. Creating Knowledge Graph of Electric Power Equipment Faults Based on BERT–BiLSTM–CRF Model. *J. Electr. Eng. Technol.* **2022**, *17*, 2507–2516. [CrossRef]
11. Ren, X.; Li, Y.; Wu, T.Y.; Qu, S.; Li, M. Fault Diagnosis of Complex Electric Power System Using the Improved Grey Incidence Degree Model. In Proceedings of the 2017 5th International Conference on Machinery, Materials and Computing Technology (ICMMCT 2017), Busan, Republic of Korea, 25–27 August 2017.
12. Zhang, Y.; Zhang, J.; Ma, J.; Wang, Z. Fault Diagnosis Based on BFS in Electric Power System. In Proceedings of the International Conference on Measuring Technology & Mechatronics Automation, Hunan, China, 11–12 April 2009.
13. Zhang, Z.; Jian, H.; Jiang, Y.; Geng, W.; Xu, Y. Overview and analysis of PM starter/generator for aircraft electrical power systems. *CES Trans. Electr. Mach. Syst.* **2017**, *1*, 117–131. [CrossRef]
14. Wang, B.; Vakil, G.; Liu, Y.; Yang, T.; Zhang, Z.; Gerada, C. Optimization and Analysis of a High Power Density and Fault Tolerant Starter-Generator for Aircraft Application. *Energies* **2020**, *14*, 113. [CrossRef]
15. Arumugam, P.; Dusek, J.; Aigbomian, A.; Vakil, G.; Bozhko, S.; Hamiti, T.; Gerada, C.; Fernando, W. Comparative design analysis of Permanent Magnet rotor topologies for an aircraft starter-generator. In Proceedings of the 2014 IEEE International Conference on Intelligent Energy and Power Systems, Kyiv, Ukraine, 2–6 June 2014.
16. Setlak, L.; Kowalik, R. Mathematical Modeling and Simulation Studies of Selected Components of the Electricity Generation, Processing and Distribution System of Aircrafts According to the Concept of More Electric Aircraft. In Proceedings of the 2018 International Symposium on Electrical Machines (SME), Andrychów, Poland, 10–13 June 2018.
17. Hoffelder, T. Equivalence analyses of dissolution profiles with the Mahalanobis distance. *Biom. J.* **2019**, *61*, 1120–1137. [CrossRef] [PubMed]
18. Xu, K. Fault Diagnosis Method of Power System Based on Neural Network. In Proceedings of the 2018 International Conference on Virtual Reality and Intelligent Systems (ICVRIS), Hunan, China, 10–11 August 2018.
19. Zhang, Y.; Shi, J.; Wang, S.; Zhan, Y. A Multi-source Information Fusion Fault Diagnosis Method for Vectoring Nozzle Control System Based on Bayesian Network. In Proceedings of the 2020 Asia-Pacific International Symposium on Advanced Reliability and Maintenance Modeling (APARM), Vancouver, BC, Canada, 20–23 August 2020.
20. Rao, T.S.; Ram, S.T.; Subrahmanyam, J. Neural network with adaptive evolutionary learning and cascaded support vector machine for fault localization and diagnosis in power distribution system. *Evol. Intell.* **2022**, *15*, 1171–1182.
21. Cai, B.; Lei, H.; Lin, J.; Xie, M. Bayesian Networks in Fault Diagnosis: Some research issues and challenges. In Proceedings of the 6th International Conference on Maintenance Performance Measurement and Management, Luleå, Sweden, 28 November 2016.
22. Gan, L.; Wu, H.; Fang, W. Bayesian network approach based on fault isolation for power system fault diagnosis. In Proceedings of the International Conference on Power System Technology, Chengdu, China, 20–22 October 2014.
23. Xu, L.; Zhou, Y. Fault diagnosis for BLDCM system used FFT algorithm and support vector machines. In Proceedings of the IEEE International Conference on Aircraft Utility Systems, Beijing, China, 10–12 October 2016.
24. Odavic, M.; Sumner, M.; Wheeler, P.; Jing, L. Real-time fault diagnostics for a permanent magnet synchronous motor drive for aerospace applications. In Proceedings of the Energy Conversion Congress & Exposition, Atlanta, GA, USA, 12–16 September 2010.
25. Chen, Q.; Li, W. Research on Fault Diagnosis Method of Aircraft Secondary Distribution System Based on Multi-valued Logic. In Proceedings of the International Conference on Sensing, San Diego, CA, USA, 12–14 June 2017.
26. Li, W.; Li, H.; Gu, S.; Chen, T. Process fault diagnosis with model- and knowledge-based approaches: Advances and opportunities. *Control Eng. Pract.* **2020**, *105*, 104637. [CrossRef]
27. Wang, C.; Li, J.; Zhu, X.; Xu, C.; Cheng, X. Adaptive Neural Fuzzy Petri Net Algorithm for Motor Fault Diagnosis. *IOP Conf. Ser. Earth Environ. Sci.* **2020**, *446*, 042063. [CrossRef]
28. Jiang, L.; Hua, Y.; Li, Q.; Zhang, R. Fault diagnosability qualitative analysis of spacecraft based on temporal fault signature matrix. In Proceedings of the Guidance, Navigation & Control Conference, Nanjing, China, 12–14 August 2016.
29. Liu, C.; Wu, G.; Yang, C.; Li, Y.; Wu, Q. A Fault Diagnosis Method Based on Signed Directed Graph and Correlation Analysis for Nuclear Power Plants. In Proceedings of the 2020 International Conference on Nuclear Engineering Collocated with the ASME 2020 Power Conference, Virtual, 4–5 August 2020.
30. Yu, J.; Wang, K.; Ye, L.; Song, Z. Accelerated Kernel Canonical Correlation Analysis with Fault Relevance for Nonlinear Process Fault Isolation. *Ind. Eng. Chem. Res.* **2019**, *58*, 18280–18291. [CrossRef]
31. Ye, Z.; Yan, H.; Zhao, Z.; Chen, Y.; Yang, Z. Research on Comprehensive Cascade Fault Diagnosis Technology for Vehicle Management System Actuator Control Subsystem Based on Associated Fault Mode Library. In Proceedings of the 2020 Prognostics and Health Management Conference (PHM-Besançon), Besançon, France, 4–7 May 2020.
32. Chai, Z.; Liu, C.; Zhu, M.; Han, Y. Fault Detection in Power Plant Equipment Based on Multi-sensor Data Correlation Analysis. *Comput. Digit. Eng.* **2019**, *47*, 682–688. [CrossRef]

33. Jun-Jie, X.U.; Chen, R. Probabilistic Diagnosis Approach to Diagnosing Multiple-fault Programs with Fault Correlation. *Comput. Sci.* **2017**, *44*, 124–130. [CrossRef]
34. Qi, H.; Xie, Q.; Yang, W.; Kan, S. Failure Mode, Effect and Criticality Analysis of Controllable Pitch Propeller Based on Fault Correlation. *Mech. Sci. Technol. Aerosp. Eng.* **2014**, *33*, 399–403.
35. Liu, H.; Pi, D.; Qiu, S.; Wang, X.; Guo, C. Data-driven identification model for associated fault propagation path. *Measurement* **2022**, *188*, 110628. [CrossRef]
36. Aini, A.; Salehipour, A. Speeding up the Floyd-Warshall algorithm for the cycled shortest path problem. *Appl. Math. Lett.* **2012**, *25*, 1–5. [CrossRef]
37. Kasa, Z. Warshall's algorithm-survey and applications. *Ann. Math. Et Inform.* **2021**, *54*, 17–31. [CrossRef]
38. Hadi, A.S.; Nyquist, H. Frechet distance as a tool for diagnosing multivariate data. *Linear Algebra Its Appl.* **1999**, *289*, 183–201. [CrossRef]
39. Gudmundsson, J.; Valladares, N. A GPU Approach to Subtrajectory Clustering Using the Fréchet Distance. *IEEE Trans. Parallel Distrib. Syst.* **2015**, *26*, 924–937. [CrossRef]
40. Tang, B.; Yiu, M.L.; Mouratidis, K.; Zhang, J.; Wang, K. On discovering motifs and frequent patterns in spatial trajectories with discrete Frechet distance. *Geoinformatica Int. J. Adv. Comput. Sci. Geogr.* **2022**, *26*, 29–66. [CrossRef]
41. Chua, L.O.; Roska, T. The CNN paradigm. *Circuits Syst. I Fundam. Theory Appl. IEEE Trans.* **1993**, *40*, 147–156. [CrossRef]
42. Lei, Y.; Yang, B.; Jiang, X.; Jia, F.; Li, N.; Nandi, A.K. Applications of machine learning to machine fault diagnosis: A review and roadmap. *Mech. Syst. Signal Process.* **2020**, *138*, 106587. [CrossRef]
43. Pan, L.; Ji, B.; Xi, P.; Wang, X.; Chongcheawchamnan, M.; Peng, S. FEDI: Few-shot learning based on Earth Mover's Distance algorithm combined with deep residual network to identify diabetic retinopathy. In Proceedings of the 2021 IEEE International Conference on Bioinformatics and Biomedicine (BIBM), Houston, TX, USA, 9–12 December 2021.
44. Yu, L.; Hao, C.; Duo, Q.; Qin, J.; Heng, P. Automated Melanoma Recognition in Dermoscopy Images via Very Deep Residual Networks. *IEEE Trans. Med. Imaging* **2016**, *36*, 994–1004. [CrossRef]
45. Shi, D.; Wu, Z.; Zhang, L.; Hu, B.; Meng, K. Multi-Scale Deep Residual Shrinkage Network for Atrial Fibrillation Recognition. *Int. J. Comput. Intell. Appl.* **2022**, *21*, 2250015. [CrossRef]
46. Pan, H.; You, X.; Liu, S.; Zhang, D. Pearson correlation coefficient-based pheromone refactoring mechanism for multi-colony ant colony optimization. *Appl. Intell.* **2021**, *51*, 752–774. [CrossRef]
47. Cui, F.; Tu, Y.; Gao, W. A Photovoltaic System Fault Identification Method Based on Improved Deep Residual Shrinkage Networks. *Energies* **2022**, *15*, 3961. [CrossRef]
48. Cw, A.; Jing, S.; Ld, A.; Yang, L.; Jia, C. Comprehensive benefit evaluation of solar PV projects based on multi-criteria decision grey relation projection method: Evidence from 5 counties in China. *Energy* **2021**, *238*, 121654.
49. Li, G.; Zhang, A.; Zhang, Q.; Wu, D.; Zhan, C. Pearson Correlation Coefficient-Based Performance Enhancement of Broad Learning System for Stock Price Prediction. *IEEE Trans. Circuits Syst. Ii-Express Briefs* **2022**, *69*, 2413–2417. [CrossRef]
50. Li, Z.; Zhao, H.; Zeng, R.; Xia, K.; Guo, Q.; Li, Y. Fault Identification Method of Diesel Engine in Light of Pearson Correlation Coefficient Diagram and Orthogonal Vibration Signals. *Math. Probl. Eng.* **2019**, *2019*, 2837580.
51. Liu, Y.; Mu, Y.; Chen, K.; Li, Y.; Guo, J. Daily Activity Feature Selection in Smart Homes Based on Pearson Correlation Coefficient. *Neural Process. Lett.* **2020**, *51*, 1771–1787. [CrossRef]
52. Garcez, T.V.; Cavalcanti, H.T.; Almeida, A. A hybrid decision support model using Grey Relational Analysis and the Additive-Veto Model for solving multicriteria decision-making problems: An approach to supplier selection. *Ann. Oper. Res.* **2021**, *304*, 199–231. [CrossRef]
53. Qu, W.; Chen, Z.; Wang, P.; Sun, J. A Grey Qualitative Based Approach for Environmental Information Analysis. *J. Grey Syst.* **2017**, *29*, 1–13.
54. Shi, C.-Z.; Zhao, Q.; Luo, L.-P. Application of Gray-scale Texture Feature In the Diagnosis of Pulmonary Nodules. In *SREE Workshop on Medical Materials and Engineering (WMME 2011)*; Trans Tech Publications Ltd.: Macau, China, 2012.
55. Xue, W.; Kuang, T. Image Edge Detection Based on Krisch Operator and Gray Correlation Analysis. In Proceedings of the 13th International Conference on Graphics and Image Processing (ICGIP), Kunming, China, 18–20 August 2021; Yunnan University: Kunming, China, 2022.
56. Cabana, E.; Lillo, R.E.; Laniado, H. Multivariate outlier detection based on a robust Mahalanobis distance with shrinkage estimators. *Stat. Pap.* **2021**, *62*, 1583–1609. [CrossRef]
57. Kwak, B.I.; Han, M.L.; Kim, H.K. Cosine similarity based anomaly detection methodology for the CAN bus. *Expert Syst. Appl.* **2021**, *166*, 114066. [CrossRef]
58. Deepa, N.; Khan, M.Z.; Prabadevi, B.; Vincent, D.R.P.M.; Maddikunta, P.K.R.; Gadekallu, T.R. Multiclass Model for Agriculture Development Using Multivariate Statistical Method. *IEEE Access* **2020**, *8*, 183749–183758. [CrossRef]
59. El Bendadi, K.; Lakhdar, Y.; Sbai, E.H. An Improved Kernel Credal Classification Algorithm Based on Regularized Mahalanobis Distance: Application to Microarray Data Analysis. *Comput. Intell. Neurosci.* **2018**, *2018*, 7525786. [CrossRef]
60. Omara, I.; Hagag, A.; Ma, G.; Abd El-Samie, F.E.; Song, E. A novel approach for ear recognition: Learning Mahalanobis distance features from deep CNNs. *Mach. Vis. Appl.* **2021**, *32*, 38. [CrossRef]
61. Keogh, E. Exact Indexing of Dynamic Time Warping—Science Direct. VLDB'02. In Proceedings of the 28th International Conference on Very Large Databases, Hong Kong, China, 20–23 August 2002; pp. 406–417.

62. Abdulhussain, M.I.; Gan, J.Q. An Experimental Investigation on PCA Based on Cosine Similarity and Correlation for Text Feature Dimensionality Reduction. In Proceedings of the 7th Computer Science and Electronic Engineering Conference (CEEC), England, UK, 24–25 September 2015.
63. Buciu, I.; Kotropoulos, C.; Pitas, I. Comparison of ICA approaches for facial expression recognition. *Signal Image Video Process.* **2009**, *3*, 345–361. [CrossRef]
64. Li, G.; Shen, J.; Dai, C.; Wu, H.; Becker, S.I. ShVEEGc: EEG Clustering With Improved Cosine Similarity-Transformed Shapley Value. *IEEE Trans. Emerg. Top. Comput. Intell.* **2022**, 1–15. [CrossRef]
65. Zhao, M.; Zhong, S.; Fu, X.; Tang, B.; Pecht, M. Deep Residual Shrinkage Networks for Fault Diagnosis. *IEEE Trans. Ind. Inform.* **2020**, *16*, 4681–4690. [CrossRef]
66. Adachi, Y.; Kawamoto, S.; Morishima, S.; Nakamura, S. Acoustic features for estimation of perceptional similarity. In Proceedings of the 8th Pacific Rim Conference on Multimedia, Hong Kong, China, 11–14 December 2007; City University of Hong Kong: Hong Kong, China.
67. Kim, S.-H.; Yang, H.-J.; Ng, K.S. Temporal Sign Language Analysis Based on DTW and Incremental Model. In Proceedings of the 9th IEEE Malaysia International Conference on Communications, Kuala Lumpur, Malaysia, 15–17 December 2009.
68. Wu, H.; Peng, Q.; Huang, Y. Features Extraction and Correlation Analysis of Stock Index. In Proceedings of the 8th World Congress on Intelligent Control and Automation (WCICA), Jinan, China, 6–9 July 2010.
69. Liu, Y.; She, G.-R.; Chen, S.-X. Magnetic resonance image diagnosis of femoral head necrosis based on ResNet18 network. *Comput. Methods Programs Biomed.* **2021**, *208*, 106254. [CrossRef] [PubMed]
70. Petrov, D.; Marshall, N.; Vancoillie, L.; Cockmartin, L.; Bosmans, H. Anthropomorphic ResNet18 for multi-vendor DBT image quality evaluation. In Proceedings of the Conference on Medical Imaging—Image Perception, Observer Performance, and Technology Assessment, Medical Imaging, Houston, TX, USA, 19–20 February 2020.
71. Zhou, Z.; Ma, Z.; Wang, Y.; Zhu, Z. Fabric wrinkle rating model based on ResNet18 and optimized random vector functional-link network. *Text. Res. J.* **2022**. [CrossRef]
72. Du, T.; Zhang, H.; Wang, L. Analogue circuit fault diagnosis based on convolution neural network. *Electron. Lett.* **2019**, *55*, 1277–1278. [CrossRef]
73. Senanayaka, J.S.L.; Van Khang, H.; Robbersmvr, K.G. CNN based Gearbox Fault Diagnosis and Interpretation of Learning Features. In Proceedings of the 30th IEEE International Symposium on Industrial Electronics (ISIE), Kyoto, Japan, 20–23 June 2021.

Article

A Unified Multi-Objective Optimization Framework for UAV Cooperative Task Assignment and Re-Assignment

Xiaohua Gao [1], Lei Wang [1], Xichao Su [2], Chen Lu [3,4,5], Yu Ding [3,4,5], Chao Wang [3,4,5,*], Haijun Peng [6] and Xinwei Wang [6,*]

1 School of Mathematical Science, Dalian University of Technology, Dalian 116024, China
2 Department of Airborne Vehicle Engineering, Naval Aeronautical and Astronautical University, Yantai 264001, China
3 Science and Technology on Reliability and Environmental Engineering Laboratory, Beijing 100191, China
4 Institute of Reliability Engineering, Beihang University, Beijing 100191, China
5 School of Reliability and Systems Engineering, Beihang University, Beijing 100191, China
6 State Key Laboratory of Structural Analysis for Industrial Equipment, Department of Engineering Mechanics, Dalian University of Technology, Dalian 116024, China
* Correspondence: wangchaowork@buaa.edu.cn (C.W.); wangxinwei@dlut.edu.cn (X.W.)

Abstract: This paper focuses on cooperative multi-task assignment and re-assignment problems when multiple unmanned aerial vehicles (UAVs) attack multiple known targets. A unified multi-objective optimization framework for UAV cooperative task assignment and re-assignment is studied in this paper. In order to simultaneously optimize the losses and benefits of the UAVs, we establish a multi-objective optimization model. The amount of tasks that each UAV can perform and the number of attacks on each target are limited according to the ammunition capacity of each UAV and the value of each target. To solve this multi-objective optimization problem, a multi-objective genetic algorithm suitable for UAV cooperative task assignment is constructed based on the NSGA-II algorithm. At the same time, a selection strategy is used to assist decision-makers in choosing one or more solutions from the Pareto-optimal front. Moreover, to deal with emergencies such as UAV damage and to detect of new targets, a task re-assignment algorithm based on the contract network protocol (CNP) is developed. It can be implemented in real-time while only slightly sacrificing the ability to seek the optimal solution. Simulation results demonstrate that the methods developed in this paper are effective.

Keywords: unmanned aerial vehicle; cooperative task assignment; multi-objective optimization; genetic algorithm; contract network protocol

MSC: 90C29

Citation: Gao, X.; Wang, L.; Su, X.; Lu, C.; Ding, Y.; Wang, C.; Peng, H.; Wang, X. A Unified Multi-Objective Optimization Framework for UAV Cooperative Task Assignment and Re-Assignment. *Mathematics* **2022**, *10*, 4241. https://doi.org/10.3390/math10224241

Academic Editor: Ioannis G. Tsoulos

Received: 15 September 2022
Accepted: 4 November 2022
Published: 13 November 2022

1. Introduction

Unmanned aerial vehicles (UAVs) refer to aircraft without pilots; such aircraft can fly autonomously or can be remotely controlled by an operator [1]. They can completely reduce casualties and costs when performing high-risk missions [2]. At present, UAVs have become very popular in many fields, such as infrastructure inspection, coastal border surveillance, military applications, and others fields [3–6]. In the increasingly complex battlefield situation, a single UAV cannot quickly adapt to the changing battlefield environment due to lack of information interaction. At the same time, the effectiveness of a single UAV in perform tasks is not high due to the limited ammunition capacity of a single UAV. However, when a team composed of multiple UAVs performs tasks cooperatively it can overcome the shortcomings of a single UAV. The UAV team can share information and fully allocate internal resources, allowing tasks to be completed efficiently [7,8].

In order to take the advantage of multiple UAVs when performing tasks realize improvements in efficiency, cooperative task assignment is important. In recent years, results have been achieved in research on task assignment in different fields [9,10]. According to the different factors considered by researchers, the task assignment problem of multiple UAVs can be categorized into different models, and many related algorithms have been proposed as well. Swarm intelligence optimization algorithms are widely used in this field, particularly genetic algorithms [11]. The UAV team can be composed of either homogeneous UAVs or heterogeneous UAVs. For cooperative task assignment of homogeneous UAVs considering the limitations on the total flight distance of UAVs, Wang et al. [12] established a combinatorial optimization problem with the total weighted cost of target value and distance cost as the objective, and presented an improved genetic algorithm based on the beetle antennae search algorithm. Venugopalan et al. [13] presented a team search-based decentralized task assignment scheme for homogeneous UAVs. Velhal et al. [14] formulated the restricted airspace protection problem as a multi-UAV spatio-temporal multi-task allocation problem, and proposed a modified consensus-based bundled auction method to solve it. For cooperative task assignment of heterogeneous UAVs, Fatemeh Afghah et al. [15] proposed a coalition formation approach to solve the problem of adversary target detection and subsequent task completion. Schwarzrock et al. [16] proposed a method to increase the amount of tasks performed within the problem of task allocation among agents representing UAVs. Taking the minimization of the task execution time of UAVs as the objective, Ye et al. [17] established a task assignment model and proposed a modified genetic algorithm with a multi-type-gene chromosome encoding method. Considering a coupled task allocation and path planning problem, Yan et al. [18] proposed a task allocation algorithm and a cooperative particle swarm algorithm. Uncertain factors are considered in the cooperative task assignment problem as well. Considering the parameter and time-sensitive uncertainties in the task assignment problem, Chen et al. [19] proposed an algorithm that combines the interior point method and the modified two-part wolf pack search algorithm. Jia et al. [20] established a two-stage stochastic programming model of the cooperative task assignment problem incorporating the stochastic velocities of UAVs, and proposed a novel metaheuristic based on a modified genetic algorithm.

However, only a single goal is considered by the above task assignment problems. In order to simultaneously optimize the losses and benefits of the UAV team, it is necessary to study the multi-objective optimization problem for multi-UAV task assignment. NSGA-II and its variants are widely used in the study of multi-objective optimization for UAV mission assignment [21,22]. Cheng et al. [23] considered the multi-objective optimization of task assignment, with minimization of cost and maximization of the value of destroyed targets regarded as the objectives. Taking into account the relationship between the UAVs and the ground control stations, Cristian et al. [24] proposed a new multi-objective genetic algorithm for solving complex mission planning problems be formulating mission planning as a constraint satisfaction problem [25]. Chen et al. [26] studied the task assignment problem for UAVs with different sensor capacities, and proposed a modified multi-objective symbiotic organism search algorithm. Wang et al. [27] considered a high-dimensional multi-objective optimization problem containing four objectives for task assignment, then used an improved multi-objective quantum-behaved particle swarm optimization algorithm to solve the problem. Pohl et al. [28] developed an innovative algorithm for multi-UAV mission routing. Phiboon et al. [29] studied multi-fidelity multi-objective airfoil design optimization for fixed-wing UAVs. However, the above studies have not explained how decision-makers are to choose a solution from the Pareto-optimal front. At the same time, the above literature does not consider the emergencies that may occur on the battlefield. The complexity of the battlefield environment inevitably causes emergencies; for example, damage to UAVs, the appearance of new targets, etc. The problem of UAV task re-assignment needs to be considered when such emergencies occur. Unlike the general task assignment problem, task re-assignment in emergencies must be completed in a short time. Therefore, the task re-assignment problem has higher requirements with respect to the calculation speed of the algorithm. A contract network algorithm [30] based on the auction mechanism has been applied to the real-time task assignment problem. Zhen et al. [31] proposed an improved contract network protocol-based cooperative target assignment scheme to deal with heterogeneous overloading and time sequence problems. Zhang et al. [32] established a model of real-time assignment of tasking based on reconnaissance benefits and reconnaissance costs, and proposed an improved contract network algorithm. Xiang et al. [33] studied the cooperation target assignment of multiple agents, and proposed an improved contract network protocol according to the characteristics and restrictions of target assignment.

The contributions of the present article are provided as follows:

(1) Based on the idea of the NSGA-II algorithm, an algorithm suitable for solving the multi-objective optimization problem of multi-UAV task assignment is presented, and the encoding format and genetic operators therein are specially designed.
(2) A method for aiding commanders in choosing an operation plan from among the Pareto solution set is provided.
(3) A highly efficient CNP-based algorithm is developed for real-time task re-assignment in emergencies.

The remainder of this paper is organized as follows. Section 2 presents a multi-objective optimization model of cooperative task assignment. Section 3 provides the multi-objective optimization strategy. Section 4 provides the method of selecting solutions from the Pareto solution set. The problem of task re-assignment in emergencies is studied in Section 5. Numerical examples are provided in Section 6. Finally, Section 7 concludes the paper.

2. Multi-Objective Optimization Model of Cooperative Task Assignment

For convenience, let $I_n := \{1, 2, \cdots, n\}$, $\bar{I}_n := \{0\} \cup I_n$, $n \in \mathbb{N}_+$. On the battlefield, UAVs with attack capabilities are required to attack multiple known targets in coordination to improve efficiency. Assume that N_U ($N_U \in \mathbb{N}_+$) UAVs coordinately attack N_T ($N_T \in \mathbb{N}_+$) targets in the combat area. Let $U := \{U_1, U_2, \cdots, U_{N_U}\}$ be the set of UAVs, where U_i ($i \in I_{N_U}$) represents the i-th UAV. The target set is recorded as $T := \{T_1, T_2, \cdots, T_{N_T}\}$, where T_j ($j \in I_{N_T}$) represents the j-th target. When a UAV attacks a target, the UAV may be destroyed, and different UAVs have different probabilities of being destroyed when they attack different targets. Let P_{ij}, K_{ij} respectively denote the probability that U_i ($i \in I_{N_U}$) and T_j ($j \in I_{N_T}$) are destroyed when U_i attacks T_j. Let V_{T_j} ($j \in I_{N_T}$) and W_{U_i} ($i \in I_{N_U}$) represent the value of T_j and U_i, respectively.

Because the previous single-objective optimization cannot achieve simultaneous optimization of two conflicting objectives, i.e., simultaneous optimization of the costs and benefits in terms of UAVs, it is necessary to establish a multi-objective optimization model for the cooperative task assignment problem. Considering the respective probabilities of UAVs and targets being destroyed, the following two objectives are used to maximize the value of the destroyed targets while incurring the minimum cost in damaged UAVs.

(i) Maximizing the total value of the targets destroyed by UAVs:

$$\max\ f_1(x) = \sum_{i=1}^{N_U} \sum_{j=1}^{N_T} K_{ij} V_{T_j} x_{ij}, \tag{1}$$

(ii) Minimizing the total cost of the damaged UAVs:

$$\min\ f_2(x) = \sum_{i=1}^{N_U} \sum_{j=1}^{N_T} P_{ij} W_{U_i} x_{ij}, \tag{2}$$

where $x_{ij} \in \{0, 1\}$, $i \in I_{N_U}$, and $j \in I_{N_T}$. If $x_{ij} = 1$, this means that U_i attacks T_j,; otherwise, T_j is not attacked by U_i.

The UAVs have a limited amount of ammunition, which makes it impossible to allocate more tasks to each UAV than its ammunition capacity. Targets have different values, and are divided into high-value targets and low-value targets. In this paper, the values of enemy targets are known in advance. Multiple attack missions are assigned to the same high-value target in order to increase the probability of success. To decrease the time that UAVs must stay within the enemy's threat range, the following assumption is made.

Hypothesis 1 (H1). *Different tasks for the same target are performed by different UAVs.*

The implicit constraint in **H1** is that the same UAV can only attack the same target once. This constraint not being taken into account can cause the limited ammunition to be distributed unevenly, which can affect efficiency. For this reason, the number of high-value targets to be attacked needs to be limited. According to the above description, the task assignment problem needs to satisfy the following constraints.

(i) The amount of tasks assigned to each UAV cannot exceed its own ammunition capacity:

$$\sum_{j=1}^{N_T} x_{ij} \leq n_i, \ \ i \in I_{N_U}, \tag{3}$$

(ii) The number of tasks for each target is limited:

$$\sum_{i=1}^{N_U} x_{ij} \leq m_j, \ \ j \in I_{N_T}, \tag{4}$$

(iii) The same UAV can only attack the same target once:

$$a_{ij} \leq 1, \ \ i \in I_{N_U}, \ j \in I_{N_T}, \tag{5}$$

where n_i $(i \in I_{N_U})$ represents the ammunition capacity of U_i, m_j $(j \in I_{N_T})$ represents the maximum number of T_j being attacked, and a_{ij} $(i \in I_{N_U}, \ j \in I_{N_T})$ represents the number of tasks performed by U_i on T_j.

Let $F(x) := \big(-f_1(x), f_2(x)\big)^\top$. The multi-objective optimization problem of the cooperative task assignment (CTAMOP) is expressed as follows.

$$\begin{aligned} \text{(CTAMOP)} \ \min \ & F(x) \\ \text{s.t.} \ & \sum_{j=1}^{N_T} x_{ij} \leq n_i, \\ & \sum_{i=1}^{N_U} x_{ij} \leq m_j, \\ & a_{ij} \leq 1, \ \ i \in I_{N_U}, \ j \in I_{N_T}, \\ & x_{ij} \in \{0,1\}, \ i \in I_{N_U}, \ j \in I_{N_T}. \end{aligned} \tag{6}$$

3. Multi-Objective Optimization Strategy

In order to solve CTAMOP, an improved multi-objective genetic algorithm based on the NSGA-II algorithm [34] is constructed in this section. Based on the characteristics of the task assignment problem, the chromosome encoding method along with the crossover and mutation operators are specially designed and constructed.

3.1. Chromosome Encoding

The task assignment problem has two characteristics. First, the problem is that multiple UAVs may attack multiple targets; second, whether U_i $(i \in I_{N_U})$ attacks T_j $(j \in I_{N_T})$ is represented by 0 and 1. Considering the above factors, we use the binary matrix encoding method to encode the chromosomes in order to accurately describe the situation of UAVs performing tasks.

For the scenario of N_U UAVs attacking N_T targets, the generated chromosomes should be $N_U \times N_T$ order matrices, which only contain 0 and 1 elements. Constraints (3)–(5) need to be satisfied, i.e., the sum of the i-th row $(i \in I_{N_U})$ of each generated matrix is less than or equal to n_i, and the sum of the j-th $(j \in I_{N_T})$ column is less than or equal to m_j. The i-th row represents the situation of the targets attacked by U_i, and the j-th column represents the situation of UAVs attacking T_j.

The chromosome encoding method is suitable for all combat situations, i.e., when ammunition is sufficient and when ammunition is insufficient. In order to ensure randomness, the chromosomes are generated in the following way. First, a UAV U_i $(i \in I_{N_U})$ and a target T_j $(j \in I_{N_T})$ are randomly selected; then, it is determined whether constraints (3)–(5) are satisfied. If both constraints are satisfied, a variable (0 or 1) is randomly assigned to x_{ij}; otherwise, $x_{ij} = 0$. This process is executed repeatedly. When all UAVs do not satisfy constraint (3) or all targets do not satisfy constraint (4) or (5), the process is terminated. At the same time, all x_{ij} $(i \in I_{N_U},\ j \in I_{N_T})$ that have not been assigned a value receive a value of 0.

Here, a specific example is provided to illustrate how chromosomes are encoded considering the case of $N_U = 4$ and $N_T = 10$. The ammunition capacity of UAVs is $n_1 = n_2 = n_3 = 3$ and $n_4 = 2$, and the maximum number of targets that can be attacked is $m_1 = m_2 = \cdots = m_{10} = 2$. For the scenario in Figure 1a, T_4, T_5, T_9 are assigned to U_1, T_1, T_2, T_7 are assigned to U_2, T_3, T_9, T_{10} are assigned to U_3, and T_6, T_8 are assigned to U_4. The values of the corresponding positions of the chromosome are set to 1, and the remaining positions are set to 0, as shown in Figure 1b.

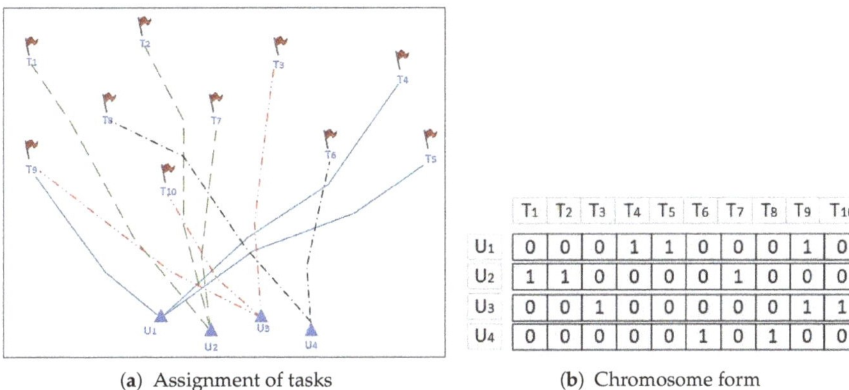

	T1	T2	T3	T4	T5	T6	T7	T8	T9	T10
U1	0	0	0	1	1	0	0	0	1	0
U2	1	1	0	0	0	0	1	0	0	0
U3	0	0	1	0	0	0	0	0	1	1
U4	0	0	0	0	0	1	0	1	0	0

(**a**) Assignment of tasks (**b**) Chromosome form

Figure 1. Assignment of tasks and the chromosome encoding method.

In the evolution process, the offspring are composed of the retained elite individuals and the individuals obtained by crossover and mutation operations. The crossover and mutation operators play key roles. Because the chromosomes are binary matrix, it is necessary to design the crossover and mutation operators for algorithm.

3.2. The Crossover Operator

Two chromosomes F_1 and F_2 are selected from the parents, then a crossover operation is performed on F_1 and F_2 with crossover probability P_c. The specific crossover steps are as follows. First, the l_1-th ($l_1 \in I_{N_U}$) row and the l_2-th ($l_2 \in I_{N_U}$) row from F_1 and F_2, respectively, are randomly selected. Then, the l_1-th row of F_1 and the l_2-th row of F_2 are swapped to obtain two new chromosomes O_1 and O_2. If the task assignment of the obtained chromosome satisfies constraints (3) and (4) and there is no idle UAV, then the obtained chromosome is the crossover offspring. It is common that O_1 and O_2 do not satisfy the constraints, and the following cases may exist as well.

- Task assignment satisfies constraint (4) while not satisfying constraint (3). If the l_1-th ($l_1 \in I_{N_U}$) row of O_1 does not satisfy constraint (3), that is, the number of tasks assigned to U_{l_1} exceeds the ammunition capacity n_{l_1} of U_{l_1}, we sort the tasks of U_{l_1} according to the number of tasks attacked, then delete the corresponding tasks from the task set of U_{l_1} according to their number, from high to low. When the l_1-th ($l_1 \in I_{N_U}$) row satisfies constraint (3), then the operation is stopped.
- Task assignment satisfies constraint (3) while not satisfying constraint (4). If the j-th ($j \in I_{N_T}$) column of O_2 does not satisfy constraint (4), that is, the number of attacks on T_j exceeds the upper limit m_j, the attack task of T_j is randomly deleted from the rows that have not been exchanged. If T_j satisfies the constraint (4), then the operation is stopped.
- Task assignment satisfies neither constraint (3) nor (4). In this case, the same method as in case 1 is first used to change the chromosome and then to determine whether constraint (4) is satisfied. If constraint (4) is not satisfied, then the method from case 2 is used to change the chromosome.

If both constraints (3) and (4) are satisfied and there is an idle UAV, then as many tasks as possible are assigned to the idle UAV under the premise that constraints (3)–(4) are satisfied; targets that have not yet been attacked are prioritized.

The example provided in Section 3.1 is used to illustrate the construction of the crossover operator. The two selected parent chromosomes are shown in Figure 2. Let the rows randomly selected from F_1 and F_2 be the second and fourth rows, respectively. It can be seen from Figure 2 that T_3 (i.e., the third column marked in yellow) in the offspring chromosome obtained by F_1 does not satisfy constraint (4). As this scenario belongs to the first case, an attack task of T_3 is randomly deleted from the first or fourth row. If the task of U_1 (i.e., the first row marked in yellow) is randomly deleted, U_1 becomes an idle UAV. Thus, as many tasks as possible are assigned to U_1 under the premise that the constraints are satisfied, and the crossover offspring C_1 can be obtained. Here, T_4 and U_4 (i.e., the fourth column and fourth row marked in yellow) in the offspring chromosome obtained by F_2 fail to satisfy constraints (4) and (3), respectively. This belongs to the third case. According to the method used in the third case, the attack task of U_4 is deleted. Then, as the chromosome satisfies the constraints and there are no idle UAVs, we have the crossover offspring C_2.

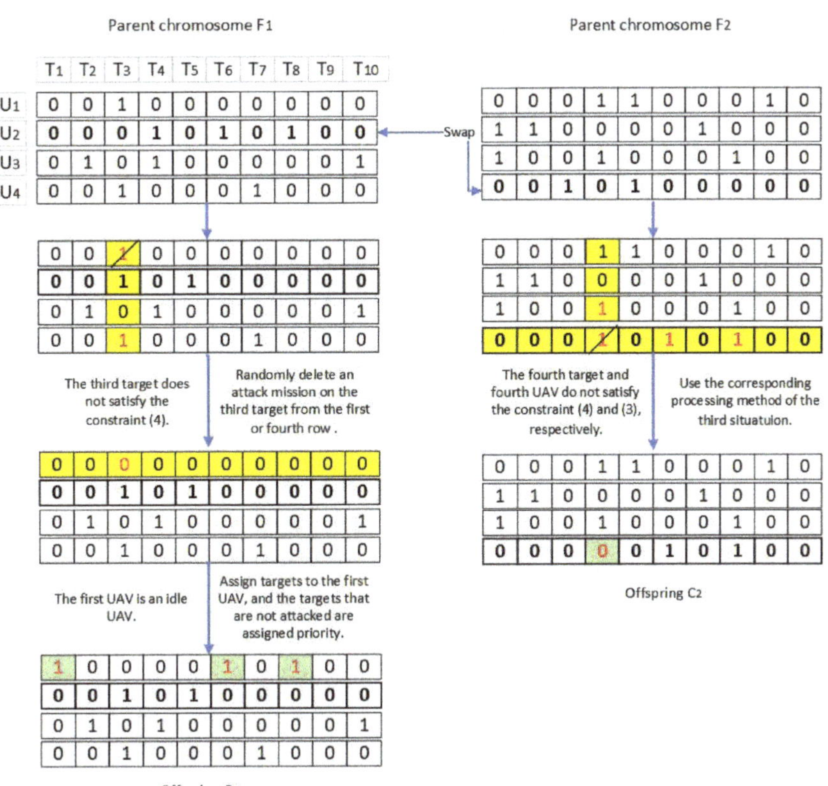

Figure 2. Example of crossover operator.

3.3. The Mutation Operator

A mutation operation is performed on crossover offspring with a mutation probability of P_m. There are three situations that may occur with respect to the crossover offspring, and different mutation operations are used for different situations.

- If there are targets in the chromosome that have not been attacked and there are UAVs with ammunition that can perform tasks, then the mutation operation seeks to assign the targets to these UAVs under the premise that constraint (3) is satisfied.
- If there are targets in the chromosome that have not been attacked and the UAVs have no remaining ammunition, then the mutation operation randomly selects the task sets of two UAVs from the chromosome and exchanges them.
- If all targets are attacked, then the task sets of two UAVs from the chromosome are randomly selected and exchanged.

3.4. The Improved Multi-Objective Genetic Algorithm

Based on the methods used to construct the chromosomes, crossover operators and mutation operators, the following multi-objective optimization algorithm (i.e., Algorithm 1) suitable for UAV cooperative task assignment is developed.

Algorithm 1 Multi-objective optimization algorithm.

```
1: Initialize the values of the following parameters: the population size N, crossover probability P_c, mutation probability P_m, and maximum number of evolutions G;
2: g ⇐ 0;
3: Randomly generate an initial population P_g of size N. The chromosome encoding method and chromosome generation method are based on the methods described in Section 3.1;
4: while g < G do
5:     Calculate the objective function values of each chromosome in population P_g using (1) and (2);
6:     Sort population P_g using the fast non-dominated sorting approach, then determine the front of each chromosome;
7:     Perform crossover operations on the selected parents according to the crossover probability P_c, then mutate the obtained crossover offspring with probability P_m. Proceed to the next step when a progeny population S_g with N chromosomes is obtained;
8:     Combine the parent population P_g with the offspring population S_g to obtain a new population Q_g; then, the size of population Q_g is 2N;
9:     Perform the process in lines 5–6 on population Q_g to obtain the front of each chromosome in Q_g;
10:    Select chromosomes from the front;
11:    while the number of chromosomes selected is less than N do
12:        First, the chromosome is selected from the first front, then, the chromosome is selected from the second front, and so on;
13:        if the number of chromosomes required is less than the number of chromosomes in the l-th front then
14:            Calculate the crowded distances;
15:            Select the chromosomes based on the crowding distance from large to small;
16:        end if
17:    end while
18:    g ⇐ g + 1 and q ⇐ g
19:    if g = G then
20:        Sort P_g using the fast non-dominated sorting approach, then output the chromosomes in the first front;
21:    end if
22: end while
```

4. Selection Strategy

Because the decision-maker needs to select one or more solutions from the Pareto solution set in order to perform specific operations, it is necessary to have a strategy for selecting non-dominated solutions from the Pareto-optimal front. Let f_j denote the j-th objective function, n denote the number of objective functions, and m denote the number of non-dominated solution on the Pareto-optimal front. The specific selection steps are shown in Algorithm 2.

The specific value of α_j $(j \in I_n)$ depends on the degree of preference of the decision-maker for the objective function f_j. Let $C = \{c_1, c_2, \cdots, c_n\}$, where c_j $(j \in I_n)$ represents the degree of preference of the decision-maker for f_j. The rules for setting the value of α_j $(j \in I_n)$ are as follows:

- If $c_{j_1} > c_{j_2} > \cdots > c_{jn}$, then $\alpha_{j_1} > \alpha_{j_2} > \cdots > \alpha_{jn}$, and $\sum_{l=j_1}^{j_n} \alpha_l = 1$, $j_i \in I_n$, $i \in I_n$.
- If $c_{j_1} = c_{j_2}$, then $\alpha_{j_1} = \alpha_{j_2}$, $\forall\, j_1, j_2 \in I_n$. In particular, if $c_{j_1} = c_{j_2} = \cdots = c_{jn}$, then $\alpha_{j_1} = \alpha_{j_2} = \cdots = \alpha_{jn} = \frac{1}{n}$.

Finally, the flowchart diagram of the improved genetic algorithm together with the selection strategy is shown in Figure 3.

Algorithm 2 The strategy for selecting solutions.

1: Convert all objective functions f_j $(j \in I_n)$ into a form that minimizes or maximizes the function F_j $(j \in I_n)$.
2: Solve the problem using the improved NSGA-II algorithm to obtain the Pareto-optimal front.
3: If the dimensions of any two objective functions are different or the orders of magnitude of the values of any two objective functions are different, then normalize the objective function values; otherwise, the objective function values are not normalized. The j-th objective function of the i-th non-dominated solution on the Pareto-optimal front is denoted as $\bar{F}_j^i$ $(j \in I_n,\ i \in I_m)$.
4: Weight and sum each group of objective function values obtained in step 3 to obtain the following set:

$$S = \left\{ S_i | S_i = \sum_{j=1}^{n} \alpha_j \bar{F}_j^i,\ \sum_{j=1}^{n} \alpha_j = 1,\ i \in I_m \right\}.$$

5: In step 1, if the objective functions are transformed into the form of seeking the minimum value, then the solution corresponding to the minimum value in set S obtained in step 4 is selected; otherwise, the solution corresponding to the maximum value in set S is selected.

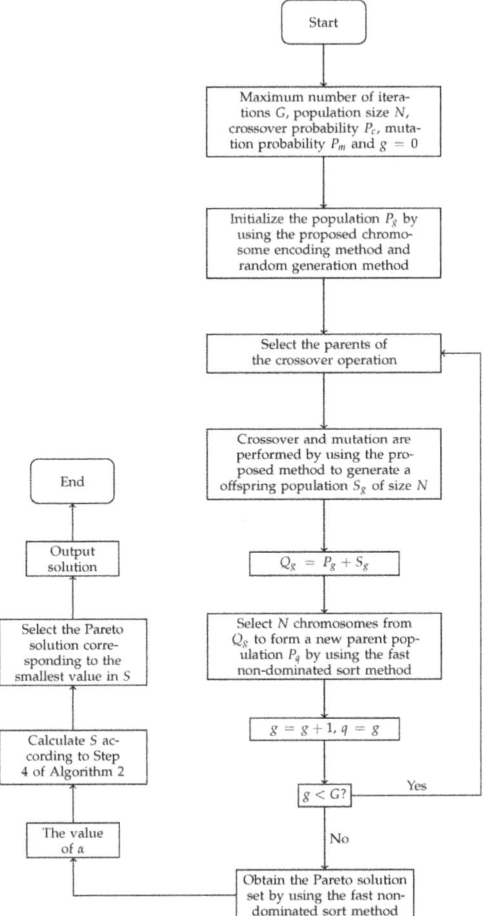

Figure 3. The flowchart of task assignment.

5. Task Re-Assignment For Emergencies

The task assignment process is carried out on the enemy targets found on the battlefield. However, there are many uncertain factors due to the complexity of the battlefield environment. For example, after assigning the discovered targets, new enemy targets may be found on the battlefield again, or certain UAVs in the task assignment may suddenly malfunction and be unable to continue performing combat tasks. Both new targets and targets in the task sets of damaged UAVs need to be re-assigned. There are two methods of assigning tasks. The first method is to assign all tasks according to the current health status of the UAVs, and the second is to assign tasks that need to be assigned based on the obtained task assignment plan. In combat, efficiency issues are more important when solving unexpected situations. Compared with the first method, the second method takes less time and has a higher task assignment efficiency.

In this paper, the re-assignment strategy for new tasks is constructed based on the idea of the contract network protocol and the characteristics of the task assignment problem. Smith first proposed the idea of a contract network protocol [30]. The principle idea of a contract network protocol is to assign tasks through a process of tendering and bidding between agents. There are three types of agents in a contract network protocol: the tender agent, bidding agent, and winning agent. In the problem of UAV task re-assignment, the tender agent is the reconnaissance UAV that discovers a new task or the UAVs that becomes damaged, the bidding agents are UAVs with the ability to perform the newly available tasks, and the winning agent is the UAV corresponding to the bid with the best function value.

5.1. Task Re-Assignment Model

Based on the above description, there are two trigger conditions for task reassignment: (1) new enemy targets are discovered and (2) one or more UAVs are damaged. Suppose that the number of new targets found on the battlefield is s_1, and the number of destroyed UAVs is s_2. Let $\bar{T}$ denote the set of targets that need to be assigned,

$$\bar{T} := \{T_{N_T+1}, T_{N_T+2}, \cdots, T_{N_T+s_1}\},$$

where T_{N_T+i} $(i \in I_{s_1})$ represents the i-th task that needs to be assigned. Let $\bar{U}$ denote the set of UAVs that can perform tasks,

$$\bar{U} := \{U_{l_1}, U_{l_2}, U_{l_{N_U-s_2}}\} = U - \{U_{\bar{l}_1}, U_{\bar{l}_2}, \cdots, U_{\bar{l}_{s_2}}\},$$

where $U_{\bar{l}_j}$ $(j \in I_{s_2})$ represents the $\bar{l}_j$-th damaged UAV. Based on (1) and (2), an objective function is constructed with the following form:

$$\begin{aligned} \max \bar{f} &= \alpha_1 \sum_{i=l_1}^{l_{N_U-s_2}} K_{i(N_T+j)} V_{T_{N_T+j}} x_{i(N_T+j)} \\ &+ \alpha_2 \sum_{i=l_1}^{l_{N_U-s_2}} (1 - P_{i(N_T+j)}) W_{U_i} x_{i(N_T+j)} - \alpha_1 \sum_{i=l_1}^{l_{N_U-s_2}} K_{ij_r} V_{T_{j_r}} x_{ij_r} \\ &- \alpha_2 \sum_{i=l_1}^{l_{N_U-s_2}} (1 - P_{ij_r}) W_{U_i} x_{ij_r}, \end{aligned} \tag{7}$$

where $j \in I_{s_1}$ and T_{j_r} $(j_r \in I_{N_T+j-1})$ represents the target replaced by T_{N_T+j}; T_{j_r} is only considered in an interchange contract, which is described along with sales contracts in the next section. The values of α_1 and α_2 are the same as the values of α_1 and α_2 in Algorithm 2 in Section 4. Thus, the model of task re-assignment (TRAM) is as follows:

$$\begin{aligned}
(\text{TRAM})\ \max\ & \bar{f} \\
\text{s.t.}\ & \sum_{\tilde{j}=1}^{N_T+j} x_{i\tilde{j}} \le n_i, \\
& \sum_{i=l_1}^{l_{N_U-s_2}} x_{i(N_T+j)} \le m_j, \\
& a_{i(N_T+j)} \le 1,\ \ i \in \{l_1, l_2, \cdots, l_{N_U-s_2}\}, \\
& x_{i(N_T+j)} \in \{0,1\},\ \ i \in \{l_1, l_2, \cdots, l_{N_U-s_2}\},
\end{aligned} \tag{8}$$

where $j \in I_{s_1}$.

5.2. Task Re-Assignment Algorithm

In the CNP-based algorithm, sales contracts and interchange contracts are considered. The idea of a sales contract is that a new task is added to the task set of the bidding agent. The specific form of a sales contract of a UAV U_i for a target T_{N_T+j} is represented as follows:

$$< U_i,\ T_{N_T+j},\ 0,\ \bar{f} >, \tag{9}$$

where, $i \in \{l_1, l_2, \cdots, l_{N_U-s_2}\}$, $j \in I_{s_1}$. The sales contract (9) indicates that the revenue obtained by adding target T_{N_T+j} to the task set of U_i is $\bar{f}$. An interchange contract, on the other hand, replaces a target in the UAV task set with a target that needs to be assigned. The specific form of an interchange contract of a UAV U_i for a target T_{N_T+j} is represented as follows:

$$< U_i,\ T_{N_T+j},\ T_{j_r},\ \bar{f} >, \tag{10}$$

where $i \in \{l_1, l_2, \cdots, l_{N_U-s_2}\}$, $j \in I_{s_1}$, and $j_r \in I_{N_T+j-1}$. The interchange contract (10) indicates that the revenue obtained by replacing T_{j_r} in the task set of U_i with T_{N_T+j} is $\bar{f}$. If UAV U_i ($i \in \{l_1, l_2, \cdots, l_{N_U-s_2}\}$) has ammunition remaining, then U_i can execute both the sales contract and the interchange contract; otherwise, U_i can only execute the interchange contract. The steps for assigning target T_{N_T+j} ($j \in I_{s_1}$) are provided in Algorithm 3.

Algorithm 3 Task re-assignment algorithm T_{N_T+j} ($j \in I_{s_1}$).

1: Initialize the information of UAV U_i, the values of parameters $K_{i(N_T+j)}$, $P_{i(N_T+j)}$, $V_{T_{N_T+j}}$ ($i \in \{l_1, l_2, \cdots, l_{N_U-s_2}\}$, $j \in I_{s_1}$), and the number of iterations of interchange contract G_{ic}.
2: Calculate the remaining ammunition R_i^m ($i \in \{l_1, l_2, \cdots, l_{N_U-s_2}\}$) of U_i.
3: If $R_i^m \neq 0$, then U_i executes the interchange contract and sales contract for T_{N_T+j}; otherwise, U_i only executes the interchange contract for T_{N_T+j}. Then, bidding agent U_i chooses the contract with the largest value of $\bar{f}$.
4: The bidding agent evaluates the received contracts and selects the contract with the largest value of $\bar{f}$ as the winning contract, then broadcasts the information of winning agent.

The flowchart diagram of the CNP-based algorithm is shown in Figure 4.

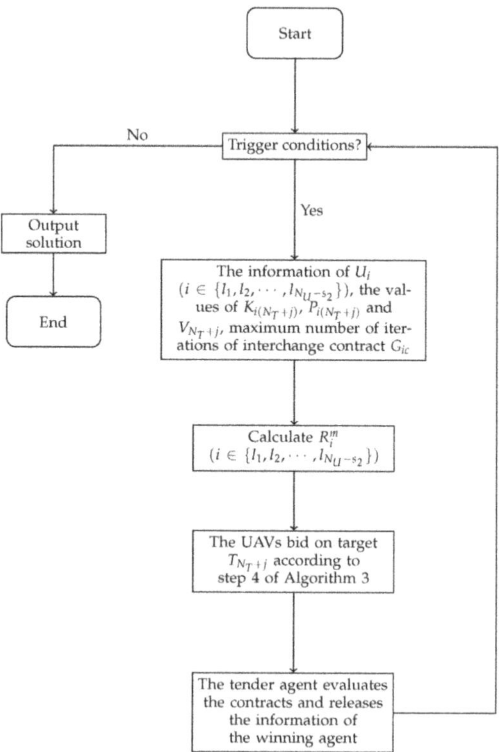

Figure 4. The flowchart of task re-assignment

6. Numerical Experiments

In order to verify the effectiveness of Algorithms 1–3, simulation examples of various battle situations are analyzed in this section. Examples of the improved multi-objective genetic algorithm and selection strategy are provided in Section 6.1. In Sections 6.1.1 and 6.1.2, examples where the total amount of ammunition is less than or equal to the total number of tasks are considered, and the effectiveness of Algorithm 1 is verified. In Section 6.1.3, a large-scale example where the total amount of ammunition is greater than the total number of tasks is provided. Examples of task re-assignment in emergencies are laid out in Section 6.2. In Section 6.2.1, an example is used to illustrate the process of Algorithm 3. A large-scale example considering emergencies is provided in Section 6.2.2 to verify the effectiveness and advantages of Algorithm 3. In Section 6.2.3, we analyze why the CNP-based method is not directly used to solve the task assignment problem. All numerical experiments were implemented using Python 3.8 on a computer with an Intel Core i5-10210U CPU @ 1.60GHz, 2.11 GHz, and 4.00 GB RAM. The code for the algorithms can be found at the URL (accessed on 6 November 2022) https://github.com/gaoxh-github/multi-objetive-task-assignment-source-code. For the different examples provided in this paper, the reader only needs to change the corresponding parameters in the code.

6.1. Test of the Improved Multi-Objective Genetic Algorithm

6.1.1. Case 1: Total Amount of Ammunition = Total Number of Tasks

First, we consider a case in which $N_U = 4$ and $N_T = 8$. The ammunition capacity of each UAV is $n_i = 2$ $(i \in I_4)$, and the upper limit of each target being attacked is $m_j = 1$ $(j \in I_8)$. When U_i $(i \in I_4)$ attacks T_j $(j \in I_8)$, the probability P_{ij} of U_i being destroyed and the probability K_{ij} of T_j being destroyed are shown in Table 1. The values of U_i and T_j are shown in Table 2. To verify the effectiveness of Algorithm 1, we compare it with the Multiple Objective Particle Swarm Optimization (MOPSO) algorithm using the example in this section. In Algorithm 1, the crossover probability is $P_c = 0.8$ and the mutation probability is $P_m = 0.2$. In MOPSO, the values of the parameters are $\omega = 0.7298$, $c_1 = 1.49618$ and $c_2 = 1.49618$. The population size and maximum number of iterations of the two algorithms are $N = 100$ and $G = 200$, respectively.

The comparison results of the obtained Pareto-optimal fronts and CPU runtime are shown in Figure 5. According to the definition of the Pareto solution [34], it can be seen from Figure 5a that all the non-dominated solutions obtained by Algorithm 1 dominate the non-dominated solution obtained by MOPSO. As can be seen from Figure 5b, the CPU runtime of GA-CTAP is significantly shorter than that of MOPSO. The convergence curves of the objective functions are shown in Figure 6. Clearly, thte GA-CTAP algorithm achieves better convergence performance compared to MOPSO. For convenient description, the task assignment corresponding to the non-dominated solutions A, B, and C are provided in Table 3.

Table 1. Probabilities of UAVs and targets being destroyed.

		T_1	T_2	T_3	T_4	T_5	T_6	T_7	T_8
U_1	P_{1j}	0.16	0.65	0.14	0.16	0.44	0.14	0.35	0.25
	K_{1j}	0.5	0.8	0.3	0.4	0.5	0.6	0.6	0.7
U_2	P_{2j}	0.14	0.16	0.44	0.14	0.65	0.16	0.45	0.35
	K_{2j}	0.8	0.4	0.4	0.8	0.7	0.6	0.8	0.6
U_3	P_{3j}	0.44	0.14	0.16	0.16	0.14	0.65	0.35	0.18
	K_{3j}	0.6	0.5	0.8	0.3	0.8	0.3	0.7	0.7
U_4	P_{4j}	0.65	0.14	0.16	0.44	0.08	0.16	0.55	0.48
	K_{4j}	0.6	0.4	0.2	0.3	0.3	0.6	0.5	0.6

Table 2. Values of UAVs and targets.

Target	T_1	T_2	T_3	T_4	T_5	T_6	T_7	T_8
Value	0.62	0.65	0.68	0.7	0.73	0.78	0.81	0.85
UAV	U_1	U_2	U_3	U_4				
Value	0.8	1.1	0.9	1.3				

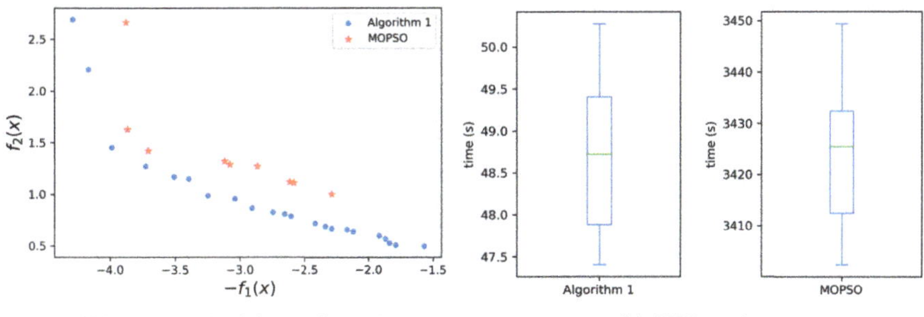

(**a**) Pareto-optimal front of case 1

(**b**) CPU runtime

Figure 5. Comparison of results.

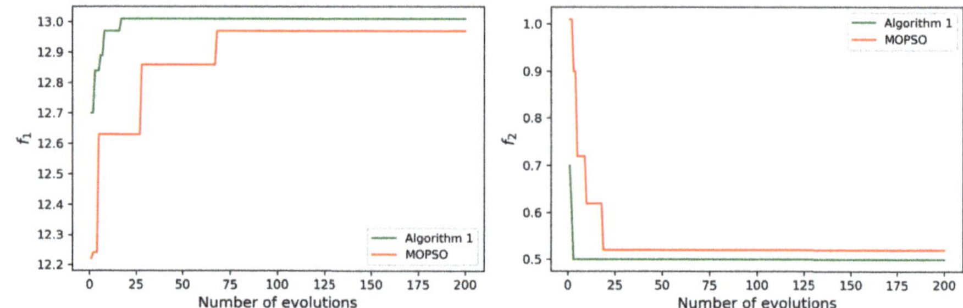

Figure 6. Convergence curves of objective functions for case 1.

Table 3. Specific task assignment of non-dominated solutions A, B, C.

	A	B	C
x	0 0 0 0 0 0 1 1 1 0 0 1 0 0 0 0 0 0 1 0 1 0 0 0 0 1 0 0 0 1 0 0	0 0 0 0 0 0 0 1 1 0 0 1 0 0 0 0 0 0 1 0 1 0 0 0 0 0 0 0 0 1 0 0	0 0 0 0 0 1 0 0 1 0 0 1 0 0 0 0 0 1 0 0 0 0 0 1 0 0 0 0 1 0 0 0

Case 1 considers a situation in which the total amount of ammunition is equal to the number of tasks. However, in actual combat it is possible that the number of tasks is more or less than the amount of ammunition.

6.1.2. Case 2: Total Amount of Ammunition < Total Number of Tasks

In this section, we analyze a case in which four UAVs attack twenty targets. For convenience of calculation, it is assumed that each UAV has the same amount of ammunition $n_i = 4$ $(i \in I_4)$. At the same time, in order to simplify the description, the parameter information of multiple UAVs carrying out attacking tasks on the first eight targets takes the values in Tables 1 and 2. When U_i $(i \in I_4)$ attacks T_j $(j \in \{9, 10, \cdots, 20\})$, the probability P_{ij} of U_i being destroyed, the probability K_{ij} of T_j being destroyed, and the value of T_j $(j \in \{9, 10, \cdots, 20\})$ are provided in Table 4.

Table 4. Probabilities of UAVs and targets being destroyed and target values.

		T$_9$	T$_{10}$	T$_{11}$	T$_{12}$	T$_{13}$	T$_{14}$	T$_{15}$	T$_{16}$	T$_{17}$	T$_{18}$	T$_{19}$	T$_{20}$
U$_1$	P_{1j}	0.21	0.15	0.32	0.18	0.46	0.23	0.55	0.14	0.35	0.16	0.26	0.25
	K_{1j}	0.7	0.6	0.5	0.6	0.4	0.6	0.4	0.3	0.3	0.8	0.3	0.7
U$_2$	P_{2j}	0.30	0.24	0.51	0.44	0.44	0.30	0.42	0.15	0.16	0.18	0.08	0.48
	K_{2j}	0.6	0.7	0.7	0.3	0.3	0.5	0.3	0.5	0.3	0.7	0.3	0.6
U$_3$	P_{3j}	0.53	0.16	0.44	0.68	0.14	0.25	0.50	0.48	0.14	0.09	0.13	0.60
	K_{3j}	0.7	0.4	0.6	0.5	0.3	0.5	0.4	0.6	0.3	0.8	0.4	0.8
U$_4$	P_{4j}	0.65	0.30	0.42	0.08	0.50	0.18	0.48	0.15	0.16	0.20	0.15	0.60
	K_{4j}	0.7	0.6	0.6	0.7	0.4	0.7	0.6	0.5	0.4	0.8	0.4	0.8
Target	value	0.72	0.78	0.62	0.65	0.76	0.88	0.63	0.7	0.68	0.82	0.75	0.81

The obtained Pareto-optimal front is shown in Figure 7. It can be seen that the non-dominated solutions are evenly distributed and the population diversity is good. Figure 8 shows the changes of the maximum value of f_2 and the minimum value of f_1 in each iteration over the course of the entire iteration when $n_i = 4$ $(i \in I_4)$. It can be seen that as the evolutionary algebra increases, the values of the two functions converge.

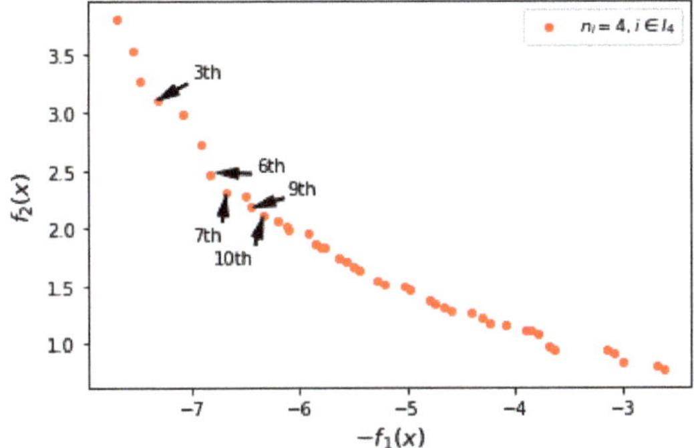

Figure 7. Pareto-optimal front of case 2.

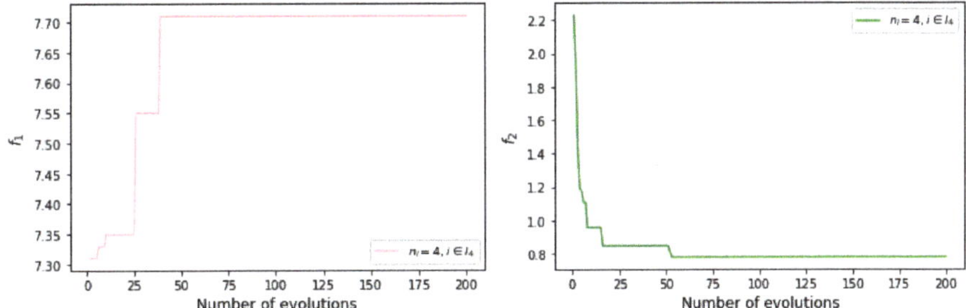

Figure 8. Convergence curves of objective functions for case 2.

The process of selecting solutions from the Pareto solution set using the selection strategy is as follows. Let $S := \{S_0, S_1, \cdots, S_{44}\}$ represent the result obtained in Step 4 of Algorithm 2, where $S_i = \alpha_1 F_1^i + \alpha_2 F_2^i$, $F_1^i = -f_1^i$, $F_2^i = f_2^i$ $(i \in \bar{I}_{44})$, α_1, and α_2 represent the weights and (F_1^i, F_2^i) represents the i-th non-dominated solution in the Pareto-optimal front. Based on this example and the description of weights in Section 4, the rules for setting the values of α_i $(i \in I_2)$ are as follows:

- If $c_1 > c_2$, then $\alpha_1 \in (0.5, 1]$.
- If $c_1 = c_2$, then $\alpha_1 = \alpha_2 = 0.5$.
- If $c_1 < c_2$, then $\alpha_1 \in [0, 0.5)$.

For the Pareto-optimal front shown in Figure 7, the solutions from the upper left corner to the lower right corner are the 0th to the 44th non-dominated solutions. In this example, the objective function values are not normalized because the dimensions of f_1 and f_2 are the same, and the order of magnitude of the values of f_1 and f_2 is the same at $2.62 \leq f_1 \leq 7.71$ and $0.78 \leq f_2 \leq 3.81$, respectively. Assuming the weights $\alpha_1 = 0.5$, $\alpha_2 = 0.5$, the results obtained by selection strategy are shown in Table 5.

As can be seen from Table 5, the sixth and seventh non-dominated solutions on the Pareto-optimal front are the best choices, while the 44th non-dominated solution is the worst choice. For the sake of simplifying the description, only the non-dominated solution information and the specific task assignment corresponding to the first five choices are shown. The positions of the five solutions are shown in Figure 7, and the corresponding specific task assignments are shown in Table 6.

The above description represents the process of selecting solutions of the multi-objective task assignment problem containing two objective functions. For general multi-objective optimization problems, the process of selecting solutions from the Pareto-optimal front is similar to the above process, and the values of weights are set according to the rules in Section 4.

Table 5. The order of selection of non-dominated solutions.

S_i	−2.185	−2.185	−2.135	−2.11	−2.105	−2.105	−2.1	−2.1	−2.065	−2.055	−2.05	−2.05
i	6	7	9	10	3	8	2	5	11	13	4	12
S_i	−2.01	−1.99	−1.99	−1.98	−1.975	−1.97	−1.95	−1.94	−1.925	−1.915	−1.9	−1.86
i	1	15	16	14	17	18	0	19	20	21	22	23
S_i	−1.85	−1.765	−1.755	−1.715	−1.7	−1.675	−1.655	−1.565	−1.545	−1.53	−1.465	−1.395
i	24	25	26	27	28	29	30	31	32	33	34	35
S_i	−1.37	−1.355	−1.355	−1.34	−1.105	−1.09	−1.08	−0.935	−0.92			
i	36	37	38	39	40	41	42	43	44			

Table 6. The information of the first five non-dominated solutions

	$(-f_1, f_2)$	x
6th	(−6.84, 2.47)	$\begin{matrix} 0&0&0&0&0&0&0&1&1&1&1&0&0&0&0&0&0&0&0&0 \\ 1&0&0&1&0&1&0&0&0&0&0&0&0&0&0&0&0&0&0&0 \\ 0&1&1&0&1&0&1&0&0&0&0&0&0&0&0&0&0&0&0&0 \\ 0&0&0&0&0&0&0&0&0&0&0&1&0&1&0&1&0&0&0&0 \end{matrix}$
7th	(−6.68, 2.31)	$\begin{matrix} 0&0&0&0&0&0&1&1&1&1&0&0&0&0&0&0&0&0&0&0 \\ 1&0&0&1&0&1&0&0&0&0&0&0&0&0&0&0&0&0&0&0 \\ 0&1&1&0&1&0&0&0&0&0&0&0&1&0&0&0&0&0&0&0 \\ 0&0&0&0&0&0&0&0&0&0&0&1&0&1&0&1&0&0&0&0 \end{matrix}$
9th	(−6.45, 2.18)	$\begin{matrix} 0&0&0&0&0&0&1&1&1&1&0&0&0&0&0&0&0&0&0&0 \\ 1&0&0&1&0&1&0&0&0&0&0&0&0&0&0&0&0&0&0&0 \\ 0&1&1&0&1&0&0&0&0&0&0&0&0&0&0&0&0&0&0&0 \\ 0&0&0&0&0&0&0&0&0&0&0&1&0&1&0&1&0&0&0&0 \end{matrix}$
10th	(−6.33, 2.11)	$\begin{matrix} 0&0&0&0&0&0&1&1&1&1&0&0&0&0&0&0&0&0&0&0 \\ 1&0&0&1&0&1&0&0&0&0&0&0&0&0&0&0&0&0&0&0 \\ 0&1&1&0&1&0&0&0&0&0&0&0&1&0&0&0&0&0&0&0 \\ 0&0&0&0&0&0&0&0&0&0&0&1&0&1&0&0&0&0&0&0 \end{matrix}$
3th	(−7.32, 3.11)	$\begin{matrix} 0&0&0&0&0&0&1&1&1&1&0&0&0&0&0&0&0&0&0&0 \\ 1&0&0&1&0&1&0&0&0&0&0&0&0&0&0&0&0&0&0&0 \\ 0&1&1&0&1&0&0&0&0&0&0&0&1&0&0&0&0&0&0&0 \\ 0&0&0&0&0&0&0&0&0&0&0&1&0&0&0&0&0&1&1&1 \end{matrix}$

Let M_{U_i} $(i \in I_{N_U})$ denote the task set of UAV U_i. According to the meaning of chromosomes, the task assignment information corresponding to the five non-dominated solutions in Table 6 is provided in Table 7.

Table 7. The task assignment schemes of the solutions in Table 6.

	UAV	Task Set		UAV	Task Set
6th	U_1	$M_{U_1} = \{T_8, T_9, T_{10}, T_{11}\}$	7th	U_1	$M_{U_1} = \{T_7, T_8, T_9, T_{10}\}$
	U_2	$M_{U_2} = \{T_1, T_4, T_6\}$		U_2	$M_{U_2} = \{T_1, T_4, T_6\}$
	U_3	$M_{U_3} = \{T_2, T_3, T_5, T_7\}$		U_3	$M_{U_3} = \{T_2, T_3, T_5, T_{13}\}$
	U_4	$M_{U_4} = \{T_{12}, T_{14}, T_{16}\}$		U_4	$M_{U_4} = \{T_{12}, T_{14}, T_{16}\}$
9th	U_1	$M_{U_1} = \{T_7, T_8, T_9, T_{10}\}$	10th	U_1	$M_{U_1} = \{T_7, T_8, T_9, T_{10}\}$
	U_2	$M_{U_2} = \{T_1, T_4, T_6\}$		U_2	$M_{U_2} = \{T_1, T_4, T_6\}$
	U_3	$M_{U_3} = \{T_2, T_3, T_5\}$		U_3	$M_{U_3} = \{T_2, T_3, T_5, T_{13}\}$
	U_4	$M_{U_4} = \{T_{12}, T_{14}, T_{16}\}$		U_4	$M_{U_4} = \{T_{12}, T_{14}\}$
3th	U_1	$M_{U_1} = \{T_7, T_8, T_9, T_{10}\}$			
	U_2	$M_{U_2} = \{T_1, T_4, T_6\}$			
	U_3	$M_{U_3} = \{T_2, T_3, T_5, T_{13}\}$			
	U_4	$M_{U_4} = \{T_{12}, T_{18}, T_{19}, T_{20}\}$			

6.1.3. Case 3: Total Amount of Ammunition > Total Number of Tasks

In this section, a large-scale task assignment example of 15 UAVs attacking 100 targets is considered. The ammunition capacity of each UAV is $n_i = 7$ $(i \in I_{15})$, and the upper limit of each target being attacked is $m_j = 1$ $(j \in I_{100})$. Considering the length of the paper, the values of parameters V_{T_j}, W_{U_i}, P_{ij}, and K_{ij} $(i \in I_{15},\ j \in I_{100})$ are not provided. The values of these parameters can be downloaded from the website (accessed on 6 November 2022) https://github.com/gaoxh-github/Values-of-parameters. In Algorithm 1, the values of the parameters are as follows: $N = 100$, $G = 200$, $P_c = 0.8$, $P_m = 0.2$. The obtained Pareto-optimal front is shown in Figure 9. The average time for this scale of experiment is about 60 min.

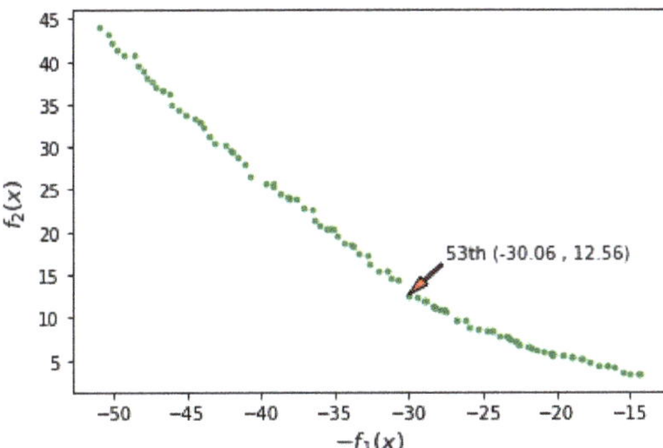

Figure 9. Pareto-optimal front of case 3.

Algorithm 2 is used to select the solution from the Pareto solution set in Figure 9. In Algorithm 2, the values of weights α_1 and α_2 are $\alpha_1 = \alpha_2 = 0.5$. The obtained results are shown in Table 8. It can be seen from Table 8 that the 53rd non-dominated solution should be selected. The information of the 53rd non-dominated solution is shown in Figure 9 and the task assignment scheme of the 53rd non-dominated solution is shown in Table 9.

To further verify the effectiveness of the proposed task assignment algorithm combined with the solution selection strategy, in this section we compare the algorithms developed in this paper with the well-developed Gurobi optimization solver. There are three methods for solving multi-objective optimization problems in the Gurobi solver, namely, Blend, Hierarchical, and a combination of these two methods. In this paper, after obtaining the Pareto front of the task assignment problem using Algorithm 1, the decision-maker can be assisted in selecting a solution from the set of non-dominated solutions based on

Algorithm 2, which is constructed based on the weights. Considering the idea behind the construction of Algorithm 2, we compared Algorithm 1 and Algorithm 2 with the Blend method in Gurobi in order to better reflect the comparison results. The comparison process is as follows. First, given nine different sets of weights, the solution of the example provided in this section is solved for each set of weights using Blend in Gurobi. Second, the Pareto front of the example is solved using Algorithm 1, then the solution is selected from the Pareto front under each set of weights using Algorithm 2. Finally, the solutions obtained by the two methods are compared for each case of weights. Table 10 shows the results of the comparison between Gurobi and the algorithms in this paper under nine sets of weights. As can be seen in Table 10, for each set of weights, the solutions developed this paper and those obtained by Gurobi are not dominated by each other, i.e., both are non-dominated solutions of the problem. Although it cannot be proven that the algorithms in this paper are better than the Gurobi solver, it can be seen that the proposed algorithms are not inferior to Gurobi in terms of solution quality.

Table 8. The order of selecting non-dominated solutions.

S_i	−8.75	−8.56	−8.555	−8.55	−8.54	−8.525	−8.515	−8.51	−8.46	−8.44	−8.375	−8.355
i	53	64	54	58	55	57	62	56	59	61	60	51
S_i	−8.355	−8.35	−8.275	−8.165	−8.14	−8.12	−8.095	−8.03	−7.995	−7.935	−7.92	−7.91
i	65	49	63	48	66	52	68	50	67	46	73	70
S_i	−7.88	−7.87	−7.865	−7.83	−7.78	−7.745	−7.745	−7.715	−7.715	−7.665	−7.655	−7.62
i	43	69	72	71	47	74	75	44	45	76	42	38
S_i	−7.61	−7.55	−7.485	−7.46	−7.405	−7.375	−7.325	−7.315	−7.155	−7.13	−7.13	−7.12
i	39	37	40	77	41	80	78	79	30	26	35	33
S_i	−7.045	−7.04	−7.025	−6.995	−6.975	−6.95	−6.915	−6.81	−6.805	−6.775	−6.605	−6.56
i	31	81	32	36	29	27	34	83	82	28	84	85
S_i	−6.525	−6.51	−6.42	−6.34	−6.335	−6.28	−6.19	−6.19	−6.165	−6.125	−6.085	−5.995
i	25	86	87	24	20	23	22	88	89	21	19	91
S_i	−5.965	−5.85	−5.815	−5.675	−5.605	−5.58	−5.57	−5.53	−5.52	−5.48	−5.06	−5.02
i	90	18	92	15	14	17	16	93	94	13	10	11
S_i	−4.965	−4.92	−4.825	−4.49	−4.4	−4.285	−4.2	−3.935	−3.915	−3.57	−3.465	
i	12	9	8	7	6	4	3	2	5	1	0	

Table 9. Task assignment of the 53rd non-dominated solution in Figure 9.

UAV	Task Set	UAV	Task Set
U_1	$M_{U_1} = \{T_8, T_{27}, T_{29}, T_{41}, T_{48}, T_{96}, T_{98}\}$	U_2	$M_{U_2} = \{T_{19}, T_{44}, T_{64}, T_{65}, T_{79}, T_{86}\}$
U_3	$M_{U_3} = \{T_{22}, T_{24}, T_{62}, T_{80}, T_{89}, T_{91}\}$	U_4	$M_{U_4} = \{T_{16}, T_{33}, T_{43}, T_{71}\}$
U_5	$M_{U_5} = \{T_{34}\}$	U_6	$M_{U_6} = \{T_3, T_{68}\}$
U_7	$M_{U_7} = \{T_{10}, T_{23}, T_{78}, T_{83}, T_{85}\}$	U_8	$M_{U_8} = \{T_{21}, T_{45}\}$
U_9	$M_{U_9} = \{T_5, T_{11}, T_{32}, T_{36}, T_{54}, T_{57}, T_{75}\}$	U_{10}	$M_{U_{10}} = \{T_7, T_{66}\}$
U_{11}	$M_{U_{11}} = \{T_{73}\}$	U_{12}	$M_{U_{12}} = \{T_{13}, T_{38}, T_{74}, T_{76}, T_{77}, T_{93}\}$
U_{13}	$M_{U_{13}} = \{T_6, T_9\}$	U_{14}	$M_{U_{14}} = \{T_{99}\}$
U_{15}	$M_{U_{15}} = \{T_{28}, T_{52}, T_{55}, T_{84}, T_{88}\}$		

Table 10. Comparison results of the proposed algorithms and the multi-objective method in Gurobi.

Weight	(α_1, α_2)	$(0.1, 0.9)$	$(0.2, 0.8)$	$(0.3, 0.7)$	$(0.4, 0.6)$	$(0.5, 0.5)$
Gurobi Algorithm 1 and 2	$(-f_1, f_2)$	$(-8.61, 0.02)$ $(-15.01, 3.38)$	$(-8.61, 0.05)$ $(-15.01, 3.38)$	$(-19.26, 3.22)$ $(-20.27, 5.52)$	$(-19.26, 3.22)$ $(-25.97, 8.85)$	$(-19.26, 3.22)$ $(-30.06, 12.56)$
Weight	(α_1, α_2)	$(0.6, 0.4)$	$(0.7, 0.3)$	$(0.8, 0.2)$	$(0.9, 0.1)$	
Gurobi Algorithm 1 and 2	$(-f_1, f_2)$	$(-19.26, 3.22)$ $(-40.73, 26.47)$	$(-19.31, 3.32)$ $(-50.94, 44.01)$	$(-19.38, 3.5)$ $(-50.94, 44.01)$	$(-19.41, 3.68)$ $(-50.94, 44.01)$	

6.2. Test of the CNP-Based Task Re-Assignment Algorithm

6.2.1. Case 1: A Small-Scale Scenario Involving the Task Re-Assignment Problem

In order to introduce the specific steps of Algorithm 3 in detail, the process of task re-assignment is explained based on the sixth non-dominated solution selected in Section 6.1.2. Suppose that four new targets T_i $(i \in \{21, 22, 23, 24\})$ are found on the battlefield. The probability of UAVs successfully attacking these targets, the probability of UAVs being destroyed, and the values of these new targets are shown in Table 11. In Algorithm 3, the value of the parameter G_{ic} is 10 and $\alpha_1 = \alpha_2 = 0.5$.

Table 11. Probabilities of UAVs and new targets being destroyed and the value of new targets.

		T_{21}	T_{22}	T_{23}	T_{24}			T_{21}	T_{22}	T_{23}	T_{24}
U_1	P_{1j} K_{1j}	0.3 0.58	0.22 0.86	0.44 0.45	0.17 0.82	U_2	P_{1j} K_{1j}	0.21 0.51	0.29 0.95	0.41 0.55	0.15 0.92
U_3	P_{1j} K_{1j}	0.34 0.69	0.2 0.86	0.21 0.54	0.32 0.82	U_4	P_{1j} K_{1j}	0.41 0.64	0.33 0.94	0.46 0.62	0.23 0.95
Target	value	0.8	0.6	0.75	0.65						

Targets T_i $(i \in \{21, 22, 23, 24\})$ are assigned using Algorithm 3; the bidding process is shown in Table 12. The results of task re-assignment are shown in Figure 10, where Figure 10a shows the results for the initial assignment and Figure 10b the results for task re-assignment in emergencies. From Figure 10 and Table 12, the following can be determined. The winning agents of T_{21} and T_{22} are U_4 and U_2, respectively, and the contracts of U_4 and U_2 are all sales contracts. The winning agents of T_{23} and T_{24} are U_3 and U_2, respectively, and the contracts of U_3 and U_2 are all interchange contracts. In the contract of U_3 and U_2, the replaced targets are T_2 and T_{22}, respectively, while in the bidding processes of T_2 and T_{22}, no UAV bids for T_2 or T_{22}.

Table 12. The bidding process and results.

	T_{21}	T_{22}	Winning contract
U_1	-	-	-
U_2	$< 2, 21, 0, 0.6385 >$	$< 2, 22, 0, 0.6755 >$	$< 2, 22, 0, 0.6755 >$
U_3	$< 3, 21, 2, 0.0235 >$	$< 3, 22, 2, 0.0685 >$	-
U_4	$< 4, 21, 0, 0.6395 >$	-	$< 4, 21, 0, 0.6395 >$

	T_{23}		T_{24}		Winning contract
		T_2		T_{22}	
U_1	-	-	$< 1, 24, 11, 0.001 >$	-	-
U_2	-	-	$< 2, 24, 22, 0.0455 >$	-	$< 2, 24, 22, 0.0455 >$
U_3	$< 3, 23, 2, 0.0085 >$	-	-	-	$< 3, 23, 2, 0.0085 >$
U_4	-	-	-	-	

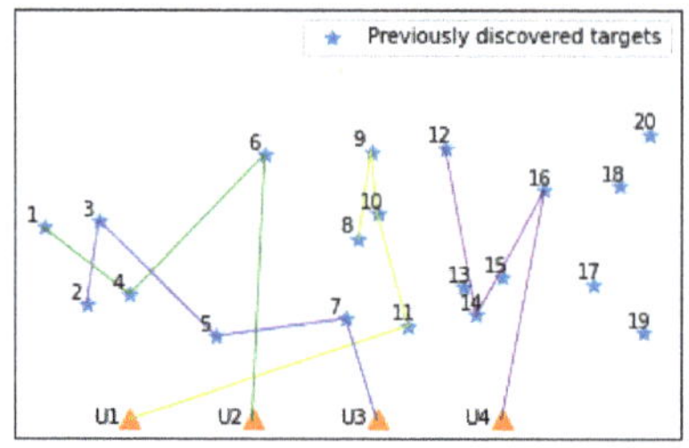

(**a**) The result of initial task assignment

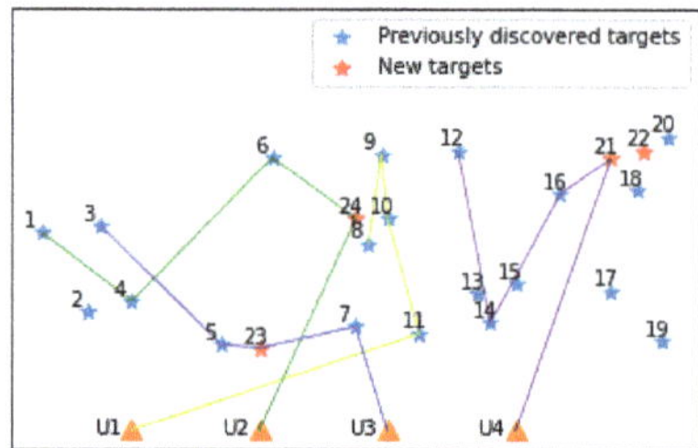

(**b**) The result of task re-assignment

Figure 10. Results of initial task assignment and task re-assignment in emergencies.

6.2.2. Case 2: A Large-Scale Scenario involving the Task Re-Assignment Problem

The primary advantage of the CNP-based method is that it can shorten the time requried for task assignment. The effectiveness of this method can be fully reflected in large-scale calculation examples. In a large-scale problem, to assign all the current tasks again takes a lot of time. However, if only new tasks are assigned using the CNP-based method, a large amount of time can be saved. In this section, the large-scale calculation example in Section 6.1.3 is used to discuss the effectiveness of the task re-assignment method in emergencies.

Suppose that ten new targets are found. The values of the parameters V_{T_j}, P_{ij}, K_{ij} ($i \in I_{15}$, $j \in \{101, 102, \cdots, 110\}$) of the new targets can be downloaded from the website (accessed on 6 November 2022) https://github.com/gaoxh-github/Values-of-parameters. In Algorithm 3, the value of the parameter G_{ic} is 50. The results of the assignment of ten new targets based on the original assignment results are shown in Table 13. It can be seen from Table 13 that the task sets of UAVs U_4, U_6, U_{11}, and U_{14} have changed. The task assignment results obtained using Algorithms 1 and 2 to assign all 110 targets are shown in Table 14. Through calculation, the values of S_1 corresponding to the task assignment schemes in Tables 13 and 14 are −8.91 and −9.42, respectively. The performance of the assignment scheme obtained using Algorithms 1 and 2 to assign all tasks is better than the performance of the assignment scheme obtained using Algorithm 3 to assign new tasks. However, the calculation time of Algorithm 3 is lower than that of Algorithm 1 combined with Algorithm 2. Figure 11 shows the time of ten task re-assignment experiments under these two assignment methods. It can be seen from Figure 11 that Algorithm 3 requires less time to solve the problem of task re-assignment in emergencies than Algorithm 1 combined with Algorithm 2. Therefore, in emergency situations, Algorithm 3 can perform real-time task re-assignment by slightly sacrificing the ability to seek global optimization.

Table 13. Results of task re-assignment using Algorithm 3.

UAV	Task Set	UAV	Task Set
U_1	$M_{U_1} = \{T_8, T_{27}, T_{29}, T_{41}, T_{48}, T_{96}, T_{98}\}$	U_2	$M_{U_2} = \{T_{19}, T_{44}, T_{64}, T_{65}, T_{79}, T_{86}\}$
U_3	$M_{U_3} = \{T_{22}, T_{24}, T_{62}, T_{80}, T_{89}, T_{91}\}$	U_4	$M_{U_4} = \{T_{16}, T_{33}, T_{43}, T_{71}, T_{103}, T_{105}, T_{106}\}$
U_5	$M_{U_5} = \{T_{34}\}$	U_6	$M_{U_6} = \{T_3, T_{68}, T_{110}\}$
U_7	$M_{U_7} = \{T_{10}, T_{23}, T_{78}, T_{83}, T_{85}\}$	U_8	$M_{U_8} = \{T_{21}, T_{45}\}$
U_9	$M_{U_9} = \{T_5, T_{11}, T_{32}, T_{36}, T_{54}, T_{57}, T_{75}\}$	U_{10}	$M_{U_{10}} = \{T_7, T_{66}\}$
U_{11}	$M_{U_{11}} = \{T_{73}, T_{107}, T_{109}\}$	U_{12}	$M_{U_{12}} = \{T_{13}, T_{38}, T_{74}, T_{76}, T_{77}, T_{93}\}$
U_{13}	$M_{U_{13}} = \{T_6, T_9\}$	U_{14}	$M_{U_{14}} = \{T_{99}, T_{101}, T_{102}, T_{104}, T_{108}\}$
U_{15}	$M_{U_{15}} = \{T_{28}, T_{52}, T_{55}, T_{84}, T_{88}\}$		

Table 14. Results of task re-assignment using Algorithm 1 and Algorithm 2.

UAV	Task Set	UAV	Task Set
U_1	$M_{U_1} = \{T_3, T_{27}, T_{106}\}$	U_2	$M_{U_2} = \{T_{108}\}$
U_3	$M_{U_3} = \{T_{14}, T_{38}, T_{39}, T_{79}, T_{80}, T_{94}\}$	U_4	$M_{U_4} = \{T_{44}, T_{57}, T_{77}, T_{84}\}$
U_5	$M_{U_5} = \{T_8\}$	U_6	$M_{U_6} = \{T_{22}\}$
U_7	$M_{U_7} = \{T_5, T_9, T_{17}, T_{34}, T_{68}, T_{74}, T_{75}\}$	U_8	$M_{U_8} = \{T_{86}\}$
U_9	$M_{U_9} = \{T_{11}, T_{48}, T_{65}, T_{73}, T_{98}\}$	U_{10}	$M_{U_{10}} = \{T_{40}, T_{52}, T_{69}\}$
U_{11}	$M_{U_{11}} = \{T_{55}, T_{66}, T_{87}\}$	U_{12}	$M_{U_{12}} = \{T_6, T_{21}, T_{32}, T_{76}, T_{100}, T_{101}, T_{103}\}$
U_{13}	$M_{U_{13}} = \{T_{24}, T_{89}\}$	U_{14}	$M_{U_{14}} = \{T_{83}\}$
U_{15}	$M_{U_{15}} = \{T_1, T_{10}, T_{33}, T_{45}, T_{78}, T_{93}, T_{99}\}$		

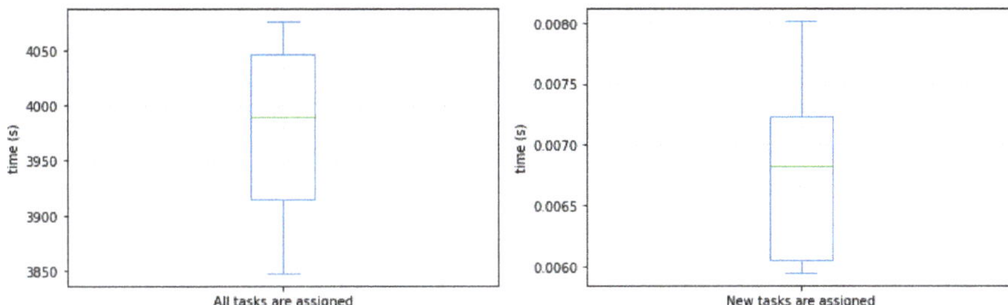

Figure 11. CPU runtime required for the task re-assignment process. (**a**) Algorithm 1 combined with Algorithm 2. (**b**) Algorithm 3.

6.2.3. Case 3: Attempting to Solve the Task Assignment Problem Directly Using the CNP-Based Method

Considering that Algorithm 3 can quickly solve the task re-assignment problem, it may be possible to use this algorithm directly to solve the task assignment problem. An analysis of this problem is provided in this section. In the task assignment problem before the battle, the main goal of assignment is to find an assignment plan that achieves better performance. Taking the 15 UAVs attacking 100 targets in Section 6.1.3 as an example. Let $\alpha_1 = \alpha_2 = 0.5$, the calculation time of Algorithm 3 is about 1 second. The task assignment plan obtained using the CNP-based algorithm is shown in Table 15. The values of S_1 corresponding to the task assignment schemes in Tables 9 and 15 are -8.75 and -5.189, respectively. Obviously, the calculation result of the improved multi-objective genetic algorithm combined with selection strategy is much better than the calculation result of the CNP-based method. For the task assignment problem, the CNP-based method is much faster than the improved multi-objective genetic algorithm combined with selection strategy. However, the result obtained by the improved multi-objective genetic algorithm combined with selection strategy is much better than the result obtained by the CNP-based algorithm. Therefore, according to the above analysis, Algorithms 1 and 2 should be used in the task assignment phase with high requirements for the performance of the task assignment scheme, and Algorithm 3 should be used in the task re-assignment phase in emergencies with high requirements related to assignment time.

Table 15. The result of Case 3 in Section 6.1.3 based on the CNP-based method.

UAV	Task Set	UAV	Task Set
U_1	$M_{U_1} = \{T_{33}, T_{40}, T_{48}, T_{52}, T_{55}, T_{64}, T_{65}\}$	U_2	$M_{U_2} = \{T_{72}, T_{73}, T_{75}, T_{76}, T_{77}, T_{78}, T_{79}\}$
U_3	$M_{U_3} = \{T_{99}, T_{100}\}$	U_4	$M_{U_4} = \{T_5, T_9, T_{10}, T_{14}, T_{16}, T_{21}, T_{22}\}$
U_5	$M_{U_5} = \{T_{36}, T_{44}, T_{46}, T_{53}, T_{54}, T_{60}, T_{61}\}$	U_6	$M_{U_6} = \{T_1, T_6, T_{18}, T_{24}, T_{26}, T_{29}, T_{31}\}$
U_7	$M_{U_7} = \{T_{74}, T_{80}, T_{82}, T_{84}, T_{85}, T_{88}, T_{96}\}$	U_8	$M_{U_8} = \{T_2, T_{42}, T_{49}, T_{50}, T_{58}, T_{59}, T_{69}\}$
U_9	$M_{U_9} = \{T_{43}, T_{51}, T_{57}, T_{62}, T_{66}, T_{68}, T_{70}\}$	U_{10}	$M_{U_{10}} = \{T_{15}, T_{17}, T_{19}, T_{20}, T_{25}, T_{30}, T_{32}\}$
U_{11}	$M_{U_{11}} = \{T_{23}, T_{27}, T_{28}, T_{34}, T_{35}, T_{38}, T_{39}\}$	U_{12}	$M_{U_{12}} = \{T_{81}, T_{86}, T_{87}, T_{90}, T_{91}, T_{97}, T_{98}\}$
U_{13}	$M_{U_{13}} = \{T_{37}, T_{41}, T_{45}, T_{47}, T_{56}, T_{63}, T_{67}\}$	U_{14}	$M_{U_{14}} = \{T_3, T_4, T_7, T_8, T_{11}, T_{12}, T_{13}\}$
U_{15}	$M_{U_{15}} = \{T_{71}, T_{83}, T_{89}, T_{92}, T_{93}, T_{94}, T_{95}\}$		

7. Conclusions

In this paper, we have provided a unified multi-objective optimization framework for the cooperative task assignment and re-assignment of multiple UAVs. First, we propose a multi-objective optimization problem in which the minimization of the cost and the maximization of the benefits are regarded as the objectives. To solve the problem, a multi-objective genetic algorithm suitable for UAV cooperative task assignment is proposed and the encoding format and genetic operators in the proposed algorithm are specially designed. Then, we provide a selection strategy to facilitate the choice of an operation plan from the Pareto solution set by the decision-maker. Finally, taking into account the possible emergencies in the complex combat environment, the task re-assignment problem in emergencies before the battle is studied and a task re-assignment algorithm based on a contract network protocol is proposed. Simulation examples are used to verify the effectiveness of the proposed algorithms.

When the battlefield environment is more complex, a single target may contain multiple different tasks. For multiple types of tasks, heterogeneous UAVs have higher efficiency in performing their tasks compared to homogeneous UAVs. At the same time, there may be multiple obstacles in the environment that affect UAV flight. In addition, it is important to study the performance of the algorithm. Therefore, in our next work we intend to focus on the performance of the algorithm and task assignment of heterogeneous UAVs in complex environments containing obstacles.

Author Contributions: Data curation, Y.D.; Funding acquisition, L.W. and X.W.; Investigation, X.S. and Y.D.; Methodology, X.G., L.W., C.W. and X.W.; Project administration, L.W. and X.W.; Resources, C.L., C.W. and X.W.; Supervision, C.L., Y.D., C.W. and H.P.; Validation, X.S.; Writing—original draft, X.G.; Writing—review and editing, X.G. and X.W. All authors have read and agreed to the published version of the manuscript.

Funding: This research was funded by the National Key Research and Development Plan (2021YFB3302501); the National Natural Science Foundation of China (12102077); and the Fundamental Research Funds for the Central Universities (DUT22LAB305, DUT22RC(3)010).

Institutional Review Board Statement: Not applicable.

Informed Consent Statement: Not applicable.

Data Availability Statement: Contact the first/corresponding author please.

Conflicts of Interest: The authors declare no conflict of interest.

References

1. Newcome, L.R. *Unmanned Aviation: A Brief History of Unmanned Aerial Vehicles*; Library of Flight Series, AIAA: Reston, VA, USA, 2004. [CrossRef]
2. Sarris, Z. Survey of UAV applications in civil markets (June 2001). In Proceedings of the IEEE Mediterranean Conference on Control and Automation, Dubrovnik, Croatia, June 2001. Available online: https://www.researchgate.net/publication/229091536_Survey_of_UAV_applications_in_civil_markets_June_2001 (accessed on 6 November 2022).

3. Nonami, K.; Kendoul, F.; Suzuki, S.; Wang, W, Nakazawa, D. *Autonomous Flying Robots: Unmanned Aerial Vehicles and Micro Aerial Vehicles*; Springer: Tokyo, Japan, 2010. Available online: https://dl.acm.org/doi/abs/10.5555/1941802 (accessed on 6 November 2022).
4. Qu, X.B.; Zhang, W.G.; Wang, X.G. Research of UAVs' attack strategy under uncertain condition. *Flight Dyn.* **2015**, *33*, 381–384. Available online: http://en.cnki.com.cn/Article_en/CJFDTOTAL-FHLX201504021.htm (accessed on 6 November 2022).
5. Máthé, K.; Busoniu, L. Vision and Control for UAVs: A Survey of General Methods and of Inexpensive Platforms for Infrastructure Inspection. *Sensors* **2015**, *15*, 14887–14916. [CrossRef] [PubMed]
6. Turner, I.L.; Harley, M.D.; Drummond, C.D. UAVs for coastal surveying. *Coast. Eng.* **2016**, *114*, 19–24. [CrossRef]
7. Fu, X.; Feng, P.; Gao, X. Swarm UAVs Task and Resource Dynamic Assignment Algorithm Based on Task Sequence Mechanism. *IEEE Access* **2019**, *7*, 41090–41100. [CrossRef]
8. Zhen, Z.; Xing, D.; Gao, C. Cooperative search-attack mission planning for multi-UAV based on intelligent self-organized algorithm. *Aerosp. Sci. Technol.* **2018**, *76*, 402–411. [CrossRef]
9. Zhang, L.; Sun, J.; Guo, C.; Zhang, H. A Multi-swarm Competitive Algorithm Based on Dynamic Task Allocation Particle Swarm Optimization. *Arab. J. Sci. Eng.* **2018**, *43*, 8255–8274. [CrossRef]
10. Issac, T.; Silas, S.; Rajsingh, E.B. Prototyping a Scalable P-system-Inspired Dynamic Task Assignment Algorithm for a Centralized Heterogeneous Wireless Sensor Network. *Arab. J. Sci. Eng.* **2020**, *45*, 10353–10380. [CrossRef]
11. Takahashi, M.; Kita, H. A crossover operator using independent component analysis for real-coded genetic algorithms. In Proceedings of the 2001 Congress on Evolutionary Computation (IEEE Cat. No. 01TH8546), Seoul, Korea, 27–30 May 2001; Volume 1, pp. 643–649. [CrossRef]
12. Wang, Z.Y.; Wang, B.; Wei, Y.L.; Liu, P.F.; Zhang, L. Cooperative multi-task assignment of multiple UAVs with improved genetic algorithm based on beetle antennae search. In Proceedings of the 2020 39th Chinese Control Conference, Shenyang, China, 27–29 July 2020; pp. 1065–1610. [CrossRef]
13. Venugopalan, T.K.; Subramanian, K.; Sundaram, S. Multi-UAV task allocation: A team-based approach. In Proceedings of the 2015 IEEE Symposium Series on Computational Intelligence, Cape Town, South Africa, 7–10 December 2015; pp. 45–50. [CrossRef]
14. Velhal, S.; Sundaram, S. Restricted airspace protection using multi-UAV spatio-temporal multi-task allocation. *arXiv* **2020**, arXiv:2011.11247.
15. Afghah, F.; Zaeri-Amirani, M.; Razi, A.; Chakareski, J.; Bentley, E. A coalition formation approach to coordinated task allocation in heterogeneous UAV networks. In Proceedings of the 2018 Annual American Control Conference, Milwaukee, WI, USA, 27–29 June 2018; pp. 5968–5975. [CrossRef]
16. Schwarzrock, J.; Zacarias, I.; Bazzan, A.L.; Fernandes, R.Q.D.A.; Moreira, L.H.; de Freitas, E.P. Solving task allocation problem in multi Unmanned Aerial Vehicles systems using Swarm intelligence. *Eng. Appl. Artif. Intell.* **2018**, *72*, 10–20. [CrossRef]
17. Ye, F.; Chen, J.; Tian, Y.; Jiang, T. Cooperative Multiple Task Assignment of Heterogeneous UAVs Using a Modified Genetic Algorithm with Multi-type-gene Chromosome Encoding Strategy. *J. Intell. Robot. Syst.* **2020**, *100*, 615–627. [CrossRef]
18. Yan, F.; Zhu, X.; Zhou, Z.; Tang, Y. Real-time task allocation for a heterogeneous multi-UAV simultaneous attack. *Sci. Sin. Informationis* **2019**, *49*, 555–569. [CrossRef]
19. Chen, Y.; Yang, D.; Yu, J. Multi-UAV Task Assignment With Parameter and Time-Sensitive Uncertainties Using Modified Two-Part Wolf Pack Search Algorithm. *IEEE Trans. Aerosp. Electron. Syst.* **2018**, *54*, 2853–2872. [CrossRef]
20. Jia, Z.; Yu, J.; Ai, X.; Xu, X.; Yang, D. Cooperative multiple task assignment problem with stochastic velocities and time windows for heterogeneous unmanned aerial vehicles using a genetic algorithm. *Aerosp. Sci. Technol.* **2018**, *76*, 112–125. [CrossRef]
21. Singh, M.K.; Choudhary, A.; Gulia, S.; Verma, A. Multi-objective NSGA-II optimization framework for UAV path planning in an UAV-assisted WSN. *J. Supercomput.* **2022**, 1–35.
22. Zhu, J.; Wang, X.; Huang, H.; Cheng, S.; Wu, M. A NSGA-II Algorithm for Task Scheduling in UAV-Enabled MEC System. *IEEE Trans. Intell. Transp. Syst.* **2021**, *23*, 9414–9429. [CrossRef]
23. Cheng, C.; Wu, X.Q.; Liu, M.; Chen, M. Research on task allocation for UCAVs cooperatively attacking multiple targets. *J. Jilin Univ. (Inf. Sci. Ed.)* **2012**, *30*, 609–615.
24. Ramirez-Atencia, C.; Bello-Orgaz, G.; R-Moreno, M.; Camacho, D. Solving complex multi-UAV mission planning problems using multi-objective genetic algorithms. *Soft Comput.* **2016**, 21, 4883–4900. [CrossRef]
25. Ramirez-Atencia C, Camacho D () Constrained multi-objective optimization for multi-UAV planning. *J. Ambient. Intell. Humaniz. Comput.* **2019**, *10*, 2467–2484. [CrossRef]
26. Chen, H.-X.; Nan, Y.; Yang, Y. Multi-UAV Reconnaissance Task Assignment for Heterogeneous Targets Based on Modified Symbiotic Organisms Search Algorithm. *Sensors* **2019**, 19, 734. [CrossRef]
27. Wang, J.-F.; Jia, G.-W.; Lin, J.-C.; Hou, Z.-X. Cooperative task allocation for heterogeneous multi-UAV using multi-objective optimization algorithm. *J. Central South Univ.* **2020**, *27*, 432–448. [CrossRef]
28. Pohl, A.J.; Lamont, G.B. Multi-objective UAV mission planning using evolutionary computation. In Proceedings of the 2008 Winter Simulation Conference, Miami, FL, USA, 7–10 December 2008; pp. 1268–1279. [CrossRef]
29. Phiboon, T.; Khankwa, K.; Petcharat, N.; Phoksombat, N.; Kanazaki, M.; Kishi, Y.; Bureerat, S.; Ariyarit, A. Experiment and computation multi-fidelity multi-objective airfoil design optimization of fixed-wing UAV. *J. Mech. Sci. Technol.* **2021**, 35, 4065–4072. [CrossRef]

30. Smith, R.G. The contract net protocol: High-level communication and control in a distributed problem solver. IEEE Transactions on Computers, 1980, 29, 1104–1113.
31. Zhen, Z.; Wen, L.; Wang, B.; Hu, Z.; Zhang, D. Improved contract network protocol algorithm based cooperative target allocation of heterogeneous UAV swarm. *Aerosp. Sci. Technol.* **2021**, *119*, 107054. [CrossRef]
32. Zhang, K.W.; Zhao, X.L.; Li, Z.Z.; Zhao, B.X.; Xiao, Z.H. Real-time reconnaissance task assignment of multi-UAV based on improved contract network. In Proceedings of the 2020 International Conference on Artificial Intelligence and Computer Engineering, Beijing, China, 23–25 October 2020.
33. Xiang, J.Q.; Dong, X.W.; Li, Q.D.; Ren, Z. Cooperation target assignment of missiles based on multi-agent technique and improved contract net protocol. In Proceedings of the 2018 IEEE CSAA Guidance, Navigation and Control Conference, Xiamen, China, 10–12 August 2018. [CrossRef]
34. Deb, K.; Pratap, A.; Agarwal, S.; Meyarivan, T. A fast and elitist multiobjective genetic algorithm: NSGA-II. *IEEE Trans. Evol. Comput.* **2002**, 6, 182–197. [CrossRef]

 mathematics

Article

An Improved Optimization Algorithm for Aeronautical Maintenance and Repair Task Scheduling Problem

Changjiu Li [1], Yong Zhang [1,2], Xichao Su [1,*] and Xinwei Wang [3,*]

1 School of Basic Science for Aviation, Naval Aviation University, Yantai 264001, China
2 Department of Precision Instrument, Tsinghua University, Beijing 100084, China
3 State Key Laboratory of Structural Analysis for Industrial Equipment, Department of Engineering Mechanics, Dalian University of Technology, Dalian 116024, China
* Correspondence: suxich@126.com (X.S.); wangxinwei@dlut.edu.cn (X.W.)

Abstract: The maintenance of carrier-based aircraft is a critical factor restricting the availability of aircraft fleets and their capacity to sortie and operate. In this study, an aeronautical maintenance and repair task scheduling problem for carrier-based aircraft fleets in hangar bays is investigated to improve the maintenance efficiency of aircraft carrier hangar bays. First, the operational process of scheduling aeronautical maintenance tasks is systematically analyzed. Based on maintenance resource constraints and actual maintenance task requirements, a wave availability index and load balance index for the maintenance personnel are proposed for optimization. An aeronautical maintenance task scheduling model is formulated for carrier-based aircraft fleets. Second, model abstraction is performed to simulate a multi-skill resource-constrained project scheduling problem, and an improved teaching-learning-based optimization algorithm is proposed. The algorithm utilizes a serial scheduling generation scheme based on resource constraint advancement. Finally, the feasibility and effectiveness of the modeling and algorithm are verified by using simulation cases and algorithm comparisons. The improved teaching-learning-based optimization algorithm exhibits improved solution stability and optimization performance. This method provides theoretical support for deterministic aeronautical maintenance scheduling planning and reduces the burden associated with manual scheduling and planning.

Keywords: carrier-based aircraft; maintenance scheduling; resource-constrained; teaching-learning-based optimization; scheduling optimization

MSC: 90-10; 90B25

Citation: Li, C.; Zhang, Y.; Su, X.; Wang, X. An Improved Optimization Algorithm for Aeronautical Maintenance and Repair Task Scheduling Problem. *Mathematics* **2022**, *10*, 3777. https://doi.org/10.3390/math10203777

Academic Editor: Yue-Jiao Gong

Received: 13 September 2022
Accepted: 11 October 2022
Published: 13 October 2022

1. Introduction

As the core combat unit of an aircraft carrier formation, carrier-based aircraft play an essential role in air control, air-to-submarine defense, electronic countermeasures, and strikes against ships. Aeronautical maintenance is necessary and indispensable in military operations to restore the fleet to excellent technical conditions and provide flight safety guarantees for various combat and training missions [1]. The efficiency of aeronautical maintenance significantly affects the availability and sustained combat capabilities of a fleet. As the scale of combat or training increases, the impact of such constraints becomes more prominent. A hangar bay is required to execute an efficient scheduling scheme for maintenance tasks to shorten the time for maintaining the fleet. Compared with land-based maintenance workshops, hangar bays have the following characteristics: (i) a smaller workspace and complex environment; (ii) complicated processes for fleet-aeronautical maintenance tasks; (iii) the need for a high degree of coordination among maintenance personnel; (iv) limited resources for maintenance personnel, equipment, and workshops; and (v) strict requirements for task timelines. These characteristics make maintenance tasks challenging to execute. In this context, meeting reliability and timeliness requirements using a manual scheduling scheme based on experience is difficult. Based on the environmental characteristics of the hangar bay and the actual needs of combat and training missions, a scientific time-series scheduling scheme and resource allocation approach for limited maintenance personnel, equipment, and workshops can shorten the duration of operations and enable the fleet to quickly return to a usable and combat-ready state. This is a critical and urgent issue that needs to be addressed to maintain the availability of the fleet. It is also a core consideration restricting the overall effectiveness of maritime operations, an essential aspect of future military efforts. This is vital to the evolution of future warfare.

For several years, the process scheduling of carrier-based aircraft has relied heavily on manual empirical approaches for formulating plans. The U.S. Navy has evolved to use an aviation data management and control system [2], known as the "electronic Ouija board", to simulate the locations and statuses of carrier-based aircraft and associated maintenance personnel. Compared with the old Ouija board, this system incorporates multiple interaction modes, and the operator interacts with the system by pointing at the aircraft and gesturing to make decisions. However, a considerable amount of the corresponding work [3] relies on manual completion because a mechanism that can generate autonomous and intelligent scheduling solutions is lacking. Ryan et al. [4] developed a decision system for carrier deck operations based on the concept of human-computer interaction and designed a set of experiments for comparing automatic planning algorithms with manual empirical decisions [5]; this enabled the development of automatic scenario planning and rapid decision-making capabilities for carrier-based aircraft scheduling. However, current research on maintenance scheduling remains limited. A lack of transparency within naval fleet aviation maintenance, complex constraints, special research areas, and the confidentiality of information or data [6] cause challenges to the development of this field.

By contrast, research on civil aeronautical maintenance and management is more established and centered on aircraft maintenance planning (AMP) problems [7]. In the context of optimization problems, AMP is a complex decision problem [8] that involves resource allocation to maintenance tasks but may also involve distributed maintenance area selection. For maintenance tasks in a certain area, the scheduling allocation problem involves assigning maintenance operations to the maintenance equipment/workshops performing the task, assigning maintenance personnel to the tasks of the corresponding operation, and determining the start and end times of the operation [9]. The shortcomings arise from the limitations in maintenance resources or the number of tasks that can be performed simultaneously. The focus of maintenance assurance tasks in naval aircraft fleet aviation differs from that in civil aviation in the following ways:

i. Slack of distributed constraints. Commercial airlines must manage a complex network of routes and the complex coupling between distributed workshops and routes, whereas the majority of military aeronautical maintenance tasks are concentrated in ship-based hanging bays on large sea platforms;
ii. Differences in the maintenance cycles, civil aeronautical maintenance optimization models, and methods applied to solve problems in fleet decision optimization. A commercial fleet is highly stable and has longer maintenance cycle intervals than a military naval aircraft fleet. The carrier-based aircraft fleet aeronautical maintenance tasks investigated in this study involve military tasks with urgent task requirements [10];
iii. Differences in maintenance goals. The literature on civil aeronautical maintenance mainly focuses on profitability, and the optimizations mainly consider economic benefits [11], such as balancing the maintenance cost of the fleet with the amount of hangar resources [12] or the labor costs of maintenance personnel [13]. By contrast, military aviation maintenance tasks are optimized to avoid delaying military response and to ensure appropriate conduct in both combat and training tasks. In other words, the goal is to positively impact operational effectiveness and subsequent warfare.

These differences make the direct application of civil aviation maintenance mission scheduling models to the maritime military domain difficult. Moreover, because of the characteristics of a cluster wave sortie in fleet combat and training missions, the downtime caused by preventive maintenance and failure repairs within a specified flight interval can significantly impact a wave sortie mission [14], thus requiring the redesign of models and optimization requirements applicable to fleet aviation maintenance assurances. The following attempts have been made in the military domain to address these issues:

i. Mission maintenance aspects: Han et al. [15] simulated mission maintenance for deck crews, with the number of aircraft ranging from five to nine. However, they considered only a single maintenance mode and not multimode/hybrid situations, such as preventative maintenance and failure repairs, and realistic constraints, such as maintenance coverage, parallel maintenance capacity, and maintenance workstation space. Thus, the simulation differs substantially from an actual task;
ii. Optimization/scheduling of fleet maintenance tasks: Most studies on optimizing fleet maintenance tasks have focused on minimizing the maintenance completion time [16]. However, Raju et al. [17] defined a military aircraft availability index for fleet wave sortie availability; the index comprised the ratio of the number of aircraft in mission-capable states to the total number of aircraft in the fleet at a given time point. The military maintenance and operational characteristics of naval aircraft were used for closer integration by the index;
iii. Optimization/Scheduling of resources: The main considerations in terms of resources have involved personnel and personnel scheduling strategies [18], resource constraints for maintenance personnel [19], and maintenance personnel time balancing [20]. No studies have been conducted to integrate limited maintenance resources, such as maintenance equipment, workshops, and space, in the models.

Moreover, differences exist in the selection of optimization models in previous studies, in which maintenance scheduling planning was typically treated as a mixed integer linear program (MILP) [21]. The scheduling problem in naval aircraft fleet maintenance involves the coordination of related personnel, equipment, and workshops; in addition, it incorporates complex and highly constrained operational processes and resources and a long makespan. This is the core of the challenge in scheduling the entire process of aircraft carriers and amphibious ships. It is also a typical resource-constrained project scheduling problem (RCPSP) [20]. The RCPSP differs from the MILP in that it emphasizes resource constraints [19]. The RCPSP can be studied to combine the classical RCPSP with the maintenance scheduling task, particularly for the scheduling of resources, such as multi-skill personnel or multifunctional equipment. Based on this feature, the maintenance scheduling problem has been classified as a multi-skill resource-constrained project scheduling problem (MS-RCPSP) to better approximate the actual situation [22]. The MS-RCPSP rationalizes scheduling in terms of time and resources to optimize the objectives while optimizing the use of skills and resources. Because the RCPSP has been proven to be an NP-hard problem, exact algorithms, such as the branch-and-bound method [19] and linear programming [23], treat the maintenance state or the working state of the object as the decision variable, and the value of the variable is usually 0 or 1. These approaches can precisely and efficiently find the optimal solution for a small-scale RCPSP within a reasonable time frame [24,25]. However, most mathematical models are oversimplified, less scalable, and still have limitations in solving large-scale problems. In addition, the solutions for integer decision variables and linear constraints rely heavily on optimization solvers, such as CPLEX [26]. However, as the problem scale increases, the complexity of the corresponding solution space increases significantly. Hence, an exact algorithm cannot complete the solution within an acceptable time frame [27]. Studies have shown that the current best exact methods can solve instances with up to only 60 activities and low resource constraints. As real projects often exceed this size and usually require fast scheduling solutions, exact algorithms are not suitable [28]. Common optimization methods, such as sequential games [29] and multi-agent approaches [18], involve the same issue. Recent developments to improve the solutions for large-scale MS-RCPSPs have been based on classical mathematical techniques. Peschiera [30] proposed a new approach based on a new mixed integer program, highlighting a good trade-off between optimality and infeasibility degradation in the performance search process. Another approach is the use of metaheuristic algorithms. Metaheuristic algorithms have been widely used to quickly obtain approximate optimal solutions for project scheduling, as they achieve the best trade-offs between accuracy, computation time, ease of implementation, and flexibility [31]. The literature is more abundant in this regard. Teaching-learning-based optimization (TLBO) is a population-based algorithm that is similar to the genetic algorithm, particle swarm optimization (PSO), and differential evolution (DE) algorithms [32]. However, TLBO differs from other algorithms in that it does not require algorithm-specific parameter settings. This avoids different optimization effects owing to different parameter settings. The algorithm has been successfully applied to problems such as flow shop scheduling [33], job shop scheduling [34], steelmaking-continuous casting scheduling [35], and RCPSP [36,37], showing good optimization performance and problem adaptability.

Overall, the current research on naval aeronautical maintenance and repair tasks is limited owing to the unique characteristics of the field, such as its complexity and confidentiality.

Above all, the unique characteristics of the naval aeronautical maintenance and repair tasks, such as complexity and confidentiality, make current research on it quite limited. In contrast, the research on civil aviation maintenance and management is more established. However, because the maintenance and repair tasks in naval aeronautics differ from those in civil aviation, the models and optimization objectives need to be redesigned. Some research attempts have been made in the field of military maintenance, but some shortcomings still remain. Moreover, various characteristics of the scheduling problem in naval fleet maintenance are consistent with those of the RCPSP. Therefore, to solve the aeronautical maintenance and repair task scheduling problem (AMRSP), we propose a mathematical formulation model based on the RCPSP using the currently popular metaheuristic algorithm.

The contributions of this study are as follows. First, a comprehensive mathematical model is proposed for the AMRSP of a carrier-based aircraft fleet for the requirements of carrier-based aircraft wave sorties. This model considers constraints regarding personnel, equipment, workshop, workspace, and operational processes, allowing the model to approximate situations in the military aviation maintenance field. Second, an improved teaching-learning-based optimization algorithm with a serial scheduling generation scheme (ITLBO-S) is proposed for solving the model. The algorithm includes a new assistant teaching phase and serial scheduling generation scheme (SSGS) based on resource constraint advancement. Third, simulation cases for method comparisons are used to verify the feasibility and effectiveness of the model and algorithm for large-scale tasks and highly resource-constrained conditions, thereby providing a scheduling scheme for the maintenance process, personnel, and equipment/workshop.

The remainder of this paper is outlined as follows. Section 2 describes the AMRSP. Section 3 presents the mathematical model of the AMRSP. Section 4 describes the process and improvement measures of the ITLBO-S. Section 5 presents a case analysis and details of the simulations. Finally, Section 6 provides conclusions and suggestions for future studies. The research content and framework of this study are shown in Figure 1.

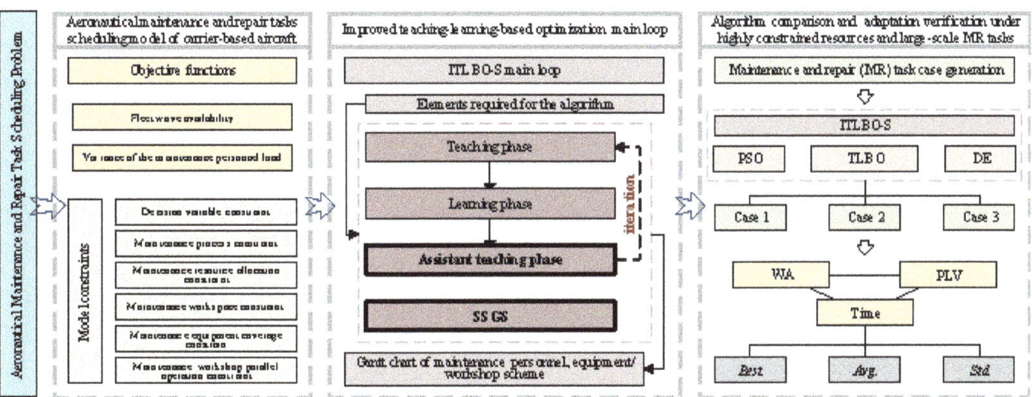

Figure 1. Research content and framework.

2. Problem Statement

The most common military aeronautical maintenance tasks include preventive maintenance, failure repair, and overhaul. Overhaul is the detailed inspection of airborne equipment and accessories of carrier-based aircraft. Generally, this task must be transferred to a land-based repair workshop for standard land-level maintenance. The ship-based hangar bay is responsible for carrier-based aircraft maintenance and repair (MR) tasks. These two types of tasks are the main focus of this study and are collectively called MR tasks. Carrier-based aircraft must be tested for failure before and after a mission. If losses are detected, the aircraft must be recovered to the hanging bay and queued for repair after entering the parking spots. After a repair, failures are fixed within certain limits, and the structural shape and performance are restored. In addition to unplanned repair tasks, both scheduled and preventive maintenance must be completed. Maintenance activities are typically conducted after an aircraft has been operational for a certain number of flight hours. Carrier-based aircraft maintenance activities are also performed after an aircraft has been operational for a certain number of flight hours [38]. Periodic inspections are usually conducted after 25, 50, and 100 flight hours, seven days, three months, and six months, respectively. The hangar is subject to extensive MR tasks to maintain high fleet availability. Figure 2 shows the maintenance resources and environment of the Kuznetsov aircraft carrier hangar bay. The involved constraints are described in more detail below.

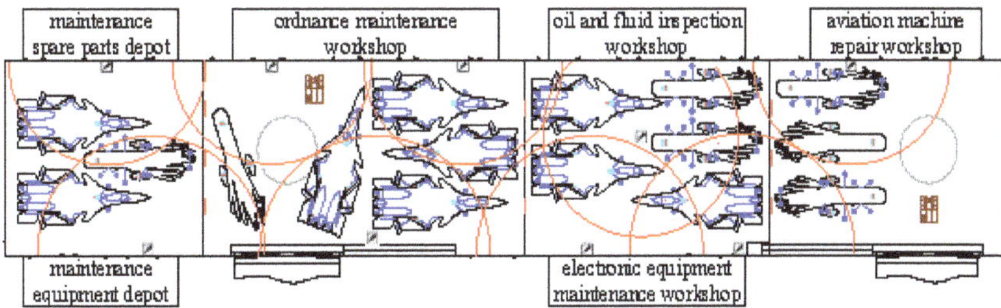

Figure 2. Maintenance resources and environment of the Kuznetsov aircraft carrier hangar bay.

2.1. Maintenance Process

The MR task operations of carrier-based aircraft have a precedence-based logical relations constraint. For the repair tasks of carrier-based aircraft, the sequential order of operations is as follows: failure location, failure repair, and re-inspection. For preventive maintenance tasks, the operations are in networked precedence relations, and any immediately preceding operation is not unique. In the case of the RCPSP, the maintenance task of a single aircraft can be regarded as a project, and the precedence constraints of the maintenance operations can be described by the activity-on-node (AoN) network node, where an operation is represented by a node, and the precedence constraints between activities are denoted by the arcs. I represents a set of carrier-based aircraft, $I = \{1, 2, \cdots, i, \cdots, |I|\}$. J_i represents the set of all maintenance operations of the ith carrier-based aircraft, $J_i = \{1, 2, \cdots, j, \cdots, |J_i|\}$, and J represents the set of all maintenance operations of the fleet, $J = \{(i, j)|i \in I, j \in J_i\}$. A maintenance operation starts after its tethering completion time Ex_i in parking spot p_i. An AoN diagram for preventive maintenance operations is shown in Figure 3. O_{ij} represents the jth maintenance operation of the ith aircraft in the fleet to be maintained. O_S and O_E refer to the virtual start and end of the virtual operation, respectively; these do not consume any resources, have zero operation durations, and serve to integrate all maintenance operations. O_S has no immediately preceding operations, and O_E has no immediately subsequent operations. The dotted line represents the process and virtual process connections.

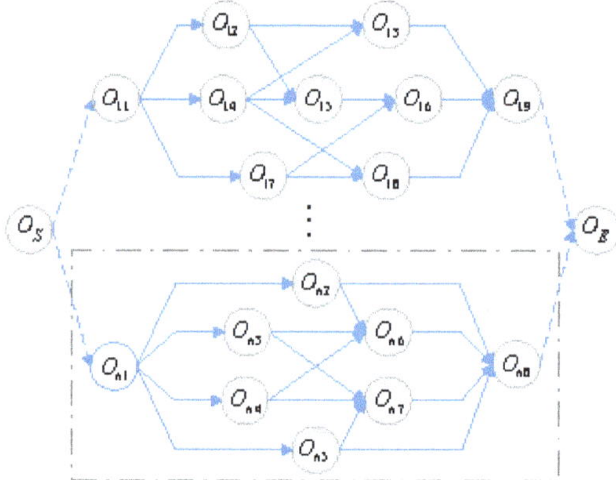

Figure 3. Activity-on-node (AoN) diagram of preventive maintenance operations.

2.2. Maintenance Personnel and Skills

In the AMRSP, the maintenance skills represent the direct operational demands, and the operations correspond to specific skill categories. As the number of maintenance personnel is a constraint, it is common to allocate personnel with multiple skills to enhance the flexibility of task execution. In other words, a set of maintenance personnel is established as a flexible resource with multiple skills. Each person is equipped to perform cross-professional maintenance work in a compatible manner. Different maintenance operations usually require different skills, and a competent professional is identified according to their maintenance skills to complete the task. Lp indicates the set of maintenance personnel. Kc indicates the set of skill categories of the maintenance personnel, $Kc = \{1, 2, \cdots, |Kc|\}$. Figure 4 shows the matching relationship between maintenance operations, skills, and personnel. It represents a further refinement of the maintenance skills and personnel requirements corresponding to the operations.

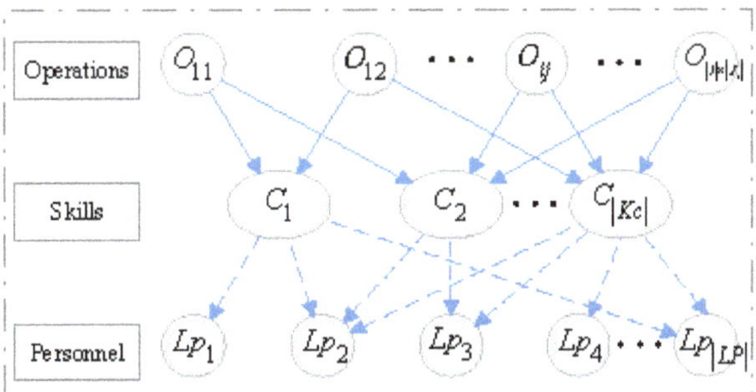

Figure 4. Matching relationship between maintenance operations, skills, and personnel.

2.3. Maintenance Equipment, Workshop, and Workspace

The maintenance equipment of hangar bays can be divided into fixed resource stations and maintenance workshops. Fixed resource stations support the tasks of carrier-based aircraft at the parking spots within the coverage area. Workshops are distributed around the hanging bay and provide regular maintenance and off-site repair of aviation components. This study focuses on a power supply station among the fixed resource stations, as represented by the red line in Figure 2. Maintenance workshops are also located around the hangar bay. They are used to provide scheduled maintenance and off-site repair for aviation components. These workshops consist of aeronautical machine repair, oil and fluid inspection, ordnance, and electronic equipment maintenance workshops. Le indicates a set of maintenance equipment or workshops. Ke indicates the set of skill categories for a piece of maintenance equipment/workshop, and $Ke = \{1, 2, \cdots, |Ke|\}$.

Given the aeronautical MR process for carrier-based aircraft, owing to space constraints, some operations, such as cockpit operations, can accommodate only a certain number of personnel for parallel operations. Ks indicates the set of skill categories for the maintenance workspace, and $Ks = \{1, 2, \cdots, |Ks|\}$.

3. Mathematical Model for Aeronautical Maintenance and Repair Task Scheduling Problem (AMRSP)

3.1. Problem Assumptions

The AMRSP mathematical modeling includes the following simplifications.

i. The MR tasks are known with certainty and do not consider the interference of dynamic factors.
ii. The MR process cannot be preempted or interrupted once started.
iii. The maintenance skills are adapted to each aircraft's MR task mode.
iv. The transit time in the hangar bay is ignored.
v. An adequate reserve of fixed-resource station resources is available.

3.2. Constraints

The related notations and descriptions of the AMRSP mathematical modeling are formulated in Table 1.

Table 1. Related notations and description of the AMRSP mathematical model.

Notations	Descriptions
I	The set of carrier-based aircraft, $I = \{1, 2, \cdots, i, \cdots, \|I\|\}$.
p_i	The parking spot of the ith carrier-based aircraft.
J_i	The set of maintenance operations of the ith carrier-based aircraft, $J_i = \{1, 2, \cdots, j, \cdots, \|J_i\|\}$.
J	The set of all maintenance operations of the fleet, $J = \{(i, j) \| i \in I, j \in J_i\}$.
A_t	The set of all maintenance operations of the fleet in the execution state at time point t.
A_{it}	The set of maintenance operations of the ith carrier-based aircraft in the execution state at time point t.
O_{ij}	The jth maintenance operation of the ith carrier-based aircraft.
Ps_{ij}	The set of immediately preceding operations of O_{ij}.
Ex_i	The tethering completion time of the ith carrier-based aircraft.
d_{ij}	The operation duration of O_{ij}.
BM	A sufficiently large real number.
Lp	The set of maintenance personnel.
Le	The set of maintenance equipment/workshops.
Kc	The set of skill categories of the maintenance personnel, $Kc = \{1, 2, \cdots, \|Kc\|\}$.
Ke	The set of skill categories for maintenance equipment/workshops, $Ke = \{1, 2, \cdots, \|Ke\|\}$.
Ks	The set of skill categories at the maintenance workspace, $Ks = \{1, 2, \cdots, \|Ks\|\}$.
rc_{ijk}	An indicator variable valued 0 or 1, where 1 indicates that O_{ij} has a demand for the kth skill category, whereas 0 indicates otherwise.
re_{ijk}	An indicator variable valued 0 or 1, where 1 indicates that O_{ij} has a demand for the kth maintenance equipment/workshop category, whereas 0 indicates otherwise.
rs_{ijk}	An indicator variable valued 0 or 1, where 1 indicates that O_{ij} has a demand for the kth maintenance workspace, whereas 0 indicates otherwise.
λ_{kl}^{p}	An indicator variable valued 0 or 1, where 1 indicates that the lth of the kth maintenance equipment/workshop category has a reachability relation with p, whereas 0 indicates otherwise.
ns_{ik}	The number of personnel who can work in parallel with the ith carrier-based aircraft kth workspace category.
Ne_{kl}	The number of operations that can be accommodated in parallel in the lth workshop of the kth category.
Sm_{ij}	A decision variable indicating the start time of O_{ij}.
Em_{ij}	A decision variable indicating the end time of O_{ij}.
Xp_{ijkl}	A decision variable valued 0 or 1, where 1 indicates that O_{ij} is assigned to the lth maintenance personnel using the kth skill category, whereas 0 indicates otherwise.
Xe_{ijkl}	A decision variable valued 0 or 1, where 1 indicates that O_{ij} is assigned to the lth of the kth maintenance equipment/workshop category, whereas 0 indicates otherwise.
Yp_{ijeg}	A decision variable valued 0 or 1, where 1 indicates that O_{ij} is assigned to the same maintenance personnel as O_{eg}, and O_{ij} is prioritized over O_{eg}, whereas 0 indicates otherwise.
Ye_{ijeg}	A decision variable valued 0 or 1, where 1 indicates that O_{ij} is assigned to the same maintenance equipment/ workshop as O_{eg}, and O_{ij} is prioritized over O_{eg}, whereas 0 indicates otherwise.

Constraints:

The first constraint concerns the starting time sequence for an MR task operation after tethering in the parking spot is completed. Sm_{i1} is the maintenance start time of the first maintenance operation of aircraft $i (i \in I)$. Aircraft i must start the first maintenance operation after the tethering completion time Ex_i. This constraint is expressed as follows:

$$Sm_{i1} \geq Ex_i, \forall i \in I \tag{1}$$

The MR task process for each aircraft must be performed sequentially by following the established workflow and precedence relations. Em_{ih} denotes the end time of maintenance operation O_{ih}, where $(i, h) \in Ps_{ij}$; Ps_{ij} denotes the set of processes immediately preceding maintenance operation O_{ij}. This constraint is expressed as follows:

$$Sm_{ij} \geq Em_{ih}, \forall (i, h) \in Ps_{ij}, \forall (i, j) \in J \tag{2}$$

When different operations require the same resources and because the number of maintenance personnel and maintenance equipment/workshops are limited, it is necessary to determine the order of maintenance according to priority. BM denotes a sufficiently large positive number; d_{ih} denotes the operation duration of a maintenance operation O_{ij}. $Yp_{ijeg} = 1$ indicates that the maintenance operation O_{ij} is assigned to the same maintenance personnel as O_{eg} and that O_{ij} takes priority over O_{eg}. $Ye_{ijeg} = 1$ indicates that the maintenance operation O_{ij} is assigned to the same maintenance equipment/workshop as O_{eg} and that O_{ij} takes priority over O_{eg}. This constraint is expressed as follows:

$$Sm_{ij} + d_{ij} \le Sm_{eg} + BM \cdot (1 - Yp_{ijeg}), \forall (i,j), (e,g) \in J \tag{3}$$

$$Sm_{ij} \le Sm_{eg} + BM \cdot (1 - Ye_{ijeg}), \forall (i,j), (e,g) \in J \tag{4}$$

Skills are direct demand resources for MR task operations. The number of skills demanded by any MR task operation should match the number of personnel assigned to that operation. $rc_{ijk} = 1$ indicates that the maintenance operation O_{ij} has a demand for the kth category skill. $Xp_{ijkl} = 1$ indicates that the maintenance operation O_{ij} is assigned to the lth$(l \in Lp)$ personnel and that the personnel performs the operation using the kth$(k \in Kc)$ skill category. This constraint is expressed as follows:

$$\sum_{l \in Lp} Xp_{ijkl} = rc_{ijk}, \forall (i,j) \in J, \forall k \in Kc \tag{5}$$

The demand for various types of maintenance equipment/workshops should match the number of resources assigned to that operation. $re_{ijk} = 1$ indicates that O_{ij} has a demand for the kth maintenance equipment/workshop category (which can accommodate a certain number of parallel operations). $Xe_{ijkl} = 1$ indicates that O_{ij} is assigned to the lth of the kth maintenance equipment/workshop category. The constraint is expressed as follows:

$$\sum_{l \in Le} Xe_{ijkl} = re_{ijk}, \forall (i,j) \in J, \forall k \in Ke \tag{6}$$

Each person uses at most one skill for any operation. This constraint is expressed as follows:

$$\sum_{k \in Kc} Xp_{ijkl} \le 1, \forall (i,j) \in J, \forall l \in Lp \tag{7}$$

Constraint (8) represents the coverage of the fixed resource stations. $\lambda_{kl}^{p} = 1$ indicates that the maintenance equipment/workshop has a reachability relationship with p. Constraint (8) is expressed as follows:

$$\sum_{(i,j) \in J} \sum_{k \in Ke} \sum_{l \in Le} Xe_{ijkl} \cdot \left(1 - \lambda_{kl}^{p_i}\right) = 0, \forall (i,j) \in J \tag{8}$$

Constraint (9) concerns the number of resources in a parallel workspace, and constraint (10) is used for the maintenance workshop. A_{it} indicates the set of maintenance operations of the ith carrier-based aircraft in the execution state at time point t. A_t indicates the set of all maintenance operations when the fleet is in the execution state at time point t. $\mathrm{rs}_{ijk} = 1$ indicates that O_{ij} has a demand for the kth maintenance workspace. ns_{ik} indicates the number of personnel that can work in parallel with the ith carrier-based aircraft kth category workspace. Ne_{kl} indicates the number of operations that can be accommodated in parallel in the lth workshop in the kth category. This constraint is expressed as follows:

$$\sum_{j \in A_{it}} rs_{ijk} \le ns_{ik}, \forall i \in I, \forall k \in Ks, \forall t > 0 \tag{9}$$

$$\sum_{j \in A_t} re_{ijk} \cdot Xe_{ijkl} \le Ne_{kl}, \forall i \in I, \forall k \in Ke, \forall l \in Le, \forall t > 0 \tag{10}$$

Constraint (11) states that Xp_{ijkl}, $Xe_{ijk'l'}$, Yp_{ijeg}, and Ye_{ijeg} are Boolean variables.

$$Xp_{ijkl}, Xe_{ijk'l'}, Yp_{ijeg}, Ye_{ijeg} \in \{0,1\}, \\ \forall k \in Kc, \forall l \in Lp, \forall k' \in Ke, \forall l' \in Le, \forall (i,j), (e,g) \in J \tag{11}$$

3.3. Objective Function

The optimization objectives for fleet wave availability and maintenance personnel load variance are constructed based on the requirements of aircraft fleet combat and training missions. The optimization objectives for the maintenance of existing equipment or support mission studies are usually set to minimize the maximum makespan (min$C_{\max}$). However, owing to the operational characteristics of carrier-based aircraft (which usually attack in clusters), the aircraft sorties are mainly focused on fleet wave sorties with the prerequisite of maximizing the number of available fleets in the sortie plan. After a command to launch the fleet is received, if the number of aircraft in good condition is insufficient for the wave, there will be aircraft with incomplete preventive maintenance or failure repair tasks. This situation can severely affect operational effectiveness if the available fleet cannot be replenished in time. In this study, the wave availability index is defined as the weighted availability of the fleet before each subsequent wave. The increased wave availability means that MR tasks can provide more intact aircraft for each wave. That is, MR tasks can meet the numbers for the wave sorties' requirements. Another consideration is to minimize the load variance of the maintenance personnel to increase the sustainability of personnel operations.

(1) Maximizing fleet-wave availability (WA)

$$\text{maxWA} = \sum_{w \in W} v_w \frac{Nm - \sum\limits_{i \in I} \text{pcf}(ET_i - SW_w)}{Nm} \tag{12}$$

Here, W denotes the set of wave sorties, SW_w the start time of the waves, v_w the weight for wave availability, and ET_i the makespan of the maintenance of carrier-based aircraft i. Moreover, pcf$(\cdot)$ is an indicator function, where pcf$(x) = 1$ when $x > 0$, and pcf$(x) = 0$ when $x \leq 0$. The purpose of the WA function is to maximize the sum of the weighted availability in the set of waves.

(2) Minimizing the personnel load variance (PLV) results in

$$\text{minPLV} = \frac{\sum\limits_{l \in Lp} \left(TB_l - \overline{TB}\right)^2}{|Lp|} \tag{13}$$

Here, TB_l denotes the total number of task hours spent by the $l(l \in Lp)$ maintenance personnel, and $\overline{TB}$ represents the mean value of the maintenance task hours for all personnel. PLV defines the personnel load variance in hours, and the objective is to minimize it.

4. Algorithm for AMRSP

4.1. Encoding and Serial Scheduling Generation Scheme (SSGS)

The encoding strategy is an essential factor affecting the effectiveness and efficiency of an algorithm search. The primary encoding strategies for solving an RCPSP problem include the task list, random number, and priority rules. Owing to the precedence relations between the operations of a task, the encoding forms from the task list and priority rules may be used to obtain combinations of operations that do not conform to the relations in the next crossover and mutation; therefore, random number encoding is used. The Gth generation population $\mathbf{P}_G$,$\mathbf{P}_G = [\mathbf{X}_{1,G}, \mathbf{X}_{2,G}, \cdots, \mathbf{X}_{n,G}], n = 1, 2, \cdots, Np$, where Np denotes the number of individuals in the population and $\mathbf{X}_{n,G}$ denotes the nth individual code of the Gth generation, can be defined as $\mathbf{X}_{n,G} = [x_{11,n,G}, x_{12,n,G}, \cdots, x_{ij,n,G}, \cdots]$, $\forall i \in I, j \in J_i$. Here, $x_{ij,n,G}$ denotes the priority number of the jth maintenance operation of the ith carrier-based aircraft in the nth individual of the Gth generation. Each aircraft is sequentially arranged in order of operation and assigned a random priority number in the interval $(0, 1)$. The smaller the priority number, the higher the priority of the corresponding operation. Integration and stitching form an individual encoding matrix with $\sum_{i \in I} |I| \times |J_i|$ dimensions for each $\mathbf{X}_{n,G}$. A schematic representation of the encoding structure is shown in Figure 5. The discrete encoding matrix avoids illegal generation in subsequent operations.

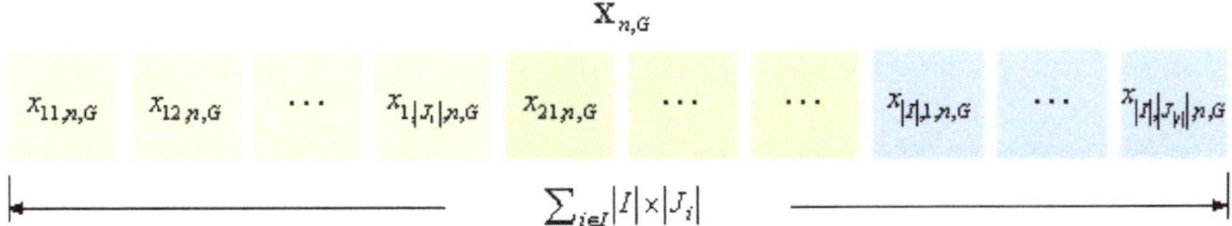

Figure 5. Schematic diagram of the encoding structure.

The schedule generation scheme (SGS) is at the core of most RCPSP metaheuristic algorithms. The SGS can generate a feasible scheduling scheme by incrementally extending the partial schedule from the start of the project. A partial schedule for a project with J tasks contains only l ($l < J$) tasks. Depending on the generated method, the SGS can be classified into task-based and time-based phase variables [39]. The SGS with task-based phase variables is also called a serial schedule generation scheme (SSGS), whereas that with time-based phase variables is called a parallel schedule generation scheme (PSGS). Hartmann [40] pointed out that the search space of the PSGS is a subset of the solution space, and using the PSGS can find a better solution in a short time, but it may not contain the optimal solution. Therefore, using an SSGS remains the optimal choice.

Unlike the conventional SSGS, to address the MS-RCPSP, the ITLBO-S is used for any waiting scheduling maintenance operation O_{ij}. The search phase of the schedule advancement, which includes constraints on the maintenance personnel, equipment, and workspace requirements, has an embedded function for matching the skills required for O_{ij} with suitable personnel. In other words, the allocation of personnel and selection of skills occur simultaneously during the progressive expansion of the schedule. A set of scheduled operations S_g is defined, along with a set of schedulable operations D_g. In the scheduling generation scheme, operation O_{ij} is selected from D_g according to the precedence relations, and the start time for O_{ij} is equal to the tethering completion time. D_g is determined by the sequence constraints and precedence relations from the AoN diagram. Next, O_{ij} is selected from D_g, and resources, such as personnel, equipment, and workshops, are then allocated to O_{ij}. After the allocation is completed, O_{ij} is added to set S_g. The iteration moves to the next selection stage and gradually expands the scheduling scheme until all operations are scheduled. Figure 6 shows the flowchart of the SSGS.

The following heuristic rules are added to the SSGS. First, considering that multi-skilled personnel are more flexible than regular personnel, priority is given to personnel with fewer skills to improve the scheduling scheme's robustness and ensure that the availability of the skills required for subsequent maintenance processes is maximized. Second, a tie-breaking priority rule is added; if the same numbers of skills are available, the personnel with fewer accumulated work hours are assigned to perform the task first to maintain the load balance. Third, the minimum total processing time remaining in the covering area rule is used for the allocation of the maintenance equipment. Fourth, in assigning maintenance workshops, a resource concentration rule is used, which assigns the tasks to the workshops with the highest number of maintenance operations in execution.

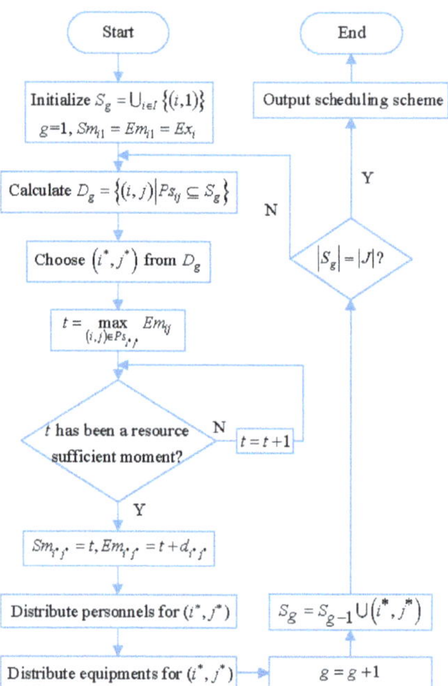

Figure 6. Flowchart of serial scheduling generation scheme (SSGS).

A decoding process is used to facilitate individual evaluation. For simplicity, this study utilizes a weighted sum approach [41] to construct the fitness function f. Several objectives are multiplied, according to their importance, by a set of weight coefficients $\alpha_1, \alpha_2, \ldots, \alpha_n$, which are then summed as the final objective function, thus simplifying the multi-objective problem to a single-objective problem. This significantly simplifies the computational process. The objective functions WA and PLV are combined linearly with weight coefficients as a single fitness function. Thus, f is formulated as follows:

$$\min f = \alpha_1 \cdot (1 - \mathrm{WA}) + \alpha_2 \cdot \mathrm{LBM} \tag{14}$$

In the above, α_1 and α_2 are the weight coefficients, and the weights can be adjusted according to the task requirements. According to this method, a set of single-objective optimization subproblems can be constructed, and the smaller the result, the better the individual fitness function.

By integrating the above preparations, a solution strategy for the algorithm is proposed, where the encoding of each individual in the population represents the order priority of all maintenance operations, and the operation of the SSGS maps this encoding to the actual operation order. In this process, a judgment that includes all types of resources (personnel, equipment, space) and the logical relations of the precedence operation order (AoN diagram) is required. This is because although some operations of a high priority level should be prioritized, if they do not meet the constraints, they are held back until the resources meet the conditions and then prioritized if they are still of a high priority. After applying the SSGS for all individuals, we obtained a population with a variety of operational orderings that meet the constraints. The quality of these operational sequences can be good or bad. We need to evaluate and evolve the population such that the quality of the operational order improves until the set conditions are met; these steps are achieved by the ITLBO main loop.

4.2. Improved Teaching-Learning-Based Optimization (ITLBO) Main Loop

Similar to other nature-inspired algorithms, TLBO is a population-based approach that uses population evolution for globally optimal solutions [31]. It simulates a teacher-student teaching-learning process in the classroom, and the optimization process consists of a teaching phase and a learning phase. The teaching phase refers to learning from the teacher, and the learning phase refers to learning through student interaction. The individual with the optimal fitness value in the population is the teacher (i.e., the optimal individual in the population). The other individuals in the population are students. The TLBO uses an objective function to evaluate an individual's performance and to determine a solution for the individual's optimal global performance. The learning results will increase in "fitness", similar to other population-based optimization algorithms.

Traditional TLBOs used in optimization problems have the following disadvantages. In the teaching phase, all individuals gain knowledge from the teacher based on the difference between the teacher and the individuals' overall average position. Therefore, in the teaching phase, all individuals gather around the teacher, ensuring a quick convergence. However, as the teacher approaches the local optimal solution, the population inevitably converges early. In the learning phase, individuals learn from each other to escape the local optima [42]. However, without the injection of new knowledge, the search space in the learning phase remains limited, and the diversity of the population can hardly increase further.

Therefore, the TLBO is still very likely to fall into a local convergence phenomenon when dealing with complex optimization problems [43]. To solve this problem, this study proposes the ITLBO-S, which is based on the TLBO, with an assistant teaching phase based on the optimal fitness-distance ranking ratio. This guides all individuals to learn from the teachers and assistant teachers according to the differential law. The exploitation and exploration abilities of the TLBO are improved by the differential knowledge between students and teachers and between students and assistant teachers. A balance between local and global exploitation is achieved, improving the performance of the algorithm [44]. Meanwhile, to capture the characteristics of the AMRSP, an SSGS based on resource constraint advancement is added to the algorithm to enable it to solve the MS-RCPSP.

4.2.1. Teaching Phase

In the teaching phase, the individual with the best fitness from the Gth generation population is selected as the individual teacher $\mathbf{X}_{t,G}$. According to the instructional guidance mechanism, all individuals (students) $\mathbf{X}_{n,G}$ learn from the Gth generation population and teacher $\mathbf{X}_{t,G}$ (their encoding numbers will be closer to the teacher's encoding number). Each individual produces a new individual $\mathbf{X}_{n,G}^{\text{new}}$ after the teaching phase, as shown in Equation (15).

$$\begin{cases} \mathbf{X}_{n,G}^{\text{new}} = \mathbf{X}_{n,G} + r_n \cdot (\mathbf{X}_{t,G} - T_F \cdot \mathbf{M}_G) \\ T_F = \text{ round}(1 + \text{ rand}(0\ ,\ 1)) \end{cases} \tag{15}$$

Here, $\mathbf{M}_G$ represents the average encoding matrix for the Gth generation of individuals, r_n denotes a random number between $(0\ ,\ 1)$, and T_F denotes the learning weight. From Equation (15), it can be seen that T_F takes a value of 1 or 2. The two random parameters r_n and T_F perform the teaching phase randomization. Comparing $\mathbf{X}_{n,G}$ with $\mathbf{X}_{n,G}^{\text{new}}$ in the one-to-one method for adaptation evaluation, the individual with the better adaptation is selected to update and replace the original individual. Updating is performed using Equation (16).

$$\mathbf{X}_{n,G} = \begin{cases} \mathbf{X}_{n,G}, & if\ f(\mathbf{X}_{n,G}) \le f\left(\mathbf{X}_{n,G}^{\text{new}}\right) \\ \mathbf{X}_{n,G}^{\text{new}}, & otherwise \end{cases} \tag{16}$$

4.2.2. Learning Phase

In the learning phase, new individuals $\mathbf{X}_{n,G}^{\text{new}}$ are generated among the students in the Gth generation population through mutual learning according to the learning guidance mechanism described by Equation (17), as follows:

$$\mathbf{X}_{n,G}^{\text{new}} = \begin{cases} \mathbf{X}_{n_1,G} + r_{n_1} \cdot \left(\mathbf{X}_{n_1,G} - \mathbf{X}_{n_2,G}\right), & if\ f(\mathbf{X}_{n_1,G}) \leq f(\mathbf{X}_{n_2,G}) \\ \mathbf{X}_{n_1,G} + r_{n_1} \cdot \left(\mathbf{X}_{n_2,G} - \mathbf{X}_{n_1,G}\right), & otherwise \end{cases} \tag{17}$$

In the above, r_{n_1} denotes a random number between $(0\ ,\ 1)$, $\mathbf{X}_{n_1,G}$ and $\mathbf{X}_{n_2,G}$ are two randomly selected student individuals in the current generation population, and $n_1 \neq n_2$. After the learning phase has generated the new individual $\mathbf{X}_{n,G}^{\text{new}}$, the same adaptation assessment is performed for $\mathbf{X}_{n,G}$ and $\mathbf{X}_{n,G}^{\text{new}}$. An individual with better adaptation is selected to update and replace the original individual. The updating method is shown in Equation (16).

4.2.3. Assistant Teaching Phase

In the teaching phase, because the individual population learns from the teacher, the algorithm achieves better convergence. However, when the individual teacher is located near the local optimal solution, it causes all individuals to move closer to the local optimal solution position, leading to the premature convergence of the algorithm. A subsequent learning phase in which students learn from each other can be used to prevent the population from falling into the local optimum. However, this is limited by the inherent knowledge of students in the population, which leads to unsatisfactory results from the algorithm exploration in the learning phase and makes it challenging to jump out of the local optimum.

To solve these problems, an assistant teacher teaching phase is proposed to guide students to learn from both the teacher and the assistant teacher. The assistant-teaching phase is based on an optimal fitness-distance ranking ratio method. Subsequently, the algorithm can balance the local exploitation and global exploration abilities of the solution space in the assistant-teaching phase.

(1) Fitness-distance ranking ratio

In any Gth generation, a fitness sorting matrix $\mathbf{F} = [F_1\ ,\ F_2\ ,\ \ldots\ ,\ F_n]$ is defined. $\mathbf{F}$ is obtained using $[f(\mathbf{X}_{1,G})\ ,\ f(\mathbf{X}_{2,G})\ ,\ \cdots\ ,\ f(\mathbf{X}_{n,G})]$ after sorting the fitness values $f(\mathbf{X}_{n,G})$ of the individuals $\mathbf{X}_{n,G}$ from best to worst. F_n corresponds to the index value of $[f(\mathbf{X}_{1,G})\ ,$ $f(\mathbf{X}_{2,G})\ ,\ \cdots\ ,\ f(\mathbf{X}_{n,G})]$ after sorting so that the individual $\mathbf{X}_{n,G}$ with the best fitness is used as the Gth generation teacher; that is, the individual $\mathbf{X}_{n,G}$ corresponding to $F_n = 1$ is used as the individual teacher $\mathbf{X}_{t,G}$.

The Euclidean distance sorting matrix is defined as $\mathbf{D} = [D_1\ ,\ D_2\ ,\ \cdots\ ,\ D_n]$. $\mathbf{D}$ is obtained after sorting in ascending order using $[E(\mathbf{X}_{1,G})\ ,\ E(\mathbf{X}_{2,G})\ ,\ \cdots\ ,\ E(\mathbf{X}_{n,G})]$ (Euclidean distance from near to far), where $E(\mathbf{X}_{n,G})$ is the Euclidean distance between an individual $\mathbf{X}_{n,G}$ and teacher individual $\mathbf{X}_{t,G}$. D_n corresponds to the index value of $[E(\mathbf{X}_{1,G})\ ,\ E(\mathbf{X}_{2,G})\ ,\ \cdots\ ,\ E(\mathbf{X}_{n,G})]$ after sorting. The fitness-distance ranking ratio is defined as $\mathbf{FD} = [FD_1\ ,\ FD_2\ ,\ \cdots\ ,\ FD_n]$, $FD_n = \frac{F_n}{D_n}$. The sorting ratio FD_n of the smallest fitness distance corresponds to the individual $\mathbf{X}_{n,G}$ as the Gth generation of assistant teacher individual $\mathbf{X}_{a,G}$. In other words, the individual $\mathbf{X}_{n,G}$ corresponding to the minor value FD_n in $\mathbf{FD}$ is $\mathbf{X}_{a,G}$. To illustrate the relative positions, fitness levels, and distance distributions of the teachers and assistant teachers, a two-dimensional population with 20 individuals in the Gth generation is selected as an example. Figure 7a shows a schematic of the distribution of the individual positions. Figure 7b shows the fitness levels of the population individuals and distances between the population individuals and teacher individuals; these can be used to determine the individuals with the best fitness $\mathbf{X}_{4,G}$ as $\mathbf{X}_{t,G}$. The sorting matrices $\mathbf{F}$ and $\mathbf{D}$ can be obtained after sorting the information in Figure 7b, and the fitness-distance ranking ratio $\mathbf{FD}$ can then be calculated. From this, the individual $\mathbf{X}_{17,G}$ can be determined as the assistant teacher's individual $\mathbf{X}_{a,G}$.

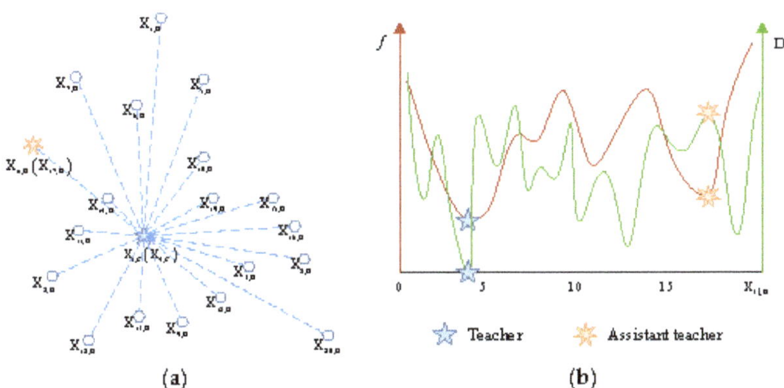

Figure 7. Example of fitness-distance ranking ratio. (**a**) Individual position distribution; (**b**) Fitness and distance distribution between teachers and assistant teachers.

(2) Assistant Teacher Teaching

In this phase, based on the difference operators $r_{1,n} \cdot (\mathbf{X}_{t,G} - \mathbf{X}_{n,G})$ and $r_{2,n} \cdot (\mathbf{X}_{a,G} - \mathbf{X}_{n,G})$, the individual $\mathbf{X}_{n,G}$ learns from teachers and assistant teachers to form new individuals. Equation (18) represents the generation of new individuals, as follows:

$$\mathbf{X}_{n,G}^{\text{new}} = \mathbf{X}_{n,G} + r_{1,n} \cdot (\mathbf{X}_{t,G} - \mathbf{X}_{n,G}) + r_{2,n} \cdot (\mathbf{X}_{a,G} - \mathbf{X}_{n,G}) \tag{18}$$

where $r_{1,n}$ and $r_{2,n}$ are random numbers between $(0, 1)$. When $r_{1,n} \geq r_{2,n}$, the position of the new individual $\mathbf{X}_{n,G}^{\text{new}}$ leans toward the teacher $\mathbf{X}_{t,G}$ to improve the algorithm's local search capability. When $r_{1,l} < r_{2,l}$, the position of the new individual $\mathbf{X}_{n,G}^{\text{new}}$ leans toward the assistant teacher $\mathbf{X}_{a,G}$ to improve the algorithm's global search capability. Taking the two-dimensional space as an example, a new individual $\mathbf{X}_{n,G}^{\text{new}}$ is generated, as shown in Figure 8.

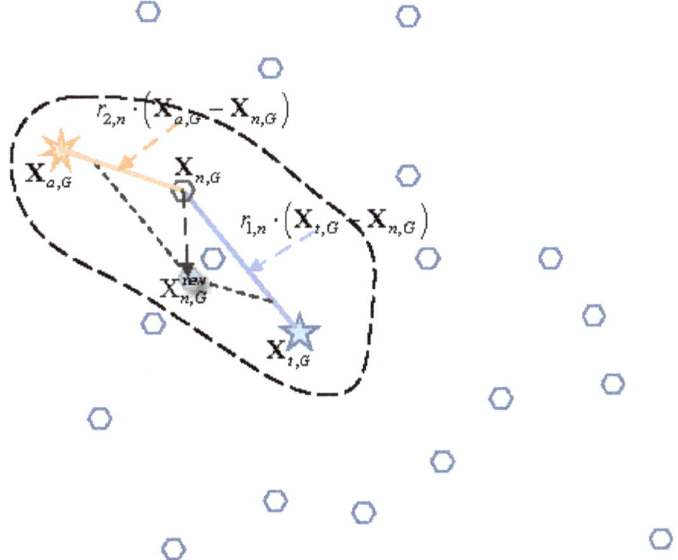

Figure 8. Schematic diagram of the two-dimensional new individual generation.

The Gth assistant teaching phase is defined to generate population $\mathbf{P}_G^{\text{new}}$ and $\mathbf{P}_G^{\text{new}} = \left[\mathbf{X}_{1,G}^{\text{new}}, \mathbf{X}_{2,G}^{\text{new}}, \cdots, \mathbf{X}_{n,G}^{\text{new}}\right]$. After the assistant teaching phase, the population generation is $G+1$. NP individuals with optimal fitness from $\{\mathbf{P}_G \cup \mathbf{P}_G^{\text{new}}\}$ are selected as the new population $\mathbf{P}_{G+1}$. A flowchart for the ITLBO-S is shown in Figure 9.

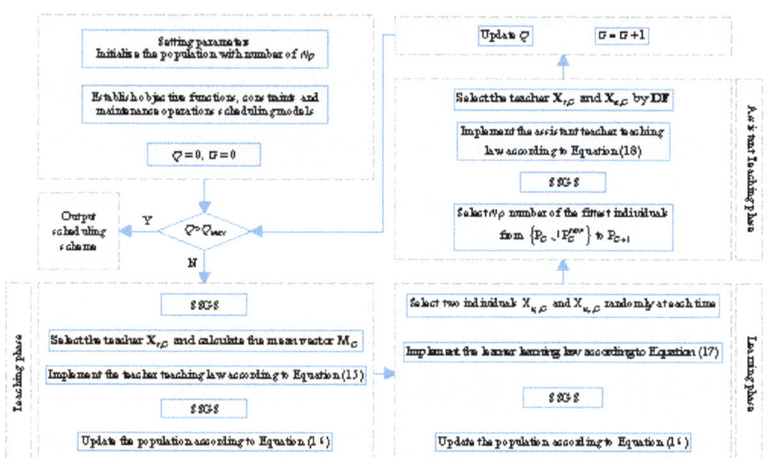

Figure 9. Flowchart for improved teaching-learning-based optimization algorithm with a serial scheduling generation scheme (ITLBO-S).

4.3. Complexity Analysis

The complexity of the ITLBO-S is reflected in two aspects. First, it is reflected in the teaching phase, learning phase, and assistant teaching phase, where each individual is coded with the dimension $\sum_{i \in I} |I| \times |J_i|$, and the complexity of the teaching phase is $O(Np \times \sum_{i \in I} |I| \times |J_i|)$. This indicates that Np individuals learn from the teacher. The complexity of the learning phase is also $O(Np \times \sum_{i \in I} |I| \times |J_i|)$. This indicates that Np individuals learn from each other. The complexity of the assistant teaching phase is $O(Np \times \sum_{i \in I} |I| \times |J_i|) + O(Np \times \log_2(2Np))$, indicating that Np individuals learn simultaneously from the teacher and assistant teacher and that Np individuals are selected from $2Np$ individuals as the next generation of the population.

However, the computational complexity of the ITLBO-S is also reflected in the SSGS process. According to the literature [39,45], the complexity of an SSGS is $O(|J|^2 R)$, where R is the number of reproducible resource types. In the AMRSP, three resource states must be considered when finding feasible resources, and the complexities of finding the spaces for the maintenance personnel, maintenance equipment/workshops, and maintenance station space are $O(|J|^2|Lp|)$, $O(|J|^2|Le|)$, and $O(|J|^2 \times |Ks|)$, respectively.

5. Simulation Case Analysis

5.1. Maintenance and Repair (MR) Task Case Generation

The simulation case in this study is based on the hangar-bay environment shown in Figure 2. Multimode mixed situations, such as preventive maintenance and failure repair, were considered, and 10, 12, and 14 carrier-based aircraft numbered A–N were set for the MR tasks. The task settings for the fleet MR are shown in Table 2. In the table, maintenance modes 1–6 correspond to six maintenance modes: mechanical failure, avionics system failure, special equipment failure, and maintenance after 25, 50, and 100 h flight hours. The maintenance process of the AoN diagram for preventive maintenance is shown in Figure 10. The subsequent outgoing wave was set as $|W| = 3$. The earlier the wave is deployed, the more critical the impact on the battlefield and the greater its importance. The wave weight was set as $[v_1, v_2, v_3] = [0.5, 0.3, 0.2]$. The wave interval period was 100 min; that is, the starting times were $[SW_1, SW_2, SW_3] = [100, 200, 300]$ min.

Table 2. MR tasks for fleet.

P.	1	2	3	4	5	6	7	8	9	10	11	12	13	14
MR Tasks	Carrier-based aircraft no.; Ex (min) MR tasks modes													
Case 1	A; 2 2	B; 8 3	C; 0 5	D; 0 4	E; 9 1	F; 16 1	G; 0 6	H; 0 5	I; 3 1	J; 15 2	-	-	-	-
Case 2	A; 2 2	B; 8 3	C; 0 5	D; 0 4	E; 9 1	F; 16 1	G; 0 6	H; 0 5	I; 3 1	J; 15 2	K; 21 5	L; 22 3	-	-
Case 3	A; 2 2	B; 8 3	C; 0 5	D; 0 4	E; 9 1	F; 16 1	G; 0 6	H; 0 5	I; 3 1	J; 15 2	K; 21 3	L; 22 4	M; 27 4	N; 29 4

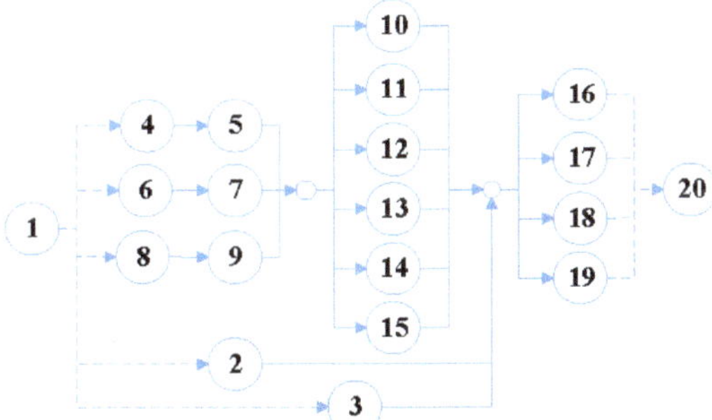

Figure 10. Process AoN diagram for preventive maintenance.

The reachability relation between parking spots (*P.*) and equipment is shown in Table 3. In Table 3, Ke_1 indicates the type of power supply station. As for the configuration of the maintenance workshops, owing to the space limitations of the compartment around the hangar bay, each workshop is equipped with one maintenance workshop covering the entire hangar bay. $Ke_{2\text{-}5}$ denote the aeronautical machine repair, oil and fluid inspection, ordnance maintenance, and electronic equipment maintenance workshops, respectively, and the number of parallel operations are $[Ne_1, Ne_2, Ne_3, Ne_4, Ne_5] = [\infty, 3, 2, 1, 4]$ for each workshop. The number of resources in this category usable for the parking space is indicated by [.]. The operation duration, resources, and skills required for each maintenance operation are shown in Table 4. In Table 4, $Kc_{1\text{-}4}$ denote special equipment, avionics, ordnance, and machinery specialties, respectively. In addition, the number of personnel is configured as $[5, 6, 4, 10]$. Special equipment is set to be compatible with avionics, ordnance, and machinery. The first four personnel in each profession have corresponding and compatible skills. Bold numbers indicate that the operation needs two personnel. The workstation space constraint *Ks* considers the cockpit space; "1" indicates that the number of personnel able to work in parallel is one, and "-" indicates that there is no demand for such resources.

Table 3. Reachability relation between parking spots and equipment.

P.	1	2	3	4	5	6	7	8	9	10	11	12	13	14
Ke_1	[3]	[4]	[3,5]	[5]	[9]	[10]	[9]	[10]	[6]	[1]	[3]	[7]	[2]	[8]
$Ke_{2\text{-}5}$	[1]	[1]	[1]	[1]	[1]	[1]	[1]	[1]	[1]	[1]	[1]	[1]	[1]	[1]

Table 4. Duration and requirements of maintenance and repair operations for carrier-based aircraft.

MR Task Modes		Operation No.																			
		1	**2**	**3**	**4**	**5**	**6**	**7**	**8**	**9**	**10**	**11**	**12**	**13**	**14**	**15**	**16**	**17**	**18**	**19**	**20**
		Operation Duration (min)																			
Mechanical failure		0	0	0	0	24	0	0	0	0	44	0	0	0	0	0	12	0	0	0	0
Avionics system failure		0	0	0	0	19	0	0	0	0	53	0	0	0	0	0	22	0	0	0	0
Special equipment failure		0	0	0	0	26	0	0	0	0	47	0	0	0	0	0	17	0	0	0	0
Maintenance after 25 flight hours		0	18	30	8	6	8	10	6	8	15	20	0	16	18	0	3	10	8	6	0
Maintenance after 50 flight hours		0	25	45	8	8	8	12	6	8	30	30	26	26	28	16	8	18	10	10	0
Maintenance after 100 flight hours		0	34	66	10	12	10	15	10	12	48	40	45	33	44	46	16	26	18	14	0
Required resource type	*Kc*	-	4	**4**	3	1,2,3,4	2	2	1	1	1,2,4	4	**4**	**2**	**1**	**3**	1,2,4	2	1	3	-
	Ke	-	-	-	-	1	-	1	-	1	2,5	3	3	5	5	4	1	1	1	1	-
	Ks	-	-	-	-	1	-	1	-	1	-	-	-	-	-	-	1	1	1	1	-

5.2. Simulation Comparison Analysis

5.2.1. Algorithm Comparison

To verify the effectiveness of the proposed ITLBO-S algorithm and its performance in solving the AMRSP, the TLBO, DE, and PSO were selected for the performance comparison. The parameters of each algorithm were set as follows. An $Np = 30$ was selected as the population size for both the ITLBO-S and the TLBO. In the PSO, the number of particles was set as $N = 30$; the learning factors were $c_1 = 2$ and $c_2 = 2$; and the linear decreasing weight strategy was $\omega = (\omega_{ini} - \omega_{end})(Q - q)/Q + \omega_{\mathrm{end}}$, where ω indicates the variable inertia weight, Q indicates the maximum number of evaluations, q is the current number of evaluations, ω_{ini} is the initial weight, and ω_{end} represents the end-of-iteration weight. The ω_{ini} and ω_{end} were 1.2 and 0.1, respectively. In the DE, the population size was set as $Np = 30$, the crossover rate as $cr = 0.1$, and the mutation probability as $F = 0.1$. A weight coefficient of $\alpha = 10^{-6}$ was used for the variance of the maintenance personnel load in the above algorithm fitness function f. Because the MR task demand prioritizes the number of intact aircraft provided for each sortie wave, the weight coefficients were selected as $\alpha_1 = 1$ and $\alpha_2 = 10^{-6}$. In all methods, an evaluation number of $Q = 3000$ was used to mark the end of the iteration.

Each algorithm was programmed using MATLAB 2020a and a personal computer (Windows 7 64-bit operating system, Intel Xeon Gold 5122 CPU @ 3.60 GHz, 32G of RAM). Each algorithm was run 15 times independently, and the results were recorded. After the optimization simulation, a statistical comparison between the algorithms of the optimization functions, WA and PLV, for the three groups of hangar MR task scheduling cases was conducted, and the results are listed in Table 5. The evaluation indicators were the optimal solution (*Best.*), average solution (*Avg.*), and standard deviation (*Std.*). In Table 5, the bold numbers indicate the optimal solutions for the algorithm comparison. A box plot of the distribution of the solutions for the repeated calculations is shown in Figure 11. The convergence trend of each algorithm is shown in Figure 12 (the result of one iteration when the WA achieves the optimal value in Case 1 is considered).

Table 5. Statistical comparison of algorithmic results.

Cases	Objective Functions	Evaluating Indicators	Algorithms			
			ITLBO-S	TLBO	DE	PSO
Case 1	WA	*Best.*	**0.750**	0.720	0.720	0.720
		Avg.	**0.750**	0.709	0.714	0.713
		Std.	**0**	0.010	0.008	0.009
	PLV	*Best.*	**52.382**	59.380	66.107	65.866
		Avg.	**53.720**	64.663	69.068	69.424
		Std.	**1.264**	3.383	1.999	1.802
Case 2	WA	*Best.*	**0.710**	0.690	0.600	0.620
		Avg.	**0.702**	0.648	0.592	0.598
		Std.	**0.012**	0.021	0.019	0.028
	PLV	*Best.*	**5.626**	16.186	25.946	20.026
		Avg.	**10.612**	33.983	51.695	55.754
		Std.	**5.113**	13.326	21.837	26.416
Case 3	WA	*Best.*	**0.650**	0.620	0.600	0.600
		Avg.	**0.627**	0.620	0.582	0.584
		Std.	0.015	**0**	0.031	0.018
	PLV	*Best.*	**19.280**	24.480	66.582	60.720
		Avg.	**45.088**	54.560	83.964	100.624
		Std.	**12.503**	21.056	16.966	31.059

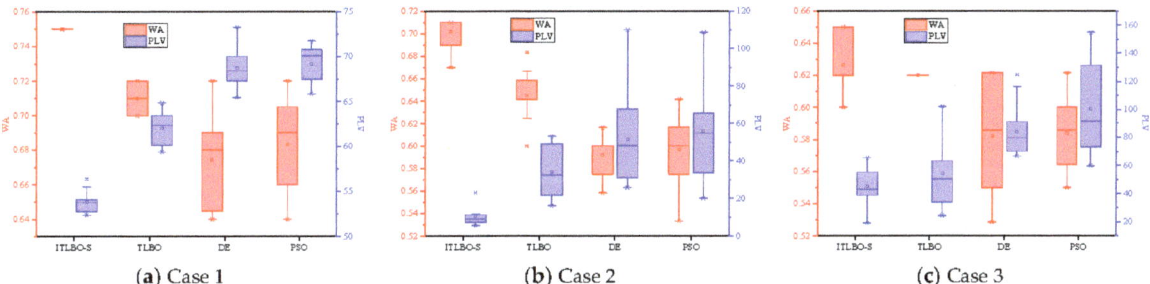

Figure 11. Box plot of the repeated calculation results.

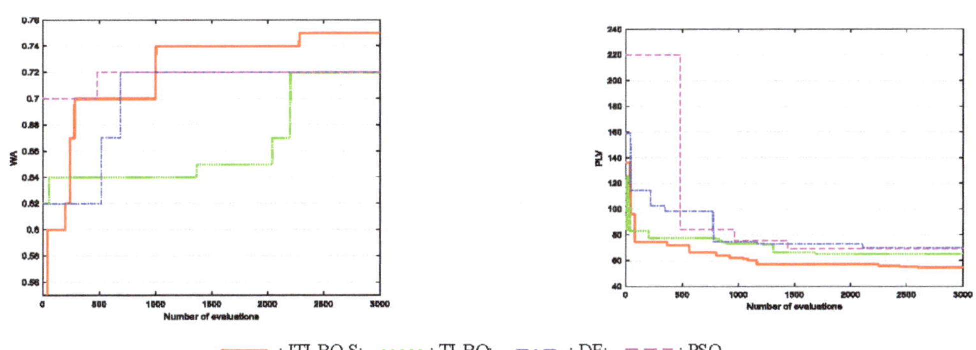

Figure 12. Change trend of wave availability (WA) and personnel load variance (PLV).

The shapes of this Pareto front are presented in Figure 13 to validate the feasibility of the solutions' distribution. The distribution of the solutions shows that the feasible solutions are scattered throughout the two-dimensional plane and that the number of points gathered in the Pareto front is small. Meanwhile, note that for the case set in this paper, the area of greatest concern is the feasible solution at the bottom right corner of Figure 13 (the maximum WA and the minimum PLV); therefore, the other Pareto front points are not of high priority.

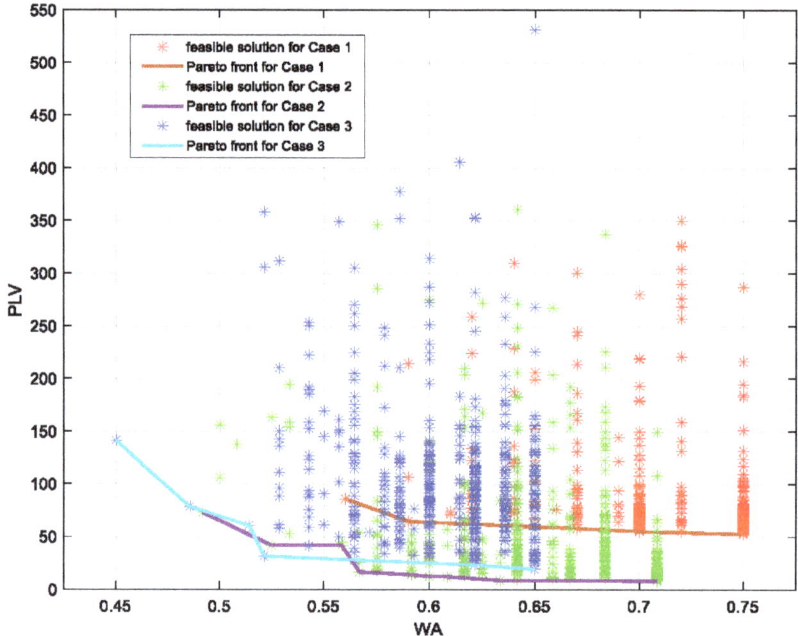

Figure 13. Pareto front and feasible solution for ITLBO-S.

First, the results in Table 5 show that based on the quality of the solutions, the ITLBO-S exhibits the best performance among the four algorithms in the three sets of experiments comprising three evaluation indicators and two objective functions. Notably, in Case 1, the ITLBO-S has the best convergence effect, and the indicators for WA converge to 0.750 for the 15 independent operations. By contrast, the other algorithms do not have sufficient search depths and are unable to search for a better solution. The box plot in Figure 11 shows the stability of the distribution of the observed results; with regard to the WA and PLV, the ITLBO-S reaches the highest median, upper quartile, and maximum value for all three sets of simulations compared to the other three classical metaheuristic algorithms while showing strong stability. By contrast, the DE and PSO perform poorly in the three sets of cases, either failing to find the optimal result or resulting in the WA having a more scattered distribution of solutions, indicating that the DE and PSO are less adaptable in finding the solution to this problem. In Case 3, the indicator WA for the TLBO converges to 0.620 for the 15 independent operations, whereas the optimal value of the ITLBO-S reaches 0.650. This is the most intuitive and evident indication that the conventional TLBO falls into a local optimum in the process of solving the problem. Owing to the enhanced global and local search operations in the assistant teaching phase, the ITLBO-S can explore better solutions in the local search process. This improves the diversity of populations and the accuracy and stability of the local optimal solutions, and the optimization effect of the algorithm is improved. However, one problem reflected in the results is that the stability of the algorithm tends to decrease as the problem scale increases; therefore, it is necessary to continue to test the adaptability of the algorithm for increasing problem scales. In summary, the ITLBO-S proposed herein is the optimal solution compared with other optimization algorithms, such as the TLBO, under the premise of considering the quality and stability of the solution.

The optimal Gantt charts for scheduling maintenance personnel and maintenance equipment/workshops, obtained from the Case 1 results, are shown in Figure 14. In Figure 14a, the vertical coordinate "$Lp - l$" indicates the lth personnel, and the order is numbered according to the special equipment, avionics, ordnance, and machinery specialties. The maintenance operations are indicated on the Gantt chart bars, where $i - j$ (hyphen in the Figure) represents the maintenance operationof O_{ij}. In Figure 14b, when the vertical coordinate is $k = 1$, Le_1^l refers to the lth power supply station. For consistency, aeronautical machine repair, oil and fluid inspection, ordnance, and electronic equipment maintenance workshops are indicated by $k = 2 - 5$, respectively. Le_{2-5}^l denotes the lth parallel maintenance operation line for the corresponding workshop. Owing to length constraints, the maintenance scheduling schemes for Cases 2 and 3 are not provided. After testing, the scheduling schemes shown in each Gantt chart were proven to satisfy all constraints, thereby verifying the correctness of the proposed model and scheduling method.

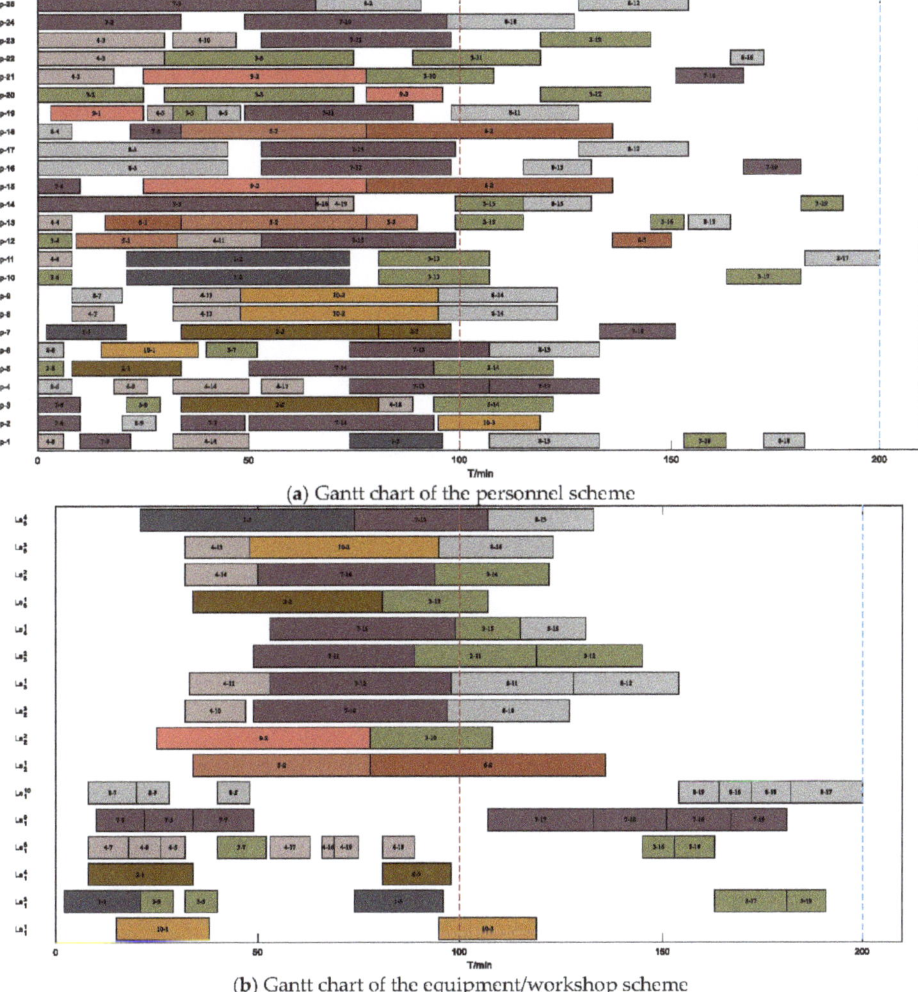

(**a**) Gantt chart of the personnel scheme

(**b**) Gantt chart of the equipment/workshop scheme

Figure 14. Gantt chart of maintenance and repair (MR) task scheduling schemes.

5.2.2. Adaptation Verification of Algorithms

To verify the performance of the ITLBO-S for highly constrained resources and large-scale fleet MR tasks, the sortie wave interval was shortened to 80 min, and a test simulation was conducted with the other algorithm parameters kept constant. The algorithm was independently run 15 times, resulting in the statistics shown in Table 6.

Table 6. Statistics of high-intensity task simulation results.

Objective Functions	Evaluating Indicators	MR Tasks			
		Case 1	Case 2	Case 3	
WA	*Best.* *Avg.* *Std.*	0.520 0.520 0	0.492 0.461 0.023	0.450 0.430 0.008	(a) WA
PLV	*Best.* *Avg.* *Std.*	57.862 65.7 3.276	16.580 21.337 2.789	6.400 11.447 2.686	(b) PLV
Time/s	*Avg.*	173.2	240.8	321.8	(c) Time

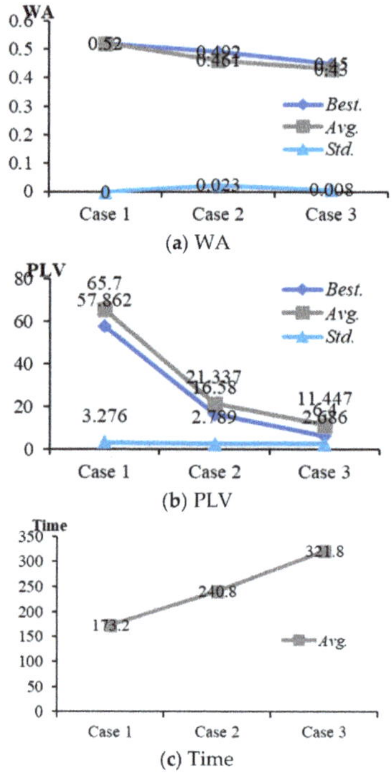

The comparison results from the simulation reveal the following three conclusions. First, after the wave interval period is shortened, the WA gradually decreases, and the PLV gradually decreases with an increase in the fleet scale. This is because completing these MR tasks within the specified time is difficult, and the ratio of a sufficient number of aircraft at the start time of the wave gradually decreases owing to the highly constrained resource situation of tight MR tasks. Furthermore, the large number of MR tasks completed by the personnel results in inter-task idle times, a short gap between the work hours of the maintenance personnel, and a minor load variance. The stability aspect was considered under index *Std.* The results in Table 6 show that increasing the scale of the problem can improve the stability of the algorithm. However, the results also indicate that the algorithm's adaptability to the problem is an advantage. The computation time of the algorithm for solving the scheduling tasks gradually increases as the problem scale increases but remains within the acceptable solution time. In summary, the proposed ITLBO-S algorithm performs well in solving the AMRSP under high resource constraints.

6. Conclusions and Future Work

In this study, for the AMRSP, we first analyzed the maintenance process, personnel, equipment, workshop, workspace, skills, and other constraints in MR task scheduling. Next, using the WA and PLV as optimization indexes, we constructed a mathematical model for aeronautical MR task scheduling problems in carrier-based aircraft fleets. An

ITLBO-S algorithm was proposed to solve the model. Finally, after case simulations and comparative experiments were performed, an optimal scheduling scheme was provided for maintenance personnel and equipment/workshops. After verification, the scheduling scheme obtained by employing the ITLBO-S algorithm was proven to comply with the constraints of the model. The improved algorithm shows advantages in terms of the quality and stability of the solution. In other words, the algorithm has strong adaptability in solving large-scale scheduling problems.

However, in this study, the model and optimization of carrier-based aircraft MR tasks were applied only to deterministic tasks. The assumption that the interference of unexpected factors, such as task changes, can be excluded is inconsistent with an actual and complex maintenance environment. Failures in aircraft systems or components often appear to be random, and maintenance activities are tightly coupled in a sequential manner. Any delay in performing a task may have a snowball effect on subsequent maintenance activities, eventually leading to maintenance delays [46]. With appropriate modifications, this model can be used for a dynamic MR system or to optimize other factors.

Subsequent research will improve the algorithm to achieve dynamic scheduling and to cope with unforeseen situations, unpredictability, and different organizational scenarios, thereby making it more relevant to the AMRSP. Moreover, according to the "no free lunch" theory [47], each algorithm has its applicable problem scope. The applicable scope is related to the characteristics of the algorithm. In this context, by considering the scale of the problem, we can select the best algorithm based on its actual performance on a particular problem.

Author Contributions: Methodology, Writing—original draft, C.L.; Software, Y.Z.; Data curation, X.S.; Formal analysis, X.W. All authors have read and agreed to the published version of the manuscript.

Funding: This research did not receive any specific grant from any funding agencies in the public, commercial, or not-for-profit sectors.

Data Availability Statement: Not applicable.

Acknowledgments: The authors highly appreciate the valuable comments provided by the reviewers, which will greatly contribute to the improvement of the paper.

Conflicts of Interest: The authors declare no conflict of interest.

References

1. Shafiee, M.; Chukova, S. Maintenance Models in Warranty: A Literature Review. *Eur. J. Oper. Res.* **2013**, *229*, 561–572. [CrossRef]
2. Johnston, J.S. A Feasibility Study of a Persistent Monitoring System for the Flight Deck of US Navy Aircraft Carriers. Doctoral Dissertation, Air Force Air University, Maxwell, AL, USA, 2009.
3. Uzun, B. A Multimodal Ouija Board for Aircraft Carrier Deck Operations. Doctoral Dissertation, Massachusetts Institute of Technology, Cambridge, MA, USA, 2016.
4. Ryan, J.; Cummings, M.; Roy, N.; Banerjee, A.; Schulte, A. Designing an Interactive Local and Global Decision Support System for Aircraft Carrier Deck Scheduling. In *Infotech@ Aerospace 2011*; AIAA: Reston, VA, USA, 2011; p. 1516.
5. Ryan, J.C.; Banerjee, A.G.; Cummings, M.L.; Roy, N. Comparing the Performance of Expert User Heuristics and an Integer Linear Program in Aircraft Carrier Deck Operations. *IEEE Trans. Cybern.* **2013**, *44*, 761–773. [CrossRef]
6. Tsarouhas, P.; Makrygianni, M. A Framework for Maintenance and Combat Readiness Management of a Jet Fighter Aircraft. *Int. J. Syst. Assur. Eng. Manag.* **2017**, *8*, 1895–1909. [CrossRef]
7. Liang, Z.; Feng, Y.; Zhang, X.; Wu, T.; Chaovalitwongse, W.A. Robust Weekly Aircraft Maintenance Routing Problem and the Extension to the Tail Assignment Problem. *Transp. Res. Part B Methodol.* **2015**, *78*, 238–259. [CrossRef]
8. Deng, Q.; Santos, B.F.; Curran, R. A Practical Dynamic Programming Based Methodology for Aircraft Maintenance Check Scheduling Optimization. *Eur. J. Oper. Res.* **2020**, *281*, 256–273. [CrossRef]
9. Kowalski, M.; Izdebski, M.; Żak, J.; Gołda, P.; Manerowski, J. Planning and Management of Aircraft Maintenance Using a Genetic Algorithm. *Eksploat. Niezawodn.* **2021**, *23*, 143–153. [CrossRef]
10. Witteman, M.; Deng, Q.; Santos, B.F. A Bin Packing Approach to Solve the Aircraft Maintenance Task Allocation Problem. *Eur. J. Oper. Res.* **2021**, *294*, 365–376. [CrossRef]
11. Eltoukhy, A.E.E.; Chan, F.T.S.; Chung, S.H.; Niu, B. A Model with a Solution Algorithm for the Operational Aircraft Maintenance Routing Problem. *Comput. Ind. Eng.* **2018**, *120*, 346–359. [CrossRef]

12. Lin, L.; Wang, F.; Luo, B. An Optimization Algorithm Inspired by Propagation of Yeast for Fleet Maintenance Decision Making Problem Involving Fatigue Structures. *Appl. Soft Comput.* **2019**, *85*, 105755. [CrossRef]
13. de Bruecker, P.; van den Bergh, J.; Beliën, J.; Demeulemeester, E. A Model Enhancement Heuristic for Building Robust Aircraft Maintenance Personnel Rosters with Stochastic Constraints. *Eur. J. Oper. Res.* **2015**, *246*, 661–673. [CrossRef]
14. Verhoeff, M.; Verhagen, W.J.C.; Curran, R. Maximizing Operational Readiness in Military Aviation by Optimizing Flight and Maintenance Planning. *Transp. Res. Procedia* **2015**, *10*, 941–950. [CrossRef]
15. Han, Q.T.; Cao, W.J.; Zhang, Y. Research on Maintenance Resources Distribution Based on Queuing Theory. *Trans. Tech. Publ.* **2013**, *239*, 1428–1431. [CrossRef]
16. Zhaodong, H.; Wenbing, C.; Yiyong, X.; Rui, L. Optimizing Human Resources Allocation on Aircraft Maintenance with Predefined Sequence. In Proceedings of the 2010 International Conference on Logistics Systems and Intelligent Management (ICLSIM), Harbin, China, 9–10 January 2010; Volume 2, pp. 1018–1022.
17. Raju, V.R.S.; Gandhi, O.P.; Deshmukh, S.G. Maintenance, Repair, and Overhaul Performance Indicators for Military Aircraft. *Def. Sci. J.* **2012**, *62*, 83–89. [CrossRef]
18. Feng, Q.; Li, S.; Sun, B. A Multi-Agent Based Intelligent Configuration Method for Aircraft Fleet Maintenance Personnel. *Chin. J. Aeronaut.* **2014**, *27*, 280–290. [CrossRef]
19. Safaei, N.; Banjevic, D.; Jardine, A.K.S. Workforce-Constrained Maintenance Scheduling for Military Aircraft Fleet: A Case Study. *Ann. Oper. Res.* **2011**, *186*, 295–316. [CrossRef]
20. Zhang, Y.; Li, C.; Su, X.; Cui, R.; Wan, B. A Baseline-Reactive Scheduling Method for Carrier-Based Aircraft Maintenance Tasks. *Complex Intell. Syst.* **2022**. [CrossRef]
21. Mollahassani-Pour, M.; Abdollahi, A.; Rashidinejad, M. Application of a Novel Cost Reduction Index to Preventive Maintenance Scheduling. *Int. J. Electr. Power Energy Syst.* **2014**, *56*, 235–240. [CrossRef]
22. Lin, J.; Zhu, L.; Gao, K. A Genetic Programming Hyper-Heuristic Approach for the Multi-Skill Resource Constrained Project Scheduling Problem. *Expert Syst. Appl.* **2020**, *140*, 112915. [CrossRef]
23. Cui, R.; Dong, X.; Lin, Y. Models for Aircraft Maintenance Routing Problem with Consideration of Remaining Time and Robustness. *Comput. Ind. Eng.* **2019**, *137*, 106045. [CrossRef]
24. Moukrim, A.; Quilliot, A.; Toussaint, H. An Effective Branch-and-Price Algorithm for the Preemptive Resource Constrained Project Scheduling Problem Based on Minimal Interval Order Enumeration. *Eur. J. Oper. Res.* **2015**, *244*, 360–368. [CrossRef]
25. Chakrabortty, R.K.; Sarker, R.; Essam, D. Resource Constrained Project Scheduling: A Branch and Cut Approach. In Proceedings of the 45th International Conference on Computers and Industrial Engineering, Metz, France, 28–30 October 2015.
26. Kiefer, A.; Schilde, M.; Doerner, K.F. Scheduling of Maintenance Work of a Large-Scale Tramway Network. *Eur. J. Oper. Res.* **2018**, *270*, 1158–1170. [CrossRef]
27. Đumić, M.; Jakobović, D. Using Priority Rules for Resource-Constrained Project Scheduling Problem in Static Environment. *Comput. Ind. Eng.* **2022**, *169*, 108239. [CrossRef]
28. Pellerin, R.; Perrier, N.; Berthaut, F. A Survey of Hybrid Metaheuristics for the Resource-Constrained Project Scheduling Problem. *Eur. J. Oper. Res.* **2020**, *280*, 395–416. [CrossRef]
29. Feng, Q.; Bi, W.; Chen, Y.; Ren, Y.; Yang, D. Cooperative Game Approach Based on Agent Learning for Fleet Maintenance Oriented to Mission Reliability. *Comput. Ind. Eng.* **2017**, *112*, 221–230. [CrossRef]
30. Peschiera, F.; Dell, R.; Royset, J.; Haït, A.; Dupin, N.; Battaïa, O. A Novel Solution Approach with ML-Based Pseudo-Cuts for the Flight and Maintenance Planning Problem. *OR Spectrum* **2021**, *43*, 635–664. [CrossRef]
31. Blum, C.; Puchinger, J.; Raidl, G.R.; Roli, A. Hybrid Metaheuristics in Combinatorial Optimization: A Survey. *Appl. Soft Comput.* **2011**, *11*, 4135–4151. [CrossRef]
32. Rao, R.V.; Savsani, V.J.; Vakharia, D.P. Teaching–Learning-Based Optimization: A Novel Method for Constrained Mechanical Design Optimization Problems. *Comput. Aided Des.* **2011**, *43*, 303–315. [CrossRef]
33. Shao, W.; Pi, D.; Shao, Z. An Extended Teaching-Learning Based Optimization Algorithm for Solving No-Wait Flow Shop Scheduling Problem. *Appl. Soft Comput.* **2017**, *61*, 193–210. [CrossRef]
34. Buddala, R.; Mahapatra, S.S. Two-Stage Teaching-Learning-Based Optimization Method for Flexible Job-Shop Scheduling under Machine Breakdown. *Int. J. Adv. Manuf. Technol.* **2019**, *100*, 1419–1432. [CrossRef]
35. Ji, X.; Ye, H.; Zhou, J.; Yin, Y.; Shen, X. An Improved Teaching-Learning-Based Optimization Algorithm and Its Application to a Combinatorial Optimization Problem in Foundry Industry. *Appl. Soft Comput.* **2017**, *57*, 504–516. [CrossRef]
36. Joshi, D.; Mittal, M.L.; Sharma, M.K.; Kumar, M. An Effective Teaching-Learning-Based Optimization Algorithm for the Multi-Skill Resource-Constrained Project Scheduling Problem. *J. Model. Manag.* **2019**, *14*, 1064–1087. [CrossRef]
37. Joshi, D.; Mittal, M.L.; Kumar, M. A Teaching–Learning-Based Optimization Algorithm for the Resource-Constrained Project Scheduling Problem. In *Harmony Search and Nature Inspired Optimization Algorithms*; Springer: Berlin/Heidelberg, Germany, 2019; pp. 1101–1109.
38. Deng, Q.; Santos, B.F.; Verhagen, W.J.C. A Novel Decision Support System for Optimizing Aircraft Maintenance Check Schedule and Task Allocation. *Decis. Support Syst.* **2021**, *146*, 113545. [CrossRef]
39. Kolisch, R. Serial and Parallel Resource-Constrained Project Scheduling Methods Revisited: Theory and Computation. *Eur. J. Oper. Res.* **1996**, *90*, 320–333. [CrossRef]

40. Hartmann, S.; Kolisch, R. Experimental Evaluation of State-of-the-Art Heuristics for the Resource-Constrained Project Scheduling Problem. *Eur. J. Oper. Res.* **2000**, *127*, 394–407. [CrossRef]
41. Fu, Y.; Zhou, M.; Guo, X.; Qi, L. Scheduling Dual-Objective Stochastic Hybrid Flow Shop With Deteriorating Jobs via Bi-Population Evolutionary Algorithm. *IEEE Trans. Syst. Man Cybern. Syst.* **2020**, *50*, 5037–5048. [CrossRef]
42. Zou, F.; Chen, D.; Xu, Q. A Survey of Teaching–Learning-Based Optimization. *Neurocomputing* **2019**, *335*, 366–383. [CrossRef]
43. Neri, F.; Tirronen, V. Recent Advances in Differential Evolution: A Survey and Experimental Analysis. *Artif. Intell. Rev.* **2010**, *33*, 61–106. [CrossRef]
44. Xu, Y.; Peng, Y.; Su, X.; Yang, Z.; Ding, C.; Yang, X. Improving Teaching-Learning-Based-Optimization Algorithm by a Distance-Fitness Learning Strategy. *Knowl. Based Syst.* **2022**, *257*, 108271. [CrossRef]
45. Cui, R.; Han, W.; Su, X.; Liang, H.; Li, Z. A Dual Population Multi-Operator Genetic Algorithm for Flight Deck Operations Scheduling Problem. *J. Syst. Eng. Electron.* **2021**, *32*, 331–346.
46. Deng, Q.; Santos, B.F. Lookahead Approximate Dynamic Programming for Stochastic Aircraft Maintenance Check Scheduling Optimization. *Eur. J. Oper. Res.* **2022**, *299*, 814–833. [CrossRef]
47. Wolpert, D.H.; Macready, W.G. No Free Lunch Theorems for Optimization. *IEEE Trans. Evol. Comput.* **1997**, *1*, 67–82. [CrossRef]

 *mathematics*

Article

The Fast Generation of the Reachable Domain for Collision-Free Asteroid Landing

Yingjie Zhao, Hongwei Yang * and Jincheng Hu

College of Astronautics, Nanjing University of Aeronautics and Astronautics, Nanjing 211106, China
* Correspondence: hongwei.yang@nuaa.edu.cn

Abstract: For the mission requirement of collision-free asteroid landing with a given time of flight (TOF), a fast generation method of landing reachable domain based on section and expansion is proposed. First, to overcome the difficulties of trajectory optimization caused by anti-collision path constraints, a two-stage collision-free trajectory optimization model is used to improve the efficiency of trajectory optimization. Second, the velocity increment under a long TOF is analyzed to obtain the distribution law of the reachable domain affected by the TOF, and the generation problem of the reachable domain is transformed into the solution problem of the initial boundary and the continuous boundary. For the initial boundary, the section method is used to acquire a point on the boundary as the preliminary reachable domain boundary. The solution of continuous boundary is based on the initial boundary continuously expanding the section into the reachable domain until the boundary is continuous. Finally, the proposed method is applied to the asteroids 101955 Bennu and 2063 Bacchus. The simulation results show that this method can quickly and accurately obtain the reachable domain of collision-free asteroid landing in a given TOF and is applicable to different initial positions.

Keywords: collision-free asteroid landing; given time of flight; reachable domain; section and expansion method; trajectory optimization

MSC: 70F05

Citation: Zhao, Y.; Yang, H.; Hu, J. The Fast Generation of the Reachable Domain for Collision-Free Asteroid Landing. *Mathematics* **2022**, *10*, 3763. https://doi.org/10.3390/math10203763

Academic Editor: Akemi Galvez Tomida

Received: 7 September 2022
Accepted: 10 October 2022
Published: 12 October 2022

1. Introduction

Asteroid exploration is the main way to understand the formation and evolution of the solar system, which is of great significance to the development and utilization of space resources and the defense against asteroid impact threats [1–3]. Asteroid sample return missions have attracted the attention of space-faring powers, such as the ongoing OSIRIS-Rex mission [4] of the United States and the Japanese Hayabusa2 mission [5] that landed on the surface of the near-Earth asteroid Ryugu and has successfully sampled and returned. The landing of the spacecraft on the asteroid surface to collect the high-resolution data and soil samples is a crucial step of the asteroid sample return mission. In the OSIRIS-REx mission, in order to select the most suitable landing site, the ground personnel screened and compared four sampling areas on the surface of the asteroid Bennu. These landing sites are controllable within the landing range that the spacecraft can reach, so they can be regarded as feasible candidate landing sites [6]. Therefore, the generation and analysis of the reachable domain of the asteroid surface are of great significance in landing site selection and mission planning [7]. The reachable domain refers to the set of terminal positions that the spacecraft can reach under given initial conditions and constraints. At present, it is mainly obtained by solving a series of trajectory optimization problems [8]. Benito and Mease [9] defined the reachable set and the controllable set and introduced the calculation method. The reachable set is obtained by the grid detection method. By defining boundary constraints, control constraints, path constraints, and cost functions, a large number of trajectory optimization is performed according to the resolution of each mesh. Arslantaş and Oehlschlägel [10] used the optimization-based method to calculate the reachable set of nonlinear system dynamics with constraints, which was used in the terminal landing phase for the lunar mission. The state space is discretized by equidistant grid points, and a distance function is defined for each grid point as the objective function to solve the feasible trajectory. The above two methods [9,10] need a lot of time to solve the reachable domain. Chen and Qiao [11] used an improved method to solve the envelope of the reachable domain of spacecraft after a gravity-assist flyby. It is determined whether the reachable domain intersects with the orbit of a planet to indicate whether the spacecraft can fly over the planet. Lee and Hwang [12] proposed a new algorithm for calculating the reachable set of spacecraft relative motion with energy-limited low thrust. By deriving the analytical solution of the optimal control problem, and applying the ellipsoid approximation method, the inner and outer two ellipsoids approaching the exact boundary of the reachable set are obtained, which effectively solves the problem of large computational complexity in solving the reachable set. It should be noted that the application of the analytical solution is any relative dynamic model in which the transfer matrix is available and analytically integrable. The reachable domain can be used not only to solve reachable terminal positions but also to design the low-thrust trajectory. Kulumani and Lee [13] designed continuous low-thrust transfers between asteroid periodic orbits by using reachable sets generated on a lower dimensional Poincare surface. The calculation of the reachable set reduces the need to generate accurate initial guesses for optimization and only needs to select a trajectory with the smallest distance to the target from the reachable set as the optimal transfer trajectory.

At present, the existing generation methods of reachable domain mainly take Earth, Mars, and the moon as landing objects, and the relevant research on the landing reachable domain of asteroid surface is less [8]. Wen and Zeng [14] obtained the landing reachable domain of the hopping rover after one maneuver on the asteroid surface and when it naturally evolves to rest through numerical simulation. This is different from the case of solving the reachable domain of soft landing on the asteroid surface under thrust control in this study. Huang and Liang [8] proposed a reachable domain generation method based on a dynamic neighborhood search. Specifically, the optimization problem of the reachable domain is transformed into three subproblems: the calculation of the landing point with minimum fuel consumption, the calculation of the landing point when fuel is exhausted, and the dynamic neighborhood search for the reachable domain boundary. This method can obtain the landing reachable domain of the asteroid surface with high efficiency. However, the landing trajectory optimization process in this method [8] does not consider the anti-collision path constraint.

The choice of landing trajectory optimization method is important for solving the reachable domain. When the initial state of the spacecraft is known, it is necessary to quickly obtain the reachable domain on the asteroid surface in a given time of flight (TOF) before the powered descending. Therefore, it is necessary not only to optimize the solution method of the reachable domain but also to select an energy-efficient landing trajectory optimization method. In the existing research, the energy-optimal problem is mostly studied by the optimal control theory and has various applications. In the transport mission, the minimum-energy trajectory can maximize the energy efficiency of the transport [15]. For robots working in special environments, energy consumption must be considered in the design phase to ensure the completion of tasks. Energy consumption caused by both motion and communication belongs to the field of energy-optimal problems [16]. Additionally, it is important to minimize energy consumption and extend the network life cycle in wireless networks [17]. The optimal energy control problem is also widely studied in astrophysics. In recent years, fast trajectory optimization methods for collision-free asteroid landing in the gravitational field have been studied [18–23]. The algorithm based on convex optimization [18–20] has the problem that as the flight distance increases, the variables of the optimization model also increase significantly, resulting in the low efficiency of long-distance trajectory optimization [19]. The anti-collision path constraints [19,20] are expressed as the combined constraints of ellipsoid/sphere and glide slope. Zhang and

Zhang [21] designed a saturated adaptive six-degree-of-freedom control law suitable for collision-free asteroid landing by separating the spacecraft from the asteroid using the designed curved surface to avoid collision. However, the control is not optimal. Zhu and Yang [22] proposed a new guidance method for avoiding danger by improving the artificial potential function and designed an anti-collision zone with continuity and rapid numerical change rate that can effectively prevent the spacecraft from falling into the local minimum area in complex terrain. The authors [23] proposed a new two-stage collision-free trajectory optimization method based on the indirect method by using the two-stage anti-collision path constraint composed of the ellipsoid and the glide slope [20] that can quickly generate the energy optimal trajectory. According to the anti-collision path constraint, the whole flight process is divided into the descent stage and the final landing stage, and the trajectory optimization problem is transformed into a two-stage energy optimal control problem with the given TOF. The approximate analytical solution of the initial costate [24] provides the guess of the initial costate for the trajectory optimization in the descent stage and directly serves as the initial costate of the final landing stage, which simplifies the complexity of the path constraint and improves the efficiency of trajectory optimization.

Before the powered descending, it is needed to generate and analyze the landing reachable domain with different flight times to determine whether the landing site can be reached. This requires trajectory optimization for all points on the asteroid surface, and every time the TOF is changed, the trajectory optimization of all surface points must be solved again, resulting in low efficiency. To this end, a method was proposed for quickly generating the landing reachable domain within a given TOF. To overcome the difficulty of landing trajectory optimization caused by anti-collision path constraints, a two-stage collision-free trajectory optimization method [23] was used to improve the efficiency and convergence of the optimization problem. Here, by analyzing the velocity increment under a long TOF, the distribution law of the reachable domain affected by TOF is obtained, so the generation of the reachable domain is simplified to the solution of the initial boundary and the continuous boundary. The initial boundary is defined as the boundary of the reachable domain preliminarily obtained by the section method. In view of the irregular shape of asteroids and the uneven gravitational field, the reachable domain usually presents a complex shape, and the boundary obtained by a one-time solution is usually difficult to clearly describe the boundary of the reachable domain. Therefore, it is proposed that the initial boundary is continuously extended to the interior of the reachable domain until the boundary is continuous to obtain the final continuous boundary. Finally, the proposed method is applied to the asteroids Bennu and Bacchus to verify the effectiveness and efficiency of the method.

2. Trajectory Optimization for Collision-Free Landing

2.1. Dynamic Models and Constraints

An asteroid-fixed coordinate system o-xyz with the mass center o of the asteroid as the coordinate origin is defined, of which the three axes are aligned with the three principle axes. Assume that asteroids uniformly rotate around the axis of maximum moment of inertia, and the motion equations of a spacecraft in the frame o-xyz are [24]

$$\begin{cases} \dot{\boldsymbol{r}} = \boldsymbol{v} \\ \dot{\boldsymbol{v}} = -2\boldsymbol{\omega} \times \dot{\boldsymbol{r}} - \boldsymbol{\omega} \times (\boldsymbol{\omega} \times \boldsymbol{r}) + \boldsymbol{g}(\boldsymbol{r}) + \frac{T_{\max} u \boldsymbol{\alpha}}{m} \\ \dot{m} = -\frac{T_{max} u}{I_{sp} g_0} \end{cases}, \tag{1}$$

where $\boldsymbol{r} = [x, y, z]^T$ is the position vector, $\boldsymbol{v} = [v_x, v_y, v_z]^T$ is the velocity vector, and m is the mass of the spacecraft system, respectively. Vector $\boldsymbol{\omega} = [0, 0, \omega]^T$ is the angular velocity of the asteroid, $\boldsymbol{g}(\boldsymbol{r})$ is the gravitational acceleration, $T_{\max}$ represents the maximum magnitude of the thrust, $u \in [0, 1]$ is the thrust ratio, $\boldsymbol{\alpha}$ is the direction of the thrust, I_{sp} is the specific impulse, and $g_0 = 9.80665\ \mathrm{m/s^2}$ is the standard gravity.

Assume that the initial state vector of the spacecraft is known and expressed as

$$\boldsymbol{r}(0) = \boldsymbol{r}_0 \ \boldsymbol{v}(0) = \boldsymbol{v}_0 \ m(0) = m_0. \tag{2}$$

In this study, the reachable domain is defined as a set of points on the surface of an asteroid that can be reached. Based on the used polyhedron model, points on the surface of an asteroid are represented by the center of the surface triangle on the polyhedron, that is

$$(\boldsymbol{r}_c)_i = \frac{(\boldsymbol{r}_1)_i + (\boldsymbol{r}_2)_i + (\boldsymbol{r}_3)_i}{3} \ i = 1, 2, \ldots N_f, \tag{3}$$

where $\boldsymbol{r}_1$, $\boldsymbol{r}_2$, and $\boldsymbol{r}_3$ are three vertexes of a triangle, i stands for the i-th triangle, and N_f represents the total number of surface triangles of the selected polyhedral model. Then, for the soft landing problem with a given flight time t_f, the final state vector of the spacecraft is known and written as

$$\boldsymbol{r}(t_f) = \boldsymbol{r}_c \ \boldsymbol{v}(t_f) = 0. \tag{4}$$

Due to the irregular gravity field and the rotation of the asteroid, it is necessary to set anti-collision path constraints to prevent the spacecraft from colliding with the asteroid's surface during landing. The anti-collision path constraints are defined as the combination of external ellipsoid constraint and glide-slope constraint [20], which are respectively expressed as

$$\boldsymbol{r}(t)^T \boldsymbol{R}_e \boldsymbol{r}(t) \geq 1\,, \tag{5}$$

$$\frac{[\boldsymbol{r}(t) - \boldsymbol{r}_c]^T \boldsymbol{n}}{\|\boldsymbol{r}(t) - \boldsymbol{r}_c\| \|\boldsymbol{n}\|} \geq \cos`, \tag{6}$$

where $\boldsymbol{R}_e$ means diagonal matrix, with $\boldsymbol{R}_e = \mathrm{diag}(\frac{1}{a^2}, \frac{1}{b^2}, \frac{1}{c^2})$, and a, b and c are the semiaxis of the ellipsoid. Vector $\boldsymbol{n}$ is the outer normal vector of the triangle on the asteroid surface, and θ is the conical angle of the glide-slope constraint.

2.2. Two-Stage Simplified Method for Collision-Free Trajectory Optimization

In this study, the energy-optimal trajectory optimization problem for collision-free asteroid landing is considered, and the two-stage simplified solution method [23] proposed by authors in the previous research is used to solve this problem. In this method, the asteroid landing process is divided into the descent stage that satisfies the ellipsoid constraint and the final landing stage that flies in the ellipsoid and meets the glide-slope constraint. In the descent stage, the approximate initial costate of the generalized gravity-free energy-optimal control problem [24] is employed as the initial guess. In the final landing stage, the approximate analytical solution [24] can directly provide initial costate and the energy consumption for the optimal trajectories.

To plan the two-stage energy-optimal trajectory, the performance index is [23]

$$J = J_1 + J_2 = \lambda_0 \int_0^{t_p} u^2 \, \mathrm{d}t + \frac{1}{2}\int_{t_p}^{t_f} \boldsymbol{a}^{\mathrm{T}} \boldsymbol{a} \, \mathrm{d}t, \tag{7}$$

where J_1 and J_2 are the performance index of the energy-optimal control problem in the descent stage and the gravity-free energy-optimal control problem [24] in the final landing stage, respectively, $\lambda_0 = T_{\max}{}^{2/} 2m_0{}^2$ is a positive numerical factor that does not inherently change the optimal problem [25], m_0 is the initial mass of the spacecraft, t_p is the flight time of the descent stage, and $\boldsymbol{a}$ is the control acceleration of the final landing stage.

For the energy-optimal control problem in the descent stage, the costate $\boldsymbol{\lambda}(t)$ satisfies

$$\begin{cases} \dot{\boldsymbol{\lambda}}_r = \boldsymbol{\omega} \times (\boldsymbol{\omega} \times \boldsymbol{\lambda}_v) - \frac{\partial}{\partial \boldsymbol{r}}(\boldsymbol{\lambda}_v \cdot \boldsymbol{g}(\boldsymbol{r})) \\ \dot{\boldsymbol{\lambda}}_v = -\boldsymbol{\lambda}_r + 2\boldsymbol{\lambda}_v \times \boldsymbol{\omega} \\ \dot{\lambda}_m = \boldsymbol{\lambda}_v \cdot \frac{T_{\max} u \boldsymbol{\alpha}}{m^2} \end{cases}, \tag{8}$$

where the costate $\boldsymbol{\lambda}(t) = [\boldsymbol{\lambda}_r, \boldsymbol{\lambda}_v, \lambda_m]^T$ correspond to the state $\mathbf{X}(t) = [\boldsymbol{r}, \boldsymbol{v}, m]^T$. The optimal thrust direction $\boldsymbol{\alpha}$ and the optimal thrust magnitude u are

$$\boldsymbol{\alpha} = -\frac{\boldsymbol{\lambda}_v}{\|\boldsymbol{\lambda}_v\|}, \tag{9}$$

$$u = \begin{cases} æ & if\, æ < 1 \\ 1 & if\, æ \geq 1 \end{cases}, \tag{10}$$

where ρ is the switching function, expressed by

$$\rho = \frac{1}{2\lambda_0}\left(\frac{T_{\max}\lambda_m}{I_{\text{sp}}g_0} + \frac{T_{\max}\|\boldsymbol{\lambda}_v\|}{m}\right). \tag{11}$$

In addition, according to the transversality condition, the final mass costate of the descent stage can be written as

$$\lambda_m(t_f) = 0. \tag{12}$$

For the gravity-free energy-optimal control problem [24] in the final landing stage, the initial costate $\boldsymbol{\lambda}(t_0) = [\boldsymbol{\lambda}_{r0}, \boldsymbol{\lambda}_{v0}, \lambda_{m0}]$ can be solved by

$$\begin{cases} \boldsymbol{\lambda}_{r0} = \frac{6\left(t_{pf}\boldsymbol{v}_p + 2\boldsymbol{r}_p - 2\boldsymbol{r}_c\right)}{t_{pf}^3} \\ \boldsymbol{\lambda}_{v0} = \frac{2\left(2t_{pf}\boldsymbol{v}_p + 3\boldsymbol{r}_p - 3\boldsymbol{r}_c\right)}{t_{pf}^2} \\ \lambda_{m0} = \frac{1}{m_0}\left(\frac{1}{3}\boldsymbol{\lambda}_{r0}\cdot\boldsymbol{\lambda}_{r0}t_{pf}^3 - \boldsymbol{\lambda}_{r0}\cdot\boldsymbol{\lambda}_{v0}t_{pf}^2 + \boldsymbol{\lambda}_{v0}\cdot\boldsymbol{\lambda}_{v0}t_{pf}\right) \end{cases}, \tag{13}$$

and the optimal-control acceleration $\boldsymbol{a}^*$ is obtained as

$$\boldsymbol{a}^* = \frac{6\left(t_{pf}\boldsymbol{v}_p + 2\boldsymbol{r}_p - 2\boldsymbol{r}_f\right)}{t_{pf}^3}t - \frac{2\left(2t_f\boldsymbol{v}_p + 3\boldsymbol{r}_p - 3\boldsymbol{r}_f\right)}{t_{pf}^2}, \tag{14}$$

where t_{pf} is the flight time of the final landing stage, $\boldsymbol{r}_p$ and $\boldsymbol{v}_p$ are the final position and velocity of the descent stage, respectively. When $\boldsymbol{r}_p$ and $\boldsymbol{v}_p$ are determined, by solving Equations (13) and (14), the energy consumption J_2 and initial costate of the final landing stage can be analytically obtained, while the trajectory is required to satisfy the glide-slope constraint given by Equation (6). Since the landing state and flight time are fixed, the trajectory only changes with $\boldsymbol{r}_p$ and $\boldsymbol{v}_p$, i.e., the trajectory satisfying the glide-slope constraint can be obtained by changing $\boldsymbol{r}_p$ and $\boldsymbol{v}_p$. In the descent stage, known the initial state in Equation (2) and flight time t_p, if the initial costates of this stage are given, the trajectory and $\boldsymbol{r}_p$ and $\boldsymbol{v}_p$ can be obtained by integrating Equations (1) and (8), thereby generating the trajectory of the final landing stage by $\boldsymbol{r}_p$ and $\boldsymbol{v}_p$. Under the conditions that the trajectory satisfies the path constraint of the descent stage, and $\boldsymbol{r}_p$ and $\boldsymbol{v}_p$ make the final landing stage satisfy the anti-collision path constraint, the initial costate that minimizes the energy consumption J of the two stages is found. Then, the problem can be solved.

The numerical integration method used above is the fourth-order Runge–Kutta algorithm with fixed step size. The optimal trajectories of anti-collision landing fulfill the following constraints: the dynamic constraints described by Equations (1), (8), and (13), initial-final state constraints described by Equations (2)–(4), anti-collision path constraints in Equations (5) and (6), the transversal condition described by Equation (12), and thrust magnitude constraint. The gradient descent method [26] is used to solve this problem, which can be performed by a nonlinear programming solver such as *fmincon* of the Matlab functions. Using the *fmincon* algorithm to solve this problem can be expressed as finding the initial costates that make the objective function, i.e., the two-stage energy consumption J, obtain the minimum value under the conditions of satisfying the above nonlinear inequality and equality constraints.

The feasibility of the trajectory optimization method depends on the error between the approximate analytical solution and the optimal solution in the final landing stage. The simulation results [23] show that the mean absolute error between them is less than 0.05, which means that the trajectories obtained by these two solutions are very close, and the convergence rate of the optimal trajectories can reach 96.4%. Because the anti-collision trajectory optimization problem has strong nonlinearity, compared with the traditional random guess method which is difficult to converge, the trajectory optimization algorithm has excellent performance.

3. Generation Method of the Reachable Domain

Through the above trajectory optimization method, the set of landing points with feasible solutions within a given TOF constitutes the landing reachable domain, which is expressed as $U_c(t_f)$. The obtained $U_c(t_f)$ is a set of terminal positions $r(t_f)$ satisfying constraints described in the previous section.

Solving times of feasible solution of landing trajectory depends on the number of surface triangles of the polyhedron model. The higher the model accuracy, the finer the division of surface triangles, that is, the more triangles, which leads to a large amount of computation and time-consuming to obtain the feasible solution of all surface points to obtain the reachable domain. To improve the efficiency of solving the reachable domain, this paper proposes to obtain the reachable domain boundary based on the distribution law of the reachable domain. The boundary roughly divides the asteroid surface into two parts with and without feasible solutions, and the former is the reachable domain of the required solution.

The reachable boundary is solved based on the section method and the expansion method. The section method is used to determine the rough boundary preliminarily. Since the boundary extracted by the section method is located at the edge of the reachable domain, it is difficult for the landing sites with the feasible solution to accurately describe the boundary contour. In order to improve the accuracy of the obtained reachable domain, an expansion method is proposed, that is, by expanding the initial boundary to the region with the feasible solution in the form of the section, the final continuous boundary is obtained. The method transforms the trajectory optimization problem of a large number of points in the region into that of a few points constituting the boundary, which avoids solving the feasible solutions of all points on the asteroid surface, and greatly reduces the amount of calculation on the premise of satisfying the high-precision solution of the reachable domain.

3.1. Initial Boundary of the Reachable Domain

The strategy of solving the boundary to obtain the reachable domain is based on the analysis of the distribution law of the reachable domain. By solving the distribution of the velocity increment of points with the feasible solution on the asteroid surface under the long TOF, the distribution law of the reachable domain affected by the TOF is obtained. The longer TOF is chosen to ensure that most of the points on the asteroid's surface have feasible solutions. Velocity increment refers to the initial and final velocity variation of the landing trajectory with the feasible solution. It can be seen from Figure 1 that the velocity increment increases with the increase in the distance between the initial position and the landing site of the spacecraft. At the same time, the change in the velocity increment depends on the flight time; that is, when the flight time is short and it is difficult to reach a large velocity increment, it can be considered that the landing site in the region with large velocity increment does not have a feasible solution. Therefore, the numerical variation law of velocity increment can be regarded as the variation law of the asteroid surface region that the spacecraft can reach limited by the TOF. In Figure 1, taking Bacchus as an example, the distribution of the velocity increment of the spacecraft landing on the asteroid surface from different initial positions and the same longer TOF is described. The initial velocity of the spacecraft is assumed to be 0, and the black dot in the figure represents the initial position.

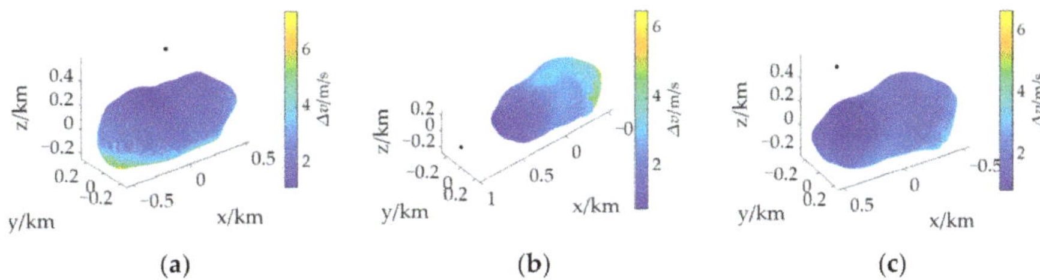

Figure 1. Velocity increment distributions at different initial positions. (**a**) Over the North Pole. (**b**) Over the Equator. (**c**) Over the mid-latitude region.

According to the above analysis, it is concluded that the landing reachable domain increases with increasing flight time, and its distribution on the asteroid surface is closely related to the initial position of the spacecraft. The reachable domain boundary is determined by the position of any point on the boundary. Specifically, taking the distance from the point to the initial position as the radius, applying an upper and lower deviation to the radius to obtain a radius range, taking out the points on the asteroid surface within the radius range, and obtaining the reachable domain boundary by solving the feasible solution. At this time, the key to the problem is to determine the position of any point on the boundary.

Take out a group of asteroid surface points that change with the distance from the initial position, expressed as P(d), as shown by the yellow dot in Figure 2a. Then obtain a point on the reachable domain boundary by successively calculating the feasible solutions of these points. Since the reachable domain boundary refers to the edge of the region composed of the asteroid surface points with feasible solutions, the last point with feasible solutions in P(d) is the point on the boundary. In order to obtain uniformly and continuously distributed P(d), a plane section method is proposed that is defined as a method of obtaining two parallel planes after a plane is translated by the same distance along the normal vector of the plane in two opposite directions. The translation distance is determined by the size of the triangle on the asteroid surface and is generally taken as one half of the height h of the triangle to ensure the uniform and continuous distribution of points between the two planes. Thereby, the plane passes through the mass center of the asteroid, and the normal vector of the plane is perpendicular to the vector from the initial point to the mass center of the asteroid. As shown in Figure 2a, the two parallel planes are obtained by the plane section method, and the yellow dot between the planes is P(d). The points with feasible solutions in this group of points are shown as yellow "o" in Figure 2b. It should be pointed out that landing points with feasible but scattered solutions will be ignored when taking a point on the boundary. This is because the gravitational field near the asteroid is irregular, and the surface points of the asteroid with feasible solutions are not strictly within a certain region. Inevitably, some points fall outside the reachable domain obtained by the distribution law, and these points are scattered and small in number. Therefore, the scattered points are all ignored in this study. After removing the scattered points "o" in Figure 2b, the point "o" farthest from the initial position is a point on the boundary. The basis for determining whether a point is a scattered point is whether the distance between adjacent points exceeds $3h$.

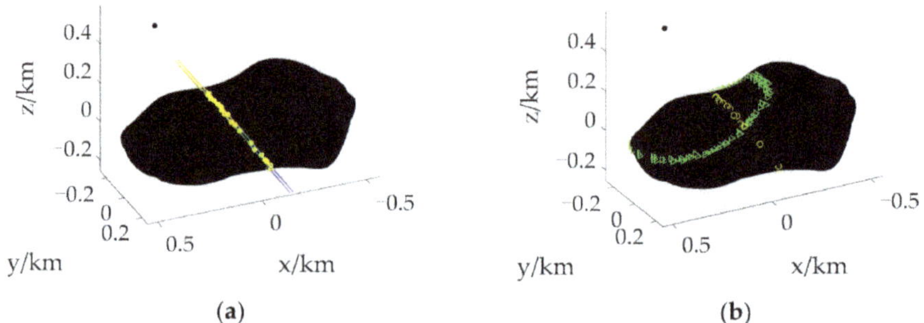

Figure 2. Use of the section method. (**a**) Solving a point on the initial boundary by the section method. (**b**) A group of asteroid surface points used to solve the initial boundary. The yellow "o" stand for points with feasible solutions between parallel planes. The green "Δ"stand for points between parallel planes when solving initial boundary.

After determining a point on the boundary, the radius r_0 is calculated, and the reachable domain boundary is obtained by using the circle section method, which is a method of obtaining the asteroid surface points between large and small radii by increasing and decreasing the radius by the same size. The size of increase and decrease is generally taken as one half of h, that is, the value range of radius r obtained is $\{r|r_0 - h/2 \leq r \leq r_0 + h/2\}$. This makes the number of points needed to solve the reachable domain boundary less and evenly distributed, and it greatly reduces the time consumption for solving the optimization problem. The obtained group of asteroid surface points is expressed as P(r), as shown by the green "Δ" in Figure 2b. The reachable domain boundary can be obtained by taking out the points with feasible solutions.

However, since this group of points is located at the boundary between the points with feasible solutions and those without feasible solutions, the probability of occurrence of the two cases with and without feasible solutions is the same, which leads to the possibility that the points with feasible solutions may be discontinuous as the reachable domain boundary and the boundary description may not be clear. Discontinuity means that the distance between adjacent points is too large. In order to ensure computational efficiency and improve the accuracy of the boundary, the obtained boundary is defined as the initial boundary, and on this basis, the continuous boundary is obtained by extending to the region with the feasible solution.

3.2. Continuous Boundary of the Reachable Domain

The specific process of extending the initial boundary to the continuous boundary is as follows. First, the distance between adjacent points on the initial boundary is used to determine whether it is continuous. When the distance is less than $3h$, it is continuous; otherwise, it is discontinuous. If any adjacent points are continuous, the initial boundary is the required final continuous boundary, and the reachable domain can be obtained. If it is not continuous, the extension method is used. Since the region composed of points with feasible solutions is the region close to the initial position in the two-part region divided by the boundary, the expansion method is to reduce the radius r to obtain a continuous boundary composed of points with feasible solutions.

The radius r_1 is obtained by reducing r by h, and the value range obtained by the circular section method is $\{r_{r_1}|r_0 - 3h/2 \leq r_{r_1} \leq r_0 - h/2\}$, so as to obtain a group of asteroid surface points after the first expansion, expressed as P(r_1). Points between all discontinuous points on the initial boundary are extracted from P(r_1) along the vector direction from the asteroid centroid to the initial position. Through trajectory optimization, the obtained points with feasible solutions and the initial boundary form the boundary after the first expansion. Judge whether the boundary is continuous or not. If it is continuous, the final continuous boundary is obtained; otherwise, it continues to expand. The radius r_2

is obtained by reducing r_1 by h, and the value range obtained by using the circular section method is $\{r_{r_2}|r_0 - 5h/2 \leq r_{r_2} \leq r_0 - 3h/2\}$, so as to obtain a group of asteroid surface points $P(r_2)$ after the second expansion. The points between discontinuous points in the boundary are taken out along the vector direction. The obtained feasible solution and the boundary after the first expansion form the boundary after the second expansion. Repeat the above process until the obtained boundary is continuous. From the above expansion process, it can be seen that the height h of the triangle on the asteroid surface is taken as an expansion unit because this expansion unit can appropriately take out a layer of asteroid surface points, and its number and distribution state are the most suitable for solving the boundary.

Figure 3 shows the expansion process that the initial boundary is expanded twice to obtain a continuous boundary. In Figure 3a, "0" represents the initial boundary, and "1" and "2" represent the boundary obtained after the first and second expansion, respectively. Judging that "2" is a continuous boundary by the distance between adjacent points, the expansion stops and the reachable domain is obtained. Figure 3b highlights the specific expansion process of discontinuous adjacent points. Taking the extension of the "a" part with the discontinuous initial boundary as an example, after $P(r_1)$ is obtained, the points between green planes perpendicular to the paper surface are taken out according to the direction indicated by the arrow, and the points with feasible solutions form the boundary of this part. The direction indicated by the arrow is the vector direction from the mass center of the asteroid to the initial position. After determining the discontinuity of the "b" part in the boundary according to the distance, it continues to expand to obtain $P(r_2)$, and then takes out the points between red planes perpendicular to the paper according to the direction indicated by the arrow. At this time, the points with feasible solutions are continuous, and we can know that the continuous boundary of the "a" part is obtained after expanding it twice. The red dot in Figure 3b represents the points with the feasible solution obtained by trajectory optimization of all points on the asteroid surface.

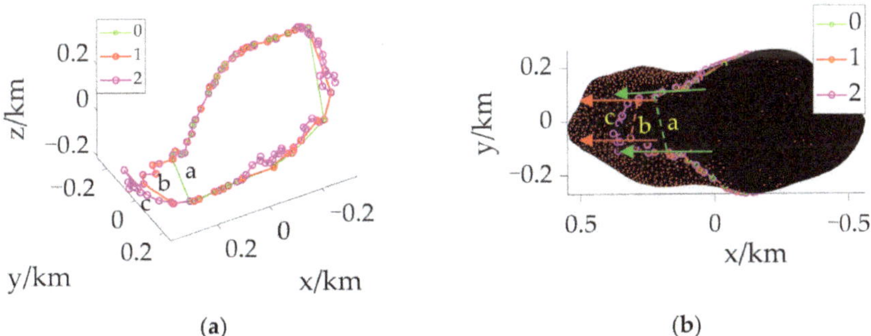

Figure 3. Use of the extension method. (**a**) The extension from the initial boundary to the continuous boundary. (**b**) The extension of the "a" part. "0" represents the initial boundary, and "1" and "2" represent the boundary obtained after the first and second expansion, respectively.

4. Simulation Results and Analysis

The section and extension method is applied to obtain the reachable domain of the top-shaped asteroid Bennu and the elongated asteroid Bacchus to verify the effectiveness of the proposed method. All the simulations are implemented on a desktop computer with Intel Core i9-7920X CPU @2.90 GHz. To quickly calculate the gravitational field of the asteroids, the 2nd order spherical harmonic model and the rotating mass dipole model [27] be applied, respectively. For the spacecraft, the initial mass is 2000 kg, the maximum thrust T_{max} = 20 N, the engine specific impulse I_{sp} = 400 s, and the scaling is used, where the length scaling factor LU is set to 246 m and 1 km, respectively, and the time scaling factor $TU = \sqrt{\frac{LU^3}{\mu_0}}$s [24].

4.1. Applications to 101,955 Bennu

The rotation period of Bennu is 4.288 h and the average diameter is 492 m. A polyhedron model with 1348 vertices and 2692 faces is used in this paper. The number of faces is the number of target landing points. Taking energy optimization as the performance index, the trajectory optimization problem of collision-free asteroid landing is solved. 2692 trajectories need to be optimized when solving the landing reachable domain, which is extremely time-consuming. Therefore, the section and expansion method is used to obtain the boundary to improve the efficiency of the reachable domain under the given TOF. In order to fully reflect the effectiveness and applicability of the proposed reachable domain generation method, the initial positions of the spacecraft are selected to be above the North Pole, the Equator, and the mid-latitude region of the asteroid, which are $[0\ 0\ 0.8]^T$ km, $[0.8\ 0\ 0]^T$ km and $[0.6\ 0\ 0.5]^T$ km respectively. The initial velocity is set to 0 m/s.

4.1.1. Initial Boundary

The initial boundary is determined according to the distribution of velocity increment with a long TOF. As shown in Figure 4, the velocity increment distribution at different initial positions when t_f = 1200 s and the TOF of the final landing stage is 200 s. It can be seen from the figure that at different initial positions, the velocity increment increases with the increase of the distance from the initial position. Therefore, the section method can be used to obtain a point on the initial boundary of the reachable domain.

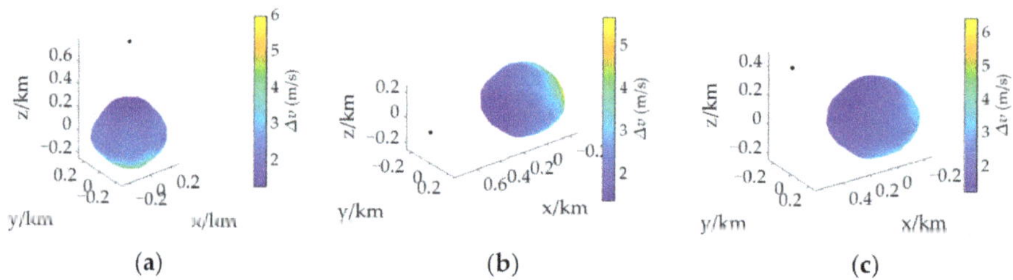

Figure 4. Distribution of velocity increment with different initial positions at t_f = 1200 s. (**a**) Over the North Pole. (**b**) Over the Equator. (**c**) Over the mid-latitude region.

The process of taking a point on the boundary using the section method is shown by the yellow connecting line in Figure 5. Yellow "o" represents the points with feasible solutions between planes. After ignoring the scattered points, the remaining points are connected as lines. The far endpoint of the line relative to the initial position is the point on the initial boundary, and the distance from this point to the initial position is taken as the radius r_0. Taking Figure 5a as an example, the radius r_0 = 625 m, and the height h of the triangle on the asteroid surface is taken as 25 m. Using the circular section method, the surface points of the asteroid with a radius of more than 612.5 m but less than 637.5 m are taken out, and the points with feasible solutions form the initial boundary, as shown in green "o". Figure 5a–f display the reachable domains of the asteroid surface at different initial positions when t_f = 700 s and t_f = 900 s. Among them, the purple dots indicate the points with feasible solutions obtained after trajectory optimization of all points on the asteroid surface, which are used as the references of the reachable domain to verify the effectiveness and accuracy of the reachable domain boundary solution.

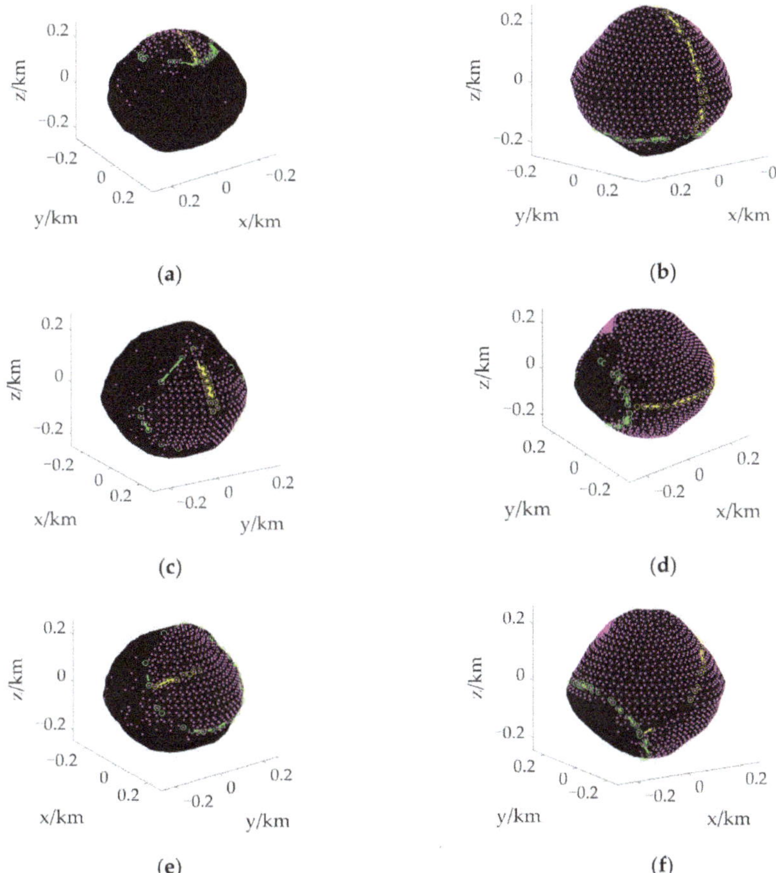

Figure 5. Initial boundary of the reachable domain under different initial states. (**a**) Initial boundary for landing from over the North Pole with $t_f = 700$ s. (**b**) Initial boundary for landing from over the North Pole with $t_f = 900$ s. (**c**) Initial boundary for landing from over the Equator with $t_f = 700$ s. (**d**) Initial boundary for landing from over the Equator with $t_f = 900$ s. (**e**) Initial boundary for landing from over the mid-latitude region with when $t_f = 700$ s. (**f**) Initial boundary for landing from over the mid-latitude region with when $t_f = 900$ s. The yellow "o" stand for points with feasible solutions between parallel planes. The green "o" stand for points that make up the initial boundary. The purple dots indicate the points with feasible solutions on the asteroid surface.

It can be seen from Figure 5 that the range of the reachable domain is related to the initial position and the TOF of the spacecraft, and the proposed solution of the reachable domain can be applied to different situations. When the initial position is the same, the longer the given flight time, the larger the reachable range. In addition, Figure 5 shows that the initial boundary can effectively surround most of the purple points, and only a few scattered points are not within the boundary.

When $t_f = 900$ s, histories of the position, velocity, mass, and descent trajectory of the energy optimal control problem landing on the asteroid surface from above the North Pole are shown in Figure 6. These results show that the two-stage simplified solution method based on the anti-collision path constraint enables the spacecraft to land safely at the target landing site. In the figure, the red "Δ" and "•" respectively indicate the transition position and landing position. In addition, the time consumption for solving an optimal landing trajectory is about 60 s.

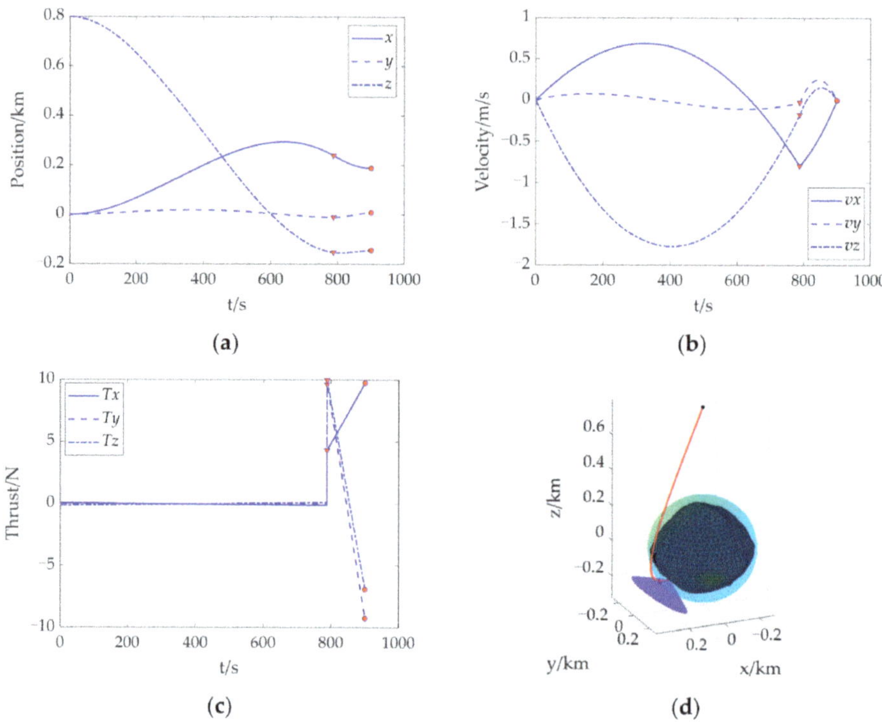

Figure 6. Trajectory optimization results of landing on the asteroid Bennu from above the North Pole. (**a**) Histories of the position. (**b**) Histories of the velocity. (**c**) Histories of the thrust. (**d**) History of the descent trajectory. The red "Δ" and "•" indicate the transition position and landing position, respectively. "•" indicate the transition position and landing position, respectively.

4.1.2. Continuous Boundary

Based on the initial boundary obtained, judge whether it is continuous by the distance between adjacent points. When the distance is greater than $3h$, i.e., 75 m, it is considered discontinuous, and the radius r needs to be reduced. Taking Figure 5a as an example, the radius $r_0 = 625$ m at the initial boundary is obtained, and the radius $r_1 = r_0 - h = 600$ m after the first expansion. The surface point $P(r_1)$ of the asteroid after the first expansion is obtained using the circular section method. Along the vector direction from the asteroid centroid to the initial position, the points between all discontinuous points on the initial boundary are taken from $P(r_1)$ for trajectory optimization, and the obtained points with feasible solutions are connected with the initial boundary to become the boundary after the first expansion. Judge the distance of the boundary, repeat the above expansion process until the distance between all adjacent points is less than 75 m, and then obtain the final continuous boundary to determine the reachable domain.

Figure 7 shows the boundary at different initial positions when $t_f = 700$ s, where the green connecting line represents the initial boundary, and the purple connecting line represents the continuous boundary. It can be seen that most of the initial boundary and the continuous boundary are coincident, and only when the distance between adjacent points is too large to describe the boundary is expansion required. In Figure 5, the initial boundary can basically surround the actual reachable domain, while the continuous boundary further improves the accuracy of the reachable domain boundary on the premise of a small increase in calculation.

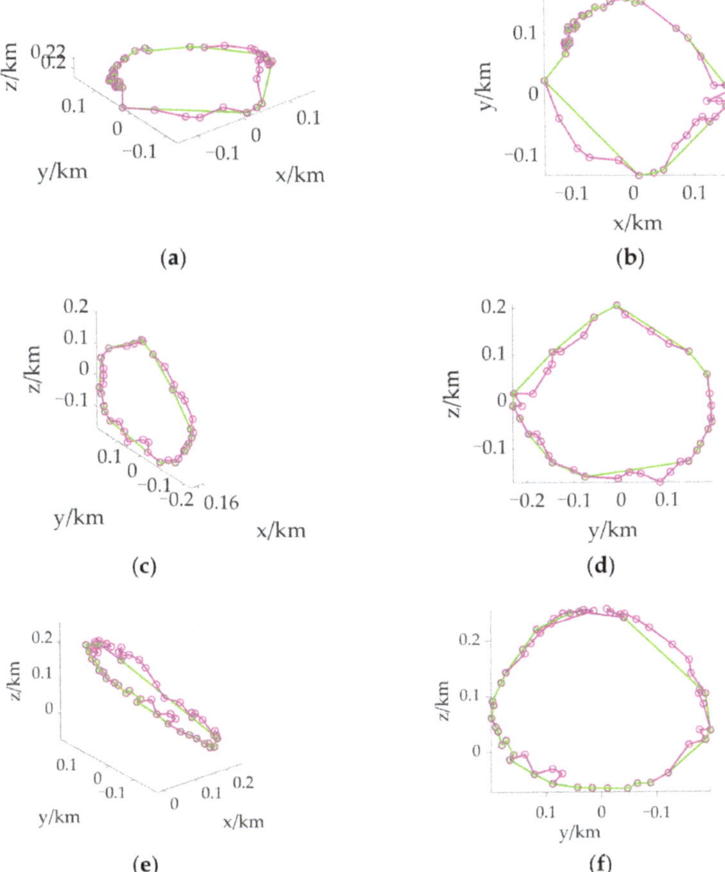

Figure 7. Boundary of the reachable domain under different initial states with $t_f = 700$ s. (**a**) 3D view of the boundary when the initial position is over the North Pole. (**b**) Supplementary view of the boundary when the initial position is over the North Pole. (**c**) 3D view of the boundary when the initial position is over the Equator. (**d**) Supplementary view of the boundary when the initial position is over the Equator. (**e**) 3D view of the boundary when the initial position is over the mid-latitude region. (**f**) Supplementary view of the boundary when the initial position is over the mid-latitude region. The green connecting line stands for the initial boundary. The purple connecting line stands for the continuous boundary.

In this study, considering the anti-collision path constraint and improving the trajectory optimization efficiency, the trajectory optimization methods used are two-stage simplified solutions [23]. Whether it is the traditional method of optimizing the trajectory of all points on the surface of the asteroid to obtain the reachable domain or the method of solving the boundary of the reachable domain proposed in this study, the time consumption for the trajectory optimization of a single point is basically the same. Therefore, the time-consuming ratio of the proposed method to the traditional method is approximated by comparing the number of points where the two methods need trajectory optimization, which illustrates the efficiency of trajectory optimization.

Table 1 lists the total number of points N of trajectory optimization required by the proposed method for obtaining a continuous boundary under different initial states, the total number of points N_f on the asteroid surface, and their ratio, i.e., the time-consuming ratio. In the table, P(d) represents the number of points needed for trajectory optimization when solving a point on the boundary; P(r) represents the number of points needed for trajectory optimization when solving the initial boundary; P(e) represents the number of points needed for trajectory optimization to obtain a continuous boundary by expanding the initial boundary and n represents the number of extension times.

Table 1. Time-consuming statistics.

Initial Condition	Over the North Pole		Over the Equator		Over the Mid-Latitude Region	
	700 s	900 s	700 s	900 s	700 s	900 s
P(d)	39		33		34	
P(r)	97	77	49	78	61	115
P(e)	22	39	51	40	40	0
n	2	2	2	2	2	0
N	158	155	133	151	135	149
N_f	2692					
Time-consuming ratio (%)	5.8692	5.7578	4.9406	5.6092	5.0149	5.5349

It can be seen that the ratio of N to N_f is not more than 6%, that is, the time-consuming ratio of the proposed method and the traditional method for solving the reachable domain is less than 6%. Therefore, the reachable domain solution method based on the section and expansion method proposed in this study can reduce the solution time by more than 94%, and greatly improve the solution efficiency. It should be pointed out that the use of the parfor greatly improves the efficiency of trajectory optimization.

We also verify that the more the number of faces on the surface of asteroid is, the smaller the time-consuming ratio is, and the advantages of the proposed method are more prominent. This is because the number of points taken by the section method for trajectory optimization can be determined manually, and the less the better under the condition of uniform and continuous distribution. Therefore, when the number of faces increases, the number of points in the section is almost unchanged, so the reduction of the time consumption ratio is the multiple of the increase of the number of faces.

4.2. Applications to 2063 Bacchus

In order to further prove the effectiveness of the proposed method, Bacchus was selected to solve the reachable domain. The rotation period of the asteroid is 14.9 h, and the polyhedron model with 2048 vertices and 4092 faces was adopted; that is, the number of triangle center points on the asteroid surface was 4092. Therefore, the number of trajectories that needed to be optimized with the two-stage simplified solution method was 4092. To further verify the effectiveness and applicability of the proposed method, it was also considered that the initial positions of the spacecraft are above the North Pole, the Equator, and the mid-latitude region of the asteroid, which were chosen as $[0\ 0\ 0.6]^T$ km, $[1\ 0\ 0]^T$ km and $[0.4\ 0\ 0.6]^T$ km, respectively. The initial velocity was set to 0 m/s.

4.2.1. Initial Boundary

The velocity increment of Bacchus at different initial positions when $t_f = 1600$ s and the TOF of the final landing stage is 300 s is shown in Figure 1. It can be clearly seen that the velocity increment increases with the increase of the distance from the initial position. The process of obtaining a point on the initial boundary by using the section method is shown by the yellow connecting line in Figures 8–10. The yellow "o" represents the point with the feasible solution in P®. After ignoring the scattered points, the yellow point "o" farthest from the initial position is the point on the initial boundary. Use this point to determine the radius to obtain the initial boundary, as shown by the green connecting line.

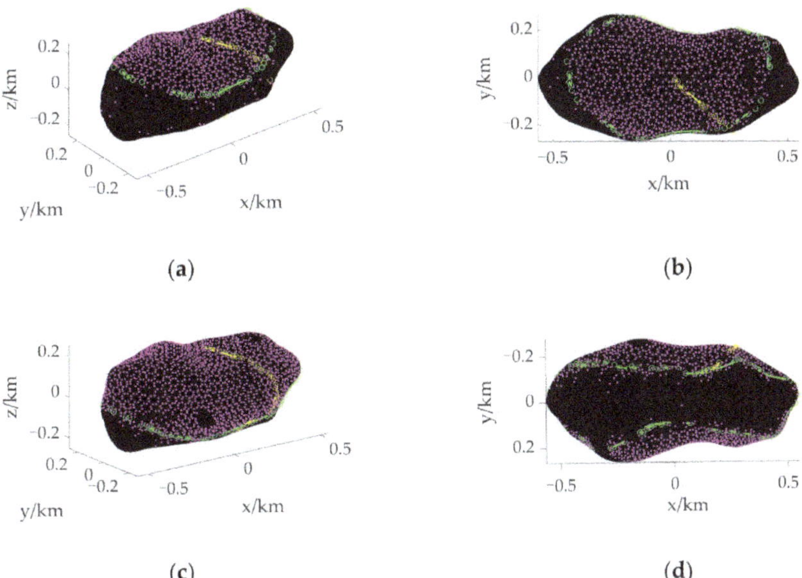

Figure 8. Initial boundary when the initial position is above the North Pole. (**a**) 3D view of the initial boundary with t_f = 900 s. (**b**) Supplementary view of the initial boundary with t_f = 900 s. (**c**) 3D view of the initial boundary with t_f = 1000 s. (**d**) Supplementary view of the initial boundary with t_f = 1000 s. The yellow "o" stand for points with feasible solutions between parallel planes. The green "o" stand for points that make up the initial boundary. The purple dots indicate the points with feasible solutions on the asteroid surface.

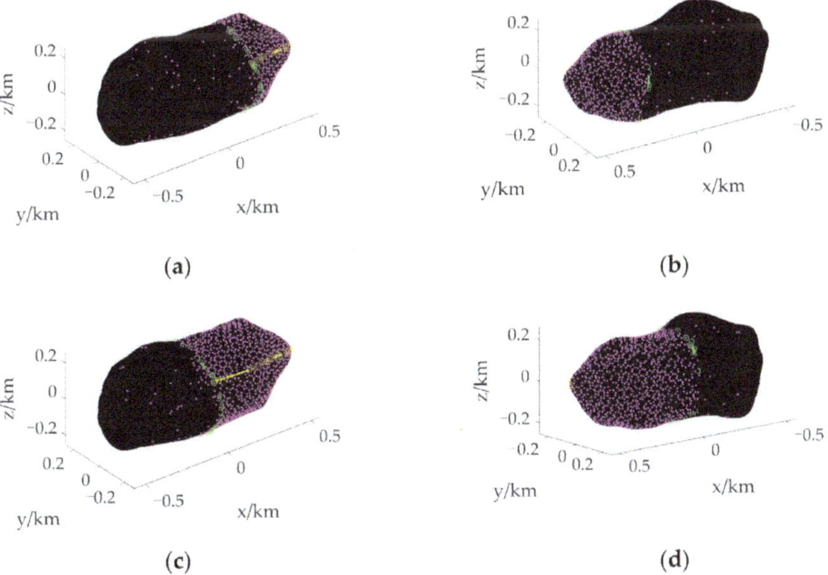

Figure 9. Initial boundary when the initial position is above the Equator. (**a**) 3D view of the initial boundary with t_f = 1000 s. (**b**) Supplementary view of the initial boundary with t_f = 1000 s. (**c**) 3D view of the initial boundary with t_f = 1100 s. (**d**) Supplementary view of the initial boundary with t_f = 1100 s.

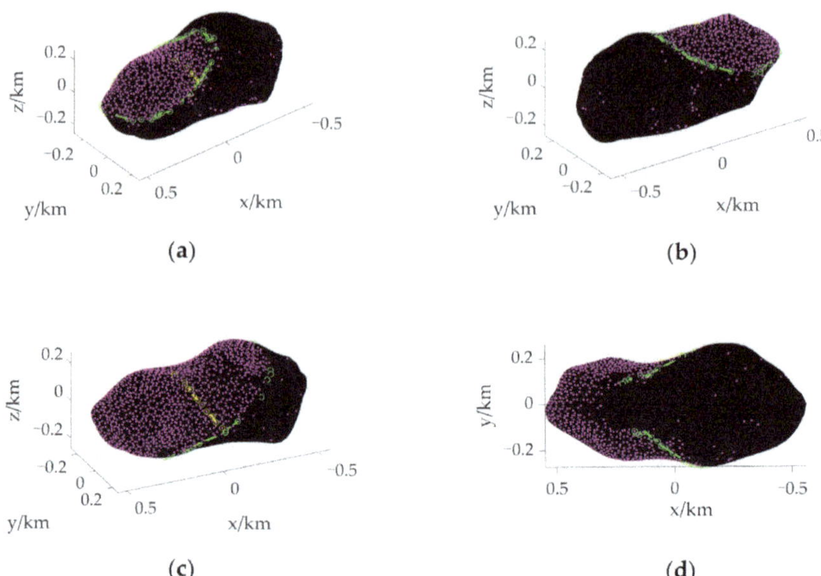

Figure 10. Initial boundary when the initial position is above the mid-latitude region. (**a**) 3D view of the initial boundary with $t_f = 900$ s. (**b**) Supplementary view of the initial boundary with $t_f = 900$ s. (**c**) 3D view of the initial boundary with $t_f = 1000$ s. (**d**) Supplementary view of the initial boundary with $t_f = 1000$ s.

Taking Figure 8a as an example, the radius r_0 and the height h of the triangle on the asteroid surface are taken as 620 m and 40 m, respectively. Using the circular section method, the asteroid surface points with radius r greater than 600 m but less than 640 m are extracted, and the initial boundary is obtained by trajectory optimization of these points. Figures 8–10 show the initial boundaries of the reachable domain with different TOF when the initial positions of the spacecraft are over the North Pole, the Equator, and the mid-latitude region.

It can be seen from Figures 8–10 that the reachable range is related to the initial position and the TOF of the spacecraft, and the proposed boundary method can be applied to different initial states. When the initial position is the same, the longer the given TOF, the larger the reachable range. The initial boundary can effectively surround most of the purple points, which further shows the effectiveness of the proposed method for solving the reachable domain boundary.

When $t_f = 1000$ s, histories of the position, velocity, mass, and descent trajectory of the energy optimal control problem landing on the asteroid surface from above the North Pole are shown in Figure 11. These results show that the two-stage simplified solution method enables the spacecraft to land on the target point without collision. Similarly, the time consumption for solving an optimal landing trajectory is about 60 s.

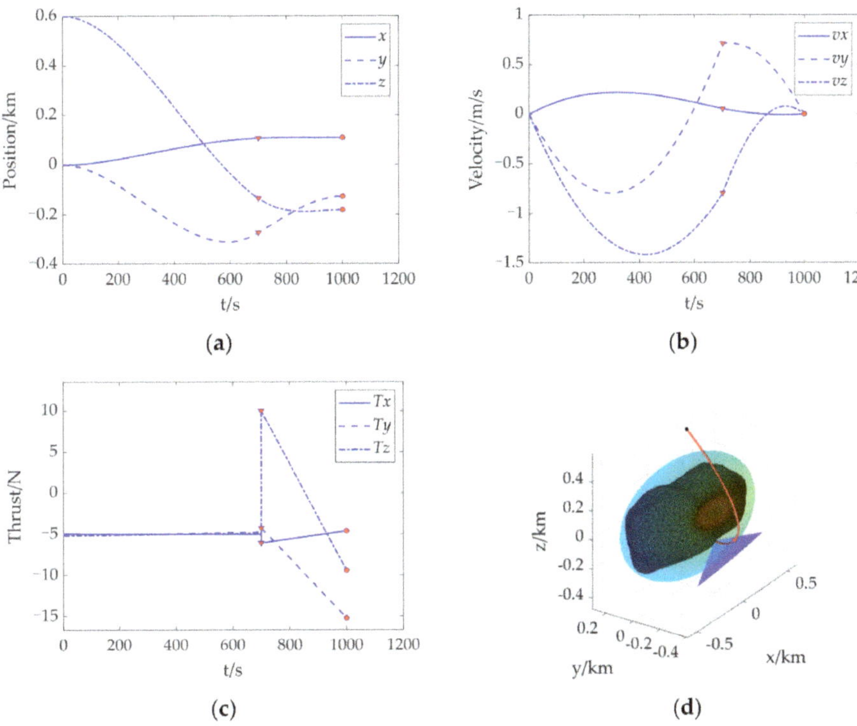

Figure 11. Trajectory optimization results of landing on the asteroid Bacchus from above the North Pole. (**a**) Histories of the position. (**b**) Histories of the velocity. (**c**) Histories of the thrust. (**d**) History of the descent trajectory. The red "Δ" and "•" indicate the transition position and landing position, respectively.

4.2.2. Continuous Boundary

Judge whether the distance between adjacent points meets the continuity condition based on the initial boundary, that is, when the distance between adjacent points is greater than $3h$, i.e., 120 m, it is considered discontinuous. In this case, the radius r needs to be reduced. Taking Figure 12a as an example, when the initial boundary is obtained, the radius r_0 = 620 m, and the radius $r_1 = r_0 - h$ = 580 m after the first expansion. Based on r_1, asteroid surface points P(r_1) after the first expansion is obtained by using the circular section method. Along the vector direction from the asteroid centroid to the initial position, the points between all discontinuous points on the initial boundary are taken from P(r_1) for trajectory optimization, and the obtained points with feasible solutions are connected with the initial boundary to become the boundary after the first expansion. Judge the distance of the boundary, repeat the above expansion process until the distance between all adjacent points is less than 120 m, and then obtain the final continuous boundary to determine the reachable domain.

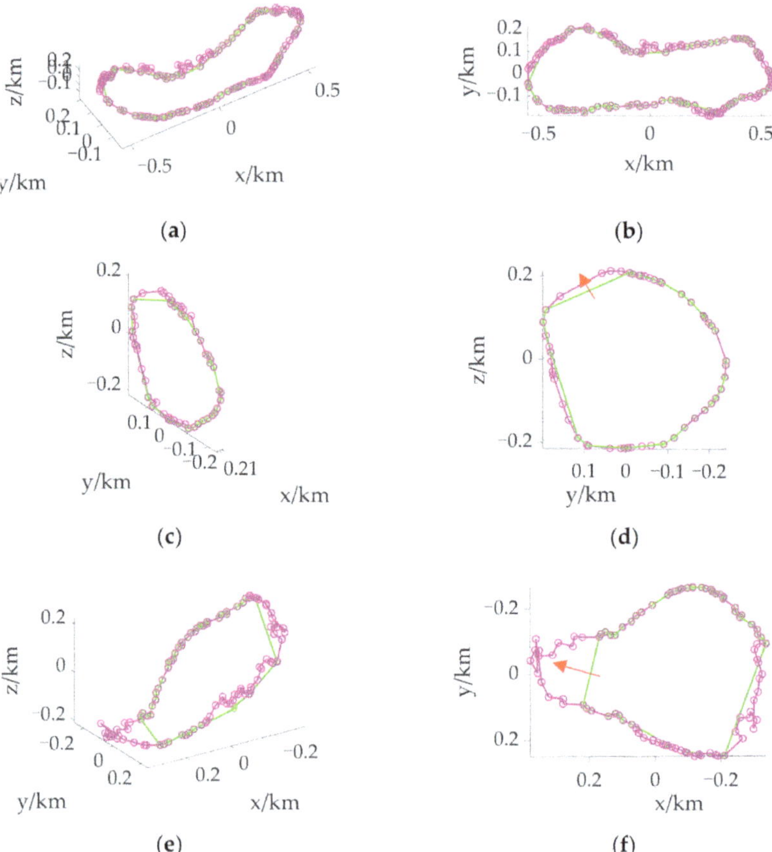

Figure 12. Boundary of the reachable domain under different initial states with t_f = 1000 s. (**a**) 3D view of the boundary when the initial position is over the North Pole. (**b**) Supplementary view of the boundary when the initial position is over the North Pole. (**c**) 3D view of the boundary when the initial position is over the Equator. (**d**) Supplementary view of the boundary when the initial position is over the Equator. (**e**) 3D view of the boundary when the initial position is over the mid-latitude region. (**f**) Supplementary view of the boundary when the initial position is over the mid-latitude region. The green connecting line stands for the initial boundary. The purple connecting line stands for the continuous boundary. The red arrow stands for the direction of expansion.

Figure 12 shows the boundary at different initial positions when t_f = 1000 s, where the green connecting line represents the initial boundary and the purple connecting line represents the continuous boundary. It can be seen that most of the initial boundary and the continuous boundary are coincident, and only when the distance between adjacent points is too large to describe the boundary, expansion is required. From Figures 8–10, it can be seen that the initial boundary can basically surround the actual reachable domain, while the continuous boundary further improves the accuracy of the reachable domain boundary on the premise of increasing a small amount of calculation. The expansion indicated by the red arrows in Figure 12d, f clearly illustrates the necessity of solving the continuous boundary.

Table 2 lists the total number of points N of trajectory optimization required for the proposed method to obtain the continuous boundary, the total number of points N_f on the asteroid surface, and their ratio, i.e., time-consuming ratio. It can be seen from Table 2 that the ratio of N to N_f is not more than 10%, that is, the time-consuming ratio of the proposed method and the traditional method to solve the reachable domain is less than 10%. Therefore, the reachable domain solution method based on the section and expansion method proposed in this study can reduce the solution time by more than 90%, and greatly improve the solution efficiency.

Table 2. Time-consuming statistics.

Initial Condition	Over the North Pole		Over the Equator		Over the Mid-Latitude Region	
	900 s	1000 s	1000 s	1100 s	900 s	1000 s
P(d)	49		53		29	
P(r)	139	126	84	54	102	157
P(e)	65	94	76	53	56	153
n	3	2	1	3	1	3
N	254	269	213	160	187	339
N_f	4092					
Time-consuming ratio (%)	6.210	6.574	5.2053	3.9101	4.5699	8.2845

5. Conclusions

In this paper, a fast generation method based on section and expansion is proposed to generate the reachable domain of collision-free asteroid landing with the given TOF. Considering the anti-collision requirements, a two-stage simplified solution method is used, which improves the efficiency and convergence of the trajectory optimization problem. By analyzing the velocity increment, the distribution law of the reachable domain is obtained. The generation problem of the reachable domain is transformed into three subproblems and solved in turn: the solution of a point on the initial boundary, the calculation of the initial boundary, and the calculation of the continuous boundary. The section and expansion method is used to solve these problems. Finally, the generation of the reachable domain on the asteroid surface is realized, and the efficiency of solving is greatly improved. Compared with the traversal algorithm, the time-consuming ratio is reduced by more than 90%. The effectiveness and applicability of the proposed method are verified by simulation analysis with asteroids of different shapes and spacecraft with different initial positions and different flight times.

Author Contributions: Conceptualization and methodology, Y.Z. and H.Y.; software, Y.Z. and J.H.; validation, Y.Z. and J.H.; formal analysis, Y.Z. and J.H.; writing—original draft preparation and supervision, Y.Z.; writing—review and editing, Y.Z. and H.Y.; visualization, Y.Z. All authors have read and agreed to the published version of the manuscript.

Funding: This research was funded by the National Natural Science Foundation of China under No. 12102177 and Natural Science Foundation of Jiangsu Province under No. BK20220130.

Institutional Review Board Statement: Not applicable.

Informed Consent Statement: Not applicable.

Data Availability Statement: All data generated or analyzed during this study are included in this published article in the form of figures and tables.

Conflicts of Interest: The authors declare no conflict of interest.

References

1. Zhang, Y.; Michel, P. Shapes, structures, and evolution of small bodies. *Astrodynamics* **2021**, *5*, 293–329. [CrossRef]
2. Zhang, Y.; Yu, Y.; Baoyin, H.X. Dynamical behavior of flexible net spacecraft for landing on asteroid. *Astrodynamics* **2021**, *5*, 249–261. [CrossRef]
3. Zhang, X.; Luo, Y.; Xiao, Y.; Liu, D.; Guo, F.; Guo, Q. Developing Prototype Simulants for Surface Materials and Morphology of Near Earth Asteroid 2016 HO3. *Space Sci. Technol.* **2021**, *2021*, 9874929. [CrossRef]

4. Rozitis, B.; Ryan, A.J.; Emery, J.P.; Nolan, M.C.; Green, S.F.; Christensen, P.R.; Lauretta, D.S. High-Resolution Thermophysical Analysis of the OSIRIS-REx Sample Site and Three Other Regions of Interest on Bennu. *J. Geophys. Res. Planets* **2022**, *127*, e2021JE007153. [CrossRef]
5. Yada, T.; Abe, M.; Okada, T.; Nakato, A.; Yogata, K.; Miyazaki, A.; Hatakeda, K.; Kumagai, K.; Nishimura, M.; Hitomi, Y.; et al. Preliminary analysis of the Hayabusa2 samples returned from C-type asteroid Ryugu. *Nat. Astron.* **2021**, *6*, 214–220. [CrossRef]
6. Ploen, S.R.; Seraji, H.; Kinney, C.E. Determination of spacecraft landing footprint for safe planetary landing. *IEEE Trans. Aerosp. Electron. Syst.* **2009**, *45*, 3–16. [CrossRef]
7. Cui, P.; Ge, D.; Zhu, S.; Zhao, D. Research progress of autonomous planetary landing site assessment and selection. *Sci. Sin. Technol.* **2021**, *51*, 1315–1325. (In Chinese) [CrossRef]
8. Huang, M.; Liang, Z.; Cui, P. Reachable zone generation for irregularly shaped asteroid landing. *J. Astronaut.* **2021**, *42*, 1550–1558. (In Chinese)
9. Benito, J.; Mease, K.D. Reachable and controllable sets for planetary entry and landing. *J. Guid. Control Dyn.* **2010**, *33*, 641–654. [CrossRef]
10. Arslantaş, Y.E.; Oehlschlägel, T.; Sagliano, M. Safe landing area determination for a moon lander by reachability analysis. *Acta Astronaut.* **2016**, *128*, 607–615. [CrossRef]
11. Chen, Q.; Qiao, D.; Wen, C. Reachable domain of spacecraft after a gravity-assist flyby. *J. Guid. Control Dyn.* **2019**, *42*, 931–940. [CrossRef]
12. Lee, S.; Hwang, I. Reachable set computation for spacecraft relative motion with energy-limited low-thrust. *Aerosp. Sci. Technol.* **2018**, *77*, 180–188. [CrossRef]
13. Kulumani, S.; Lee, T. Low-thrust trajectory design using reachability sets near asteroid 4769 castalia. In Proceedings of the AIAA/AAS Astrodynamics Specialist Conference, Long Beach, CA, USA, 13–16 September 2016. [CrossRef]
14. Wen, T.; Zeng, X.; Circi, C.; Gao, Y. Hop reachable domain on irregularly shaped asteroids. *J. Guid. Control Dyn.* **2020**, *43*, 1269–1283. [CrossRef]
15. Kim, H.; Kim, B. Energy-optimal transport trajectory planning and online trajectory modification for holonomic robots. *Asian J. Control* **2021**, *23*, 2185–2200. [CrossRef]
16. Zhang, Y.; Wang, J.; Xu, Y.; Yang, D. Energy-optimal problem of multiple nonholonomic wheeled mobile robots via distributed event-triggered optimization algorithm. *Chin. Phys. B* **2019**, *28*, 030501. [CrossRef]
17. Neely, M. Energy optimal control for time-varying wireless networks. *IEEE Trans. Inf. Theory* **2006**, *52*, 2915–2934. [CrossRef]
18. Yang, H.; Bai, X.; Baoyin, H. Rapid generation of time-optimal trajectories for asteroid landing via convex optimization. *J. Guid. Control Dyn.* **2017**, *40*, 628–664. [CrossRef]
19. Liu, X.; Yang, H.; Li, S. Collision-free trajectory design for long distance hopping transfer on asteroid surface using convex optimization. *IEEE Trans. Aerosp. Electron. Syst.* **2021**, *57*, 3071–3083. [CrossRef]
20. Zhang, Y.; Huang, J.; Cui, H. Trajectory optimization for asteroid landing with two-phase free final time. *Adv. Space Res.* **2020**, *65*, 1210–1224. [CrossRef]
21. Zhang, B.; Zhang, Y.; Bai, J. Twistor-Based Adaptive Pose Control of Spacecraft for Landing on an Asteroid with Collision Avoidance. *IEEE Trans. Aerosp. Electron. Syst.* **2021**, *58*, 152–167. [CrossRef]
22. Zhu, S.; Yang, H.; Cui, P.; Xu, R.; Liang, Z. Anti-collision zone division based hazard avoidance guidance for asteroid landing with constant thrust. *Acta Astronaut.* **2022**, *190*, 377–387. [CrossRef]
23. Zhao, Y.; Yang, H.; Li, S. Real-time trajectory optimization for collision-free asteroid landing based on deep neural networks. *Adv. Space Res.* **2022**, *70*, 112–124. [CrossRef]
24. Yang, H.; Li, S.; Bai, X. Fast homotopy method for asteroid landing trajectory optimization using approximate initial costates. *J. Guid. Control Dyn.* **2019**, *42*, 585–597. [CrossRef]
25. Jiang, F.; Baoyin, H.; Li, J. Practical techniques for low-thrust trajectory optimization with homotopic approach. *J. Guid. Control Dyn.* **2012**, *35*, 245–258. [CrossRef]
26. Ma, H.; Xu, S. Optimization of bounded low-thrust rendezvous with terminal constraints by interval analysis. *Aerosp. Sci. Technol.* **2018**, *79*, 58–69. [CrossRef]
27. Zeng, X.; Jiang, F.; Li, J.; Baoyin, H. Study on the connection between the rotating mass dipole and natural elongated bodies. *Astrophys. Space Sci.* **2015**, *356*, 29–42. [CrossRef]

 mathematics

Article

Stability Analysis on the Moon's Rotation in a Perturbed Binary Asteroid

Yunfeng Gao [1], Bin Cheng [2], Yang Yu [1,*], Jing Lv [1] and Hexi Baoyin [2]

[1] School of Aeronautic Science and Engineering, Beihang University, D411 New Main Building, Beijing 100191, China
[2] School of Aerospace Engineering, Tsinghua University, Mengminwei Science & Technology Building, Beijing 100084, China
* Correspondence: yuyang.thu@icloud.com

Abstract: Numerical calculation provides essential tools for deep space exploration, which are indispensable to mission design and planetary research. In a specific case of binary asteroid defense such as the DART mission, an accurate understanding of the possible dynamical responses and the system's stability and engineers' prerequisite. In this paper, we discuss the numeric techniques for tracking the year-long motion of the secondary after being perturbed, based upon which its rotational stability is analyzed. For long-term simulations, we compared the performances of several integrating schemes in the scenario of a post-impact full two-body system, including low- and high-order Runge–Kutta methods, and a symplectic integrator that combines the finite element method with a symplectic integral format. For rotational stability analysis of the secondary, we focus on the rotation of the secondary around its long-axis. We calculated a linearised error propagation matrix and found that, in the case of tidal locking of the secondary to the primary, the rotation is stable; as the perturbation amplitude of the spin angular velocity of the secondary increases, the rotation will lose stability and will be prone to being unstable in the long-axis direction of the secondary. Furthermore, we investigated the one-year-long influences of the non-spherical perturbations of the primary and the secondary.

Keywords: motion stability; numerical simulation scheme; binary asteroid; dynamics

MSC: 85-10

Citation: Gao, Y.; Cheng, B.; Yu, Y.; Lv, J.; Baoyin, H. Stability Analysis on the Moon's Rotation in a Perturbed Binary Asteroid. *Mathematics* **2022**, *10*, 3757. https://doi.org/10.3390/math10203757

Academic Editor: Rami Ahmad El-Nabulsi

Received: 26 August 2022
Accepted: 5 October 2022
Published: 12 October 2022

1. Introduction

The dynamics of binary asteroid systems is a hot topic in the field of astronomy, and the ongoing NASA's Double Asteroid Redirection Test (DART) mission has sparked profound and heated discussions on this topic. NASA's DART mission launched on 24 November 2021, with plans to impact the secondary (Dimorphos) of binary asteroid system 65,803 Didymos on 26 September 2022, using a 563 kg impactor at 6.14 km/s [1–7]. Four years later, ESA's Hera mission will arrive at the Didymos system to observe the results of the impact [7]. This mission will obtain important information, including the surface as well as the internal properties of the binary asteroid system, which will have a significant impact on our understanding of the history of the solar system [2].

For the prediction of the dynamic state of the Didymos system after the impact, the mission team has organized related research [7]. In [8], it was determined that Dimorphos is prone to unstable rotation in its long-axis direction after DART's impact, which would introduce significant uncertainty in the evolution of the rotational state of the secondary [9]. The unstable rotation poses challenges for understanding the state of motion of the binary system at the time of HERA's arrival, especially over a years-long period of time. In this paper, we investigate the year-long rotational stability of the secondary through mathematical and non-linear theoretical methods.

The description of the gravitational field between two rigid bodies is the foundation for the study of binary asteroid dynamics. There are some well-established methods, such as [10–12], for describing the rigid body using the polyhedral method, and [13] for describing rigid body using agglomerates of grains of multiple spherical particles, etc. Reference [14] proposed a finite element method (FEM) for computing the gravitational interactions between two arbitrarily shaped rigid bodies that has no restrictions on the shape and internal mass distribution of the asteroid. This method differs from the polyhedral approach, which divides two polyhedra into a series of elongated tetrahedra, each connecting the centre of the rigid body to the triangular face of the polyhedron. The finite element method divides the polyhedra into smaller tetrahedral meshes, so that the internal structure of the two rigid bodies can be reconstructed by defining the density of each tetrahedron. Therefore, we chose the finite element method to describe the gravitational field between two asteroids. For calculating the dynamical states of binary asteroids, numerical simulation schemes are indispensable tools. Especially when considering the long-term evolution, many commonly used schemes may encounter the problem of numerical error accumulation.

There have been many studies on numerical algorithms for the long-term simulation of a Hamiltonian system [15–18]. For the orbital problem of celestial bodies, Kosmas [19–23] has proposed some numerical simulation methods that are excellent for the long-term simulation of two-body and N-body problems. In terms of the motion of rigid bodies, many studies have investigated the Sintegrator [24–28]. The symplectic algorithm is a difference method which preserves the Hamiltonian system based on the basic principle of Hamiltonian mechanics. It makes the discretized difference equations keep the symplectic structure of the original system and has long time stability. Applying the finite element method and the symplectic integrator, we study the stability of the rotational motion of the secondary, which has not been studied much. [8] used fast Lyapunov indicators to investigate the rotation stability of the secondary, and found that the secondary is prone to become unstable near the resonance locations. Ref. [29] analyzed the rotation of the secondary around its long axis through a large set of short numerical simulations and referred to it as "barrel instability".

The paper is organized as follows. In Section 2, we compare the conservation of total mechanical energy, total momentum, and total angular momentum in several numerical integrators for the full two-body problem, in order to find the suitable numerical simulation scheme for our work. Based on the numerical simulation scheme presented, we propose an error propagation matrix to study the stability of the motion of the secondary rotating from its long axis, and we evaluate the effect of the non-spherical gravitational perturbation term of the primary and the shape of the secondary on its stability, which we discuss in Section 3. Our conclusions are given in Section 4. Our simulations were performed on a large-scale computing cluster using CUDA and OpenMP parallelism techniques.

2. Comparison of Numerical Schemes for Long Assessment

We used numerical methods to simulate the motion of the binary asteroid. Therefore, before analyzing the stability of the tumbling motion, it is necessary to discuss whether the results of the numerical simulation scheme are reasonable. This section discusses numerical simulation schemes for the full two-body problem. Three coordinate systems were adopted: The world coordinate system $\mathcal{T}$, the primary body-fixed frame $\mathcal{P}$, and the secondary body-fixed frame $\mathcal{S}$. Assuming two rigid bodies P and S, the full two-body problem is a conservative system with three conserved quantities, which are the total mechanical energy (represented by T.M.E), the total momentum (represented by T.M), and the total moment of momentum (represented by T.M.O.M). The former is a scalar, while the latter two are vectors, which can be calculated as follows:

$$
\begin{aligned}
&E = \frac{1}{2}m_P \boldsymbol{v}_P^T \boldsymbol{v}_P + \frac{1}{2}m_S \boldsymbol{v}_S^T \boldsymbol{v}_S + \frac{1}{2}\boldsymbol{\omega}_P^T \boldsymbol{J}_P \boldsymbol{\omega}_P + \frac{1}{2}\boldsymbol{\omega}_S^T \boldsymbol{J}_S \boldsymbol{\omega}_S + U_{PS}, \\
&\boldsymbol{p} = m_P \boldsymbol{v}_p + m_S \boldsymbol{v}_S, \\
&\boldsymbol{\pi} = \boldsymbol{r}_P \times m_P \boldsymbol{v}_P + \boldsymbol{r}_S \times m_S \boldsymbol{v}_S + \boldsymbol{J}_P \boldsymbol{\omega}_P + \boldsymbol{J}_S \boldsymbol{\omega}_S,
\end{aligned} \tag{1}
$$

where E is the T.M.E., $\boldsymbol{p}$ is the T.M., $\boldsymbol{\pi}$ is the T.M.O.M., m_P is the total mass of P, $\boldsymbol{r}_P = [r_{Px}, r_{Py}, r_{Pz}]^T$ is the position of P, $\boldsymbol{v}_P = [v_{Px}, v_{Py}, v_{Pz}]^T$ is the velocity of P, $\boldsymbol{\omega}_P = [\omega_{Px}, \omega_{Py}, \omega_{Pz}]^T$ is the angular velocity of P, $\boldsymbol{J}_P = \mathrm{diag}(J_{Px}, J_{Py}, J_{Pz})$ is the moment of inertia matrix of P, replacing the angle labels with S corresponds to the body S, and U_{PS} is the gravitational potential between P and S.

The critical evaluation criterion of the numerical schemes is that the cumulative error of the above three conserved quantities can be kept within an acceptable range. For short-term simulations, the Runge–Kutta integrator is widely used, due to its mature development and ease of use. Meanwhile, for long-term simulations, the Runge–Kutta integrator may not perform well, in terms of the cumulative error of the above conserved quantities. In this section, we perform a decade-long simulation of the Didymos system and compare the performance of three integrators. The binary asteroid shape model constructed by [30] was adopted to describe the primary (Didymos), while the shape model constructed by [2] was adopted to describe the secondary (Dimorphos). We chose the classic fourth-order Runge–Kutta integrator (represented by RK4) and a high-order Runge–Kutta integrator (represented by RK78) as the first two integrators. The task of these two integrators is to solve the differential equations of the system numerically. For the full two-body problem, the dynamical equations of the system are:

$$
\begin{aligned}
\dot{\boldsymbol{r}}_P &= \boldsymbol{v}_P, \\
\dot{\boldsymbol{v}}_P &= \frac{\boldsymbol{F}_P}{m_P}, \\
\dot{\boldsymbol{\lambda}}_P &= \frac{1}{2}\boldsymbol{\lambda}_P \diamond \boldsymbol{\omega}_P, \\
\dot{\boldsymbol{\pi}}_P &= \boldsymbol{\pi}_P \times \boldsymbol{\omega}_P + \boldsymbol{T}_P,
\end{aligned} \tag{2}
$$

where $\boldsymbol{\lambda}_P$ is the attitude quaternions of the body P; $\diamond$ is the Grassmann product operator ([31]), which defines multiplication between a quaternion and a vector; $\boldsymbol{\pi}_P = \boldsymbol{J}_P \boldsymbol{\omega}_P$ is the angular momentum of P; replacing the angle labels with S corresponds to the rigid body S. It should be noted that the unity of quaternions can not naturally preserve, therefore, the quaternions need to be renormalized at each time step. In Equation (2), $\boldsymbol{F}_P$ is the gravitational force of the rigid body P from S, and $\boldsymbol{T}_P$ is the torque of gravitation from S to P, calculated by the finite method proposed by [14]:

$$
\begin{aligned}
\boldsymbol{F}_P &= \mathrm{G}\sum_{\alpha=1}^{N_P}\sum_{\beta=1}^{N_S} w_\alpha w_\beta \sigma(\boldsymbol{\rho}_{P\alpha})\sigma\left(\boldsymbol{\rho}_{S\beta}\right)\frac{\boldsymbol{r}_{S\beta} - \boldsymbol{r}_{P\alpha}}{|\boldsymbol{r}_{S\beta} - \boldsymbol{r}_{A\alpha}|^3}, \\
\boldsymbol{T}_P &= \mathrm{G}\sum_{\alpha=1}^{N_P}\sum_{\beta=1}^{N_S} w_\alpha w_\beta \sigma(\boldsymbol{\rho}_{P\alpha})\sigma\left(\boldsymbol{\rho}_{S\beta}\right)\frac{\boldsymbol{\rho}_{P\alpha} \times \left(\boldsymbol{r}_{P\alpha} - \boldsymbol{r}_{S\beta}\right)}{|\boldsymbol{r}_{P\alpha} - \boldsymbol{r}_{S\beta}|^3}, \\
\boldsymbol{T}_S &= \mathrm{G}\sum_{\alpha=1}^{N_P}\sum_{\beta=1}^{N_S} w_\alpha w_\beta \sigma(\boldsymbol{\rho}_{P\alpha})\sigma\left(\boldsymbol{\rho}_{S\beta}\right)\frac{\boldsymbol{\rho}_{S\beta} \times \left(\boldsymbol{r}_{P\alpha} - \boldsymbol{r}_{S\beta}\right)}{|\boldsymbol{r}_{P\alpha} - \boldsymbol{r}_{S\beta}|^3},
\end{aligned} \tag{3}
$$

where the parameters are explained as follows:

N_P	The number of the nodes of the rigid body P
$\boldsymbol{r}_{P\alpha}$	The position of node α in body P in the world coordinate system $\mathcal{T}$
$\boldsymbol{\rho}_{P\alpha}$	The position of node α in body P in the body-fixed frame $\mathcal{P}$
$\boldsymbol{w}_{P\alpha}$	The nodal weights of node α in body P
$\sigma(\boldsymbol{\rho}_{P\alpha})$	The density at node α in body P

Replacing the angle labels with S and β corresponds to body S and the node in body S, while $\boldsymbol{F}_P$ and $\boldsymbol{F}_S$ are equal in modulus and opposite in direction.

Combining the symplectic integration scheme proposed by [24] and the finite method to calculate the full two-body problem, we used a symplectic integrator (represented by SI) as the third tested integrator. Some of its parameters are detailed as follows:

- $\boldsymbol{q}_P$ position of body P
- $\boldsymbol{Q}_P$ orientation matrix of body P
- $\boldsymbol{p}_P$ momentum of body P
- $\boldsymbol{\pi}_P$ angular momentum of body P

Replacing the angle labels with S corresponds to body S. The states $\boldsymbol{q}_P^t$, $\boldsymbol{q}_S^t$, $\boldsymbol{Q}_P^t$, $\boldsymbol{Q}_S^t$, $\boldsymbol{p}_P^t$, $\boldsymbol{p}_S^t$, $\boldsymbol{\pi}_P^t$, and $\boldsymbol{\pi}_S^t$ of the two rigid bodies are at time t, the step size of the integrator is taken as Δt and the states $\boldsymbol{q}_P^{t+\Delta t}$, $\boldsymbol{q}_S^{t+\Delta t}$, $\boldsymbol{Q}_P^{t+\Delta t}$, $\boldsymbol{Q}_S^{t+\Delta t}$, $\boldsymbol{p}_P^{t+\Delta t}$, $\boldsymbol{p}_S^{t+\Delta t}$, $\boldsymbol{\pi}_P^{t+\Delta t}$, and $\boldsymbol{\pi}_S^{t+\Delta t}$ of the two rigid bodies are obtained after integration. The specific calculation process used in one integration step is given below.

First, calculate the gravitational attraction forces $\boldsymbol{F}_P^t$ on P and $\boldsymbol{F}_S^t$ and S, as well as the torques $\boldsymbol{T}_P^t$ on P and $\boldsymbol{T}_P^t$ on S, using the finite method (Equation (3)). Then, perform the following calculations for the momentum and angular momentum of each of the two rigid bodies (here, only the formula of the body P is given, replace the angle labels with S for that of the body S):

$$
\begin{aligned}
\boldsymbol{p}_P^{t+\frac{1}{2}\Delta t} &= \boldsymbol{p}_P^t + \frac{1}{2}\Delta t \boldsymbol{F}_P^t \\
\boldsymbol{\pi}_P^{t+\frac{1}{2}\Delta t} &= \boldsymbol{\pi}_P^t + \frac{1}{2}\Delta t \boldsymbol{T}_P^t.
\end{aligned} \tag{4}
$$

$\boldsymbol{Q}_P$ can be written as:

$$
\boldsymbol{Q}_P^T = [\boldsymbol{s}_{P1}, \boldsymbol{s}_{P2}, \boldsymbol{s}_{P3}] \tag{5}
$$

Second, the angular momentum and rotation matrices of the rigid body are then transformed five times in the order R_{P1}, R_{P2}, R_{P3}, R_{P2}, R_{P1} respectively, with the first transformation given below:

$$
\boldsymbol{\pi}_P^{t+\frac{1}{2}\Delta t} = R_{P1}\boldsymbol{\pi}_P^{t+\frac{1}{2}\Delta t}, \boldsymbol{s}_{Pj}^t = R_{P1}\boldsymbol{s}_{Pj}^t, (j = 1, 2, 3), \tag{6}
$$

where

$$
\begin{aligned}
R_{P1} &= \begin{bmatrix} 1 & 0 & 0 \\ 0 & \cos\left(\frac{\pi_{Px}}{J_{Px}}\Delta t\right) & \sin\left(\frac{\pi_{Px}}{J_{Px}}\Delta t\right) \\ 0 & -\sin\left(\frac{\pi_{Px}}{J_{Px}}\Delta t\right) & \cos\left(\frac{\pi_{Px}}{J_{Px}}\Delta t\right) \end{bmatrix}, \\
R_{P2} &= \begin{bmatrix} \cos\left(\frac{\pi_{Py}}{J_{Py}}\Delta t\right) & 0 & -\sin\left(\frac{\pi_{Py}}{J_{Py}}\Delta t\right) \\ 0 & 1 & 0 \\ \sin\left(\frac{\pi_{Py}}{J_{Py}}\Delta t\right) & 0 & \cos\left(\frac{\pi_{Py}}{J_{Py}}\Delta t\right) \end{bmatrix}, \\
R_{P3} &= \begin{bmatrix} \cos\left(\frac{\pi_{Pz}}{J_{Pz}}\Delta t\right) & \sin\left(\frac{\pi_{Pz}}{J_{Pz}}\Delta t\right) & 0 \\ -\sin\left(\frac{\pi_{Pz}}{J_{Pz}}\Delta t\right) & \cos\left(\frac{\pi_{Pz}}{J_{Pz}}\Delta t\right) & 0 \\ 0 & 0 & 1. \end{bmatrix}
\end{aligned} \tag{7}
$$

Third, update the positions of the two bodies:

$$
\boldsymbol{q}_P^{t+\Delta t} = \boldsymbol{q}_P^t + \Delta t \frac{\boldsymbol{p}_P^{t+\frac{1}{2}\Delta t}}{m_P}. \tag{8}
$$

Fourth, according to the positions $q_P^{t+\Delta t}$, $q_S^{t+\Delta t}$ and attitudes $Q_P^{t+\Delta t}$, $Q_S^{t+\Delta t}$ of the two rigid bodies at moment $t + \Delta t$, calculate $F_P^{t+\Delta t}$, $F_S^{t+\Delta t}$, $T_P^{t+\Delta t}$, and $T_S^{t+\Delta t}$ using Equation (3). Then, update the momentum and angular momentum, as follows:

$$\begin{aligned} p_P^{t+\Delta t} &= p_P^{t+\frac{1}{2}\Delta t} + \frac{1}{2}\Delta t F_P^{t+\Delta t} \\ \pi_P^{t+\Delta t} &= \pi_P^{t+\frac{1}{2}\Delta t} + \frac{1}{2}\Delta t T_P^{t+\Delta t}. \end{aligned} \tag{9}$$

Note that the forces and torques calculated here can be used in the next time step, such that they only need to be calculated once per time step.

Regarding the selection of step size for the integrator, our principle was to ensure the same computational cost for the three integrators. In this simulation, the most computationally expensive step was the calculation of the full two-body gravitational potential, for which we used the GPU parallelization method proposed by [32] to accelerate the calculation. For RK4, the gravitational potential needs to be calculated four times per time step; for RK78, it needs to be calculated 12 times; and, for SI, it needs to be calculated once. Therefore, we set the step size of RK4 to be 4 s, RK78 to be 12 s, and SI to be 1 s. In terms of setting system parameters, in order to ensure generality, we arbitrarily set the rotation states of the two asteroids (not a tidal locking state, the angular velocity had components in all three directions), in order to test the performance of all integrators in a relatively terrible simulation environment.

We performed simulations of the binary asteroid Didymos system over 10 years, using the step settings mentioned above, with a calculation time of 14 days for all three integrators. Figures 1–3 show the simulation results of the relative errors (represented by RelErr) for the three conserved quantities of the three integrators over 10 years. The first part of each figure represents the relative error T.M.E. varying with time, the second represents the modulus of T.M., the third represents the modulus of T.M.O.M., and the fourth to sixth parts represent the relative error change of T.M.O.M. in the three directions of X, Y, and Z (represented by T.M.O.M.X, T.M.O.M.Y, and T.M.O.M.Z, respectively).

By analyzing the relative error curves of the conserved quantities of the three integrators, we find that the performance of the different integrators varies considerably. In terms of the T.M.E, the two Runge–Kutta integrators performed better than the symplectic integrator. The relative error of RK4 and RK78 was on the order of 10^{-13}, and RK78 performed slightly better than RK4. That of SI was on the order of 10^{-9}, and partial magnification shows the change of a chord curve with no significant change in amplitude with time. Regarding the T.M., the relative error of RK4 and SI was on the order of 10^{-12}, while that of RK78 was on the order of 10^{-13}, thus showing better performance. As the three components of T.M. had no more obvious characteristics, we do not show them in the figure, but only give the variation of the modulus. For the T.M.O.M., an obvious difference between three integrators was that the relative errors of the components of T.M.O.M. with the Runge–Kutta methods were monotonically varying, which was not the case for SI. SI also performed better in terms of the order of magnitude of relative error for the T.M.O.M. Considering the possible reason for the choice of step size, we reduced the step size to 0.1 s for both RK4 and RK78, and the results show that the relative errors of components of angular momentum still show monotonic variations. Monotonically variation in the relative error can lead to the accumulation of errors, reducing the accuracy of the integrator under long simulation periods. As the integration time increases, the truncation error introduced by the RK method accumulates, resulting in a constant decrease in the relative error accuracy of the conserved quantities. The relative errors in the conserved quantities of the SI show a long-term stable trend. Therefore, SI only has a truncation error, not a cumulative error, in the case of long integration time is required, SI relies on its stability and has some potential and advantages in terms of numerical solution accuracy. Therefore, a higher-order RK integrator can be used if the relative error of mechanical energy is to be minimized, while the symplectic integrator can be used if the conservativeness of the conserved quantities of the system is pursued. Considering the above, we use the symplectic integrator for further simulations.

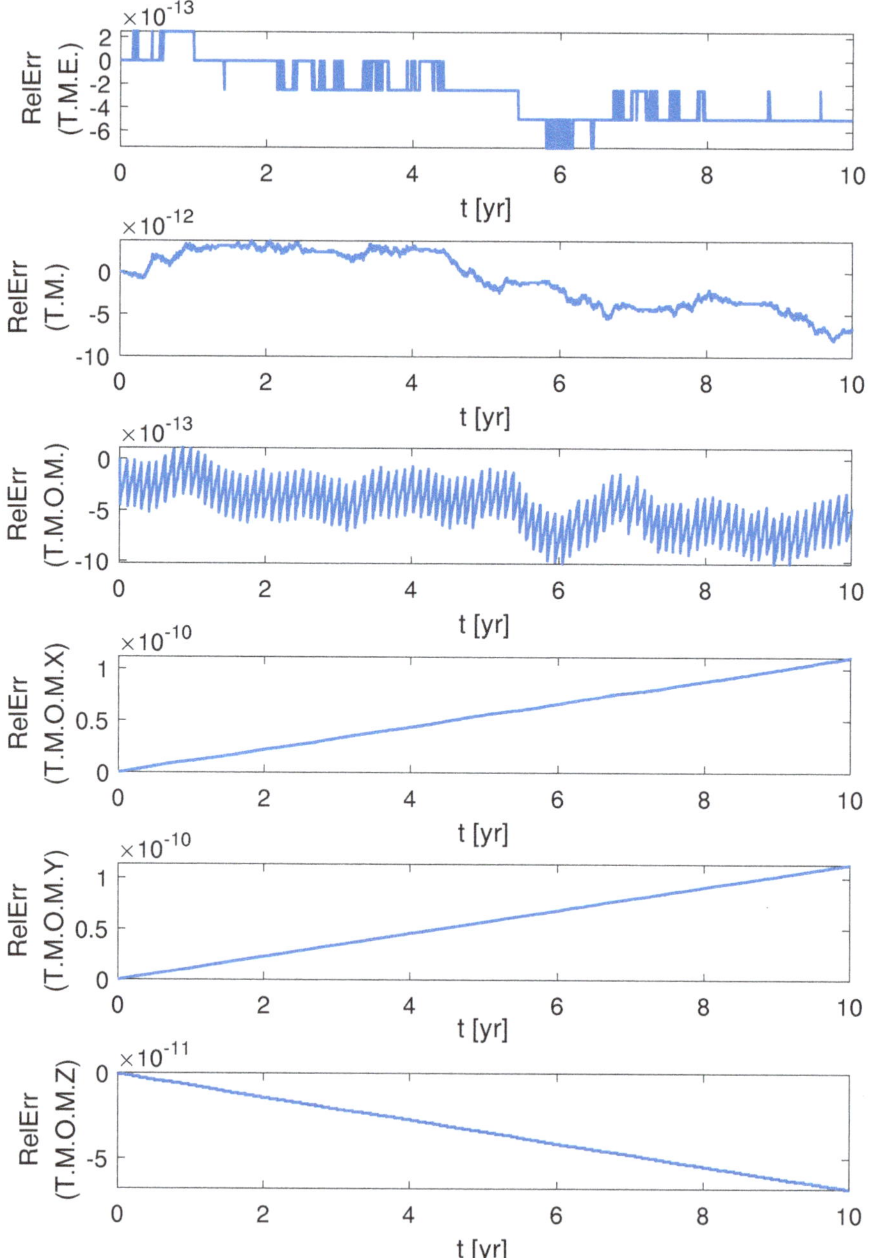

Figure 1. Variation of the relative error of the conserved quantities over ten years for simulations of the full two-body problem using the RK4 integrator.

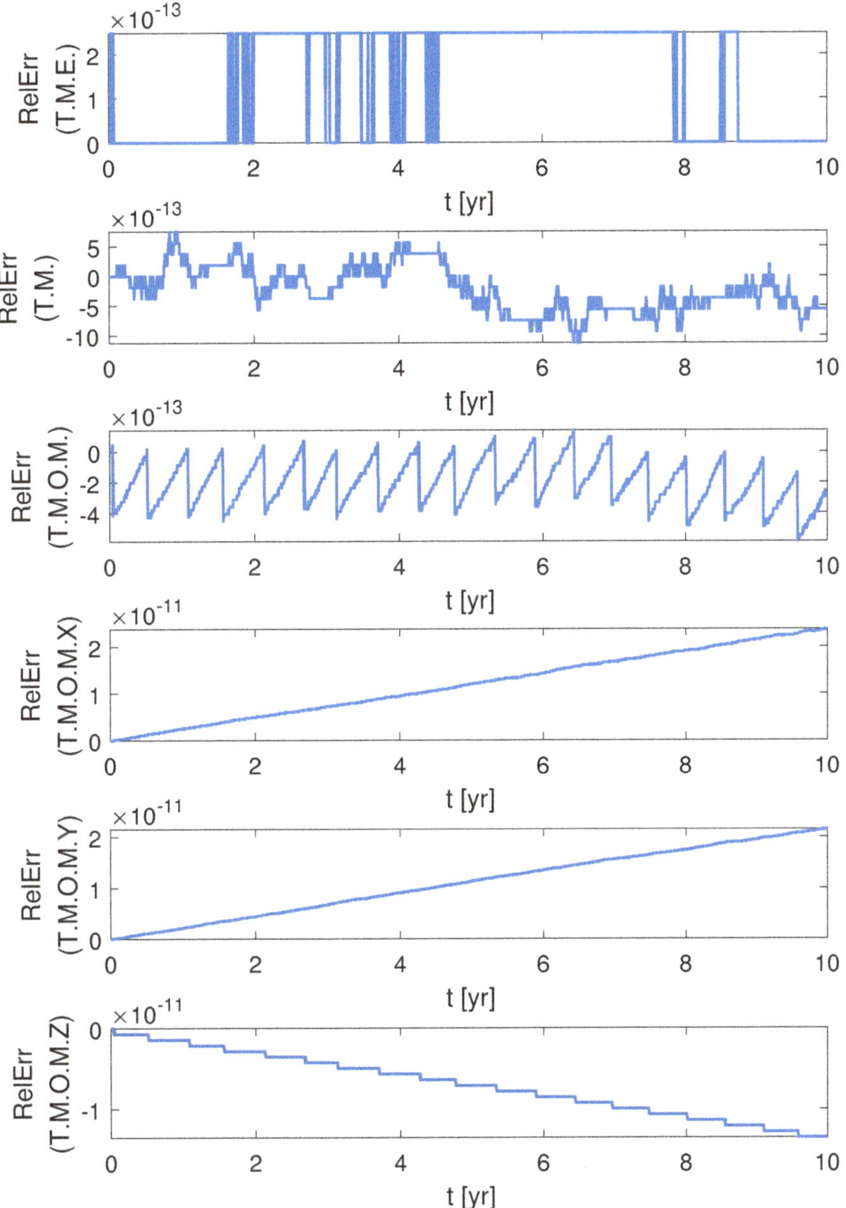

Figure 2. Variation of the relative error of the conserved quantities over ten years for simulations of the full two-body problem using the RK78 integrator.

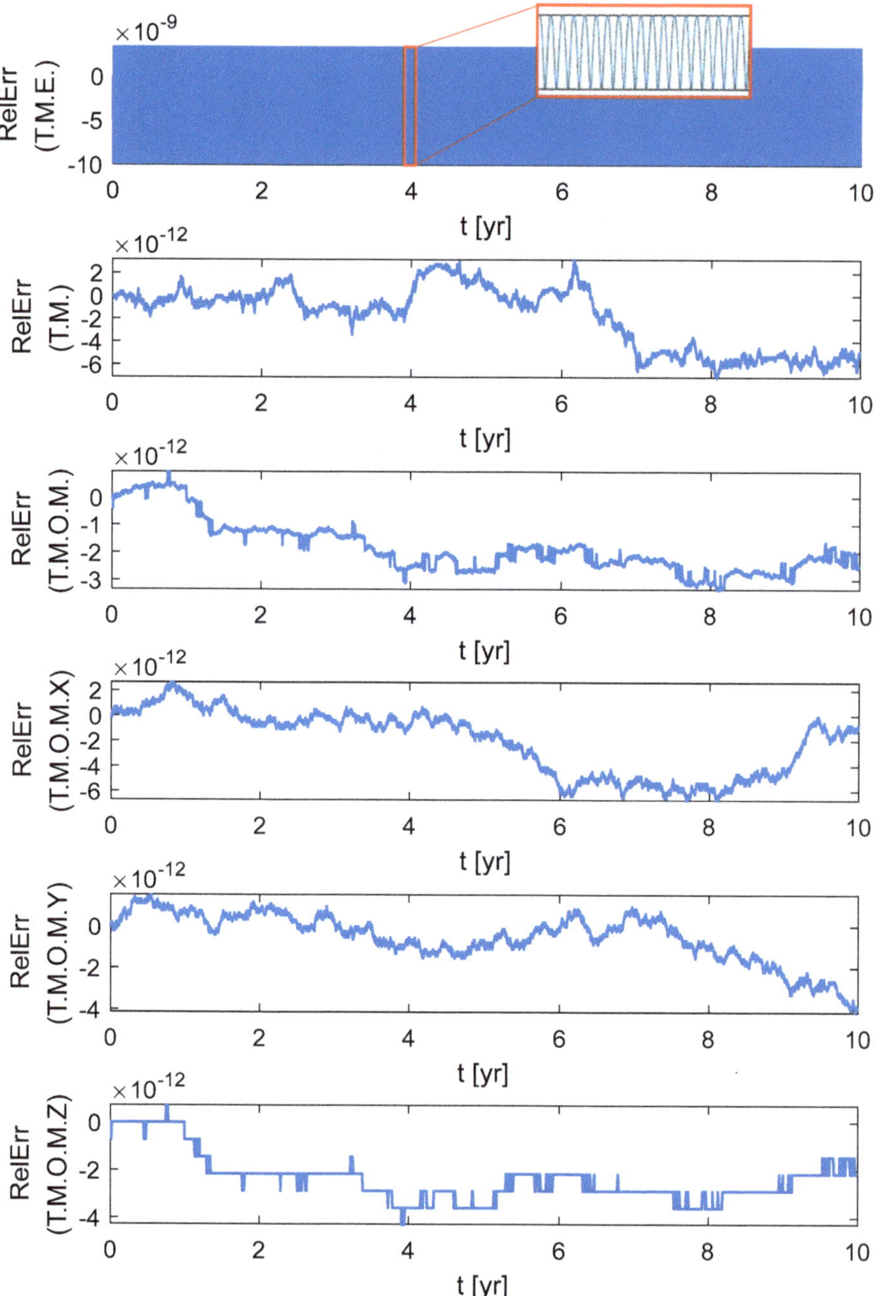

Figure 3. Variation of the relative error of the conserved quantities over ten years for simulations of the full two-body problem using the SI integrator.

3. Stability of the Excited Spin State of the Secondary

Using the SI integrator mentioned in Section 2, we investigated the stability of motion of the secondary rotating around its long axis. Observation showed that the secondary (Dimorphos) of the Didymos system is in a state of tidal locking to the primary (Didymos); that is, the rotational angular velocity of the secondary is equal to the orbital angular velocity around the primary. The impact of DART on the secondary is expected to change this state. The study of [8] showed that the secondary is prone to unstable spins in its long axis. In this section, we study this phenomenon using a linearised error propagation matrix.

3.1. Definition of the Linearised Error Propagation Matrix $M(t)$

We also determined the unstable tumbling rotation of the secondary in the long-axis direction in a simplified model. In this section, we use a mass point–seven mass points model, in which the primary is simplified to a single mass point whose mass is equal to the total mass of the primary, while the secondary is simplified to seven mass points whose positions are at the centre of mass of the secondary and the endpoints of the three axes of the ellipsoid, each mass being $1/7$ of the total mass of the secondary (Figure 4). For the parameters of the binary system, please refer to [33]. We used the 1-2-3 Euler angle to describe the attitude of the secondary, as shown in Figure 4. We denote the rotational angular velocity (around the axis perpendicular to the orbit surface) of the tidal locking of the secondary as ω_0. When the disturbance of the system is 0, no matter the rotational angular velocity of the secondary, the attitude of the secondary will only vary in the direction of ψ. However, in practice, disturbances are unavoidable due to the irregular shape and the uneven distribution of the internal mass of two asteroids, as well as various other forces in the Solar system. Here, we consider a small perturbation in the direction of ϕ. Figure 5 shows the variation in the three Euler angles when the rotational angular velocity is $1.0\omega_0$ and $1.5\omega_0$. It can be seen that when the rotation angular velocity was $1.5\omega_0$, ϕ exceeded 90 degrees on the third day, and we denote this phenomenon as secondary "flips" in the direction of ϕ. Meanwhile, when the rotation angular velocity was $1.0\omega_0$, this situation did not occur. Therefore, this tumbling rotation may be related to the rotational angular velocity of the secondary. In order to study the characteristics of the motion of the secondary, we defined a linearised error propagation matrix $M(t)$, the specific calculation method of which is described below.

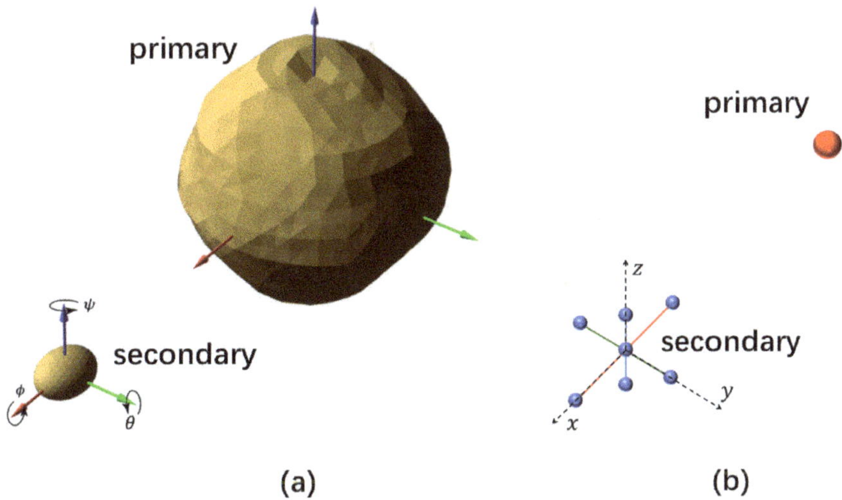

Figure 4. Diagram of the 1-2-3 Euler angles of the secondary: (**a**) diagram of the Didymos system; and (**b**) the simplified model.

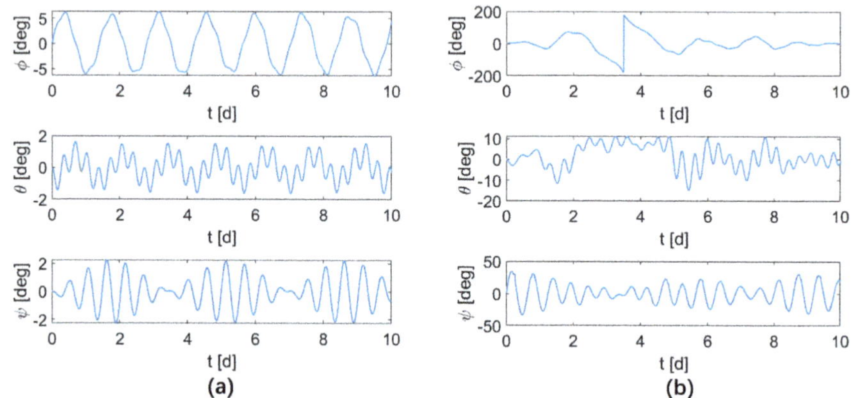

Figure 5. Variation of the three Euler angles of the secondary over time: (**a**) initial spin angular velocity = $1.0\omega_0$ and (**b**) initial spin angular velocity = $1.5\omega_0$.

There are 12 quantities in the motion of the secondary: three components each of position, velocity, attitude, and angular velocity, which are denoted as:

$$s = \left[x, y, z, v_x, v_y, v_z, \phi, \theta, \psi, \omega_x, \omega_y, \omega_z\right]^{\mathrm{T}}, \tag{10}$$

We denote an undisturbed system state as:

$$s_0 = \left[x_0, y_0, z_0, v_{x0}, v_{y0}, v_{z0}, \phi_0, \theta_0, \psi_0, \omega_{x0}, \omega_{y0}, \omega_{z0}\right]^{\mathrm{T}}. \tag{11}$$

The state at the initial time is denoted by $s(0)$, while the state at time t is denoted by $s(t)$. Then, we introduce a disturbance to each state at the initial moment, and perform 12 calculations. The disturbance is defined as:

$$\begin{aligned}\delta s(0) = [&\delta x_1(0), \delta y_2(0), \delta z_3(0), \delta v_{x4}(0), \delta v_{y5}(0), \delta v_{z6}(0),\\ &\delta\phi_7(0), \delta\theta_8(0), \delta\psi_9(0), \delta\omega_{x10}(0), \delta\omega_{y11}(0), \delta\omega_{z12}(0)]^{\mathrm{T}}.\end{aligned} \tag{12}$$

The specific process for these twelve calculations is as follows. The first calculation only introduces a disturbance $\delta x_1(0)$ at the initial moment, and the initial state of the system becomes:

$$\begin{aligned}s_1(0) = [&x_0(0) + \delta x_1(0), y_0(0), z_0(0), v_{x0}(0), v_{y0}(0), v_{z0}(0),\\ &\phi_0(0), \theta_0(0), \psi_0(0), \omega_{x0}(0), \omega_{y0}(0), \omega_{z0}(0)]^{\mathrm{T}}.\end{aligned} \tag{13}$$

Then, the state of the system at time t becomes:

$$\begin{aligned}s_1(t) = [&x_0(t) + \delta x_1(t), y_0(t) + \delta y_1(t), z_0(t) + \delta z_1(t),\\ &v_{x0}(t) + \delta v_{x1}(t), v_{y0}(t) + \delta v_{y1}(t), v_{z0}(t) + \delta v_{z1}(t),\\ &\phi_0(t) + \delta\phi_1(t), \theta_0(t) + \delta\theta_1(t), \psi_0(t) + \delta\psi_1(t),\\ &\omega_{x0}(t) + \delta\omega_{x1}(t), \omega_{y0}(t) + \delta\omega_{y1}(t), \omega_{z0}(t) + \delta\omega_{z1}(t)]^{\mathrm{T}}.\end{aligned} \tag{14}$$

The second calculation only introduces disturbance $\delta y_2(0)$ at the initial moment, and the initial state of the system becomes:

$$\begin{aligned}s_2(0) = [&x_0(0), y_0(0) + \delta y_2(0), z_0(0), v_{x0}(0), v_{y0}(0), v_{z0}(0),\\ &\phi_0(0), \theta_0(0), \psi_0(0), \omega_{x0}(0), \omega_{y0}(0), \omega_{z0}(0)]^{\mathrm{T}}.\end{aligned} \tag{15}$$

Then, the state of the system at time t becomes:

$$\begin{aligned} s_2(t) = [&x_0(t) + \delta x_2(t), y_0(t) + \delta y_2(t), z_0(t) + \delta z_2(t), \\ &v_{x0}(t) + \delta v_{x2}(t), v_{y0}(t) + \delta v_{y2}(t), v_{z0}(t) + \delta v_{z2}(t), \\ &\phi_0(t) + \delta\phi_2(t), \theta_0(t) + \delta\theta_2(t), \psi_0(t) + \delta\psi_2(t), \\ &\omega_{x0}(t) + \delta\omega_{x2}(t), \omega_{y0}(t) + \delta\omega_{y2}(t), \omega_{z0}(t) + \delta\omega_{z2}(t)]^{\mathrm{T}}. \end{aligned} \tag{16}$$

The third to twelfth calculations are carried out similarly. Therefore, when a small disturbance is introduced at the initial time, the error of the system at time t is:

$$\begin{bmatrix} \delta x(t) \\ \delta y(t) \\ \vdots \\ \delta\omega_z(t) \end{bmatrix}_{12\times 1} = M(t) \begin{bmatrix} \delta x_1(0) \\ \delta y_2(0) \\ \vdots \\ \delta\omega_{z12}(0) \end{bmatrix}_{12\times 1}, \tag{17}$$

where

$$M(t) = \begin{bmatrix} \frac{\delta x_1(t)}{\delta x_1(0)} & \frac{\delta x_2(t)}{\delta y_2(0)} & \cdots & \frac{\delta x_{12}(t)}{\delta\omega_{z12}(0)} \\ \frac{\delta y_1(t)}{\delta x_1(0)} & \frac{\delta y_2(t)}{\delta y_2(0)} & \cdots & \frac{\delta y_2(t)}{\delta\omega_{z12}(0)} \\ \vdots & \ddots & \vdots & \\ \frac{\delta\omega_{z1}(t)}{\delta x_1(0)} & \frac{\delta\omega_{z2}(t)}{\delta y_2(0)} & \cdots & \frac{\delta\omega_{z12}(t)}{\delta\omega_{z12}(0)} \end{bmatrix}_{12\times 12}. \tag{18}$$

Equation (17) can be written as

$$\delta(t) = M(t)\delta(0) \tag{19}$$

Diagonalize $M(t)$, then

$$\delta(t) = \boldsymbol{P}^{-1}\boldsymbol{\Lambda}\boldsymbol{P}\delta(0). \tag{20}$$

Transform the perturbation vector to the eigenvector coordinate system, and we have

$$\boldsymbol{P}\delta(t) = \delta_e(t) = [e_1(t), e_2(t), \ldots, e_{12}(t)]^{\mathrm{T}}. \tag{21}$$

Then,

$$\delta_e(t) = \boldsymbol{\Lambda}\delta_e(0). \tag{22}$$

The full form of Equation (22) is:

$$\begin{bmatrix} e_1(t) \\ e_2(t) \\ \vdots \\ e_{12}(t) \end{bmatrix}_{12\times 1} = \begin{bmatrix} m_1(t) & 0 & \cdots & 0 \\ 0 & m_2(t) & \cdots & 0 \\ \vdots & \vdots & \ddots & \vdots \\ 0 & 0 & 0 & m_{12}(t) \end{bmatrix}_{12\times 12} \begin{bmatrix} e_1(0) \\ e_2(0) \\ \vdots \\ e_{12}(0) \end{bmatrix}_{12\times 1}. \tag{23}$$

At each moment, the error of the system (in the eigenvector coordinate system) is:

$$e_i(t) = m_i(t)e_i(0), \quad \mathrm{i} = 1, 2, \ldots, 12. \tag{24}$$

It should be noted that in the calculation of $M(t)$, the initial minutely perturbation should be chosen to be as small as possible (but needs to be greater than the accuracy of the computer) so that the calculated $M(t)$ can be guaranteed to be consistent. $M(t)$ is a linearised error propagation matrix, representing the transfer properties of an initial minutely perturbation vector on an unperturbed system. The implication is that an initial minutely perturbation vector $\delta s(0)$ is transformed to $\delta s(t)$ after time t by the effect of the $M(t)$. This transformation relationship can be determined by analyzing the eigenvalues and eigenvectors of $M(t)$. There are 12 eigenvalues of $M(t)$, representing a combination of a series of scaling and rotation actions on $\delta s(0)$. If an eigenvalue of the matrix is a real eigenvalue, then the transformation represented by this eigenvalue is scaled in the direction of the eigenvector corresponding to this eigenvalue, and the scaling factor is equal to the eigenvalue. If two eigenvalues of the matrix are complex (and, consequently, appear as a pair), then the pair of eigenvalues represents a rotation plus a scaling, where the angle of rotation is the argument of the complex eigenvalue, the rotation occurs in the plane formed by the real and imaginary vectors of the complex eigenvectors, and the scaling factor is the modulus of the complex eigenvalues. For our calculations, scaling greater than 1 indicates that the initial error is scaled up over time.

3.2. Analysis of $M(t)$ with the Initial Angular Velocity from $1.0\omega_0$ to $1.5\omega_0$

We calculated the eigenvalue distribution of $M(t)$ in 10^6 seconds considering the state of the secondary with the spin angular velocity of $1.0\omega_0$ (i.e., tidal locking to the primary). Figure 6 shows the distribution of the $M(t)$ eigenvalues at four moments: 8000 s, 110,000 s, 623,000 s, and 990,000 s. For each diagram, we sampled every 1 s, giving the distribution of eigenvalues for the 2000 s before the given moment. The arrow indicates the direction of the change of this next eigenvalue. The results show that there were 12 eigenvalues of $M(t)$. One eigenvalue varied around 0, which means that this eigenvalue did not magnify the initial error; another 10 eigenvalues basically varied on or near the unit circle, which means that the initial error was not magnified unrestrictedly by these ten eigenvalues; however, there was also one eigenvalue that varied with time, where its modulus became larger (always a real eigenvalue), which means that, in this eigenvalue, the initial error of the system is continuously amplified with time. Here, we call this eigenvalue the maximum eigenvalue. Figure 7 shows the distribution of all eigenvalues over 10^6 s. Due to the sampling frequency, some of the eigenvalues are discontinuous. There were 12 eigenvalues at each moment, and cool colours represent the initial moment, while warm colours represent the later moments. The results indicate that the modulus of the largest eigenvalue reached more than 800, demonstrating that the error was amplified.

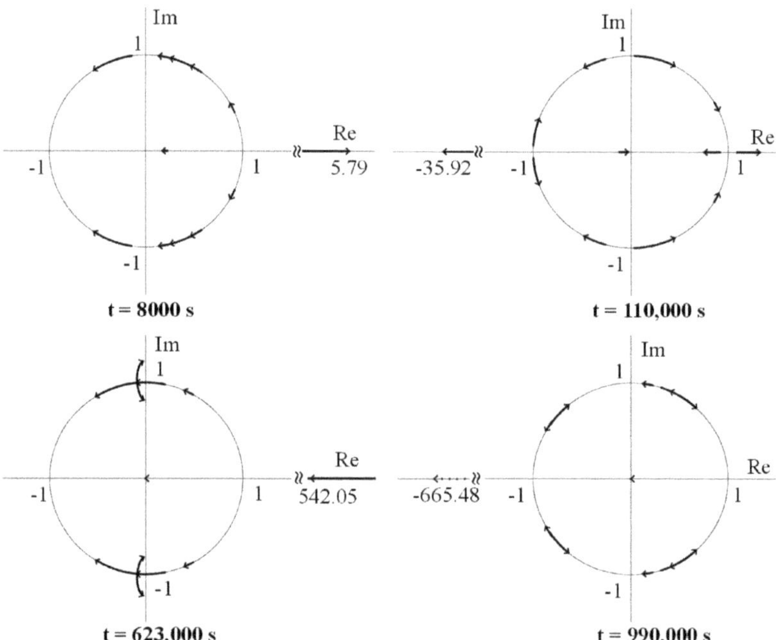

Figure 6. The distribution of the eigenvalues of $M(t)$ at $t = 8000$ s, 110,000 s, 623,000 s, and 990,000 s, where the initial angular velocity of the secondary is $1.0\omega_0$.

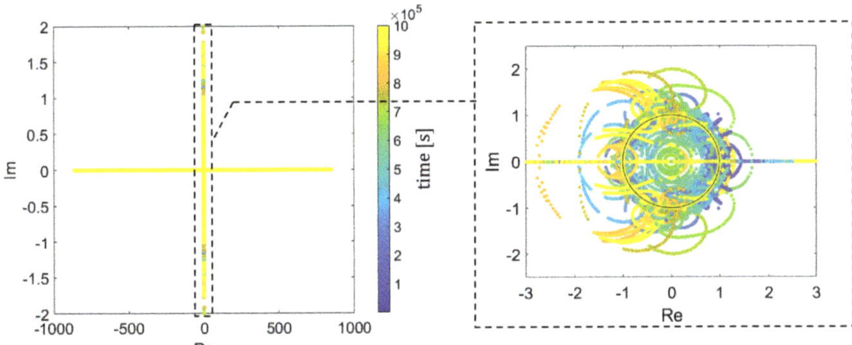

Figure 7. The distribution of the eigenvalues of $M(t)$ in 10^6 s, with initial angular velocity of the secondary of $1.0\omega_0$.

Next, we focused on the maximum eigenvalue at each time step and the corresponding eigenvectors, in which the error scaling was maximal in this direction. Figure 8a shows the variation in the modulus of the maximum eigenvalue with time, and the results show that the modulus basically showed an increasing trend as time progressed. As we are concerned with the error propagation from the secondary in the ϕ-direction, we also analyzed the variation of the component of the corresponding eigenvectors in the ϕ-direction, as shown in Figure 8b. These results show that the components of the eigenvectors in this direction were of particularly low order in magnitude, and the errors did not diverge in this direction.

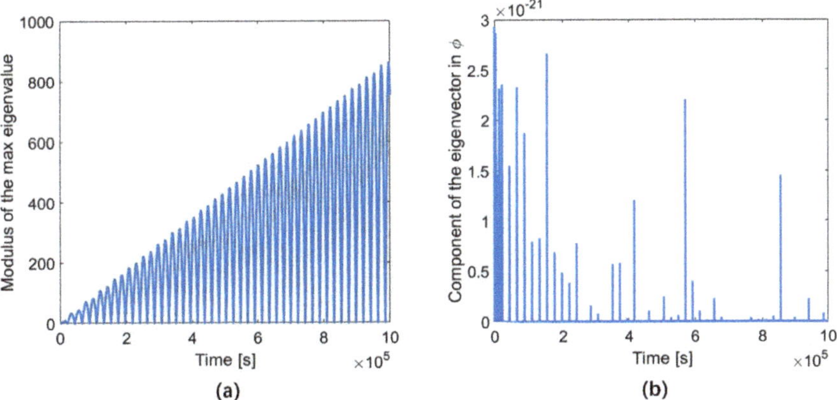

Figure 8. The maximum eigenvalue of $M(\mathbf{t})$ and the corresponding eigenvector component in the ϕ-direction, where the initial angular velocity of the secondary is $1.0\omega_0$: (**a**) Variation of the modulus of the maximum eigenvalue over 10^6 s seconds; and (**b**) the component of the eigenvector in the ϕ-direction corresponding to the maximum eigenvalue.

We observed the 12 components of the eigenvector corresponding to the maximum eigenvalue at each time step, and found that the largest components of the eigenvector were in the x and y directions, and the components of the other directions were all much smaller than these two directions. Figure 9 shows the variation of these two components, so the error amplification caused by the maximum eigenvalue was mainly concentrated in the x and y directions of the orbital position of the secondary. Therefore, at the angular velocity of $1.0\omega_0$, the error accumulation is mainly in the x and y axes of the orbit, and not in the attitude of the secondary.

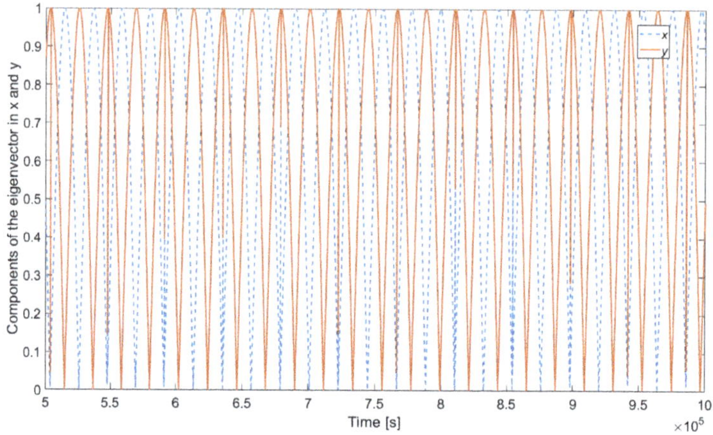

Figure 9. Components of the eigenvector in the x-direction and y-direction corresponding to the maximum eigenvalue.

Next, we increased the initial angular velocity and repeated the analysis above. The distributions of the eigenvalues of $M(t)$ for initial spin angular velocities of $1.1\omega_0$, $1.2\omega_0$, and $1.3\omega_0$ are shown in Figure 10, where (a) and (b) are the results of $1.1\omega_0$, (c) and (d) are the results of $1.2\omega_0$, (e) and (f) are the results of $1.3\omega_0$. (a), (c) and (e) indicate the overall distribution of eigenvalues within the simulation time (with a sampling step of 10 s), while (b), (d) and (f) indicate the trend of each eigenvalue towards the end of the simulation. The results in (a)–(d) show that the distribution of eigenvalues of $M(t)$ for initial angular velocities of $1.1\omega_0$ and $1.2\omega_0$ were similar to those with an initial angular velocity of $1.0\omega_0$, with one eigenvalue moving away from the unit circle and all other eigenvalues distributed near the unit circle, indicating that the motion in the direction of interest is relatively stable for these two initial conditions.

Unlike the previous two cases, the results with an initial angular velocity of $1.3\omega_0$ presented three eigenvalues moving away from the unit circle during the simulation time (through further analysis, the eigenvalue shown in Figure 10f around 5.5 was found not to move away from the unit circle, instead varying around it). Therefore, we further analyzed the eigenvectors corresponding to these three eigenvalues. These three eigenvalues are real eigenvalues, Figure 11a–c shows the variation of the modulus of these eigenvalues with time, while (d)–(f) depict the components of the eigenvectors in the ϕ-direction corresponding to these three eigenvalues, respectively.

The results show that, similar to the first three cases, for the first eigenvalue, the component of its corresponding eigenvector in the ϕ-direction was extremely small, indicating that this eigenvalue does not amplify the error of motion in the ϕ-direction. In contrast, the second and third eigenvectors correspond to eigenvectors with large components in the ϕ-direction, indicating that these two eigenvectors amplify the error of the motion in the ϕ-direction. As time passes, the cumulative error in this direction will exceed the defined stability range (90°).

In addition, we provide the components of the eigenvectors in the θ-direction corresponding to these three eigenvalues in Figure 11g–i. The eigenvector corresponding to the first eigenvalue had a tiny component in the θ-direction, while the second and third eigenvectors had significantly smaller components in the θ-direction than in the ϕ-direction, suggesting that errors accumulated significantly more in the ϕ-direction than in the θ-direction and, therefore, the motion is more prone to become unstable in the ϕ-direction.

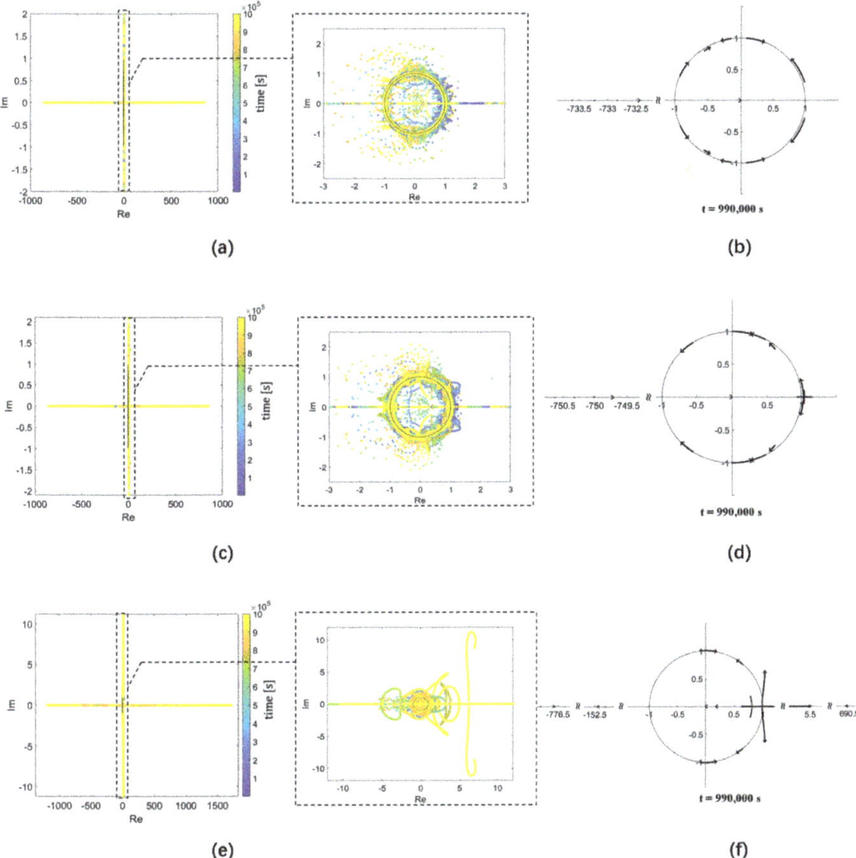

Figure 10. Distribution of the eigenvalues of $M(t)$ over 10^6 s seconds. (**a**,**b**) The initial angular velocity of the secondary is $1.1\omega_0$. (**c**,**d**) The initial angular velocity of the secondary is $1.2\omega_0$. (**e**,**f**) The initial angular velocity of the secondary is $1.3\omega_0$.

Figure 12 shows the distribution of the eigenvalues of $M(t)$ with initial spin angular velocities of $1.4\omega_0$ and $1.5\omega_0$. The results show that, in these two cases, most of the eigenvalues have moved away from the unit circle, indicating that large initial angular velocities lead to more error amplification and a more unstable motion of the secondary than in the previous cases.

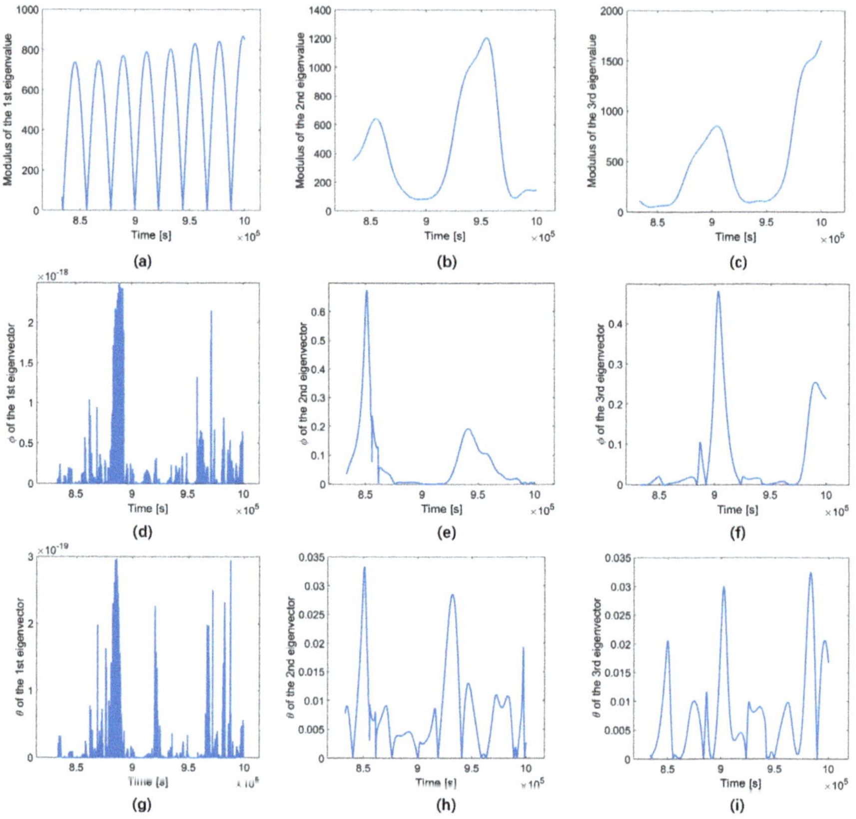

Figure 11. The variation of the modulus of the eigenvalues of $M(t)$ and the components of the eigenvector in the ϕ- and θ-directions corresponding to the eigenvalues over 10^6 s, where the initial angular velocity of the secondary is $1.3\omega_0$. (**a**) Modulus of the 1st eigenvalue. (**b**) Modulus of the 2nd eigenvalue. (**c**) Modulus of the 3rd eigenvalue. (**d**) ϕ of the 1st eigenvector. (**e**) ϕ of the 2nd eigenvector. (**f**) ϕ of the 3rd eigenvector. (**g**) θ of the 1st eigenvector. (**h**) θ of the 2nd eigenvector. (**i**) θ of the 3rd eigenvector.

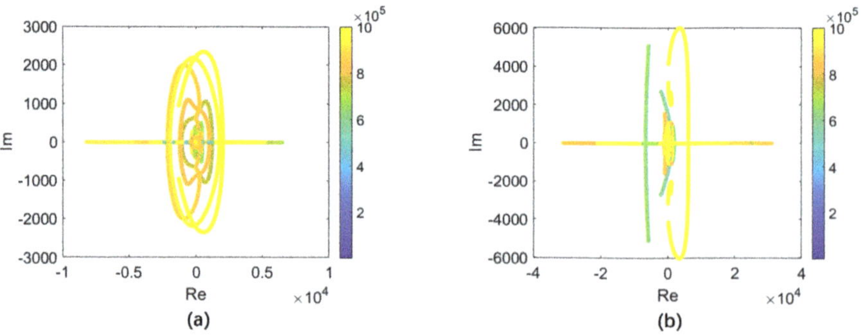

Figure 12. The distribution of the eigenvalues of $M(t)$ over 10^6 seconds, where the initial angular velocity of the secondary is $1.4\omega_0$ (**a**) and $1.5\omega_0$ (**b**).

3.3. Effect of the Non-Spherical Gravitational Field of the Primary and the Shape of the Secondary on the Tumbling Motion of the Secondary

Based on the above analysis, an increase in the spin angular velocity can lead to unstable tumbling motion of the secondary. Next, we discuss the perturbation factors leading to the tumbling rotation of the secondary, focusing on the non-spherical gravitational potential of the primary and the shape of the secondary.

In terms of the non-spherical gravitational potential, we used the homogeneous polyhedron model constructed by [30] as the model for the primary and calculated the non-spherical gravitational terms $J2$–$J7$ of the model (please refer to the Appendix A for the specific calculation method and the values of $J2$–$J7$). In order to study the influence of each disturbance term of $J2$–$J7$ on the stability of ϕ of the secondary, we chose the gravitational field of the primary as the particle gravitational field plus the gravitational field generated by the disturbance term. For the secondary, we chose the model proposed by [2]. Taking the $J2$ term as an example, we calculated the maximum ϕ values under 0 perturbation to 5 times the current $J2$ perturbation under different initial spin angular velocities of the secondary within one year.

Figure 13 shows the influences of these six disturbance terms on ϕ, in which the colour represents the magnitude of the maximum ϕ value within a year. In terms of the range of angular velocity, we chose $1.0\omega_0$ to $1.5\omega_0$. When the angular velocity was greater than $1.36\omega_0$, ϕ_{max} was 90 degrees, and when the angular velocity was less than $1.2\omega_0$, ϕ_{max} was very small. Therefore, in the figure, we only show the results with the angular velocity ranging from $1.2\omega_0$ to $1.36\omega_0$. The results show that as the six non-spherical perturbation terms increase, ϕ_{max} becomes larger, making it easier to "flip". However, this change was not very obvious; therefore, the non-spherical perturbation terms are not the main factor affecting the "flip" of the secondary in the ϕ direction.

In terms of the shape of the secondary, we used a mass point to model the primary, while the model of the secondary was still that proposed by [2]; however, we changed the shape of the ellipsoid. Assuming that the three semi-long axes of the ellipsoid were a, b, c ($a > b > c$), we performed two sets of simulations by varying the values of a/b and b/c, respectively, while keeping the total mass of the ellipsoid constant. Taking the first set of simulations as an example, we calculated the maximum ϕ for a/b ranging from 1 to 1.5 under different initial spin angular velocities of the secondary within one year (Figure 14). The results show that this unstable tumbling rotation of the secondary was related to the shape of the ellipsoid, with the most unstable cases occurring at a/b = 1.16 and b/c = 1.22.

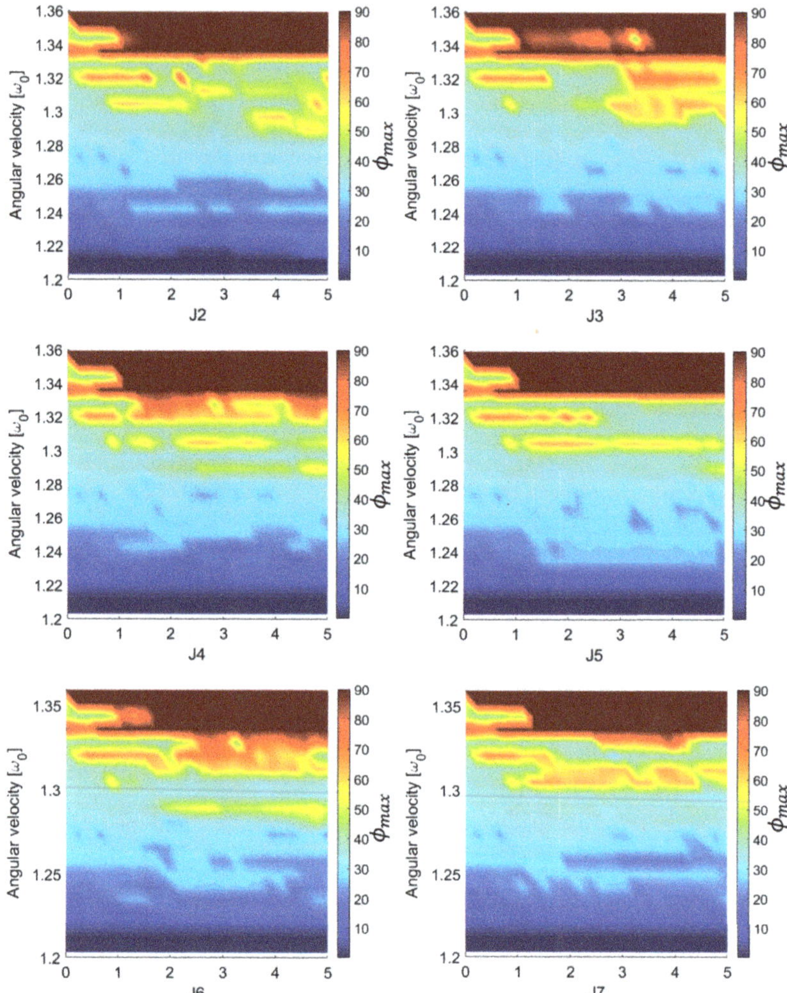

Figure 13. The maximum ϕ value under different perturbation terms and initial angular velocities within 1 year.

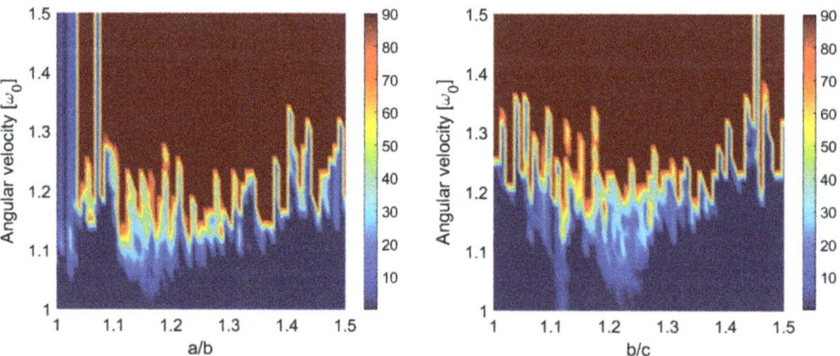

Figure 14. The maximum ϕ value under different a/b, b/c, and initial angular velocity within 1 year.

4. Conclusions

In this paper, we discussed the stability of the excited spin state of the secondary in a binary asteroid system over one year. For long-term numerical simulation schemes, we combined the finite element method with a symplectic integral format for the simulation of the full two-body problem, and compared it with low- and high-order Runge–Kutta methods. We analyzed the rotation stability of the secondary using a linearised error propagation matrix, and discussed the influence of the non-spherical perturbation terms $J2 - J7$ of the primary and the shape of the secondary on the rotation stability of the secondary.

The results of the numerical simulation schemes over 10 years show that the Runge–Kutta methods led to a monotonic increase in the relative error of the components of the angular momentum, which can be avoided by the symplectic integrator. Therefore, we chose the symplectic integrator as the numerical scheme for the long-term simulation of the full two-body system. For the rotation stability of the secondary, the results demonstrate that the secondary is prone to losing stability in rotation around its long-axis, which is related to the post-impact spin angular velocity of the secondary. The rotation of the secondary is stable when the spin angular velocity of the secondary satisfies the tidal locking state to the primary; as the spin angular velocity of the secondary increases, errors caused by the irregular gravitational field of the primary or by other reasons are more prone to accumulating in the rotation direction of the secondary around its long axis, so as to lose stability. For the non-spherical gravitational perturbation of the primary, the results show that the rotation stability of the secondary does not change significantly even if we amplify each perturbation term by a maximum of five times, which indicates that the non-spherical perturbation term of the primary is not the main factor affecting the rotation stability of the secondary under the current model of the primary. Furthermore, we varied the ratio of the semi-major axis a/b and b/c ($a > b > c$) of the ellipsoid model of the secondary, and the results show significant differences in the critical spin angular velocity at which the secondary loses rotational stability for different a/b and b/c, suggesting that the shape abnormality of the secondary has a more significant effect on the rotating stability of the secondary.

In the next work, it will be necessary to compare more numerical simulation methods in order to find the most suitable numerical simulation scheme for the full two body problem. In addition, in the simplified model of the binary asteroid system, we used a model with seven masses as the model of the secondary for computational reasons, and in the future, further studies can be carried out using more refined models of the secondary after solving the computational consumption problem.

Author Contributions: Conceptualization, Y.G. and Y.Y.; methodology, Y.G. and Y.Y.; software, Y.G. and Y.Y; validation, Y.G., Y.Y. and J.L.; formal analysis, Y.G., B.C. and Y.Y.; investigation, Y.G. and Y.Y.; resources, Y.G. and Y.Y.; data curation, Y.G. and Y.Y.; writing—original draft preparation, Y.G.; writing—review and editing, B.C., Y.Y., J.L. and H.B.; The research work is discussed by all authors. All authors have read and agreed to the published version of the manuscript.

Funding: This research was funded by the National Natural Science Foundation of China Grant No. 12022212.

Data Availability Statement: Not applicable.

Acknowledgments: We thank the members of Hera WG3 group for the constructive conversations. Y.Y. acknowledges financial support provided by the National Natural Science Foundation of China Grant No. 12022212.

Conflicts of Interest: The authors declare no conflict of interest.

Appendix A

This appendix provides the method for calculating the coefficients of the spherical harmonic function using the finite element method. The spherical harmonic function method is a mature and effective method for dealing with the gravitational field of planets, and has been widely used in determining the dynamics of near-Earth satellite orbits. This method can also be used to describe the non-spherical perturbation of the gravitational field near small celestial bodies. The advantage of this method is that it is computationally efficient and requires few parameters. Here, we combine the spherical harmonic function method and the finite element method to calculate the orbit of a mass point around the small celestial body, such that the irregular shape and non-homogeneous internal structure of asteroids can be taken into account, while ensuring efficient computational efficiency.

In another work [34], we have given a calculation method for the gravitational force of a small irregular celestial body on a mass point by FEM. The gravitational field can be described as

$$U = G\sum_{\alpha}^{N_1} \frac{w_\alpha \sigma_\alpha}{|\boldsymbol{r}_\alpha - \boldsymbol{r}|} \tag{A1}$$

where N_1 represents the number of nodes described by the finite element method of the small celestial body, ω_α represents the weight of the αth node, σ_α represents the density of the αth node, $\boldsymbol{r}_\alpha$ represents the position of the node, and $\boldsymbol{r}$ represents the position of the mass point (please refer to [14] for explanations of the specific parameters). The advantages of this method have been described above, while the key disadvantage is that the computational effort increases as the grid of the primary model is divided approximately finely. Even if it is accelerated by various means, it still cannot change the fact that the gravitational potential between each node and the mass point needs to be calculated. Therefore, we desire to combine the spherical harmonic function method to improve the computational efficiency in orbit calculation.

The general method for calculating the gravitational field by the spherical harmonic function method is

$$\begin{aligned} U = \frac{GM_a}{R}\Bigg[1 + \sum_{l=1}^{\infty} C_{l0}\left(\frac{a_a}{R}\right)^l P_{l0}(\sin\varphi) \\ + \sum_{l=1}^{\infty}\sum_{m=1}^{l}\left(\frac{a_a}{R}\right)^l P_{lm}(\sin\varphi)(C_{lm}\cos m\lambda + S_{lm}\sin m\lambda)\Bigg] \end{aligned} \tag{A2}$$

where M_a is the mass of the small celestial body, a_a is the equatorial radius of the reference ellipsoid of the small celestial body, $P_{lm}(\sin\varphi')$ is the Associated Legendre polynomial of $\sin\varphi'$,$\delta = 0\,(m = 0)$ or $\delta = 1\,(m \neq 0)$, and R is the distance from the mass point to the centre of the small celestial body. For the spherical harmonics method to describe the gravitational field, the parameters describing the irregularity of the shape and the inhomogeneity of the internal mass distribution of the small celestial body are

$$\begin{aligned} C_{lm} &= 2^\delta \frac{(l-m)!}{(l+m)!}\left(\frac{1}{M_a a_a^l}\right)\iiint \rho^l P_{lm}(\sin\varphi')\cos m\lambda' \mathrm{d}M \\ S_{lm} &= 2^\delta \frac{(l-m)!}{(l+m)!}\left(\frac{1}{M_a a_a^l}\right)\iiint \rho^l P_{lm}(\sin\varphi')\sin m\lambda' \mathrm{d}M \end{aligned} \tag{A3}$$

where λ' and φ' are the longitude and latitude of the volume element $\mathrm{d}M$, respectively, and ρ is the distance from the volume element $\mathrm{d}M$ to the centre of mass of the small celestial body. In Equation (A2), the term with $m = 0$ is independent of longitude and is called the zonal harmonic term; while the term with $m \neq 0$ is related to longitude and is called the tesseral harmonic term. Using the finite element method, replacing the body element $\mathrm{d}M$ with the node, the integral number of Equation (A3) can be split. Then,

$$\begin{aligned} C_{lm} &= 2^\delta \frac{(l-m)!}{(l+m)!}\left(\frac{1}{M_a a_a^l}\right)\sum_{\alpha} w_\alpha \sigma_\alpha \rho^l P_{lm}(\sin\varphi')\cos m\lambda' \\ S_{lm} &= 2^\delta \frac{(l-m)!}{(l+m)!}\left(\frac{1}{M_a a_a^l}\right)\sum_{\alpha} w_\alpha \sigma_\alpha \rho^l P_{lm}(\sin\varphi')\sin m\lambda' \end{aligned} \tag{A4}$$

Now, if we learn about the information of the shape and internal mass distribution of a small body, we can model it using the finite element method, then calculate the corresponding spherical harmonic function coefficients using the above method. Below, we explain the accuracy of this method using the primary model of Didymos as an example. We keep the mass constant and adjust the internal structure of the primary using four models: (a) Uniform internal density distribution. (b) The density decreases from the inside to the outside, with the centre density set to 3.2 g/cm^2 (equivalent to the density of granite) and the surface density set to 1.6 g/cm^2 (equivalent to the density of sandy soil); (c) The internal structure is hollow. (d) The internal structure contains some holes (we implement this by removing some elements and replacing them with voids). The four models correspond to Figure A1a–d, respectively. Then, the spherical harmonic function coefficients are calculated using the above method. Some of these coefficients are shown in Table A1.

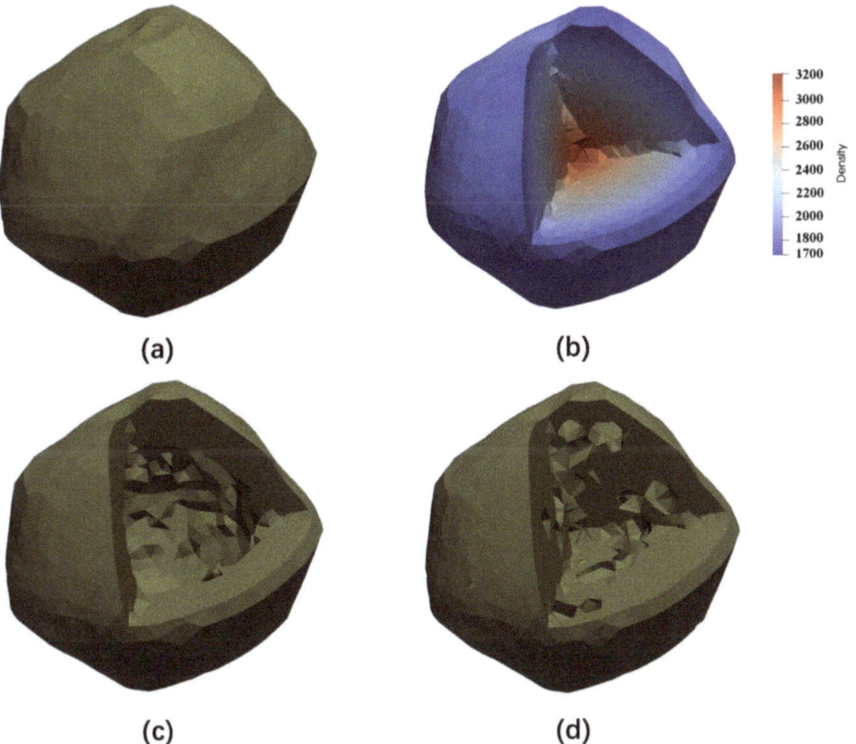

Figure A1. The internal structure of the primary: (**a**) Uniform internal mass distribution; (**b**) density decreases from inside to outside; (**c**) hollow structure; and (**d**) randomly distributed internal holes.

We calculated the orbits of the mass point around the primary over one month using the finite element method and the spherical harmonic function method, respectively. We set a random initial position and velocity for the mass point, with a distance 1200 m from the primary and whose velocity kept it in a circular orbit.

Table A1. The coefficients of the partial spherical harmonic functions of the four models corresponding to Figure A1.

	Model (a)	Model (b)	Model (c)	Model (d)
J_2	1.1806016×10^{-2}	9.8940464×10^{-3}	1.6734636×10^{-2}	1.5034951×10^{-2}
J_3	1.6620303×10^{-3}	1.5130812×10^{-3}	2.4893284×10^{-3}	1.3309408×10^{-3}
J_4	$-8.2823689 \times 10^{-3}$	$-6.5632877 \times 10^{-3}$	$-1.1255250 \times 10^{-3}$	$-8.4519822 \times 10^{-3}$
J_5	1.3132394×10^{-3}	1.0301008×10^{-3}	1.9799122×10^{-3}	1.7177357×10^{-3}
J_6	5.0458902×10^{-3}	4.3363831×10^{-3}	7.6811147×10^{-3}	5.0889960×10^{-3}
C_{22}	1.4205710×10^{-3}	1.2214748×10^{-3}	2.0914078×10^{-3}	1.3592346×10^{-3}
S_{22}	$-1.4884062 \times 10^{-17}$	$-6.5408149 \times 10^{-17}$	$3.4962132 \times 10^{-17}$	$2.7487490 \times 10^{-17}$
C_{31}	1.4205710×10^{-3}	8.2970092×10^{-4}	1.4993794×10^{-3}	1.3687619×10^{-3}
C_{32}	4.5358186×10^{-4}	3.1217587×10^{-4}	5.1968086×10^{-4}	6.2947825×10^{-4}
C_{33}	$-7.3986272 \times 10^{-5}$	$-6.7329189 \times 10^{-5}$	$-1.3757727 \times 10^{-4}$	$-1.1369448 \times 10^{-4}$
S_{31}	$-1.7122335 \times 10^{-3}$	4.1793971×10^{-3}	7.1960664×10^{-3}	$-4.8583376 \times 10^{-3}$
S_{32}	$-5.5112926 \times 10^{-4}$	5.0319504×10^{-4}	8.1352188×10^{-4}	$-5.2487380 \times 10^{-4}$
S_{33}	4.3490667×10^{-5}	$-8.4002799 \times 10^{-5}$	$-1.5102661 \times 10^{-4}$	7.3761001×10^{-5}
C_{41}	8.2756971×10^{-4}	4.8424441×10^{-4}	$7.54612325 \times 10^{-4}$	8.8267016×10^{-4}
C_{42}	$-3.6264708 \times 10^{-5}$	$-5.1243370 \times 10^{-6}$	$-7.8521454 \times 10^{-5}$	5.8103214×10^{-5}
C_{43}	$-4.9772428 \times 10^{-5}$	$-6.6087746 \times 10^{-5}$	$-9.8008247 \times 10^{-5}$	$-4.0274728 \times 10^{-5}$
C_{44}	2.2303289×10^{-5}	1.8673576×10^{-5}	$3.19242917 \times 10^{-5}$	$2.40624550 \times 10^{-5}$
S_{41}	1.7122335×10^{-3}	1.4349064×10^{-3}	2.4430001×10^{-3}	$-1.1834871 \times 10^{-3}$
S_{42}	1.4850440×10^{-4}	$-1.4613356 \times 10^{-4}$	$-2.4425241 \times 10^{-4}$	1.9224648×10^{-4}
S_{43}	$-1.4255166 \times 10^{-4}$	1.0462180×10^{-4}	1.8717446×10^{-4}	$-1.4832237 \times 10^{-4}$
S_{44}	3.7897508×10^{-6}	2.1443836×10^{-6}	-5.813172×10^{-7}	$4.12749518 \times 10^{-6}$
C_{51}	$-3.1272871 \times 10^{-5}$	$-3.4821246 \times 10^{-5}$	$-6.8427557 \times 10^{-5}$	5.3334476×10^{-5}
C_{52}	$-1.3763895 \times 10^{-5}$	$-9.4857243 \times 10^{-6}$	$-1.8897903 \times 10^{-5}$	1.2900471×10^{-5}
C_{53}	1.5176728×10^{-5}	1.0813339×10^{-5}	1.9819451×10^{-5}	2.3163710×10^{-5}
C_{54}	$-1.3104122 \times 10^{-6}$	$-1.7654773 \times 10^{-6}$	$-3.5584973 \times 10^{-6}$	$-1.5303503 \times 10^{-6}$
C_{55}	1.1230563×10^{-7}	$-3.5638557 \times 10^{-8}$	$-2.0440055 \times 10^{-8}$	4.6177160×10^{-7}
S_{51}	$-3.0555771 \times 10^{-4}$	2.5269240×10^{-4}	3.9629143×10^{-4}	$-1.9158968 \times 10^{-4}$
S_{52}	$-8.3027337 \times 10^{-5}$	5.5164301×10^{-5}	1.0287761×10^{-4}	$-6.4137630 \times 10^{-5}$
S_{53}	$-2.1025676 \times 10^{-5}$	1.9801873×10^{-5}	3.2486021×10^{-5}	$-1.9990395 \times 10^{-5}$
S_{54}	$-8.5562671 \times 10^{-7}$	4.0510217×10^{-7}	9.9360799×10^{-7}	$-3.4240771 \times 10^{-7}$
S_{55}	$-5.6674802 \times 10^{-7}$	7.9659473×10^{-7}	1.3832809×10^{-6}	$-1.2130380 \times 10^{-6}$
C_{61}	7.4598908×10^{-5}	1.0254846×10^{-5}	1.3039376×10^{-4}	$-1.0657605 \times 10^{-4}$
C_{62}	$-2.2087532 \times 10^{-5}$	$-8.6100296 \times 10^{-6}$	$-2.6696073 \times 10^{-5}$	$-1.5985003 \times 10^{-5}$
C_{63}	$-8.0428517 \times 10^{-6}$	$-7.3253673 \times 10^{-6}$	$-1.1413149 \times 10^{-5}$	$-9.1612740 \times 10^{-6}$
C_{64}	$-4.0554689 \times 10^{-7}$	$-4.0401878 \times 10^{-8}$	$-1.9263216 \times 10^{-7}$	$-2.1994592 \times 10^{-7}$
C_{65}	1.2221950×10^{-7}	8.2412156×10^{-8}	$1.54076076 \times 10^{-7}$	2.1036180×10^{-7}
C_{66}	$-3.6108293 \times 10^{-8}$	-5.009707×10^{-8}	$-8.8044116 \times 10^{-8}$	$-6.2420189 \times 10^{-8}$
S_{61}	$-2.6668643 \times 10^{-4}$	1.8252031×10^{-4}	1.7433184×10^{-4}	$-4.6283910 \times 10^{-4}$
S_{62}	9.1296564×10^{-5}	$-8.4002799 \times 10^{-5}$	$-1.2608227 \times 10^{-4}$	$7.36740260 \times 10^{-5}$
S_{63}	$-8.4915327 \times 10^{-6}$	$-8.4002799 \times 10^{-5}$	1.4218991×10^{-5}	$-1.0994466 \times 10^{-5}$
S_{64}	4.3587887×10^{-7}	$-8.4002799 \times 10^{-7}$	$-6.6267905 \times 10^{-7}$	$4.28696097 \times 10^{-8}$
S_{65}	$-1.4568412 \times 10^{-7}$	$-8.4002799 \times 10^{-7}$	$1.94633108 \times 10^{-7}$	$-1.1636263 \times 10^{-7}$
S_{66}	$-1.4975725 \times 10^{-8}$	$-8.4002799 \times 10^{-8}$	$-1.4714211 \times 10^{-8}$	$5.34328597 \times 10^{-9}$

Figure A2 shows the distance between the orbital position of the mass point calculated by the spherical harmonic function method considering different perturbation terms and the position calculated by the finite element method; that is, the error in the calculated orbital positions of the spherical harmonic function method. The four figures correspond to the four models of the primary in Figure A1. Here, we take Figure A2a as an example to explain. The blue line indicates that only $J2$, $J3$, and $J4$ of the zonal harmonic terms and $T2$ of the tesseral harmonic terms were considered, which are the main perturbation terms for the calculation of the Earth's gravitational field. The result shows bad performance in error maintenance, with a maximum error of 520.02 m within one month. The light blue line indicates that we added the tesseral harmonic terms $T3$ and $T4$ to the blue one, and the results show a significant reduction in the error, with a maximum error of 12.43 m within 30 days. The yellow line indicates that we added $J5$ and $T5$ to the light blue one, with a maximum error of 5.40 m within 30 days. The red line indicates the addition of $J6$ and $T6$ to the yellow case, and the calculation error was significantly reduced, with a maximum error of 2.35 m within 30 days.

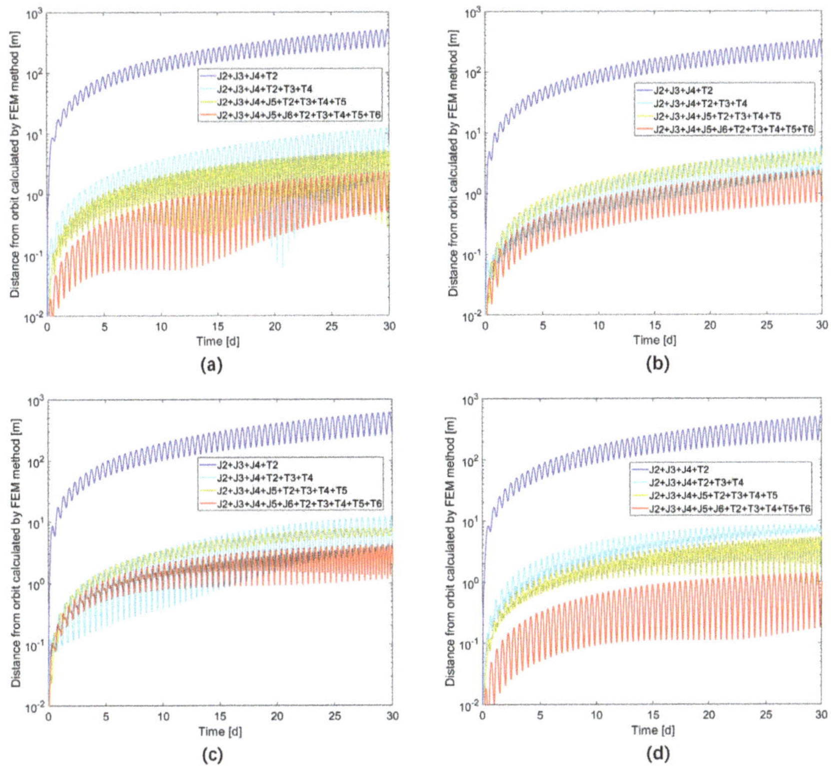

Figure A2. The distance error between the orbit calculated by the spherical harmonic function method and the finite element method. (**a–d**) correspond to the four models of the primary in Figure A1, and the different coloured lines indicate that different perturbation terms are considered, where JX indicates the expansion to the Xth order of the zonal harmonic term and TX indicates the expansion to the Xth tesseral harmonic term.

The results show that our method is effective. For longer simulation times, we can further calculate higher-order zonal and tesseral harmonic terms, such that the errors can be maintained within acceptable accuracy. This method imposes no restrictions on the shape and internal mass distribution of the small body. Furthermore, using this method, we can calculate the coefficients of the spherical harmonic function of any finite element model at once and call them in the orbit calculation, thus avoiding the high computational cost of the finite element method when calculating high-precision models.

References

1. Cheng, A.; Michel, P.; Jutzi, M.; Rivkin, A.; Stickle, A.; Barnouin, O.; Ernst, C.; Atchison, J.; Pravec, P.; Richardson, D.; et al. Asteroid impact & deflection assessment mission: Kinetic impactor. *Planet. Space Sci.* **2016**, *121*, 27–35.
2. Michel, P.; Cheng, A.; Küppers, M.; Pravec, P.; Blum, J.; Delbo, M.; Green, S.; Rosenblatt, P.; Tsiganis, K.; Vincent, J.B.; et al. Science case for the asteroid impact mission (AIM): A component of the asteroid impact & deflection assessment (AIDA) mission. *Adv. Space Res.* **2016**, *57*, 2529–2547.

3. Cheng, A.F.; Rivkin, A.S.; Michel, P.; Atchison, J.; Barnouin, O.; Benner, L.; Chabot, N.L.; Ernst, C.; Fahnestock, E.G.; Kueppers, M.; et al. AIDA DART asteroid deflection test: Planetary defense and science objectives. *Planet. Space Sci.* **2018**, *157*, 104–115. [CrossRef]
4. Rainey, E.S.; Stickle, A.M.; Cheng, A.F.; Rivkin, A.S.; Chabot, N.L.; Barnouin, O.S.; Ernst, C.M.; Group, A.I.S.W. Impact Modeling for the Double Asteroid Redirection Test Mission. In Proceedings of the Hypervelocity Impact Symposium, Destin, FL, USA, 16–20 April 2019; Volume 883556, p. HVIS2019-038.
5. Rainey, E.S.; Stickle, A.M.; Cheng, A.F.; Rivkin, A.S.; Chabot, N.L.; Barnouin, O.S.; Ernst, C.M.; AIDA/DART Impact Simulation Working Group. Impact modeling for the Double Asteroid Redirection Test (DART) mission. *Int. J. Impact Eng.* **2020**, *142*, 103528. [CrossRef]
6. Rivkin, A.S.; Chabot, N.L.; Stickle, A.M.; Thomas, C.A.; Richardson, D.C.; Barnouin, O.; Fahnestock, E.G.; Ernst, C.M.; Cheng, A.F.; Chesley, S.; et al. The double asteroid redirection test (DART): Planetary defense investigations and requirements. *Planet. Sci. J.* **2021**, *2*, 173. [CrossRef]
7. Agrusa, H.; Richardson, D.; Barbee, B.; Bottke, W.; Cheng, A.; Eggl, S.; Ferrari, F.; Hirabayashi, M.; Karatekin, O.; McMahon, J.; et al. Predictions for the Dynamical State of the Didymos System Before and After the Planned DART Impact. *LPI Contrib.* **2022**, *2678*, 2447.
8. Agrusa, H.F.; Gkolias, I.; Tsiganis, K.; Richardson, D.C.; Meyer, A.J.; Scheeres, D.J.; Ćuk, M.; Jacobson, S.A.; Michel, P.; Karatekin, Ö.; et al. The excited spin state of Dimorphos resulting from the DART impact. *Icarus* **2021**, *370*, 114624. [CrossRef]
9. Agrusa, H.; Ballouz, R.; Meyer, A.J.; Tasev, E.; Noiset, G.; Karatekin, Ö.; Michel, P.; Richardson, D.C.; Hirabayashi, M. Rotation-induced granular motion on the secondary component of binary asteroids: Application to the DART impact on Dimorphos. *Astron. Astrophys.* **2022**, *664*, L3. [CrossRef]
10. Werner, R.A.; Scheeres, D.J. Mutual potential of homogeneous polyhedra. *Celest. Mech. Dyn. Astron.* **2005**, *91*, 337–349. [CrossRef]
11. Hirabayashi, M.; Scheeres, D.J. Recursive computation of mutual potential between two polyhedra. *Celest. Mech. Dyn. Astron.* **2013**, *117*, 245–262. [CrossRef]
12. Hou, X.; Scheeres, D.J.; Xin, X. Mutual potential between two rigid bodies with arbitrary shapes and mass distributions. *Celest. Mech. Dyn. Astron.* **2017**, *127*, 369–395. [CrossRef]
13. Richardson, D.C.; Quinn, T.; Stadel, J.; Lake, G. Direct large-scale N-body simulations of planetesimal dynamics. *Icarus* **2000**, *143*, 45–59. [CrossRef]
14. Yu, Y.; Cheng, B.; Hayabayashi, M.; Michel, P.; Baoyin, H. A finite element method for computational full two-body problem: I. The mutual potential and derivatives over bilinear tetrahedron elements. *Celest. Mech. Dyn. Astron.* **2019**, *131*, 51. [CrossRef]
15. Ruth, R.D. A canonical integration technique. *IEEE Trans. Nucl. Sci.* **1983**, *30*, 2669–2671. [CrossRef]
16. Marsden, J.E.; West, M. Discrete mechanics and variational integrators. *Acta Numer.* **2001**, *10*, 357–514. [CrossRef]
17. Feng, K.; Qin, M. *Symplectic Geometric Algorithms for Hamiltonian Systems*; Springer: Berlin/Heidelberg, Germany, 2010; Volume 449.
18. Karamali, G.; Shiri, B. Numerical solution of higher index DAEs using their IAE's structure: Trajectory-prescribed path control problem and simple pendulum. *Casp. J. Math. Sci. CJMS* **2018**, *7*, 1–15.
19. Kosmas, O.T.; Vlachos, D. Phase-fitted discrete Lagrangian integrators. *Comput. Phys. Commun.* **2010**, *181*, 562–568. [CrossRef]
20. Kosmas, O.T.; Vlachos, D. Local path fitting: A new approach to variational integrators. *J. Comput. Appl. Math.* **2012**, *236*, 2632–2642. [CrossRef]
21. Kosmas, O.; Leyendecker, S. Analysis of higher order phase fitted variational integrators. *Adv. Comput. Math.* **2016**, *42*, 605–619. [CrossRef]
22. Kosmas, O.; Leyendecker, S. Variational integrators for orbital problems using frequency estimation. *Adv. Comput. Math.* **2019**, *45*, 1–21. [CrossRef]
23. Kosmas, O. Energy minimization scheme for split potential systems using exponential variational integrators. *Appl. Mech.* **2021**, *2*, 431–441. [CrossRef]
24. Leimkuhler, B.; Reich, S. *Simulating Hamiltonian Dynamics*; Cambridge University Press: Cambridge, UK, 2004; Number 14.
25. Dullweber, A.; Leimkuhler, B.; McLachlan, R. Symplectic splitting methods for rigid body molecular dynamics. *J. Chem. Phys.* **1997**, *107*, 5840–5851. [CrossRef]
26. Kol, A.; Laird, B.B.; Leimkuhler, B.J. A symplectic method for rigid-body molecular simulation. *J. Chem. Phys.* **1997**, *107*, 2580–2588. [CrossRef]
27. van Zon, R.; Schofield, J. Symplectic algorithms for simulations of rigid-body systems using the exact solution of free motion. *Phys. Rev. E* **2007**, *75*, 056701. [CrossRef] [PubMed]
28. Celledoni, E.; Fassò, F.; Säfström, N.; Zanna, A. The exact computation of the free rigid body motion and its use in splitting methods. *SIAM J. Sci. Comput.* **2008**, *30*, 2084–2112. [CrossRef]
29. Ćuk, M.; Jacobson, S.A.; Walsh, K.J. Barrel Instability in Binary Asteroids. *Planet. Sci. J.* **2021**, *2*, 231. [CrossRef]
30. Benner, L.A.; Margot, J.; Nolan, M.; Giorgini, J.; Brozovic, M.; Scheeres, D.; Magri, C.; Ostro, S. Radar imaging and a physical model of binary asteroid 65803 Didymos. In Proceedings of the AAS/Division for Planetary Sciences Meeting Abstracts# 42, Pasadena, CA, USA, 4–8 October 2010; Volume 42, pp. 13–17.
31. Hand, L.N.; Finch, J.D. *Analytical Mechanics*; Cambridge University Press: Cambridge, UK, 1998.

32. Gao, Y.; Yu, Y.; Cheng, B.; Baoyin, H. Accelerating the finite element method for calculating the full 2-body problem with CUDA. *Adv. Space Res.* **2022**, *69*, 2305–2318. [CrossRef]
33. Naidu, S.; Benner, L.; Brozovic, M.; Nolan, M.; Ostro, S.; Margot, J.; Giorgini, J.; Hirabayashi, T.; Scheeres, D.; Pravec, P.; et al. Radar observations and a physical model of binary near-Earth asteroid 65803 Didymos, target of the DART mission. *Icarus* **2020**, *348*, 113777. [CrossRef]
34. Gao, Y.; Cheng, B.; Yu, Y. The interactive dynamics of a binary asteroid and ejecta after medium kinetic impact. *Astrophys. Space Sci.* **2022**, *367*, 84. [CrossRef]

 mathematics

Article

Simultaneous-Fault Diagnosis of Satellite Power System Based on Fuzzy Neighborhood ζ-Decision-Theoretic Rough Set

Laifa Tao [1,2,3], Chao Wang [1,2,3], Yuan Jia [4], Ruzhi Zhou [5], Tong Zhang [6], Yiling Chen [1,2,3], Chen Lu [1,2,3] and Mingliang Suo [1,2,3,*]

1 Institute of Reliability Engineering, Beihang University, Beijing 100191, China
2 Science & Technology on Reliability & Environmental Engineering Laboratory, Beijing 100191, China
3 School of Reliability and Systems Engineering, Beihang University, Beijing 100191, China
4 Beijing Institute of Radio Metrology and Measurement, China Aerospace Science and Industry Corporation Limited, Beijing 100039, China
5 Shanghai Institute of Satellite Engineering, China Aerospace Science and Technology Corporation, Shanghai 201109, China
6 Marine Design and Research Institute of China, China State Shipbuilding Corporation Limited, Shanghai 200011, China
* Correspondence: suozi@buaa.edu.cn

Abstract: Due to the increasing complexity of the entire satellite system and the deteriorating orbital environment, multiple independent single faults may occur simultaneously in the satellite power system. However, two stumbling blocks hinder the effective diagnosis of simultaneous-fault, namely, the difficulty of obtaining the simultaneous-fault data and the extremely complicated mapping of the simultaneous-fault modes to the sensor data. To tackle the challenges, a fault diagnosis strategy based on a novel rough set model is proposed. Specifically, a novel rough set model named FNζDTRS by introducing a concise loss function matrix and fuzzy neighborhood relationship is proposed to accurately mine and characterize the relationship between fault and data. Furthermore, an attribute rule-based fault matching strategy is designed without using simultaneous-fault data as training samples. The numerical experiments demonstrate the effectiveness of the FNζDTRS model, and the diagnosis experiments performed on a satellite power system illustrate the superiority of the proposed approach.

Keywords: simultaneous-fault diagnosis; rough set; attribute reduction; satellite power system

MSC: 94C12

Citation: Tao, L.; Wang, C.; Jia, Y.; Zhou, R.; Zhang, T.; Chen, Y.; Lu, C.; Suo, M. Simultaneous-Fault Diagnosis of Satellite Power System Based on Fuzzy Neighborhood ζ-Decision-Theoretic Rough Set. *Mathematics* **2022**, *10*, 3414. https://doi.org/10.3390/math10193414

Academic Editor: Denis N. Sidorov

Received: 12 August 2022
Accepted: 7 September 2022
Published: 20 September 2022

1. Introduction

The power system is regarded as the heart of a satellite, whose health management is critical to the on-orbit operation of the entire satellite. The satellite power system is mainly composed of a solar array and battery pack. The solar array exposes in the outer space environment for a long time, and is very vulnerable to external environment intrusion. The battery pack is in a frequent and long-term working state with the periodic operation of the satellite. Therefore, with the increasing probability of space junk collisions, intense radiation of space particles, and striking temperature differences in space, the satellite power system may have multiple independent single faults occurring at the same time, which is called simultaneous-fault [1]. Accurate fault diagnosis is the basis for the health management of a satellite. At present, the research on the diagnosis of single-fault has achieved great success [2,3]. However, as satellites become more complex in their functional composition and longer in their mission time, the mode of simultaneous-fault has become the key factor affecting the normal on-orbit operation of satellites, and the risk and influence caused by such a fault mode cannot be ignored, because the development speed and destructive power of such a fault mode are far more than that of a single-fault mode. Therefore, it is necessary to diagnose the simultaneous-fault precisely to make sound decisions to enable satellites to perform their missions smoothly and safely. This is the core motivation of our work, namely, we try to solve the diagnosis problem of simultaneous-fault, which is more complex and more harmful than that of single-fault.

With respect to the diagnosis of simultaneous-fault, there are two major challenges that can be listed as follows: (1) The historical simultaneous-fault data are scarce, which greatly limits the effectiveness of data-driven models; (2) The simultaneous-faults would involve multiple sensors, and the mapping between sensor data and fault modes is complicated, which leads to the uncertainty in the diagnosis process. Therefore, new cognitive methods and further research are needed for simultaneous-fault cognition and diagnosis. These can be considered as the technical motivation of our research.

Regarding the first challenge issue, the absence of historical simultaneous-fault data is a thorny problem that needs to be solved urgently. Unlike the traditional fault diagnosis studies that require all kinds of samples during the training phase [4–6], some literature has shown that multi-label classification is expected to achieve simultaneous-fault diagnosis without historical simultaneous-fault data [1,7–10]. The multi-label classification task focuses on the problem where each training simple is represented by a single instance with a single label, and the task is to yield a model that can predict the proper label sets for unseen instances [11]. Multi-label classification methods can be divided into two categories, one of which is the problem transformation methods, including Binary Relevance [12], Classifier Chains [13], Calibrated Label Ranking [14], and other classical methods; the other includes the algorithm adaptation methods, including multi-label K-nearest neighbor (ML-KNN) [15], multi-label decision tree (ML-DT) [16], etc. However, in the face of complex problems, the above methods cannot effectively deal with the problem of insufficient data, and there is still a need for long-term and in-depth research.

For the second challenge issue, some data mining methods are good solutions. In terms of the cognition of things, rough set theory provides a perspective of knowledge and data fusion. This is the main reason why this paper chooses the rough set model as the basic model. The setting of condition attribute and decision attribute can provide multiple information for the characterization of fault, which is conducive to extracting the mapping information between sensor data and fault modes. Rough set theory initiated by Pawlak [17] provides an authoritative mathematical framework for analyzing and handling ambiguous and uncertain data, which can be used to attribute reduction [18–22], rule extraction [23–26], and uncertainty reasoning [22,27–29]. Among kinds of rough set models, the decision-theoretic rough set (DTRS) model has been proved to be a generalized model of many other rough set models [30,31]. At present, there have been related studies on various decision-theoretic rough set models for fault diagnosis, which have proved that the models can effectively select the fault attributes when the pair of the threshold parameters is set appropriately [30,31]. Nevertheless, how to determine the appropriate threshold parameters is the biggest difficulty in the research and application of DTRS. In our previous work [32], we have presented a single-parameter decision-theoretic rough set (SPDTRS) model by setting only one parameter named compensation coefficient rather than two or six, which facilitates the convenient application of the DTRS model. However, the setting of the compensation coefficient in this model is still not clear enough, and the setting of the loss function matrix is defective. In addition, this model lacks the consideration of uncertain information in data description, which makes it unable to deal with continuous data directly. Therefore, in order to make the rough set model (i.e., SPDTRS) more effective in dealing with the simultaneous-fault problem, we need to carry out more targeted improvement work. The details are as follows.

Motivated by the analyses mentioned above, in this work, we propose a fault matching strategy for simultaneous-fault diagnosis based on a revised DTRS named fuzzy neighborhood ζ-decision-theoretic rough set model (FNζDTRS). Since there is a coupling relationship of fault characteristics between a single-fault and its associated simultaneous-fault, this paper proposes the fault matching strategy based on this principle. The main idea of the proposed strategy is that when an unknown simultaneous-fault occurs, its fault attributes are first selected by the FNζDTRS and then classified according to the correlation between the obtained fault attributes and the fault attributes of each single-fault selected by the FNζDTRS model beforehand. Therefore, the main novelties and contributions of this study can be listed as follows.

(1) A novel and concise data-driven loss function matrix is designed for DTRS.
(2) A fuzzy neighborhood ζ-decision-theoretic rough set model is proposed with the help of the fuzzy neighborhood relationship and the proposed loss function matrix, which can deal with hybrid data common in engineering.
(3) The proposed FNζDTRS model, used for attribute reduction, has a significant advantage in classification accuracy compared with other existing rough sets. This proves that it is more suitable for real fault diagnosis.
(4) A diagnosis strategy of simultaneous-fault is put forward based on a coupling mapping relationship between single-fault and its associated simultaneous-fault. This ensures that our strategy can handle both single-fault and simultaneous-fault.
(5) The proposed strategy is successfully applied to the simultaneous-fault diagnosis of the satellite power system and only requires single-fault samples in the training phase, which is highly feasible for practical applications.

The remainder of this paper starts with some preliminaries and related work, then puts forward the presentation of the FNζDTRS model in Section 2 and presents the basic framework of simultaneous-fault diagnosis in Section 3. The effectiveness and superiority of the FNζDTRS model is verified through some numerical experiments in Section 4, and further demonstrated by a comparative analysis with several baseline algorithms for simultaneous-fault diagnosis in Section 5. The paper closes with main conclusions in Section 6.

2. Preliminaries and Related Work

This subsection will review some notions about rough sets that are relevant to the development of our theory.

Definition 1. *(Decision system) A binary group: $DS = (U, C \cup D)$ can describe a decision system. Among them, $U = \{x_1, x_2, \cdots, x_m\}$ is called the universe, which is a finite and nonempty set. D is the set of decision attributes which is a nonempty set. C is the collection of conditional attributes, $C \cap D = \varnothing$, $D \neq \varnothing$ 31. Therefore, the relationship between each element in a decision system can be represented as shown in Figure 1. To better understand the above definition, we describe the above-mentioned elements in combination with the fault diagnosis problem. C represents the parameters output by the sensor or the extracted feature attributes, D represents the category of the failure mode, and U denotes the collected data.*

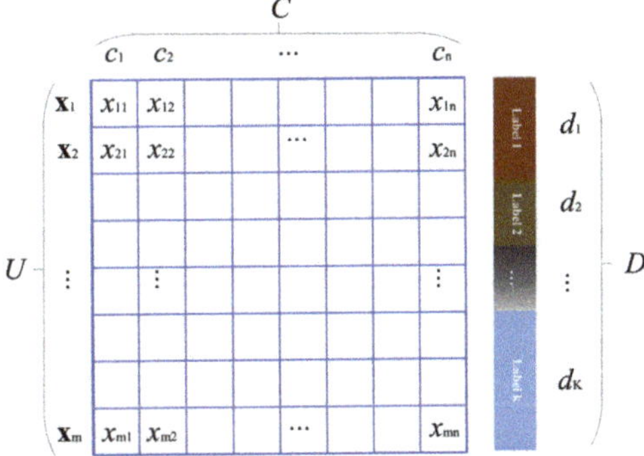

Figure 1. The illustration of a decision system.

The decision-theoretic rough set (DTRS) presented by Yao et al. [33]. provides a concise semantic interpretation through a loss function matrix. The loss function matrix is described in Table 1.

Table 1. The detailed information of a loss function matrix.

	Q	Q^c
a_P	λ_{PP}	λ_{PN}
a_B	λ_{BP}	λ_{BN}
a_N	λ_{NP}	λ_{NN}

Consider that X is the subset of samples with the same label d_k. The state Q suggests that a related sample defined as x is in X, and the state Q^c suggests that x is not in X. The set of actions a_P, a_B, and a_N indicate the classification of x into three regions, which are $x \in POS(X)$, $x \in BND(X)$, $x \in NEG(X)$. $POS(X)$ denotes the acceptance of the event $x \in X$. $BND(X)$ denotes the deferment of the event $x \in X$, also considers $BND(X)$ denotes the non-commitment of the event $x \in X$. $NEG(X)$ denotes the rejection of $x \in X$. Furthermore, $\lambda_{\bullet P}$ denotes the loss caused by taking actions (a_P, a_B, a_N) while $x \in X$. $\lambda_{\bullet N}$ is the loss caused by taking actions (a_P, a_B, a_N) while $x \notin X$.

Consider this scenario: the risk of delaying the execution of the correct action is increased compared to that of the correct action, and both are less than the loss of taking the wrong action, the DTRS model therefore made a reasonable assumption: $0 \leq \lambda_{PP} \leq \lambda_{BP} < \lambda_{NP}$ and $0 \leq \lambda_{NN} \leq \lambda_{BN} < \lambda_{PN}$, which is the basis for generating this rough set model.

Thanks to the above assumption, a pair of threshold parameters is used to define the positive region $POS(X)$, the boundary region $BND(X)$ and the negative region $NEG(X)$ to construct the DTRS model, which is guided by the Bayesian risk minimization principle and the three-way decision theory. Thus, we have the form of a DTRS model as follows 31:

$$POS_{(\alpha,\beta)}(X) = \{x \in U | P(X|[x]) \geq \alpha\}, \tag{1}$$

$$BND_{(\alpha,\beta)}(X) = \{x \in U | \beta < P(X[x]) < \alpha\}, \tag{2}$$

$$NEG_{(\alpha,\beta)}(X) = \{x \in U | P(X|[x]) \leq \beta\}. \tag{3}$$

The following equations represent the relationship between the two threshold parameters and the six loss functions:

$$\alpha = \frac{(\lambda_{PN} - \lambda_{BN})}{(\lambda_{PN} - \lambda_{BN}) + (\lambda_{BP} - \lambda_{PP})}, \tag{4}$$

$$\beta = \frac{(\lambda_{BN} - \lambda_{NN})}{(\lambda_{BN} - \lambda_{NN}) + (\lambda_{NP} - \lambda_{BP})}. \tag{5}$$

The key parts of the DTRS model are the loss function or threshold parameter (α, β). To study and employ the DTRS model, an important issue is how to determine these parameters. Inspired by the idea of being data-driven, our previous work proposed a single-parameter decision-theoretic rough set (SPDTRS) model [32] that simplifies the traditional DTRS model. Specifically, the model requires only one parameter to be preset rather than the pair of (α, β) or the six parameters in the loss function matrix. However, the solution of employing two truncation functions utilized in the model calculation makes the model relatively complex. Moreover, the interpretability of the loss function matrix in the SPDTRS model is slightly insufficient. The above two disadvantages are the focus of this paper in proposing a new rough set model.

3. Fuzzy Neighborhood ζ-Decision-Theoretic Rough Set

3.1. Granular Computing Based on Fuzzy Neighborhood Relationship

In order to be more applicable to practical problems, rough set models need to be able to handle a hybrid dataset, including continuous and discrete data. Fuzzy relationship and neighborhood relationship are two effective means to deal with the spatial relationship of samples. Their combined form is used by a variety of models [34]. The fuzzy neighborhood relationship can analyze the relationship between the entities in the decision system more precisely. Therefore, to overcome the inability of the SPDTRS model to handle the hybrid dataset, we introduce this fuzzy neighborhood relationship.

Definition 2. *(Fuzzy neighborhood relationship) Given a decision system $DS = (U, C \cup D)$, for an arbitrary sample $x \in U$, the fuzzy neighborhood subset of x* is defined as:

$$[x]^{\delta} = \{y \in U | r(x,y) \geq \delta\}, \tag{6}$$

where δ is fuzzy neighborhood radius. The range of δ is $0 \leq \delta \leq 1$. If x and y are continuous data, we have $r(x,y) = 1 - \frac{1}{n}\sqrt{\left(\sum_{i=1}^{n}(x_i - y_i)^2\right)}$. While the two elements x and y are discrete data, we have

$$r(x,y) = \begin{cases} 1, \text{ if } x_i = y_i \\ 0, \text{ if } x_i \neq y_i \end{cases}, \tag{7}$$

Thus, the fuzzy neighborhood subset is also called equivalence class. On this basis, the fuzzy conditional probability of x could be described as:

$$\widetilde{P}\left(X|[x]^{\delta}\right) = \frac{\sum\left\{r(x,y)|y \in \left(X \cap [x]^{\delta}\right)\right\}}{\sum\left\{r(x,z)|z \in [x]^{\delta}\right\}}, \tag{8}$$

where X is the subset of samples with the same label d_k. Under the assumption of the fuzzy neighborhood subset $[x]^{\delta} \cap X \neq \varnothing$, we have $0 < \widetilde{P}\left(X|[x]^{\delta}\right) \leq 1$, while $\widetilde{P}\left(X|[x]^{\delta}\right) = 1$ if and only if $[x]^{\delta} \subseteq X$. $\sum\{\}$ represents the sum of all elements in its set.

3.2. Determination of the Two Threshold Parameters

Considering the disadvantage of the SPDTRS model, a new loss function matrix is proposed, which is under fuzzy neighborhood relationship by a concise loss function relationship to avoid introducing the truncation functions. The novel SPDTRS model avoids the discussion of multiple situations and reduces the computational complexity of the SPDTRS model.

In the new loss function matrix, the data-driven loss functions under fuzzy neighborhood relationship is shown in Table 2. Besides, $\widetilde{P}\left(X|[x]^{\delta}\right)$ is the fuzzy neighborhood conditional probability, which can be calculated by Equation (8). The compensation coefficient is ζ with $0 \leq \zeta < 1$. $\widetilde{S}\left(X|[x]^{\delta}\right)$ and $\widetilde{S^c}\left(X|[x]^{\delta}\right)$ are the significance coefficients, which can be described as follows:

$$\widetilde{S}\left(X|[x]^{\delta}\right) = \frac{\sum\left\{\widetilde{P}\left(X|[y]^{\delta}\right)|y \in \left(X \cap [x]^{\delta}\right)\right\}}{\sum\left\{\widetilde{P}\left(X|[z]^{\delta}\right)|z \in X\right\}}, \tag{9}$$

$$\widetilde{S^c}\left(X|[x]^{\delta}\right) = \frac{\sum\left\{\widetilde{P}\left(X^c|[y]^{\delta}\right)|y \in \left(X^c \cap [x]^{\delta}\right)\right\}}{\sum\left\{\widetilde{P}\left(X|[z]^{\delta}\right)|z \in X\right\}}. \tag{10}$$

where $\sum\{\}$ represents the sum of all elements in its set.

Under the assumption of the equivalence class $[x]^\delta \cap X \neq \varnothing$, the relationships $\widetilde{S}\left(X|[x]^\delta\right) > 0$ and $\widetilde{S}^c\left(X|[x]^\delta\right) \geq 0$ hold, and $\widetilde{S}^c\left(X|[x]^\delta\right) = 0$ if and only if $[x]^\delta \subseteq X$.

Table 2. The fuzzy neighborhood data-driven loss function matrix.

	Q	Q^c
a_p	$\lambda_{PP} = 0$	$\lambda_{PN} = \widetilde{S}^c\left(X\|[x]^\delta\right)$
a_B	$\lambda_{BP} = \widetilde{S}\left(X\|[x]^\delta\right)\widetilde{P}\left(X\|[x]^\delta\right)\zeta$	$\lambda_{BN} = \widetilde{S}^c\left(X\|[x]^\delta\right)\left(1 - \widetilde{P}\left(X\|[x]^\delta\right)\right)\zeta$
a_N	$\lambda_{NP} = \widetilde{S}\left(X\|[x]^\delta\right)$	$\lambda_{NN} = 0$

Subsequently, we can conclude the pair of threshold parameters according to the fuzzy neighborhood data-driven loss function matrix, which can be represented as follows. In addition, we rewrite $\widetilde{S}\left(X|[x]^\delta\right) = S, \widetilde{S}^c\left(X|[x]^\delta\right) = S^c, \widetilde{P}\left(X|[x]^\delta\right) = P$ for the sake of convenience.

$$\begin{aligned} \alpha^{fn} &= \frac{(\lambda_{PN}-\lambda_{BN})}{(\lambda_{PN}-\lambda_{BN})+(\lambda_{BP}-\lambda_{PP})} \\ &= \frac{\left(S^C-S^C(1-P)\zeta\right)}{\left(S^C-S^C(1-P)\zeta\right)+(SP\zeta-0)}, \\ &= \frac{S^C(1-\zeta+P\zeta)}{S^C(1-\zeta+P\zeta)+SP\zeta} \end{aligned} \tag{11}$$

$$\begin{aligned} \beta^{fn} &= \frac{(\lambda_{BN}-\lambda_{NN})}{(\lambda_{BN}-\lambda_{NN})+(\lambda_{NP}-\lambda_{BP})} \\ &= \frac{\left(S^C(1-P)\zeta-0\right)}{\left(S^C(1-P)\zeta-0\right)+(S-SP\zeta)}. \\ &= \frac{S^C(1-P)\zeta}{S^C(1-P)\zeta+S(1-P\zeta)} \end{aligned} \tag{12}$$

Subsequently, we can set up three-way decision rules as follows:
Rule (P): Decide $x \in POS(X)$ while $\widetilde{P}\left(X|[x]^\delta\right) \geq \alpha^{fn}$;
Rule (B): Decide $x \in BND(X)$ while $\beta^{fn} < \widetilde{P}\left(X|[x]^\delta\right) < \alpha^{fn}$;
Rule (N): Decide $x \in NEG(X)$ while $\widetilde{P}\left(X|[x]^\delta\right) \leq \beta^{fn}$.

According to the decision rules, the following roots about α^{fn} and β^{fn} can be described in the following two cases.

Case 1: $0 < \zeta < 1$

From the rule (P), we can obtain

$$P \leq \frac{(2\zeta S^C - S^C) - \sqrt{S^C(-4\zeta^2 S + 4\zeta S + S^C)}}{2\zeta(S + S^C)},$$

$$P \geq \frac{(2\zeta S^C - S^C) + \sqrt{S^C(-4\zeta^2 S + 4\zeta S + S^C)}}{2\zeta(S + S^C)}. \tag{13}$$

From the rule (N), we can obtain

$$P \leq \frac{(2\zeta S^C + S) - \sqrt{S(-4\zeta^2 S^C + 4\zeta S^C + S)}}{2\zeta(S + S^C)},$$

$$P \geq \frac{(2\zeta S^C + S) + \sqrt{S(-4\zeta^2 S^C + 4\zeta S^C + S)}}{2\zeta(S + S^C)}. \tag{14}$$

From these results, we can only accept two roots because of the relationship $0 < P \leq 1$. Thus, we can rewrite these two roots:

$$\alpha_1^{fn} = \frac{(2\zeta S^C - S^C) + \sqrt{S^C(-4\zeta^2 S + 4\zeta S + S^C)}}{2\zeta(S + S^C)}, \tag{15}$$

$$\beta_1^{fn} = \frac{(2\zeta S^C + S) - \sqrt{S(-4\zeta^2 S^C + 4\zeta S^C + S)}}{2\zeta(S + S^C)}. \tag{16}$$

Case 2: $\zeta = 0$

The values of these two parameters are as follows:

$$\alpha_2^{fn} = 1, \tag{17}$$

$$\beta_2^{fn} = 0. \tag{18}$$

The model arising from this case corresponds to the Pawlak model. Both boundary loss functions are equal to 0. Therefore the model clearly exhibits a two-way decision-making characteristic. Thus, the Pawlak model is one of the specific examples of our model, and $\zeta = 0$ is a necessary non-sufficient condition for it.

Theorem 1. *For the fuzzy neighborhood data-driven loss function matrix, assuming the equivalence class $[x]^\delta \cap X \neq \varnothing$, when $[x]^\delta \not\subseteq X$ holds, namely, the concerned equivalence class is not a consistent class, then we have:*
(a_1) $\lambda_{PP} \leq \lambda_{BP} < \lambda_{NP}$,
(a_2) $\lambda_{NN} \leq \lambda_{BN} < \lambda_{PN}$.
When $[x]^\delta \subseteq X$ holds, i.e., the concerned equivalence class is a consistent class, then we have:
(b_1) $\lambda_{PP} \leq \lambda_{BP} < \lambda_{NP}$
(b_2) $\lambda_{NN} = \lambda_{BN} = \lambda_{PN} = 0$

Proof.
(a_1) If $[x]^\delta \not\subseteq X$, then $\widetilde{S}\left(X|[x]^\delta\right) > 0$, $0 < \widetilde{P}\left(X|[x]^\delta\right) < 1$. Since $0 \leq \zeta < 1$, $\lambda_{BP} = \widetilde{S}\left(X|[x]^\delta\right)\widetilde{P}\left(X|[x]^\delta\right)\zeta$, then $0 \leq \lambda_{BP} < \widetilde{S}\left(X|[x]^\delta\right)$. Due to $\lambda_{PP} = 0$ and $\lambda_{NP} = \widetilde{S}\left(X|[x]^\delta\right)$, hence $\lambda_{PP} \leq \lambda_{BP} < \lambda_{NP}$.

(a_2) If $[x]^\delta \not\subseteq X$, then $\widetilde{S^c}\left(X|[x]^\delta\right) > 0$, $0 < \widetilde{P}\left(X|[x]^\delta\right) < 1$. Since $0 \leq \zeta < 1$, $\lambda_{BN} = \widetilde{S^c}\left(X|[x]^\delta\right)\left(1 - \widetilde{P}\left(X|[x]^\delta\right)\right)\zeta$, then $0 \leq \lambda_{BN} < \widetilde{S^c}\left(X|[x]^\delta\right)$. Due to $\lambda_{NN} = 0$ and $\lambda_{PN} = \widetilde{S^c}\left(X|[x]^\delta\right)$, hence $\lambda_{NN} \leq \lambda_{BN} < \lambda_{PN}$.

(b_1) If $[x]^\delta \subseteq X$, then $\widetilde{S}\left(X|[x]^\delta\right) > 0$, $\widetilde{P}\left(X|[x]^\delta\right) = 1$. Since $0 \leq \zeta < 1$, $\lambda_{BP} = \widetilde{S}\left(X|[x]^\delta\right)\widetilde{P}\left(X|[x]^\delta\right)\zeta$, then $0 \leq \lambda_{BP} < \widetilde{S}\left(X|[x]^\delta\right)$. Due to $\lambda_{PP} = 0$ and $\lambda_{NP} = \widetilde{S}\left(X|[x]^\delta\right)$, hence $\lambda_{PP} \leq \lambda_{BP} < \lambda_{NP}$.

(b_2) If $[x]^\delta \subseteq X$, then $\widetilde{S^c}\left(X|[x]^\delta\right) = 0$, and $\widetilde{P}\left(X|[x]^\delta\right) = 1$. Since $0 \leq \zeta < 1$, $\lambda_{BN} = \widetilde{S^c}\left(X|[x]^\delta\right)\left(1 - \widetilde{P}\left(X|[x]^\delta\right)\right)\zeta$, then $\lambda_{BN} = 0$. Due to $\lambda_{NN} = 0$ and $\lambda_{PN} = \widetilde{S^c}\left(X|[x]^\delta\right)$, hence $\lambda_{NN} = \lambda_{BN} = \lambda_{PN} = 0$. QED. □

3.3. Establishment of FNζDTRS

Reasoning by Section 3.2, the expressions of these two threshold functions lead to the following results:$\alpha^{fn} = f(S, S^c, \zeta)$ and $\beta^{fn} = f(S, S^c, \zeta)$ under the above two conditions, where $\alpha^{fn} = \left\{\alpha_1^{fn}, \alpha_2^{fn}\right\}$ and $\beta^{fn} = \left\{\beta_1^{fn}, \beta_2^{fn}\right\}$. Based on Equations (9) and (10), it is easily to obtain S and S^c by confirming the parameter δ and analyzing the distribution information of the original data. In summary, we can change these two threshold parameters to $\alpha^{fn} = f(\delta,\zeta)$, $\beta^{fn} = f(\delta,\zeta)$. The rough set model below, which is including parameters δ and ζ is defined as fuzzy neighborhood ζ-decision-theoretic rough set (FNζDTRS):

$$\widetilde{POS} = \left\{x \in U | \widetilde{P}\left(X|[x]^{\delta}\right) \geq \alpha^{fn}\right\}, \tag{19}$$

$$\widetilde{BND} = \left\{x \in U | \beta^{fn} < \widetilde{P}\left(X|[x]^{\delta}\right) < \alpha^{fn}\right\}, \tag{20}$$

$$\widetilde{NEG} = \left\{x \in U | \widetilde{P}\left(X|[x]^{\delta}\right) \leq \beta^{fn}\right\}, \tag{21}$$

where both threshold parameters have different descriptions under the following two conditions:

Case 1: $0 < \zeta < 1$, then

$$\alpha_1^{fn} = \frac{(2\zeta S^C - S^C) + \sqrt{S^C(-4\zeta^2 S + 4\zeta S + S^C)}}{2\zeta(S + S^C)}, \tag{22}$$

$$\beta_1^{fn} = \frac{(2\zeta S^C + S) - \sqrt{S(-4\zeta^2 S^C + 4\zeta S^C + S)}}{2\zeta(S + S^C)}. \tag{23}$$

Case 2: $\zeta = 0$, then

$$\alpha_2^{fn} = 1, \tag{24}$$

$$\beta_2^{fn} = 0. \tag{25}$$

In the above FNζDTRS model, there are only two cases to discuss, in contrast to the SPDTRS model that requires four cases to discuss, which greatly reduces the computational complexity of the SPDTRS model due to the concise setting of loss functions.

Theorem 2. *In the FNζDTRS model, given two compensation coefficients ζ_1 and ζ_2 with $0 \leq \zeta_1 < 1$ and $0 \leq \zeta_2 < 1$, and the parameter δ is fixed, if there exists $\zeta_1 \geq \zeta_2$, then $\alpha^{fn}(\zeta_1) \leq \alpha^{fn}(\zeta_2)$ and $\beta^{fn}(\zeta_1) \geq \beta^{fn}(\zeta_2)$ hold.*

Proof. If the equivalence class $[x]^{\delta} \subseteq X$, then $S^C = 0$, according to Equations (22)–(25), when $0 < \zeta < 1$, $\alpha^{fn}(\zeta_1) = \alpha^{fn}(\zeta_2) = 0$, $\beta^{fn}(\zeta_1) = \beta^{fn}(\zeta_2) = 0$, when $\zeta = 0$, $\alpha^{fn}(\zeta_1) = \alpha^{fn}(\zeta_2) = 1$, $\beta^{fn}(\zeta_1) = \beta^{fn}(\zeta_2) = 0$. If the equivalence class $[x]^{\delta} \nsubseteq X$, then its monotonicity relations will be proved by the following derivations.

Part I: For $\zeta_1 \geq \zeta_2 \Rightarrow \alpha^{fn}(\zeta_1) \leq \alpha^{fn}(\zeta_2)$, two cases need to be considered.

Case 1: $0 < \zeta < 1$

Since $\alpha_1^{fn} = \frac{(2\zeta S^C - S^C) + \sqrt{S^C(-4\zeta^2 S + 4\zeta S + S^C)}}{2\zeta(S + S^C)}$, we set $\eta = 1/\zeta$, due to $0 < \zeta < 1$, then $\eta > 1$ and $\alpha_1^{fn} = \frac{(2S^C - \eta S^C) + \sqrt{\eta^2 (S^C)^2 + 4\eta S S^C - 4 S S^C}}{2(S + S^C)}$. Due to $S > 0$, $S^C > 0$, we can set $\overline{\alpha}_1^{fn} = (2S^C - \eta S^C) + \sqrt{\eta^2 (S^C)^2 + 4\eta S S^C - 4 S S^C}$ for simplicity of derivation. We can find the partial derivative of it, denoted as f_{α}^1, which is

$$f_{\alpha}^1 = \frac{\partial \overline{\alpha}_1^{fn}}{\partial \eta} = -S^C + \frac{\eta (S^C)^2 + 2 S S^C}{\sqrt{\eta^2 (S^C)^2 + 4\eta S S^C - 4 S S^C}}.$$

Its second-order partial derivative is denoted as f_{α}^{2}:

$$f_{\alpha}^{2} = \frac{\partial^2 \overline{\alpha}_1^{fn}}{\partial^2 \eta} = \frac{-4S(S^C)^2(S+S^C)}{\left(\eta^2(S^C)^2 + 4\eta S S^C - 4S S^C\right)^{3/2}} < 0.$$

Because f_{α}^{2} is less than 0, f_{α}^{1} is monotonically decreasing. Since $\eta > 1$, $f_{\alpha}^{1} \to 2S > 0(1 \leftarrow \eta)$, $f_{\alpha}^{1} \to 0(\eta \to +\infty)$, then $f_{\alpha}^{1} > 0$. Therefore, α_1^{fn} grows monotonically with respect to η. Hence, α_1^{fn} decreases monotonically with respect to ζ, that is $\zeta_1 \geq \zeta_2 \Rightarrow \alpha_1^{fn}(\zeta_1) \leq \alpha_1^{fn}(\zeta_2)$.
Case 2: $\zeta = 0$

In this case, we have $\alpha_2^{fn} = 1$. Thus, for $\zeta_1 \geq \zeta_2$, we have $\alpha_2^{fn}(\zeta_1) = \alpha_2^{fn}(\zeta_2)$.

Part II: For $\zeta_1 \geq \zeta_2 \Rightarrow \beta^{fn}(\zeta_1) \geq \beta^{fn}(\zeta_2)$, two cases need to be considered as well.

Case 1: $0 < \zeta < 1$

Since $\beta_1^{fn} = \frac{(2\zeta S^C + S) - \sqrt{S(-4\zeta^2 S^C + 4\zeta S^C + S)}}{2\zeta(S+S^C)}$, we also set $\eta = 1/\zeta$, due to $0 < \zeta < 1$, then $\eta > 1$ and $\beta_1^{fn} = \frac{(2S^C + \eta S) - \sqrt{\eta^2 S^2 + 4\eta S S^C - 4S S^C}}{2(S+S^C)}$. Due to $S > 0$, $S^C > 0$, we have the simple form $\beta_1^{fn} = (2S^C + \eta S) - \sqrt{\eta^2 S^2 + 4\eta S S^C - 4S S^C}$. We describe partial derivatives of β_1^{fn} like:

$$f_{\beta}^{1} = \frac{\partial \overline{\beta}_1^{fn}}{\partial \eta} = S - \frac{\eta S^2 + 2S S^C}{\sqrt{\eta^2 S^2 + 4\eta S S^C - 4S S^C}},$$

$$f_{\beta}^{2} = \frac{\partial^2 \overline{\beta}_1^{fn}}{\partial^2 \eta} = \frac{4S^2 S^C(S+S^C)}{(\eta^2 S^2 + 4\eta S S^C - 4S S^C)^{3/2}} > 0.$$

From $f_{\beta}^{2} > 0$, we know that f_{β}^{1} increases monotonously along with η. Since $\eta > 1$, $f_{\beta}^{1} \to -2S^C < 0(1 \leftarrow \eta)$, $f_{\beta}^{1} \to 0(\eta \to +\infty)$, then $f_{\alpha}^{1} < 0$, and β_1^{fn} is monotonously decreasing with regard to η. Therefore, β_1^{fn} is monotonously increasing with ζ, that is $\zeta_1 \geq \zeta_2 \Rightarrow \beta_1^{fn}(\zeta_1) \geq \beta_1^{fn}(\zeta_2)$. QED. □

Theorem 3. *In the FNζDTRS model, the relationship* $0 \leq \beta^{fn} \leq \alpha^{fn} \leq 1$ *holds.*

Proof. If the equivalence class $[x]^{\delta} \subseteq X$, then $S^C = 0$, according to Equations (22)–(25), when $0 < \zeta < 1$, $\alpha^{fn} = \beta^{fn} = 0$, when $\zeta = 0$, $\alpha^{fn} = 0$, $\beta^{fn} = 1$, satisfying the inequality $0 \leq \beta^{fn} \leq \alpha^{fn} \leq 1$. If the equivalence class $[x]^{\delta} \nsubseteq X$, then in following three parts we intend to prove the inequality.

Part I: Proof of $0 \leq \beta^{fn}$ under two cases.

Case 1: $0 < \zeta < 1$

According to Equation (23), we could get $\beta_1^{fn} = \frac{(2\zeta S^C + S) - \psi}{2\zeta(S+S^C)}$, $\psi = \sqrt{(S + 2\zeta S^C)^2 - 4\zeta^2 S^C(S+S^C)}$, and then we only need to prove $4\zeta^2 S^C(S+S^C) > 0$. Since $S > 0$, $S^C > 0$, then $4\zeta^2 S^C(S+S^C) > 0$, so $\beta_1^{fn} > 0$.

Case 2: $\zeta = 0$

In this case, we have $\beta_2^{fn} = 0$.

Part II: Proof of the inequality $\beta^{fn} \leq \alpha^{fn}$ in two cases.

Case 1: $0 < \zeta < 1$

According to Equations (22) and (23), we could get

$$\alpha_1^{fn} - \beta_1^{fn} = \frac{-S^C - S + \sqrt{S^C(-4\zeta^2 S + 4\zeta S + S^C)} + \sqrt{S(-4\zeta^2 S^C + 4\zeta S^C + S)}}{2\zeta(S + S^C)}.$$

Since $S > 0$, $S^C \geq 0$, then

$$\sqrt{S^C(-4\zeta^2 S + 4\zeta S + S^C)} = \sqrt{4\zeta S S^C(1-\zeta) + (S^C)^2} > \sqrt{(S^C)^2} = S^C,$$
$$\sqrt{S(-4\zeta^2 S^C + 4\zeta S^C + S)} = \sqrt{4\zeta S S^C(1-\zeta) + S^2} > \sqrt{S^2} = S,$$

so $\alpha_1^{fn} - \beta_1^{fn} > 0$, that is $\beta_1^{fn} < \alpha_1^{fn}$.

Case 2: $\zeta = 0$

In this case, we have $\alpha_2^{fn} = 1$, $\beta_2^{fn} = 0$, so $\beta_2^{fn} < \alpha_2^{fn}$.

Part III: Proof of the inequality $\alpha^{fn} \leq 1$ in two cases.

Case 1: $0 < \zeta < 1$

According to Equation (22), if we want to prove $\alpha_1^{fn} \leq 1$, then we need to prove $\sqrt{S^C(-4\zeta^2 S + 4\zeta S + S^C)} - (2\zeta S + S^C) < 0$, which means we need to prove $S^C(-4\zeta^2 S + 4\zeta S + S^C) - (2\zeta S + S^C)^2 < 0$. Since $S > 0$, $S^C \geq 0$, then

$$S^C\left(-4\zeta^2 S + 4\zeta S + S^C\right) - (2\zeta S + S^C)^2 = -4\zeta^2 S S^C - 4\zeta^2 S^2 = -4\zeta^2 S\left(S^C + S\right) < 0.$$

Therefore, we have $\alpha_1^{fn} < 1$.

Case 2: $\zeta = 0$

In this case, we have $\alpha_2^{fn} = 1$. QED. □

Theorem 4. *For a decision system, which is described as $DS = (U, C \cup D)$ with a fixed parameter δ, and two parameters ζ_1 and ζ_2 with $0 \leq \zeta_1 \leq \zeta_2 < 1$, we have $\widetilde{POS}_1 \subseteq \widetilde{POS}_2$, $\widetilde{NEG}_1 \subseteq \widetilde{NEG}_2$, $\widetilde{BND}_1 \supseteq \widetilde{BND}_2$.*

Proof. At the very beginning of the proof, we assume an arbitrary sample y to facilitate the proof of the theorem. While $y \in \widetilde{POS}_1$, we have $P(X|[y]) \geq \alpha^{fn}(\zeta_1)$. Since $0 \leq \zeta_1 \leq \zeta_2 < 1$, the relation $\alpha^{fn}(\zeta_1) \geq \alpha^{fn}(\zeta_2)$ holds according to Theorem 2. Thus, $P(X|[y]) \geq \alpha^{fn}(\zeta_2)$ and $y \in \widetilde{POS}_2$ hold. Hence, we conclude that $\widetilde{POS}_1 \subseteq \widetilde{POS}_2$.

Likewise, to conclude that $\widetilde{NEG}_1 \subseteq \widetilde{NEG}_2$ and $\widetilde{BND}_1 \supseteq \widetilde{BND}_2$ is easy via Theorem 2. From the above, we can find that ζ is inversely correlated with the range of neutrality and positively correlated with the uncertainty of the decision. QED. □

3.4. FNζDTRS-Based Attribute Reduction Algorithm

Jia et al. [35] presented a reduction principle in response to the problem of attribute reduction by using the DTRS model. The core idea of it is minimizing the risk of the reduction subset. On this principle, our previous work has designed an attribute reduction algorithm based on the SPDTRS model [32,34]. It is built on minimizing the risk of overall decisions, which can be utilized for the attribute reduction in our proposed FNζDTRS model. Therefore, the detailed attribute reduction algorithm is not repeated in this paper. For details, the readers could refer to our previous work [32,34].

4. Strategy of Simultaneous-Fault Diagnosis

Under the assumption that the data in all single-fault modes are fully available, when an unknown fault occurs, we use the FNζDTRS model to mine the fault attributes of the unknown fault. If the fault attributes of the unknown fault are different from the fault attributes of the existing single-fault, then the unknown fault can be considered as a simultaneous-fault. Furthermore, we can use the attribute reduction results obtained from the FNζDTRS model to analyze and identify the corresponding fault modes of the simultaneous-fault. Finally, a strategy of simultaneous-fault diagnosis called fault matching strategy is formed, as shown in Figure 2.

The proposed fault matching strategy consists of two main parts, prior knowledge acquisition and rule matching. In the first part, the single-fault data with abnormal labels and normal data with normal labels are sent into the FNζDTRS model as the training data set, and the optimal fault attribute subsets of each single-fault are obtained by attribute reduction, used as the prior knowledge for subsequent diagnosis. In the second part, the simultaneous-fault data with abnormal labels and normal data with normal labels are combined to form the data to be diagnosed, and then the data are fed into the FNζDTRS model to obtain the optimal fault attribute subset. The optimal fault attribute subset is then obtained here and the optimal fault attribute subsets obtained in the first part are measured by using the Jaccard similarity coeffective. It is worth noting that there may be some single faults with the same fault attributes, therefore we set some rules based on the differences between attribute data to subdivide the faults and complete the fault matching, which can be seen in the subsequent experiments based on the satellite power system.

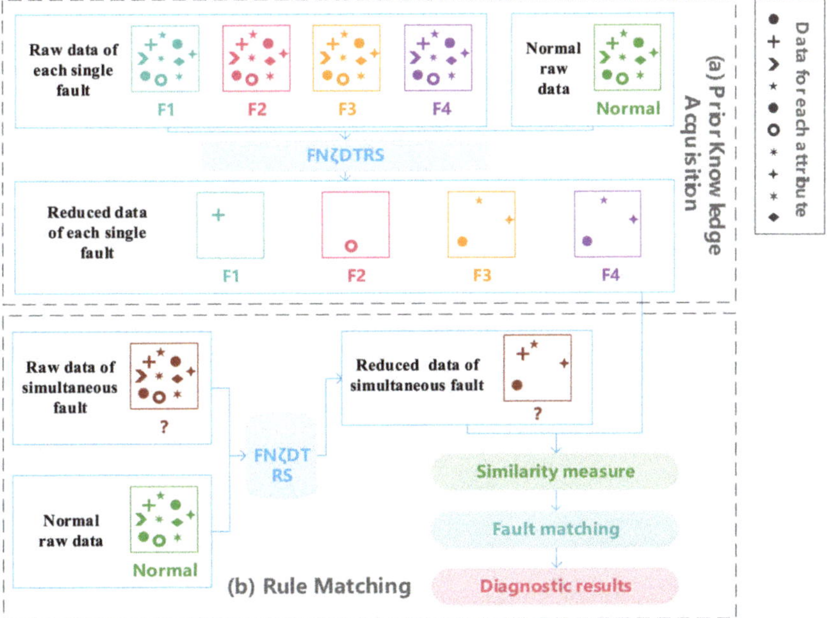

Figure 2. The procedure of fault diagnosis strategy for simultaneous-fault.

Based on the above description, we can write the core pseudo code in the above process, as shown in Table 3.

Table 3. The core pseudo code of the diagnosis strategy.

Input:	Raw data of each single fault and normal state
Output:	Fault mode

Part I	**Prior Knowledge Acquisition**
	For each DS regarding to single fault or state
	Initialized: $red = \varnothing$, $Cl = C$, $Rred = H$, //H is a large positive number.
	While $Cl \neq \varnothing$
	For $c \in Cl$
	$a = c \cup red$, //a is a temporary set.
	Compute the risk generated by a.
	End For
	Find such a subset $a = c \cup red$ with the minimum risk, i.e., Ra.
	If $Ra < Rred$
	The subset a is the selected set
	End If
	End While
	End For, return the reduction *red* set of each state.

Part II	**Rule Matching** Utilize the above code to obtain the reduction set r of the given fault data to be diagnosed. For each *red* Compute the similarity between *red* and r. End For Find such a *red* with the maximum similarity, which could be considered as the similar fault mode f. Return f

5. Numerical Experiment of Attribute Reduction

The effectiveness and advantage of the proposed FNζDTRS model is verified on several hybrid decision systems from the UCI (http://archive.ics.uci.edu/ml/index.php, accessed on 21 July 2021) and KEEL (https://sci2s.ugr.es/keel/datasets.php, accessed on 21 July 2021) datasets. As shown in Table 4, the test datasets include both discrete and continuous data. Specific comparative experiments regarding parameters test and attribute reduction are conducted on the same hard and soft platforms. Ten baseline classifiers, including NaiveBayes, REPTree, LogitBoost, SMO, Filtered, Bagging, PART, IBk, J48 and JRip, are employed with a 10-fold cross-validation in Weka (https://waikato.github.io/weka-wiki/downloading_weka/, accessed on 21 July 2021) software to demonstrate the accuracy of attribute selection. The input data are normalized into the range of [0, 1] during preprocessing.

Table 4. The information of the employed datasets.

ID	Full Name	Name	Samples	Attribute	Discrete	Continuous	Class	Source
1	Mutagenesis-Atoms	Atoms	1618	10	8	2	2	KEEL
2	Australian Credit Approval	Australian	690	14	8	6	2	UCI
3	Breast Cancer	Breast	277	9	6	3	2	UCI
4	Heart Disease Cleveland	Cleve	296	13	7	6	2	UCI
5	Statlog Heart	Heart	270	13	6	7	2	UCI
6	Iris	Iris	150	4	0	4	3	UCI
7	Website Phishing	Phishing	1353	10	10	0	3	UCI
8	South African Hearth	Saheart	462	9	1	8	2	UCI
9	Seismic-Bumps	Seismic	2584	18	12	6	2	UCI
10	Congressional Voting Records	Vote	435	16	16	0	2	UCI

5.1. Parameters Test for FNζDTRS

For the FNζDTRS model, two parameters ζ and δ need to be set in advance. As described in Section 2, the theoretic value field of ζ is $[0, 1)$, and δ is $[0, 1]$. Therefore, ζ is sampled with an interval of 0.05, and end at 0.99. δ is also sampled with an interval of 0.05, but end at 1. Figure 3 shows the experimental results.

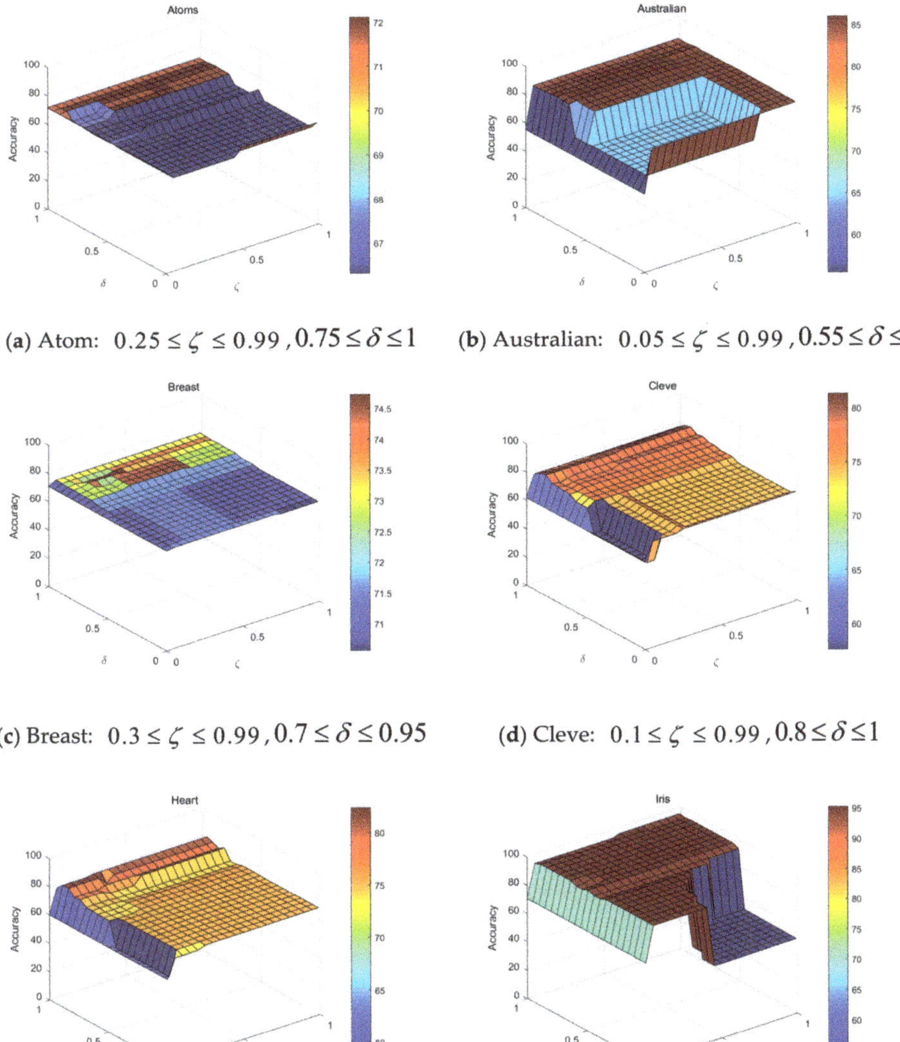

(e) Heart: $0.3 \le \zeta \le 0.99, 0.8 \le \delta \le 1$ (f) Iris: $0.05 \le \zeta \le 0.99, 0.6 \le \delta \le 1$

Figure 3. *Cont.*

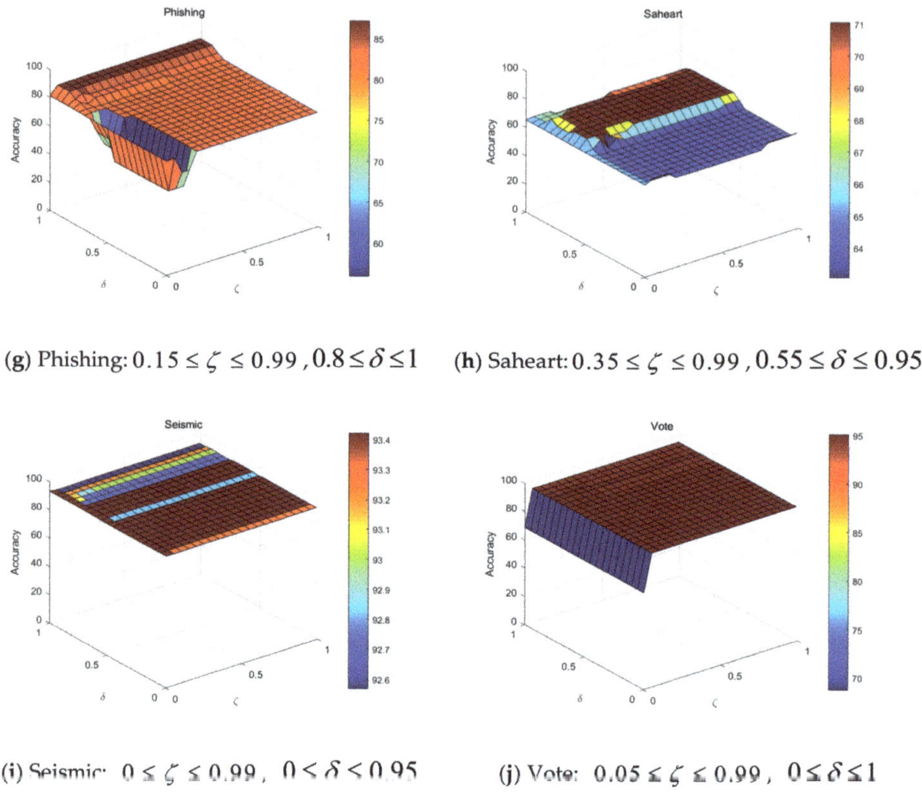

Figure 3. The accuracy results of ζ and δ with respect to FNζDTRS.

The results show that the appropriate settings of ζ and δ range in [0.3, 0.99] and [0.85, 0.95], respectively. It could be explained by the fact that a smaller ζ will result in a larger boundary region, marking more samples as uncertain state. It means setting a smaller ζ for the FNζDTRS decision system will lead to greater uncertainty. When applied in real world, ζ should be adjusted appropriately according to the risk of wrong decision. When the danger of making a bad decision is low, ζ can be set larger, and vice versa. On the other hand, with the fuzzy neighborhood threshold δ closer to 1, the fuzzy neighborhood granules will be finer, allowing for the samples to be classified accurately into the appropriate regions. The above two parameters are the core parameters of the model proposed in this paper, and their setting values directly affect the test results. Therefore, when setting the above parameters, the values of the two parameters need to be adjusted according to the actual needs with the above principles.

5.2. Comparison Experiments on Attribute Reduction

In this part, seven related models, DTRS-EF [36], DTRS-SMDNS [37], SPDTRS-EF [32], SPDTRS-SMDNS [32], NDTRS [38], FDTRS [39] and FN3WD [34], are introduced into a contrastive analysis on the attribute reduction to demonstrate the superiority of the proposed FNζDTRS. The settings of the relevant parameters in these comparison models are the same as those of the corresponding models. The number of reduction attributes and the classification accuracy are the common evaluation indicators of the comparison experiment of attribute reduction [40,41]. The standard deviations of ten trials are also calculated, and the results are shown in Tables 5 and 6.

Table 5. The classification accuracy of the reduction subset.

ID	Name	DTRS-EF	DTRS-SMDNS	SPDTRS-EF	SPDTRS-SMDNS	NDTRS	FDTRS	FN3WD	FNζDTRS
1	Atoms	69.65 ± 2.38	71.08 ± 1.66	70.94 ± 1.20	71.27 ± 1.14	70.42 ± 1.61	70.87 ± 2.07	71.71 ± 1.00	**72.08 ± 1.13**
2	Australian	81.34 ± 5.09	82.39 ± 5.64	82.27 ± 2.87	83.46 ± 0.85	83.31 ± 2.76	72.06 ± 12.31	84.56 ± 0.39	**84.97 ± 0.42**
3	Breast	72.31 ± 1.06	72.53 ± 0.82	72.67 ± 0.70	72.65 ± 0.72	72.72 ± 0.67	70.38 ± 0.75	73.21 ± 0.29	**74.01 ± 0.81**
4	Cleve	79.13 ± 1.09	78.34 ± 5.02	78.99 ± 1.01	79.37 ± 0.61	77.69 ± 6.68	66.64 ± 11.29	80.13 ± 0.78	**81.34 ± 0.37**
5	Heart	78.34 ± 3.38	78.72 ± 5.20	79.99 ± 1.87	79.95 ± 0.88	76.31 ± 7.16	68.37 ± 10.42	80.27 ± 2.25	**80.99 ± 1.23**
6	Iris	94.85 ± 0.50	94.85 ± 0.62	94.93 ± 0.47	94.87 ± 0.55	94.95 ± 0.41	62.96 ± 17.98	94.82 ± 0.40	**95.27 ± 0.33**
7	Phishing	84.23 ± 9.62	86.05 ± 6.11	87.08 ± 1.10	87.08 ± 1.10	86.40 ± 5.08	69.93 ± 14.06	**87.15 ± 1.06**	87.14 ± 1.07
8	Saheart	69.23 ± 0.99	69.01 ± 1.29	69.49 ± 0.38	69.51 ± 0.43	69.35 ± 0.40	67.93 ± 1.99	69.63 ± 1.61	**70.35 ± 1.06**
9	Seismic	92.64 ± 0.80	92.33 ± 0.90	92.53 ± 0.46	91.94 ± 0.69	91.91 ± 0.70	92.01 ± 0.76	92.56 ± 0.48	**93.21 ± 0.15**
10	Vote	94.66 ± 0.38	**94.67 ± 0.38**	94.63 ± 0.36	94.63 ± 0.36	94.65 ± 0.38	83.86 ± 15.36	94.63 ± 0.36	94.65 ± 0.31
	Average	81.64 ± 2.53	82.00 ± 2.76	82.35 ± 1.04	82.47 ± 0.73	81.77 ± 2.59	72.50 ± 8.70	82.87 ± 0.86	**83.40 ± 0.69**

* Bolded indicates that the model achieves the best performance on this dataset.

Table 6. The number of reduction attributes.

ID	Name	DTRS-EF	DTRS-SMDNS	SPDTRS-EF	SPDTRS-SMDNS	NDTRS	FDTRS	FN3WD	FNζDTRS
1	Atoms	5.5 ± 1.8	6.4 ± 1.8	6.8 ± 0.4	7.8 ± 0.4	5.2 ± 1.2	4.5 ± 1.3	**1.2 ± 0.4**	2.0 ± 0.0
2	Australian	11.2 ± 1.9	12.2 ± 3.0	11.3 ± 0.6	13.0 ± 0.1	12.7 ± 1.4	**4.7 ± 2.7**	10.8 ± 0.6	8.4 ± 0.5
3	Breast	7.7 ± 2.7	8.5 ± 2.0	9.0 ± 0.0	9.0 ± 0.1	9.0 ± 0.2	**3.6 ± 1.0**	8.0 ± 0.0	6.9 ± 0.6
4	Cleve	9.8 ± 0.5	12.5 ± 2.4	9.9 ± 0.5	13.0 ± 0.2	10.2 ± 2.6	4.1 ± 2.7	7.1 ± 1.6	**3.0 ± 0.0**
5	Heart	7.1 ± 2.0	12.1 ± 2.6	7.9 ± 0.6	12.7 ± 0.4	10.0 ± 3.0	4.8 ± 3.1	6.8 ± 1.3	**3.0 ± 0.0**
6	Iris	3.8 ± 0.7	3.6 ± 0.8	3.6 ± 0.5	4.0 ± 0.1	4.0 ± 0.0	1.7 ± 1.3	2.6 ± 0.5	**1.0 ± 0.0**
7	Phishing	8.3 ± 2.3	8.8 ± 1.4	9.0 ± 0.0	9.0 ± 0.0	8.8 ± 1.4	**1.1 ± 0.2**	9.0 ± 0.0	9.0 ± 0.0
8	Saheart	8.7 ± 1.6	8.5 ± 1.9	9.0 ± 0.0	9.0 ± 0.0	9.0 ± 0.0	6.4 ± 2.8	4.8 ± 0.4	**2.6 ± 0.3**
9	Seismic	6.6 ± 4.8	10.9 ± 6.3	4.0 ± 0.2	13.4 ± 0.9	13.8 ± 0.5	8.3 ± 0.7	2.0 ± 0.0	**1.0 ± 0.0**
10	Vote	8.5 ± 0.6	8.5 ± 0.6	8.5 ± 0.5	8.5 ± 0.5	8.5 ± 0.8	**1.1 ± 0.3**	8.5 ± 0.5	8.1 ± 0.3
	Average	7.7 ± 1.9	9.2 ± 2.3	7.9 ± 0.3	9.9 ± 0.3	9.1 ± 1.1	**4.0 ± 1.6**	6.1 ± 0.5	4.5 ± 0.2

* Bolded indicates that the model achieves the best performance on this dataset.

According to the results in Tables 4 and 5, the following analysis can be obtained:

(a) The analysis based on the classification accuracy indicates that the FNζDTRS model is superior to other rough set models. The main reason may lie in the different methods to describe spatial granules. Discretization methods such as EF and SMDNS are commonly introduced to process continuous data in the traditional DTRS models, which results in the destruction of the spatial structure of granules. Using special measures (such as fuzzy relationship, neighborhood relationship, etc.) can avoid the distortion of the discretization method, but it also has some disadvantages, such as simple measurement, insufficient description ability, etc. The proposed FNζDTRS model utilizes fuzzy neighborhood relationships to overcome the above shortcomings. Compared with other DTRS models, the description of spatial granules is more precise in our model and results in the higher classification accuracy.

(b) With respect to the number of reduction attributes, the FDTRS model has the least number of reduction attributes, but it fails to achieve a desired classification accuracy, whereas the FNζDTRS model can maintain high classification accuracy while keeping the number of reduction attributes small. The results show that the classification ability can be maintained or improved only when the reduction attributes are accurately selected. The above conclusion also conforms to the basic principle of attribute reduction, that is, in the operation of reduction, we want to get a relatively concise set, which can ensure that the original classification accuracy is not reduced, and the purpose is to improve the operation efficiency.

(c) The standard deviation is used to measure the robustness of models. It is obvious that the standard deviation of the FNζDTRS model is the smallest regardless of the classification accuracy or the number of reduced attributes, which directly proves that the robustness of the FNζDTRS model is the highest compared to other models. The above robustness characteristics also show that we have a large selection range when setting our two parameters, which is conducive to the wide application of the model in practical projects.

6. Simultaneous-Fault Diagnosis of Satellite Power System

In-orbit faults of the power system should be avoided to the maximum extent for satellites. Therefore, simulation is the best platform to mine fault diagnosis knowledge. In this section, the effectiveness of the proposed simultaneous-fault diagnosis scheme is verified with the simulation model of a geosynchronous (GEO) satellite power system [3]. As shown in Figure 4, the power system works in a direct energy transfer mode during the simulation, and ten telemetry parameters can be measured in the marked position. The information of the telemetry parameters is shown in Table 7.

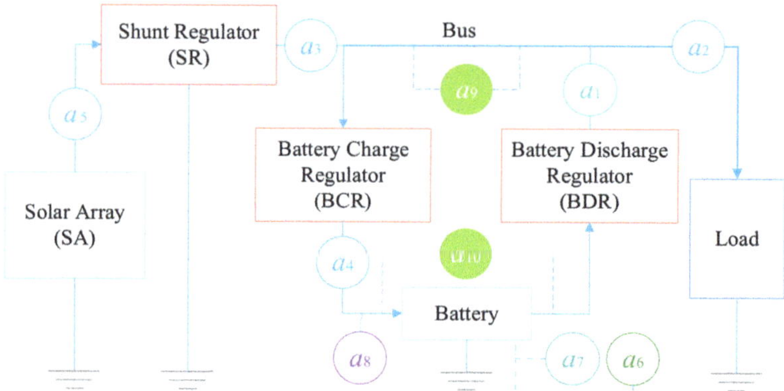

Figure 4. The schematic diagram of the power system.

Table 7. Information of the telemetry parameters.

ID	Attribute	Rate Range	Data Type	Unit
a_1	Duty cycle	0–1	Continuous	-
a_2	Bus current	13.5–17.3	Continuous	A
a_3	Shunt current	5.3–12.4	Continuous	A
a_4	Battery current	3.6–19.4	Continuous	A
a_5	Output power	1070–1090	Continuous	W
a_6	Battery pressure	2.0–5.4	Continuous	MPa
a_7	Battery quantity	54.3–71.2	Continuous	Ah
a_8	Status word	−1 0 1	Discrete	-
a_9	Bus voltage	40.5–43.1	Continuous	V
a_{10}	Battery voltage	33.0–40.5	Continuous	V

The raw data used for simultaneous-fault diagnosis is composed of the above-mentioned ten kinds of attributes, and all the data are selected in the stationary period. The dataset is stored in a time-series format, with each subset representing one of the scenarios shown in Table 8. There are a total of 12 scenarios, where scenario 0 represents the system without any fault. F1 represents open-circuit failure in solar array. F2 represents the short-circuit failure in the battery. F3 represents shunt regulator failure without shunt. F4 represents shunt regulator failure with constant shunt. The remaining 7 scenarios are concurrent failures composed of the above 4 single failures occurring at the same time, where F3 and F4 cannot occur simultaneously.

Table 8. Different scenarios for faults in satellite power system.

Scenario	Fault Name	Scenario	Fault Name
0	—	6	F1-F3
1	F1	7	F1-F4
2	F2	8	F2-F3
3	F3	9	F2-F4
4	F4	10	F1-F2-F3
5	F1-F2	11	F1-F2-F4

It can be seen that this means can effectively solve the problem of insufficient data in the simultaneous-fault diagnosis, which also responds to one the difficulties in the simultaneous-fault diagnosis introduced at the beginning of this paper.

6.1. Simultaneous-Fault Diagnosis Based on the Fault Matching Strategy

The two main parts of the simultaneous-fault diagnosis strategy, namely prior knowledge acquisition and rule matching, are equivalent to the training and testing process. We choose 4 kinds of single-fault data as the training set and the remaining 7 kinds of simultaneous-fault data as the testing set. The results obtained through the first step of prior knowledge acquisition are shown in Table 9. It can be found that the results of the output attribute subset of F3 and F4 are the same. Therefore, in order to distinguish F3 and F4, further information needs to be excavated. For attribute a_3, its corresponding shunt current data can directly distinguish F3 from F4. The shunt current value of F3 fluctuates between 6.42–8.67 and that of F4 is between 12.45–14.77. Therefore, F3 and F4 can be distinguished by setting the threshold value of the shunt current average.

Table 9. The results of the training process.

Fault Name	The Output Attribute Subset	Average Value of the Data for Attribute a_3
F1	a_5	-
F2	a_7	-
F3	a_2, a_3, a_9	7.46
F4	a_2, a_3, a_9	13.47

The results obtained through the second step of rule matching are shown in Table 10. For a simultaneous-fault, the Jaccard similarity coefficient between its output attribute subset and the output attribute subset of each single-fault obtained in the training process can be calculated in turn. If the Jaccard similarity coefficient is 0, the corresponding single fault can be eliminated preliminarily. Since F3 and F4 cannot be distinguished by the Jaccard similarity coefficient, it is necessary to further distinguish F3 and F4 through the set shunt current threshold and to finally obtain the matching result. Through the final matching result, it can be found that the diagnostic accuracy of the fault matching strategy is 100%. The above fault matching process comprehensively utilizes the similarity of attributes and expert knowledge, which can ensure that the obtained diagnosis results are more accurate.

Table 10. The results of the testing process.

Fault Name	The Output Attribute Subset	Jaccard Similarity Coefficient				Average Value of the Data for Attribute a_3	Matching Result
		F1	F2	F3	F4		
F1-F2	a_5, a_7	0.50	0.50	0	0	-	F1-F2
F1-F3	a_2, a_3, a_5, a_9	0.25	0	0.75	0.75	6.63	F1-F3
F1-F4	a_2, a_3, a_5, a_9	0.25	0	0.75	0.75	12.62	F1-F4
F2-F3	a_2, a_3, a_7, a_9	0	0.25	0.75	0.75	7.47	F2-F3
F2-F4	a_2, a_3, a_7, a_9	0	0.25	0.75	0.75	13.46	F2-F4
F1-F2-F3	a_2, a_3, a_5, a_7, a_9	0.20	0.20	0.60	0.60	6.63	F1-F2-F3
F1-F2-F4	$a_2, a_3, a_5, a_6, a_7, a_9$	0.17	0.17	0.50	0.50	12.63	F1-F2-F4

6.2. Comparison Experiment on Simultaneous-Fault Diagnosis

6.2.1. Experimental Setup

The superiority of the proposed fault matching strategy is demonstrated through comparison experiments of simultaneous-fault diagnosis with several multi-label classification algorithms (Binary Relevance, Classifier Chain, Calibrated Label Ranking, ML-KNN, and ML-DT). In these comparison algorithms, the classifiers of the first three algorithms are all set to Random Forest, which is the best classifier after the pretest, and the value of k for ML-KNN is 12. Subset accuracy, hamming loss, precision, recall, and F1 are introduced as the metrics of the multi-label classification performance [11].

$$\text{Subset Accuracy} = \frac{1}{n}\sum_{i=1}^{n} I(y_i = \hat{y}_i).,\tag{26}$$

$$\text{Hamming Loss} = \frac{1}{nL}\sum_{i=1}^{n}\sum_{j=1}^{L} I\left(y_i^j \neq \hat{y}_i^j\right),\tag{27}$$

$$\text{Precision} = \frac{1}{n}\sum_{i=1}^{n}\frac{\left|y_i^j = 1 \cap \hat{y}_i^j = 1\right|}{\left|y_i^j = 1\right|},\tag{28}$$

$$\text{Recall} = \frac{1}{n}\sum_{i=1}^{n}\frac{\left|y_i^j = 1 \cap \hat{y}_i^j = 1\right|}{\left|\hat{y}_i^j = 1\right|},\tag{29}$$

$$F_1 = \frac{1}{n}\sum_{i=1}^{n}\frac{2\left|y_i^j = 1 \cap \hat{y}_i^j = 1\right|}{\left|y_i^j = 1\right| + \left|\hat{y}_i^j = 1\right|},\tag{30}$$

where y_i represents the ground-truth label vector of the i sample, $\hat{y}_i$ represents the predicted label vector, y_i^j represents the ground-truth label of j position in i sample, $\hat{y}_i^j$ represents the predicted label of j position in i sample. Intuitively, subset accuracy, precision, recall, F1 perform as the multi-label counterparts of traditional metrics. Hamming lose performs as a special metric of multi-label.

The training set of all algorithms uses single-fault data, while the test set uses simultaneous-fault data. Ten-fold cross validation is also employed in this part.

6.2.2. Experimental Results and Analysis

The results are shown in Table 11. It is obvious that the proposed method outperforms other methods in the simultaneous-faults diagnosis of a satellite power system, which benefits from both the FNζDTRS model and the fault matching strategy (FNζDTRS-FMS). Fundamentally, on the one hand, the attribute reduction results obtained from the FNζDTRS model can accurately represent the fault information, and on the other hand, the proposed matching rules are reasonable and reliable.

Table 11. The results of the simultaneous-fault diagnosis.

Algorithm	Accuracy/Subset Accuracy	Hamming Loss	Precision	Recall	F1
FNζDTRS–FMS	100.0 ± 0.0	-	**100.0 ± 0.0**	**100.0 ± 0.0**	**100.0 ± 0.0**
Binary Relevance	82.34 ± 5.39	4.43 ± 1.35	**100.0 ± 0.0**	93.88 ± 1.87	96.28 ± 1.14
Classifier Chain	65.78 ± 8.93	9.30 ± 2.63	**100.0 ± 0.0**	86.42 ± 4.45	91.31 ± 3.07
Calibrated Label Ranking	0.0 ± 0.0	32.14 ± 7.11	**100.0 ± 0.0**	45.24 ± 0.0	61.90 ± 0.0
ML-KNN	0.0 ± 0.0	32.15 ± 0.0	99.98 ± 0.0	45.23 ± 7.11	61.89 ± 0.0
ML-DT	0.0 ± 0.0	32.35 ± 0.31	99.59 ± 0.62	45.03 ± 0.31	61.63 ± 0.42

* Bolded indicates that the model achieves the best performance on this metric.

In addition to the results of our method, as for multi-label classification methods, the false alarm rate performs satisfactorily, while the missed diagnosis rate performs poorly. It can be seen that the recall rates have been lower than 50%, which is unacceptable in engineering applications. At the same time, the results of the F1 index generated by the multi-label classification methods are relatively low, only slightly higher than 60%. Similarly, the results obtained by the Calibrated Label Ranking method are similar to those of ML-KNN and ML-DT. The results obtained by the Classifier Chain method are in the middle level. In addition, Binary Relevance has the best performance among the multi-label classification methods, which means that there are no relevant dependencies between the single faults.

7. Conclusions

In this work, a novel DTRS model called FNζDTRS is proposed and the fault match strategy (FMS) based on the FNζDTRS model is designed to overcome three fundamental hurdles faced by simultaneous-fault diagnosis. The effectiveness and superiority of our methodology is demonstrated by both numerical experiments conducted on several standard datasets and comparison analysis of simultaneous-fault diagnosis performed on a simulation model of a satellite power system. Consequently, two main conclusions can be drawn, as follows.

(1) The proposed FNζDTRS model performs attribute reduction more effectively compared with other models, and it has strong generalization ability. This benefits from the concise loss functions and the introduction of the fuzzy neighborhood relationships. The advantages of our model can greatly promote the smooth implementation of the model in simultaneous-fault diagnosis, which reflects the effectiveness and superiority of our selection of this model.

(2) The proposed FNζDTRS–FMS does not require simultaneous-fault samples to accomplish training and performs excellently in simultaneous-fault diagnosis compared to classic multi-label classification algorithms. This is completely consistent with the real situation, that is, the existing data cannot completely cover all the imagined failure modes. Therefore, the diagnostic strategy proposed in this paper has stronger application value.

Although the model we proposed has the above advantages, it still has the problem of low computational efficiency compared with the classical rough set because of the use of fuzzy neighborhood computing. This is one of our future research directions. Furthermore, our future work will also focus on fusing rough set models and multi-label learning algorithms to make the simultaneous-fault diagnosis framework more general.

Author Contributions: Data curation, R.Z.; Formal analysis, Y.J. and T.Z.; Funding acquisition, C.L. and M.S.; Methodology, L.T. and C.W.; Writing—original draft, Y.C., Y.J. and M.S.; Validation, Y.J.; Investigation, T.Z.; Supervision, M.S. All authors have read and agreed to the published version of the manuscript.

Funding: This study was supported by the National Natural Science Foundation of China (Grant Nos. 61903015 and 61973011), the Fundamental Research Funds for the Central Universities (Grant No. KG21003001), National key Laboratory of Science and Technology on Reliability and Environmental Engineering (Grant No. WDZC2019601A304), as well as the Capital Science & Technology Leading Talent Program (Grant No. Z191100006119029).

Data Availability Statement: The public data can be accessed through the following two websits: the UCI (http://archive.ics.uci.edu/ml/index.php, accessed on 21 July 2021) and KEEL (https://sci2s.ugr.es/keel/datasets.php, accessed on 21 July 2021). However, the data set of the satellite power system is not convenient for public display. If necessary, researchers can make further consultation via email.

Acknowledgments: Thank the reviewers for their comments on improving the quality of our papers, and thank the journal editors for their enthusiastic work.

Conflicts of Interest: The authors declare no conflict of interest.

Nomenclature

$U = \{x_1, x_2, \cdots, x_m\}$	the universe, which is a finite and nonempty set.
D	the set of decision attributes that is a nonempty set.
C	the collection of conditional attributes.
X	the subset of samples with the same label d_k.
a_P, a_B, and a_N	the classification of x into three regions, which are $x \in POS(X)$, $x \in BND(X), x \in NEG(X)$.
$POS(X)$	the acceptance of the event $x \in X$.
$BND(X)$	the non-commitment of the event $x \in X$, denotes the deferment of the event $x \in X$.
$NEG(X)$	the rejection of $x \in X$.
$\lambda_{\bullet P}$	the loss caused by taking actions (a_P, a_B, a_N) while $x \in X$.
$\lambda_{\bullet N}$	the loss caused by taking actions (a_P, a_B, a_N) while $x \notin X$.
α, β	the threshold parameters of the DTRS model.
δ	fuzzy neighborhood radius.
ζ	the compensation coefficient.

References

1. Li, S.; Cao, H.; Yang, Y. Data-driven simultaneous fault diagnosis for solid oxide fuel cell system using multi-label pattern identification. *J. Power Sources* **2018**, *378*, 646–659. [CrossRef]
2. Suo, M.; Tao, L.; Zhu, B.; Chen, Y.; Lu, C.; Ding, Y. Soft decision-making based on decision-theoretic rough set and Takagi-Sugeno fuzzy model with application to the autonomous fault diagnosis of satellite power system. *Aerosp Sci. Technol.* **2020**, *106*, 106108. [CrossRef]
3. Suo, M.; Zhu, B.; An, R.; Sun, H.; Xu, S.; Yu, Z. Data-driven fault diagnosis of satellite power system using fuzzy Bayes risk and SVM. *Aerosp Sci. Technol.* **2019**, *84*, 1092–1105. [CrossRef]
4. Asgari, S.; Gupta, R.; Puri, I.K.; Zheng, R. A data-driven approach to simultaneous fault detection and diagnosis in data centers. *Appl. Soft Comput.* **2021**, *110*, 107638. [CrossRef]
5. Liang, P.; Deng, C.; Wu, J.; Yang, Z.; Zhu, J.; Zhang, Z. Single and simultaneous fault diagnosis of gearbox via a semi-supervised and high-accuracy adversarial learning framework. *Knowl.-Based Syst.* **2020**, *198*, 105895. [CrossRef]
6. Zhang, Z.; Li, S.; Xiao, Y.; Yang, Y. Intelligent simultaneous fault diagnosis for solid oxide fuel cell system based on deep learning. *Appl. Energ.* **2019**, *233*, 930–942. [CrossRef]
7. Pooyan, N.; Shahbazian, M.; Salahshoor, K.; Hadian, M. Simultaneous Fault Diagnosis using multi class support vector machine in a Dew Point process. *J. Nat. Gas. Sci. Eng.* **2015**, *23*, 373–379. [CrossRef]
8. Vong, C.; Wong, P.; Ip, W. A New Framework of Simultaneous-Fault Diagnosis Using Pairwise Probabilistic Multi-Label Classification for Time-Dependent Patterns. *Ieee T Ind. Electron.* **2013**, *60*, 3372–3385. [CrossRef]
9. Wong, P.K.; Zhong, J.; Yang, Z.; Vong, C.M. Sparse Bayesian extreme learning committee machine for engine simultaneous fault diagnosis. *Neurocomputing* **2016**, *174*, 331–343. [CrossRef]

10. Wu, B.; Cai, W.; Chen, H.; Zhang, X. A hybrid data-driven simultaneous fault diagnosis model for air handling units. *Energy Build.* **2021**, *245*, 111069. [CrossRef]
11. Zhang, M.; Zhou, Z. A Review on Multi-Label Learning Algorithms. *IEEE Trans. Knowl. Data Eng.* **2014**, *26*, 1819–1837. [CrossRef]
12. Boutell, M.R.; Luo, J.B.; Shen, X.P.; Brown, C.M. Learning multi-label scene classification. *Pattern Recognit.* **2004**, *37*, 1757–1771. [CrossRef]
13. Read, J.; Pfahringer, B.; Holmes, G.; Frank, E. Classifier chains for multi-label classification. *Mach. Learn.* **2011**, *85*, 333–359. [CrossRef]
14. Fuernkranz, J.; Huellermeier, E.; Mencia, E.L.; Brinker, K. Multilabel classification via calibrated label ranking. *Mach. Learn.* **2008**, *73*, 133–153. [CrossRef]
15. Zhang, M.; Zhou, Z. ML-KNN: A lazy learning approach to multi-label leaming. *Pattern Recognit.* **2007**, *40*, 2038–2048. [CrossRef]
16. Clare, A.; King, R.D. Knowledge Discovery in Multi-label Phenotype Data. In *European Conference on Principles of Data Mining and Knowledge Discovery*; Springer: Berlin/Heidelberg, Germany, 2001; pp. 42–53.
17. Pawlak, Z. Rough sets. *Int. J. Comput. Inf. Sci.* **1982**, *11*, 341–356. [CrossRef]
18. Dong, L.; Chen, D.; Wang, N.; Lu, Z. Key energy-consumption feature selection of thermal power systems based on robust attribute reduction with rough sets. *Inf. Sci.* **2020**, *532*, 61–71. [CrossRef]
19. Su, L.; Yu, F. Matrix approach to spanning matroids of rough sets and its application to attribute reduction. *Theor. Comput. Sci.* **2021**, *893*, 105–116. [CrossRef]
20. Sahu, R.; Dash, S.R.; Das, S. Career selection of students using hybridized distance measure based on picture fuzzy set and rough set theory. *Decis. Mak. Appl. Manag. Eng.* **2021**, *4*, 104–126. [CrossRef]
21. Dash, S.R.; Dehuri, S.; Sahoo, U.K. Interactions and Applications of Fuzzy, Rough, and Soft Set in Data Mining. *Int. J. Fuzzy Syst. Appl.* **2015**, *3*, 37–50. [CrossRef]
22. Zhang, P.; Li, T.; Wang, G.; Luo, C.; Chen, H.; Zhang, J.; Wang, D.; Yu, Z. Multi-source information fusion based on rough set theory: A review. *Inf. Fusion* **2021**, *68*, 85–117. [CrossRef]
23. Bai, H.; Ge, Y.; Wang, J.; Li, D.; Liao, Y.; Zheng, X. A method for extracting rules from spatial data based on rough fuzzy sets. *Knowl.-Based Syst.* **2014**, *57*, 28–40. [CrossRef]
24. Landowski, M.; Landowska, A. Usage of the rough set theory for generating decision rules of number of traffic vehicles. *Transp. Res. Procedia* **2019**, *39*, 260–269. [CrossRef]
25. Sharma, H.K.; Kumari, K.; Kar, S. A rough set theory application in forecasting models. *Decis. Mak. Appl. Manag. Eng.* **2020**, *3*, 1–21. [CrossRef]
26. Guo, Y.; Tsang, E.C.C.; Xu, W.; Chen, D. Adaptive weighted generalized multi-granulation interval-valued decision-theoretic rough sets. *Knowl.-Based Syst.* **2020**, *187*, 104804. [CrossRef]
27. Wang, T.; Liu, W.; Zhao, J.; Guo, X.; Terzija, V. A rough set-based bio-inspired fault diagnosis method for electrical substations. *Int. J. Electr. Power Energy Syst.* **2020**, *119*, 105961. [CrossRef]
28. Sang, B.; Yang, L.; Chen, H.; Xu, W.; Guo, Y.; Yuan, Z. Generalized multi-granulation double-quantitative decision-theoretic rough set of multi-source information system. *Int. J. Approx. Reason.* **2019**, *115*, 157–179. [CrossRef]
29. Zhang, P.F.; Li, T.R.; Yuan, Z.; Luo, C.; Liu, K.Y.; Yang, X.L. Heterogeneous Feature Selection Based on Neighborhood Combination Entropy. *IEEE Trans. Neural Netw. Learn. Syst.* **2022**, 1–14. [CrossRef]
30. Wang, L.; Shen, J.; Mei, X. Cost Sensitive Multi-Class Fuzzy Decision-theoretic Rough Set Based Fault Diagnosis. In Proceedings of the 2017 36th Chinese Control Conference (CCC), Dalian, China, 26–28 July 2017; pp. 6957–6961.
31. Yu, J.; Ding, B.; He, Y. Rolling bearing fault diagnosis based on mean multigranulation decision-theoretic rough set and non-naive Bayesian classifier. *J. Mech. Sci. Technol.* **2018**, *32*, 5201–5211. [CrossRef]
32. Suo, M.; Tao, L.; Zhu, B.; Miao, X.; Liang, Z.; Ding, Y.; Zhang, X.; Zhang, T. Single-parameter decision-theoretic rough set. *Inf. Sci.* **2020**, *539*, 49–80. [CrossRef]
33. Yao, Y.Y.; Wong, S.K.M. A decision theoretic framework for approximating concepts. *Int. J. Man Mach. Stud.* **1992**, *37*, 793–809. [CrossRef]
34. Suo, M.; Cheng, Y.; Zhuang, C.; Ding, Y.; Lu, C.; Tao, L. Extension of labeled multiple attribute decision making based on fuzzy neighborhood three-way decision. *Neural Comput. Appl.* **2020**, *32*, 17731–17758. [CrossRef]
35. Jia, X.; Liao, W.; Tang, Z.; Shang, L. Minimum cost attribute reduction in decision-theoretic rough set models. *Inf. Sci.* **2013**, *219*, 151–167. [CrossRef]
36. Yao, Y. Three-way decisions with probabilistic rough sets. *Inf. Sci.* **2010**, *180*, 341–353. [CrossRef]
37. Jiang, F.; Sui, Y. A novel approach for discretization of continuous attributes in rough set theory. *Knowl.-Based Syst.* **2015**, *73*, 324–334. [CrossRef]
38. Li, W.; Huang, Z.; Jia, X.; Cai, X. Neighborhood based decision-theoretic rough set models. *Int. J. Approx. Reason.* **2016**, *69*, 1–17. [CrossRef]
39. Song, J.; Tsang, E.C.C.; Chen, D.; Yang, X. Minimal decision cost reduct in fuzzy decision-theoretic rough set model. *Knowl.-Based Syst.* **2017**, *126*, 104–112. [CrossRef]

40. Wang, C.; Qi, Y.; Shao, M.; Hu, Q.; Chen, D.; Qian, Y.; Lin, Y. A Fitting Model for Feature Selection with Fuzzy Rough Sets. *IEEE Trans. Fuzzy Syst.* **2017**, *25*, 741–753. [CrossRef]
41. Wang, C.; Shao, M.; He, Q.; Qian, Y.; Qi, Y. Feature subset selection based on fuzzy neighborhood rough sets. *Knowl.-Based Syst.* **2016**, *111*, 173–179. [CrossRef]

 *mathematics*

Article

SMoCo: A Powerful and Efficient Method Based on Self-Supervised Learning for Fault Diagnosis of Aero-Engine Bearing under Limited Data

Zitong Yan and Hongmei Liu *

School of Reliability and Systems Engineering, Beihang University, Beijing 100191, China
* Correspondence: liuhongmei@buaa.edu.cn

Abstract: Vibration signals collected in real industrial environments are usually limited and unlabeled. In this case, fault diagnosis methods based on deep learning tend to perform poorly. Previous work mainly used the unlabeled data of the same diagnostic object to improve the diagnostic accuracy, but it did not make full use of the easily available unlabeled signals from different sources. In this study, a signal momentum contrast for unsupervised representation learning (SMoCo) based on the contrastive learning algorithm—momentum contrast for unsupervised visual representation Learning (MoCo)—is proposed. It can learn how to automatically extract fault features from unlabeled data collected from different diagnostic objects and then transfer this ability to target diagnostic tasks. On the structure, SMoCo increases the stability by adding batch normalization to the multilayer perceptron (MLP) layer of MoCo and increases the flexibility by adding a predictor to the query network. Using the data augmentation method, SMoCo performs feature extraction on vibration signals from both time and frequency domains, which is called signal multimodal learning (SML). It has been proved by experiments that after pre-training with artificially injected fault bearing data, SMoCo can learn a powerful and robust feature extractor, which can greatly improve the accuracy no matter the target diagnostic data with different working conditions, different failure modes, or even different types of equipment from the pre-training dataset. When faced with the target diagnosis task, SMoCo can achieve accuracy far better than other representative methods in only a very short time, and its excellent robustness regarding the amount of data in both the unlabeled pre-training dataset and the target diagnosis dataset as well as the strong noise demonstrates its great potential and superiority in fault diagnosis.

Keywords: self-supervised learning; data augmentation; limited data; fault diagnosis; aero-engine; rolling bearing

MSC: 90B25

Citation: Yan, Z.; Liu, H. SMoCo: A Powerful and Efficient Method Based on Self-Supervised Learning for Fault Diagnosis of Aero-Engine Bearing under Limited Data. *Mathematics* **2022**, *10*, 2796. https://doi.org/10.3390/math10152796

Academic Editors: Yu Jiang, Haijun Peng and Hongwei Yang

Received: 15 July 2022
Accepted: 4 August 2022
Published: 6 August 2022

1. Introduction

As the key component of the aero-engine rotor system, rolling bearings often work in the environment of large load and high-speed rotation, which will inevitably cause huge economic losses or safety accidents [1–3]. Therefore, it is of great significance to improve the diagnostic accuracy and efficiency of rolling bearings for the healthy and stable operation of aero-engines.

With the continuous development of artificial intelligence technology, deep learning has been widely used in rolling bearing fault diagnosis to ensure the high reliability of aero-engines [4]. However, in practical industrial situations, it is very difficult to obtain a sufficient amount of labeled data, which greatly affects the performance of fault diagnosis methods based on deep learning [5].

In this case, researchers mainly use semi-supervised learning and transfer learning to solve this problem. Semi-supervised learning uses both a large amount of unlabeled data and a small amount of labeled data for training, thereby improving the performance of the model. A three-stage semi-supervised method using data augmentation was proposed by Yu et al. [6] for bearing fault diagnosis. Zhang et al. [7] proposed a deep generative model based on a variational autoencoder (VAE) for semi-supervised learning of bearing fault diagnosis, which can effectively utilize the dataset when only a limited part of the data has labels. Transfer learning transfers the knowledge obtained from the source domain to the target domain to improve the diagnostic performance of the target domain. Wen et al. [8] adopted a three-layer sparse autoencoder to extract the features of the original data and forced the autoencoder to create a latent feature space containing the representations of the source and target domain data by adding a maximum mean difference (MMD), thereby predicting the failure of the target domain data. Wang et al. [9] proposed a deep adversarial domain adaptation network to transfer fault diagnosis knowledge, which learns domain-invariant features from raw signals using domain adversarial training based on Wasserstein distance.

Although the above methods have achieved good results, they are still only for limited application scenarios. Specifically, for semi-supervised learning, previous work mainly uses unlabeled data of the same object, which is often difficult to obtain in practical situations. For transfer learning, it requires that the distribution difference between the source and target domain data is limited, and it requires the source domain data to be labeled [10]. In addition, when faced with different diagnostic tasks, these two methods need to use all the additional data and target diagnostic data for training, which is computationally expensive and cannot be quickly and efficiently used for various diagnostic tasks.

Unlike the above algorithms, self-supervised learning provides a new solution [11]. From the perspective of data, self-supervised learning can automatically extract meaningful features from unlabeled data for fault classification, thus making full use of the easily available unlabeled data from different sources [12–15]. From the perspective of computational efficiency, self-supervised learning can be applied to various downstream diagnostic tasks with only fine-tuning after the training is completed [16]. There is no need to reuse unlabeled data for training on various downstream tasks, so that different downstream diagnostic tasks can be quickly solved.

Contrastive learning has been successfully applied to the field of computer vision as a state-of-the-art method for self-supervised learning [17–20] by reducing the distance between different augmented views of the same image (positive pairs) and increasing the distance between augmented views of different images (negative pairs) for representation learning [21]. However, there are few studies on self-supervised learning in the field of fault diagnosis. Wang et al. [16] performed self-supervised learning by having the model identify the categories that augment the signal and convert it into a classification model. The methods based on contrastive learning include: Wei et al. [22] used the data augmentation method in the image field to perform representation learning by transforming the signal through a simple reshape based on SimCLR [18]. Ding et al. [23] used momentum contrastive learning for instance-level discrimination based on MoCo [24] for representation learning. Peng et al. [25] proposed an automatic fault feature extractor based on BYOL [21] to explore some transformations of signal time-domain features.

The above methods have made attempts to apply self-supervised learning in fault diagnosis, but the problems they address are still limited to self-supervised learning using unlabeled data from the same diagnostic object and do not take full advantage of unlabeled data that are easier to obtain in other operating conditions or even other devices. In addition, their data augmentation method is still limited to morphological changes in time-domain signals and does not take advantage of the natural multi-modal characteristics of signals, such as time-domain information and frequency-domain information.

In response to the above problems, this paper proposes a new self-supervised learning method called signal momentum contrast for unsupervised representation learning (SMoCo). It improves the original MoCo in structure and designs a sufficiently difficult task by adopting the time-domain and frequency-domain cross-learning in the data augmentation stage, which helps the model to learn the essential characteristics of the signal. For more details on SMoCo, please refer to Section 3.

This paper focuses on the problem of fault diagnosis of aero-engine bearing under limited data. Based on this background, a fault diagnosis method based on SMoCo is proposed. It first performs self-supervised learning on easily accessible unlabeled data to obtain a powerful and robust feature extractor. It is worth noting that the unlabeled data can be obtained from a wide range of sources, such as laboratory data of the same model under different operating conditions, or even from completely different types of products, which greatly improves the feasibility of the method. Subsequently, the feature extractor can obtain the easily classifiable features of the target diagnostic object, thus solving the difficult problem that it is difficult to diagnose aero-engine bearing faults with little data in the actual industry. Despite its good performance, SMoCo requires a relatively long training time to learn how to extract the essential features of the signal during the self-supervised learning phase. The main contributions of this paper are summarized as follows:

1. In terms of structure, based on MoCo, this paper increases the performance of the model and the stability of training by introducing a predictor to the query network and adding batch normalization (BN) [26] to the multilayer perceptron (MLP) layer.
2. In terms of data augmentation method, this paper proposes signal multimodal learning (SML), which enables the model to learn the signal representation from both the time domain and the frequency domain, thereby characterizing the signal from two dimensions.
3. The unlabeled pre-training data used by SMoCo comes from a wide range of sources and is no longer limited to the same diagnostic object, which makes it more feasible in the real task.
4. Experiments show that SMoCo can be used as a feature extractor with fixed weights to extract robust features after pre-training on artificially injected fault bearings, whether it is a bearing with different failure modes under different working conditions or a completely different type of rolling bearing. Aero-engine high-speed rolling bearings can achieve extremely high diagnostic accuracy with very few samples, providing timelier and more robust fault diagnosis than other state-of-the-art techniques.
5. Further studies have shown that SMoCo can still achieve excellent performance with a much-reduced data volume and in the presence of strong noise, further broadening its applicability.

The paper is structured as follows. In Section 2, the structure and idea of the original MoCo are introduced. In Section 3, the SMoCo algorithm proposed in this paper is introduced in detail, including the entire fault diagnosis process and its improvements in structure and data augmentation methods. In Section 4, the performance of SMoCo is verified via experiments on two datasets. In Section 5, this paper further explores the sensitivity of SMoCo to the size of the unlabeled pre-training dataset and its robustness to target diagnostic objects under different noise conditions. Section 6 summarizes the paper and looks at future work.

2. MoCo Network

MoCo [24] is a contrastive learning method with good training stability; the structure is shown in Figure 1. It performs representation learning in the latent space by minimizing the distance between different augmented views of the same data and rejecting augmented views of other samples.

MoCo uses two neural networks, query network f_q and key network f_k, with the same structure for training, and its goal is to learn the convolutional layers in the query network to serve as feature extractors for downstream tasks. Since negative pair-based contrastive learning relies on the number of negative samples for representation learning, MoCo maintains a queue, which contains a single positive sample and multiple negative samples, the model learns representations by finding the corresponding positive samples.

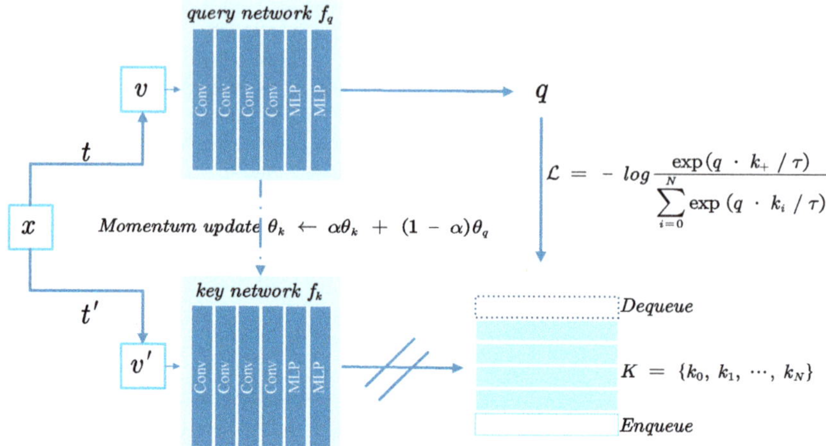

Figure 1. The framework of the MoCo network.

Specifically, for a given sample x and the distribution T of its data augmentation methods, the data augmentation methods $t \sim T$ and $t' \sim T$ are adopted respectively to generate two different augmented views of the same instance, denoted as v and v', and treat these two as a positive pair. Input v to the f_q produces a query batch q, and input v' to the f_k produces the features in the queue. It uses a dynamically updated queue to store the representations of multiple batches recently used for training. After a new batch enters the queue, the oldest training batch is out of the queue, thereby maintaining a large number of negative samples to help model training. For a given set of queues, $K = \{k_0, k_1, \cdots, k_N\}$ contains N + 1 encoding keys, where the encoder f_k produces a positive sample k_+ for the current v', and the others are negative samples, thus transforming the contrastive learning task into positive and negative samples corresponding to a given query q. Finally, InfoNCE [27] is used as the loss function:

$$\mathcal{L} = -\log \frac{\exp(q \cdot k_+ / \tau)}{\sum_{i=0}^{N} \exp(q \cdot k_i / \tau)} \tag{1}$$

where τ is the temperature parameter.

During the training process, only the parameters of the f_q are updated via gradient back-propagation, while the parameters of the f_k are updated via a momentum update. Specifically, denoting the parameters of f_k as θ_k and the parameters of f_q as θ_q, it updates θ_k by:

$$\theta_k \leftarrow \alpha\theta_k + (1-\alpha)\theta_q \tag{2}$$

where $\alpha \in [0, 1)$ is the momentum update parameter.

MoCo builds a dynamic dictionary by using queues and momentum updates, which enables it to learn in a wider range of negative samples, making the network learn better and train more stably.

3. SMoCo

The framework of fault diagnosis based on SMoCo is shown in Figure 2, which is mainly composed of three key steps: (1) data acquisition, (2) self-supervised on unlabeled data, (3) fault diagnosis on labeled data. Given the difficulty of fault diagnosis of aero-engines in the case of limited data, we use unlabeled vibration signals that are easily obtained from different working conditions or even different equipment. Self-supervised learning is first employed with unlabeled signals, using our proposed signal multimodal learning (SML) as the data augmentation method. After the training is completed, the convolutional layers of the query network are selected as the feature extractor for the downstream task, and it is worth noting that its weights remain unchanged. Finally, for the downstream labeled aero-engine bearing dataset, the feature extractor is used to extract features, and then support vector machines (SVMs) are used to classify the extracted features, and finally, the diagnostic model is obtained. The SVM is a classifier that classifies data in a supervised learning manner, where the decision boundary is the maximum-margin hyperplane solved for the learned samples.

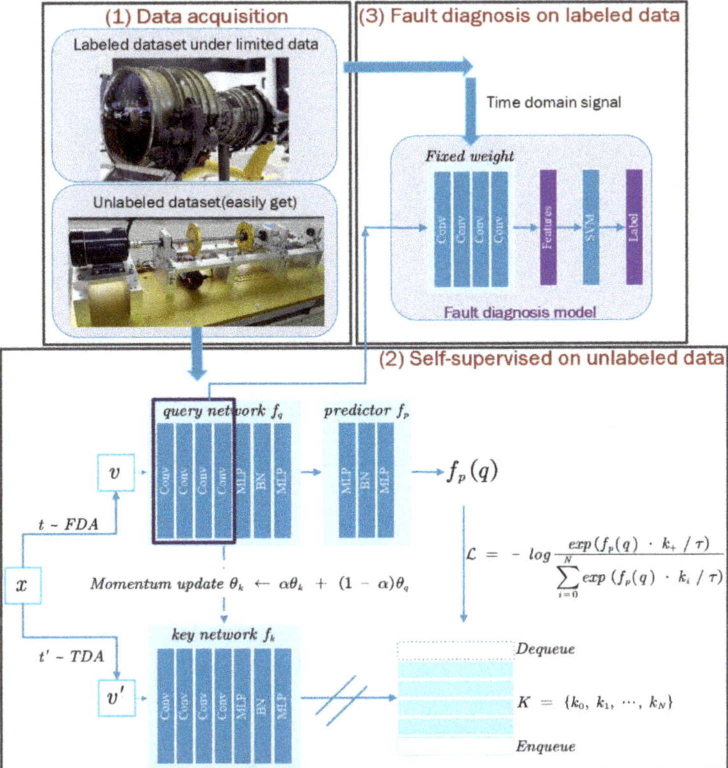

Figure 2. The framework of fault diagnosis based on SMoCo.

In this section, we first describe our unique data augmentation approach, signal multimodal learning (SML). Then, the network structure of SMoCo is proposed through several improvements based on MoCo. Finally, we specify an implementation detail based on SMoCo for fault diagnosis.

3.1. Signal Multimodal Learning (SML)

The representation learning ability of contrastive learning depends greatly on the design and optimization of data augmentation methods [18]. Aero-engine rolling bearings diagnosis has difficult problems such as variable working conditions, strong noise, and weak faults in a real task. If a model can be unaffected by these factors, then the essential characteristics of the signal can be well characterized. The previous work was only limited to making some morphological changes to the time-domain signal when designing data augmentation methods. This paper proposes SML from the perspective of the time domain and the frequency domain according to the characteristics of vibration signals, including six basic data augmentation transformations as shown in Figure 3. The following describes in detail how these methods transform a given vibration signal $x = [x_1, x_2, \cdots, x_N]$.

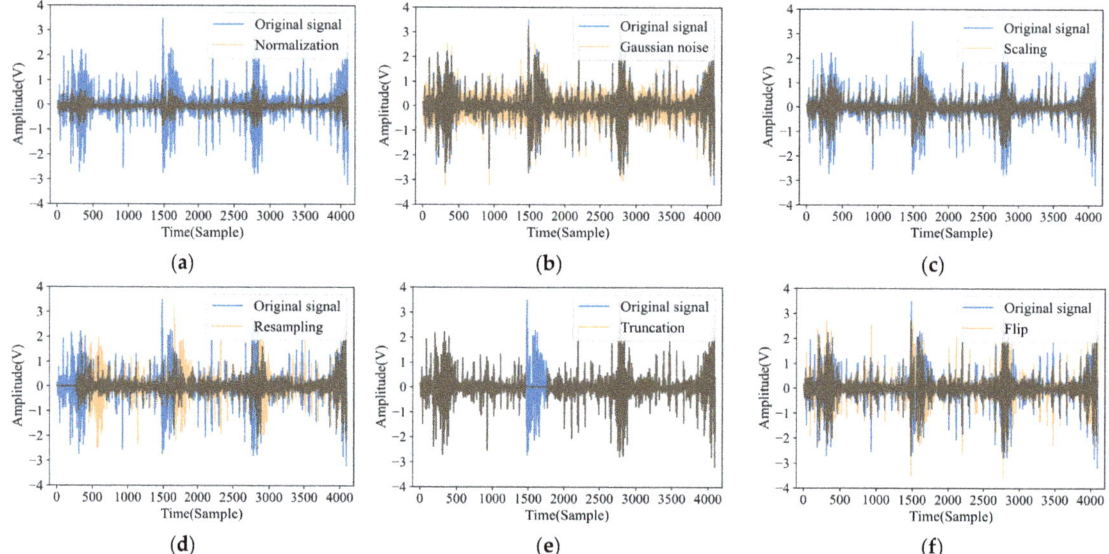

Figure 3. Data augmentation of sampled signals. (**a**) Normalization; (**b**) Gaussian noise; (**c**) scaling; (**d**) resampling; (**e**) truncation; (**f**) flip.

1. Normalization: There are differences in the measurement range of different sensors. This strategy normalizes the signal to a uniform range, which is also beneficial for model training. The formula is as follows:

$$\tilde{x} = -1 + 2 * \frac{x - x_{min}}{x_{max} - x_{min}} \tag{3}$$

2. Gaussian noise: There is an inevitable environmental noise problem during the operation of the device. This strategy adds Gaussian noise to the original signal to mimic this phenomenon. The formula is as follows:

$$\tilde{x} = x + n, n \sim N(0, \sigma_n) \tag{4}$$

where n is generated by the Gaussian distribution $N(0, \sigma_n)$.

3. Scaling: This strategy increases the sensitivity of the model to signals of different amplitudes by directly amplifying or reducing the amplitude of the signal without losing the semantics contained in the original data. The formula is as follows:

$$\tilde{x} = x * s, s \sim N(1, \sigma_s) \tag{5}$$

where s is generated from a Gaussian distribution $N(1, \sigma_s)$.

4. Resampling: This strategy improves the robustness of the model to variable speed scenarios by resampling and transforming the signal length to $s \sim N(1, \sigma_s)$ times the original length.
5. Truncation: This strategy randomly covers part of the signal, and its formula is as follows:

$$\tilde{x} = x * mask \tag{6}$$

where *mask* is a binary sequence with subsequence zeros at random positions.

6. Flip: The vibration signal usually vibrates up and down with 0 as the mean value. This strategy randomly flips the signal to increase the diversity of the signal. The formula is as follows:
$$\widetilde{x} = -x \tag{7}$$

Since the signal naturally has multi-modal characteristics, our proposed SML treats the time-domain signal and the frequency-domain signal using fast Fourier transform (FFT) as a positive pair, as shown in Figure 4. If the model can correspond the augmented time-domain signal to the augmented frequency-domain signal, it can characterize the signal more comprehensively from both the time-domain and frequency-domain dimensions. Specifically, according to the characteristics of the time-domain signal, the order of normalization, Gaussian noise, scaling, resampling, truncation, and flip is used as the data augmentation method, which is called time-domain augmentation (TDA). For the frequency-domain signal, the order of normalization and Gaussian noise is used as the data augmentation method, which is called frequency-domain augmentation (FDA).

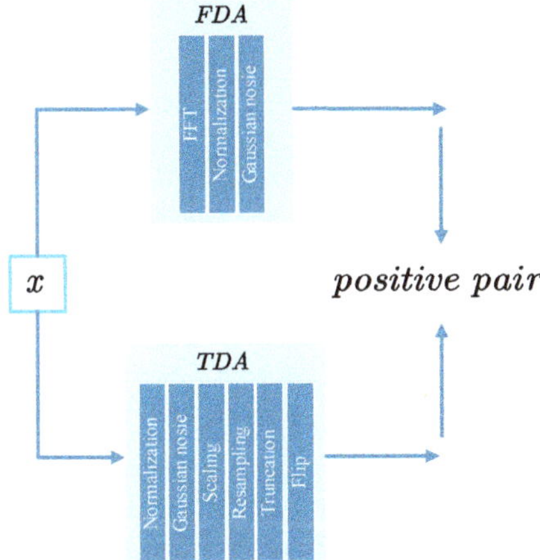

Figure 4. Signal multimodal learning (SML).

3.2. Fault Diagnosis Based on SMoCo

The network structure of SMoCo is shown in Figure 5, which includes query network f_q, predictor f_p, key network f_k, and *queue*. The query network and the key network have the same structure. To increase the stability of model training, we add BN to the MLP projection layer based on MoCo. In addition, we add a predictor to the query network, which greatly increases the flexibility, so that the characteristics of the query network do not need to be the same as those of the key network, but only need to be matched by another predictor, which greatly improves the effect of representation learning. Like MoCo, SMoCo maintains a dynamically updated queue, using only the gradient to update f_q, and using the parameter of f_q to momentum update the parameters of f_k. Specifically, denoting the parameters of f_k as θ_k and the parameters of f_q as θ_q, it updates θ_k according to the Equation (2).

Given a vibration signal x, the data augmentation distribution of the time-domain signal is TDA, and the data augmentation distribution of the frequency-domain signal is FDA. By adopting the data augmentation strategies $t \sim FDA$ and $t' \sim TDA$ for x, two augmented time series $v = t(FFT(x))$ and $v' = t'(x)$ are generated. For v, use the query network to output the feature $q = f_q(v)$, and then use the predictor to predict q to get $f_p(q)$. For v', the key network outputs $k_+ = f_k(v')$. Therefore, for a given queue, for $f_p(q)$, except for k_+, which is a positive pair, all other features in the queue are negative pairs. Its loss function is formulated as:

$$\mathcal{L} = -log\frac{exp\left(f_p(q) \cdot k_+/\tau\right)}{\sum_{i=0}^{N} exp\left(f_p(q) \cdot k_i/\tau\right)} \tag{8}$$

where τ is the temperature parameter.

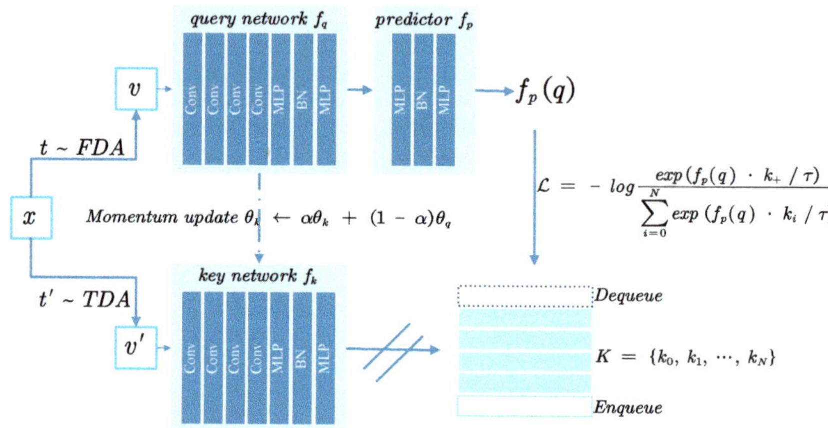

Figure 5. The structure of SMoCo.

It gets the symmetric loss function $\widetilde{\mathcal{L}}$ by feeding v' to the query network and v to the key network. Finally, the network updates the query network f_q by minimizing the loss $\mathcal{L}_{SMoCo}$:

$$\mathcal{L}_{SMoCo} = 0.5 \times \left(\mathcal{L} + \widetilde{\mathcal{L}}\right) \tag{9}$$

The detailed SMoCo is shown in Algorithm 1.

Algorithm 1. The detailed SMoCo.

Input:
Structure of f_q, f_p, f_k, temperature τ, momentum update α, *queue* size N
batch size n_b, learning rate η, total number of optimization steps K,
distributions of transformations TDA, FDA, set of signals D
Initialize parameters, $\theta_k \leftarrow \theta_q$, and *queue*
for $k = 1$ to K **do**
  Batch $\leftarrow \{x_i \sim D\}_{i=1}^{n_b}$
  for $x_i \in$ Batch **do**
    $t \in FDA$ and $t' \in TDA$
    $q^1 \leftarrow f_q(t(x_i))$ and $k_+^1 \leftarrow f_k(t'(x_i))$
    $q^2 \leftarrow f_q(t'(x_i))$ and $k_+^2 \leftarrow f_k(t(x_i))$
    $l_i \leftarrow 0.5 \times (-\log \frac{\exp\left(f_p(q^1) \cdot k_+^1/\tau\right)}{\sum_{i=0}^{N}\exp\left(f_p(q^1) \cdot k_i/\tau\right)} - \log \frac{\exp\left(f_p(q^2) \cdot k_+^2/\tau\right)}{\sum_{i=0}^{N}\exp\left(f_p(q^2) \cdot k_i/\tau\right)})$
  end
    // Back-propagation
  $\theta_q \leftarrow \theta_q - \eta \cdot \frac{\partial \frac{1}{n_b}\sum_{i=1}^{n_b} l_i}{\theta_q}$
    // Momentum update without back-propagation
  $\theta_k \leftarrow \alpha\theta_k + (1-\alpha)\theta_q$
    // Update dictionary
    Enqueue and dequeue with $\{k_+^1\}_{i=1}^{n_b}$ and $\{k_+^2\}_{i=1}^{n_b}$
end
Output: query network parameters θ_q

After training, the convolutional layers in the query network are extracted to perform feature extraction on downstream tasks. When performing downstream tasks, the weights of the convolutional layers remain fixed and only serve as a function of feature extraction. Since the SVM is the classifier with the largest interval in the feature space, the SVM is adopted to classify the extracted features, which is more robust in the problem under limited data.

4. Performance Verification of SMoCo

To verify the effectiveness and superiority of SMoCo, as proposed in this paper, the bearing dataset of Paderborn University and the aero-engine bearing dataset of the Polytechnic University of Turin are used for experimental verification. SMoCo is first pre-trained on the unlabeled laboratory data of artificially injected faults from Paderborn University. The learned feature extractors are then transferred to products of the same type but with failures generated in natural operation from Paderborn University, and these two datasets are characterized using different working conditions, different failure levels, and different failure modes. It is further transferred to the aero-engine bearing dataset from the Polytechnic University of Turin, which is a completely different model compared to the pre-training dataset, and the data distributions of these two datasets differ significantly and thus can effectively verify the validity of aero-engine bearing fault diagnosis under limited data. The purpose of using two cases is to verify the effect of the proposed method on different diagnostic subjects.

4.1. Self-Supervised on Artificially Damaged Bearing Data

The Paderborn University dataset [28] is a public dataset collected by the Paderborn University Bearing Data Center in 2016 with high diagnostic difficulty [29]. In this dataset, bearing damages are rich and can be divided into three categories: 6 healthy bearings, 12 artificially damaged bearings, and 14 real damaged bearings. Among them, the real damaged data were obtained through the accelerated life test. The vibration signal was obtained at a sampling rate of 64 khz, including 4 working conditions, as shown in Table 1, and the test rig is shown in Figure 6.

Table 1. Operating parameters.

Name of Setting	Rotational Speed [rpm]	Load Torque [Nm]	Radial Force [N]
N09_M07_F10	900	0.7	1000
N15_M07_F10	1500	0.7	1000
N15_M01_F10	1500	0.1	1000
N15_M07_F04	1500	0.7	400

Figure 6. Test rig of Paderborn dataset.

To better represent the easy-to-obtain unlabeled data, the artificially injected fault bearing data in the Paderborn University dataset is used as the unlabeled pre training dataset, as shown in Table 2. There are 13 types of bearings including one type of health status; 4096 is selected as the sample length to contain enough information, and the working condition is N15_M01_F10. The number of samples in each category is 2000, and all data are kept as raw time-domain data without any signal pre-processing.

Table 2. Dataset 1: Unlabeled artificially damaged bearing dataset under N15_M01_F10.

Bearing Code	Damaged Element	Damaged Extent	Damage Method
K001	Health state	/	Run-in 50 h before test
KA01	Outer ring	Level 1	Made by EDM
KA03	Outer ring	Level 2	Made by electric engraver
KA05	Outer ring	Level 1	Made by electric engraver
KA06	Outer ring	Level 2	Made by electric engraver
KA07	Outer ring	Level 1	Made by drilling
KA08	Outer ring	Level 2	Made by drilling
KA09	Outer ring	Level 2	Made by drilling
KI01	Inner ring	Level 1	Made by EDM
KI03	Inner ring	Level 1	Made by electric engraver
KI05	Inner ring	Level 1	Made by electric engraver
KI07	Inner ring	Level 2	Made by electric engraver
KI08	Inner ring	Level 2	Made by electric engraver

The original MoCo used ResNet50 [30] as the backbone network and achieved excellent results. However, as the number of network layers increases, the computational complexity of the network gradually increases and it is difficult to converge. The original MoCo uses a deep ResNet network because it is used to solve computer vision tasks, while the feature learning task of bearings is less difficult than the feature learning task of images, so the backbone network of SMoCo adopts the ResNet18 [30].

The output dimension of the query network and the key network is 128 in line with MoCo, thus ensuring that there is enough space to represent the extracted features. Since the convolutional layer output of ResNet18 has a dimension of 512, the MLP layers in the query network, key network, and predictor have the same structure with a hidden layer dimension of 512 and an output layer dimension of 128, and this structure has also been shown to be very effective for representation learning [21,24].

The initial learning rate η is set to 0.1 because using a larger learning rate can [24,25] accelerate the convergence and allows the model to try multiple directions at the early stage of optimization to prevent the model from getting stuck at the saddle point or the local minimum due to the small learning rate. In addition, since this paper uses both time-domain and frequency-domain data for learning, the data distribution between the two differs greatly and the learning task is more complex, therefore, 0.1 is chosen as the initial learning rate. The learning rate is updated via the cosine learning rate scheduler with the following equation.

$$\eta_t = \frac{1}{2}\left(1 + cos\left(\frac{t\pi}{T}\right)\right)\eta \tag{10}$$

where η is the initial learning rate, η_t is the current learning rate, T is the maximum number of epochs, and t is the current epoch.

It has been shown in MoCo that the model performs better when the value of momentum α is in the range 0.99~0.9999, showing that a slowly progressing (i.e., relatively large momentum) key encoder is beneficial, while when α is too small (e.g., 0.9), the accuracy drops considerably [24]. This is because MoCo relies on a consistent dictionary for training, which is the data in the queue generated by the key encoder [24]. Therefore, SMoCo chooses to keep the same parameter selection as MoCo, i.e., 0.999. See Table 3 for other hyperparameters. In addition, the data augmentation methods in Table 3 are all implemented with a probability of 50%, thereby increasing the variety of the transformation. The variation of the loss values during the training process is shown in Figure 7; it can be found that the loss value becomes smooth in the late training period, indicating that the training has reached the fitting state. The experiment was conducted under Windows 11 and PyTorch1.11, running on a computer with the following configurations: i5-12400F, NVIDIA RTX 3060, and 16GB RAM. The training time for self-supervised learning is about 6.5 h.

Table 3. Hyperparameter setting.

Hyperparameter	Value	Data Augmentation	Value
Batch size	64	Normalization	/
Optimizer	SGD	Gaussian noise	Noise coefficient $\sigma_n = 0.05$
Learning rate	0.1	Scaling	Scale coefficient $\sigma_s = 0.05$
Momentum	0.9	Resampling	Stretch coefficient $\sigma_s = 0.3$
Weight decay	0.0001	Truncation	Truncation length = 100
Epochs	350	Flip	/
Learning rate schedule	Cosine		
Queue size	65536		
Momentum update	0.999		
Temperature	0.07		

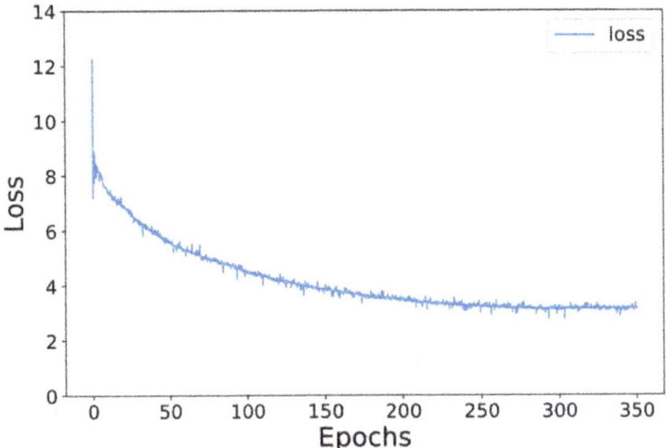

Figure 7. Loss history of self-supervised on unlabeled dataset 1.

Other self-supervised learning methods, Wang, SimCLR, BYOL, and MoCo, are carried out for comparison. To exclude the influence of other factors, the backbone network of all methods is ResNet18, which is trained using time-domain signals. In addition, to prove the great superiority of SMoCo, as a comparison, the labeled dataset 1 is used for supervised learning, and the network structure is also ResNet18, which is called labeled pretraining. The feature extractors of all methods, that is, the convolutional layers of ResNet18, are used to perform feature extraction on part of the data in dataset 1 and T-SNE is used to reduce it to 2D for visualization. The results are shown in Figure 8. SMoCo can achieve an excellent feature extraction performance without using labels and achieves the aggregation of each category and the separation of different categories from each other, which greatly exceeds all other self-supervised learning methods, even reaching the level of labeled pretraining. Other self-supervised methods perform poorly, specifically for Wang, which only identifies the corresponding data augmentation categories without instance-level self-supervised learning and therefore does not perform feature extraction well. For SimCLR, its reliance on learning in large batches, via comparing data within a batch without other techniques such as momentum updates, makes its training less stable and less performant. For BYOL and MoCo, although they achieve relatively good results without labels, they lack the unique SML proposed in this paper, so the results are not as good as SMoCo.

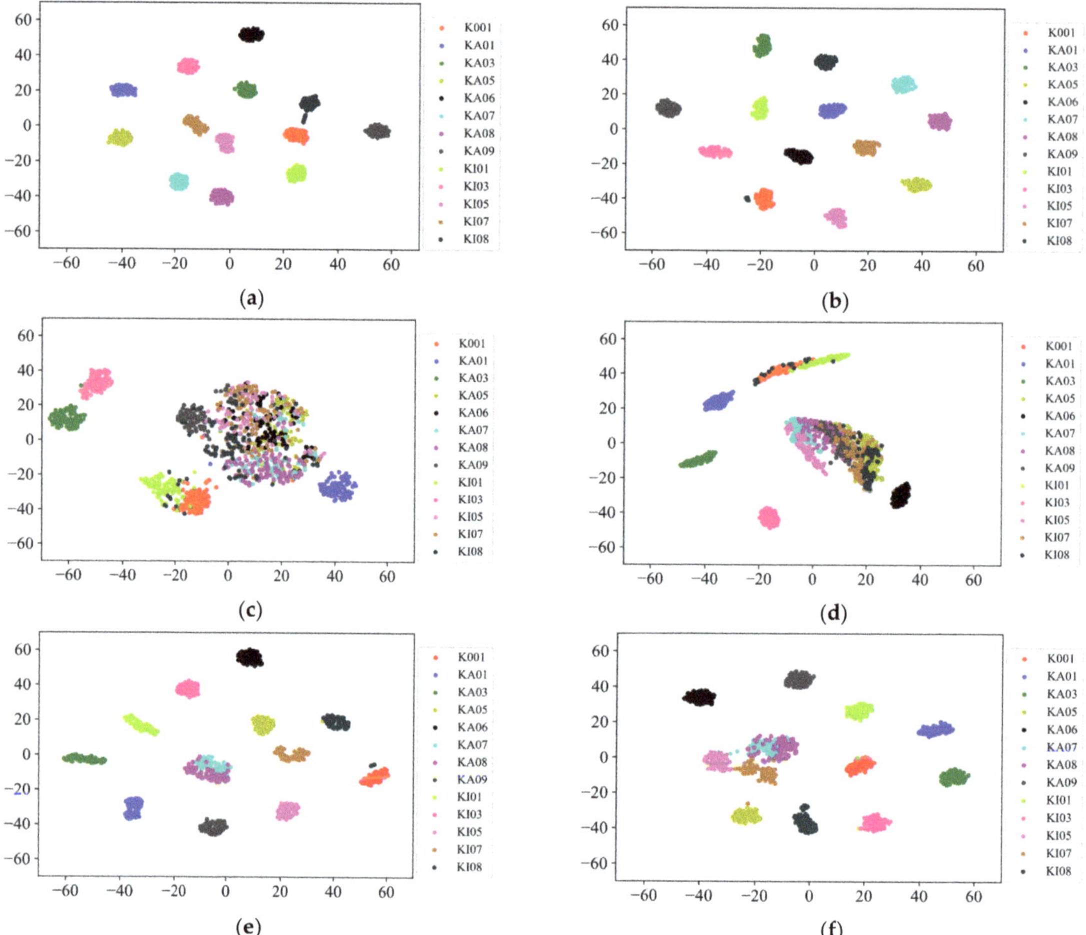

Figure 8. The visualization of feature extractors on unlabeled bearing dataset 1. (**a**) SMoCo; (**b**) labeled pretraining; (**c**) Wang; (**d**) SimCLR; (**e**) BYOL; (**f**) MoCo.

4.2. Fault Diagnosis on Same Products under Different Fault Characteristic Distributions

To verify the diagnostic performance of SMoCo for the same products under different failure levels, different failure models, and different working conditions, 10 types of real damaged bearings in the Paderborn University dataset, including a healthy state bearing and 2 mixed fault bearings with the working condition of N15_M07_F04, are selected as the target diagnosis dataset. The specific information is shown in Table 4. To reflect the limited data problem faced in the actual diagnosis task, the training set uses 5 samples per class, and the testing set uses 50 samples per class.

To demonstrate the performance of the feature extractor obtained in the self-supervised learning stage, the feature extractors trained in Section 4.1 are used to perform feature extraction on the testing set without any training, and T-SNE is used for visualization. The results are shown in Figure 9. The SMoCo proposed in this paper can achieve an excellent feature extraction performance on target diagnostic data without using training data. It not only greatly outperforms other self-supervised learning methods, but also outperforms labeled pretraining. Compared to the result of extracting from dataset 1, other methods are less capable of extracting features from the target diagnostic data at this time due to the difference between the distribution of the pre-training dataset and the target diagnostic dataset.

Table 4. Dataset 2: Real damaged bearing dataset under N15_M07_F04.

Bearing Code	Damaged Element	Fault Mode	Damage Form	Arrangement	Damaged Extent
K001	Health state	/	/	/	/
KA04	Outer ring	Fatigue: pitting	Single damage	No repetition	Level 1
KA15	Outer ring	Plastic deform: Indentations	Single damage	No repetition	Level 1
KA16	Outer ring	Fatigue: pitting	Repetitive damage	Random	Level 2
KB23	Outer ring and inner ring	Fatigue: pitting	Multiple damage	Random	Level 2
KB24	Outer ring and inner ring	Fatigue: pitting	Multiple damage	No repetition	Level 3
KI14	Outer ring	Fatigue: pitting	Multiple damage	No repetition	Level 1
KI16	Outer ring	Fatigue: pitting	Single damage	No repetition	Level 3
KI17	Inner ring	Fatigue: pitting	Repetitive damage	Random	Level 1
KI18	Inner ring	Fatigue: pitting	Single damage	No repetition	Level 2

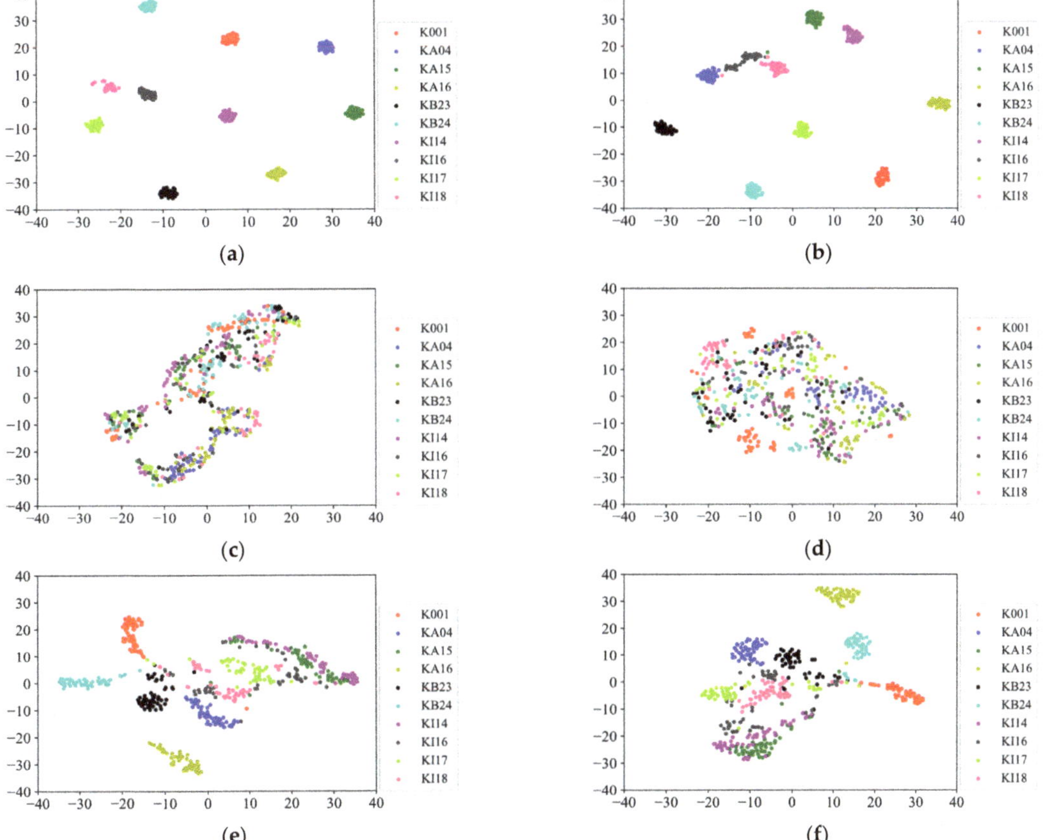

Figure 9. The visualization of feature extractors on labeled bearing dataset 2. (**a**) SMoCo; (**b**) labeled pretraining; (**c**) Wang; (**d**) SimCLR; (**e**) BYOL; (**f**) MoCo.

To more fully demonstrate the superiority of our method, in addition to the methods in Section 4.1, we also use MixMatch [31], ResNet18, and FFT + SVM as a comparison for the diagnosis task. Among them, MixMatch is one of the best-performing semi-supervised methods, which uses the unlabeled dataset 1 and the training set of dataset 2 for training. ResNet18 is trained using only the training set of dataset 2. The diagnostic accuracy of each method is shown in Table 5 and Figure 10. FFT + SVM is a classical and effective fault diagnosis method for small sample cases, which first performs FFT transformation on the original signal and then uses SVM to classify the FFT transformed features.

Table 5. Comparison of diagnostic results on dataset 2 under 5 samples per class.

Method	Accuracy (%)	Time (s)
SMoCo	99.68 ± 0.26	1.47
MixMatch	89.96 ± 4.84	411.24
Labeled Pretraining	97.16 ± 1.80	25.11
Wang	73.88 ± 3.40	29.93
SimCLR	73.76 ± 1.35	30.44
BYOL	89.48 ± 3.29	30.72
MoCo	89.68 ± 2.16	30.75
ResNet18	71.96 ± 3.13	26.26
FFT + SVM	79.14 ± 7.86	0.16

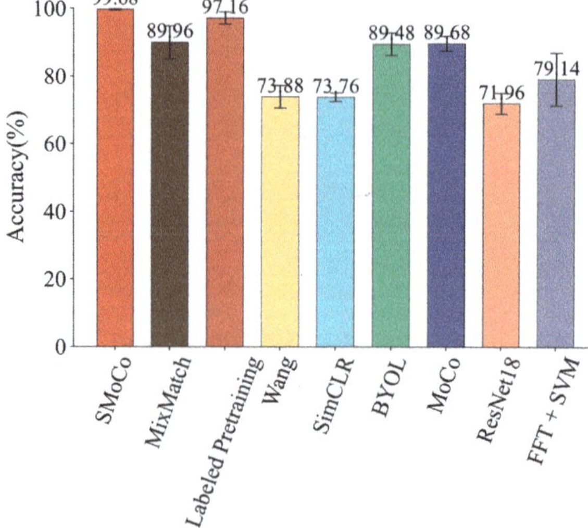

Figure 10. Comparison of diagnostic results on dataset 2 under 5 samples per class.

It can be seen from Table 5 and Figure 10 that SMoCo benefits from its unique SML and structural improvements to MoCo; its accuracy reaches an astonishing 99.68%, while the time it takes is only 1.47 s, which even significantly exceeds the results of labeled pretraining. This is also consistent with the visualization results in Figure 9. SMoCo can distinguish each class well before training, so it only needs to use very few samples to build an excellent classification surface. Labeled pretraining uses labels for pre-training, but the obtained feature extractor is only adapted to the pre-training dataset. When faced with new diagnostic tasks, although its diagnostic accuracy is improved, the effect is still limited. Other self-supervised learning methods lack our unique SML and gaps in the structure, so their performance falls far short of SMoCo. For FFT + SVM, it performs better than ResNet18 using only time-domain features in the case of small samples; however, its diagnostic accuracy is not high in the face of complex diagnostic problems under real faults.

The confusion matrix for SMoCo and labeled pretraining with the best diagnostic performance is plotted as shown in Figure 11. SMoCo only misclassified one sample of KI17 as KI16, which is consistent with the results visualized in Figure 9. The interval between

KI17 and KI16 is relatively close, which may cause errors in the classification plane due to the special training samples. Nonetheless, our SMoCo outperforms labeled pretraining in every category.

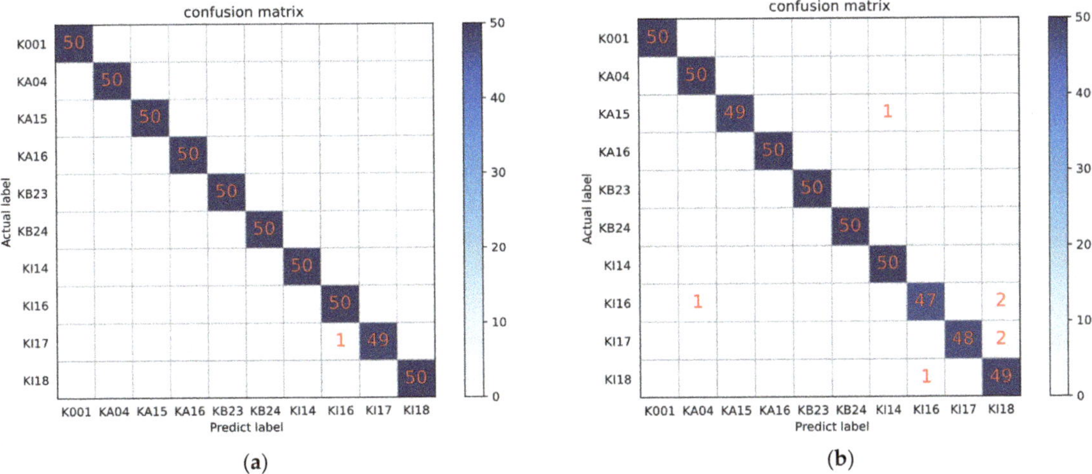

Figure 11. Confusion matrix of the two best-performing methods on dataset 2. (**a**) SMoCo; (**b**) labeled pretraining.

The diagnostic accuracy of SMoCo in the case of fewer samples is also further explored by selecting the best performing SMoCo and labeled pretraining as a comparison. For the training set, a total of 5 groups of samples from 1 to 5 per class were used to explore the results, as shown in Figure 12. It can be seen from Figure 12 that SMoCo is far better than labeled pretraining in all cases. SMoCo can achieve 99.16% accuracy with only 3 samples per class and its accuracy only drops more in the case of one sample per class. It is demonstrated that our method has strong performance and robustness for diagnosis in limited data.

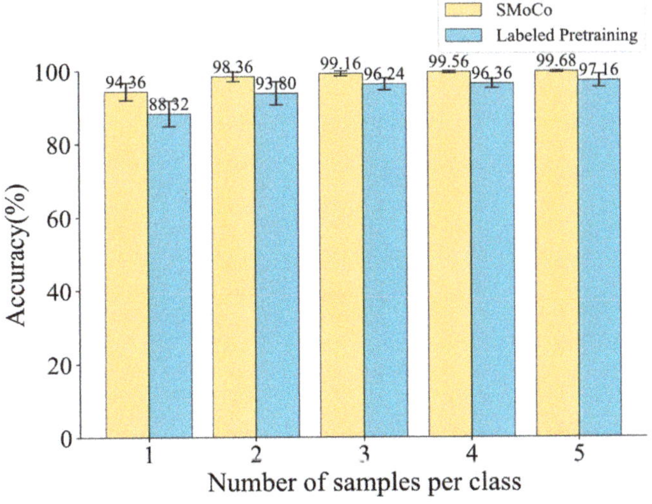

Figure 12. Comparison of results under different training set sizes on dataset 2.

4.3. Fault Diagnosis on Different Products of Aero-Engine Bearing

To verify the diagnostic effectiveness of SMoCo on aero-engine rolling bearings, this paper uses the dataset of aero-engine high-speed bearings from the Department of Mechanical and Aeronautical Engineering of the Polytechnic University of Turin [32]. The test rig is shown in Figure 13. For the dataset, we use the vibration acceleration data of aero-engine bearings at different rotational speeds and different degrees of damage. The length of a single sample is still 4096, and the y-direction channel data at A1 is used. To reflect the extremely limited data situation in the actual diagnosis process, only 3 samples per class are used in the training set, and 50 samples per class are used in the testing set. The specific dataset information is shown in Table 6. At this point, the unlabeled pre-training dataset 1 and the target diagnostic dataset 3 have completely different device types, working conditions, and failure modes.

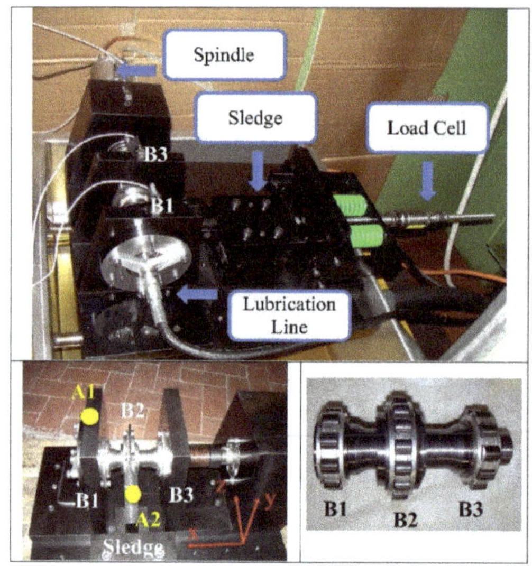

Figure 13. Test rig of the aero-engine bearing dataset from Polytechnic University of Turin.

Table 6. Dataset 3: Aero-engine bearing dataset from Polytechnic University of Turin.

Damaged Element	Diameter (μm)	Fault Mode Rotation Speed (r/min)	Load (N)	Training Samples	Testing Samples	Label
Healthy	/	24,000	1400	3	50	0
Inner ring	450	24,000	1400	3	50	1
Inner ring	250	24,000	1400	3	50	2
Inner ring	150	24,000	1400	3	50	3
Roller	450	24,000	1400	3	50	4
Roller	250	24,000	1400	3	50	5
Roller	150	24,000	1400	3	50	6
Inner ring	450	18,000	1400	3	50	7
Inner ring	250	18,000	1400	3	50	8
Inner ring	150	18,000	1400	3	50	9
Roller	450	18,000	1400	3	50	10
Roller	250	18,000	1400	3	50	11
Roller	150	18,000	1400	3	50	12

As in Section 4.2, the feature extractors trained in Section 4.1 are used to perform feature extraction on the testing set data and visualize it using T-SNE. It's worth noting that this was done without any training on dataset 3. The results are shown in Figure 14. The SMoCo proposed in this paper still achieves amazing feature extraction results in the face of completely different devices without using any training data, greatly surpassing other methods.

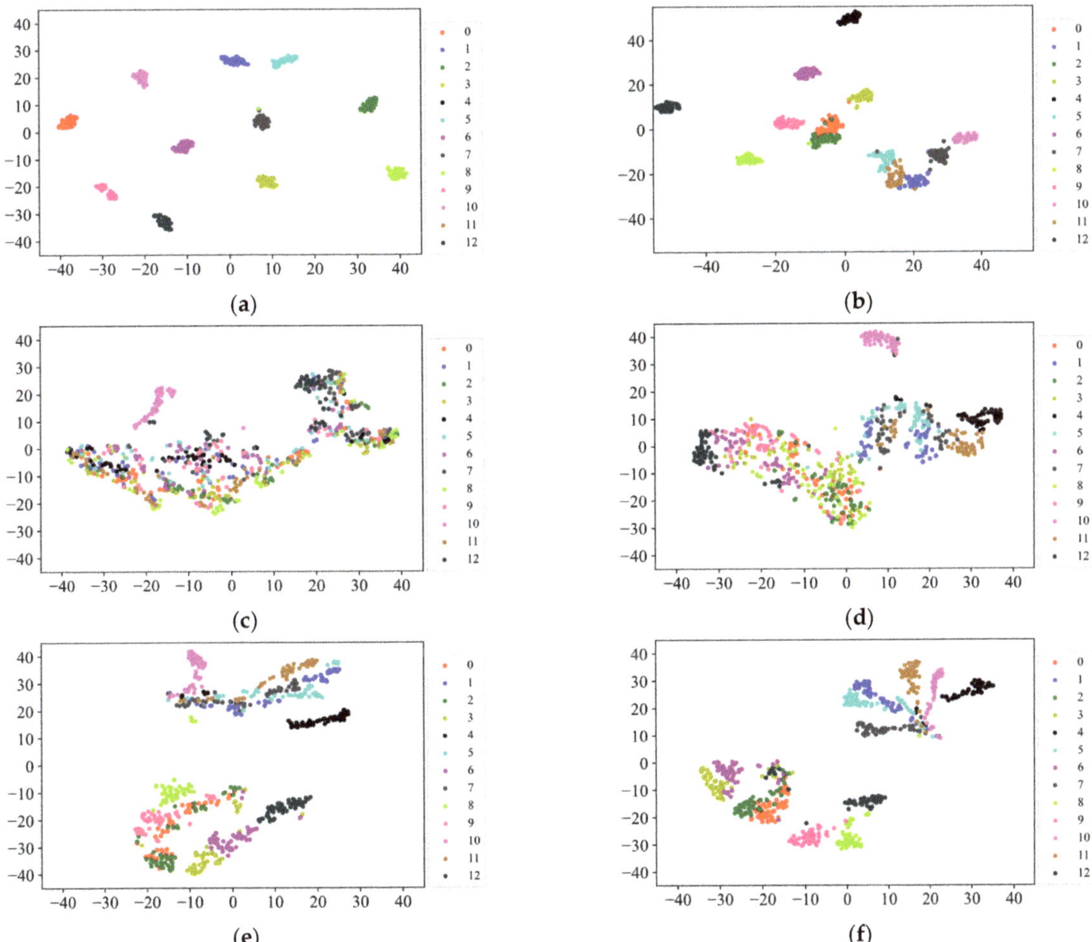

Figure 14. The visualization of feature extractors on labeled aero-engine bearing dataset 3. (**a**) SMoCo; (**b**) labeled pretraining; (**c**) Wang; (**d**) SimCLR; (**e**) BYOL; (**f**) MoCo.

The methods trained in Section 4.1, MixMatch, ResNet18, and FFT + SVM are used for comparison on dataset 3, and the results are shown in Table 7 and Figure 15.

It can be seen from Table 7 and Figure 15 that SMoCo achieves 100% diagnostic accuracy when faced with diagnostic problems of different devices, and its training and inference time is only 1.6 s. Both the accuracy and efficiency achieved the best results, greatly surpassing other methods. Although labeled pretraining can still improve the accuracy at this time, in the case of different devices, due to the large difference between the distribution of the pre-training data and the data to be diagnosed, namely dataset 1 and dataset 3, its effect is greatly reduced at this time. Since MixMatch uses both dataset 1 and dataset 3 for training, it can adapt the target diagnostic data with unlabeled data and thus obtain better diagnostic accuracy, but even so it is not as good as SMoCo. In addition, it needs to be trained from scratch for each diagnostic task, so its training time is far inferior to SMoCo. The performance of other self-supervised methods is still far from that of ours. FFT + SVM has achieved good results in the face of relatively simple diagnostic tasks, but there is still a big gap compared with SMoCo.

Table 7. Comparison of diagnostic results on dataset 3 under 3 samples per class.

Method	Accuracy (%)	Time (s)
SMoCo	100.00 ± 0.00	1.60
MixMatch	98.55 ± 0.65	469.06
Labeled Pretraining	90.92 ± 2.11	30.62
Wang	74.65 ± 4.56	36.04
SimCLR	81.85 ± 4.06	37.32
BYOL	85.66 ± 2.82	35.12
MoCo	84.00 ± 4.10	40.42
ResNet18	82.83 ± 2.88	29.78
FFT + SVM	94.94 ± 4.19	0.15

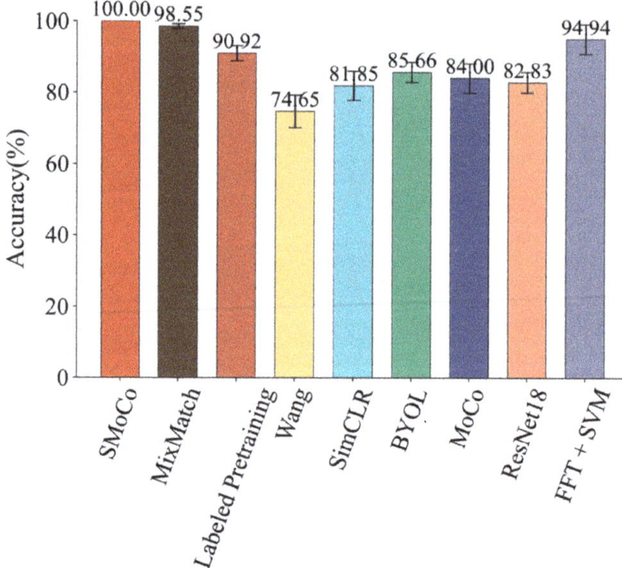

Figure 15. Comparison of diagnostic results on dataset 3 under 3 samples per class.

To further explore the effectiveness of SMoCo, MixMatch is also used as a comparison, which is the best performing method among the other methods. For the training set of dataset 3, one sample per class to three samples per class are used for training, and the results are shown in Figure 16. SMoCo can achieve a diagnostic accuracy of 99.15% with only one sample per class, which is also consistent with the results of feature visualization. It is proven that SMoCo is efficient and robust in the face of diagnostic tasks of different devices, which greatly reflects its superiority. In the case of extremely limited data, MixMatch's diagnostic accuracy drops sharply. This is due to the lack of a stable and efficient feature extractor, and it will encounter the common problem of deep learning, that is, the performance will be greatly reduced when the amount of data is extremely limited.

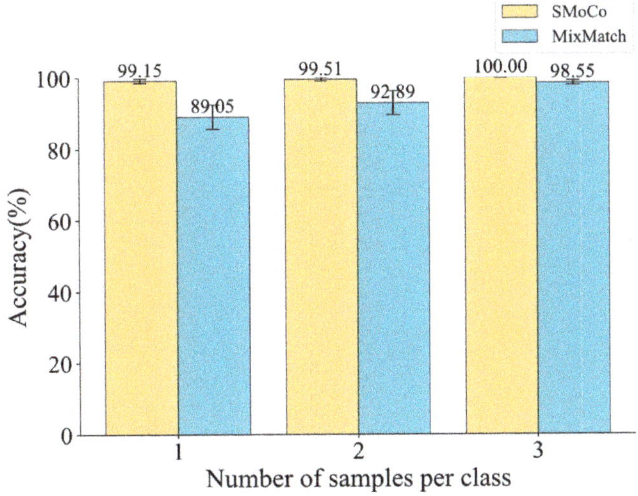

Figure 16. Comparison of results under different training set sizes on dataset 3.

5. Robustness Verification of SMoCo

5.1. Sensitivity to the Size of the Pre-Training Dataset

To further explore the sensitivity of SMoCo to the size of the unlabeled pre-training dataset, in this section, five different data volumes of 2000, 1500, 1000, 500, and 100 for each class are used for self-supervised learning on unlabeled dataset 1. After the self-supervised training is completed, all feature extractors are used to perform fault diagnosis on the labeled dataset 2 and dataset 3, respectively. In addition, to further explore their performance with different numbers of labeled training sets, this paper varies the number of samples per class from 1 to 5 for the training set of dataset 2 and from 1 to 3 for dataset 3. For each dataset, an additional method that performs the best except SMoCo in Sections 4.2 and 4.3 is performed as a comparison. Finally, to better evaluate their diagnostic performance, the F1 score is used as the evaluation criterion [33], and the results are shown in Table 8, Figure 17, Table 9, and Figure 18. Where SMoCo + 2000 means self-supervised learning using 2000 unlabeled samples per class in dataset 1, the meaning of SMoCo + 1500, etc. can be deduced accordingly. Labeled pretraining + 2000 means pre-training with labels using 2000 samples per class in dataset 1. MixMatch + 2000 means semi-supervised learning using both the 2000 unlabeled samples per class in dataset 1 and the labeled target diagnostic dataset.

Table 8. Experimental results of the sensitivity to the size of the data set on dataset 2.

Method	Number of Samples Per Class on Dataset 2				
	1 (F1/%)	2 (F1/%)	3 (F1/%)	4 (F1/%)	5 (F1/%)
SMoCo + 2000	94.39	97.86	98.92	99.60	99.64
SMoCo + 1500	92.35	95.43	97.79	98.52	98.76
SMoCo + 1000	91.80	94.90	96.76	98.07	98.51
SMoCo + 500	89.85	94.26	96.46	97.00	97.95
SMoCo + 100	89.33	94.19	96.26	96.65	97.61
Labeled Pretraining + 2000	88.33	94.24	96.20	96.84	97.20

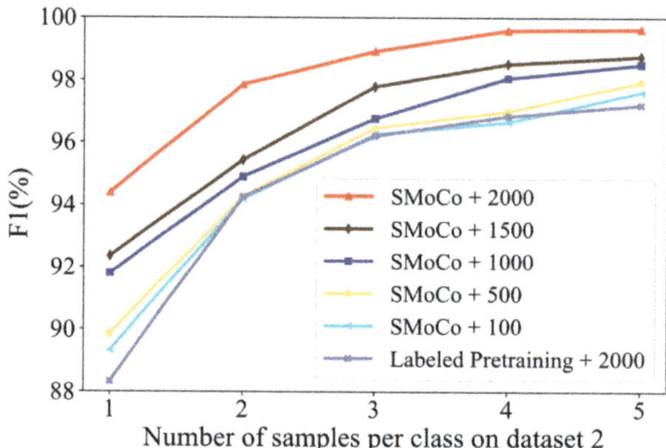

Figure 17. Experimental results of the sensitivity to the size of the data set on dataset 2.

Table 9. Experimental results of the sensitivity to the size of the data set on dataset 3.

Method	Number of Samples Per Class on Dataset 3		
	1 (F1/%)	2 (F1/%)	3 (F1/%)
SMoCo + 2000	99.46	99.84	99.94
SMoCo + 1500	98.31	99.11	99.54
SMoCo + 1000	98.01	99.04	99.38
SMoCo + 500	97.74	98.86	99.20
SMoCo + 100	97.04	98.21	98.89
MixMatch + 2000	88.51	94.27	97.43

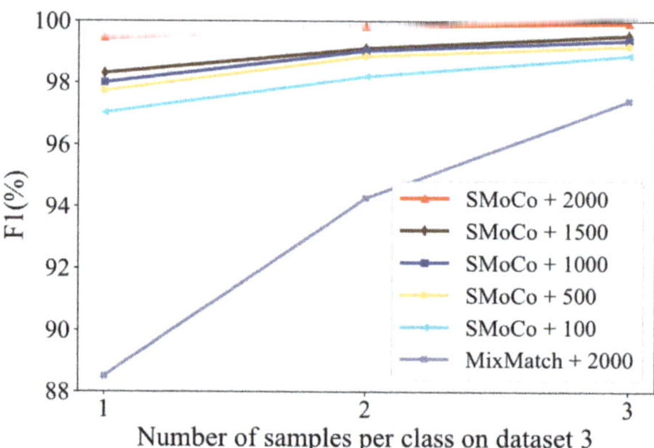

Figure 18. Experimental results of the sensitivity to the size of the data set on dataset 3.

From Table 8 and Figure 17, it can be seen that for dataset 2 when using 5 labeled training samples per class, all SMoCo with different unlabeled data sizes achieved excellent results. When using 1 labeled training sample per class, even SMoCo + 100 achieved a score of nearly 90%. SMoCo + 100 achieved a similar level of performance as with labeled pretraining and even reached the leading performance in the case of 1 sample per class and 5 samples per class, demonstrating the superior performance and robustness of SMoCo regarding the size of the unlabeled dataset. With the increase in data volume, SMoCo can achieve feature extractors with better performance via self-supervised learning.

As can be seen from Table 9 and Figure 18, SMoCo + 100 achieves excellent diagnostic performance even in the face of diagnostic problems across different devices and surprisingly greatly outperforms MixMatch + 2000. The progressive improvement in diagnostic performance from SMoCo + 100 to SMoCo + 2000 proves that the performance of SMoCo can be increased gradually with the increase of the amount of data.

5.2. Sensitivity to Aero-Engine Bearing Dataset under Different Noise Levels

In this section, noise stress tests are carried out to demonstrate the robustness and effectiveness of SMoCo with different signal-to-noise ratio (SNR) values on dataset 3. As a comparison, MixMatch and FFT + SVM are also used to perform diagnosis on dataset 3 with 3 samples per class at different noise levels, which are the best performing methods except SMoCo. SMoCo and MixMatch both use the full unlabeled dataset 1, i.e., 2000 samples per class. In this paper, we also further increase the difficulty of the experiment by training SMoCo from 1 sample per class to 3 samples per class of the labeled datasets, to verify the robustness of SMoCo under severe conditions, which are denoted as SMoCo + 1, SMoCo + 2, and SMoCo + 3. The evaluation criterion is the F1 score, and the results are shown in Table 10 and Figure 19.

Table 10. Experimental results of the sensitivity to the SNR on the aero-engine bearing dataset.

Method	SNR										
	0 dB	1 dB	2 dB	3 dB	4 dB	5 dB	6 dB	7 dB	8 dB	9 dB	10 dB
SMoCo + 3	96.61	97.60	97.90	98.03	98.65	98.74	99.23	99.53	99.56	99.69	99.75
SMoCo + 2	95.50	95.61	96.64	97.63	98.00	98.15	98.43	98.98	99.10	99.29	99.35
SMoCo + 1	91.54	92.03	92.74	93.75	94.92	96.06	96.68	97.08	97.32	97.93	98.58
MixMatch	54.84	67.54	72.41	79.27	85.79	90.95	92.94	93.56	93.72	94.99	95.58
FFT + SVM	83.28	85.46	87.15	88.55	89.98	90.85	91.41	91.95	92.89	93.11	94.09

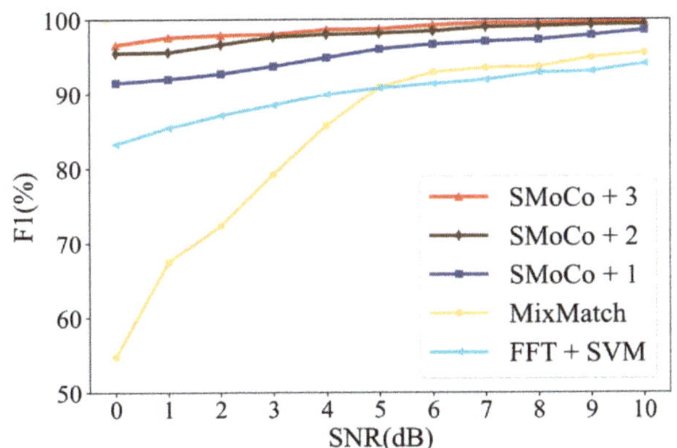

Figure 19. Experimental results of the sensitivity to the SNR on the aero-engine bearing dataset.

From Table 10 and Figure 19, it can be seen that SMoCo achieves the best result compared to the other two methods, even SMoCo + 1 can achieve a score of 91.54 at 0 dB, showing its strong robustness against noise. Although SMoCo + 1 achieves good diagnostic accuracy, the gap between it and SMoCo + 2 is large compared to the gap between SMoCo + 2 and SMoCo + 3, which is especially obvious in the case of strong noise. This is because, in the case of extremely small samples, there is a deviation in the decision boundary between the training and testing data sets due to interference of noise. In addition, MixMatch performs worse than FFT + SVM in the case of higher noise due to the fact that the gap between its data distribution and that of the unlabeled dataset gradually widens when the noise of the target diagnostic data increases, resulting in MixMatch not being able to make good use of the unlabeled data to improve the diagnostic accuracy of the target labeled data.

6. Conclusions

Under complex and harsh actual working conditions, there is a limited data problem in the fault diagnosis of aero-engine rolling bearings, which seriously affects the performance of intelligent diagnosis methods. Based on MoCo, this paper proposes a new intelligent diagnosis method based on SMoCo through improvement of the structure and innovation of the data augmentation method. SMoCo first performs self-supervised learning on easily available unlabeled data and then utilizes the trained feature extractor for downstream diagnostic tasks under limited data. Experimental results show that SMoCo not only has high diagnostic accuracy and training efficiency, but also has good generalization ability. The experimental results show that SMoCo can have high diagnostic accuracy and training efficiency under limited data, whether the target data are from the same model but with different failure modes and different working conditions or from a completely different type from the pre-training data, which proves its good generalization ability. The main conclusions are as follows:

1. In this paper, BN and a predictor are introduced to solve the deficiency of the MoCo structure, and SML is innovatively proposed according to the time domain and frequency domain of the signal, which regards the time-domain signal and frequency-domain signal as a positive pair. Therefore, a fault diagnosis method based on SMoCo is proposed.
2. SMoCo uses easily available unlabeled data for self-supervised learning, the sources of which can be diverse and are not limited to objects that need to be diagnosed. Therefore, its acquisition range is wider, and its feasibility in practical diagnostic tasks is much greater than that of previous work.
3. This paper uses two independent bearing datasets from Paderborn University and the Polytechnic University of Turin for experimental verification. In the experiment, three important problems of aero-engine bearing fault diagnosis under the condition of limited data are studied, which are different working conditions, different failure modes, and different equipment. After SMoCo performs self-supervised learning on artificially injected faulted bearings, the trained feature extractor can be used to solve the above problems. The results show that the proposed SMoCo method can effectively solve the diagnosis problem in the case of limited data, it greatly exceeds the existing state-of-the-art methods both in accuracy and speed and is very little affected by limited data, even requiring only one sample per class to achieve high diagnostic accuracy for aero-engine bearing.
4. Compared with representative methods, SMoCo still achieves good performance in the case of limited unlabeled pre-training data and less labeled training data with strong noise, demonstrating the robustness of SMoCo regarding data volume and noise.

Although the SMoCo proposed in this paper has achieved good results, there is still some work that deserves further exploration, especially in relation to the time and efficiency of self-supervised learning. SMoCo takes a relatively long time to learn the essential features of the signal in the self-supervised learning phase, and future research could be conducted to improve the training efficiency. In addition, in this paper, only Gaussian noise is explored as the data augmentation method, while there are often other non-Gaussian noises and mixed noises in the actual industry [34,35], which could be further investigated in the future to be more robust regarding the complex conditions in actual industry. Future work could also try to change the structure of the encoder to use a convolutional network with better performance or a transformer network, which is currently performing extremely well in the field of deep learning [36]. A larger pre-trained dataset with different data sources, not just from one bearing dataset, could be used to try to build a unified feature extractor for all rotating machinery problems.

Author Contributions: Conceptualization, Z.Y.; methodology, Z.Y. and H.L.; software, Z.Y.; validation, Z.Y.; writing—original draft, Z.Y.; writing—review and editing, H.L. All authors have read and agreed to the published version of the manuscript.

Funding: This study was supported by the National Natural Science Foundation of China (Grant No. 61973011).

Institutional Review Board Statement: Not applicable.

Informed Consent Statement: Not applicable.

Data Availability Statement: Not applicable.

Conflicts of Interest: The authors declare no conflict of interest.

References

1. Wang, B.; Zhang, X.; Sun, C.; Chen, X. A Quantitative Intelligent Diagnosis Method for Early Weak Faults of Aviation High-Speed Bearings. *ISA Trans.* **2019**, *93*, 370–383. [CrossRef] [PubMed]
2. Jiang, X.; Huang, Q.; Shen, C.; Wang, Q.; Xu, K.; Liu, J.; Shi, J.; Zhu, Z. Synchronous Chirp Mode Extraction: A Promising Tool for Fault Diagnosis of Rolling Element Bearings under Varying Speed Conditions. *Chin. J. Aeronaut.* **2022**, *35*, 348–364. [CrossRef]
3. Wang, Y.; Tse, P.W.; Tang, B.; Qin, Y.; Deng, L.; Huang, T. Kurtogram Manifold Learning and Its Application to Rolling Bearing Weak Signal Detection. *Measurement* **2018**, *127*, 533–545. [CrossRef]
4. Lei, Y.; Yang, B.; Jiang, X.; Jia, F.; Li, N.; Nandi, A.K. Applications of Machine Learning to Machine Fault Diagnosis: A Review and Roadmap. *Mech. Syst. Signal Process.* **2020**, *138*, 106587. [CrossRef]
5. Feng, Y.; Chen, J.; Zhang, T.; He, S.; Xu, E.; Zhou, Z. Semi-Supervised Meta-Learning Networks with Squeeze-and-Excitation Attention for Few-Shot Fault Diagnosis. *ISA Trans.* **2022**, *120*, 383–401. [CrossRef] [PubMed]
6. Yu, K.; Lin, T.R.; Ma, H.; Li, X.; Li, X. A Multi-Stage Semi-Supervised Learning Approach for Intelligent Fault Diagnosis of Rolling Bearing Using Data Augmentation and Metric Learning. *Mech. Syst. Signal Process.* **2021**, *146*, 107043. [CrossRef]
7. Zhang, S.; Ye, F.; Wang, B.; Habetler, T.G. Semi-Supervised Bearing Fault Diagnosis and Classification Using Variational Autoencoder-Based Deep Generative Models. *IEEE Sens. J.* **2021**, *21*, 6476–6486. [CrossRef]
8. Wen, L.; Gao, L.; Li, X. A New Deep Transfer Learning Based on Sparse Auto-Encoder for Fault Diagnosis. *IEEE Trans. Syst. Man Cybern. Syst.* **2019**, *49*, 136–144. [CrossRef]
9. Wang, Y.; Sun, X.; Li, J.; Yang, Y. Intelligent Fault Diagnosis With Deep Adversarial Domain Adaptation. *IEEE Trans. Instrum. Meas.* **2021**, *70*, 3035385. [CrossRef]
10. Zheng, H.; Wang, R.; Yang, Y.; Yin, J.; Li, Y.; Li, Y.; Xu, M. Cross-Domain Fault Diagnosis Using Knowledge Transfer Strategy: A Review. *IEEE Access* **2019**, *7*, 129260–129290. [CrossRef]
11. Jing, L.; Tian, Y. Self-Supervised Visual Feature Learning With Deep Neural Networks: A Survey. *IEEE Trans. Pattern Anal. Mach. Intell.* **2021**, *43*, 4037–4058. [CrossRef]
12. Zhang, R.; Isola, P.; Efros, A.A. Colorful Image Colorization. In *Computer Vision–ECCV 2016*; Leibe, B., Matas, J., Sebe, N., Welling, M., Eds.; Lecture Notes in Computer Science; Springer International Publishing: Cham, Switzerland, 2016; Volume 9907, pp. 649–666; ISBN 978-3-319-46486-2.
13. Pathak, D.; Krähenbühl, P.; Donahue, J.; Darrell, T.; Efros, A.A. Context Encoders: Feature Learning by Inpainting. In Proceedings of the 2016 IEEE Conference on Computer Vision and Pattern Recognition (CVPR), Las Vegas, NV, USA, 27–30 June 2016; pp. 2536–2544.
14. Noroozi, M.; Favaro, P. Unsupervised Learning of Visual Representations by Solving Jigsaw Puzzles. In *Computer Vision–ECCV 2016*; Leibe, B., Matas, J., Sebe, N., Welling, M., Eds.; Springer International Publishing: Cham, Switzerland, 2016; pp. 69–84.
15. Ledig, C.; Theis, L.; Huszár, F.; Caballero, J.; Cunningham, A.; Acosta, A.; Aitken, A.; Tejani, A.; Totz, J.; Wang, Z.; et al. Photo-Realistic Single Image Super-Resolution Using a Generative Adversarial Network. In Proceedings of the 2017 IEEE Conference on Computer Vision and Pattern Recognition (CVPR), Honolulu, HI, USA, 21–26 July 2017; pp. 105–114.
16. Wang, H.; Liu, Z.; Ge, Y.; Peng, D. Self-Supervised Signal Representation Learning for Machinery Fault Diagnosis under Limited Annotation Data. *Knowl. Based Syst.* **2022**, *239*, 107978. [CrossRef]
17. Tian, Y.; Sun, C.; Poole, B.; Krishnan, D.; Schmid, C.; Isola, P. What Makes for Good Views for Contrastive Learning? In *Advances in Neural Information Processing Systems*; Curran Associates, Inc.: New York, NY, USA, 2020; Volume 33, pp. 6827–6839.
18. Chen, T.; Kornblith, S.; Norouzi, M.; Hinton, G. A Simple Framework for Contrastive Learning of Visual Representations. In Proceedings of the 37th International Conference on Machine Learning, PMLR, Vienna, Austria, 21 November 2020; pp. 1597–1607.
19. Chen, T.; Kornblith, S.; Swersky, K.; Norouzi, M.; Hinton, G.E. Big Self-Supervised Models Are Strong Semi-Supervised Learners. In *Advances in Neural Information Processing Systems*; Curran Associates, Inc.: New York, NY, USA, 2020; Volume 33, pp. 22243–22255.
20. Caron, M.; Misra, I.; Mairal, J.; Goyal, P.; Bojanowski, P.; Joulin, A. Unsupervised Learning of Visual Features by Contrasting Cluster Assignments. In *Advances in Neural Information Processing Systems*; Curran Associates, Inc.: New York, NY, USA, 2020; Volume 33, pp. 9912–9924.

21. Grill, J.-B.; Strub, F.; Altché, F.; Tallec, C.; Richemond, P.H.; Buchatskaya, E.; Doersch, C.; Pires, B.A.; Guo, Z.D.; Azar, M.G.; et al. Bootstrap Your Own Latent: A New Approach to Self-Supervised Learning. *Adv. Neural Inf. Processing Syst.* **2020**, *33*, 21271–21284.
22. Wei, M.; Liu, Y.; Zhang, T.; Wang, Z.; Zhu, J. Fault Diagnosis of Rotating Machinery Based on Improved Self-Supervised Learning Method and Very Few Labeled Samples. *Sensors* **2021**, *22*, 192. [CrossRef]
23. Ding, Y.; Zhuang, J.; Ding, P.; Jia, M. Self-Supervised Pretraining via Contrast Learning for Intelligent Incipient Fault Detection of Bearings. *Reliab. Eng. Syst. Saf.* **2022**, *218*, 108126. [CrossRef]
24. He, K.; Fan, H.; Wu, Y.; Xie, S.; Girshick, R. Momentum Contrast for Unsupervised Visual Representation Learning. In Proceedings of the 2020 IEEE/CVF Conference on Computer Vision and Pattern Recognition (CVPR), Seattle, WA, USA, 13–19 June 2020.
25. Peng, T.; Shen, C.; Sun, S.; Wang, D. Fault Feature Extractor Based on Bootstrap Your Own Latent and Data Augmentation Algorithm for Unlabeled Vibration Signals. *IEEE Trans. Ind. Electron.* **2022**, *69*, 9547–9555. [CrossRef]
26. Ioffe, S.; Szegedy, C. Batch Normalization: Accelerating Deep Network Training by Reducing Internal Covariate Shift. *arXiv* **2015**, arXiv:1502.03167.
27. Oord, A.; van den Li, Y.; Vinyals, O. Representation Learning with Contrastive Predictive Coding. *arXiv* **2018**, arXiv:1807.03748.
28. Lessmeier, C.; Kimotho, J.K.; Zimmer, D.; Sextro, W. Condition Monitoring of Bearing Damage in Electromechanical Drive Systems by Using Motor Current Signals of Electric Motors: A Benchmark Data Set for Data-Driven Classification. In Proceedings of the PHM Society European Conference, Bilbao, Spain, 5–8 July 2016; Volume 3. [CrossRef]
29. Zhao, Z.; Li, T.; Wu, J.; Sun, C.; Wang, S.; Yan, R.; Chen, X. Deep Learning Algorithms for Rotating Machinery Intelligent Diagnosis: An Open Source Benchmark Study. *ISA Trans.* **2020**, *107*, 224–255. [CrossRef]
30. He, K.; Zhang, X.; Ren, S.; Sun, J. Deep Residual Learning for Image Recognition. In Proceedings of the 2016 IEEE Conference on Computer Vision and Pattern Recognition (CVPR), Las Vegas, NV, USA, 27–30 June 2016; pp. 770–778.
31. Berthelot, D.; Carlini, N.; Goodfellow, I.; Papernot, N.; Oliver, A.; Raffel, C.A. MixMatch: A Holistic Approach to Semi-Supervised Learning. In *Advances in Neural Information Processing Systems*; Curran Associates, Inc.: New York, NY, USA, 2019; Volume 32.
32. Daga, A.P.; Fasana, A.; Marchesiello, S.; Garibaldi, L. The Politecnico Di Torino Rolling Bearing Test Rig: Description and Analysis of Open Access Data. *Mech. Syst. Signal Process.* **2019**, *120*, 252–273. [CrossRef]
33. Forouzanfar, M.; Safaeipour, H.; Casavola, A. Oscillatory Failure Case Detection in Flight Control Systems via Wavelets Decomposition. In *ISA Transactions*; Elsevier: Amsterdam, The Netherlands, 2021. [CrossRef]
34. Safaeipour, H.; Forouzanfar, M.; Ramezani, A. Incipient Fault Detection in Nonlinear Non-Gaussian Noisy Environment. *Measurement* **2021**, *174*, 109008. [CrossRef]
35. Ortiz Ortiz, F.J.; Rodríguez-Ramos, A.; Llanes-Santiago, O. A Robust Fault Diagnosis Method in Presence of Noise and Missing Information for Industrial Plants. In *Proceedings of the Pattern Recognition*; Springer International Publishing: Cham, Switzerland, 2022; pp. 35–45.
36. Fang, H.; Deng, J.; Bai, Y.; Feng, B.; Li, S.; Shao, S.; Chen, D. CLFormer: A Lightweight Transformer Based on Convolutional Embedding and Linear Self-Attention With Strong Robustness for Bearing Fault Diagnosis Under Limited Sample Conditions. *IEEE Trans. Instrum. Meas.* **2022**, *71*, 3132327. [CrossRef]

Article

Semi-Analytical Search for Sun-Synchronous and Planet Synchronous Orbits around Jupiter, Saturn, Uranus and Neptune

Biao Yang [1], Yu Jiang [1,*], Hengnian Li [1,2], Chunsheng Jiang [1], Yongjie Liu [1], Chaojin Zhan [1], Hongbao Jing [1] and Yake Dong [1]

[1] State Key Laboratory of Astronautic Dynamics, Xi'an Satellite Control Center, Xi'an 710043, China; yangbiao-1995@163.com (B.Y.); henry_xscc@mail.xjtu.edu.cn (H.L.); csjiang1990@163.com (C.J.); liuyongjie_xian@163.com (Y.L.); cjzhan_xian@163.com (C.Z.); jinghongbao@163.com (H.J.); 18991922017@163.com (Y.D.)

[2] School of Electronic and Information Engineering, Xi'an Jiaotong University, Xi'an 710049, China

* Correspondence: jiangyu_xian_china@163.com

Abstract: With the development of aerospace science and technology, more and more probes are expected to be deployed around extraterrestrial planets. In this paper, some special orbits around Jupiter, Saturn, Uranus, and Neptune are discussed and analyzed. The design methods of some special orbits are sorted out, considering the actual motion parameters and main perturbation forces of these four planets. The characteristics of sun-synchronous orbits, repeating ground track orbits, and synchronous planet orbits surrounding these plants are analyzed and compared. The analysis results show that Uranus does not have sun-synchronous orbits in the general sense. This paper also preliminarily calculates the orbital parameters of some special orbits around these planets, including the relationship between the semi-major axis, the eccentricity and the orbital inclination of the sun-synchronous orbits, the range of the regression coefficient of the sun-synchronous repeating ground track orbits, and the orbital parameters of synchronous planet orbits, laying a foundation for more accurate orbit design of future planetary probes.

Keywords: exoplanet; sun-synchronous orbit; repeating ground track orbit; planet-synchronous orbit

MSC: 70M20; 70F15

Citation: Yang, B.; Jiang, Y.; Li, H.; Jiang, C.; Liu, Y.; Zhan, C.; Jing, H.; Dong, Y. Semi-Analytical Search for Sun-Synchronous and Planet Synchronous Orbits around Jupiter, Saturn, Uranus and Neptune. *Mathematics* **2022**, *10*, 2684. https://doi.org/10.3390/math10152684

Academic Editor: Paolo Mercorelli

Received: 15 June 2022
Accepted: 27 July 2022
Published: 29 July 2022

1. Introduction

Moving towards deep space is an important goal for the development of human civilization, and the exploration of extraterrestrial planets is also the litmus test of human technology. At present, many countries are actively exploring the planets in the solar system. Mars, as a close neighbor of the Earth, already has a number of artificial satellites in its orbit, such as the Odyssey [1], Mars Express [2], Mars Reconnaissance Orbiter [3], and Mars Atmosphere and Volatile Evolution (MAVEN) [4]. In addition, China's tianwen-1 [5], the US Curiosity [6], InSight [7], and other landers have carried out various tests on the surface of Mars.

The success of the exploration of Mars has further stimulated human enthusiasm for the exploration of other planets: Jupiter, Saturn, Uranus, and Neptune. As early as half a century ago, Voyager 1 was the first to provide detailed photos of Jupiter and Saturn [8]; after that, Voyager 2 [9] made a flyby exploration of all these four planets. However, with the progress of space technology and the in-depth study of the solar system, human beings have long been dissatisfied with this fleeting glimpse.

The new close-range planetary exploration mission has achieved great success. The Juno Jupiter probe launched in 2016 has greatly promoted our understanding of Jupiter's magnetic field model [10], core composition [11] and dynamic tides [12]. The data from the Cassini Saturn probe [13] has also accelerated our research progress on Saturn's upper atmosphere [14], satellite system [15], interior structure [16], and ring system [17].

Although Uranus and Neptune are more distant from us, research about them is also of great significance. Guillot's research shows that Uranus and Neptune are the key to understanding planets with hydrogen atmospheres [18]. Voosen et al. [19] said that Uranus should be the primary goal of NASA. However, at present, our understanding of these two planets is still relatively limited. Helled R. [20] pointed out that Uranus and Neptune are still mysterious planets, and it is obvious that these planets need to be further explored in theory and observation. Brozović's research [21] shows that the satellite systems of Uranus and Neptune are extremely complex and need further and more detailed observation. Hofstadter et al. [22] pointed out that some key measurements can only be carried out by orbiters of giant planets and detectors falling into their atmospheres.

It is obvious that probes dedicated to exclusive and focused study of Uranus and Neptune are needed. Research on the detection of Uranus and Neptune has been carried out. Rohan et al. [23] have designed the incident orbit of the Neptune detector. Cohen et al. [24] have begun to study the detector design of Uranus. Deniz et al. [25] discussed how to effectively use the time when the detector flies to Uranus and Neptune to detect gravitational waves.

2. Dynamic Model and Symbols

According to previous experience, in order to complete the detection task more efficiently, these orbiting probes often work in some special orbits [26], such as sun-synchronous orbit, repeating ground track orbit, and planet-synchronous orbit. Therefore, it is necessary to analyze and compare some special orbits around these four planets.

This paper uses some traditional symbols to represent the dynamic parameters and the orbital elements: a is the semi-major axis of the orbit. e is the orbital eccentricity. p is the semi-latus rectum and $p = a(1 - e^2)$. i is the orbital inclination. Ω is the right ascension of the ascending node. ω is the argument of perigee. M is the mean anomaly. f is the true anomaly. n is the mean angular velocity. The geometric interpretations of these elements are shown in Figure 1. The space coordinate system shown in Figure 1 is a right-hand coordinate system, where O is the center of mass of the planet and a focal point of an elliptical orbit, the x-axis points in the direction of the ascending node of the Sun, the z-axis points in the direction of the angular momentum direction of the planet's rotation. O′ is the center of the ellipse, C is the perigee of the orbit, A is the apogee of the orbit, B is the ascending node of the orbit and O′ is at the center of the ellipse ABC.

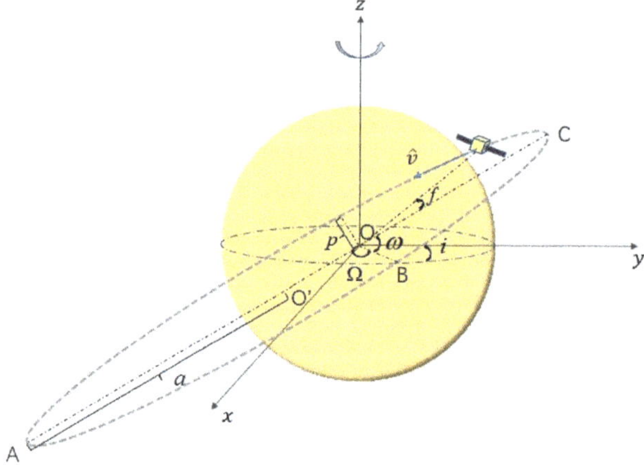

Figure 1. Schematic diagram of some orbital elements.

Some relevant dynamic parameters of the four giant planets are shown in the table below:

For a planet, J2 is the second-order zonal harmonic coefficient. Additionally, J4 is the fourth-order zonal harmonic coefficient. All parameters shown in Table 1 can be obtained from the public website of NASA [27]. To make it convenient for readers to verify the calculation results of this paper, the codes of this paper are available and can be obtained through private communication.

Table 1. Main dynamic parameters of each planet [27].

Parameters	Jupiter	Saturn	Uranus	Neptune
Mass(10^{24} kg)	1898.13	568.32	86.81	102.41
Equatorial radius(km)	71,492	60,268	25,559	24,764
Tropical orbit period(days)	4330.59	10,746.94	30,588.74	59,799.90
Sidereal rotation period(hours)	9.92	10.65	17.24	16.11
Inclination of equator(deg)	3.13	26.73	97.77	28.32
J_2 (10^{-6})	14,736	16,298	3343	3411
J_4 (10^{-6})	−586.61	−935.31	−34.52	−38.01

The gravitational field functions of the four giant planets are established in the planet centroid system shown in Figure 1. References [28,29] show that the magnitude of the non-spherical perturbation coming from the central body (irregular shape) is usually much larger than the ones coming from the moons, but they give a zero net result concerning variations of energy. Therefore, from this point of view, it is important to study those perturbations individually [28,29].

The main non-spherical perturbation terms of these four planets are J_2 and J_4, and therefore, their gravitational field functions can be expressed as [30,31]:

$$U = \frac{\mu_p}{r}\left[1 - \frac{J_2}{2}\left(\frac{R_p}{r}\right)^2\left(3\sin^2\varphi - 1\right) - \frac{J_4}{8}\left(\frac{R_p}{r}\right)^4\left(35\sin^4\varphi - 30\sin^2\varphi + 3\right)\right] \quad (1)$$

where μ_p is the gravitational field coefficient, R_p is the equatorial radius, φ is the geographic latitude, λ is the geographic longitude, ω_p is the rotational angular velocity, and r is the distance between the probe and the centroid of the planet.

3. Sun-Synchronous Orbits

A remarkable feature of a sun-synchronous orbit is that the solar angle of the orbital plane can maintain long-term stability, which is not only conducive to energy management. However, it also can ensure the relative stability of the light conditions for the observation [32].

In terms of the present technology, the service life of an artificial satellite generally does not exceed ten years [33]. For a planet with a very long tropical orbit period like Neptune, the change in the orbit's solar angle caused by the planet's revolution is not significant during the life cycle of the probe. However, with the continuous development of satellite manufacturing and propulsion system technology, the service life of a probe will become longer and longer, especially for a planetary probe, and its service life would be much longer than that of the Earth's probe. Therefore, it is still necessary to study the sun-synchronous orbits around planets with a long tropical period.

Taking the orbit design of the Earth satellite as a reference, the realization of sun-synchronous orbits mainly utilizes the perturbation of the non-spherical gravitational field of the planet. There will be a long-term drift of the right ascension of the ascending node under the influence of the gravitational field described in Equation (1). $\dot{\Omega}$, which represents the drift rate of Ω, can be described as follows [32]:

$$\dot{\Omega} = -\frac{3R_p^2}{2p^2}nJ_2\cos i - \left(\frac{3J_2R_p}{2p^2}\right)^2 n\cos i\left[\frac{1}{6}e^2\left(1+\frac{5}{4}\sin^2 i\right) + \sqrt{1-e^2}\left(1-\frac{3}{2}\sin^2 i\right) + \left(\frac{3}{2}-\frac{5}{3}\sin^2 i\right)\right] - \left(\frac{35}{8}\right)\frac{(-J_4)R_p^4}{p^4}n\cos i\left[e^2\left(\frac{9}{7}-\frac{9}{4}\sin^2 i\right) + \left(\frac{6}{7}-\frac{3}{2}\sin^2 i\right)\right] \tag{2}$$

To achieve the characteristics of sun synchronization, it is necessary to use the gravitational field characteristics of different planets to design different semi-major axis, eccentricity, and orbital inclination, so that the following relationship is established:

$$\dot{\Omega} = \dot{M}_s, \tag{3}$$

where $\dot{M}_s$ is the mean angular velocity during one sidereal rotation period of the planet. When combining Equation (2) and Equation (3), we get:

$$\frac{9nJ_2^2R_p^4}{4p^4}\left[e^2\left(-\frac{5}{24}-\frac{105J_4}{24J_2^2}\right)+\frac{3}{2}\sqrt{1-e^2}+\frac{5}{3}-\frac{35J_4}{12J_2^2}\right]\cos^3 i + \frac{9J_2^2R_p^4}{4p^4}\left[\frac{2np^2}{3J_2R_p^2}+e^2\left(\frac{3}{8}+\frac{15J_4}{8J_2^2}\right)-\frac{1}{2}\sqrt{1-e^2}-\frac{1}{6}+\frac{5J_4}{4J_2^2}\right]\cos i + \dot{M}_s = 0 \tag{4}$$

It can be seen from Equation (4) that with preset a and e, i can be obtained by solving the cubic equation with cos$i$ as the independent variable. The solution of a cubic equation probably has one, two, or three distinct roots.

The properties of the solution of the cubic equation can be obtained by calculating the following discriminant:

$$\Delta = \frac{\dot{M}_s{}^2}{4\Gamma_3{}^2} + \frac{\Gamma_1{}^3}{27\Gamma_3{}^3}, \tag{5}$$

where Γ_1 is the coefficient of cos$i$ and Γ_3 is the coefficient of $\cos^3 i$.

In combination with the dynamic parameters shown in Table 1, the discriminant is calculated, and the results are shown in Figure 2:

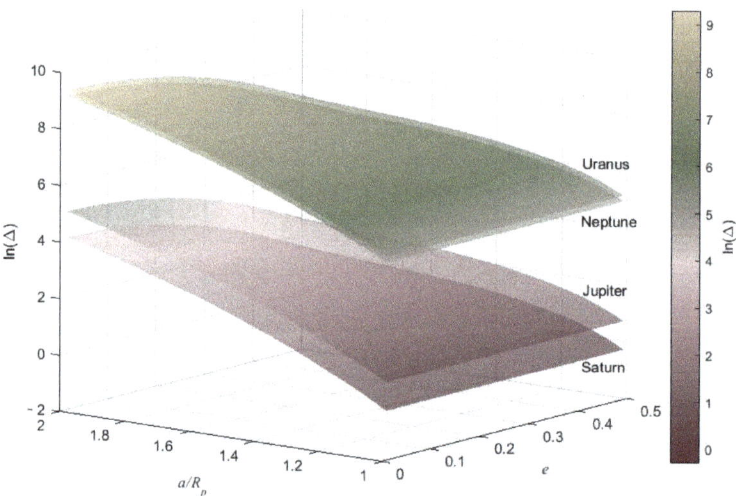

Figure 2. Calculation results of discriminant under different semi-major axes and eccentricities.

As can be seen from Figure 2, the corresponding discriminant of the four giant planets is always greater than zero, which indicates that the equation will have only one real root. That is, for a given a and e, all four planets will be able to find a unique orbital inclination i to meet the requirements of solar synchronous orbit.

Combined with the physical parameters of the four giant planets shown in Table 1, the semi-major axis, eccentricity, and orbital inclination of their solar synchronous orbit are further calculated in this paper. To more intuitively show the change relationship among the three parameters, the value range is wide, and the results are shown in Figure 3.

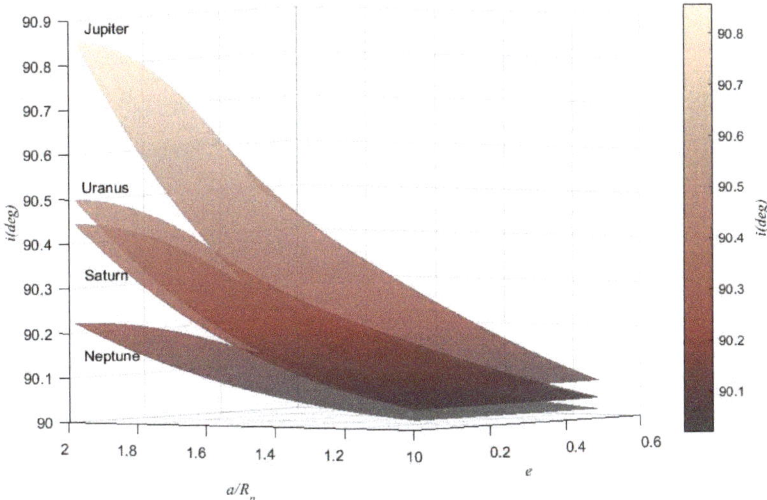

Figure 3. The relationship between the orbital inclination, semi-major axis, and eccentricity of sun-synchronous orbits.

Calculations show that the orbital inclinations for the sun-synchronous orbits around the four giant planets are greater than 90 degrees, which belong to retrograde orbits. Jupiter's sun-synchronous orbital inclination varies most significantly with the change of its semi-major axis, while Neptune's sun-synchronous orbit has the smallest orbital inclination. In addition, for all four planets, when the semi-major axis is larger, and the eccentricity is smaller, the orbital inclination changes more significantly, which indicates that when deploying a probe to near-circular orbits with high orbit altitude, more attention should be paid to the injection accuracy.

For a probe orbiting Uranus, this paper believes that running in this orbit does not mean that it has the characteristics of sun-synchronization, although Equation (4) still has a solution.

As mentioned above, the fundamental feature of a sun-synchronous orbit is that the angle between the orbit plane normal vector and the direction vector of the Sun remains relatively fixed. In the planetary equatorial coordinate system, the motion of the Sun can be described by orbital elements introduced in Section 2, and the unit direction vector of the Sun is [31]:

$$\hat{r}_s = \begin{bmatrix} \cos\Omega_s\cos(f_s+\omega_s) - \sin\Omega_s\cos i_s\sin(f_s+\omega_s) \\ \sin\Omega_s\cos(f_s+\omega_s) + \cos\Omega_s\cos i_s\sin(f_s+\omega_s) \\ \sin i_s\sin(f_s+\omega_s) \end{bmatrix} \tag{6}$$

where Ω_s is the right ascension of the ascending node of the Sun, f_s is the true anomaly of the Sun, ω_s is the argument of perigee of the Sun, and i_s is the orbital inclination of the Sun.

Under the same coordinate system, the orbit plane normal vector of the probe is [31]:

$$\hat{h} = \begin{bmatrix} \sin\Omega\sin i \\ -\cos\Omega\sin i \\ \cos i \end{bmatrix}. \tag{7}$$

Therefore, the cosine value of the orbital solar angle is:

$$\cos\Psi = \hat{r}_s \cdot \hat{h}, \tag{8}$$

where Ψ is the angle between vector $\hat{r}_s$ and vector $\hat{h}$, and Ψ is called the orbital solar angle.

Figure 4 shows the relationship between the location of the Sun and the orbital solar angle Ψ under the coordinate system centered on Uranus. The outer circle represents the trajectory of the Sun during a cycle of Uranus' revolution.

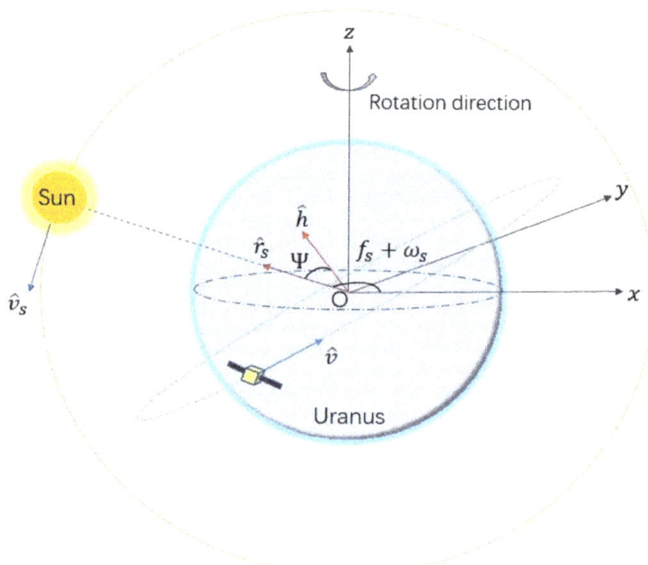

Figure 4. Right-hand coordinate system centered on Uranus, where O is the center of mass of Uranus, the x-axis points in the direction of the ascending node of the Sun, the z-axis points in the direction of the angular momentum direction of Uranus' rotation.

Considering the long-term stability of planetary revolution and the physical meaning of the right ascension of ascending node, the following simplification can be made [31]:

$$\begin{cases} \Omega_s = 0 \\ f_s = M_s \end{cases}, \tag{9}$$

then Equation (8) can be expressed as:

$$\cos\Psi = \sin\Omega\sin i\cos u_s - \cos\Omega\sin i\cos i_s\sin u_s + \cos i\sin i_s\sin u_s, \tag{10}$$

where $u_s = f_s + M_s$. When taking the derivative of the above equation with respect to time, we get:

$$\begin{aligned} \tfrac{d}{dt}(\cos\Psi) =& \dot{\Omega}(\cos\Omega\sin i\cos u_s + \sin\Omega\sin i\cos i_s\sin u_s) \\ &+\dot{i}(\sin\Omega\cos i\cos u_s - \cos\Omega\cos i\cos i_s\sin u_s - \sin i\sin i_s\sin u_s) \\ &-\dot{M}_s(\cos\Omega\sin i\cos i_s\cos u_s + \sin\Omega\sin i\sin u_s - \cos i\sin i_s\cos u_s) \end{aligned} \tag{11}$$

where $\dot{i}$ is the drift rate of i. The ideal sun-synchronous orbit should meet the following requirements:

$$\frac{d}{dt}(\cos\Psi) = 0. \tag{12}$$

For Earth, Mars, Jupiter, and Saturn, further simplifications tend to be made when designing the sun-synchronous orbits around these planets [27,31,32]:

$$\begin{cases} \dot{i} = 0 \\ \dot{i}_s = 0 \end{cases}, \tag{13}$$

Equation (12) is therefore reduced to:

$$\left(\dot{\Omega} - \dot{M}_s\right)(\cos\Omega \sin i \cos u_s + \sin\Omega \sin i \sin u_s) = 0. \tag{14}$$

It is easy to see that the above equation can be established if $\dot{\Omega} = \dot{M}_s$. However, due to the existence of ecliptic obliquity i_s and the non-uniform speed of the planetary revolution, even if Equation (14) is established, it only ensures that the angle between the orbital plane and the mean Sun remains unchanged, the angle between the orbital plane and the real Sun will still change within one revolution period. In the case of a sun-synchronous satellite orbiting Earth, the solar angle will still change by about 20 degrees within a year, which shows that i_s has a significant influence on the solar angle of the sun-synchronous orbit.

For Uranus, whose ecliptic obliquity is 97.7 degrees, the i_s = 0 simplification is no longer an option.

Learning from the design of Earth's sun-synchronous orbits [27,31,32], we introduce a mean Sun under the coordinate system shown in Figure 3. The mean Sun orbiting Uranus has the same ascending node and orbital period with the apparent Sun. Furthermore, its motion plane is perpendicular to the equatorial plane of Uranus. Under this ideal model, there is i_s = 90(deg), Equation (11) is simplified to:

$$\begin{aligned} \tfrac{d}{dt}(\cos\Psi) &= \dot{\Omega}\cos\Omega \sin i \cos u_s \\ &+\dot{i}(\sin\Omega \cos i \cos u_s - \sin i \sin u_s) \\ &-\dot{M}_s(\sin\Omega \sin i \sin u_s - \cos i \cos u_s) \end{aligned} \tag{15}$$

According to the perturbation theory [34], the long-term perturbation of the orbital inclination mainly comes from the influence of the third-body gravitational force. When considering the Sun's gravity as the main third-body gravitational perturbation term, the long-term average change rate of the orbital inclination angle is [35]:

$$\begin{aligned} \dot{i} &= \tfrac{3\dot{M}_s^2}{8n}(\sin 2\Omega \sin i + \sin 2i_s \sin\Omega \cos i - \sin 2\Omega \cos^2 i_s \sin i) \\ &= \tfrac{3\dot{M}_s^2}{8n}(\sin i \sin 2\Omega \sin^2 i_s + \cos i \sin\Omega \sin 2i_s). \end{aligned} \tag{16}$$

It can be seen from above that when n is smaller, $\dot{i}$ is larger. Taking the planet-synchronous orbits around Uranus for example, n is taken as the rotation angular velocity of Uranus, and with different orbital inclination and right ascension of ascending node, $\dot{i}$ is calculated as shown in Figure 5.

As can be seen from Figure 5, the drift rate of orbital inclination $\dot{i}$ will change periodically with the change of orbital inclination i and right ascension of ascending node Ω. The right ascension of ascending node Ω mainly determines the direction of the orbital inclination drift rate $\dot{i}$, and its magnitude is mainly determined by the orbital inclination i. In addition, the maximum value of $\dot{i}$ is only on the order of 10^{-14}, while the angular velocity of Uranus's revolution $\dot{M}_s$ is on the order of 10^{-9}. There is a big difference in magnitude between the two, so Equation (15) can be further simplified as:

$$\frac{d}{dt}(\cos\Psi) = \dot{\Omega}\cos\Omega \sin i \cos u_s - \dot{M}_s(\sin\Omega \sin i \sin u_s - \cos i \cos u_s). \tag{17}$$

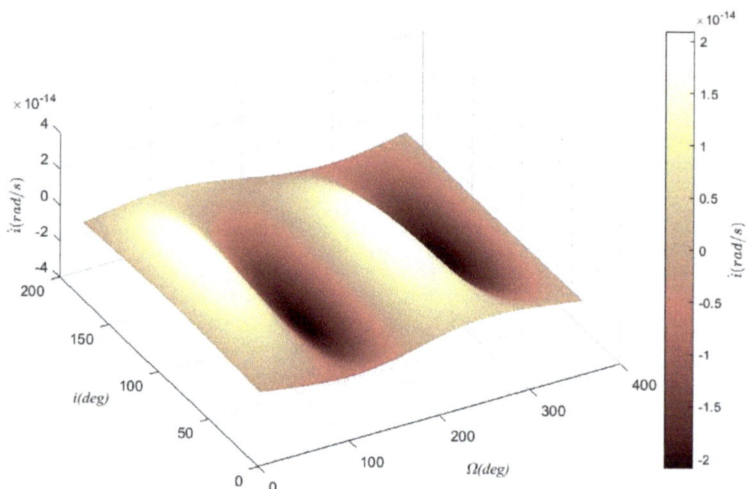

Figure 5. The relationship between the orbital inclination, right ascension of ascending node, and long-term perturbation of the orbital inclination around Uranus.

Therefore, the following relationships are required in a sun-synchronous orbit:

$$\dot{\Omega} = \frac{\sin\Omega\sin i\sin u_s - \cos i\cos u_s}{\cos\Omega\sin i\cos u_s}\dot{M}_s. \tag{18}$$

For Uranus' sun-synchronous orbits, $\dot{\Omega}$ should be a periodic function, which indicates that there is no long-term constant $\dot{\Omega}$ to achieve the stability of the solar angle. However, relevant studies have shown that $\dot{\Omega}$ is a secular term in a tropical period [30]; for a probe orbiting Uranus, the long-term stability of solar angle would not be realized by orbit design. Therefore, based on the above analysis, this paper believes that Uranus does not have a natural sun-synchronous orbit.

Nevertheless, with the development of new technologies such as electric propulsion, we do not rule out the possibility of achieving long-term stability of the solar angle of Uranus probes through orbit control. After all, for a probe running in Earth's sun-synchronous orbit, regular orbit control is also essential to achieve the stability of solar angle [32].

4. Repeating Ground Track Orbits

Orbits with periodically repeated ground trajectory are called repeating ground track orbits [36]. For a probe running in such orbits, after each regression period, the probe will repass over specific places on the planet, which is conducive to the repeated observation of specific targets and the dynamic monitoring of relevant areas. It is conceivable that if we can have planetary probes running in such orbits, we can make more detailed observations of specific targets on the surface of these planets, such as Jupiter's mysterious Great Red Spot, Saturn's peculiar Great White Spot [37], and so on.

According to the definition, the repeating ground track orbits should meet the following requirement [38]:

$$RT_N = ND_N, \tag{19}$$

where R and N are positive integers, T_N is the orbital period of the probe, D_N is the node period of the planet's rotation relative to the orbital plane. The physical meaning of the above equation is as follows: when the probe moves around the planet R times, the planet just rotates N times relative to the orbital plane. Specifically [31]:

$$T_N = \frac{2\pi}{\dot{M} + \dot{\omega}}, \tag{20}$$

where $\dot{M}$ is the angular velocity of the probe's mean anomaly, and $\dot{\omega}$ is drift velocity of argument of perigee. The detailed form of $\dot{M}$ and $\dot{\omega}$ are shown in Appendix A. D_N can be derived from:

$$D_N = \frac{2\pi}{\omega_p - \dot{\Omega}}. \tag{21}$$

When the precession direction of the ascending node is the same as the rotation direction of the planet, $\dot{\Omega}$ is positive, otherwise it is negative.

Many repeating ground track orbits can be designed around a planet. To better distinguish these orbits, this paper uses the parameter Q to describe the different regression characteristics between them, which is defined as:

$$Q = \frac{R}{N} = \frac{\dot{M} + \dot{\omega}}{\omega_p - \dot{\Omega}}. \tag{22}$$

The physical meaning of the above equation is as follows: after N planetary rotation periods, the probe flies in R circles, and its trajectory on the planetary surface is closed.

Through adding the detailed form of $\dot{M}$ and $\dot{\omega}$ into the above equation, the univariate quadratic equation with $\sin^2 i$ as the independent variable is obtained:

$$A\sin^4 i + B\sin^2 i + C - Q\left(\omega_J - \dot{\Omega}\right) = 0, \tag{23}$$

the detailed form of A, B and C are shown in Appendix B.

According to the quadratic equation, Equation (23) has a solution only when the following inequality is true:

$$\Delta = B^2 - 4A\left(C - Q\left(\omega_p - \dot{\Omega}\right)\right) \geq 0. \tag{24}$$

Solving this inequality yields the minimum value of Q:

$$Q_{\min} = \frac{C - \frac{B^2}{4A}}{\omega_p - \dot{\Omega}}. \tag{25}$$

By analyzing Equation (22), it can be found that for a certain planet, since $\dot{\Omega}$ and $\dot{\omega}$ are both small quantities relative to $\dot{M}$, the maximum value of Q is basically determined by the maximum value of $\dot{M}$, that is, the lower the orbit is, the greater the maximum value of Q. Therefore, the choice of the Q value is not arbitrary when designing the repeating ground track orbits, and different planets have different Q value ranges [35,39].

In addition, a semi-major axis and eccentricity must be preset for the solution of the Q value range; otherwise the inequality cannot be solved. In the actual exploration process, the orbit altitude needs to be determined in combination with the instrument performance carried by the probe, the atmospheric environment of the planet, and the specific exploration task. Therefore, the accurate Q value range of each planet is not given in this paper.

It should be noted that when designing the repeating ground track orbits, the orbital parameters, such as the semi-major axis a and eccentricity e, cannot be completely determined only based on the given Q value. In combination with the characteristics of the Earth's repeating ground track orbit, it is common that the orbits of this kind basically meet the sun-synchronous characteristics at the same time [27,40], and the orbit altitude fluctuates very little within an orbit period so that the detection instrument can achieve observation of specific targets under stable illumination conditions. Assuming that the repeating ground track orbits around the four Giant planets are also sun-synchronous orbits, Equation (3) is established.

In this paper, the relationship between the a, e, and Q values of the sun-synchronous repeating ground track orbits around these four planets is calculated, as shown in Figure 5. It should be noted that although Uranus does not have a sun-synchronous orbit, to better compare the general characteristics of the repeating ground track orbits around the four giant planets, the analysis of Uranus is also carried out under the condition that Equation (3) is established.

It can be seen from Figure 6 that under the same orbit altitude, the Q value from large to small is Neptune, Uranus, Jupiter, and Saturn. The larger the Q value is, the more times the probe moves around the planet in a sidereal day. Moreover, the Q value of the sun-synchronous repeating ground track orbits around the four giant planets is mainly affected by a. When a is determined, the change of e has little effect on the Q value.

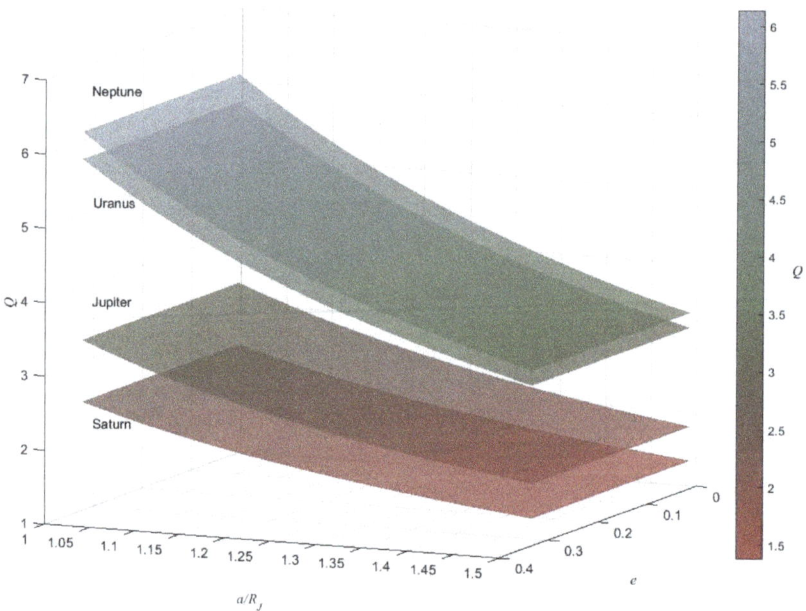

Figure 6. The relationship between the semi-major axis, eccentricity, and Q value of the sun-synchronous repeating ground track orbits.

In practical engineering applications, the orbital design of the sun-synchronous repeating ground track orbits around these three planets can be carried out as follows [41]:

First, calculate the intersection period T_N. According to the Equation (22), the probe rotates R times around the planet in a regression period, and rotates Q times around the planet every day, thus:

$$T_N = \frac{D_N}{Q}. \tag{26}$$

After that, taking the initial values of a and the orbital inclination i, and more accurate values can be obtained through iteration. The selection of the initial value needs to be combined with the physical parameters of different planets:

$$\begin{cases} a = R_p + H \\ i = \pi/2 \end{cases}. \tag{27}$$

where H represents the estimated orbit altitude. Since the orbital inclination of the sun-synchronous orbits around the four giant planets is close to 90 degrees, $\pi/2$ could be a suitable initial value of i. Then, the initial value is carried into the following equation:

$$\begin{cases} T_0 = \frac{T_N}{1+\frac{3J_2R_p^2}{2a^2}(1-4\cos^2 i)} \\ a = \left[\frac{\mu_p T_0^2}{4\pi^2}\right]^{\frac{1}{3}} \\ i = \arccos\left[-\dot{M}_s^2 \times \frac{\pi}{180} \times \frac{1}{86400} \times 2 \times \frac{a^2}{3nJ_2R_p^2}\right] \times \frac{180}{\pi} \end{cases}. \tag{28}$$

Every calculation of Equation (28) gets a new value of a and i. Repeat this process until the accuracy meets the requirements of the mission.

5. Planet-Synchronous Orbits

In a broad sense, a planet-synchronous orbit refers to an orbit with the same orbital period as the planetary rotation period. According to Kepler's third law, the square of the orbit period is inversely proportional to the cube of the semi-major axis of the orbit. Therefore, theoretically, the design of planet-synchronous orbit is mainly constrained by the semi-major axis of the orbit, and there are no special requirements for parameters such as orbit eccentricity and orbital inclination.

However, in practical engineering applications, it is often not enough to only meet the requirements that the orbital period is the same as the planetary rotation period. The main value of planet-synchronous orbits is to keep the longitude and latitude of the sub-satellite point of the probe basically unchanged, which is extremely advantageous in relay communication and other application scenarios [42]. A planet-synchronous orbit with such characteristics is called a stationary orbit.

If generalized coordinates $q = [r, \lambda, \varphi]$ are defined, the Lagrange equation can be established [29]:

$$\frac{d}{dt}\left(\frac{\partial T}{\partial \dot{q}}\right) - \frac{\partial T}{\partial q} = \frac{\partial U}{\partial q}, \tag{29}$$

where $T = \frac{1}{2}\left(\dot{r}^2 + r^2\dot{\varphi}^2 + r^2\cos^2\varphi\dot{\lambda}^2\right)$, substituting the potential function shown in Equation (1) into Equation (29), we get:

$$\begin{cases} \ddot{r} - r\dot{\varphi}^2 - r\cos^2\varphi\dot{\lambda}^2 = -\frac{\mu}{r^2} + \frac{3\mu_p J_2 R_p^2}{2r^4}(3\sin^2\varphi - 1) + \frac{5\mu_p J_4 R_p^4}{8r^6}\left(35\sin^4\varphi - 30\sin^2\varphi + 3\right) \\ \frac{d}{dt}\left(r^2\cos^2\varphi\dot{\lambda}\right) = 0 \\ \frac{d}{dt}(r^2\dot{\varphi}) + \frac{1}{2}r^2\sin(2\varphi)\dot{\lambda}^2 = -\left[\frac{3\mu_p J_2 R_p^2}{2r^3} + \frac{\mu_p J_4 R_p^4}{8r^5}(70\sin^2\varphi - 30)\right]\sin 2\varphi \end{cases}. \tag{30}$$

According to the physical meaning of stationary orbit, the motion equation should satisfy:

$$\begin{cases} \dot{\lambda} = \omega_p, \ddot{\lambda} = 0 \\ \varphi = \dot{\varphi} = \varphi = 0 \\ \dot{r} = \ddot{r} = 0 \end{cases}, \tag{31}$$

The function $f(r)$ is defined as:

$$f(r) = \sqrt{\frac{\mu_p}{r^3} + \frac{3\mu_p J_2 {R_p}^2}{2r^5} - \frac{15\mu_p J_4 {R_p}^4}{8r^7}} - \omega_p. \tag{32}$$

Taking different r values and calculating the $f(r)$ of the four giant planets respectively, the resulting values are shown in Figure 7.

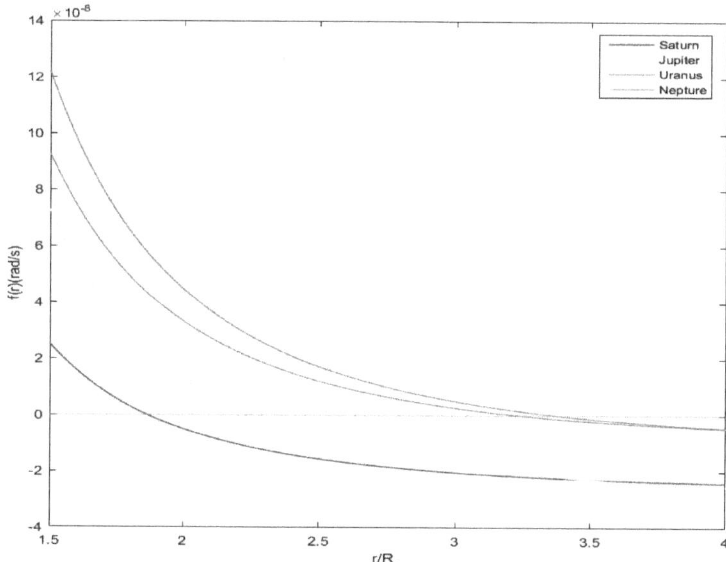

Figure 7. The relationship between r and $f(r)$.

According to the definition, the abscissas corresponding to the intersections of the curves and $f(r) = 0$ are the semi-major axes of each planets' stationary orbit. The orbital semi-major axes of the stationary orbits around Jupiter, Saturn, Uranus, and Neptune are obtained using the method above, as shown in Table 2.

Table 2. Parameters of the stationary orbits around each planet.

Parameters	Jupiter	Saturn	Uranus	Neptune
r/Rp	2.241	1.867	3.235	3.373
Centroid distance (km)	160,247	112,506	82,700	83,520
Orbit altitude (km)	88,755	52,238	57,141	58,756

The results show that the orbit altitude of Jupiter's stationary orbit is much higher than that of the other three planets. Although the volume of Saturn is much larger than that of Uranus and Neptune, its stationary orbit altitude is very close to that of the latter two planets. If sorted according to the value of r/Rp, Neptune, Uranus, Jupiter, and Saturn are in order from the largest to the smallest, which is also not proportional to the volume of the planets. Combined with the planetary parameters shown in Table 1, it can be found that for the two planets with similar rotation angular velocity, the value of r/Rp is likely to be positively related to planet density.

6. Conclusions

In this paper, considering the perturbation of J_2 and J_4 terms, the sun-synchronous orbits, the repeating ground track orbits, and the planet-synchronous orbits around Saturn, Jupiter, Uranus, and Neptune are analyzed.

First, the sun-synchronous orbits around the four giant planets are studied. The calculation results of the discriminant show that for a given semi-major axis and eccentricity, the four giant planets can find a unique orbital inclination, making the declination drift rate of the right ascension of ascending node equal to the planet revolution rate, which satisfies the theoretical requirements of the sun-synchronous orbits design. The numerical relationship between these three orbital parameters is then calculated. Since Uranus' ecliptic obliquity is close to 90 degrees, this paper defines a mean Sun moving around Uranus with an orbital inclination of 90 degrees. Under this motion model, the variation law of the solar angle of the probe orbiting around Uranus is theoretically analyzed. The results show that, unlike the other three planets, considering the long-term invariance of the semi-major axis, eccentricity, and orbital inclination, Uranus does not have a natural sun-synchronous orbit in theory.

After that, this paper analyzes the repeating ground track orbits around these four planets in combination with the parameter Q. Relevant studies have shown that for the design of the repeating ground track orbits around a specific planet, the Q value cannot be taken arbitrarily. This paper describes the calculation method of the Q value range. This paper calculates the relationship between the orbital parameters of the sun-synchronous repeating ground track orbits around each planet and gives the design methods except for that of Uranus, aiming at the most probable application scenario.

Then, the planet-synchronous orbits around the four giant planets are analyzed, and the parameters of the most typical representative, the stationary orbits, are calculated. The results show that the altitudes of stationary orbits around Jupiter, Neptune, Uranus, and Saturn are in descending order. A planet with a larger volume does not necessarily have a higher stationary orbit altitude, while a fast-rotating and dense planet tends to have this feature.

Furthermore, the real perturbation environments of the four giant planets are extremely complex under the influence of their ring system and satellite system [28,29]. How to conduct a more precise and long-term analysis of the special orbits around the four giant planets in a more realistic and complex perturbation environment is a work that needs further exploration. It would be worth it to learn even more from the "Integral Indexes" and the perturbation maps used as references [28,29] to study the dynamical behavior of the orbits around planets analysis methods.

Finally, to make the planetary probe work in designed orbits throughout its life cycle, orbit control is usually indispensable [23,32,39–41]; the orbit control methods applicable to the four giant planets' probes are also worthy of in-depth study.

Author Contributions: Conceptualization, B.Y. and Y.J.; methodology, B.Y.; software, C.J.; validation, B.Y., C.J. and Y.L.; formal analysis, H.L.; resources, Y.J.; data curation, C.Z.; writing—original draft preparation, B.Y.; writing—review and editing, H.J.; visualization, Y.D.; supervision, H.L.; project administration, H.L.; funding acquisition, H.L. All authors have read and agreed to the published version of the manuscript.

Funding: This research was funded by the National Natural Science Foundation of China (Grant No. 11772356).

Acknowledgments: The authors gratefully acknowledge the anonymous reviewers for their careful work and thoughtful suggestions that have helped improve this paper substantially.

Conflicts of Interest: The authors declare no conflict of interest.

Appendix A

Under the gravitational field described in Equation (1), we have:

$$
\begin{aligned}
\dot{M} = {} & n + \frac{3nJ_2R_J^2}{2p^2}\left(1 - \tfrac{3}{2}\sin^2 i\right)\sqrt{1-e^2} \\
& + \frac{9nJ_2^2R_J^4}{4p^4}\sqrt{1-e^2}\left[\tfrac{1}{2}\left(1-\tfrac{3}{2}\sin^2 i\right)^2\sqrt{1-e^2} + e^2\left(\tfrac{10}{3} - \tfrac{26}{3}\sin^2 i + \tfrac{103}{12}\sin^4 i\right)\right. \\
& + \left(\tfrac{5}{2} - \tfrac{19}{3}\sin^2 i + \tfrac{233}{48}\sin^4 i\right) + \tfrac{e^4}{1-e^2}\left(\tfrac{35}{12} - \tfrac{35}{4}\sin^2 i + \tfrac{315}{32}\sin^4 i\right) \\
& \left. - \tfrac{35J_4}{18J_2^2}e^2\left(\tfrac{9}{14} - \tfrac{45}{14}\sin^2 i + \tfrac{45}{16}\sin^4 i\right)\right]
\end{aligned}
$$

and:

$$
\begin{aligned}
\dot{\omega} = {} & -\frac{3nJ_2R_J^2}{2p^2}\left(\tfrac{5}{2}\sin^2 i - 2\right) + \frac{9nJ_2^2R_J^4}{p^4}\left\{e^2\left(\tfrac{7}{12} - \tfrac{3}{8}\sin^2 i - \tfrac{15}{32}\sin^4 i\right)\right. \\
& + \sqrt{1-e^2}\left(2 - \tfrac{11}{2}\sin^2 i + \tfrac{15}{4}\sin^4 i\right) + \left(4 - \tfrac{103}{12}\sin^2 i + \tfrac{215}{48}\sin^4 i\right) \\
& \left. - \tfrac{35J_4}{18J_2^2}\left[e^2\left(\tfrac{27}{14} - \tfrac{27}{4}\sin^2 i + \tfrac{81}{16}\sin^4 i\right) + \left(\tfrac{12}{7} - \tfrac{93}{14}\sin^2 i + \tfrac{21}{4}\sin^4 i\right)\right]\right\}
\end{aligned}
$$

Appendix B

The detailed form of A, B and C are:

$$
\begin{aligned}
A = {} & \frac{9nJ_2^2R_p^4}{4p^4}\left[\sqrt{1-e^2}\left(\tfrac{9}{8}\sqrt{1-e^2} + \tfrac{413}{48} + \tfrac{103}{12}e^2 + \tfrac{315e^4}{32(1-e^2)} - \tfrac{105J_4}{32J_2^2}e^2\right)\right. \\
& \left. + \tfrac{215}{48} - \tfrac{15}{32}e^2 - \tfrac{35J_4}{18J_2^2}\left(\tfrac{21}{4} + \tfrac{81}{16}e^2\right)\right]
\end{aligned}
$$

$$
\begin{aligned}
B = {} & \frac{9nJ_2^2R_p^4}{4p^4}\left[\sqrt{1-e^2}\left(-\tfrac{3}{2}\sqrt{1-e^2} - \tfrac{71}{6} - \tfrac{26}{3}e^2 - \tfrac{35e^4}{4(1-e^2)} + \tfrac{25J_4}{4J_2^2}e^2 - \tfrac{p^2}{J_2}\right)\right. \\
& \left. - \tfrac{103}{12} - \tfrac{3}{8}e^2 + \tfrac{35J_4}{6J_2^2}\left(\tfrac{31}{14} + \tfrac{9}{4}e^2\right) - \tfrac{5p^2}{3J_2}\right]
\end{aligned}
$$

$$
\begin{aligned}
C = {} & \frac{9nJ_2^2R_p^4}{4p^4}\left[\sqrt{1-e^2}\left(\tfrac{1}{2}\sqrt{1-e^2} + \tfrac{9}{2} + \tfrac{10}{3}e^2 - \tfrac{35e^4}{12(1-e^2)} - \tfrac{5J_4}{4J_2^2}e^2 - \tfrac{2p^2}{3J_2}\right)\right. \\
& \left. + 4 + \tfrac{7}{12}e^2 - \tfrac{5J_4}{6J_2^2}\left(4 + \tfrac{9}{2}e^2\right) + \tfrac{4p^2}{3J_2}\right] + n
\end{aligned}
$$

References

1. Konopliv, A.S.; Park, R.S.; Rivoldini, A.; Baland, R.; Le Maistre, S.; Van Hoolst, T.; Yseboodt, M.; Dehant, V. Detection of the Chandler Wobble of Mars From Orbiting Spacecraft. *Geophys. Res. Lett.* **2020**, *47*, e2020GL090568. [CrossRef]
2. Ma, M.; Calvés, G.M.; Cimò, G.; Zhang, P.; Xiong, M.; Li, P.; Kummamuru, P.; Chu, Z.; Jiang, T.; Xia, B.; et al. VLBI Data Processing on Coronal Radio-sounding Experiments of Mars Express. *Astron. J.* **2021**, *162*, 141–153. [CrossRef]
3. Mcewen, A.S.; Eliason, E.M.; Bergstrom, J.W. Special Section: Mars Reconnaissance Orbiter Mission and Science Investigations-E05S02-Mars Reconnaissance Orbiter's High Resolution Imaging Science Experiment (HiRISE). *J. Geophys. Res.* **2007**, *112*, E05S02.
4. Jakosky, B.M.; Jakosky, B.M. Preface: The Mars Atmosphere and Volatile Evolution (MAVEN) Mission. *Space Sci. Rev.* **2015**, *195*, 1–2. [CrossRef]
5. Li, C.; Zhang, R.; Yu, D.; Dong, G.; Liu, J.; Geng, Y.; Sun, Z.; Yan, W.; Ren, X.; Su, Y.; et al. China's Mars Exploration Mission and Science Investigation. *Space Sci. Rev.* **2021**, *217*, 57–80. [CrossRef]
6. Vasavada, A.R. Mission Overview and Scientific Contributions from the Mars Science Laboratory Curiosity Rover after Eight Years of Surface Operations. *Space Sci. Rev.* **2022**, *218*, 14. [CrossRef]
7. Chatain, A.; Spiga, A.; Banfield, D.; Forget, F.; Murdoch, N. Seasonal Variability of the Daytime and Nighttime Atmospheric Turbulence Experienced by InSight on Mars. *Geophys. Res. Lett.* **2021**, *48*, e2021GL095453. [CrossRef]
8. Martin, V. On the location of the Io plasma torus: Voyager 1 observations. *Ann. Geophys.* **2018**, *36*, 831–839.
9. Hammel, H.B. Lessons learned from (and since) the Voyager 2 flybys of Uranus and Neptune. *Philos. Trans. R. Soc. A* **2020**, *378*, 20190485. [CrossRef]
10. Connerney, J.E.P.; Timmins, S.; Oliversen, R.J.; Espley, J.R.; Joergensen, J.L.; Kotsiaros, S.; Joergensen, P.S.; Merayo, J.M.G.; Herceg, M.; Bloxham, J.; et al. A New Model of Jupiter's Magnetic Field at the Completion of Juno's Prime Mission. *J. Geophys. Res. Planets* **2022**, *127*, e2021JE007055. [CrossRef]
11. Ni, D. Empirical models of Jupiter's interior from Juno data. *Astron. Astrophys.* **2018**, *613*, a32. [CrossRef]

12. Idini, B.; Stevenson, D.J. The Gravitational Imprint of an Interior–Orbital Resonance in Jupiter–Io. *Planet. Sci. J.* **2022**, *3*, 89. [CrossRef]
13. Ingersoll, A.P. Cassini Exploration of the Planet Saturn: A Comprehensive Review. *Space Sci. Rev.* **2020**, *216*, 122. [CrossRef]
14. Chadney, J.M.; Koskinen, T.; Hu, X.; Galand, M.; Lavvas, P.; Unruh, Y.; Serigano, J.; Hörst, S.; Yelle, R. Energy deposition in Saturn's equatorial upper atmosphere. *Icarus* **2022**, *372*, 114724. [CrossRef]
15. Filacchione, G.; Ciarniello, M.; D'Aversa, E.; Capaccioni, F.; Clark, R.N.; Buratti, B.J.; Helfenstein, P.; Stephan, K.; Plainaki, C. Saturn's icy satellites investigated by Cassini-VIMS. V. Spectrophotometry. *Icarus* **2022**, *375*, 114803. [CrossRef]
16. Koskinen, T.T.; Guerlet, S. The Atmospheric structure and helium abundance on Saturn from Cassini/UVIS and CIRS observations. *Icarus* **2018**, *307*, 161–171. [CrossRef]
17. Tiscareno, M.S.; Nicholson, P.D.; Cuzzi, J.N.; Spilker, L.J.; Murray, C.D.; Hedman, M.M.; Colwell, J.E.; Burns, J.A.; Brooks, S.M.; Clark, R.N.; et al. Close-range remote sensing of Saturn's rings during Cassini's ring-grazing orbits and Grand Finale. *Science* **2019**, *364*, eaau1017. [CrossRef]
18. Guillot, T. Uranus and Neptune are key to understand planets with hydrogen atmospheres. *Exp. Astron.* **2021**, *30*, 1–23. [CrossRef]
19. Voosen, P. Uranus should be NASA's top target, report finds. *Science* **2022**, *376*, 332–333. [CrossRef]
20. Helled, R.; Fortney, J. The interiors of Uranus and Neptune: Current understanding and open questions. *Philos. Trans. R. Soc. A* **2020**, *378*, 20190474. [CrossRef]
21. Brozović, M.; Jacobson, R.A. Orbits of the Irregular Satellites of Uranus and Neptune. *Astron. J.* **2022**, *163*, 241–252. [CrossRef]
22. Hofstadter, M.D.; Fletcher, L.N.; Simon, A.A.; Masters, A.; Turrini, D.; Arridge, C.S. Future Missions to the Giant Planets that Can Advance Atmospheric Science Objectives. *Space Sci. Rev.* **2020**, *216*, 91–107. [CrossRef]
23. Deshmukh, R.G.; Spencer, D.A.; Dutta, S. Flight control methodologies for Neptune aerocapture trajectories. *Acta Astronaut.* **2022**, *193*, 255–268. [CrossRef]
24. Cohen, I.J.; Beddingfield, C.; Chancia, R.; DiBraccio, G.; Hedman, M.; MacKenzie, S.; Mauk, B.; Sayanagi, K.M.; Soderlund, K.M.; Turtle, E.; et al. The Case for a New Frontiers–Class Uranus Orbiter: System Science at an Underexplored and Unique World with a Mid-scale Mission. *Planet. Sci. J.* **2022**, *3*, 58–71. [CrossRef]
25. Soyuer, D.; Zwick, L.; D'Orazio, D.J.; Saha, P. Searching for gravitational waves via Doppler tracking by future missions to Uranus and Neptune. *Mon. Not. R. Astron. Soc. Lett.* **2021**, *503*, 73–79. [CrossRef]
26. Paek, S.; Kim, S.; Kronig, L.; de Weck, O. Sun-synchronous repeat ground tracks and other useful orbits for future space missions. *Aeronaut. J.* **2020**, *124*, 917–939. [CrossRef]
27. Available online: https://nssdc.gsfc.nasa.gov/planetary/factsheet (accessed on 14 July 2022).
28. Dos Santos, J.C.; Prado, A.F.B.A.; Carvalho, J.P.S.; Vilhena de Moraes, R. Search for less disturbed regions for spacecrafts in planetary systems. In Proceedings of the SPACE 2016-AAS/AIAA Astrodynamics Specialist Conference, Long Beach, CA, USA, 13 September 2016.
29. Dos Santos, J.C. Study of the Dynamics around Celestial Bodies Using Analytical and Semi-Analytical Techniques. Ph.D. Thesis, Department of Physics, School of Engineering, São Paulo State University (UNESP), Guaratinguetá, Brazil, 2018.
30. Brouwer, D. Solution of the problem of artificial satellite theory without drag. *Astron. J.* **1959**, *64*, 378–395. [CrossRef]
31. Liu, L. *Orbit Theory of Spacecraft*; National Defense Industry Press: Beijing, China, 2000; pp. 58–96. (In Chinese)
32. Nazarenko, A.I. Sun synchronous orbits. predicting the local solar time of the ascending node. *Acta Astronaut.* **2021**, *181*, 585–593. [CrossRef]
33. Zeng, H.; Xia, X.W.; Liu, Z.G.; Wu, L. Navigation Satellite's Lifetime Model and Optimization Design. In *Applied Mechanics and Materials*; Trans Tech Publications Ltd.: Zurich, Switzerland, 2014; Volume 513, pp. 4346–4351.
34. Cook, G.E. Luni-Solar perturbations of the orbit of an earth satellite. *Geophys. J. Int.* **1962**, *6*, 271–291. [CrossRef]
35. Jiang, C.; Liu, Y.; Jiang, Y.; Li, H. Orbital Design and Control for Jupiter-Observation Spacecraft. *Aerospace* **2021**, *8*, 282. [CrossRef]
36. Ortore, E.; Cinelli, M.; Circi, C. A ground track-based approach to design satellite constellations. *Aerosp. Sci. Technol.* **2017**, *69*, 458–464. [CrossRef]
37. Hyman, R. Wild weather of the solar system. *Astronomy* **2022**, *50*, 16–23.
38. Liao, C.; Xu, M.; Jia, X.; Dong, Y. Semi-analytical acquisition algorithm for repeat-groundtrack orbit maintenance. *Astrodynamics* **2018**, *2*, 161–173. [CrossRef]
39. Zhan, C.; Jiang, Y.; Li, H.; Liu, Y. Dynamics and Control of Typical Orbits around Saturn. *Appl. Sci.* **2022**, *12*, 1462. [CrossRef]
40. Liu, Y.; Jiang, Y.; Li, H.; Zhang, H. Some Special Types of Orbits around Jupiter. *Aerospace* **2021**, *8*, 183. [CrossRef]
41. Jiang, Y. *Control of Satellite Formation Flying and Constellation*; National Defense Industry Press: Beijing, China, *in press*.
42. Kopp, B.; Harris, J.; Lauand, C. Utilizing Existing Commercial Geostationary Earth Orbit Fixed Satellite Services for Low Earth Orbit Satellite Communication Relays with Earth. *New Space* **2019**, *7*, 19–30. [CrossRef]

 mathematics 

Article

A Novel Decomposed Optical Architecture for Satellite Terrestrial Network Edge Computing

Xiaotao Guo [1], Ying Zhang [2,*], Yu Jiang [1], Shenggang Wu [1] and Hengnian Li [1]

[1] State Key Laboratory of Astronautic Dynamics, Xi'an Satellite Control Center, Xi'an 710043, China; guoxtchina@163.com (X.G.); jiangyu_xian_china@163.com (Y.J.); s_wu_xscc@163.com (S.W.); henry_xscc@mail.xjtu.edu.cn (H.L.)
[2] Information and Navigation School, Air Force Engineering University, Xi'an 710082, China
* Correspondence: y_zhang0505@163.com

Abstract: Aiming at providing a high-performance terrestrial network for edge computing in satellite networks, we experimentally demonstrate a high bandwidth and low latency decomposed optical computing architecture based on distributed Nanoseconds Optical Switches (NOS). Experimental validation of the decomposed computing network prototype employs a four-port NOS to interconnect four processor/memory cubes. The SOA-based optical gates provide an ON/OFF ratio greater than 60 dB, enabling none-error transmission at a Bit Error Rate (BER) of 1×10^{-9}. An end-to-end access latency of 122.3 ns and zero packet loss are obtained in the experimental assessment. Scalability and physical performance considering signal impairments when increasing the NOS port count are also investigated. An output OSNR of up to 30.5 dB and an none-error transmission with 1.5 dB penalty is obtained when scaling the NOS port count to 64. Moreover, exploiting the experimentally measured parameters, the network performance of NOS-based decomposed computing architecture is numerically assessed under larger network scales. The results indicate that, under a 4096-cube network scale, the NOS-based decomposed computing architecture achieves 148.5 ns end-to-end latency inside the same rack and zero packet loss at a link bandwidth of 40 Gb/s.

Keywords: satellite-terrestrial network; hardware decomposition; nanoseconds optical switches

MSC: 78-05; 94-10

Citation: Guo, X.; Zhang, Y.; Jiang, Y.; Wu, S.; Li, H. A Novel Decomposed Optical Architecture for Satellite Terrestrial Network Edge Computing. *Mathematics* **2022**, *10*, 2515. https://doi.org/10.3390/math10142515

Academic Editor: Pedro A. Castillo Valdivieso

Received: 17 June 2022
Accepted: 15 July 2022
Published: 19 July 2022

1. Introduction

In order to satisfy various requirements of emerging big data applications (like Internet of Things (IoT), automatic driving, and high-quality video/image processing), a novel integrated Satellite-Terrestrial Network (STN) has been proposed combing the space-based satellite communication system and terrestrial computing network [1–4]. The STN achieves stable global coverage to the user-terminal utilizing satellite networks, while relieving the limited processing performance of the satellite system by offloading the computing procedure to terrestrial computing infrastructures [5,6]. The satellites can be applied as front-end nodes and process delay sensitive tasks with less requirements of computing performance. Meanwhile, the terrestrial network coordinates with satellites as the back-end to process computing intensive tasks. This architecture requires a powerful and efficient terrestrial computing network. However, because of the integrated on-board hardware in current server-centric terrestrial computing architecture, a large amount of hardware resources (processor, memory, and storage) is frequently underutilized [7]. Moreover, the application performance can be degraded under server-centric computing architectures when limited on-board hardware resources cannot meet the application requirements. In addition, the failure or upgrade of just one kind of resource (only processor or memory) in a server causes a significant impact to the whole server.

To relieve the above issues of server-centric architectures, a novel computing architecture consisting of decomposed hardware cubes (hence, naming decomposed architecture) is developed to provide flexible resource provision and boosting performance for various processor (memory) intensive applications [8–12]. In order to implement the decomposed architecture, there are several issues to be addressed, in which the disaggregation of the processor and memory is a key challenge. Due to the hardware decomposition, the on-board high-speed point-to-point bus between the processor and memory is replaced by the network interconnection. This difference requires a network connection of high bandwidth and low latency to sustain the traffic among decomposed hardware cubes. The network switching may also lead to signal deterioration (including channel crosstalk, OSNR degradation, signal distortion, and power budget), hence, degrading the computing performance. Therefore, a stable, error-free, and low packet loss network is also significantly important for decomposed architectures.

In this paper, we design and implement an optical terrestrial computing network with decomposed hardware for STN edge computing, while hardware cubes are interconnected by an NOS-based flat network to minimize the communication delay. An independent optical packet control plane is designed to process the optical packet switching and solve the packet contention. The decomposed computing prototype is experimentally implemented with a 4 $\times$ 4 NOS and four processor/memory cubes. The hardware resource cubes (processor and memory) are implemented based on Field-Programmable Gate Array (FPGA) platforms. The physical and network performance of the optical computing prototype with decomposed hardware are experimentally assessed, while the scalability of the decomposed computing architecture (up to 4096 hardware cubes) is also numerically investigated based on experimentally measured parameters.

The article is organized as follows. Section 2 provides an overview of the existing works and describes the contributions of this work. In Section 3, the NOS-based decomposed optical computing architecture for STN and its operation are presented. In Section 4, the experimental demonstration of the NOS-based decomposed computing prototype is discussed. Section 5 shows the scalability of the NOS-based computing architecture with decomposed hardware in terms of physical performance and network performance. In addition, our proposed optical computing network with decomposed hardware is compared with current works in this section. The main results of this work are concluded in Section 6.

2. Literature Review and Contribution

2.1. Related Works

STN has been investigated as a promising solution to provide various cloud services and applications in next generation network architectures. Xie et al. [2] deployed the computing resource in multi-layer heterogeneous edge computing clusters for STN, considering the Quality of Service (QoS) requirements, computation offloading, and task scheduling. Wang et al. [3] designed a space edge computing node for STN to provide services coordinated with the terrestrial computing network, taking less computing time and consuming less energy than traditional satellite constellation. Tang et al. [5] presented a three-tier computation architecture combining hybrid terrestrial cloud computing architecture and an edge computing Low Earth Orbit (LEO) satellite network to minimize the sum power consumption of the user-terminal. Pfandzelter et al. [13] proposed a resource place method to select a subset of satellites as computing nodes with QoS constraints. A joint offloading decision and resource allocation scheme is designed in [14] considering satellites as the computing node to assist the terrestrial computing network in task processing, which minimizes the completion delay of computing tasks.

In order to implement the STN in the above studies and provide a minimal delay for the user-terminal with QoS requirements, a powerful terrestrial computing network is necessary. The decomposed computing architecture has been considered as an emerging paradigm with flexible resource provision and faster task runtime. Several experimental studies have been conducted to investigate the feasibility of decomposed architectures.

According to the analysis in [15], the low packet loss and long-term network stability are critical, but the extra network latency impacts the performance of decomposed architectures the most. Some decomposed architectures were proposed based on current servers and the hierarchical electrical network to implement decoupled memory blades [16,17]. A decomposed in-memory store framework was proposed in [18] for big data applications, utilizing theThymesisFlow memory system. A Software-Defined Networking (SDN)-based orchestration plane is designed and experimentally implemented for a decomposed computing architecture in [19] with hybrid optical switches. Decomposed architectures based on optical switches were proposed and experimentally investigated in [20,21], exploiting high aggregation bandwidths and transparent switching; however, the high switching delay (milliseconds) of the optical switch technology cannot provide nanoseconds scale communication between processor and memory cubes. An optically connected memory architecture was demonstrated in [22,23] based on micro-ring resonator switches and the Aurora 64B/66B protocol, which achieved an optical switching time of hundreds of microseconds. To provide fast optical switching, a flat optical network was developed based on tunable lasers and passive gratings [24], which may lead to unstable operation during high-speed processing. A decomposed optical computing architecture was proposed based on Nanoseconds Optical Switches (NOS) [25]. The NOS is based on a broadcast and select switch architecture employing Semiconductor Optical Amplifiers (SOA)-based optical gates. Exploiting the nanoseconds switching of SOA-based gates and parallel optical flow control, the proposed architecture can potentially provide an optical network interconnection of high bandwidth and low latency for decomposed architectures.

2.2. Motivation and Contribution

Despite the fact that the decomposed computing architecture can provide a more flexible and efficient terrestrial network with faster application runtime for STN, the interconnection and communication among hardware cubes are still challenges, which requires low access latency and high aggregated bandwidth. Existing electrical network-based solutions is based on commercially available hardware, which needs to be compatible with the current on-board bus protocol. This inherent high latency due to the on-board peripheral I/O connection and hierarchical server-to-server interconnect network leads to degraded application performance, while repeatedly photovoltaic conversions deteriorate the energy efficiency of decomposed computing architectures. The optical switches-based network can avoid photovoltaic conversions and achieve a high aggregated bandwidth of up to hundreds of gigabits. However, the long reconfiguration time (up to milliseconds) limits the flexibility of the decomposed computing architectures. A stable and fast switching interconnect network is significant for the decomposed terrestrial computing architecture of STN. Our previous work in [25] only numerically assessed the application performance of NOS-based decomposed computing architecture, and the impact of optical network switching based on NOS as well as network performance must be experimentally investigated to validate the feasibility and scalability of the proposed decomposed architecture.

The contributions of our work are summarized as follows:

(1) A four-node decomposed computing prototype is experimentally implemented in this work, consisting of two processor nodes, two memory nodes, and one four-port NOS. The hardware cubes are implemented utilizing FPGA chip, and two independent interconnect channels are designed between hardware cubes and NOS for sending optical payload and signal tags respectively.

(2) The physical and network performance of the decomposed computing prototype are investigated in experimental assessments. In the physical assessment, the SOA-based optical gates achieve ON/OFF switch ratios larger than 60 dB and ensure low interchannel optical signal interference. The implemented prototype provides a none-error transmission among decomposed hardware cubes with 0.5 dB power compensation at a BER of 1×10^{-9}. Meanwhile, in the network performance evaluation, the prototype performs an end-to-end latency of 122.3 ns and zero packet loss after link establishing.

(3) As the NOS port count directly impacts the scalability and feasibility of decomposed architectures, we further investigate the physical performance in terms of output OSNR and required power penalty as a function of the NOS port count. The proposed decomposed architecture provides an output OSNR of up to 30.5 dB under the NOS port count of 64. Scaling the NOS port count to 64, an error-free operation with a power penalty of 1.5 dB is achieved.
(4) The scalability of the NOS-based computing network with decomposed hardware is also evaluated in this work. Based on the experimentally measured parameters, the network performance of the NOS-based decomposed architecture is also numerically assessed under different network scales and link bandwidths. The results show that with a scale of 4096 hardware cubes and a memory cube access rate of 0.9, an end-to-end latency of 148.5 ns inside a rack and an end-to-end latency of 265.6 ns across racks are obtained under a link bandwidth of 40 Gb/s.

3. Decomposed Optical Network for STN Edge Computing

The satellite-terrestrial edge computing network is shown in Figure 1a with a decomposed optical network. The satellite system receives the requests from user terminals and transfers corresponding instructions to terrestrial decomposed computing architecture via downlink. The decomposed optical computing architecture consists of diverse resource pools such as processor, memory (Mem), and GPU, which can be flexibly configured based on application requirements. The hardware-to-NOS interconnection is divided into two parallel parts: optical packet sending plane and control plane. In the packet sending plane, the NOS switch port is linked to hardware cubes for sending optical payloads; while, in the packet control plane, the packet tag from the hardware cube is processed by the switch controller to forward/block optical payloads and reduced optical packet contention. It is significant for the scalability of the decomposed network to implement an NOS with large port count.

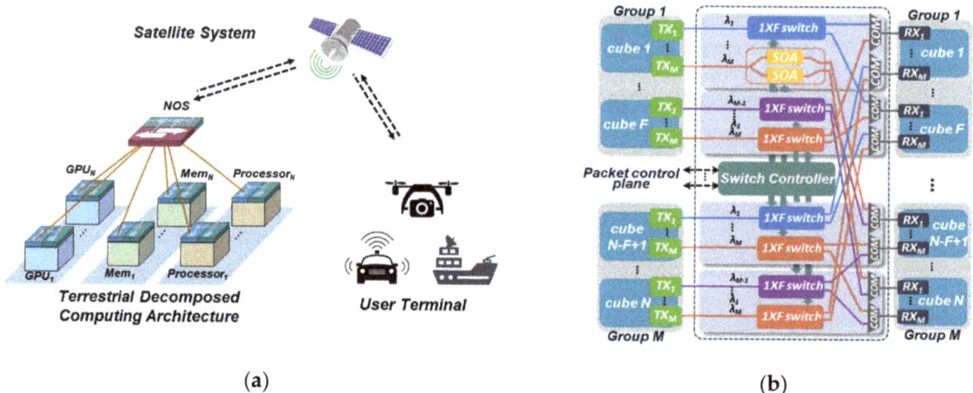

(a) (b)

Figure 1. (**a**) Satellite terrestrial network with decomposed computing architecture; (**b**) Schematic of nanoseconds optical switch.

The schematic of NOS is depicted in Figure 1b. There are N hardware cubes in total, split into M groups and F hardware cubes in each group. Leveraging distributed processing modules, the NOS can process multiple optical packets from different hardware cubes in parallel. When the FPGA-implemented switch controller analyzes the packet tag from the control-path channel, the packet payload from the data-path channel is broadcasted to SOA-based gates of the 1 × F switch using a splitter. The hardware cube grouping can scale the port count of the NOS utilizing multiple 1 × F switch with smaller port counts. SOA gates can provide nanoseconds switching time and compensate the splitting power loss. The number of cells N_{cell} that a packet payload occupied in TX is calculated as follows:

$$N_{cell} = \lceil L_p / L_b \rceil \tag{1}$$

where L_p and L_b are the length of packet and each buffer unit, respectively. After the $1 \times F$ switch, one $F \times 1$ Arrayed Waveguide Gratings (AWG) gathers F different optical wavelengths from the same group and sends packets to the corresponding receiver. According to the packet destination information in the packet tag, the controller switches the corresponding SOA gate on and rest optical gates off, then the packet payload is forwarded to the target hardware cube. Taken the group that wavelength λ_i of the hardware cube n $(1 \leq n \leq F, 1 \leq I \leq M)$ destine to as d. When M is equal to or larger than F, a feasible wavelength mapping rule is shown in the following formula:

$$d = (i + 1 - n) \bmod M \tag{2}$$

Due to the processing delay of the switch controller in the control-path channel, hardware cubes send out optical packets with the respective delay. To guarantee the alignment of the tag and packet, there is a periodic calibration in the control-path channel. The switch controller is also responsible for solving potential contentions among optical packets. If packet contention occurs, the optical payload with higher priority is transmitted at first, while the rest of the packet payloads sent in the same time slot are blocked by switching corresponding SOA gates off. The switch controller then sends the acknowledgment signals to the corresponding hardware cubes for successfully forwarding the packet (ACK) or re-transmitting the packet (NACK) [26]. Benefiting from the structure of the distributed modules and nanoseconds switching time of SOA gates, the NOS can provide a scalable network with the minimal network latency and high aggregation bandwidth for the decomposed hardware cubes interconnection. More details about the NOS can be found in [27].

Each hardware cube has three kinds of components: on-board resource, resource management module, and network interconnect module. The functional diagram of the processor cube is illustrated in Figure 2a. The on-board resource of the processor cubes is the CPU, and a small memory chunk (local memory) is still placed inside the processor cube to run the operating system and cache core data. Both the CPU and local memory are interconnected to the Memory Management Unit (MMU), which is the resource management module of the processor cube. The MMU is responsible to the translation of virtual data addresses to physical data addresses. The network interconnect module consists of a flow controller, Network Interface (NI), and transmitters (TX and RX in Figure 2a,b). The flow controller is for sending optical packets to corresponding TX and processing packets from RX, while NI can package the instructions to network packets. All the TRXs are divided into two parts: some in the packet plane for sending payloads and others in the control plane for sending optical tags. The functional diagram of the memory cube is shown in Figure 2b. The on-board resource of the memory cubes is based on the Double Data Rate 4 (DDR4) memory or Hybrid Memory Cube (HMC), connected to the memory controller (resource management module of memory cube). The memory cubes have the same network interconnect module as processor cubes, processing packets of reading/writing data from processor cubes and packets from other memory cubes for the direct memory access. Same as current server-centric architectures, the CPU first accesses the fast cache when processing application data [28]. Once data are missing in the fast cache, the instruction and logical data address are sent to the MMU. If the physical address of the target data locates in the local memory, CPU accesses the target data within the processor cube. Otherwise, the instruction and physical data address are forwarded to the flow controller. Based on the hardware cube address containing the target data address, the instruction is packaged in NI, and then sent to the corresponding TX and forwarded to destination memory cube.

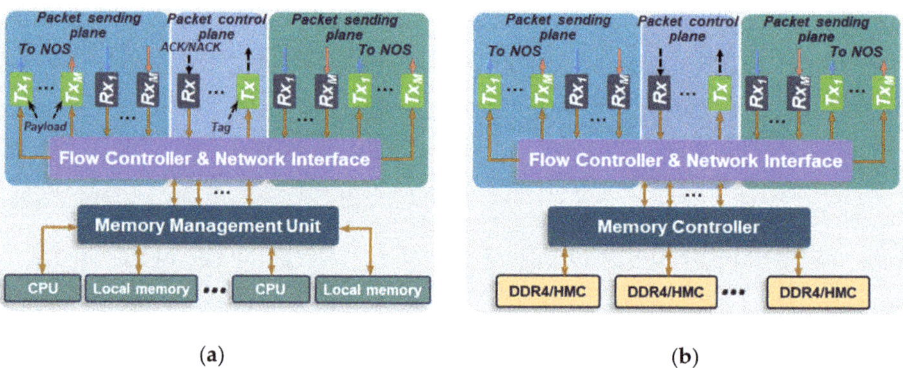

Figure 2. Functional diagram of (**a**) processor cube and (**b**) memory cube.

4. Experimental Demonstration of Decomposed Optical Architecture

4.1. Experimental Setup

The implemented experimental computing prototype with decomposed hardware is depicted in Figure 3. There are four FPGA-based hardware cubes (two processor cubes and two memory cubes) with one four-port-count NOS in the prototype. Four hardware cubes are designed via Vivado utilizing Xilinx Vertex VU095 [29], and the controller for the four-port-count optical switch is implemented with Xilinx Vertex-7 VC709 [30]. In this work, we use DDR4 memory as the on-board resource of memory cubes. All the four hardware cubes of NOS interconnections are based on two parallel commercial 10 Gb/s SFP+ transceivers (TRX). One TRX is to connect hardware cube and the NOS input/output port for the optical packet sending plane, while another TRX is for the optical packet control plane to process the packet tag. All the components in the hardware cube (including MMU, flow controller, and NI) are designed by FPGA circuit with a 322.3 MHz reference clock for data processing. In the processor cube, all the transferred data are handled via 32 bit-width format, and the payload length of each packet is set to 512 bits, as this value is the classical size of a cache line in existing computing structures. Before sending the optical payload, the packet has an eight-bit size preamble code to set up the link between hardware cube and NOS. Meanwhile, there is also an eight-bit size check code after the optical payload. Between two continuous optical packets, it has a slot to identify the start/end of packets, including 16 ns slack and 6 ns rise/fall times. The transmitter has an output of 1.2 dBm by utilizing the SFP+ transceiver, while a 2 m-length fiber is applied to connect the hardware cubes and NOS. Each SOA-based optical gate is interconnected to the input/output port of the NOS with a 1 m-length fiber. In the packet sending plane of the four-port-count NOS, there are four 1-to-4 optical signal splitters, sixteen SOA-based optical gates, and four 4-to-1 optical signal couplers in total. The switch controller distributes its reference clock to all the hardware cubes for time synchronization, and the processing of the optical packet sending plane and control plane is synchronized by utilizing the same clock and periodic calibration. At the same time, blank packets are sent to keep the link alive during periods of no data packets.

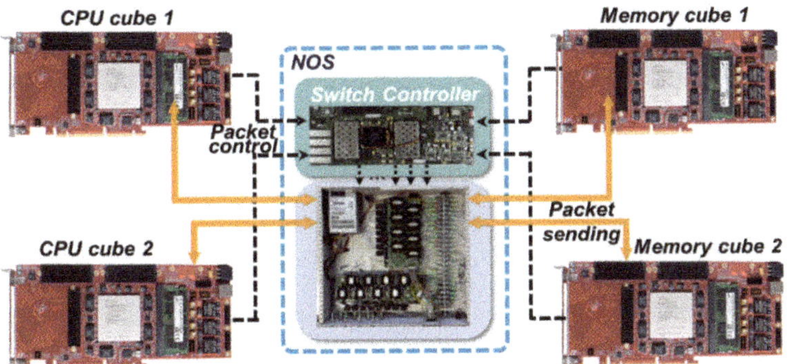

Figure 3. Experimental setup consisting of four hardware cubes and one NOS.

4.2. Physical Performance of Decomposed Prototype

Due to the broadcast and selective structure of NOS, only one of N optical gates is set to ON status during sending optical payloads to the corresponding destination hardware cube. This procedure requires the rest of the optical SOA gates to keep any optical signal from passing NOS. Otherwise, these leaked optical signals may lead to the signal interference after optical signal coupling at the output port of NOS. Therefore, in order to evaluate the implemented prototype and quantify the performance degradation due to optical signal interference, the optical power difference of SOA-based optical gates switching between ON and OFF status (ON/OFF ratio) is assessed in this part. It is depicted in Figure 4a that the SOA-based optical gate obtains a larger power difference when switching between ON and OFF status at higher SOA operation currents (better performance). When increasing the SOA operation current higher than 30 mA, the power difference of SOA-based optical gates is larger than 60 dB. The power spectra of optical signal passing through the SOA-based optical gates are shown in Figure 4b with ON and OFF status, respectively, and SOA operation current is configured as 60 mA in the assessment. With an ON/OFF ratio of higher than 60 dB, the SOA gates can block almost all the optical signals at OFF status, avoiding extra noise at output channel. Meanwhile, the target optical signal is amplified though ON SOA gate (output channel), guaranteeing a minimal signal interference across channels. Benefiting from the operation features of SOA, we can set the ON/OFF status of SOA gates within nanoseconds and achieve a rapid packet switching with good signal quality.

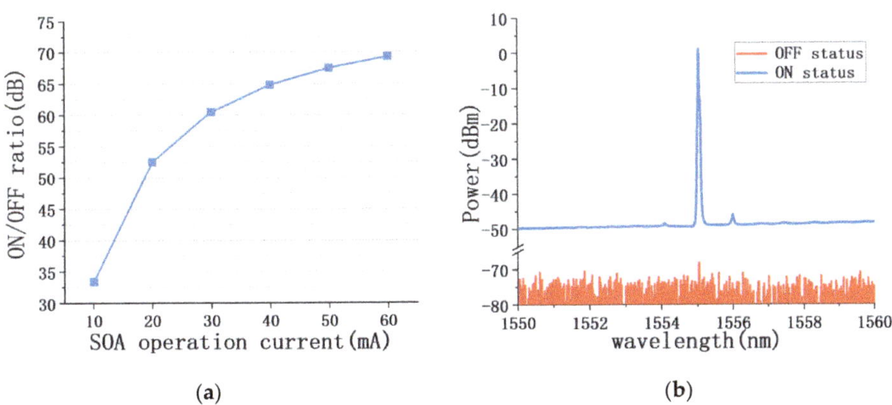

Figure 4. (**a**) Optical signal power difference with ON and OFF SOA status; (**b**) Power spectra of optical signal passing through SOA based optical gates.

To quantify the physical performance and validate the feasibility of the decomposed computing architecture with decomposed hardware, the BER of the implemented computing prototype is assessed with a SOA operation current of 60 mA, as shown in Figure 5. The Xilinx IBERT module [31] is deployed in all the four hardware cubes for calculating the BER of the computing prototype. BER is recorded when processor cubes send instructions to memory cubes. The commercially available plug-in SFP+ transceivers are applied in the assessment. The end-to-end BER without NOS (B-to-B) is measured as a criterion in the evaluation. It is shown in Figure 5 that the implemented computing prototype can perform the none-error packet transmission with 0.5 dB power compensation under a BER of 1×10^{-9} and operation current of 60 mA. This demonstrates that the implemented computing prototype can provide a feasible physical interconnection among decomposed hardware cubes

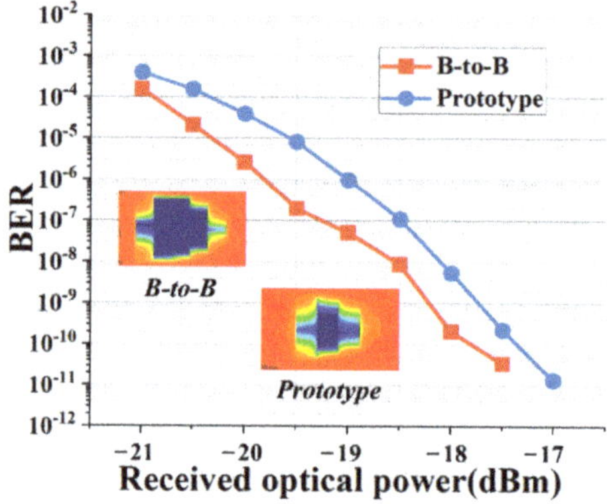

Figure 5. BER and eye diagram of decomposed computing prototype.

4.3. Network Performance of Decomposed Computing Prototype

The network performance of the decomposed computing prototype is assessed in terms of end-to-end access latency and packet loss. The network latency of the decomposed prototype includes four components: the processing delay in the flow controller and network interface of the source and destination hardware cubes, packet switching in the NOS, and fiber transmission delay. The end-to-end access latency of the implemented computing prototype with its breakdown is illustrated in Figure 6a, in which the latency is recorded when the processor cubes send instructions to the memory cubes. The customized transmission protocol is designed for the computing prototype with decomposed hardware to minimize the protocol processing delay. It is shown that, based on customized transmission protocol, the processor cube contributes 20.63 ns to handle data access instructions before sending optical packets out, while the memory cube takes 28.27 ns for receiving instructions and finding the target data. The NOS switching delay is higher compared to other components because it has more processing procedure including control signal processing, switch driver delay, and acknowledgement signal generation. Utilizing fast packet switching by NOS and customized transmission protocol for decomposed hardware, the implemented computing prototype performs minimal end-to-end access latency of 122.3 ns. By applying the Application Specific Integrated Circuit (ASIC) to implement the function of the decomposed hardware instead of the FPGA chip, the end-to-end access latency can be reduced still further.

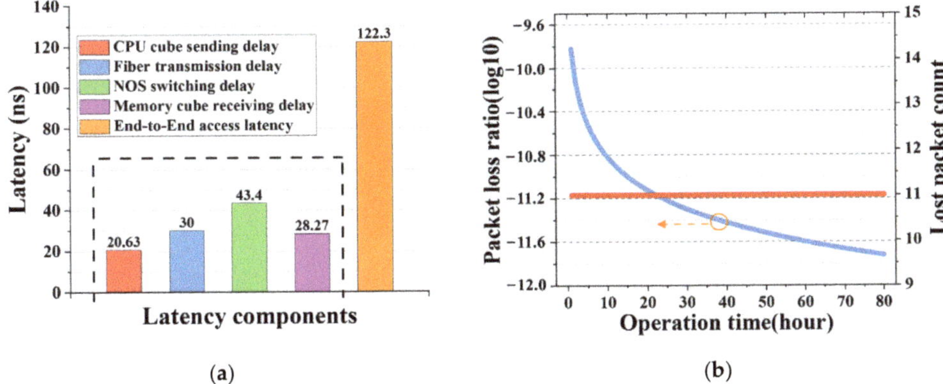

(a)

(b)

Figure 6. (**a**) Network latency components when accessing memory cube; (**b**) Cumulative network packet loss over 80 h.

To evaluate the network transmission stability of the computing prototype with decomposed hardware, the packet loss is cumulatively measured during 80-h operation time. In the assessment, the processor cube sent 5.8×10^{-11} instructions to memory cube in total. As shown in Figure 6b, the cumulative packet loss of the implemented computing prototype with decomposed hardware is less than 1.9×10^{-12} in the end. Only 11 packets are lost during initialization stage before setting up the alive link. This is because the Clock and Data Recovery (CDR) procedure is required during initialization stage at receiver part. After finishing the initial CDR procedure, the NOS based network can provide a stable and no packet loss interconnection for the decomposed hardware cubes. This is because that the link keeps active and the clock is locked by inserting blank packets, avoiding resetting up the link.

5. Scalability and Discussion

The decomposed architecture prototype has been experimentally validated in Section 4, consisting of four hardware cubes. To better investigate the scalability of decomposed optical computing architecture, the physical and network performance of decomposed architecture are evaluated in this section under different network scales. For the physical performance evaluation, the output OSNR and power penalty for error-free operation are experimentally assessed as a function of the NOS port count. Meanwhile, exploiting the experimentally measured parameters, the network latency of decomposed computing architecture is numerically investigated under different network scales and bandwidths.

5.1. Physical Performance under Different Port Counts

In the optical computing architecture with decomposed hardware, all the on-board interconnect buses are removed, and NOS based flat optical network is applied to interconnect hardware cube. Thus, the port count of NOS is significantly important for the network scale of optical computing architecture with decomposed hardware. Due to the broadcast & select structure, the input power of OSA based optical gates is dramatically reduced when port count of NOS increases. Therefore, the output Optical Signal Noise Ratio (OSNR) of NOS is evaluated with a range of NOS port counts (four-port to 64-port). The output OSNR of decomposed hardware cubes is 62.3 dB in the experiment. With four different SOA operation currents (60 mA, 90 mA, 120 mA, and 150 mA in the experiment), the received OSNR at the decomposed hardware side is measured by increasing the NOS port count from 4 to 64. It is shown in Figure 7a that, with SOA-based optical gates operated at 150 mA, the decomposed hardware cube receives optical signals of 43.3 dB OSNR utilizing a four-port NOS, and obtains optical signals of 30.5 dB OSNR utilizing a 64-port NOS. In addition, it is shown that, when deploying the NOS with small port counts in the experiment, the current values applied for SOA-based optical gates (from 60 mA to 150 mA) do not impact the received OSNR of decomposed hardware cubes too much. Meanwhile, when applying the NOS with larger port counts (>16) and a small SOA operation current (<100 mA), the received OSNR dramatically increases under a larger operation current.

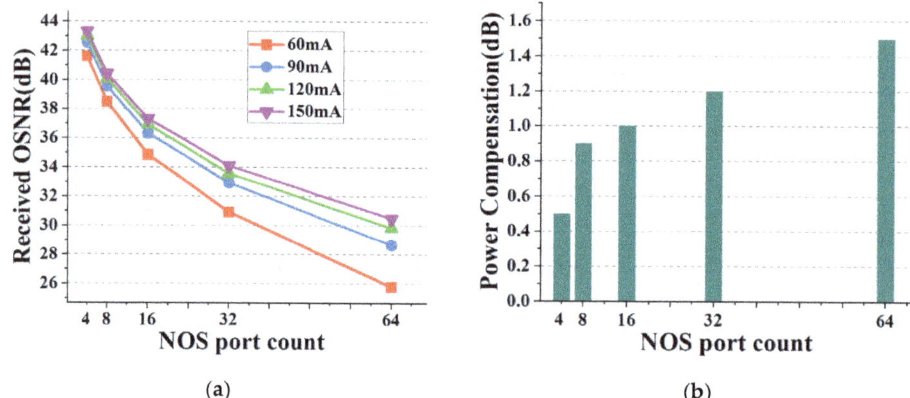

Figure 7. (**a**) Received ONSR of decomposed hardware under various operation currents; (**b**) Power compensation for none-error transmission ranging from four-port to 64-port NOS.

In order to guarantee the stable communication among decomposed hardware cubes, the required power compensation for none-error network transmission is investigated ranging from four-port NOS to 64-port NOS. In the experiment, the required power compensation is measured with a BER of 1×10^{-9}. As depicted in Figure 7b, the optical computing architecture with decomposed hardware requires a power compensation of 0.9 dB for the none-error transmission with an eight-port NOS. With a 64-port NOS, the required power compensation increases to 1.5 dB for none-error transmission. The reason is that, with the broadcast and select structure, there is much more power loss after optical signal splitters (18 dB extra loss under NOS port count of 64). When amplifying the optical signal at SOA-based optical gates, more noise is introduced under a lower input power. The experimental investigation shows that the proposed optical computing architecture with decomposed hardware is feasible and stable under a larger network scale.

5.2. Network Performance under Larger Network Scales

Due to the limitation of the hardware amount, it is not easy to experimentally evaluate the network performance of the implemented computing prototype with decomposed hardware cubes at larger scales. Thus, exploiting the experimental measurements (like the NOS switching time and processing time of processor/memory cubes), we numerically assess the network performance of optical computing architecture with decomposed hardware in this part. The discrete event simulator OMNeT++ is applied to model the NOS-based flat interconnect network and decomposed hardware cubes. Scaling the decomposed computing architecture, the network topology in [26] is applied in the assessment to interconnect hardware cubes. Four different network scales and NOS with a corresponding port count are considered in this evaluation: 64 hardware cubes (eight-port NOS), 256 hardware cubes (16-port NOS), 1024 hardware cubes (32-port NOS), and 4096 hardware cubes (64-port NOS). As analyzed in Section 3, the grouping number M is configured as 4, while each group includes two to 16 hardware cubes. Considering the network performance and cost, the TRX bandwidth in each hardware cube is configured as 40 Gb/s based on numerical investigation in [25]. Benefiting from the local memory in the processor cube and on-board resource in the memory cube, no packet loss can be measured in the experimental demonstration. Therefore, the end-to-end access latency is used as performance criterion in the assessment. To study the end-to-end access latency of the NOS-based computing architecture with decomposed hardware, the Memory Cube Access Ratio (MCAR) is defined as the ratio of required memory size in memory cubes and the overall memory size required by processor cubes. The access instruction is sent from the processor cubes following existing computing structures [32]. Based on the spatial and temporal characteristics of data access, long-tailed Pareto distribution is applied to generate access instruction. Same as the experimental investigation, each network packet is configured as 512 bit-length. While a memory cube processes the data access instruction, the target cache line is first fetched to the processor cube. Then, the remaining data of the same data page (4096 bytes) are fetched to source the processor cube to avoid repeat remote memory cube access [33]. In the assessment, the network packets carrying target data are assigned with higher priority.

Figure 8a reports the end-to-end access latency of the target data line with different network scales and different locations of decomposed hardware cubes. There are two kinds of locations: the source processor cube and destination memory cube are located inside the same rack (intra-rack) and across different racks (inter-rack). It is illustrated that, with the MCAR of less than 0.9, the intra-rack and inter-rack locations perform similar end-to-end access latency with four different scales. With a network scale of 4096 decomposed hardware cubes, intra-rack access latency of 130.8 ns and inter-rack access latency of 240.9 ns are obtained. When the MCAR is larger than 0.9, the end-to-end access latency dramatically increases scaling the optical computing architecture with decomposed hardware cubes. However, while increasing decomposed hardware from 64 cubes to 4096 cubes, the intra-rack end-to-end access latency increases by 12.6% with the MCAR of 0.9 (148.5 ns for 4096 decomposed hardware cubes), compared with 15.8% more access latency for inter-rack interconnection (265.7 ns for 4096 decomposed hardware cubes).

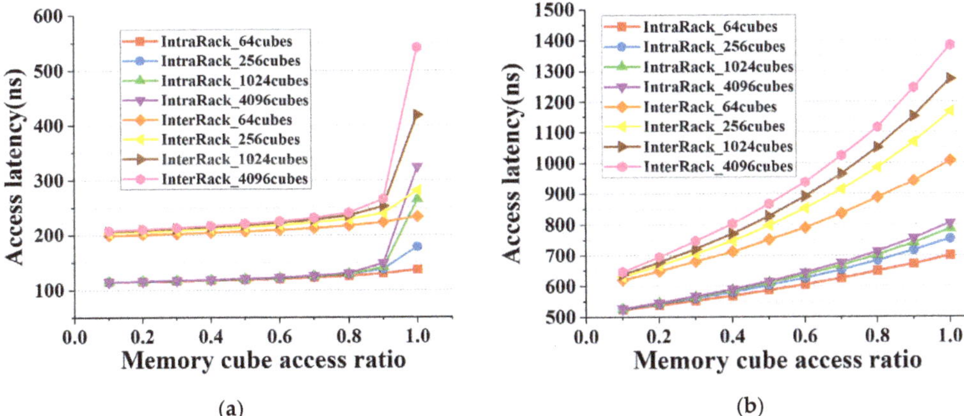

Figure 8. (**a**) End-to-end access latency of fetching (**a**) target data line and (**b**) data page with 40 Gb/s TRX bandwidth.

Besides the target data line access, the end-to-end access latency for data page access is also numerically investigated as shown in Figure 8b. Different with target data line access, the end-to-end latency for data page access increases with larger MCAR regardless of network scales. Scaling the amount of decomposed hardware from 64 cubes to 4096 cubes, the intra-rack end-to-end access latency increases by 11.1% under an MCAR of 0.9 (671.8 ns for 64-cube network and 755.8 ns for 4096-cube network). As for inter-rack interconnection, the end-to-end latency for data page access performs only a small increase of 7.4% under large network sizes (more than 256 cubes). It can be referred that the optical computing architecture keeps similar performance when increasing the port count of NOS and interconnecting more decomposed hardware cubes.

5.3. Discussion

Based on the above experimental and numerical assessments, it is shown that the NOS-based optical network can provide stable and fast switching interconnection among hardware cubes under various network scales. Compared with the microseconds access latency of current electrical network-based solutions in [16,17], the implemented decomposed optical computing architecture performs lower target data access latency of 148.5 ns under a 4096-cube network and an MCAR of 0.9. Meanwhile, the proposed NOS-based optical computing architecture can achieve a higher aggregated bandwidth (up to hundreds of gigabits) utilizing commercially available transceivers and Dense Wavelength Division Multiplexing (DWDM) technologies.

Compared with milliseconds switching time in an Optical Circuit Switch (OCS)-based network in [21] and microseconds switching time in a micro-ring resonator-based network in [23], the implemented NOS-based decomposed computing prototype can achieve nanoseconds switching time (43.4 ns), while keeping a stable interconnect link with none packet loss. These assessment results demonstrate the superiority of the proposed optical decomposed computing network based on NOS with respect to existing works.

6. Conclusions

We implement and experimentally investigate an optical computing prototype with decomposed hardware cubes for STN edge computing. In the proposed NOS-based flat terrestrial computing network, decomposed hardware cubes are interconnected, leveraging two parallel optical packet sending plane and control plane. Based on a four-cube computing prototype, the physical and network performance of the proposed computing architecture are experimentally assessed. Then, utilizing the experimentally measured parameters, the scalability of the decomposed computing network is numerically evaluated scaling up to 4096 hardware cubes. Finally, compared with the existing terrestrial computing networks, the superiority of the implemented optical computing network with decomposed hardware cubes is verified, and it is feasible to apply the proposed decomposed architecture as terrestrial infrastructures for STN edge computing.

It is shown in experimental and numerical assessments:

(1) In the physical assessment, the implemented computing prototype with decomposed hardware cubes achieves none-error packet transmission based on the power compensation of 0.5 dB. Minimal signal interference across the optical channel is ensured with larger than 60 dB ON/OFF ratio of SOA-based gates.
(2) For the network performance of the computing prototype with decomposed hardware cubes, an end-to-end access latency of 122.3 ns can be obtained in the experimental investigation, while there is zero packet loss after initial CDR procedure.
(3) When scaling the NOS port count to 64, the NOS-based interconnect network provides optical signals with 30.5 dB OSNR at the receiver part of decomposed hardware cubes, while requiring power compensation of 1.5 dB for none-error packet transmission. Under a network scale of 4096 decomposed hardware cubes, numerical studies report an end-to-end access latency of 148.5 ns inside the same rack with an MCAR of 0.9 and TRX bandwidth of 40 Gb/s.

Compared with current terrestrial computing networks, the proposed NOS-based flat decomposed computing network can provide high bandwidth optical interconnection among hardware cubes (even higher than hundreds of gigabits) and low access latency (tens nanoseconds). Benefiting from the parallel and flat structure, the performance is maintained when scaling the network (up to thousands of hardware cubes).

Due to the broadcast and select structure of NOS, the SOA-based gates receive much lower optical power input when further increasing the port count of NOS. This limitation may introduce more noise when amplifying the optical signals and degrade the performance of the NOS-based decomposed computing network. Meanwhile, if the target data are non-uniformly distributed among hardware cubes, there are more potential optical packet contentions, leading to higher access latency. Therefore, it is necessary to design the corresponding data management algorithm and packet routing policy to minimize the packet contention and access latency.

Author Contributions: Conceptualization, X.G. and Y.J.; methodology, X.G.; software, X.G.; formal analysis, X.G., Y.Z., Y.J., S.W. and H.L.; resources, X.G. and Y.Z.; data curation, X.G.; writing—original draft preparation, X.G.; writing—review and editing, X.G.; visualization, X.G.; supervision, X.G.; project administration, X.G. All authors have read and agreed to the published version of the manuscript.

Funding: This research was funded by National Natural Science Foundation of China, grant number U21B2050.

Institutional Review Board Statement: Not applicable.

Informed Consent Statement: Not applicable.

Data Availability Statement: Not applicable.

Conflicts of Interest: The authors declare no conflict of interest.

References

1. Kim, T.; Kwak, J.; Choi, J.P. Satellite Edge Computing Architecture and Network Slice Scheduling for IoT Support. *IEEE Internet Things J.* **2021**, *8*, 1. [CrossRef]
2. Xie, R.; Tang, Q.; Wang, Q.; Liu, X.; Yu, F.R.; Huang, T. Satellite-Terrestrial Integrated Edge Computing Networks: Architecture, Challenges, and Open Issues. *IEEE Netw.* **2020**, *34*, 224–231. [CrossRef]
3. Wang, Y.; Yang, J.; Guo, X.; Qu, Z. Satellite edge computing for the internet of things in aerospace. *Sensors* **2019**, *19*, 4375. [CrossRef] [PubMed]
4. Li, C.; Zhang, Y.; Xie, R.; Hao, X.; Huang, T. Integrating edge computing into low earth orbit satellite networks: Architecture and prototype. *IEEE Access* **2021**, *9*, 39126–39138. [CrossRef]
5. Tang, Q.; Fei, Z.; Li, B.; Han, Z. Computation offloading in LEO satellite networks with hybrid cloud and edge computing. *IEEE Internet Things J.* **2021**, *8*, 9164–9177. [CrossRef]
6. Wang, Y.; Zhang, J.; Xing, Z.; Peng, W.; Liu, L. A Computation Offloading Strategy in Satellite Terrestrial Networks with Double Edge Computing. In Proceedings of the 2018 IEEE International Conference on Communication Systems (ICCS), Chengdu, China, 19–21 December 2018; pp. 450–455. [CrossRef]
7. Guo, J.; Chang, Z.; Wang, S.; Ding, H.; Feng, Y.; Mao, L.; Bao, Y. Who limits the resource efficiency of my datacenter: An analysis of alibaba datacenter traces. In Proceedings of the ACM 27th International Symposium on Quality of Service, Phoenix, AZ, USA, 24–25 June 2019; pp. 1–10.
8. Lin, R.; Cheng, Y.; Andrade, M.D.; Wosinska, L.; Chen, J. Disaggregated data centers: Challenges and trade-offs. *IEEE Commun. Mag.* **2020**, *58*, 20–26. [CrossRef]
9. Han, S.; Egi, N.; Panda, A.; Ratnasamy, S.; Shi, G.; Shenker, S. Network support for resource disaggregation in next generation datacenters. In Proceedings of the 12th ACM Workshop on Hot Topics in Netwworks (HotNets-XII), College Park, MD, USA, 21–22 November 2013.
10. Li, C.-S.; Franke, H.; Parris, C.; Abali, B.; Kesavan, M.; Chang, V. Composable architecture for rack scale big data computing. *Futur. Gener. Comp. Syst.* **2017**, *67*, 180–193. [CrossRef]
11. Bielski, M.; Syrigos, I.; Katrinis, K.; Syrivelis, D.; Reale, A.; Theodoropoulos, D.; Alachiotis, N.; Pnevmatikatos, D.; Pap, E.; Zervas, G.; et al. dReDBox: Materializing a full-stack rack-scale system prototype of a next-generation disaggregated datacenter. In Proceedings of the 2018 Design, Automation & Test in Europe Conference & Exhibition (DATE), Dresden, Germany, 19–23 March 2018; pp. 1093–1098. [CrossRef]
12. Alexoudi, T.; Terzenidis, N.; Pitris, S.; Moralis-Pegios, M.; Maniotis, P.; Vagionas, C.; Mitsolidou, C.; Mourgias-Alexandris, G.; Kanellos, G.T.; Miliou, A.; et al. Optics in Computing: From Photonic Network-on-Chip to Chip-to-Chip Interconnects and Disintegrated Architectures. *J. Light. Technol.* **2019**, *37*, 363–379. [CrossRef]
13. Pfandzelter, T.; Bermbach, D. QoS-Aware Resource Placement for LEO Satellite Edge Computing. In Proceedings of the 6th International Conference on Fog and Edge Computing (ICFEC), Messina, Italy, 16–19 May 2022; pp. 66–72.
14. Tong, M.; Wang, X.; Li, S.; Peng, L. Joint Offloading Decision and Resource Allocation in Mobile Edge Computing-Enabled Satellite-Terrestrial Network. *Symmetry* **2022**, *14*, 564. [CrossRef]
15. Gao, P.X. Network requirements for resource disaggregation. In Proceedings of the 12th USENIX Symposium on Operating Systems Design and Implementation (OSDI), Savannah, GA, USA, 2–4 November 2016; pp. 249–264.
16. Lim, K.; Turner, Y.; Santos, J.R.; AuYoung, A.; Chang, J.; Ranganathan, P.; Wenisch, T.F. System-level implications of disaggregated memory. In Proceedings of the IEEE International Symposium on High-Performance Comp Architecture, New Orleans, LA, USA, 25–29 February 2012; pp. 1–12.

17. Shan, Y.; Huang, Y.; Chen, Y.; Zhang, Y. LegoOS: A Disseminated, Distributed OS for Hardware Resource Disaggregation. In Proceedings of the 13th USENIX Symposium on Operating Systems Design and Implementation (OSDI '18), Carlsbad, CA, USA, 8–10 October 2018; pp. 69–87.
18. Abrahamse, R.; Hadnagy, A.; Al-Ars, Z. Memory-Disaggregated In-Memory Object Store Framework for Big Data Applications. *arXiv* **2022**, arXiv:2204.12889.
19. Guo, X.; Xue, X.; Yan, F.; Pan, B.; Exarchakos, G.; Calabretta, N. DACON: A reconfigurable application-centric optical network for disaggregated data center infrastructures [Invited]. *J. Opt. Commun. Netw.* **2022**, *14*, A69–A80. [CrossRef]
20. Ali, H.M.M.; El-Gorashi, T.E.H.; Lawey, A.Q.; Elmirghani, J.M.H. Future energy efficient data centers with disaggregated servers. *J. Light. Technol.* **2017**, *35*, 5361–5380.
21. Saljoghei, A.; Yuan, H.; Mishra, V.; Enrico, M.; Parsons, N.; Kochis, C.; De Dobbelaere, P.; Theodoropoulos, D.; Pnevmatikatos, D.; Syrivelis, D.; et al. MCF-SMF Hybrid Low-Latency Circuit-Switched Optical Network for Disaggregated Data Centers. *J. Light. Technol* **2019**, *37*, 4017–4029. [CrossRef]
22. Zhu, Z.; Di Guglielmo, G.; Cheng, Q.; Glick, M.; Kwon, J.; Guan, H.; Carloni, L.P.; Bergman, K. Photonic Switched Optically Connected Memory: An Approach to Address Memory Challenges in Deep Learning. *J. Light. Technol* **2020**, *38*, 2815–2825. [CrossRef]
23. Gonzalez, J.; Palma, M.G.; Hattink, M.; Rubio-Noriega, R.; Orosa, L.; Mutlu, O.; Bergman, K.; Azevedo, R. Optically connected memory for disaggregated data centers. *J. Parallel Distrib. Comput.* **2022**, *163*, 300–312. [CrossRef]
24. Ballani, H.; Costa, P.; Behrendt, R.; Cletheroe, D.; Haller, I.; Jozwik, K.; Karinou, F.; Lange, S.; Shi, K.; Thomsen, B.; et al. Sirius: A flat datacenter network with nanosecond optical switching. In Proceedings of the Conference of the ACM Special Interest Group on Data Communication (SIGCOMM'20), Association for Computing Machinery, New York, NY, USA, 10–14 August 2020; pp. 782–797.
25. Guo, X.; Yan, F.; Wang, J.; Exarchakos, G.; Peng, Y.; Xue, X.; Pan, B.; Calabretta, N. RDON: A rack-scale disaggregated data center network based on a distributed fast optical switch. *J. Opt. Commun. Netw.* **2020**, *12*, 251–263. [CrossRef]
26. Yan, F.; Miao, W.; Raz, O.; Calabretta, N. OPSquare: A flat DCN architecture based on flow-controlled optical packet switches. *J. Opt. Commun. Netw.* **2017**, *9*, 291–303. [CrossRef]
27. Miao, W.; Luo, J.; Lucente, S.D.; Dorren, H.; Calabretta, N. Novel flat datacenter network architecture based on scalable and flow controlled optical switch system. *Opt. Express* **2014**, *22*, 2465–2472. [CrossRef] [PubMed]
28. Drepper, U. What Every Programmer Should Know about Memory. Available online: http://people.redhat.com/drepper/cpumemory.pdf (accessed on 9 February 2015).
29. Xilinx. UltraScale Architecture and Product Data Sheet: Overview. Available online: https://www.xilinx.com/products/silicon-devices/fpga/virtex-ultrascale.html (accessed on 20 May 2022).
30. Xilinx. VC709 Evaluation Board for the Virtex-7 FPGA. Available online: https://www.xilinx.com/products/boards-and-kits/dk-v7-vc709-g.html (accessed on 11 March 2019).
31. Xilinx. IBERT for UltraScale/UltraScale+ GTH Transceivers. Available online: https://www.xilinx.com/products/intellectual-property/ibert_ultrascale_gth.html (accessed on 4 February 2021).
32. Hennessy, J.L.; Patterson, D.A. *Computer Architecture: A Quantitative Approach*, 6th ed.; Elsevier: Amsterdam, The Netherlands, 2018.
33. Matani, D.; Shah, K.; Mitra, A. An O(1) Algorithm for Implementing the lfu CACHE eviction Scheme. *arXiv* **2021**, arXiv:2110.11602.

 mathematics

Article

Neural Network-Based Approximation Model for Perturbed Orbit Rendezvous

Anyi Huang * and Shenggang Wu

Xi'an Satellite Control Center, Xi'an 710043, China; wushenggangxscc@163.com
* Correspondence: hay04@foxmail.com; Tel.: +86-029-8476-2399

Abstract: An approximation of orbit rendezvous is usually used in the global optimization of multi-target rendezvous missions, which can greatly affect the efficiency of optimization process. A fast neural network-based surrogate model is proposed to approximate the optimal velocity increment of perturbed orbit rendezvous in low Earth orbits. According to a dynamic analysis, the initial and target orbits together with the flight time are transformed into a nine-dimensional normalized vector that is used as the input layer of the neural network. An existing approximation method is introduced to quickly generate the training data. In simulations, different numbers of layer nodes and hidden layers are tested to choose the best parameters. The proposed neural network model demonstrates high precision and high efficiency compared with previous approximation methods and neural network models. The mean relative error is less than 1%. Finally, a case of an optimization of a multi-target rendezvous mission is tested to prove the potential application of the neural network model.

Keywords: neural network; perturbed orbit rendezvous; trajectory optimization

MSC: 85-08

Citation: Huang, A.; Wu, S. Neural Network-Based Approximation Model for Perturbed Orbit Rendezvous. *Mathematics* **2022**, *10*, 2489. https://doi.org/10.3390/math10142489

Academic Editors: Yu Jiang, Haijun Peng and Hongwei Yang

Received: 7 June 2022
Accepted: 15 July 2022
Published: 18 July 2022

1. Introduction

The fast approximation of orbit rendezvous is a basis for the global optimization of a multi-target rendezvous mission [1]. Due to the drift of the right ascension of the ascending node (RAAN) and argument of perigee [2], the rendezvous velocity increment is closely related to the flight time for perturbed orbit rendezvous in low Earth orbits (LEOs), which makes it difficult to obtain an analytical solution. Numerical methods based on evolutionary algorithms can obtain a high-precision solution, but applying them for the global optimization of a multi-target rendezvous sequence is time-consuming [3,4] because the global search needs to evaluate the velocity increments required for orbit transfers between the different targets at different times for many instances to find the global optimal order and arrival time of each target.

To obtain efficient methods that quickly calculate the optimal velocity increment, several studies have focused on analytical methods based on dynamic approximations. A simple strategy is to calculate the orbit differences between the initial and target orbits and add them to the velocity increment separately [5,6]. It is fast enough, but cannot deal with the coupling terms between the different components of the orbit elements. As differences in the semi-major axis and inclination may cause the RAAN to drift due to perturbations, it can be used to indirectly change the RAAN instead of a normal impulse maneuver. Cerf [7] proposed a traversal method to search for the optimal RAAN drift rate to minimize the total impulses. Huang [8,9] established an equal constraint optimization model of different impulse components and derived an extremality condition based on the minimum principle. Shen [10] and Chen [11] separately proposed similar methods by rewriting the objective function to obtain the analytical expression of the optimal solution.

With the development of artificial neural networks [12–14], several studies have employed neural networks to approximate the solution of complex dynamic equations.

Li [15] proposed a surrogate model of low-thrust transfer between asteroids in deep space. Zhu [16,17] also studied the application of artificial neural networks in low-thrust and impulsive orbit transfers. Due to the effect of perturbations on the orbit elements in low Earth orbits, it is more difficult to find all the features that determine the optimal velocity increment of the rendezvous. In [15,16], the residuals of the neural networks for transfers in deep space were less than 1%. By contrast, in [17], the residual of the neural network for perturbed rendezvous with a similar structure was more than 2%. Moreover, in [17], multiple man-made combinations of characteristic parameters were tested to find the optimal input layer of the neural network for perturbed orbit rendezvous. However, a few of the candidate parameters lacked physical meanings and the orbit rendezvous was divided into three types corresponding with three different neural networks to be trained, which made the process more time-consuming. Therefore, we focused on a neural network structure that precisely reflected the optimization of orbit rendezvous using the fewest parameters.

The major contribution of this study is the proposition of a novel neural network model for the approximation of long-duration perturbed orbit rendezvous. According to the existing analytical methods, the feature vector that completely determines the optimal velocity increment was exacted and normalized to be used as the input layer. The efficiency of the training data generation processes was also improved. The simulation results indicated that the relative error of the neural network was less than 1% and the calculation time was much less. It can be reasonably applied to the global optimization of multi-target rendezvous sequences.

2. Problem Description of Orbit Rendezvous

In this study, we addressed time-fixed impulsive orbit rendezvous in low Earth orbits with small eccentricities. The spacecraft was deemed to be in an initial orbit and needed to transfer to a given target orbit. The rendezvous time and flight time were fixed. Thus, the optimal velocity increment was the minimum summary of impulses that transferred the spacecraft to the target orbit under the gravity of the Earth and other perturbations. The dynamics equations can be described as follows [8]:

$$\begin{aligned} \dot{\mathbf{r}} &= \mathbf{v} \\ \dot{\mathbf{v}} &= -\tfrac{\mu}{r^3}\mathbf{r} + \mathbf{a}_p \end{aligned} \tag{1}$$

where $\mathbf{r}$ and $\mathbf{v}$ are the position and velocity of the spacecraft, respectively; r is the magnitude of $\mathbf{r}$; μ is the gravity constant of the Earth; and $\mathbf{a}_p$ is the acceleration of perturbations, which included the non-sphere perturbation of the Earth, the gravities of the sun and the moon, solar radial pressure, and the drag of the atmosphere [2].

The model of the impulsive maneuver was expressed as:

$$\begin{aligned} \mathbf{r}(t_m{}^+) &= \mathbf{r}(t_m{}^-) \\ \mathbf{v}(t_m{}^+) &= \mathbf{v}(t_m{}^-) + \Delta\mathbf{v} \end{aligned} \tag{2}$$

where $t_m{}^-$ and $t_m{}^+$ are the instantaneous times before and after the maneuver, respectively, and $\Delta\mathbf{v}$ is the vector of impulse. Assuming that $\{\Delta\mathbf{v}_i\}, i = 1,2\ldots n$ is the sequence of impulses that ensures that the spacecraft rendezvous with a target orbit, the optimization problem is:

$$\begin{aligned} &\min J = \sum_{i=1}^{n} |\Delta\mathbf{v}_i| \\ &s.t.\ \mathbf{r}(t_f) = \mathbf{r}_f \\ &\qquad \mathbf{v}(t_f) = \mathbf{v}_f \end{aligned} \tag{3}$$

where t_f is the rendezvous time; $\mathbf{r}_f$ and $\mathbf{v}_f$ are the position and velocity of the target orbit, respectively; and n is the number of impulses.

Equation (3) is a non-linear optimization model and evolutionary algorithms are always required to obtain a high-precision solution. When searching for the best path and rendezvous times of each target in a multi-target sequence, the global optimization process needs to frequently evaluate the velocity increments of the transfers between the different targets with different flight times, which is extremely time-consuming. Most existing studies have employed different forms of approximation to improve the efficiency [5–8,11]. However, such a problem still lacks a solution that is fast enough for global optimization. In this study, we propose a new artificial neural network approach to approximate the optimal velocity increment.

3. Methodology

In this section, the semi-analytical approximation method in [8] was reviewed first. Based on this method, the features that fully determined the velocity increment were extracted and validated by the sampling data of different orbit elements and transfer durations. The feature vector was then employed as the input layer of a multi-layer neural network. Meanwhile, the numerical high-precision solution in [9] was applied to generate the sampling data for the training and validation. The process was as follows.

3.1. Approximation Method of the Perturbed Orbit Rendezvous Problem

To quickly evaluate the optimal velocity increment, Huang [8] proposed a semi-analytical model that considered both efficiency and precision in which the analytical dynamic equations of J_2 perturbation were used and the changes in the orbit elements by maneuvers were set as unknown parameters. We assumed that $\Delta a_0, \Delta i_0$ and $\Delta\Omega_0$ were the differences of the semi-major axis, inclination, and RAAN between the initial and target orbits. Δa_1, Δi_1, and $\Delta\Omega_1$ then denoted the changes in the semi-major axis, inclination, and RAAN caused by the impulses at the beginning of the transfer. Δa_2, Δi_2, and $\Delta\Omega_2$ denoted the changes in semi-major axis, inclination, and RAAN caused by the impulses at the end of the transfer. Thus, the equality constraint optimization model was obtained as:

$$\begin{aligned}
&\min\Delta v = \sqrt{\left(\frac{\Delta a_1}{2a_0}\right)^2 + (\Delta i_1)^2 + \left(\frac{\Delta\Omega_1}{\sin i_0}\right)^2} + \sqrt{\left(\frac{\Delta a_2}{2a_0}\right)^2 + (\Delta i_2)^2 + \left(\frac{\Delta\Omega_2}{\sin i_0}\right)^2} \\
&g.t.\ g_1 \triangleq \Delta a_1 + \Delta a_2 = \Delta a_0 \\
&\quad\ g_2 \triangleq \Delta i_1 + \Delta i_2 = \Delta i_0 \\
&\quad\ g_3 \triangleq \Delta\Omega_1 + \Delta\Omega_2 + \Delta\dot{\Omega}\Delta t = \Delta\Omega_0
\end{aligned} \tag{4}$$

where Δa_1, Δi_1, $\Delta\Omega_1$, Δa_2, Δi_2, and $\Delta\Omega_2$ are unknowns and g_1, g_2, and g_3 are the constraints required for rendezvous. a_0 and i_0 are the initial semi-major axis and inclination, respectively; note that, in this paper, i_0 could not be zero. In g_3, $\Delta\dot{\Omega}$ is used to denote the difference of the RAAN drift rate between the drift orbit (meaning that the orbit had been changed by Δa_1, Δi_1, and $\Delta\Omega_1$) and target orbit; $\Delta\dot{\Omega}$ can be calculated by Δa_1 and Δi_1 [8].

According to the minimum principle, $L = \Delta v + \lambda_1 g_1 + \lambda_2 g_2 + \lambda_3 g_3$ can denote the Lagrange function where λ_1, λ_2, and λ_3 are the Lagrange multipliers. The extreme condition can be derived and easily solved by a non-linear algorithm [18]. The solution is locally corrected by the differences in phase (Δu_0) and eccentricity (Δe_{x0} and Δe_{y0}) to obtain a near-optimal solution that meets all the constraints. An iterative process [9] was further developed to transfer the approximate solution into a high-precision solution of numerical dynamics via a group of analytical correction equations.

Such a method can be well-applied to the multi-target rendezvous sequence optimization of active debris removal missions. The shortcoming is that the method cannot be applied directly to global optimization because the calculation time is still not acceptable when repeating it many times. Instead, it is used to generate a data grid before the optimization and the evaluation of the velocity increment is calculated by interpolation.

3.2. Features Analysis of the Perturbed Orbit Rendezvous Problem

Equation (4) and other processes in [8] indicated that the key factors of Δv were the initial semi-major axis and inclination (a_0, i_0), the differences between the initial and target orbits (Δa_0, Δi_0, $\Delta\Omega_0$, Δu_0, Δe_{x0}, and Δe_{y0}), and the flight time Δt. To validate this assumption, the same initial orbit and target orbit given in Table 6 in [8] were used to obtain the vector $x = [a_0, i_0, \Delta a_0, \Delta i_0, \Delta\Omega_0, \Delta u_0, \Delta e_{x0}, \Delta e_{y0}]$. A group of random real numbers were then generated to represent the initial RAAN, phase, and eccentricity (Ω_0, u_0, e_{x0}, and e_{y0}) These corresponded with different orbit rendezvous problems with the same x.

$$\begin{aligned} \Omega_0 &= 2\pi c_1 \\ u_0 &= 2\pi c_2 \\ e_{x0} &= e_{\max} c_3 \cos(2\pi c_4) \\ e_{y0} &= e_{\max} c_3 \sin(2\pi c_4) \end{aligned} \tag{5}$$

where c_1, c_2, c_3, and c_4 are the real numbers in [0, 1] and $e_{\max}$ = 0.02 is the maximum eccentricity to analyze. The optimal velocity increments solved by the evolutionary algorithm are illustrated in Figure 1. It can be seen that when Δt was fixed to different values and x remained the same, the relative deviation of the optimized Δv was less than 1% although the other orbit elements were randomly generated and not equal.

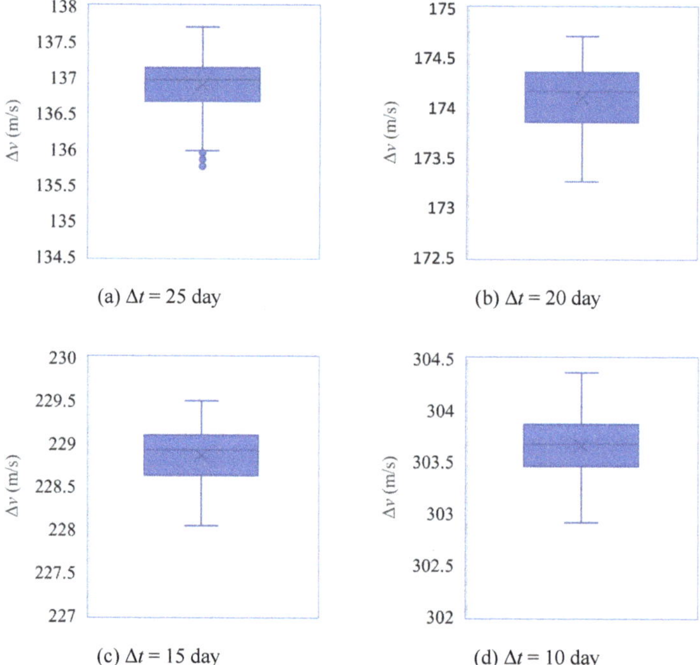

Figure 1. Box diagram of optimized velocity increments with different orbits and the same x.

According to Figure 1, the feature vector of perturbed orbit rendezvous could be defined as x together with Δt. According to the range of orbit elements, it could be normalized as $\mathbf{y}^{in}$:

$$\mathbf{y}^{in} = [\frac{a_0 - \bar{a}}{\Delta a_{\max}}, \frac{i_0 - \bar{i}}{\Delta i_{\max}}, \frac{\Delta a_0}{\Delta a_{\max}}, \frac{\Delta i_0}{\Delta i_{\max}}, \frac{\Delta e_{x0}}{e_{\max}}, \frac{\Delta e_{y0}}{e_{\max}}, \frac{\Delta\Omega_0}{\pi}, \frac{\Delta u_0}{\pi}, \frac{\Delta t}{\Delta t_{\max}}] \tag{6}$$

where $\bar{a}$ and $\bar{i}$ are the middle values of the semi-major axis and the inclination of all orbits that needed to be analyzed to obtain the approximate model of orbit rendezvous, respectively; $\Delta a_{\max}$ and $\Delta i_{\max}$ are the maximum values of the changes in the semi-major axis and inclination; and $\Delta t_{\max}$ is the maximum transfer time. Each component of $\mathbf{y}^{in}$ is then within $[-1, 1]$. $\mathbf{y}^{in}$ is used as an input layer to construct the neural network.

3.3. Neural Network and Training

In this study, we applied a multi-layer fully connected neural network [15–17] to obtain the surrogate model of the optimal velocity increment. The neural network structure is illustrated in Figure 2.

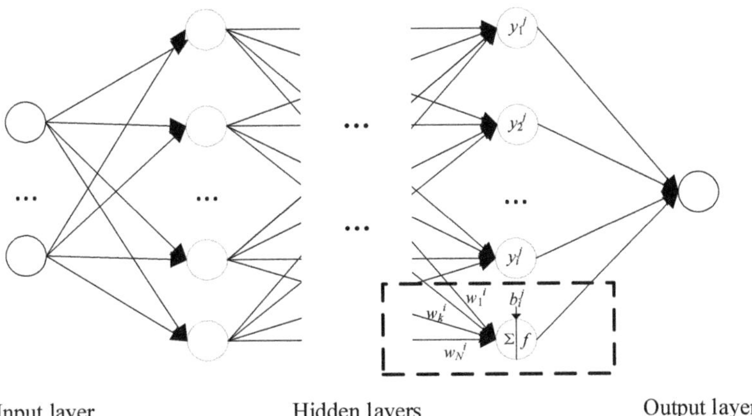

Figure 2. Structure of the multi-layer neural network.

In Figure 2, the dashed box shows the relationship between the nodes of neighboring layers. The value of the ith node in the jth layer was a weighted sum of the nodes of the previous layer and a constant bias:

$$y_i^j = f(\sum_{k=1}^{N} w_k^i y_i^{j-1} + b_i^j) \tag{7}$$

where N is the number of nodes that are connected to the current node, w_k^i is the weight, b_i^j is the bias, and f is a non-linear function named the activation function. The output was calculated by a given input through multiple layers.

In this study, the input layer was $\mathbf{y}^{in}$ and the output layer was the optimal velocity increment. The number of hidden layers was set to 2 and each layer had 60 nodes. A standard rectified linear unit function was set as the activation function. The training process was as follows.

First, a large amount of training data from different inputs was needed. Equation (8) was used to generate the random flight time and the initial and target orbits.

$$\begin{aligned}
a_0 &= \bar{a} + k_1 \Delta a_{\max} \\
i_0 &= \bar{i} + k_2 \Delta i_{\max} \\
e_{x0} &= k_3 e_{\max} \cos(k_4 \pi) \\
e_{y0} &= k_3 e_{\max} \sin(k_4 \pi) \\
\Omega_0 &= k_5 \pi \\
u_0 &= k_6 \pi \\
a_f &= \bar{a} + k_7 \Delta a_{\max} \\
i_f &= \bar{i} + k_8 \Delta i_{\max} \\
e_{xf} &= k_9 e_{\max} \cos(k_{10} \pi) \\
e_{yf} &= k_9 e_{\max} \sin(k_{10} \pi) \\
\Omega_f &= \Omega_0 + k_{11} \Delta \Omega_{\max} \\
u_f &= k_{12} \pi \\
\Delta t &= \Delta t_{\min} + k_{13} \Delta t_{\max}
\end{aligned} \tag{8}$$

where $k_i, i = 1, 2...12$ are random real numbers within $[-1, 1]$ and k_{13} is within $(0, 1]$. $\Delta\Omega_{\max}$ is the upper limit of the RAAN difference. The optimization method in [9] was applied to obtain the corresponding Δv. Each group of $\mathbf{y}^{in}$ and Δv was recorded in the dataset.

The dataset was divided into training (90%) and validating data (10%). Keras, a well-known neural network framework [19], was adopted to complete the training process. For details on the training algorithm, refer to [19]. In this paper, we did not need to adjust the hyperparameters of the neural network by the validating result. Therefore, the functions of the testing data and validating data were almost the same; the validating data could, therefore, prove the precision of the trained neural network.

The training process and the application of the trained neural network are illustrated in Figure 3. To obtain the neural network model, a dataset of optimal velocity increments with different input orbits was generated first. We then obtained the optimal input vector of such a perturbed orbit rendezvous problem and constructed the neural network. The dataset was then used to train the neural network and obtain the weights. Finally, the weights and bias in the neural network were obtained and used in Equation (7) to predict the optimal velocity increment with various input values.

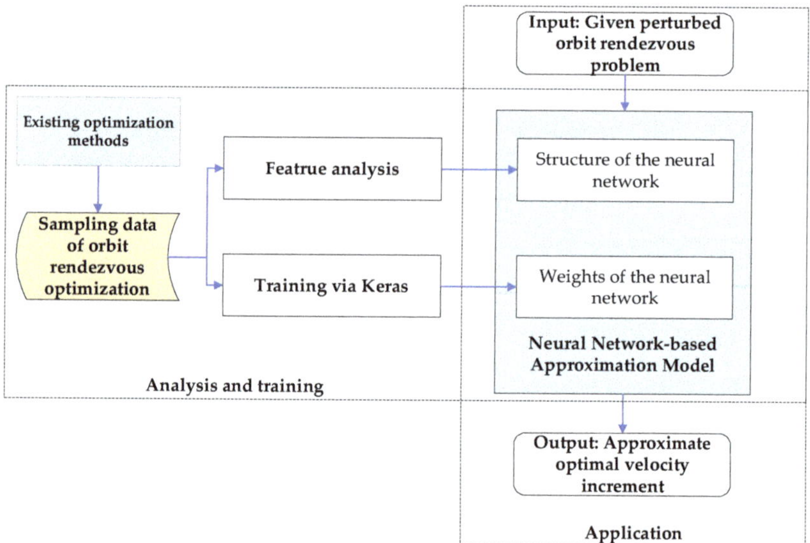

Figure 3. Flowchart of the training and application of the neural network.

4. Experiments

To validate the proposed neural network design, the problem of the ninth Global Trajectory Optimization Competition (GTOC9) [20] was tested, which provided 123 pieces of debris in LEO that must be removed by multiple orbit transfer vehicles (OTVs) within a given duration. The objective function was to minimize the total launch mass of all that OTVs. It is a complex global optimization problem that has attracted many participants even after the competition. Thus, in the simulation, we trained the neural network to help evaluate the optimal velocity increment of the transfers between the different debris.

4.1. Dataset Generalization and Training Result

In GTOC9, the orbits of the debris are near-circular, the semi-major axis is centralized at 7100 km, and the inclinations are centralized at 98°. According to Equation (8), we set $\bar{a}$ = 7100 km, $\bar{i}$ = 98°, $\Delta a_{\max}$ = 200 km, $\Delta i_{\max}$ = 2°, $\Delta\Omega_{\max}$ = 10°, and $\Delta t_{\max}$ = 30 d. A dataset consisting of 130,000 groups of input orbits and flight times was generated and the optimal Δv was calculated and recorded. The distribution of Δv is illustrated in Figure 4.

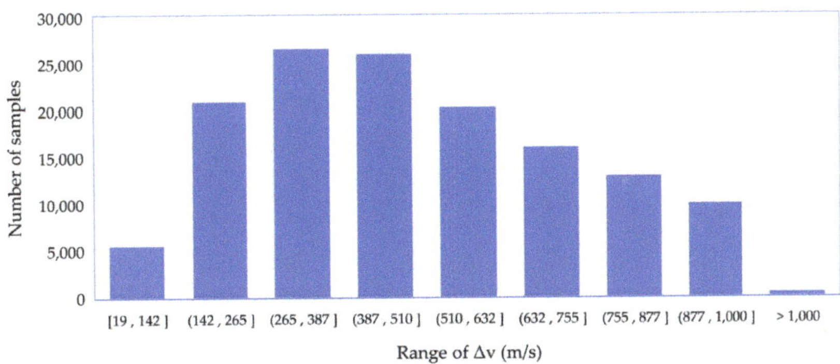

Figure 4. Distribution of sampling Δv at different ranges.

In the Keras framework, the training algorithm was set to "rmsprop" (root mean square propagation), the loss function was "mse" (mean square error), and the batch size was 32. A total of five cases with different numbers of hidden layers and nodes were tested; the results are detailed in Table 1. The results indicated that 2 hidden layers of 60 nodes were enough to obtain high precision. The mean relative error (MRE) was less than 1% and the mean absolute error (MAE) was less than 4 m/s from the validation data, which was an improvement of more than 50% compared with the results achieved in [17]. This was because the feature vector was extracted more reasonably; the training data were also more precise.

Table 1. Comparison of different neural network parameters.

Number of Hidden Layers	Number of Nodes in Each Hidden Layer	MRE (%)	MAE (m/s)	Time of Each Training Epoch (s)	Training Time (s)	Time of Δv Evaluation (s)
2	30	1.34	5.3	4.6	1380	1.2×10^{-6}
2	60	0.96	3.8	5.0	1500	4.8×10^{-6}
2	90	0.89	3.7	5.2	1560	1.1×10^{-5}
3	60	0.81	3.3	6.0	1800	8.9×10^{-6}
4	60	0.79	3.2	7.0	2100	1.3×10^{-5}

The velocity increments of all transfers using the same input orbits and durations of the solution in [20] (from the Jet Propulsion Laboratory, which won GTOC9) were recalculated by the neural network model presented in this paper. Compared with the results from the Jet Propulsion Laboratory [20], the MRE was less than 4% and close to the semi-analytical method [8].

The correlation between the Δv predicted by the neural network and the optimized Δv in [21] is illustrated in Figure 5, which indicated that the results of two methods were close and the correlation was close to the function $y = x$. Moreover, the calculation time was only 4.8×10^{-6} s using an AMD 4.2 GHz CPU, which demonstrated a higher efficiency than previous approximation methods [8–11].

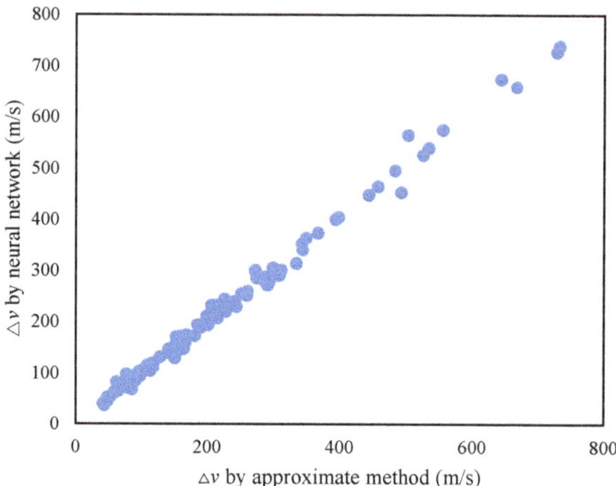

Figure 5. Correlation between the proposed neural network and approximate method in Petropoulos 2018.

4.2. Application in Global Optimization

The performance of the proposed neural network was evaluated in the global optimization of a multi-target rendezvous sequence in the GTOC9 problem. Based on the problem description, OTVs can be launched one by one to complete the debris removal mission. Each OTV starts from one debris point and then rendezvous with several targets sequentially. As the optimal velocity required for an orbit rendezvous between two debris objects changes with the orbit elements and transfer time, it is difficult to find the global optimal path of all targets. In the problem description, the maximum duration of the flight time is 25 d between every two debris points; another 5 d is required for the OTV to release a de-orbit package (Δm_{kit} = 30 kg) after a rendezvous with target debris. The specific impulse is I_{sp} = 1000 s and the dry mass of the OTV is 2000 kg. Optimizing one OTV is a sub-problem of GTOC9, which aims to find the best path and rendezvous times of given targets to minimize the objective function (the total cost of the OTV mission per unit: million Euro, also MEUR), defined as:

$$J = 2 \times 10^{-6}(m_0 - 2000)^2 + 55 \tag{9}$$

where m_0 is the launch mass and can be calculated by the velocity increments of all transfers:

$$\begin{aligned} m_{i-1} &= m_i e^{\Delta v_i/(I_{sp}g)} + \Delta m_{kit} \\ m_N &= 2000 \text{ kg} \end{aligned} \tag{10}$$

where g is the gravity acceleration at the sea level, N is the number of debris objects in sequence, m_i represents the mass after the ith transfer, and Δv_i is the velocity increment of the ith transfer. The problem is illustrated in Figure 6.

The optimization method in [21] was adopted and the neural network was employed to replace the evaluation of Δv_i corresponding with orbit rendezvous between different targets with different transfer times. In the optimization model, the dimension of the decision variables was $2N$. The integer variables $\{x_i\}, i = 1, 2 \ldots N$ represented the order of the rendezvous and the real number variables $\{\Delta t_i\}, i = 1, 2 \ldots N$ represented the flight times between two debris points. Thus, the start time t_i^{start} and arrival time t_i^{arrivel} of the ith transfer could be calculated as Equation (11) and the orbit elements of the corresponding targets could be obtained.

$$t_i^{start} = \begin{cases} t_{i-1}^{arrivel} + \Delta t_{kit}, i > 1 \\ t_0, i = 1 \end{cases}$$
$$t_i^{arrivel} = t_i^{start} + \Delta t_i \tag{11}$$

where t_0 is the given initial time of the OTV mission and Δt_{kit} = 5 d is the time required to release the de-orbit package. Equation (6) was then sequentially applied to calculate the input feature vector. The approximate Δv_i could then be obtained by the trained neural network. After all the velocity increments were known, the objective function could be calculated by Equation (9).

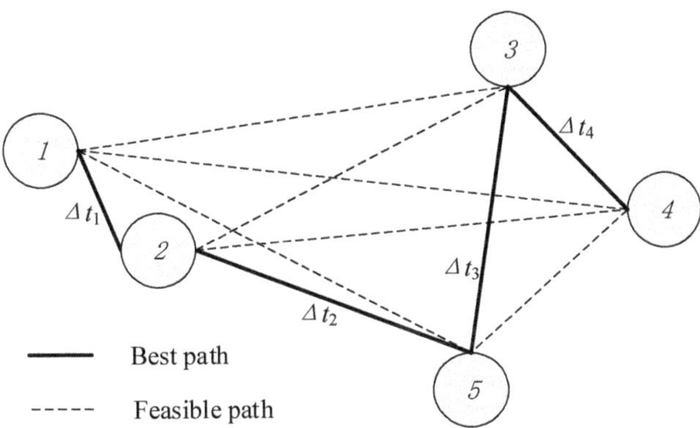

Figure 6. Optimization of a sequence (N = 5).

The differential evolutionary algorithm was then used to solve this model and obtain the optimal order of the debris and optimal rendezvous times. The results to rendezvous with the same debris objects achieved by the different approximation methods of Δv_i are listed in Table 2, which indicates that the optimal J achieved by the neural network was comparable with other results, but required less calculation using the same AMD 4.2 GHz CPU. Moreover, the test was single-threaded and could be further accelerated because a neural network is easy to parallelize.

Table 2. Comparison of different methods.

Model of Velocity Increment	Optimal Order of Debris	Total Δv (m/s)	J (MEUR)	Computational Time (s)
Method in [20]	72, 107, 61, 10, 28, 3, 64, 66, 31, 90, 73, 87, 57, 35, 69, 65, 8, 43, 71, 4, 29	3409.5	97.1	>3600
Method in [21]	72, 107, 61, 73, 3, 69, 64, 66, 31, 10, 90, 87, 57, 35, 28, 65, 8, 43, 71, 4, 29	3357.0	95.6	600
Neural network model in this paper	72, 61, 107, 73, 3, 69, 64, 66, 31, 10, 90, 87, 57, 35, 28, 65, 8, 43, 71, 4, 29	3407.5	97.1	120

5. Conclusions

In this study, we proposed a novel neural network surrogate model for orbit rendezvous between near-circular orbits in low Earth orbits. Most previous methods focused on analytical approximation forms, which require an optimization process and thus lead to an efficiency bottleneck. A few of the latest studies have employed neural networks, but the structures have a lack of theoretical references. In this study, we designed an input layer based on orbit dynamics and normalization was applied to improve the performance. Based on an efficient data generalization process, the network was constructed using a normal training process. The simulation results demonstrated the precision and efficiency of the neural network model. The relative error was less than 1% and was better than that achieved by a similar work [17] based on neural networks. Moreover, the calculation time was 5.8×10^{-6} s using an ordinary desktop processor and could be directly applied to the global optimization of multi-target rendezvous missions.

Author Contributions: Conceptualization, A.H.; methodology, A.H.; software, A.H. and S.W.; validation, S.W.; formal analysis, S.W.; investigation, A.H.; resources, S.W.; data curation, S.W.; writing—original draft preparation, A.H.; writing—review and editing, S.W.; visualization, A.H.; supervision, A.H.; project administration, A.H.; funding acquisition, A.H. All authors have read and agreed to the published version of the manuscript.

Funding: This research was funded by the National Natural Science Fund of China, grant number 12002394.

Institutional Review Board Statement: Not applicable.

Informed Consent Statement: Not applicable.

Data Availability Statement: Data are contained within the article.

Conflicts of Interest: The authors declare no conflict of interest.

Nomenclature

a_0	Semi-major axis of initial orbit
i_0	Inclination of initial orbit
Δa_0	Difference of semi-major axis between initial and target orbits
Δi_0	Difference of inclination axis between initial and target orbits
$\Delta \Omega_0$	Difference of RAAN axis between initial and target orbits
Δu_0	Difference of phase axis between initial and target orbits
Δe_{x0}	Difference of $e \cos\omega$ between initial and target orbits
Δe_{y0}	Difference of $e \sin\omega$ between initial and target orbits
$\dot{\Omega}_0$	Initial drift rate of RAAN
e_{max}	Upper limit of eccentricity
Δa_{max}	Upper limit of change in semi-major axis
Δi_{max}	Upper limit of change in inclination
$\Delta \Omega_{max}$	Upper limit of change in RAAN
Δt_{max}	Upper limit of flight time
$\bar{a}$	Mean value of semi-major axis
$\bar{i}$	Mean value of inclination
Δv	Velocity increment of orbit rendezvous
OTV	Orbit transfer vehicle
m_0	Launch mass of OTV
m_N	Dry mass of OTV
Δm_{kit}	Mass of de-orbit package released at each debris point

References

1. Li, S.; Huang, X.; Yang, B. Review of Optimization Methodologies in Global and China Trajectory Optimization Competitions. *Prog. Aerosp. Sci.* **2018**, *102*, 60–75. [CrossRef]
2. Vallado, D.A. *Fundamentals of Astrodynamics and Applications*, 2nd ed.; Microscosm Press: Torrance, CA, USA, 2001; pp. 757–800.
3. Casalino, L.; Dario, P. Active Debris Removal Missions with Multiple Targets. In Proceedings of the AIAA/AAS Astrodynamics Specialist Conference, San Diego, CA, USA, 4–7 August 2014.
4. Yang, Z.; Luo, Y.Z.; Zhang, J. Two-Level Optimization Approach for Mars Orbital Long-Duration, Large Non-Coplanar Rendezvous Phasing Maneuvers. *Adv. Space Res.* **2013**, *52*, 883–894. [CrossRef]
5. Zhang, T.J.; Shen, H.; Yang, Y. Ant Colony Optimization-Based Design of Multiple-Target Active Debris Removal Mission. *Trans. Jpn. Soc. Aeronaut. Space Sci.* **2018**, *61*, 201. [CrossRef]
6. Barea, A.; Urrutxua, H.; Cadarso, L. Large-Scale Object Selection and Trajectory Planning for Multi-Target Space Debris Removal Missions. *Acta Astronaut.* **2020**, *170*, 289–301. [CrossRef]
7. Cerf, M. Multiple Space Debris Collecting Mission: Optimal Mission Planning. *J. Optim. Theory Appl.* **2015**, *167*, 195–218. [CrossRef]
8. Huang, A.Y.; Luo, Y.Z.; Li, H.N. Fast Estimation of Perturbed Impulsive Rendezvous via Semi-Analytical Equality-Constrained Optimization. *J. Guid. Control Dyn.* **2020**, *43*, 2383–2390. [CrossRef]

9. Huang, A.Y.; Luo, Y.Z.; Li, H.N. Fast Optimization of Impulsive Perturbed Orbit Rendezvous Using Simplified Parametric Model. *Astrodynamics* **2021**, *5*, 391–402. [CrossRef]
10. Chen, S.Y.; Baoyin, H.X. Analytical Estimation of the Velocity Increment in J2-Perturbed Impulsive Transfers. *J. Guid. Control Dyn.* **2022**, *45*, 310–319. [CrossRef]
11. Shen, H.X.; Casalino, L. Simple ΔV Approximation for Optimization of Debris-to-Debris Transfers. *J. Spacecr. Rocket.* **2021**, *58*, 575–580. [CrossRef]
12. Schmidhuber, J. Deep learning in neural networks: An overview. *Neural Netw.* **2015**, *61*, 85–117. [CrossRef]
13. Izzo, D.; Märtens, M.; Pan, X. A survey on artificial intelligence trends in spacecraft guidance dynamics and control. *Astrodynamics* **2019**, *4*, 287–299. [CrossRef]
14. Diao, Y.; Pu, J.; Xu, H.; Mu, R. Orbit-Injection Strategy and Trajectory-Planning Method of the Launch Vehicle under Power Failure Conditions. *Aerospace* **2022**, *9*, 199. [CrossRef]
15. Li, H.; Chen, S.; Izzo, D. Deep networks as approximators of optimal low-thrust and multi-impulse cost in multitarget missions. *Acta Astronaut.* **2020**, *166*, 469–481. [CrossRef]
16. Zhu, Y.H.; Luo, Y.Z. Fast Evaluation of Low-Thrust Transfers via Multilayer Perceptions. *J. Guid. Control Dyn.* **2019**, *42*, 2627–2637. [CrossRef]
17. Zhu, Y.H.; Luo, Y.Z. Fast Approximation of Optimal Perturbed Long-Duration Impulsive Transfers via Artificial Neural Networks. *IEEE Trans. Aerosp. Electron. Syst.* **2021**, *57*, 123–1138. [CrossRef]
18. More, J.J.; Garbow, B.S.; Hillstrom, K.E. *User Guide for MinPack-1*; Report No. ANL-80-74; Argonne National Lab.: Lemont, IL, USA, 1980.
19. Izzo, D.; Martens, M. The Kessler Run: On the Design of the GTOC9 Challenge. *Acta Futura* **2018**, *11*, 11–24.
20. Petropoulos, A.; Grebow, D.; Jones, D. GTOC9: Methods and Results from the Jet Propulsion Laboratory Team. *Acta Futura* **2018**, *11*, 25–35.
21. Huang, A.Y.; Luo, Y.Z.; Li, H.N. Global Optimization of Multiple-Spacecraft Debris Removal Mission via Problem Decomposition and Dynamics-Guide Evolution Approach. *J. Guid. Control Dyn.* **2022**, *45*, 171–178. [CrossRef]

Article

North/South Station Keeping of the GEO Satellites in Asymmetric Configuration by Electric Propulsion with Manipulator

Lijun Ye [1,2,3,*], Chunyang Liu [2,3], Wenshan Zhu [2,3], Haining Yin [2,3], Fucheng Liu [4] and Hexi Baoyin [1]

1 School of Aerospace Engineering, Tsinghua University, Beijing 100084, China; baoyin@tsinghua.edu.cn
2 Shanghai Key Laboratory of Aerospace Intelligent Control Technology, Shanghai 201109, China; 18800235087@163.com (C.L.); 13916627214@139.com (W.Z.); yinhaining812@gmail.com (H.Y.)
3 Shanghai Aerospace Control Technology Institute, Shanghai 201109, China
4 Shanghai Academy of Spaceflight Technology, Shanghai 201109, China; liufch@126.com
* Correspondence: yelj18@mails.tsinghua.edu.cn; Tel.: +86-13611817796

Abstract: Geosynchronous orbit (GEO) is a very important strategic resource. In order to maximize the utilization of the GEO resources, the use of all-electric propulsion GEO platforms can greatly extend the service life of satellites. Therefore, this paper proposes a control scheme of the north/south station keeping (NSSK) by using electric propulsion with a manipulator. First, on the basis of the traditional calculation method of the semi-diurnal period of the orbital inclination, the calculation method of the semi-monthly period and the semi-annual period of the orbital inclination are proposed. The new method can reduce the fuel consumption and reduce the control amount and control frequency of the station keeping (SK). Secondly, a fuel-optimized NSSK algorithm by using electric propulsion with a manipulator is proposed. The algorithm can not only be applied to a large initial orbital inclination but also can unload the large angular momentum of the asymmetric satellites while keeping the north/south station, thereby avoiding the loss of control of the satellite's attitude. The research results of this paper provide a new idea for the SK control of the GEO satellites and have great engineering application value.

Keywords: GEO; asymmetric configuration satellites; NSSK; mean orbital inclination

MSC: 85-10

Citation: Ye, L.; Liu, C.; Zhu, W.; Yin, H.; Liu, F.; Baoyin, H. North/South Station Keeping of the GEO Satellites in Asymmetric Configuration by Electric Propulsion with Manipulator. *Mathematics* **2022**, *10*, 2340. https://doi.org/10.3390/math10132340

Academic Editor: António M. Lopes

Received: 13 June 2022
Accepted: 2 July 2022
Published: 4 July 2022

1. Introduction

Geosynchronous orbit (GEO) satellites [1,2] rotate in the same direction as the earth's rotation. Its orbital period is equal to the earth's rotation period, the orbital plane coincides with the earth's equatorial plane, and the orbital semi-major axis is also a constant (about 42,165.7 km). Therefore, the ideal GEO satellite is stationary relative to any point on the earth, and the continuous and uninterrupted communication can be achieved by using a fixed-point antenna at a fixed point on the ground. At the same time, due to the high orbital altitude of the GEO satellites and a wide range of ground coverage, a GEO satellite can perform long-term repeated observations on about one-third of the world's mid- and low-latitude regions. Due to these characteristics, GEO satellites can be widely used in communication, navigation and meteorological observation and other fields. Therefore, the GEO is actually a very important strategic resource.

However, under the action of various natural perturbations, satellites in GEO will gradually drift away from the original orbit, which will not only reduce the work efficiency of satellites but may also cause satellites in GEO to collide. Therefore, orbital control of the GEO satellite is required on a regular basis to keep the GEO satellite near the designed orbital position. Similarly, under the action of various natural perturbation torques, the angular momentum of the GEO satellite will gradually accumulate and may exceed the capacity of the on-board angular momentum storage device (here, the on-board angular momentum storage device generally refers to the flywheel or the control moment gyro). At the limit, it will cause the satellite's attitude to be out of control and unable to work, and it may even cause the satellite to be scrapped early and become space junk because it cannot obtain enough solar energy. Therefore, it is necessary to unload the angular momentum of the GEO satellite regularly, so that the angular momentum of the on-board angular momentum storage device is always within the limit range, and it can always have sufficient control capability of the attitude to maintain the stability of the satellite's attitude and ensure the safety of the energy of the GEO satellite.

In order to maximize the utilization of the GEO resources, large-scale high-carrying ratio and long-life satellite platforms are the future development trend [3]. Conventional station keeping (SK) of the GEO satellite uses chemical thrusters. Zhang [4] used dual tangential thrust control to realize the EWSK and NWSK. It adopts the iterative shooting method to obtain the optimal orbital control interval that meets the requirements of positional accuracy. Simulation shows that this method can achieve an SK accuracy of 0.005°. Li [5,6] combined engineering practice to introduce several kinds of strategies of the SK of the GEO satellite based on pulse thrust in detail, and they analyzed the advantages, disadvantages and uses of various SK strategies. Park [7], Li [8], Shi [9], etc. gave the co-location isolation strategy, the co-location strategy of multiple satellites and the design method of the corresponding nominal orbit based on the eccentricity vector and orbital inclination vector. Shi [10] discussed the relationship between the orbital control period and the EWSK fuel consumption and gave an EWSK control strategy based on the pulse method. Li et al. [11–13] introduced the EWSK method based on chemical thruster in detail, and they successfully applied it on the Fengyun-2 satellite. No [14] designed the mean longitude keeping strategy based on dead zone control and the mean eccentricity keeping strategy based on the orbital eccentricity control by predicting the change of the mean eccentricity vector, and they realized the EWSK of the satellite. Yang [15] adopted the LQG (Linear Quadratic Gaussian) method to achieve an accuracy of the EWSK of 0.05° and an accuracy of the NWSK of 0.02°. Yang [16] draws on the idea of a "Deep Space One" intelligent autonomous control system structure and tries to design a GEO satellite SK strategy with strong autonomy. Vinod [17] designed an EWSK strategy based on perigee pointing to the sun, which can effectively reduce the EWSK velocity increment. Chang [18] adopted the method of equally spaced pulses to divide the jet volume required for one EWSK into several smaller jets, which reduced the interference of a single jet on the satellite attitude and improved the control accuracy of the mean longitude. The control amount needs to be calculated and bet on the ground.

However, the specific impulse of chemical propellants is low, and a greater amount of propellant is consumed for the velocity increments, which makes it difficult to ensure the long life requirement of the GEO satellite. The specific impulse of electric propulsion (EP) is 5–10 times that of chemical propulsion, and the propellant consumed to generate the same velocity increment is only about 10% of that of chemical propulsion. Configuring an all-EP system can not only increase the life of the GEO satellite but also reduce the weight of the satellite, which can meet the requirement of the high load-carrying ratio and long life of the GEO satellite.

In recent years, scholars have conducted a series of studies on the SK of the GEO satellite. Weiss [19] introduced a Model Predictive Control (MPC)-based online real-time control algorithm for GEO satellite SK. Weiss developed a feedback control algorithm in the form of a linear quadratic constraint model over-policy control strategy, and through co-simulation with commercial software high-precision orbital dynamics, the satellite's angular momentum management was realized, and the accuracy of the east/west station keeping or north/south station keeping reached 0.01°, which verifies the feasibility of real-time closed-loop high-precision SK. However, he assumed that electric thrusters were installed on all six surfaces of the satellite, leaving no layout space for solar panels and payload antennas. He assumed that the electric thrusters were variable thrust, which was inconsistent with the general switch-controlled constant small thrust model. In addition, his controller uses a 15-dimensional dynamic equation, which requires high computing power. Frederik [20] used a convex optimization algorithm to study the problem of the high-precision SK of the GEO satellite based on pulse and small thrust. Gazzino [21,22] et al. decompose the SK problem into three steps to solve: the first step adopts the pulse method, and the optimal control sequence is obtained by the indirect method; the second step is to convert the pulse into a small thrust; the third step is to further optimize the moment of the low-thrust switch. Gazzino [23,24] considered the SK period and the orbital determination period as a whole, transformed the small thrust SK problem of the GEO satellite into a linear integer programming problem, and realized the sub-optimal fuel GEO SK. However, this strategy is computationally complex and can only be used on the ground. A.A. Sukhanov [25] et al. introduced a small-thrust SK optimization algorithm, based on which the SK of the GEO satellite was achieved. Roth [26] improved the optimization algorithm by taking the solar light pressure dynamics with earth shadow as one of the constraints of the global optimization of fuel for the nonlinear optimization problem of the small thrust SK of the GEO satellite.

The above-mentioned low-thrust position-keeping algorithm has a high dimension and a large amount of calculation; it needs to use a complex optimization algorithm [27]. Furthermore, some GEO satellites use asymmetric configurations (such as single-wing solar panels) due to the needs of payload work, which may cause the accumulation of the satellite's daily angular momentum to reach 100 Nms [28]. Therefore, the angular momentum unloading must be performed every day; otherwise, the satellite will be affected by the actuator (flywheel or control moment gyroscope) exceeding its control limit and losing attitude control ability [29]. This paper proposes a control method of the north/south station keeping (NSSK) by using the electric propulsion (EP) with the manipulator. By placing the electric thruster at the end of the manipulator, the active adjustment of the position and direction of the manipulator end can be used to realize the unloading of the satellite's angular momentum while keeping the north/south station.

The novel contributions of this paper are as follows:

(1) The method proposed in this paper has great advantages in control accuracy and fuel consumption.
(2) The method proposed in this paper can solve the problem that the angular momentum cannot be unloaded in the traditional NWSK method, and it prevents the satellite's attitude from running out of control.

The structure of this paper is as follows: In Section 2, the basic concepts of the vernal equinox orbital elements is introduced. The calculation method of the mean orbital inclination for semi-monthly and semi-annual periods is proposed to be suitable for satellites with different control precision or fuel requirements. The NSSK accuracy and the required velocity increments for SK corresponding to different periods of the mean orbital inclination are analyzed. Section 3 proposes a strategy of using the EP with a manipulator to unload the large-scale angular momentum while in NSSK, and it proposes a zone control method based on the angular momentum unloading requirements The correctness of the method proposed in this paper is verified through mathematical simulation in Section 4; the full text is summarized in Section 5.

2. Calculation of the Mean Orbital Inclination under Different NSSK Accuracy

2.1. The Vernal Equinox Orbital Elements

For an ideal GEO, when $i = 0°$, $e = 0$, the values of Ω and ω are uncertain; they are only singular values in the mathematical sense. In order to avoid singular values in orbital calculation, this paper adopts the following vernal equinox orbital elements [5] (pp. 61–64):

$$x = \begin{bmatrix} a & l & e_y & e_x & i_y & i_x \end{bmatrix}^T \tag{1}$$

where

a is the orbital semi-major axis, the unit is m.

l is the mean orbital longitude, the unit is rad;
e_y is the Y-component of the orbital eccentricity vector, dimensionless;
e_x is the X-component of the orbital eccentricity vector, dimensionless;
i_y is the Y-component of the orbital inclination vector, the unit is rad;
i_x is the X-component of the orbital inclination vector, the unit is rad.

The expressions in formula (1) are expanded into:

$$\begin{aligned} \Theta &= \Theta_0 + \omega_e t \\ e_y &= e\sin(\omega+\Omega) \\ e_x &= e\cos(\omega+\Omega) \\ i_y &= i\sin(\Omega) \\ i_x &= i\cos(\Omega) \end{aligned} \tag{2}$$

where

ω is the argument of perigee of the satellite in the J2000.0 coordinate system, in rad;
M is the mean anomaly of the satellite in the J2000.0 coordinate system, in rad;
Ω is the right ascending of ascension node of the satellite in the J2000.0 coordinate system, in rad;
i is the orbital inclination of the satellite in the J2000.0 coordinate system, in rad;
ω_e is the rotational angular velocity of the earth, the unit is rad/s;
Θ is the Greenwich sidereal hour angle at the current moment, the unit is rad;
Θ_0 is the Greenwich sidereal hour angle at the time of J2000.0, the value is 4.899787426069032 rad.

2.2. Calculation of the Mean Orbital Inclination

Generally speaking, the more period terms are eliminated by the mean orbital inclination vector of the GEO satellite, the lower the fuel required to keep the orbital inclination, and the lower the required accuracy of the orbital inclination keeping. Therefore, when calculating the mean orbital inclination vector, it is not enough to only deduct the semi-diurnal period term. Generally, it is necessary to select the corresponding algorithm of the mean orbital inclination vector according to the mission requirements.

The orbital inclination of the GEO satellite is mainly affected by the three-body gravitational force, and the three-body motion is approximated as follows [30]:

$$\begin{aligned} x_k &= \cos\lambda_k \cos\Omega_k - \sin\lambda_k \sin\Omega_k \cos i_k \\ y_k &= \cos\lambda_k \sin\Omega_k + \sin\lambda_k \cos\Omega_k \cos i_k \\ z_k &= \sin i_k \sin\lambda_k \end{aligned} \tag{3}$$

where

x_k, y_k, and z_k are the position of the third body (sun or moon) in the J2000 coordinate system, the units are m;
λ_k is the longitude of the third body (moon or sun) in the J2000 coordinate system, in rad;
Ω_k, is the right ascending of the ascension node of the third body (moon or sun) in the J2000 coordinate system, in rad;
i_k is the orbital inclination of the ascension node of the third body (moon or sun) in the J2000 coordinate system, in rad.

The effect of three-body gravity on the orbital inclination vector is [30]:

$$\begin{aligned} \left(\frac{di_y}{dt}\right)_k &= \frac{3}{2}\frac{n_k^2}{\omega_e}\left(y_k z_k + x_k z_k \sin 2\lambda_k - y_k z_k \cos 2\lambda_k + i_x {z_k}^2 - i_x {z_k}^2 \cos 2\lambda_k - i_y {z_k}^2 \sin 2\lambda_k\right) \\ \left(\frac{di_x}{dt}\right)_k &= \frac{3}{2}\frac{n_k^2}{\omega_e}\left(x_k z_k + y_k z_k \sin 2\lambda_k + x_k z_k \cos 2\lambda_k - i_y {z_k}^2 - i_y {z_k}^2 \cos 2\lambda_k + i_x {z_k}^2 \sin 2\lambda_k\right) \end{aligned} \tag{4}$$

where n_k is the orbital angular velocity of the third body (sun or moon), the unit is rad/s. Combining Equations (3) and (4), ignoring the short period (semi-diurnal) term, the influence of the three-body gravity on the semi-monthly period, semi-annual period and nutation period of the orbital inclination vector is obtained as follows:

$$\begin{aligned} \left(\frac{di_y}{dt}\right)_{\text{k-long+D}} &= \frac{3}{8}\frac{n_k{}^2}{\omega_e}\begin{pmatrix} \cos\Omega_k \sin 2i_k \\ +2\sin i_k \sin\Omega_k \sin 2\lambda_k \\ -\sin 2i_k \cos\Omega_k \cos 2\lambda_k \end{pmatrix} \\ \left(\frac{di_x}{dt}\right)_{\text{k-long+D}} &= \frac{3}{8}\frac{n_k{}^2}{\omega_e}\begin{pmatrix} -\sin\Omega_k \sin 2i_k \\ +2\sin i_k \cos\Omega_k \sin 2\lambda_k \\ +\sin 2i_k \sin\Omega_k \cos 2\lambda_k \end{pmatrix} \end{aligned} \tag{5}$$

where subscript "long" means long-term drift caused by the semi-monthly period term and semi-annual period term; subscript "D" means drift caused by the nutation period term.

2.2.1. Nutation Period Term Perturbation

In formula (5), the perturbation equation including the nutation period term is:

$$\begin{aligned} \left(\frac{di_y}{dt}\right)_{\text{k-D}} &= \frac{3}{8}\frac{n_k{}^2}{\omega_e}(\cos\Omega_k \sin 2i_k) \\ \left(\frac{di_x}{dt}\right)_{\text{k-D}} &= \frac{3}{8}\frac{n_k{}^2}{\omega_e}(-\sin\Omega_k \sin 2i_k) \end{aligned} \tag{6}$$

In Equation (6), considering the variation law of the ephemeris of the sun and the moon, superimposing the perturbation forces of the sun and the moon on the GEO orbital inclination, and deducting the semi-diurnal, semi-monthly and semi-annual period terms, the perturbation equation of the mean orbit inclination vector under the perturbation effect of the nutation period term can be obtained as follows [5] (p. 137):

$$\begin{aligned} \left(\frac{di_y}{dt}\right)_{\text{k-D}} &= (22.79 + 2.59\cos\Omega_{\text{sm}}) \times 10^{-4\circ}/\text{day} \\ \left(\frac{di_x}{dt}\right)_{\text{k-D}} &= -3.5\sin\Omega_{\text{sm}} \times 10^{-4\circ}/day \end{aligned} \tag{7}$$

where Ω_{sm} is the angle between the vernal equinox and the intersection of the lunar orbital plane and the ecliptic plane, in rad, and its expression is [11]

$$\Omega_{\text{sm}} = 125.04456^\circ - 1934.1362^\circ t + 0.0020767^\circ t^2 \tag{8}$$

where t is the Julian century number corresponding to the current moment.

It can be seen from Formula (8) that the ecliptic period of the ascending node of the lunar orbit is 18.6 years, which is a nutation period of the earth.

The drift angle of the mean orbital inclination vector is defined as the projection of the angle from the inertial system axis to the orbital mean inclination vector on the instantaneous equatorial plane of the earth. According to the definition, it can be seen from Equation (7) that the drift angle of the mean inclination vector under the nutation period term perturbation is:

$$\begin{aligned} \theta_{ni} &= \begin{cases} \arctan\left(\left(\frac{di_y}{dt}\right)_{\text{k-D}} \Big/ \left(\frac{di_x}{dt}\right)_{\text{k-D}}\right) & \left(\frac{di_x}{dt}\right)_{\text{k-D}} > 0 \\ \pi + \arctan\left(\left(\frac{di_y}{dt}\right)_{\text{k-D}} \Big/ \left(\frac{di_x}{dt}\right)_{\text{k-D}}\right) & \left(\frac{di_x}{dt}\right)_{\text{k-D}} < 0 \\ \frac{\pi}{2} & \left(\frac{di_x}{dt}\right)_{\text{k-D}} = 0 \end{cases} \\ &= \begin{cases} \arctan((22.79 + 2.59\cos\Omega_{\text{sm}})/(-3.5\sin\Omega_{\text{sm}})) & \sin\Omega_{\text{sm}} < 0 \\ \pi + \arctan((22.79 + 2.59\cos\Omega_{\text{sm}})/(-3.5\sin\Omega_{\text{sm}})) & \sin\Omega_{\text{sm}} > 0 \\ \pi/2 & \sin\Omega_{\text{sm}} = 0 \end{cases} \end{aligned} \tag{9}$$

It can be seen from Equation (9) that under the influence of the nutation period perturbation, the drift angle of the mean orbital inclination vector is around 90°. Equation (7) shows that the mean orbital inclination of GEO moves in an ellipse under the influence of the nutation period perturbation, and the major semi-axis of the ellipse can represent the oscillation amplitude of the mean orbital inclination under the influence of the nutation period perturbation, which is:

$$A_{\rm ni} = \frac{3.5 \times 10^{-4\circ}}{86400s} \cdot \frac{18.6 \times 365.25 \times 86400s}{2\pi} = 0.38^\circ \tag{10}$$

2.2.2. Semi-Annual and Semi-Monthly Period Term Perturbation

In Equation (5), retaining the semi-annual and semi-monthly period terms, the perturbation equation of the mean orbital inclination vector under the influence of the semi-annual and semi-monthly period terms of the sun-moon gravity can be obtained:

$$\begin{aligned} \left(\frac{{\rm d}i_y}{{\rm d}t}\right)_{\rm k-long} &= \frac{3}{8}\frac{n_{\rm k}{}^2}{\omega_{\rm e}}(2\sin i_{\rm k}\sin\Omega_{\rm k}\sin 2\lambda_{\rm k} - \sin 2i_{\rm k}\cos\Omega_{\rm k}\cos 2\lambda_{\rm k}) \\ \left(\frac{{\rm d}i_x}{{\rm d}t}\right)_{\rm k-long} &= \frac{3}{8}\frac{n_{\rm k}{}^2}{\omega_{\rm e}}(2\sin i_{\rm k}\cos\Omega_{\rm k}\sin 2\lambda_{\rm k} + \sin 2i_{\rm k}\sin\Omega_{\rm k}\cos 2\lambda_{\rm k}) \end{aligned} \tag{11}$$

The semi-annual oscillation of the mean orbital inclination vector of the GEO satellite caused by the gravity of the sun is:

$$\begin{aligned} {\rm amp}(i_y)_{\rm s-long} &= \int \left(\frac{{\rm d}i_y}{{\rm d}t}\right)_{\rm s-long} dt \\ {\rm amp}(i_x)_{\rm s-long} &= \int \left(\frac{{\rm d}i_x}{{\rm d}t}\right)_{\rm s-long} dt \end{aligned} \tag{12}$$

Substitute Equation (11) into (12), and let the solar orbital parameter $\Omega_{\rm s} = 0$, $i_{\rm s}$ be a constant; then, the semi-annual oscillation of the mean orbital inclination vector of the GEO satellite caused by the solar gravity can be calculated as:

$$\begin{aligned} {\rm amp}(i_y)_{\rm s-long} &= \frac{3}{8}\frac{n_{\rm s}}{\omega_{\rm e}}\left(-\frac{1}{2}\sin 2i_{\rm s}\sin 2\lambda_{\rm s}\right) \\ {\rm amp}(i_x)_{\rm s-long} &= \frac{3}{8}\frac{n_{\rm s}}{\omega_{\rm e}}(-\sin i_{\rm s}\cos 2\lambda_{\rm s}) \end{aligned} \tag{13}$$

By formula (13), it can be seen that the semi-annual period fluctuation of the orbital inclination of the GEO satellite under the influence of the sun's gravity is about:

$$A_{\rm syi} = \frac{3}{8}\frac{n_{\rm s}}{\omega_{\rm e}}\sin i_{\rm s} = 0.03^\circ \tag{14}$$

Similarly, the semi-monthly periodic oscillation of the orbital inclination vector of the GEO satellite under the influence of the moon's gravity is:

$$\begin{aligned} {\rm amp}(i_y)_{\rm m-long} &= \int \left(\frac{{\rm d}i_y}{{\rm d}t}\right)_{\rm m-long} dt \\ {\rm amp}(i_x)_{\rm m-long} &= \int \left(\frac{{\rm d}i_x}{{\rm d}t}\right)_{\rm m-long} dt \end{aligned} \tag{15}$$

Substitute Equation (11) into (15), and let the solar orbit parameter $i_{\rm m}$ be a constant; then, the semi-monthly oscillation of the mean orbital inclination vector of the GEO satellite caused by the moon's gravity can be calculated as:

$$\begin{aligned} {\rm amp}(i_y)_{\rm m-long} &= \frac{3}{8}\frac{n_{\rm m}{}^2}{n\omega_{\rm m}}\left(-\sin i_{\rm m}\sin\Omega_{\rm m}\cos 2\lambda_{\rm m} - \frac{1}{2}\sin 2i_{\rm m}\cos\Omega_{\rm m}\sin 2\lambda_{\rm m}\right) \\ {\rm amp}(i_x)_{\rm m-long} &= \frac{3}{8}\frac{n_{\rm m}{}^2}{n\omega_{\rm m}}\left(-\sin i_{\rm m}\cos\Omega_{\rm m}\cos 2\lambda_{\rm m} + \frac{1}{2}\sin 2i_{\rm m}\sin\Omega_{\rm m}\sin 2\lambda_{\rm m}\right) \end{aligned} \tag{16}$$

In Formula (16), $\Omega_{\mathrm{m}} \in (-13^\circ, 13^\circ)$, approximately, let $\cos\Omega_{\mathrm{m}} = 1$, $\sin\Omega_{\mathrm{m}} = 0$; then, the semi-monthly periodic oscillation amplitude of the mean orbital inclination of the GEO satellite under the influence of lunar gravity is about:

$$A_{\mathrm{mmi}} = \frac{3}{8}\frac{{n_{\mathrm{m}}}^2 \sin i_{\mathrm{m}}}{n\omega_{\mathrm{m}}} = 0.003^\circ \tag{17}$$

2.2.3. Semi-Diurnal Period Term Perturbation

The semi-diurnal periodic oscillation of the mean orbital inclination vector of the GEO satellite under the influence of the three-body gravitational perturbation is:

$$\begin{aligned} \mathrm{amp}(i_y)_{\mathrm{k-short}} &= \int \left(\frac{\mathrm{d}i_y}{\mathrm{d}t}\right)_{\mathrm{k-short}} dt \\ \mathrm{amp}(i_x)_{\mathrm{k-short}} &= \int \left(\frac{\mathrm{d}i_x}{\mathrm{d}t}\right)_{\mathrm{k-short}} dt \end{aligned} \tag{18}$$

Retaining only the semi-diurnal term in Equation (4), and substituting it into Equation (18), the short-period oscillation of the mean orbital inclination vector of the GEO satellite under the influence of three-body gravitational perturbation can be obtained as:

$$\begin{aligned} \mathrm{amp}(i_y)_{\mathrm{k-short}} &= \frac{3}{4}\frac{{n_{\mathrm{k}}}^2}{n}\frac{1}{\omega_{\mathrm{e}}-\omega_{\mathrm{k}}}\left(-x_{\mathrm{k}}z_{\mathrm{k}}\cos 2\lambda - y_{\mathrm{k}}z_{\mathrm{k}}\sin 2\lambda - i_x z_{\mathrm{k}}^2 \sin 2\lambda + i_y z_{\mathrm{k}}^2\cos 2\lambda\right) \\ \mathrm{amp}(i_x)_{\mathrm{k-short}} &= \frac{3}{4}\frac{{n_{\mathrm{k}}}^2}{n}\frac{1}{\omega_{\mathrm{e}}-\omega_{\mathrm{k}}}\left(-y_{\mathrm{k}}z_{\mathrm{k}}\cos 2\lambda + x_{\mathrm{k}}z_{\mathrm{k}}\sin 2\lambda - i_y z_{\mathrm{k}}^2 \sin 2\lambda - i_x z_{\mathrm{k}}^2\cos 2\lambda\right) \end{aligned} \tag{19}$$

According to Equation (19), the semi-diurnal oscillation amplitudes of the orbital inclination of the GEO satellite under the influence of the sun's gravitational and lunar gravitational perturbations are:

$$A_{\mathrm{sdi}} = \frac{3}{4}\frac{{n_{\mathrm{s}}}^2}{n}\frac{1}{\omega_{\mathrm{e}} - \omega_{\mathrm{s}}} = 3.6 \times 10^{-4\circ} \tag{20}$$

$$A_{\mathrm{mdi}} = \frac{3}{4}\frac{{n_{\mathrm{m}}}^2}{n}\frac{1}{\omega_{\mathrm{e}} - \omega_{\mathrm{m}}} = 7.5 \times 10^{-4\circ} \tag{21}$$

To sum up, the period term of the orbital inclination vector of the satellites is mainly affected by the three-body gravitational perturbation, which includes the semi-annual period term, semi-monthly period term, and semi-diurnal period term. Among them, the semi-annual period fluctuation of the orbital inclination of the GEO satellite under the influence of the sun's gravity is about 0.03°; the semi-monthly period oscillation amplitude of the mean orbital inclination of the GEO satellites under the influence of lunar gravity is about 0.003°; the semi-diurnal oscillation amplitudes of the orbital inclination of the GEO satellite under the influence of the sun's gravitational and lunar gravitational perturbations is about 0.0008°.

Therefore, we can draw the following conclusions:

(1) For a GEO satellite whose north/south keeping accuracy is required to be about 0.1°, it is recommended to use the calculation method of the mean orbital inclination after deducting the semi-diurnal period term, semi-monthly period term and semi-annual period term; that is, the item needed to be deducted is

$$\begin{aligned} \mathrm{amp}(i_y) &= \mathrm{amp}(i_y)_{\mathrm{k}} + \mathrm{amp}(i_y)_{\mathrm{m-long}} + \mathrm{amp}(i_y)_{\mathrm{s-long}} \\ \mathrm{amp}(i_x) &= \mathrm{amp}(i_x)_{\mathrm{k}} + \mathrm{amp}(i_x)_{\mathrm{m-long}} + \mathrm{amp}(i_x)_{\mathrm{s-long}} \end{aligned} \tag{22}$$

The remaining term is the mean orbital inclination vector under the influence of the nutation period term, as shown in Figure 1.

(2) For a GEO satellite whose north/south keeping accuracy is required to be about 0.01°, it is recommended to use the calculation method of the mean inclination after deducting the semi-monthly periodic term and semi-diurnal period term; that is, the item needed to be deducted is

$$\begin{aligned} \operatorname{amp}(i_y) &= \operatorname{amp}(i_y)_{\mathrm{k}} + \operatorname{amp}(i_y)_{\mathrm{m-long}} \\ \operatorname{amp}(i_x) &= \operatorname{amp}(i_x)_{\mathrm{k}} + \operatorname{amp}(i_x)_{\mathrm{m-long}} \end{aligned} \tag{23}$$

The remaining term is the mean orbital inclination vector under the influence of the semi-annual period term, as shown in Figure 2.

(3) For GEO satellites whose NSSK accuracy is required to be about 0.005°, it is recommended to use the calculation method of the mean orbital inclination after deducting the semi-diurnal period term; that is, the item needed to be deducted is

$$\begin{aligned} \operatorname{amp}(i_y) &= \operatorname{amp}(i_y)_{\mathrm{k}} \\ \operatorname{amp}(i_x) &= \operatorname{amp}(i_x)_{\mathrm{k}} \end{aligned} \tag{24}$$

The remaining term is the mean orbital inclination vector under the influence of the semi-monthly period term, as shown in Figure 3.

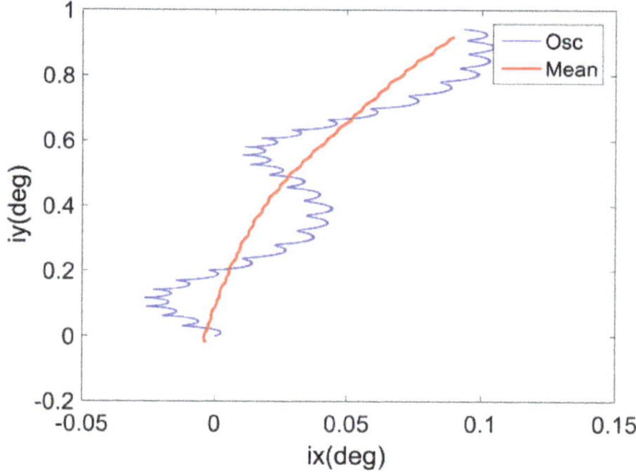

Figure 1. Mean orbital inclination vector under the influence of the nutation period term.

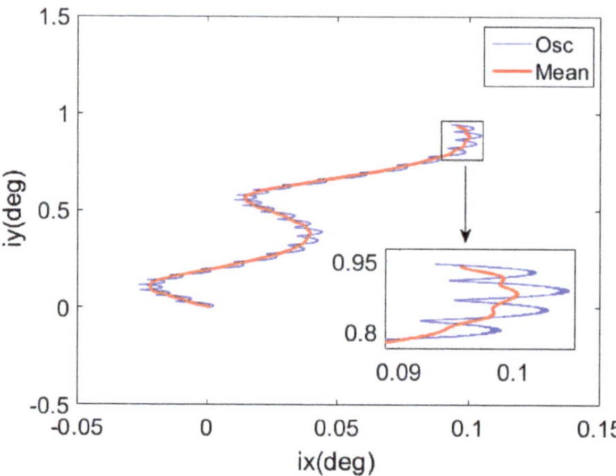

Figure 2. Mean orbital inclination vector under the influence of the semi-annual period term.

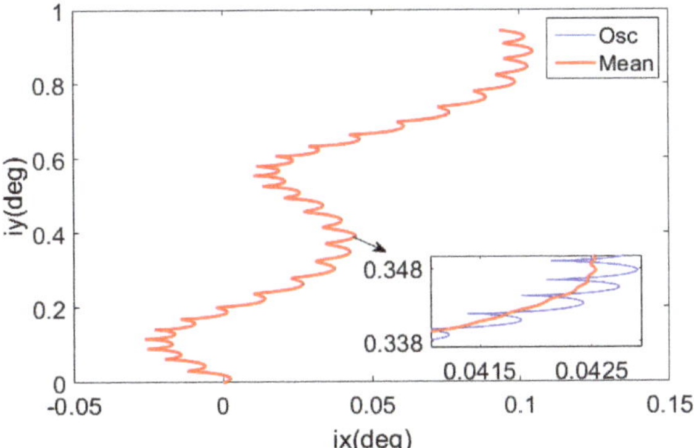

Figure 3. Mean orbital inclination vector under the influence of the semi-monthly period term.

3. North/South Station Keeping Control by Electric Propulsion with Manipulator

3.1. Basic Concepts

The SK of the GEO satellite is divided into north/south station keeping (NSSK) and east/west station keeping (EWSK). The NSSK is also called orbital inclination keeping, which is the out-of-plane control; the EWSK includes the mean longitude keeping and the eccentricity vector keeping, which is the orbital in-plane control. The required velocity increment of the satellite's orbital semi-major axis keeping is no more than 2 m/s per year; the required velocity increment of satellite's orbital eccentricity vector keeping is no more than 2 m/s per year; the required velocity increment of the satellite's orbital inclination vector keeping is no more than 51 m/s per year. Therefore, the NSSK accounts for more than 92% of the velocity increment required for the SK of the GEO satellite, and it occupies a large portion in the SK of the GEO satellite.

At this stage, chemical thrusters are used to keep the north/south station, which has low control accuracy and large fuel consumption. This paper proposes a scheme of a four-degree-of-freedom manipulator with the EP system. As shown in Figure 4, the EP points to the Y-direction of the satellite. The manipulator includes a shoulder joint, an elbow joint, a wrist joint and a double-degree-of-freedom wrist joint. Because there is no need to offset the influence of eccentricity, the electric thrust only needs to work once in an orbital period. By deflecting the thrust position and direction by the manipulator, the angular momentum can be unloaded while keeping the north/south station.

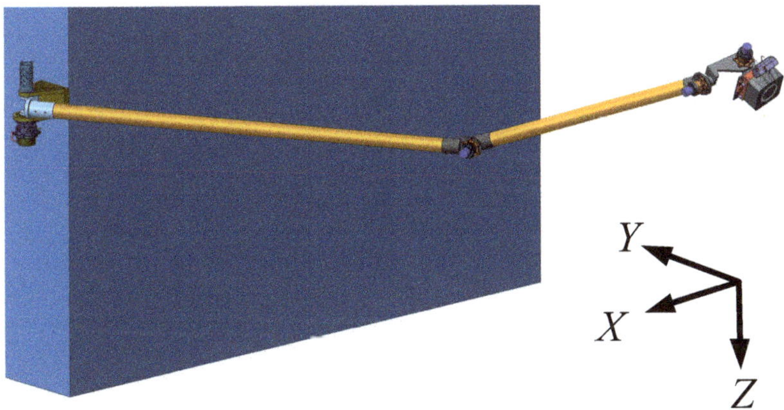

Figure 4. Four-degree-of-freedom manipulator with EP solution.

3.2. Range for North/South Station Keeping Zone

The process of the NSSK is essentially to offset the influence of the environmental perturbation force on the orbital inclination vector through the velocity increment generated by the EP. The NSSK can be regarded as keeping the orbital inclination of the satellite relative to the target orbital inclination near zero. In order to facilitate the description of the target orbit, the target orbit generally adopts constant orbital parameters. The mean orbital inclination after deducting the period term mentioned in Section 2.2 of the satellite is also used.

NSSK can be achieved by providing a negative normal velocity increment near the relative orbital ascending node, or it can provide a positive normal velocity increment near the relative orbital descending node. The magnitude of the control vector of the SK is equal to the magnitude of the mean orbital inclination vector under the influence of natural perturbation, and the direction of the control vector of the SK is opposed to the direction of the mean orbital inclination vector under the influence of natural perturbation. Because the natural drift direction of the mean orbital inclination vector is generally near the Y-axis of the inertial system, in the steady-state control, the relative orbital ascending node is generally near the inertial system Y-axis, and the relative orbital descending node is generally near the inertial system Y-axis. Figure 5 shows the drift range of the mean orbital inclination vector and the range of the SK zone.

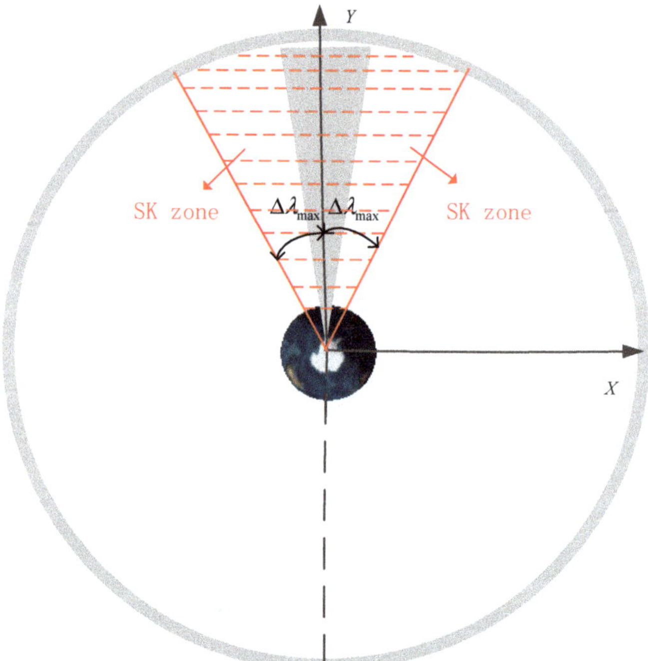

Figure 5. The range for NSSK zone of the GEO satellite.

In Figure 5, the gray zone is the envelope of the mean orbital inclination vector direction. The zone enclosed by the red dotted line is the "normal SK zone". Because the EP points to the Y-direction of the satellite, the electric thrust points to the south, producing a northward thrust. The range of the mean right ascension covered by each SK zone is $2\Delta\lambda_{max}$. During the SK, the larger $\Delta\lambda_{max}$ is, the larger interval of the optional SK point is, and the stronger the orbital control adjustment ability, but the consistency of the station between the initial position capture and steady SK may be poor. On the contrary, the smaller $\Delta\lambda_{max}$ is, the smaller interval of the optional SK point is, and the weaker the orbital control adjustment ability, but the consistency of the station between the initial station capture and steady SK may be better. Obviously, in order for the satellite to have sufficient SK ability, $\Delta\lambda_{\max}$ needs to be large enough, but in order to make the SK point more consistent, $\Delta\lambda_{\max}$ should be designed to be as small as possible.

According to Figure 5, the NSSK capability of the GEO satellite needs to cover the drift range of the mean orbit inclination vector under the influence of the natural perturbation, that is:

$$\Delta\lambda_{\max} > \max(\frac{\pi}{2} - \theta_{\text{imin}}, \theta_{\text{imax}} - \frac{\pi}{2}) \tag{25}$$

where, θ_{imax} is the maximum value of the drift angle of the mean orbital inclination vector, the unit is rad; θ_{imin} is the minimum value of the drift angle of the mean orbital inclination vector, the unit is rad.

According to the definition of the SK zone, there are:

$$\left|\frac{\Delta v_{ix}}{\Delta v_{iy}}\right| \leq \tan(\Delta\lambda_{\max}) \tag{26}$$

where Δv_{ix} is the velocity increment required to control the inclination vector in the X-direction of the inertial frame, in m/s; Δv_{iy} is the velocity increment required to control the inclination vector in the Y-direction of the inertial frame, in m /s; its calculation formula is:

$$\begin{aligned} \Delta v_{iy} &= -\delta\bar{i}_y^{C} n_0 a_0 \\ \Delta v_{ix} &= -\delta\bar{i}_x^{C} n_0 a_0 \end{aligned} \tag{27}$$

where
$(\delta\bar{i}_x^{C}, \delta\bar{i}_y^{C})$ is the mean orbital inclination used for control, and it is also the orbital inclination of the satellite's orbit relative to the target orbit, in rad;
a_0 is the initial orbital semi-major axis;
n_0 is the orbital angular velocity.

In order to achieve the lowest fuel consumption, the velocity increment generated by control needs to be opposite to the velocity increment generated by environmental perturbation. The minimum velocity increment must meet the following conditions:

$$\Delta v_{iy} < 0 \tag{28}$$

Then, when the electric thruster is used for SK, the calculation formula of the orbital argument λ_{tm} corresponding to the center point of the ignition arc segment is:

$$\begin{aligned} \lambda_{tm} &= \begin{cases} \arctan(\Delta v_{iy}/\Delta v_{ix}) & \Delta v_{ix} > 0 \\ \pi + \arctan(\Delta v_{iy}/\Delta v_{ix}) & \Delta v_{ix} < 0 \\ \pi/2 & \Delta v_{ix} = 0 \end{cases} \\ &= \begin{cases} \arctan(\delta\bar{i}_y/\delta\bar{i}_x) & \delta\bar{i}_x > 0 \\ \pi + \arctan(\delta\bar{i}_y/\delta\bar{i}_x) & \delta\bar{i}_x < 0 \\ \pi/2 & \delta\bar{i}_x = 0 \end{cases} \end{aligned} \tag{29}$$

3.3. Duration of the North/South Station Keeping

After entering the stable maintenance state, the control duration of each SK theoretically corresponds to the change rate of the mean orbital inclination, and it changes continuously. However, due to the initial orbital error, orbital control target switching (co-location configuration switching, fixed-point position switching) and other requirements, the control time of the orbit may be too long or too short. If the orbital control time is too long, the entire satellite consumes too much energy, making it difficult to achieve energy balance, and the orbital arc loss effect is obvious, reducing the efficiency of the orbital control. If the orbit control time is too short, not only the daily angular momentum cannot be fully unloaded, causing the attitude to be out of control, but also the ability to keep mean longitude may be insufficient, resulting in a decrease in the accuracy of the EWSK or an increase in the motion envelope of the manipulator. Therefore, before entering a stable maintenance state, it is hoped that the daily orbital control duration should be as uniform as possible; that is, the difference between the maximum duration $t_{\max}$ designed for the SK each time and the shortest duration $t_{\min}$ for the SK each time is minimized so as to ensure the energy consumption of the whole satellite is smooth and the angular momentum unloading capability varies smoothly.

Obviously, if we need to ensure that there is sufficient NSSK capability throughout the whole process, it needs to meet:

$$\begin{aligned} t_{\max} &> \bar{t}_{\max} \\ t_{\min} &< \bar{t}_{\min} \end{aligned} \tag{30}$$

where $t_{\max}$ is the longest orbital control time required to offset the daily drift of the mean orbital inclination vector; $t_{\min}$ is the shortest orbital control time required to offset the daily drift of the mean orbital inclination vector.

$t_{\max}$ and $t_{\min}$ can be calculated as follows:

The linear velocity of the GEO satellite is

$$V_0 = n_0 a_0 \tag{31}$$

The maximum value of the velocity increment required for daily NSSK is

$$\Delta V_{\max} = d_{i\max} V_0 \tag{32}$$

where

$d_{i\max}$ is the maximum daily drift of the mean orbital inclination vector, in rad;
V_0 is the initial velocity of the satellite.

When arc loss is not considered, the duration of the SK is

$$\Delta t_{\max} = \frac{m \Delta V_{\max}}{F} \tag{33}$$

where

m is the mass of the satellite;
F is the magnitude of the thrust acting on the satellite.

When considering the arc loss, the orbital control efficiency of the thruster is

$$\eta = \frac{\sin(\theta/2)}{\theta/2} \tag{34}$$

where θ is the orbital control arc (true anomaly) of the satellite under the action of the thrust. θ is calculated as

$$\theta = n_0 \Delta t_{\max} \tag{35}$$

In order to offset the effect of arc loss, it is necessary to extend the original orbital control arc to

$$\theta_{new} = \frac{\theta}{\eta} = \frac{\theta^2}{2\sin\frac{\theta}{2}} \tag{36}$$

Combined with Equations (35) and (36), we can obtain

$$\theta_{new} = \frac{(n_0 \Delta t_{\max})^2}{2\sin(\frac{1}{2} n_0 \Delta t_{\max})} \tag{37}$$

Therefore, the longest orbital control time $\bar{t}_{\max}$ required to offset the daily drift of the mean orbital inclination vector is:

$$\bar{t}_{\max} = \frac{\left(\frac{d_{i\max} n_0 a_0 m}{F}\right)^2 n_0}{2\sin\left(\frac{1}{2} n_0 \frac{d_{i\max} n_0 a_0 m}{F}\right)} \tag{38}$$

Similarly, the shortest orbital control time $\bar{t}_{\min}$ required to offset the daily drift of the mean orbital inclination vector

$$\bar{t}_{\min} = \frac{\left(\frac{d_{i\min} n_0 a_0 m}{F}\right)^2 n_0}{2\sin\left(\frac{1}{2} n_0 \frac{d_{i\min} n_0 a_0 m}{F}\right)} \tag{39}$$

where

$d_{i\max}$ is the maximum daily drift of the mean orbital inclination vector, in rad;
$d_{i\min}$ is the minimum daily drift of the mean orbital inclination vector, in rad;

However, it is also necessary to consider that during the SK, the thrust direction and the thrust position are slightly offset by the manipulator to achieve unloading of the three-axis angular momentum, so the daily SK time cannot be too short. Therefore, it must meet:

$$t_{\min} > t_{dump} \tag{40}$$

where t_{dump} is the daily minimum time required for angular momentum unloading.

Depending on the choice of the mean orbital inclination vector, Equations (30) and (40) may conflict. Among them, Equation (40) must be satisfied, while Equation (30) does not need to be satisfied. When Equation (30) is satisfied, it means that there is sufficient control capability of the mean orbital inclination vector in the whole SK process. It is worth noting that $d_{i\min}$ and $d_{i\max}$ are theoretical analysis values, the errors such as mean/osculating orbital inclination conversions error and orbital control error have not been considered. Therefore, margins need to be considered when designing the algorithm. When Equation (30) is not satisfied, it means that when the natural drift of the orbital inclination vector is small, and the change of the orbital inclination vector caused by the minimum orbital control amount is relatively large, the orbital inclination vector will continue to be controlled to the moving direction (mainly the inertial frame-Y direction) under the control action, and the mean orbital inclination vector cannot be normally kept near zero during this period. However, once the natural drift of the orbital inclination vector is greater than the change of the orbital inclination vector caused by the minimum orbital control amount, the orbital inclination vector will gradually approach zero under the control and return to the normal SK state.

3.4. The Control Amount of the North/South Station Keeping

The NSSK needs to meet the following five functional requirements and design constraints: (1) In order to facilitate the design of the entire satellite mission sequence and the on-board autonomous SK sequence, the initial station capture and the steady-state SK need to have a good consistency; (2) In order to have enough time to use EP for daily angular momentum management, the single SK time must be large enough; (3) In order to ensure optimal fuel during station capture and keeping, in the direction of the inclination vector, the control amount must only be used for to overcome the orbital perturbation; (4) It needs to have the ability to capture any orbital inclination angle vector within 0.1° of the initial deviation; (5) There is no constraint on the duration of capturing the target.

When the SK is in a steady state, the orbital control amount and the environmental perturbation amount cancel each other out, which can naturally meet the above functional requirements. When the initial orbital deviation is too large or the station capture is performed again, the overall design needs to be combined with the law of the environmental perturbation force and the above functional requirements.

3.4.1. Zone Control Method

For the convenience of illustration, the SK zone where the control position of the orbital is the same as the drift direction of the current mean orbital inclination vector is selected for illustration. The shaded part of the blue solid line in Figure 6 is the SK zone. The orbital inclination control is used to adjust the orbital surface. When pulse control is used, it can be understood as instantaneous control, that is, it is considered that the orbital inclination will be adjusted in the decreasing direction under the action of orbital control at the next moment. Therefore, the input of the orbital inclination control is the orbital inclination deviation during orbital control, and it is not necessary to pay attention to the orbital inclination change rate. Figure 6 shows the NSSK strategy.

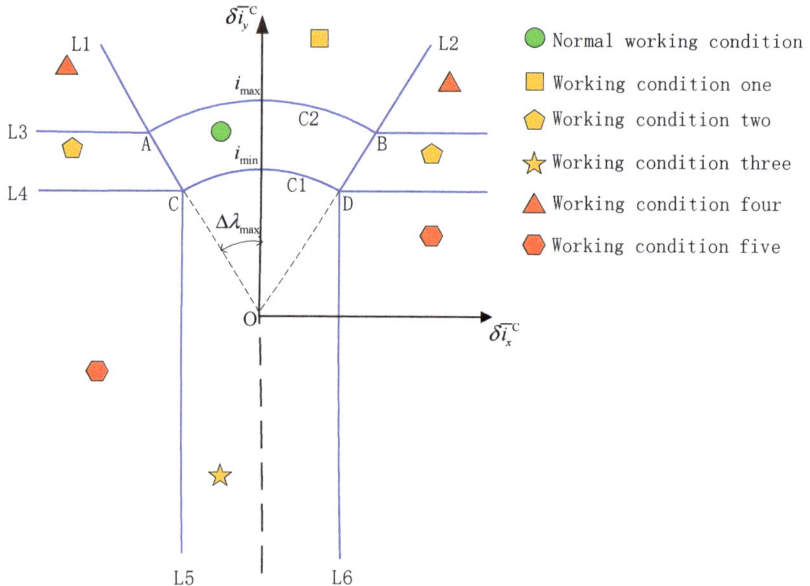

Figure 6. The NSSK strategy.

The coordinate system in Figure 6 is the inertial system, and the object described is the mean orbital inclination vector for control. i_{min} is the orbital inclination of the GEO satellite changed by the time of the EP working time i_{min}, and i_{max} is the orbital inclination of the GEO satellite changed by the EP working time i_{max}.The radius of the small circle C1 is i_{min}, and the radius of the large circle C2 is i_{max}. The straight line L1 is the boundary of the SK zone, which is greater than 90°. The straight line L2 is the boundary of the SK zone, which is less than 90°. Point A is the intersection of L1 and the circle C2, point B is the intersection of L2 and the circle C2, point C is the intersection of L1 and the circle C1, and point D is the intersection of L2 and the circle C1. L3 is a straight line passing through point A and parallel to X, L4 is a straight line passing through point C and parallel to X, L5 is a straight line passing through point C and parallel to Y, and L6 is a straight line passing through point D and parallel to Y.

L1~L6, C1 and C2 divide XOY into nine zones, corresponding to six different working conditions, namely:

(1) Normal working condition: closed zone enclosed by ABCD;
(2) Working condition one: It is a half-zone closed zone surrounded by L1, L2 and AB arcs, and the modulus of the mean orbital inclination vector corresponding to the target to the current orbit in this zone is greater than i_{max};

(3) Working condition two: It consists of two half-zone enclosed zones; one is enclosed by L1, L3 and L4, and the other is enclosed by L2, L3 and L4, and they are all outside the allowed SK zone;
(4) Working condition three: It is a half-zone closed zone surrounded by L5, L6 and CD arcs, and the component in the Y-direction of this zone is less than $i_{\min}$;
(5) Working condition four: It consists of two half-zone enclosed zones; one is enclosed by L1 and L3, the other is enclosed by L2 and L3, and both are outside the range of the allowable SK zone;
(6) Working condition five: It includes two half-zone closed zones; one is enclosed by L4 and L5, the other is enclosed by L4 and L6, and the absolute value of the components in X-direction of the two zones is greater than $i_{\min}\Delta\lambda_{\max}$.

The nine zones in Figure 6 can be divided into three categories: stable (the zone where the green geometry is located), semi-stable (the zone where the yellow geometry is located) and unstable (the zone where the red geometry is located).

(1) It contains a stable zone, namely the normal working condition. Under the normal working condition, the orbital inclination vector from the target orbit to the current orbit will continue to maintain the normal working condition, that is, the steady-state SK;
(2) It contains four semi-stable zones, including two zones of working condition two, as well as working condition one and working condition three. These zones, in the shape of pipelines, are connected to the intermediate normal working conditions, and their orbital inclination vectors in the X-axis or Y-axis are in a closed-loop stable state, so they will not leave the steady-state pipeline and will eventually enter the normal working conditions along the pipeline. The semi-stable zone is further divided into X-axis stability (condition two) and Y-axis stability (condition one and condition three). In the semi-stable zone where the X-axis is stable, the center position of the NSSK is unchanged, and the duration of the orbital control changes in real time with the orbital inclination. In the semi-stable zone where the Y-axis is stable, the duration of NSSK control is unchanged (the longest or the shortest duration), but the center of the SK will change in real time with the orbital inclination.
(3) It contains four unstable zones, including two zones in working condition four and two zones in working condition five. These zones are in the form of sectors. In these zones, the orbital inclination vector will move under the combined action of orbital control and natural perturbation. It will enter the semi-stable zone adjacent to it, and then reaches the stable zone through the semi-stable zone.

Since the control force acting on the orbital inclination vector covers the drifting of the orbital inclination vector caused by orbital perturbation, the switching between zones is theoretically irreversible. Even if the reversible zone switching occurs due to environmental perturbation changes, since the control law calculated at the junction of two adjacent zones is the same, there will be no "jitter" of the control law caused by frequent switching between two zones. In the unstable zone (working condition four and working condition five), the point and the amount of the SK are both constant, and the control strategy remains unchanged.

In the semi-stable zone (working condition one, working condition two and working condition three) and stable zone (normal working condition), the orbital control amount and orbital control position will fluctuate slightly with the motion of the mean orbital inclination vector under the influence of perturbation. It can also be seen from Figure 6 that under all orbital control strategies, the orbital control amount in the Y-axis direction of the inertial system is negative, that is to say, all the y-direction velocity increments are used to overcome the natural drift of the mean orbital inclination vector under the influence of perturbation. Therefore, the strategy of NSSK proposed in this paper is also the SK strategy with the least fuel consumption.

In Figure 6, the SK point of working condition four is located at point A (B), which means that the time of the single orbital control is the longest. The Y-axis component of the orbital inclination vector in this zone is large, so it is not only necessary to perform orbital adjustment in the X-axis direction but also to ensure that the Y-axis direction continues to decrease. In working condition one, at point A (B), the control ability in the Y-axis direction is the weakest. In order to make the Y-axis still overcome the natural drift of the orbital inclination and converge to zero, it is necessary to satisfy:

$$i_{\max} \cos \Delta\lambda_{\max} > d_{i\max} \tag{41}$$

Therefore, the maximum duration $t_{\max}$ of the single SK should satisfy:

$$t_{\max} = \frac{\left(\frac{i_{\max} n_0 a_0 m}{F}\right)^2 n_0}{2\sin\left(\frac{1}{2} n_0 \frac{i_{\max} n_0 a_0 m}{F}\right)} > \frac{\left(\frac{d_{i\max} n_0 a_0 m}{\cos \Delta\lambda_{\max} F}\right)^2 n_0}{2\sin\left(\frac{1}{2} n_0 \frac{d_{i\max} n_0 a_0 m}{\cos \Delta\lambda_{\max} F}\right)} \tag{42}$$

In Figure 6, for working condition three, it is necessary to use the environmental perturbation force to realize the movement of the X-axis of the component of the orbital inclination vector to zero. Therefore, the maximum point in the X-axis direction (the midpoint of the CD arc) should be less than the minimum daily drift of the orbital inclination vector; then, we have

$$t_{\min} = \frac{\left(\frac{i_{\min} n_0 a_0 m}{F}\right)^2 n_0}{2\sin\left(\frac{1}{2} n_0 \frac{i_{\min} n_0 a_0 m}{F}\right)} < \frac{\left(\frac{d_{\min} n_0 a_0 m}{F}\right)^2 n_0}{2\sin\left(\frac{1}{2} n_0 \frac{d_{\min} n_0 a_0 m}{F}\right)} \tag{43}$$

Combined with Equations (42) and (43), in the subsequent design and simulation of this paper, we may make:

$$\begin{aligned} t_{\max} &= 1.1 \frac{\left(\frac{d_{i\max} n_0 a_0 m}{\cos \Delta\lambda_{\max} F}\right)^2 n_0}{2\sin\left(\frac{1}{2} n_0 \frac{d_{i\max} n_0 a_0 m}{\cos \Delta\lambda_{\max} F}\right)} \\ t_{\min} &= 0.9 \frac{\left(\frac{d_{\min} n_0 a_0 m}{F}\right)^2 n_0}{2\sin\left(\frac{1}{2} n_0 \frac{d_{\min} n_0 a_0 m}{F}\right)} \end{aligned} \tag{44}$$

The detailed control amount of the SK for each working condition is described as follows.

(1) Normal working condition

The normal working condition is the stable zone (complete coverage of the natural drift range of the orbital inclination vector). The mean orbital inclination vector is moderate in the inertial system, and the control amount of the NSSK and the drifting amount of the mean orbital inclination vector are equal in magnitude and opposite in direction. The position of the orbital control is within the allowable orbital control range. The NSSK in normal working condition is shown in Figure 7.

In Figure 7 the direction of the straight arrow represents the change direction of the orbital inclination vector under the action of orbital control. The starting point of the straight arrow represents the control amount, and the starting point of the straight arrow is located in the center of the normal working condition, indicating that the orbital control duration is between the shortest and longest duration. The straight arrow is yellow, indicating that the amount of orbital control is moderate. Under normal working conditions, under the combined effect of the perturbation and control force, the orbital inclination vector from the target to the current will continue to remain within the normal working conditions.

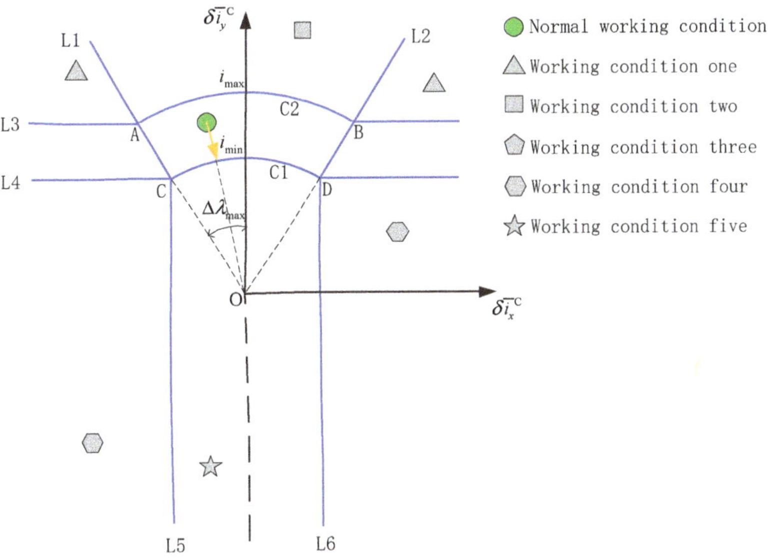

Figure 7. The NSSK in normal working condition.

To meet the normal working conditions, the following conditions must be met at the same time:

$$\begin{aligned} &\sqrt{\delta\bar{i}_x^2+\delta\bar{i}_y^2} \leq i_{\max} \\ &\sqrt{\delta\bar{i}_x^2+\delta\bar{i}_y^2} \geq i_{\min} \\ &\delta\bar{i}_y > i_{\min} \\ &\left|\frac{\delta\bar{i}_x}{\delta\bar{i}_y}\right| < \tan\Delta\lambda_{\max} \end{aligned} \tag{45}$$

Considering the arc loss, under normal working condition, the mean orbital right ascension λ_{tm} and the north/south ignition duration t_{NS} corresponding to the midpoint of the EP arc are:

$$\begin{aligned} \lambda_{tm} &= \begin{cases} \arctan(\delta\bar{i}_y/\delta\bar{i}_x) & \delta\bar{i}_x < 0 \\ \pi+\arctan(\delta\bar{i}_y/\delta\bar{i}_x) & \delta\bar{i}_x > 0 \\ \pi/2 & \delta\bar{i}_x = 0 \end{cases} \\ t_{NS} &= \frac{\left(\frac{\sqrt{\delta\bar{i}_x^2+\delta\bar{i}_y^2}\,n_0 a_0 m}{F}\right)^2 n_0}{2\sin\left(\frac{\sqrt{\delta\bar{i}_x^2+\delta\bar{i}_y^2}\,n_0 a_0 m}{2F}n_0\right)} \end{aligned} \tag{46}$$

(2) Working condition one

Working condition one is a semi-stable zone, and the orbital inclination vector is in a positive bias state. The mean orbital inclination vector has a larger absolute value in the Y-axis direction of the inertial system and a smaller absolute value in the X-axis direction of the inertial system. Therefore, it is necessary to use the maximum orbital control capability to overcome the drift of the orbital inclination vector under the perturbation, and finally make the orbital inclination vector approach the target orbital inclination. In this condition, the ignition duration of the control is longest, and the ignition position fluctuates a small amount with the current orbital inclination vector within the range of the SK zone. The NSSK in working condition one is shown in Figure 8.

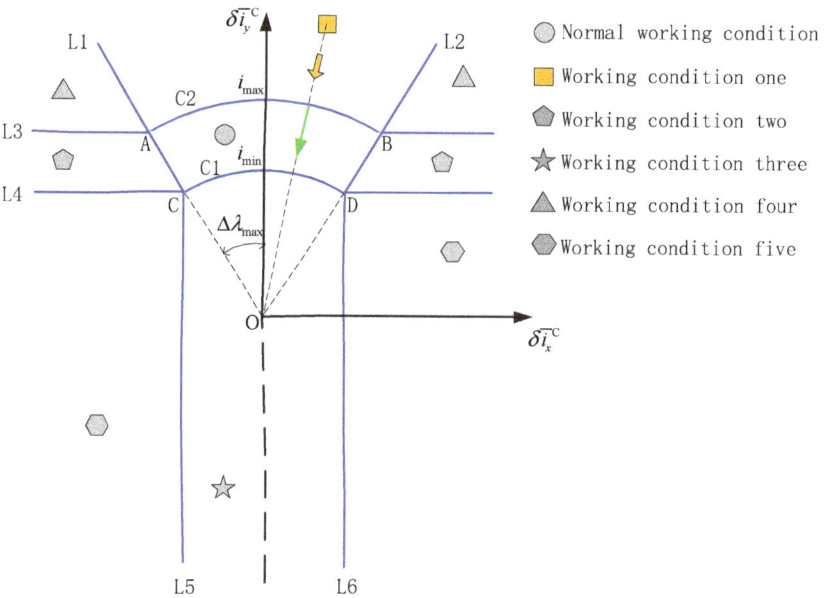

Figure 8. The NSSK in working condition one.

In Figure 8, the starting point of the straight line arrow is located on the AB arc on the C2 circle, indicating that the orbital control time is the longest and remains unchanged, which is most conducive to the management of angular momentum. The direction of the straight line arrow points to the center of the circle, indicating that the SK point is in the SK zone and needs to be adjusted in real time according to the actual orbital inclination vector. The 45° arrow describes the approximate direction of the motion of the orbital inclination vector under the combined action of the perturbation force and the control force. Because the control force on the orbital inclination vector in two directions is greater than the perturbation force on it, the working condition one will only enter the normal working condition in one direction.

To meet the working conditions one, the following conditions must be met at the same time:

$$\begin{array}{l} \sqrt{\left(\delta\bar{i}_x^C\right)^2 + \left(\delta\bar{i}_y^C\right)^2} \geq i_{\min} \\ \delta\bar{i}_y^C > i_{\max}\cos\Delta\lambda_{\max} \\ \left|\frac{\delta\bar{i}_x^C}{\delta\bar{i}_y^C}\right| < \tan\Delta\lambda_{\max} \end{array} \tag{47}$$

Considering the arc loss, under working condition one, the mean orbital right ascension λ_{tm} and the north/south ignition duration t_{NS} corresponding to the midpoint of the EP arc are:

$$\begin{array}{l} \lambda_{tm} = \begin{cases} \arctan(\delta\bar{i}_y^C/\delta\bar{i}_x^C) & \delta\bar{i}_x^C > 0 \\ \pi + \arctan(\delta\bar{i}_y^C/\delta\bar{i}_x^C) & \delta\bar{i}_x^C < 0 \\ \pi/2 & \delta\bar{i}_x^C = 0 \end{cases} \\ t_{NS} = \frac{\left(\frac{i_{\max}n_0 a_0 m}{F}\right)^2 n_0}{2\sin\left(\frac{i_{\max}n_0 a_0 m}{2F}n_0\right)} \end{array} \tag{48}$$

(3) Working condition two

Working condition two is in the semi-stable zone, and the absolute value of the mean orbital inclination vector is small in the Y-axis direction of the inertial system, which can keep stable control. The mean orbital inclination vector has a large absolute value in the X-axis direction, and it is necessary to provide the control capability in the X-axis direction as much as possible while ensuring the Y-axis control. The orbital inclination vector approaches the normal working condition along the X-axis under control. During the above process, the orbital control position of the orbital inclination does not change, and the orbital control duration is between the longest and the shortest. The orbital control position fluctuates slightly with the drift rate of the Y-axis orbital inclination. The NSSK in working condition two is shown in Figure 9.

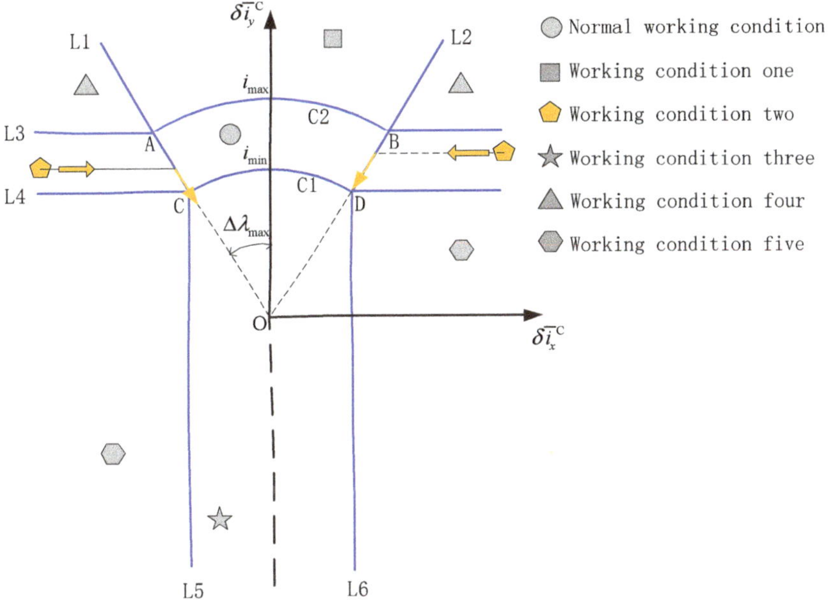

Figure 9. The NSSK in working condition two.

In Figure 9, the starting point of the straight line arrow is located on the straight line AC or BD between the C2 circle and the C1 circle, indicating that the SK duration is between the shortest and longest duration. The straight-line arrows point in the AC direction, indicating that the SK control points remain unchanged in the inertial space. The 45° arrow points to the normal zone, indicating that working condition two will enter the normal working condition in one direction.

To meet the working conditions two, the following conditions must be met at the same time:

$$\begin{gathered} i_{\max}\cos\Delta\lambda_{\max} > \delta\bar{i}_y > i_{\min}\cos\Delta\lambda_{\max} \\ \left|\frac{\delta\bar{i}_x}{\delta\bar{i}_y}\right| > \tan\Delta\lambda_{\max} \end{gathered} \tag{49}$$

Considering the arc loss, under working condition two, the mean orbital right ascension λ_{tm} and the north/south ignition duration t_{NS} corresponding to the midpoint of the EP arc are:

$$\lambda_{tm} = \begin{cases} \arctan(i_{\max}\cos\Delta\lambda_{\max}/\text{sgn}(\delta\bar{i}_x)i_{\max}\sin\Delta\lambda_{\max}) & \text{sgn}(\delta\bar{i}_x)i_{\max}\sin\Delta\lambda_{\max} > 0 \\ \pi+\arctan(i_{\max}\cos\Delta\lambda_{\max}/\text{sgn}(\delta\bar{i}_x)i_{\max}\sin\Delta\lambda_{\max}) & \text{sgn}(\delta\bar{i}_x)i_{\max}\sin\Delta\lambda_{\max} < 0 \\ \pi/2 & \text{sgn}(\delta\bar{i}_x)i_{\max}\sin\Delta\lambda_{\max} = 0 \end{cases}$$

$$t_{NS} = \frac{\left(\frac{\delta\bar{i}_y n_0 a_0 m}{\cos\Delta\lambda_{\max}F}\right)^2 n_0}{2\sin\left(\frac{\delta\bar{i}_y n_0 a_0 m}{2\cos\Delta\lambda_{\max}F}n_0\right)} \tag{50}$$

(4) Working condition three

Working condition three is a semi-stable zone, and the orbital inclination vector is in a negative bias state. It is necessary to take advantage of the natural perturbation force to make the current orbital inclination vector approach the target orbital inclination. Under this working condition, it is necessary to provide as little orbital control capability as possible, so that the orbital inclination vector can drift to the normal working condition as soon as possible under the action of natural perturbation. At the same time, the orbital control adjustment capability is used to make the X-axis component of the orbit inclination vector drift toward zero as much as possible. Under this condition, the orbital control duration is the shortest, and the ignition position fluctuates a little within the SK zone along with the current orbital inclination vector. The NSSK in working condition three is shown in Figure 10.

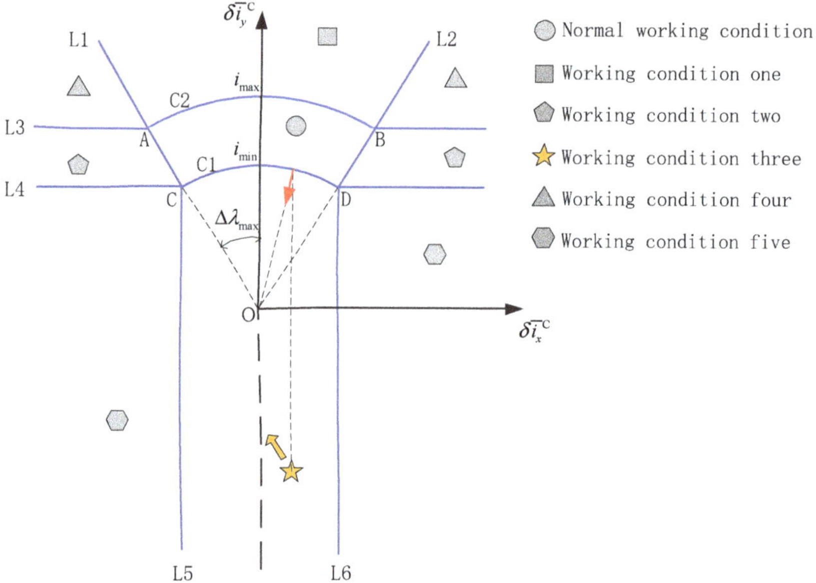

Figure 10. The NSSK in working condition three.

In Figure 10, the starting point of the straight arrow is located between the CD arc segments on the C1 circle, indicating that the duration of the SK is shortest. The control point of the SK is dynamically adjusted with the fluctuation of the current mean orbital inclination vector. The 45° arrow points to the normal zone, indicating that working condition three will enter the normal working condition in one direction. Working condition three cannot be easily described with simple mathematical expressions. However, since all six working conditions, including normal working conditions, cover all zones of a two-dimensional plane, the exclusion method can be used to complete the conditions of working condition three.

Considering the arc loss, under working condition three, the mean orbital right ascension λ_{tm} and the north/south ignition duration t_{NS} corresponding to the midpoint of the EP arc are:

$$\lambda_{tm} = \begin{cases} \arctan(\sqrt{i_{\min}{}^2 - \delta\bar{i}_x^2}/\mathrm{sgn}(\delta\bar{i}_x)\delta\bar{i}_x) & \mathrm{sgn}(\delta\bar{i}_x)\delta\bar{i}_x > 0 \\ \pi+\arctan(\sqrt{i_{\min}{}^2 - \delta\bar{i}_x^2}/\mathrm{sgn}(\delta\bar{i}_x)\delta\bar{i}_x) & \mathrm{sgn}(\delta\bar{i}_x)\delta\bar{i}_x < 0 \\ \pi/2 & \mathrm{sgn}(\delta\bar{i}_x)\delta\bar{i}_x = 0 \end{cases} \tag{51}$$

$$t_{NS} = \frac{\left(\frac{i_{\min} n_0 a_0 m}{F}\right)^2 n_0}{2\sin\left(\frac{i_{\min} n_0 a_0 m}{2F} n_0\right)}$$

(5) Working condition four

Working condition four is an unstable zone, and the absolute value of the mean orbital inclination vector in the X-axis and Y-axis directions of the inertial system is large, and it is positive in the Y-direction. In this case, it is necessary to have the orbital control capability on both the X and Y axes, the position of orbital control is at the boundary of the allowable orbital control range, and the orbital control time is the longest. The NSSK in working condition four is shown in Figure 11.

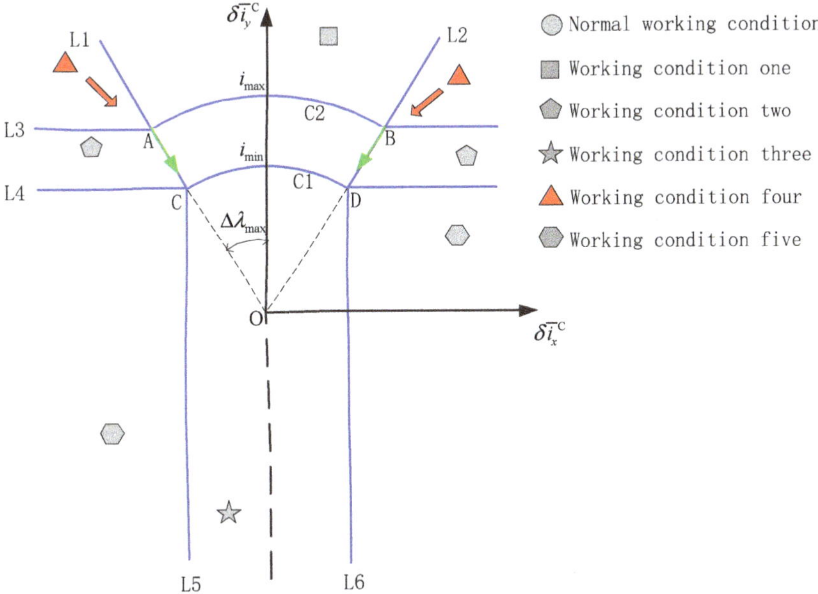

Figure 11. The NSSK in working condition four.

In Figure 11, the starting point of the straight line arrow is located at A or B on the C2 circle, indicating that the duration of the orbital control is longest. The straight arrow points in the direction of AC or BD, indicating that the orbital position is constant in the inertial frame. The 45° arrow describes the approximate movement direction of the orbital inclination vector under the combined action of the perturbation force and the control force of the SK. Since the orbital control duration remains constant, if the rate of change of the mean orbital inclination vector caused by the environmental perturbation force is also regarded as a constant value, then under the action of the orbital control force and the natural perturbation force, the mean orbital inclination vector will move in a fixed direction. Because the control force of the inclination vector in both directions is greater than the natural perturbation force, the working condition four will theoretically enter into two adjacent semi-stable zones along one direction (working condition one or working condition two, which is related to the initial stage).

To meet the working condition four, the following conditions must be met at the same time:

$$\begin{aligned} &\sqrt{\left(\delta \bar{i}_x^C\right)^2 + \left(\delta \bar{i}_y^C\right)^2} \geq i_{\min} \\ &\delta \bar{i}_y^C > i_{\max} \cos \Delta\lambda_{\max} \\ &\left|\frac{\delta \bar{i}_x^C}{\delta \bar{i}_y^C}\right| > \tan \Delta\lambda_{\max} \end{aligned} \quad (52)$$

Considering the arc loss, under working condition two, the mean orbital right ascension λ_{tm} and the north/south ignition duration t_{NS} corresponding to the midpoint of the EP arc are:

$$\lambda_{tm} = \begin{cases} \arctan(i_{\max} \cos \Delta\lambda_{\max} / \mathrm{sgn}(\delta \bar{i}_x) i_{\max} \sin \Delta\lambda_{\max}) & \mathrm{sgn}(\delta \bar{i}_x) i_{\max} \sin \Delta\lambda_{\max} > 0 \\ \pi + \arctan(i_{\max} \cos \Delta\lambda_{\max} / \mathrm{sgn}(\delta \bar{i}_x) i_{\max} \sin \Delta\lambda_{\max}) & \mathrm{sgn}(\delta \bar{i}_x) i_{\max} \sin \Delta\lambda_{\max} < 0 \\ \pi/2 & \mathrm{sgn}(\delta \bar{i}_x) i_{\max} \sin \Delta\lambda_{\max} = 0 \end{cases}$$
$$t_{NS} = \frac{\left(\frac{i_{\max} n_0 a_0 m}{F}\right)^2 n_0}{2 \sin\left(\frac{i_{\max} n_0 a_0 m}{2F} n_0\right)} \quad (53)$$

(5) Working condition five

Working condition five is an unstable zone, and the absolute value of the mean orbital inclination vector in the X-axis and Y-axis directions of the inertial system is large, and it is negative in the Y-direction. In this case, it is necessary to have orbital control capability on both the X and Y axes at the same time. The position of the orbital control is at the boundary of the allowable orbital control range, and the orbital control time is the shortest. The NSSK in working condition five is shown in Figure 11.

In Figure 12, the starting point of the head of the straight arrow is located at C or D on the C1 circle, which means that the orbital control time is the shortest. Straight arrows point in the AC or BD direction, indicating that the position of the orbit is constant in the inertial frame. The 45° arrow describes the approximate movement direction of the orbital inclination vector under the combined action of the perturbation force and the control force of the SK.

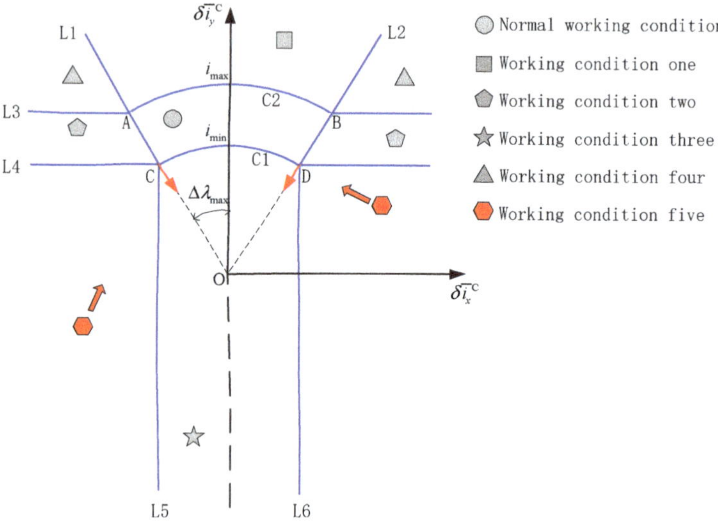

Figure 12. The NSSK in working condition five.

Since the duration of the orbital control remains constant, if the rate of change of the mean orbital inclination vector caused by the environmental perturbation force is also regarded as a constant value, then under the action of the orbit control force and the natural perturbation force, the mean orbital inclination vector will move in a fixed direction. Because the control force of the inclination vector in the two directions is greater than the natural perturbation force, working condition five will theoretically enter into two adjacent semi-stable zones along one direction (working condition two or working condition three, which is related to the initial stage).

To meet working condition five, the following conditions must be met at the same time:

$$\begin{aligned} \delta\bar{i}_y^C &< i_{\min}\cos\Delta\lambda_{\max} \\ \left|\delta\bar{i}_x^C\right| &> i_{\min}\sin\Delta\lambda_{\max} \end{aligned} \tag{54}$$

Considering the arc loss, under working condition two, the mean orbital right ascension λ_{tm} and the north/south ignition duration t_{NS} corresponding to the midpoint of the EP arc are:

$$\lambda_{tm} = \begin{cases} \arctan(i_{\min}\cos\Delta\lambda_{\max}/\mathrm{sgn}(\delta\bar{i}_x)i_{\min}\sin\Delta\lambda_{\max}) & \mathrm{sgn}(\delta\bar{i}_x)i_{\min}\sin\Delta\lambda_{\max} > 0 \\ \pi+\arctan(i_{\min}\cos\Delta\lambda_{\max}/\mathrm{sgn}(\delta\bar{i}_x)i_{\min}\sin\Delta\lambda_{\max}) & \mathrm{sgn}(\delta\bar{i}_x)i_{\min}\sin\Delta\lambda_{\max} < 0 \\ \pi/2 & \mathrm{sgn}(\delta\bar{i}_x)i_{\min}\sin\Delta\lambda_{\max} = 0 \end{cases}$$
$$t_{NS} = \frac{\left(\frac{i_{\min} n_0 a_0 m}{F}\right)^2 n_0}{2\sin\left(\frac{i_{\min} n_0 a_0 m}{2F} n_0\right)} \tag{55}$$

The five working conditions are summarized in Table 1.

Table 1. Summary of five working conditions.

Working Condition	λ_{tm}	t_{NS}
Normal	$\lambda_{tm} = \begin{cases} \arctan(\delta\bar{i}_y/\delta\bar{i}_x) & \delta\bar{i}_x < 0 \\ \pi+\arctan(\delta\bar{i}_y/\delta\bar{i}_x) & \delta\bar{i}_x > 0 \\ \pi/2 & \delta\bar{i}_x = 0 \end{cases}$	$\frac{\left(\frac{\sqrt{\delta\bar{i}_x^2+\delta\bar{i}_y^2} n_0 a_0 m}{F}\right)^2 n_0}{2\sin\left(\frac{\sqrt{\delta\bar{i}_x^2+\delta\bar{i}_y^2} n_0 a_0 m}{2F} n_0\right)}$
One	$\lambda_{tm} = \begin{cases} \arctan(\delta\bar{i}_y^C/\delta\bar{i}_x^C) & \delta\bar{i}_x^C > 0 \\ \pi+\arctan(\delta\bar{i}_y^C/\delta\bar{i}_x^C) & \delta\bar{i}_x^C < 0 \\ \pi/2 & \delta\bar{i}_x^C = 0 \end{cases}$	$\frac{\left(\frac{i_{\max} n_0 a_0 m}{F}\right)^2 n_0}{2\sin\left(\frac{i_{\max} n_0 a_0 m}{2F} n_0\right)}$
Two	$\lambda_{tm} = \begin{cases} \arctan(\sqrt{i_{\min}^2-\delta\bar{i}_x^2}/\mathrm{sgn}(\delta\bar{i}_x)\delta\bar{i}_x) & \mathrm{sgn}(\delta\bar{i}_x)\delta\bar{i}_x > 0 \\ \pi+\arctan(\sqrt{i_{\min}^2-\delta\bar{i}_x^2}/\mathrm{sgn}(\delta\bar{i}_x)\delta\bar{i}_x) & \mathrm{sgn}(\delta\bar{i}_x)\delta\bar{i}_x < 0 \\ \pi/2 & \mathrm{sgn}(\delta\bar{i}_x)\delta\bar{i}_x = 0 \end{cases}$	$\frac{\left(\frac{i_{\min} n_0 a_0 m}{F}\right)^2 n_0}{2\sin\left(\frac{i_{\min} n_0 a_0 m}{2F} n_0\right)}$
Three	$\lambda_{tm} = \begin{cases} \arctan(i_{\max}\cos\Delta\lambda_{\max}/\mathrm{sgn}(\delta\bar{i}_x)i_{\max}\sin\Delta\lambda_{\max}) & \mathrm{sgn}(\delta\bar{i}_x)i_{\max}\sin\Delta\lambda_{\max} > 0 \\ \pi+\arctan(i_{\max}\cos\Delta\lambda_{\max}/\mathrm{sgn}(\delta\bar{i}_x)i_{\max}\sin\Delta\lambda_{\max}) & \mathrm{sgn}(\delta\bar{i}_x)i_{\max}\sin\Delta\lambda_{\max} < 0 \\ \pi/2 & \mathrm{sgn}(\delta\bar{i}_x)i_{\max}\sin\Delta\lambda_{\max} = 0 \end{cases}$	$\frac{\left(\frac{i_{\max} n_0 a_0 m}{F}\right)^2 n_0}{2\sin\left(\frac{i_{\max} n_0 a_0 m}{2F} n_0\right)}$
Four	$\lambda_{tm} = \begin{cases} \arctan(i_{\min}\cos\Delta\lambda_{\max}/\mathrm{sgn}(\delta\bar{i}_x)i_{\min}\sin\Delta\lambda_{\max}) & \mathrm{sgn}(\delta\bar{i}_x)i_{\min}\sin\Delta\lambda_{\max} > 0 \\ \pi+\arctan(i_{\min}\cos\Delta\lambda_{\max}/\mathrm{sgn}(\delta\bar{i}_x)i_{\min}\sin\Delta\lambda_{\max}) & \mathrm{sgn}(\delta\bar{i}_x)i_{\min}\sin\Delta\lambda_{\max} < 0 \\ \pi/2 & \mathrm{sgn}(\delta\bar{i}_x)i_{\min}\sin\Delta\lambda_{\max} = 0 \end{cases}$	$\frac{\left(\frac{i_{\min} n_0 a_0 m}{F}\right)^2 n_0}{2\sin\left(\frac{i_{\min} n_0 a_0 m}{2F} n_0\right)}$

3.4.2. Analysis of Fuel Consumption

In the stable stage of the NSSK, the control position of the north/south station is kept at the ascending node or the descending node, which is the most ideal point of the SK. At this time, the velocity increment generated by EP is due south or due north, and the direction of the velocity increment is also optimal. Therefore, it can be considered that the velocity increment generated by EP is equal to the velocity increment generated by environmental perturbation (three-body gravitational force), and the direction is opposite, which is the optimal NSSK scheme for fuel.

In the initial state, for any initial orbital inclination vector within the allowable range, the direction of the velocity increments generated by EP is opposite to the velocity increments generated by the environmental perturbation force; that is, the velocity increments generated by EP are only used to overcome the environmental perturbation force. The change of the orbital inclination vector caused by the environmental perturbation force is mainly along the Y-axis direction, so the initial orbital inclination vector deviation in the X-direction needs to be offset by the velocity increment generated by the EP. When the initial orbital inclination vector in the Y-direction is greater than zero, it is necessary to use additional electric thrust control force to eliminate the deviation on the basis of the normal NSSK. At this time, the fuel consumption is slightly more than the fuel consumption required by the SK in a steady state. When the initial orbital inclination vector in the Y-direction is less than zero, the current orbital inclination vector can be made closer to the target orbital inclination vector by using the environmental perturbation force. At this time, the fuel consumption for the SK is slightly less than that required for the SK in a steady state.

3.5. Orbital Inclination Vector for Control

The NSSK of the satellite can be regarded as the SK of the orbital inclination of the deputy satellite relative to the chief satellite. The error between the current orbital inclination and the target orbital inclination for control should be clarified. The determination of the orbital inclination of the target orbit for control includes two aspects: first, there is the determination of the orbital inclination vector of the chief satellites. When multi-satellite formation or multi-satellite co-location is kept, the orbital inclination vector of the chief satellite is set by the ground and can be changed as required. For the SK of satellites generally located in GEO, the orbital inclination vector of the chief satellite can be regarded as (0, 0). Second, on the basis of the first point, to improve the accuracy of the keeping control of the orbital inclination, it is necessary to make the orbital inclination vector properly negatively biased on the basis of predicting the change law of the orbital inclination. The orbital inclination vector is ultimately kept within the minimum envelope radius centered on the orbital inclination vector of the chief satellite.

The orbital inclination vector for control is shown in Figure 13.

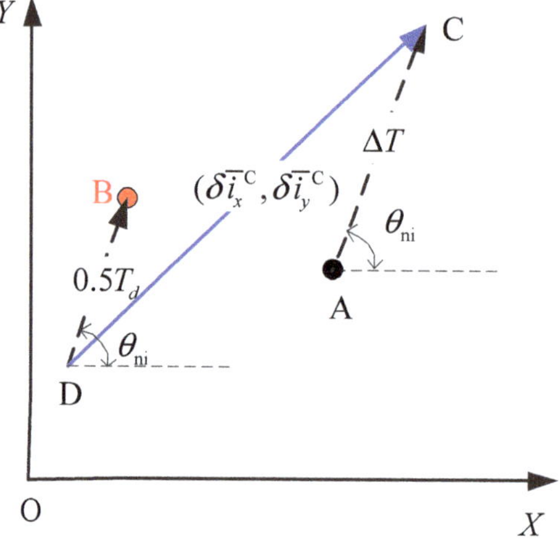

Figure 13. The orbital inclination vector for control.

In Figure 13, point A represents the coordinates of the current mean orbital inclination vector. Point C represents the coordinates of the mean orbital inclination vector under the action of the natural perturbation force at the central moment of SK. Point B represents the coordinates of the target mean orbital inclination vector. Point D represents the target of the SK. AC and DB represent the drifting direction of the mean orbital inclination vector caused by the natural perturbation force. After the orbit is controlled to point D, the mean orbital inclination vector will pass through point B under the action of natural perturbation force, and the natural drift trajectory of the orbital inclination vector will be evenly distributed at both ends of point B. Therefore, taking D point as the target of the SK can improve the keeping accuracy of the mean orbital inclination vector as much as possible. DC is the orbital inclination vector for control.

The formula for calculating the mean orbital inclination vector for control is:

$$\begin{aligned} \delta\bar{i}_y^C &= \bar{i}_y + \tfrac{\Delta T}{T} d_i \sin\theta_{ni} - \left(\bar{i}_{y0} - \tfrac{1}{2} d_i \sin\theta_{ni}\right) \\ \delta\bar{i}_x^C &= \bar{i}_x + \tfrac{\Delta T}{T} d_i \cos\theta_{ni} - \left(\bar{i}_{x0} - \tfrac{1}{2} d_i \cos\theta_{ni}\right) \end{aligned} \tag{56}$$

where

$(\bar{i}_x, \bar{i}_y)$ is the current mean orbital inclination vector of the satellite, in rad;
$(\bar{i}_{x0}, \bar{i}_{y0})$ is the target mean orbital inclination vector of the satellite, in rad;
d_i is the daily drift of the orbital inclination vector, in rad;
T is the orbital period, which is 86,400.091s.
ΔT is the time of the current position to the center of the target position.

The calculation formula of ΔT is:

$$\Delta T = \frac{\mathrm{mod}\left(\frac{\pi}{2} + \theta_{ni} - \lambda, 2\pi\right)}{\omega_e} \tag{57}$$

4. Simulation and Analysis

Let $t_{dump} = 3207$ s be the minimum time required per day for angular momentum unloading. The correctness of the SK control law under each working condition is verified based on mathematical simulation. The design principles of the example include:

(1) The control law covers all working conditions;
(2) The result of the SK of the mean orbital inclination vector under the influence of different period term perturbations is verified;
(3) The feasibility of parameter adaptation is verified.

Table 2 shows the examples used in the simulation.

Table 2. The examples used in the simulation.

Example	Perturbation Term	Working Condition
Example one	Nutation	Five → two →normal
Example two	Nutation	Five →three →normal
Example three	Nutation	Four →one →normal
Example four	Semi-annual	Four →one →normal
Example five	Semi-monthly	Four →one →normal

The results of the five working conditions are shown in Table 3.

4.1. Example One

The simulation conditions are shown in Table 2, the simulation time is 360 days, and the results are shown in Figure 14.

Table 3. Summary of Simulation.

Example	One	Two	Three	Four	Five
Perturbation term	Nutation	Nutation	Nutation	Semi-annual	Semi-monthly
Ascending node right ascension (°)	359.989	269.989	59.989	59.989	59.989
Initial orbital inclination vector (y-direction) (°)	0.000	−0.080	0.069	0.069	0.069
Initial orbital inclination vector (x-direction) (°)	0.080	0.000	0.040	0.040	0.040
$t_{\max}$ (°)	5703	5703	5703	7688	24,970
$t_{\min}$ (°)	3426	3426	3426	3207	3207
$\Delta\lambda_{\max}$ (°)	11.70	11.70	11.68	22.01	55.00
Velocity increment in one year (m/s)	44.04	41.48	46.89	47.82	54.93
Keeping accuracy of inclination (°)	0.03	0.03	0.03	0.005	0.008

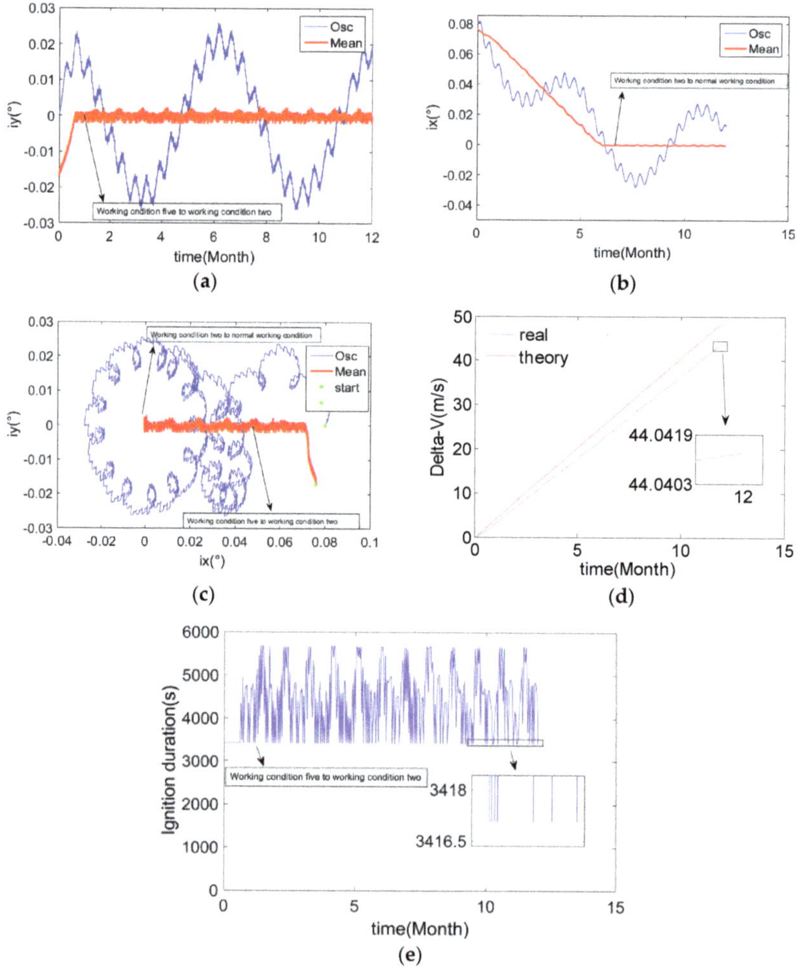

Figure 14. The results of example one. (**a**) Y-axis component of orbital inclination vector; (**b**) X-axis component of orbital inclination vector; (**c**) Orbital inclination vector; (**d**) Velocity increment for SK; (**e**) Duration of SK.

It can be seen from Figure 14a,b that under the control action, the orbital inclination vector converges and remains near zero. The keeping accuracy of the mean inclination vector is better than 0.005°.

It can be seen from Figure 14c that the initial value of the mean inclination is located in working condition five (unstable zone). Under the action of the control law of working condition five, it enters working condition two (semi-stable zone) with a certain slope, and it finally enters and stays in normal working condition (stable zone) through working condition two.

It can be seen from Figure 14d that the actual annual velocity increment used for the NSSK is about 43 m/s, which is less than the theoretical velocity increment. There are two main reasons: first, the total velocity increment calculated by the theoretical formula is slightly larger; second, the initial orbital inclination vector in the Y- direction is less than zero. According to Section 3.4.2, when the initial orbital inclination vector in the Y-direction is less than 0, the fuel consumption for the SK is slightly less than that required for the SK in a steady state.

It can be seen from Figure 14e that the duration of the orbital control of the condition five is the shortest, which is consistent with the strategy of condition five, and the shortest control duration is about 3417 s, which is consistent with the calculated value of 3426 s in formula (36). In working condition two and normal working condition, the duration of the orbital control varies between the longest and shortest according to different orbital parameters. It is worth noting that when this strategy is used to calculate the duration of the orbital control, error factors such as the semi-major axis and the eccentricity of the orbit are ignored. Therefore, the duration of the orbital control calculated by the actual control strategy will have a small error with the theoretical longest and shortest durations.

It can also be seen from Figure 14e that although the duration of the orbital control is frequently abrupt within the allowed longest and shortest durations, the result of the NSSK is good. Due to the existence of the orbital control error, the mean/osculating orbital inclination conversions error and the target position prediction error, the single orbital control amount will be too large or too small; thus, it breaks the allowable range. However, the above error can be regarded as a high-frequency error compared with the orbital control frequency, and the daily drift of the orbital inclination vector under the influence of the perturbation of the nutation period term is close to a constant value. Therefore, the limiting effect of the orbital control duration is equivalent to filtering the high-frequency error part of the constant physical quantity, thereby realizing the high-precision SK of the mean orbital inclination.

It can be seen from Figure 14a that the mean orbital inclination vector fluctuates slightly in the Y-direction about 12 times a year. The peak of the fluctuation corresponds to the longest orbital control duration in Figure 14e, indicating that there is still some residual error when calculating the perturbation of the semi-monthly period term, which causes the mean orbital inclination vector to drift and periodically exceeds the orbital control capability. Nevertheless, the control error is still small, and it can be seen from Figure 14c that the error hardly affects the accuracy of the final NSSK.

The algorithm of NSSK in this paper has the advantages of optimal fuel, fixed SK points, and wide application range. The disadvantage is that small initial errors will cause long orbital adjustment times. It can be seen from Figure 14a–c that the error of the initial orbital inclination vector is 0.08°, and it takes about six months to complete the final inclination capture and keeping.

4.2. Example Two

The initial conditions of the simulation are shown in Table 2. In order to simulate from working condition five to working condition three, the ascending node right ascension in example two is rotated 90 degrees clockwise, and the other conditions are the same as those in example one. The results are shown in Figure 15.

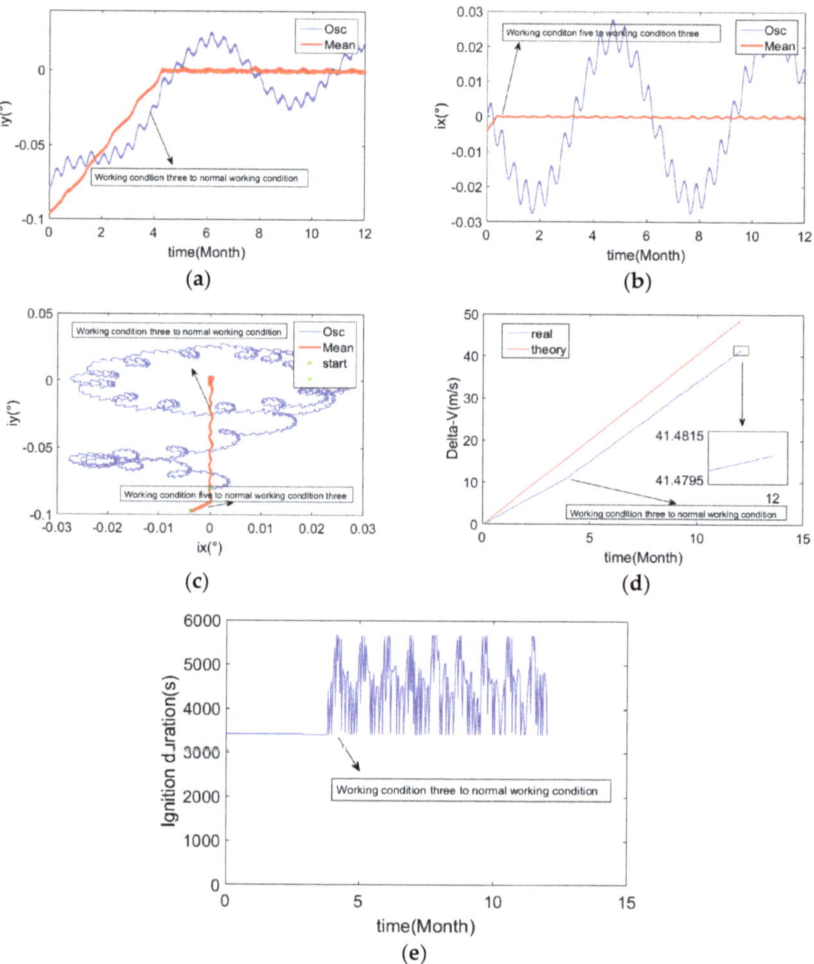

Figure 15. The results of example two. (**a**) Y-axis component of orbital inclination vector; (**b**) X-axis component of orbital inclination vector; (**c**) Orbital inclination vector; (**d**) Velocity increment for SK; (**e**) Duration of SK.

It can be seen from Figure 15a–c that under the control action, the orbital inclination vector converges and remains near zero. It can be seen from Figure 15c that the initial value of the mean orbital inclination is located in working condition five (unstable zone). Under the action of the control law of working condition five, it enters working condition three (semi-stable zone) with a certain slope, and it enters and stays in normal working condition (stable zone) through working condition three.

In Figure 15d, the actual velocity increment is significantly lower than the theoretical velocity increment, which is mainly because the Y-component of the initial inclination vector has a large negative offset in this example. The greater the negative offset of the initial orbital inclination, the more fuel is saved in NSSK. Therefore, using the NSSK algorithm proposed in this paper can reduce a lot of velocity increment requirements.

4.3. Example Three

The initial conditions of the simulation are shown in Table 2. In order to simulate from working condition four to working condition one, the right ascending of the ascension node in example two is rotated 60 degrees clockwise, and the other conditions are the same as those in example one. The results are shown in Figure 16.

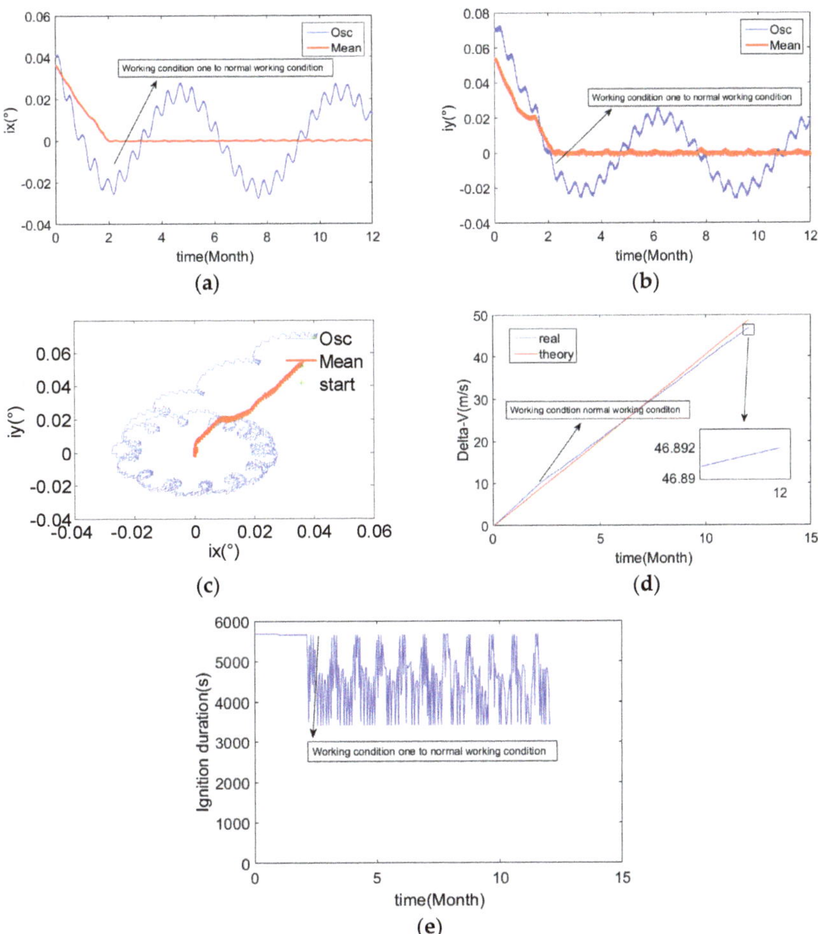

Figure 16. The results of example three. (**a**) Y-axis component of orbital inclination vector; (**b**) X-axis component of orbital inclination vector; (**c**) Orbital inclination vector; (**d**) Velocity increment for SK; (**e**) Duration of SK.

It can be seen from Figure 16a–c that under the control action, the orbital inclination vector converges and remains near zero. It can be seen from Figure 16a,c that since the control laws in working condition four and working condition one are relatively close, the ignition time is the longest, so it is not easy to clearly distinguish the switching point from working condition four to working condition one.

It can be seen from Figure 16d that in working condition four and working condition one, the daily duration of orbital control is the longest. Therefore, the increase in the actual velocity increment is faster than the theoretical velocity increment, and this part of the extra velocity increment is caused by the positive bias of the mean orbital inclination vector in the y-direction at the initial moment.

4.4. Example Four

The initial conditions of the simulation are shown in Table 2. The minimum orbital control duration calculated by Equation (30) is 2157 s, which contradicts the orbital control duration of 3207 s required by Equation (32), so the shortest orbital control duration is finally taken as 3207 s. Other conditions are the same as in example three. The results are shown in Figure 17.

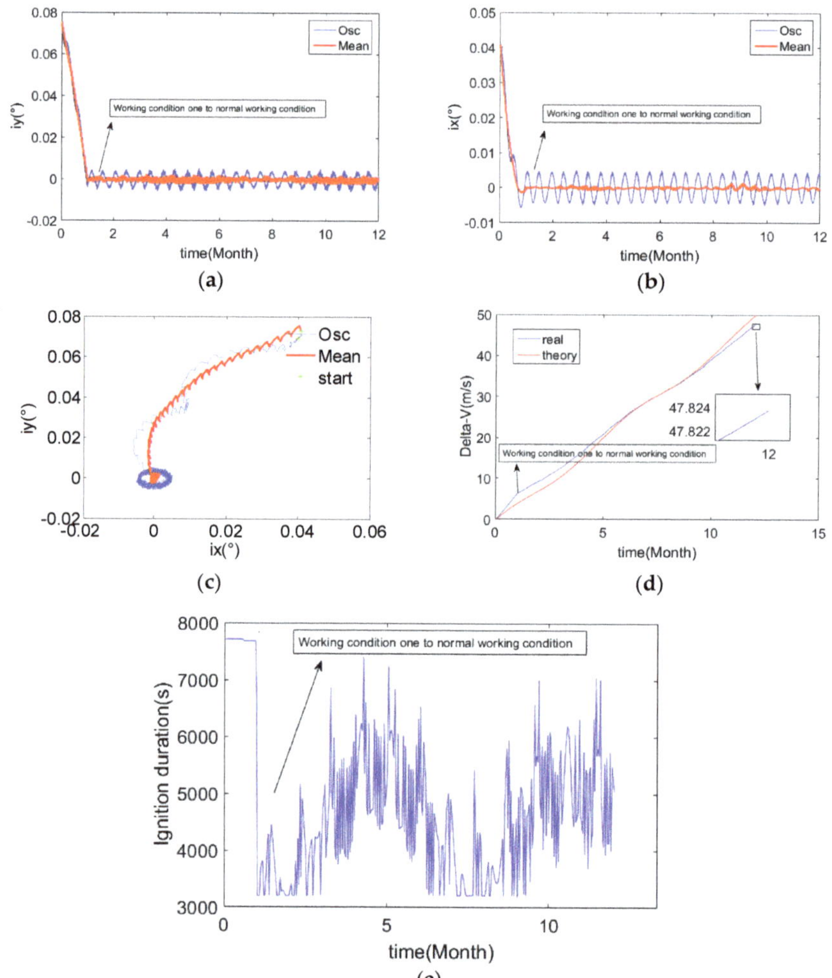

Figure 17. The results of the example four. (**a**) Y-axis component of orbital inclination vector; (**b**) X-axis component of orbital inclination vector; (**c**) Orbital inclination vector; (**d**) Velocity increment for SK; (**e**) Duration of SK.

It can be seen from Figure 17a,b that under the control action, the orbital inclination vector converges and remains near zero. It can be seen from Figure 17c that the precision of the mean orbital inclination vector is about 0.002°, and the osculating accuracy of the orbital inclination vector is about 0.005°.

It can also be seen from Figure 17b that the mean orbital inclination vector fluctuates significantly twice a year in the X-direction. This is because the mean orbital inclination vector under the influence of the semi-annual period term perturbation presents the form of semi-annual periodic fluctuation, and the orbital control capability lags behind the controlled target, resulting in the error of the system of the orbital control.

After entering the normal working condition, the fluctuation range of the duration of the SK in Figure 17e is larger than that in Figure 16e. Although the initial orbital parameters are the same as those of example three, the longest orbital control time allowed in example three is longer after using the calculation method of the mean orbital inclination vector under the influence of the semi-annual term perturbation. Therefore, in this example, the duration from working condition four to the normal working condition is shorter than that of example three. Although the fluctuation range of the SK duration in Figure 17e is larger than that of Figure 16e, the design should consider global convergence; that is, the longest time of the orbital control allowed by the design should also be larger. Therefore, the duration of the SK does not always reach the maximum allowed duration. During the stable state of the NSSK, although the minimum duration of the orbital control often touches the lower boundary of the allowed duration of the orbital control, this does not affect the stable keeping of the orbital inclination, which is consistent with the analysis in Section 3.4.

4.5. Example Five

The initial conditions of the simulation are shown in Table 2. The minimum duration of the orbital control calculated by Equation (30) is 1112 s, which contradicts the orbital control duration of 3207 s required by Equation (32), so the shortest orbital control duration is finally taken as 3207 s. According to the above analysis, in this example, it is theoretically impossible to realize the controllability of any global point. Therefore, in order to achieve the NSSK simulation, it is necessary to sacrifice the controllability of some areas and focus on the overall controllability. In this simulation, let $\Delta\lambda_{\max} = 55°$, and the other conditions are the same as those in example three. The results are shown in Figure 18.

It can be seen from Figure 18a,b that under the control action, the orbital inclination vector converges and remains near zero. It can be seen from Figure 18c that the precision of the mean orbital inclination vector is about 0.008°. It can also be seen from Figure 18b that the mean orbital inclination vector fluctuates significantly twenty-six times a year in the X-direction. This is because the mean orbital inclination vector under the influence of the semi-annual period term perturbation presents the form of semi-annual periodic fluctuation, and the orbital control capability lags behind the controlled target (flat orbital inclination), resulting in the error of the system of the orbital control.

After entering the normal working condition, the fluctuation range of the duration of the SK in Figure 18e is larger than that in Figure 17e. Although the initial orbital parameters are the same as those of example four and example three, the longest orbital control time allowed in example five is the longest after using the calculation method of the mean orbital inclination vector under the influence of the semi-monthly term perturbation. Therefore, in this example, the duration from working condition four to the normal working condition is shorter than that of example three and example three. It can also be seen from Figure 18e that the maximum SK time per day is about 14,400s, while the longest allowed orbital control duration is 24,970s, which does not trigger the limiting effect of the longest allowed orbital control duration. This is because in order to ensure that the calculation method of the mean orbital inclination vector can still achieve the convergence of the global orbital inclination under the influence of the semi-monthly period term perturbation, the boundary relationship of each zone needs to be seamlessly connected. Therefore, the conditions of Equations (26), (35) and (36) need to be satisfied at the same time, and finally, the longest and shortest allowable durations of the orbital control are obtained according to Equation (36). This longest duration of the orbital control is mainly used in the capture phase of the initial inclination, and it will not be used in the stable keeping of the orbital inclination.

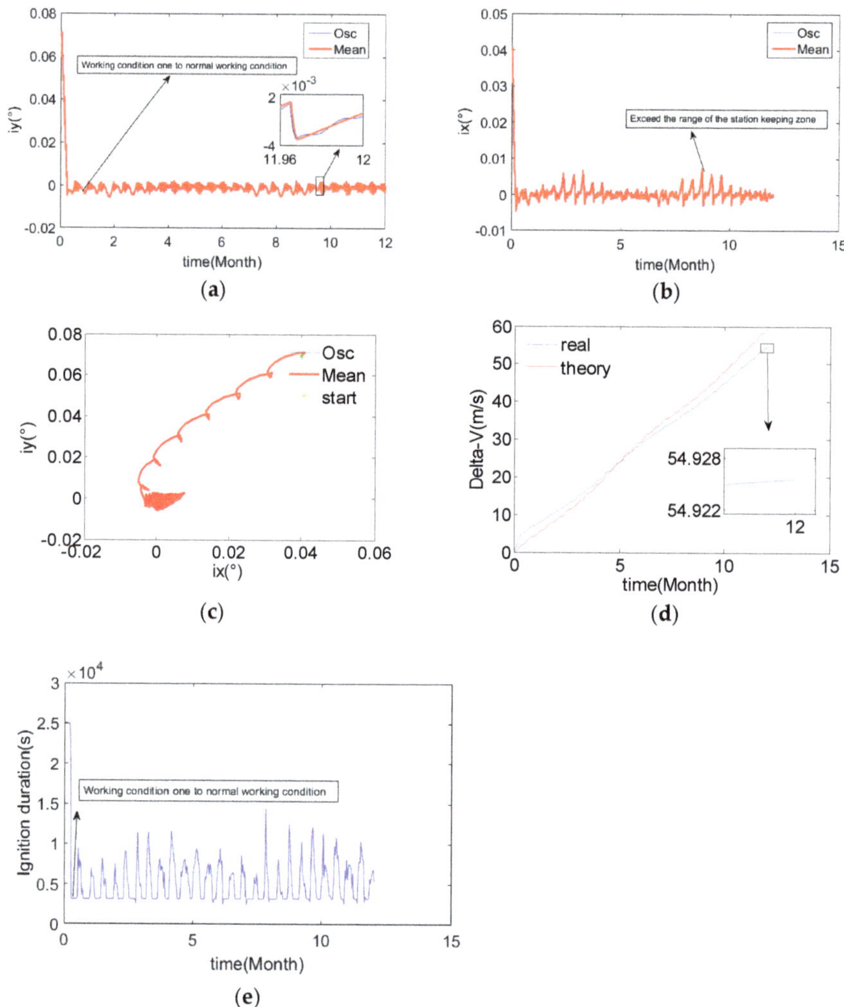

Figure 18. The results of the example five. (**a**) Y-axis component of orbital inclination vector; (**b**) X-axis component of orbital inclination vector; (**c**) Orbital inclination vector; (**d**) Velocity increment for SK; (**e**) Duration of SK.

In addition, the variation of the duration of daily SK in Figure 18e is more continuous than that in Figures 16e and 17e. Because the fluctuation of the mean orbital inclination vector is the most severe under the influence of the semi-monthly period perturbation, using the same method of the orbital control, the error in this example is the smallest. That is to say, the orbital control amount that overcomes the influence of the natural perturbation of the orbital inclination plays a more dominant role, so the daily time length of the SK is relatively continuous.

5. Conclusions

Aiming at the characteristics of low fuel utilization and weak angular momentum unloading ability of traditional all-electric satellites, semi-monthly and semi-annual inclination calculation methods for mean orbital inclination are proposed, and a low fuel consumption NSSK method based on zone control strategy is proposed. The method in this paper has the following characteristics:

(1) The longer the period of the drifting of the mean orbit inclination under the influence of perturbation, the smaller the fluctuation of the center of the SK, the shorter required duration for orbital control, and the smaller the velocity increment required for the SK, but the accuracy of the NSSK is lower;
(2) The velocity increment required for the NSSK of the mean orbital inclination for a semi-monthly period is about 45.5 m/s, and the accuracy of the NSSK is about 0.004°, which is suitable for a high-precision NSSK. The velocity increment required for the NSSK of the mean orbital inclination for the semi-annual period is about 45.5 m/s, and the accuracy of the NSSK is about 0.03°, which is suitable for the NSSK with medium precision and low fuel consumption;
(3) The zone control method of the NSSK has strong adaptability to the initial large orbital inclination;
(4) When the initial orbital inclination has a negative bias, the velocity increment required for the NSSK is less. When the initial orbital inclination has a positive bias, the velocity increment requirements for the NSSK is large;
(5) The manipulator can also be used as a despinning platform for the satellite to achieve the NSSK and angular momentum unloading during the attitude maneuver. The angular momentum unloading scheme of manipulator with an electric thruster is worthy of further study;
(6) The EWSK scheme of the manipulator with EP is worthy of further in-depth study.

The NSSK method proposed in this paper is applicable to any electric thrust and specific impulse. However, from the perspective of optimal fuel, theoretically, the larger the thrust, the better the specific impulse. From the perspective of engineering maturity, the recommended electric propulsion is 80 mN, and the specific impulse is 3000 s.

For the NWSK by EP with manipulator, further research can be conducted in the following aspects in the future:

(1) Carrying out EWSK at the same time in NWKS;
(2) Unloading angular momentum of a large number of stages (such as 50 Nms each time) while in SK;
(3) Online solution for inverse motion of manipulator.

Author Contributions: Methodology, L.Y., F.L. and H.B.; software, L.Y.; writing—original draft preparation, L.Y. and C.L.; funding acquisition, W.Z.; data curation, H.Y. All authors have read and agreed to the published version of the manuscript.

Funding: This research was funded by the National Key Basic Research and Development (973) Program, grant number 2016YFB0501003.

Institutional Review Board Statement: Not applicable.

Informed Consent Statement: Not applicable.

Data Availability Statement: Not applicable.

Conflicts of Interest: The funders had no role in the design of the study; in the collection, analyses, or interpretation of data; in the writing of the manuscript, or in the decision to publish the results.

References

1. Chao, C.C. *Applied Orbit Perturbation and Maintenance*; The Aerospace Press: Reston, VA, USA, 2005.
2. Wang, Z.C.; Xing, G.H.; Zhang, H.W. *Handbook of Geostationary Orbits*; National Defense Industry Press: Beijing, China, 1999.
3. Hu, Z.; Wang, M.; Yuan, J.G. Development and enlightenment of foreign all-EP satellite platforms. *Spacecr. Environ. Eng.* **2015**, *32*, 566–570.
4. Zhang, N. High-Precision Positioning Technology for Geostationary Orbit Satellites. Ph.D. Thesis, Tsinghua University, Beijing, China, 2017.

5. Li, H.N. *Geostationary Satellite Orbit and Co-Location Control Technology*, 1st ed.; National Defense Industry Press: Beijing, China, 2010; pp. 61–64.
6. Li, H.N.; Gao, Y.J.; Yu, P.J. Research on GEO Co-location Control Strategy. *Chin. J. Astronaut.* **2009**, *30*, 967–973.
7. Park, B.K.; Tahk, M.J.; Bang, H.C.; Choi, S.B. Station Collocation Design algorithm for Multiple Geostationary Satellites Operation. *J. Spacecr. Rockers* **2003**, *40*, 889–893.
8. Li, J.C.; An, J.W. Co-location isolation strategy based on orbital eccentricity and orbital inclination vector square root. *Spacecr. Eng.* **2009**, *18*, 20–24.
9. Shi, S.B.; Dong, G.L.; Luo, Q. Orbit maintenance strategy for GEO co-located satellites based on isolation in the tangent plane. *Shanghai Aerosp.* **2009**, *3*, 47–55.
10. Shi, S.B.; Han, Q.L.; Lv, B.T. Optimal control of east-west orbit maintenance for GEO co-located satellites. *Shanghai Aerosp.* **2011**, *2*, 43–49.
11. Li, Y.H. Principles and Implementation Strategies of Orbit Maintenance for Geostationary Communication Satellites. *J. Aircr. Meas. Control.* **2003**, *22*, 53–61.
12. Li, Y.H.; Wei, W.; Yi, K.C. Calculation and Engineering Implementation of Orbit Control Parameters of On-orbit Geostationary Satellites. *Acta Space Sci.* **2007**, *27*, 72–76.
13. Chen, Z.J.; Li, Y.H. Optimization method of east-west position keeping strategy for bias momentum satellites. *Shanghai Aerosp.* **2011**, *28*, 37–41.
14. No, T.S. Simple Approach to East-West Station Keeping of Geosynchronous spacecraft. *J. Guid. Control Dyn.* **1999**, *22*, 734–736. [CrossRef]
15. Yang, W.B.; Li, S.Y.; Li, N. Station-Keeping Control Method for GEO Satellite based on Relative Orbit Dynamics. In Proceedings of the 11th World Congress on Intelligent Control and Automation, Shenyang, China, 29 June–4 July 2014.
16. Yang, W.B.; Li, S.Y.; Li, N. Station-Keeping Control Method for High Orbit Spacecraft Based on Autonomous Control Architecture. In Proceedings of the 32nd Chinese Control Conference, Xi'an, China, 26–28 July 2013.
17. Vinod, K.; Hari, B.H. Autonomous Formation Keeping of Geostationary Satellites with Regional Navigation Satellites and Dynamics. *J. Guid. Control Dyn.* **2017**, *40*, 53–57.
18. Chang, J.S.; Li, Q.J.; Yuan, Y. East-west position keeping strategy of continuous equally spaced pulse thrust for geostationary satellites. *Space Control. Technol. Appl.* **2013**, *39*, 24–32.
19. Weiss, A.; Cairano, D. Station Keeping and Momentum Management of Low-thrust Satellites Using MPC. *Aerosp. Sci. Technol.* **2019**, *76*, 229–241. [CrossRef]
20. Frederik, J.; Bruijn, D. Geostationary Satellite Station-Keeping Using Convex Optimization. *J. Guid. Control Dyn.* **2015**, *39*, 605–616. [CrossRef]
21. Gazzino, C.; Arzelier, D.; Cerri, L.; Losa, D.; Louembet, C.; Pittet, C. A Three-step Decomposition Method for Solving the Minimum-fuel Geostationary SK of Satellites Equipped with EP. *Acta Astronaut.* **2019**, *158*, 12–22. [CrossRef]
22. Gazzino, C.; Arzelier, D.; Losa, D.; Louembet, C.; Pittet, C.; Cerri, L. Optimal Control for Minimum-fuel Geostationary SK of Satellites Equipped with EP. *IFAC Pap. Online* **2016**, *49*, 379–384. [CrossRef]
23. Gazzino, C.; Louembet, C.; Arzelier, D.; Jozefowiez, N.; Losa, D.; Pittet, C.; Cerri, L. Interger Programming for Optimal Control of Geostationary SK of Low-thrust Satellites. *IFAC-Pap. OnLine* **2017**, *50*, 8169–8174. [CrossRef]
24. Gazzino, C.; Arzelier, D.; Louembet, C.; Cerri, L.; Pittet, C.; Losa, D. Long-Term Electric-Propulsion Geostationary Station-Keeping via Integer Programming. *J. Guid. Control Dyn.* **2019**, *42*, 976–991. [CrossRef]
25. Sukhanov, A.A.; Prado, A.F. On one Approach to the Optimization of Low-thrust SK Manoeuvres. *Adv. Space Res.* **2012**, *50*, 1478–1488. [CrossRef]
26. Roth, M. Strategies for Geostationary Spacecraft Orbit SK Using Electrical Propulsion Only. Ph.D. Thesis, Czech Technical University, Prague, Czech Republic, 2020.
27. Ogawa, N.; Terui, F.; Mimasu, Y.; Yoshikawa, K.; Ono, G.; Yasuda, S.; Matsushima, K.; Masuda, T.; Hihara, H.; Sano, J.; et al. Image-based autonomous navigation of Hayabusa2 using artificial landmarks: The design and brief in-flight results of the first landing on asteroid Ryugu. *Astrodynamics* **2020**, *4*, 89–103. [CrossRef]
28. Wang, Y.; Xu, S. Non-equatorial equilibrium points around an asteroid with gravitational orbit-attitude coupling perturbation. *Astrodynamics* **2020**, *4*, 1–16. [CrossRef]
29. Zhang, T.-J.; Wolz, D.; Shen, H.-X.; Luo, Y.-Z. Spanning tree trajectory optimization in the galaxy space. *Astrodynamics* **2021**, *5*, 27–37. [CrossRef]
30. Kuai, Z. Research on GEO Satellite Orbit Maintenance and Orbit Transfer Strategy under Pulse and EP. Ph.D. Thesis, University of Science and Technology of China, Hefei, China, 2017.

 mathematics

Article

Bistatic Radar Observations Correlation of LEO Satellites Considering J_2 Perturbation

Zongbo Huyan, Yu Jiang *, Hengnian Li, Pengbin Ma and Dapeng Zhang

State Key Laboratory of Astronautic Dynamics, Xianning Road No. 462, Xi'an 710043, China; huyanzongbo@outlook.com (Z.H.); henry_xscc@mail.xjtu.edu.cn (H.L.); map_bin@163.com (P.M.); zhangdapeng12@163.com (D.Z.)

* Correspondence: jiangyu_xian_china@163.com

Abstract: Space debris near Earth severely interferes with the development of space, and cataloging space objects is increasingly important. Since optical telescopes and radars used to detect space debris only provide short-arc observations, mathematical algorithms are needed to solve problems in the correlation of observations. In this work, an efficient mathematical algorithm based on J_2 analytic solutions is put forward. Initial orbit determination (IOD) serves as the starter and orbit determination (OD) with the weighted least-squares method (WLSM) is used to improve the accuracy of the estimated orbit. Meanwhile, the effect of the weight of different observation types is analyzed. The correlation criteria for bistatic radar observations are accordingly developed. Lastly, the variation in and evolution of the error of bistatic radar ranging are discussed.

Keywords: space debris; bistatic radar; correlation; J_2 perturbation

MSC: 85-08

Citation: Huyan, Z.; Jiang, Y.; Li, H.; Ma, P.; Zhang, D. Bistatic Radar Observations Correlation of LEO Satellites Considering J_2 Perturbation. *Mathematics* **2022**, *10*, 2197. https://doi.org/10.3390/math10132197

Academic Editor: Ninoslav Truhar

Received: 22 March 2022
Accepted: 9 June 2022
Published: 23 June 2022

1. Introduction

The application of space technologies is the theme of this era. Growing uncontrolled space debris and satellites greatly increase the possibility of collisions year by year. The collision of Iridium 33 and Cosmos 2251 is believed to be the first accidental hypervelocity collision of two intact satellites [1]. In August 2016, significant orbit and attitude changes occurred to the Sentinel-1A, which were later proved to be the result of a 1 cm space debris impact [2]. Therefore, there have been many efforts to calculate collision probabilities [3], for collision avoidance [4] and to design space debris removal missions [5]. Above all, cataloging space objects with precise orbits is needed for the good performance of collision avoidance operations and space debris removal missions.

Restricted to the characteristics of current optical or radar surveys for space debris, only short-arc observations, also called as tracklets, can be obtained. If a tracklet can be correlated to one of the cataloged orbits, the tracklet can be used to update the orbit. The left tracklets that are uncorrelated (UCT) are either newly generated debris or an operational satellite after maneuvering. For UCTs, tracklet correlation is usually first needed to accomplish cataloging.

Milani [6] suggested the method of an admissible region (AR) using attributables to solve the observation correlation of asteroids. Tommei and Milani [7] applied the AR method to space debris in Earth orbit and generalized the method to radar cases. Fujimoto [8] gave circular and zero-inclination solutions to the AR method. Farnocchia [9] proposed a virtual debris algorithm based on the AR method. For many correlation works, only two-body integrals were considered. However, Reihs [10] showed that correlation without considering J_2 perturbation is effective only when the time interval between two measurements is very limited. Rehis [11] suggested a solution of the AR method considering J_2 perturbation.

The Gaussian and Laplacian methods are the most classical IOD algorithms, and they are used in this work. IOD algorithms such as Gibbs are used to deal with radar observations. Details of these algorithms can be found in Escobal [12], Vallado [13], and Liu [14]. Hill [15] took the IOD result as an initial value for an unscented Kalman filter. The calculated orbits and covariances are propagated to a common epoch to accomplish the comparison of orbits. A numerical integral has good precision in propagating orbits and covariances, but the computation requirements are heavy. It is not quite good at dealing with massive amount of tracklets considering the cost of time.

The Air Force Space Surveillance System (AFSSS) has achieved great success in the past few decades because of the wide coverage and its ability to detect high-speed LEO objects. Therefore, continuous attention is being paid to fencelike radar systems. Huang [16] investigated a large-scale distributed space surveillance radar system, and a tracklet association scheme for LEO space debris observed by the double fence radar system was produced [17].

At one step further than other UCTs correlation algorithms, J_2 analytic solutions are not only used in orbit calculation but also used in covariance propagation in this work. With J_2 analytic solutions, the lack of accuracy by Keplerian integrals can be compensated for, and the cost of time is still much less than that of the numerical integral. For monostatic radars, traditional IOD methods are accurate enough when dealing with a single tracklet. However, the same IOD methods are not quite suitable for the sum of ranges by bistatic radars; thus, an extra OD step is added, and a direct correlation criterion to the observations is raised. The effect of the weight of different observation types in the OD process is analyzed. The criteria can eliminate beforehand outliers that might lead to an error in the correlation process. Lastly, the variation in and evolution of the error of bistatic radar ranging are discussed.

2. Initial Orbit Determination for Tracklets Observed by Bistatic Radar

Given the geocentric position $\boldsymbol{r_T}$ of a transmitting station, the geocentric position $\boldsymbol{r_R}$ of the receiving station and the corresponding topocentric position of the space debris $\boldsymbol{\rho_T}, \boldsymbol{\rho_R}$, the geocentric position $\boldsymbol{r}$ of space debris can be expressed as $\boldsymbol{r} = \boldsymbol{\rho_T} + \boldsymbol{r_T}$ or $\boldsymbol{r} = \boldsymbol{\rho_R} + \boldsymbol{r_R}$. As shown in Figure 1, there are two types of observation for bistatic radars.

- angles observed by the receiving station, usually azimuth and elevation (A, E) in topocentric horizontal coordinate system for radars;
- the sum of ranges by the transmitting station and receiving station, $\rho = \rho_T + \rho_R$. $\boldsymbol{\rho_T} = \rho_T \hat{\boldsymbol{\rho_T}}$ and $\boldsymbol{\rho_R} = \rho_R \hat{\boldsymbol{\rho_R}}$, $\hat{\boldsymbol{\rho_T}}$ and $\hat{\boldsymbol{\rho_R}}$ are the unit vector of $\boldsymbol{\rho_T}$ and $\boldsymbol{\rho_R}$, ρ_T and ρ_R are the length of $\boldsymbol{\rho_T}$ and $\boldsymbol{\rho_R}$. Sum of ranges ρ can be measured directly, but ρ_T and ρ_R are unknown.

Radar ranging is based on the measurement of signal transmission time, and angles are based on the mechanical measurements of an antenna. Different measurement principles and equipment capabilities result in a difference in accuracy. In normalized units in which the unit of distance is the radius of Earth, and the unit of angles is radian, the error of angles is dozens of times larger than the error of radar ranging.

Traditional IOD methods can deal with monostatic radar ranging, but they are not quite suitable for a sum of ranges by a bistatic radar. Two approximate approaches can be used to obtain an initial orbit from bistatic radar observations.

- Angles only: Since a series of angle observations is sufficient for IOD, a sum of ranges can be temporarily put aside. With Equation (1),

$$\hat{\boldsymbol{\rho_R}} \times \boldsymbol{r} = \hat{\boldsymbol{\rho_R}} \times \boldsymbol{r_R}, \tag{1}$$

  ρ_R from the receiving station to the space debris can be eliminated; therefore, only azimuth and elevation observed by the receiving station are used. The defect of this approach is that low-accuracy measurements are used, and high-accuracy measurements are rejected.

- ρ_R calculation: Since $\boldsymbol{r}_{R2T} = \boldsymbol{r}_T - \boldsymbol{r}_R$, $\hat{\rho_R}$ and ρ are known with a simple geometric calculation, $\boldsymbol{\rho}_R$ can be obtained. Then, the position of space debris can be calculated. The problem of this approach is that the errors of angles are transferred to $\boldsymbol{\rho}_R$.

Since a tracklet is usually short-arc with initial geocentric position and velocity ($\boldsymbol{r}_0 = \boldsymbol{r}(t_0)$, $\dot{\boldsymbol{r}}_0 = \dot{\boldsymbol{r}}(t_0)$) at t_0 and prediction duration $\Delta t = t - t_0$, the geocentric position $\boldsymbol{r}(t)$ of the space debris at t could be calculated by series expansion:

$$\boldsymbol{r}(t) = F(\boldsymbol{r}_0, \dot{\boldsymbol{r}}_0, \Delta t)\boldsymbol{r}_0 + G(\boldsymbol{r}_0, \dot{\boldsymbol{r}}_0, \Delta t)\dot{\boldsymbol{r}}_0, \tag{2}$$

where F and G are the polynomial function of Δt. For the ρ_R calculation approach, Equation (2) has 6 unknown variables ($\boldsymbol{r}_0$, $\dot{\boldsymbol{r}}_0$) and a known vector $\boldsymbol{\rho}_R$. With at least 2 groups of measurements $\boldsymbol{\rho}_R(t_i)(i = 1, 2, 3...)$, ($\boldsymbol{r}_0$, $\dot{\boldsymbol{r}}_0$) would be solvable.

By substituting Equation (2) into Equation (1),

$$\hat{\rho_R} \times (F\boldsymbol{r}_0 + G\dot{\boldsymbol{r}}_0) = \hat{\rho_R} \times \boldsymbol{r}_R. \tag{3}$$

For the angles-only approach, Equation (3) has 6 unknown variables ($\boldsymbol{r}_0$, $\dot{\boldsymbol{r}}_0$) and 2 known observations (A, E). With at least 3 groups of measurements $\hat{\rho}(t_i)(i = 1, 2, 3...)$, ($\boldsymbol{r}_0$, $\dot{\boldsymbol{r}}_0$) would be solvable.

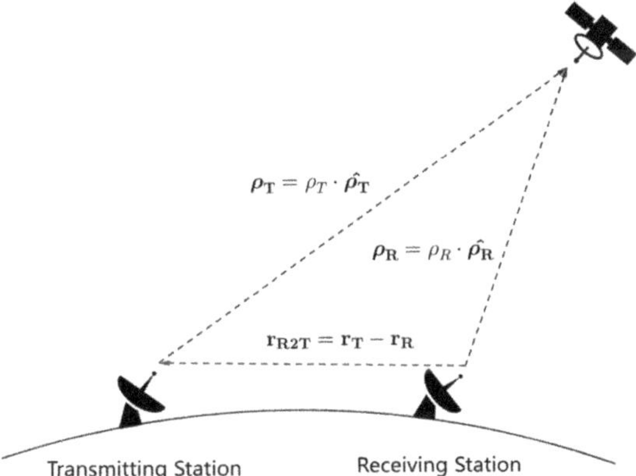

Figure 1. Bistatic radar observation.

3. Orbit Improvement with Weighted Least Square Method

The angles-only and ρ_R calculation approaches can both provide a set of the estimated state, but the accuracies of the two approaches much depend on the quality of angle measurements. For the angles-only approach, the random noise of (A, E) is directly absorbed by the estimated state. For the ρ_R calculation approach, the random noise of (A, E) is absorbed by ρ_R and also leads to a huge error in the estimated state.

With the weighted least-squares method (WLSM) and an accurate measurement model, the effects of the random noise of measurements can be reduced, measurements with large error can be stripped out, and ρ can be appropriately calculated. Therefore, the accuracy of the orbit can be improved.

3.1. *Weighted Least-Squares Method*

Suppose that z_i is the observation at t_i, $\boldsymbol{x}_i$ is the calculated state at t_i, and $h(\boldsymbol{x}_i) = h_i(\boldsymbol{x}_0)$ is the observation equation. The loss function is defined as

$$J(\boldsymbol{x}_0) = \sum_{i=1}^{N} \|z_i - h(\boldsymbol{x}_i)\|, \tag{4}$$

the result x_0^{est} should satisfy

$$J(x_0^{est}) = \min_{x_0 \in X_0} J(x_0) \tag{5}$$

where X_0 is the state-space of x_0. For the least-squares method, either the position and velocity or orbital elements could form the state vector of space debris. For analytic solutions, the state of the space debris is usually expressed by orbital elements.

Define

$$\begin{aligned} Z &= (z_1, z_2, ..., z_n)^T, && (6)\\ H(x_0) &= (h_1(x_0), h_2(x_0), ..., h_n(x_0))^T, && (7)\\ \Delta Z &= (\Delta z_1, \Delta z_2, ..., \Delta z_n)^T = (z_1 - h_1(x_0), z_2 - h_2(x_0), ..., z_n - h_n(x_0))^T. && (8) \end{aligned}$$

The loss function can also be expressed as

$$J(x_0) = (Z - H(x_0))^T (Z - H(x_0)) = \Delta Z^T \Delta Z. \tag{9}$$

Supposing that $\Delta x_0 = x_0 - x_0^{true}$ where x_0^{true} is the actual state at t_0, we have

$$J(x_0) = \sum_{i=1}^{N} \| \frac{\partial h_i(x_0)}{\partial x_0} \Delta x_0 \|. \tag{10}$$

If $\partial H(x_0)/\partial \Delta x_0$ is nonsingular, there exists a solution

$$\Delta x_0^{est} = \left[\left(\frac{\partial H(x_0)}{\Delta x_0} \right)^T \left(\frac{\partial H(x_0)}{\Delta x_0} \right) \right]^{-1} \left(\frac{\partial H(x_0)}{\Delta x_0} \right)^T \Delta Z \tag{11}$$

which leads to $\partial J(x_0)/\partial \Delta x_0 = 0$.

As mentioned in Section 2, the accuracies of ρ and (A, E) are different. Equal treatment with different types of observations would lower the accuracy of the results, and a proper weight is essential to data fusion. Thus, measurement errors $\sigma_i (i = 1, 2, 3...)$ are put into Equation (11) and form Equation (12).

$$\Delta x_0^{est} = \left[\left(\frac{\partial H(x_0)}{\Delta x_0} \right)^T W \left(\frac{\partial H(x_0)}{\Delta x_0} \right) \right]^{-1} \left[\left(\frac{\partial H(x_0)}{\Delta x_0} \right)^T W \Delta Z \right] \tag{12}$$

where

$$W = \begin{pmatrix} \sigma_1^{-2} & 0 & ... & 0 & ... & 0 \\ 0 & \sigma_2^{-2} & ... & 0 & ... & 0 \\ ... & ... & ... & ... & ... & ... \\ 0 & 0 & ... & \sigma_i^{-2} & ... & 0 \\ ... & ... & ... & ... & ... & ... \\ 0 & 0 & ... & 0 & ... & \sigma_n^{-2} \end{pmatrix}. \tag{13}$$

Since observation equation $h(x_i)$ is an equation with respect to x_i, to calculate $\partial h_i(x_0)/\partial x_0$, the state transition matrix ϕ_i is needed:

$$\begin{aligned} \frac{\partial h_i(x_0)}{\partial x_0} &= \frac{\partial h(x_i)}{\partial x_i} \phi_i, && (14)\\ \phi_i &= \frac{\partial x_i}{\partial x_0}. && (15) \end{aligned}$$

3.2. *Effect of Weight*

Theoretical weight in WLSM is the accuracy of observation, as shown in Equation (13). In practice, it is not easy to obtain the exact error of each observation while tracking and observing. The errors of observations are different since the error is affected by multiple factors. Usually, a composite weight from experience and equipment performance is set for each type of observation.

In this work, the relative weight between different types of observations could affect the accuracy of a certain orbital element. Two stations, as shown in Table 1, and a satellite, as shown in Table 2, were simulated to demonstrate the effect of observation weight. The duration of the simulated tracklet was 1 min.

Table 1. Description of two simulated stations.

Simulated Stations	Latitude (deg)	Longitude (deg)	Height (m)
Transmitting station	30	108	0
Receiving station	30	105	0

Table 2. Description of the simulated satellite.

Semi-Major Axis (m)	Eccentricity	Inclination (deg)	RAAN (deg)
6,878,137.0	0.001	60.0	60.0

As discussed in Section 2, there are mainly two types of observation for bistatic radar, and the accuracy of radar ranging is usually better than that of angles. From Equation (12), the results of estimation change with the relative weight between different observations, instead of the absolute weight of observations. In normalized units which the unit of distance is the radius of Earth, and the unit of angles is radian, variation in the relative error between the sum of ranges and azimuth (σ_ρ/σ_A) was set from 0.1 to 0.02, and variation in the relative error between elevation and azimuth (σ_E/σ_A) was set from 0.5 to 2.0. Like the relative errors of observations being used to describe weight, the relative error between different orbital elements is used to describe the accuracy of certain orbital element. By setting the error of the estimated eccentricity as the reference, the relative error between the semimajor axis and eccentricity (σ_a/σ_e) can represent the accuracy of the estimated semimajor axis, and the relative error between inclination and eccentricity (σ_i/σ_e) can represent the accuracy of the estimated inclination. The effects of weight on the accuracy of estimated orbital elements are shown in Figure 2.

Figure 2 shows that the accuracy of the estimated semimajor axis increases with the weight of radar ranging. This effect becomes stronger when $\sigma_E \neq \sigma_A$. On the other hand, the accuracy of inclination decreases with the weight of radar ranging, and increases with the weight of elevation.

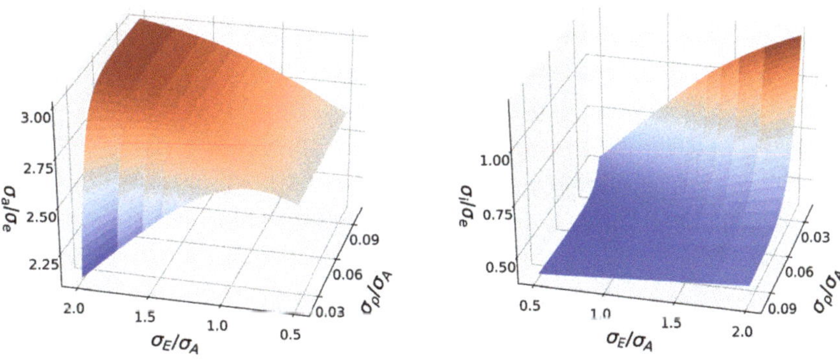

Figure 2. Effect of weight on the accuracy of estimated orbital elements.

4. Correlation Considering J_2 Perturbation

The motion of space debris in terrestrial space is affected by all kinds of perturbations, such as drag, solar radiation pressure, and the gravitational perturbations of the Sun and Moon. Among all, the J_2 term of Earth's nonspherical perturbation has the strongest influence.

The J_2 term represents the perturbation caused by the oblateness of Earth. The acceleration of J_2 perturbation is shown in Equation (16),

$$\ddot{\boldsymbol{r}}_{J2} = \begin{bmatrix} -\frac{3}{2}J_2\frac{GM_eR_e^2}{r_{ecf}^5}\left(1-5\frac{z_{ecf}^2}{r_{ecf}^2}\right)x_{ecf} \\ -\frac{3}{2}J_2\frac{GM_eR_e^2}{r_{ecf}^5}\left(1-5\frac{z_{ecf}^2}{r_{ecf}^2}\right)y_{ecf} \\ -\frac{3}{2}J_2\frac{GM_eR_e^2}{r_{ecf}^5}\left(3-5\frac{z_{ecf}^2}{r_{ecf}^2}\right)z_{ecf} \end{bmatrix}. \tag{16}$$

G is the gravitational constant, M_e is the mass of Earth, R_e is the radius of Earth, and $\boldsymbol{r}_{ecf} = (x_{ecf}, y_{ecf}, z_{ecf})$ is the position of space debris in an Earth-centered fixed coordinate system. J_2 perturbation is not only considered in orbit prediction, but also in covariance propagation in this work.

4.1. Orbit Propagation with J_2 Perturbation

J_2 perturbation causes a secular variation in the orbital plane (right ascension of ascending node, Ω) and argument of perigee (ω) as shown in Equations (17) and (18):

$$\dot{\Omega} = -\frac{3}{2}J_2\left(\frac{R_e}{p}\right)^2 n\cos i \tag{17}$$

$$\dot{\omega} = \frac{3}{2}J_2\left(\frac{R_e}{p}\right)^2 n\left(2-\frac{5}{2}\sin^2 i\right) \tag{18}$$

where R_e is the radius of Earth, n is the mean motion of a satellite, and $p = a(1-e^2)$. Equation (19) shows that the mean motion (n) of space debris is affected by J_2 perturbation, but has no secular variation:

$$n_{J_2} = n + \frac{3}{4}J_2\left(\frac{R_e}{a}\right)^2\left(\frac{2-3\sin^2 i}{p^{\frac{3}{2}}}\right). \tag{19}$$

Since $M = M_0 + n(t-t_0)$, variation in n leads to extra secular variation in mean anomaly (M). Equation (20) gives the expression of $\dot{M}$:

$$\dot{M} = n + \frac{3}{2}nJ_2\left(\frac{R_e}{p}\right)^2\left(1-\frac{3}{2}\sin^2 i\right)\sqrt{1-e^2}. \tag{20}$$

With Equations (17)–(20), analytic state transition matrix $\boldsymbol{\phi} = \boldsymbol{\phi}^{(0)} + \boldsymbol{\phi}^{(1)}$,

$$\boldsymbol{\phi}^{(0)} = \begin{pmatrix} 1 & 0 & 0 & 0 & 0 & 0 \\ 0 & 1 & 0 & 0 & 0 & 0 \\ 0 & 0 & 1 & 0 & 0 & 0 \\ 0 & 0 & 0 & 1 & 0 & 0 \\ 0 & 0 & 0 & 0 & 1 & 0 \\ \phi_{61}^{(0)} & 0 & 0 & 0 & 0 & 1 \end{pmatrix}, \tag{21}$$

$$\boldsymbol{\phi}^{(1)} = \begin{pmatrix} 0 & 0 & 0 & 0 & 0 & 0 \\ 0 & 0 & 0 & 0 & 0 & 0 \\ 0 & 0 & 0 & 0 & 0 & 0 \\ \phi_{41}^{(1)} & \phi_{42}^{(1)} & \phi_{43}^{(1)} & 0 & 0 & 0 \\ \phi_{51}^{(1)} & \phi_{52}^{(1)} & \phi_{53}^{(1)} & 0 & 0 & 0 \\ \phi_{61}^{(1)} & \phi_{62}^{(1)} & \phi_{63}^{(1)} & 0 & 0 & 0 \end{pmatrix}, \tag{22}$$

where $\phi_{61}^{(0)}$ is a function of $(a_0, \Delta t)$, and $\phi_{ij}^{(1)}$ are functions of $(a_0, e_0, i_0, \Delta t)$. $\boldsymbol{\phi}^{(0)}$ represents the state transition of Keplerian motion, and $\boldsymbol{\phi}^{(1)}$ represents the effect of J_2 perturbation.

4.2. Correlation of Tracklets

Assuming that there are n tracklets $(1, 2, \ldots j, \ldots, k, \ldots, n)$, and each tracklet has more than 3 groups of measurements, the correlation between the jth tracklet and one of the measurements in the kth tracklet is taken as an example.

After IOD and OD with WLSM, an improved state $(\boldsymbol{x}_j)$ could be obtained for the jth tracklet. Propagating $\boldsymbol{x}_j$ and the error of $\boldsymbol{x}_j$ to the kth tracklet, observation (A_k^j, E_k^j, ρ_k^j) and the error of observation $(\Delta A_k^j, \Delta E_k^j, \Delta \rho_k^j)$ can be calculated. The error of $\boldsymbol{x}_j$ by OD with only one tracklet was much smaller than the actual deviation of $\boldsymbol{x}_j$. In order to more accurately calculate $(\Delta A_k^j, \Delta E_k^j, \Delta \rho_k^j)$, the empirical error of the estimated orbit with one tracklet is needed.

Since the observation error $(\Delta A, \Delta E, \Delta \rho_R)$ of the receiving station was pairwise orthogonal, (A, E, ρ_R) should conform to the restriction of the error ellipsoid as shown in Figure 3.

If the jth and kth tracklets belong to the same satellite, $(A, E, \rho_R)_k$ should satisfy Equation (23):

$$\left(\frac{A_k - A_k^j}{m \Delta A_k^j}\right)^2 + \left(\frac{E_k - E_k^j}{m \Delta E_k^j}\right)^2 + \left(\frac{(\rho_R)_k - (\rho_R)_k^j}{m (\Delta \rho_R)_k^j}\right)^2 < 1, \tag{23}$$

m is the coefficient absorbing the inaccuracy of dynamic models and the error growth in propagation.

The error of bistatic radar ranging $(\Delta \rho)$ is affected by three factors:

$\Delta \rho_R$ the error produced by the receiving station;

$\Delta \rho_T$ the error produced by the transmitting station;

$\Delta \rho_s$ the systematic error between the receiving station and the transmitting station.

$$\Delta \rho = f(\Delta \rho_R, \Delta \rho_T, \Delta \rho_s), \tag{24}$$

$\Delta \rho_s$ is mainly decided by the performance of time synchronization between different stations. According to Guo [18], timing with a global navigation satellite system (GNSS) is about 0.1 ns. Thus, $\Delta \rho_s \ll \Delta \rho_R, \Delta \rho_T$ at present. Assuming that the variation in $\Delta \rho_R$

and $\Delta\rho_T$ is mainly affected by J_2 perturbation, and Equation (24) can be approximated to Equation (25) in one tracklet:

$$\frac{\rho_R}{\rho} \cong \frac{\Delta\rho_R}{\Delta\rho}, \tag{25}$$

Equation (23) can be transformed into Equation (26),

$$\left(\frac{A_k - A_k^j}{m\Delta A_k^j}\right)^2 + \left(\frac{E_k - E_k^j}{m\Delta E_k^j}\right)^2 + \left(\frac{\rho_k - \rho_k^j}{m\Delta\rho_k^j}\right)^2 < 1. \tag{26}$$

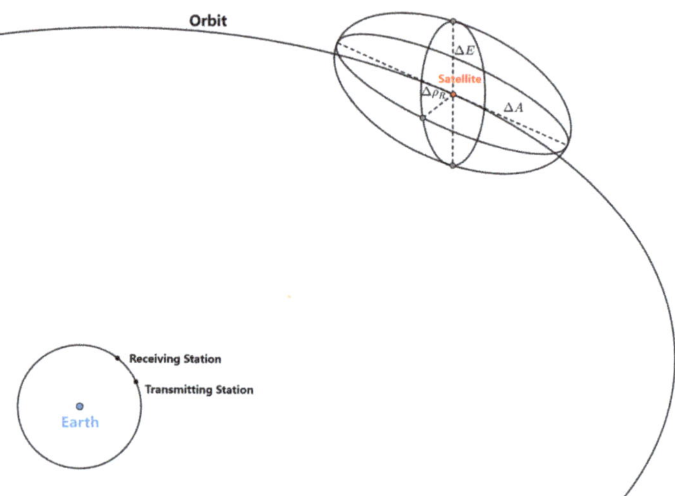

Figure 3. Error ellipsoid of observations of a receiving station.

Different from calculating the Mahalanobis distance of two orbits [11,19], each group of observations was tested with Equation (26). If 70% measurements of the tracklet were successfully correlated, the tracklet was successfully correlated. For tracklets with clean data, the effect of the proposed approach is similar to that of calculating Mahalanobis distance. However, tracklets with mixed measurements of different space debris appear now and then, and mixed measurements could lead to a failure in an OD process or an estimated orbit with huge error. With the proposed approach, correlation and data cleansing can be accomplished in one step.

There were quite a few miscorrelations only with Equation (26). Orbit determination with WLSM can also be used to screen out miscorrelations. Two tracklets were insufficient for confirmation. Tests with real data were reported by Tommei [20], who found that the correctness of correlation would be largely increased when at least 3 tracklets are confirmed by the least-square method. In this work, only correlated observations, instead of the entire tracklet, were used to implement the confirmation.

5. Discussion

Since the properties of azimuth and elevation observed by a receiving station are the same with those observed by monostatic radars, which was discussed by Cordelli [21], ΔA and ΔE are not discussed in the following. Two issues are discussed in detail:

1. the performance of orbit determination with WLSM for a single bistatic radar tracklet;
2. the effect of orbital elements' accuracy and prediction duration on $\Delta\rho$.

5.1. Accuracy of Orbit Determination

In order to test the performance of orbit determination, 4298 tracklets of 3538 LEO satellites were simulated. Detailed simulation strategies are shown in Table 3.

Table 3. Strategies of simulation.

Subject	Content
Orbital elements	Two-Line-Element (TLE)
Dynamic model	sgp4
Minimal height threshold	200 km
Maximal height threshold	1700 km
Minimal time span	20 s
Maximal time span	300 s
Mean time span	120 s
σ of azimuth noise	0.1°
σ of elevation noise	0.1°
σ of ρ noise	50 m

For the initial orbit determination demonstration, the ρ_R calculation approach was selected. Figure 4 gives the deviation between the estimated orbit elements by IOD and the true orbital elements (TLE). μ is the mathematical expectation of the deviation which represents the systematic bias of the estimated orbital elements.

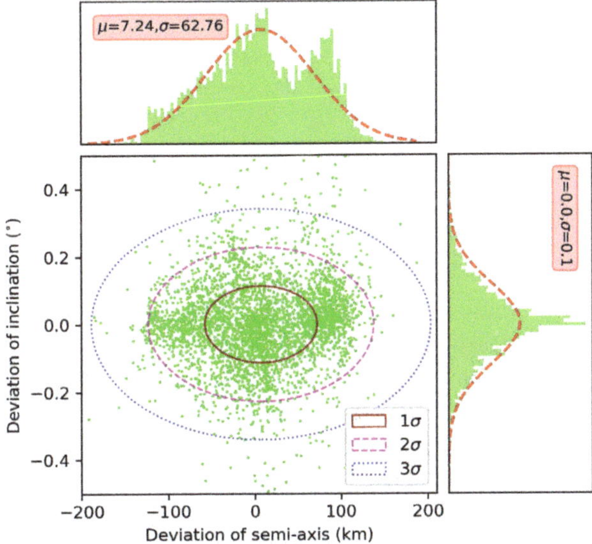

Figure 4. Accuracy of ρ_R calculation approach.

The estimated inclination by IOD barely had systematic bias, and the error reached $\sigma \sim 0.1°$. On the other hand, the systematic bias of the estimated semimajor axis by IOD was as large as several kilometers, and the standard deviation was even larger.

Figure 5 gives the deviation between the estimated orbital elements by WLSM and the true orbital elements (TLE).

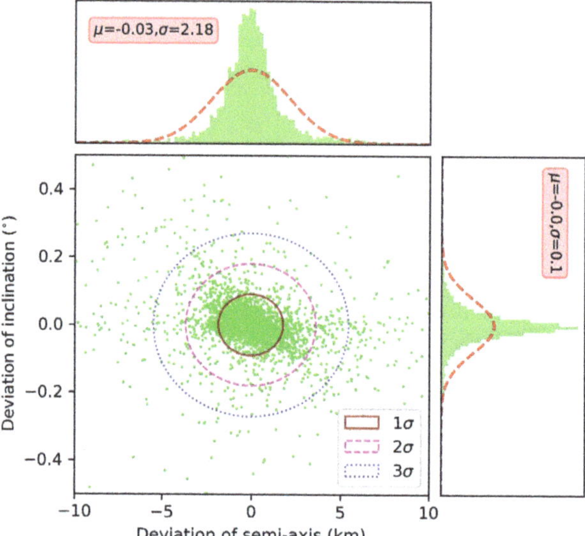

Figure 5. Accuracy of orbit determination with WLSM.

The accuracy of the estimated inclination by OD was only slightly higher than that of the estimated inclination by IOD. However, the estimated semimajor axis was significantly improved by OD with WLSM. The systematic bias of the estimated semimajor axis dropped to the order of magnitude of ten meters, and the accuracy of the estimated semimajor axis increased several dozens of times. This improvement was largely due to the proper use of ρ. ρ had a strong restriction on the estimation of the semimajor axis, and this phenomenon corresponded to the effect of weight discussed in Section 3.2.

Two more things were also noticed from the results of orbit determination:

- Orbit improvement with WLSM is indispensable. Since the error of the estimated orbit elements by IOD was too large, the number of miscorrelations would grow rapidly as the interval between tracklets increased. At the same time, the systematic bias of the estimated semimajor axis would render the orbit propagation wrong.
- As mentioned in Section 4.2, an empirical error of the estimated orbit is needed to calculate $(\Delta A_k^j, \Delta E_k^j, \Delta\rho_k^j)$ in Equation (26). From Figure 5, the empirical error can be obtained.

5.2. Variation in and Evolution of $\Delta\rho$

$\Delta\rho$ is mainly affected by the accuracy of orbit determination and the prediction duration. In order to test the effect of different factors, the two stations in Table 1 and the satellite in Table 2 were chosen to accomplish the experiment. Assuming that the prediction duration was 1 day, Figure 6 shows the variation in $\Delta\rho$ with respect to the estimated orbit element and its accuracy.

$\Delta\rho$ was easily found to always be positively associated with the absolute error of an orbital element. This feature can substantially simplify the calculation because the extreme value is sufficient for calculating the confidence zone of $\Delta\rho$ instead of traversing all possible errors of orbital elements. Figure 6 also shows that $\Delta\rho$ became smaller for the satellites of a higher altitude with the same semimajor axis error. The effect of the right ascension of the ascending node (Ω) was almost identical to that of inclination, which demonstrates that the orbit plane had no direct relationship with $\Delta\rho$.

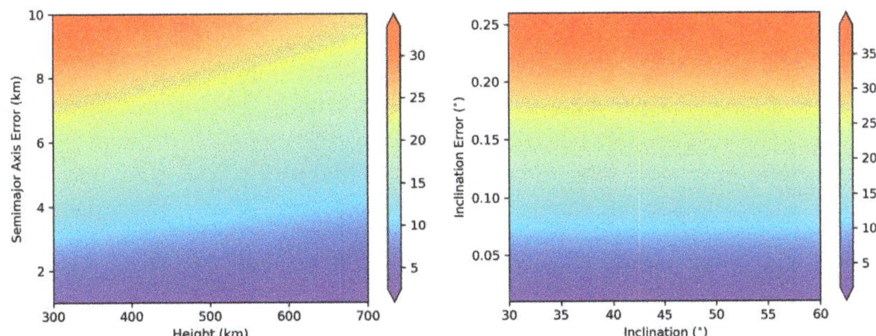

Figure 6. $\Delta\rho$ with respect to the accuracy of the estimated orbital elements.

Assuming that the orbit was calculated with the tracklet in Pass 0, the orbit and its error propagated to tracklets in Passes 1, 10, and 14. The evolution of ρ and $\Delta\rho$ is shown in Figure 7.

Figure 7 shows that ρ in one tracklet could vary by several thousand kilometers for a satellite with an altitude of 500 km, while $\Delta\rho$ only varies little. This shows that $\Delta\rho$ barely had a relationship with ρ. σ_ρ is not always positively associated with prediction duration. If σ_ρ drops, either the error of velocity or the error of azimuth and elevation grows.

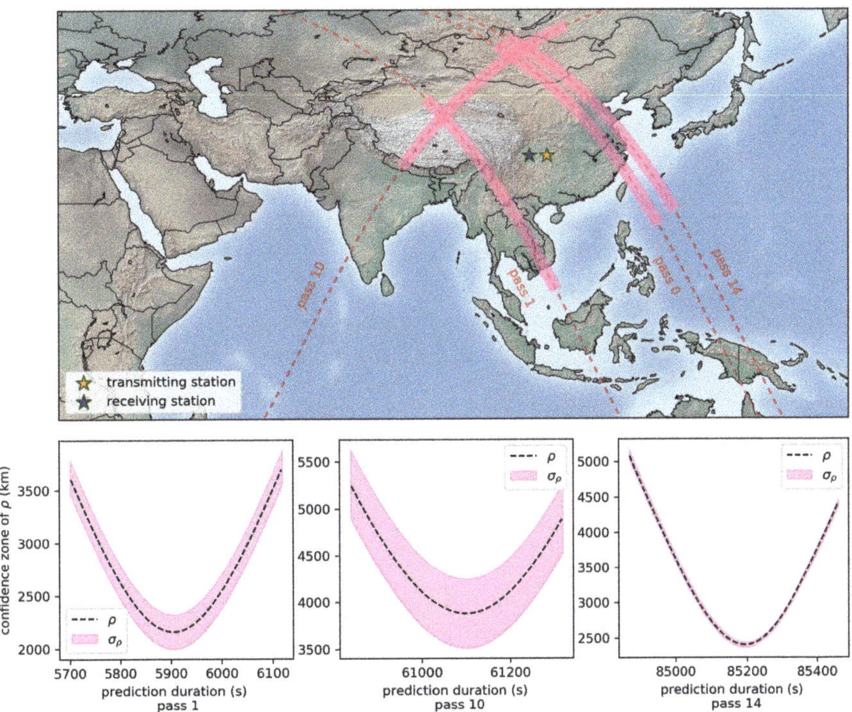

Figure 7. Evolution of ρ and $\Delta\rho$.

6. Conclusions

In this work, an efficient algorithm was presented to deal with the UCT correlation problem. The algorithm was based on J_2 analytic solutions for orbit and covariance propagation. The lack of accuracy of Keplerian integral can be compensated to a certain level by taking J_2 perturbation into consideration.

The process of correlation starts with the IOD of a tracklet, followed by obtaining an improved orbit with WLSM. An empirical error of the estimated state is used to form the covariance. The OD with an analytic orbit and covariance propagation runs fast for sparse data, which also significantly decreases the systematic bias of the estimated semimajor axis, and the accuracy of the estimated semimajor axis increases several dozens of times. The orbit and covariance are propagated to the epoch of the second tracklet, and Equation (26) was used to perform the correlation. Instead of OD for the second tracklet and comparing the estimated orbit, each pair of observations in the second tracklet were separately correlated. If 70% observations of the tracklet were successfully correlated, the tracklet was successfully correlated. With the proposed approach, correlation and data cleansing can be accomplished in one step. However, only the correlated observations in the tracklet are used in the next step to implement the confirmation, and update the orbit and covariance. The accuracy of the semimajor axis increased with the weight of radar ranging. This effect became stronger when $\sigma_E \neq \sigma_A$. On the other hand, the accuracy of inclination decreased with the weight of radar ranging, and increased with the weight of elevation. The error of bistatic radar ranging also became smaller for space debris of higher altitude with the same semimajor axis error, and the orbit plane had no direct relationship with the error of bistatic radar ranging.

Author Contributions: Conceptualization, Z.H. and P.M.; Data curation, D.Z.; Formal analysis, H.L.; Funding acquisition, Y.J.; Investigation, Z.H., Y.J. and H.L.; Methodology, Z.H. and Y.J.; Project administration, Y.J. and H.L.; Resources, Y.J.; Software, Z.H. and D.Z.; Supervision, H.L.; Validation, Y.J. and P.M.; Visualization, Z.H.; Writing—original draft, Z.H.; Writing—review & editing, Z.H., Y.J., H.L. and P.M. All authors have read and agreed to the published version of the manuscript.

Funding: This research was funded by National Natural Science Foundation of China grant number U21B2050.

Conflicts of Interest: The authors declare no conflict of interest.

References

1. Anselmo, L.; Pardini, C. Analysis of the consequences in low Earth orbit of thecollision between Cosmos 2251 and Iridium 33. In Proceedings of the 21st International Symposium on Space Flight Dynamics (ISSFD-2009), Toulouse, France, 28 September–2 October 2009.
2. Krag, H.; Serrano, M.; Braun, V.; Kuchynka, P.; Catania, M.; Siminski, J.; Schimmerohn, M.; Marc, X.; Kuijper, D.; Shurmer, I.; et al. A 1 cm space debris impact onto the Sentinel-1A solar array. *Acta Astronaut.* **2017**, *137*, 434–443. [CrossRef]
3. Wen, C.; Qiao, D. Calculating collision probability for long-term satellite encounters through the reachable domain method. *Astrodynamics* **2022**, *6*, 141–159. [CrossRef]
4. Uriot, T.; Izzo, D.; Simões, L.F.; Abay, R.; Einecke, N.; Rebhan, S.; Martinez-Heras, J.; Letizia, F.; Siminski, J.; Merz, K. Spacecraft collision avoidance challenge: Design and results of a machine learning competition. *Astrodynamics* **2021**, *6*, 121–140. [CrossRef]
5. Zhang, N.; Zhang, Z.; Baoyin, H. Timeline Club: An optimization algorithm for solving multiple debris removal missions of the time-dependent traveling salesman problem model. *Astrodyn* **2021**, *6*, 219–234. [CrossRef]
6. Milani, A.; Gronchi, G.F.; Vitturi, M.d.M.; Knezevic, Z. Orbit determination with very short arcs. i admissible regions. *Celestial Mech. Dyn. Astron.* **2004**, *90*, 57–85. [CrossRef]
7. Tommei, G.; Milani, A.; Rossi, A. Orbit determination of space debris: Admissible regions. *Celestial Mech. Dyn. Astron.* **2004**, *97*, 289–304. [CrossRef]
8. Fujimoto, K.; Maruskin, J.M.; Scheeres, D.J. Circular and zero-inclination solutions for optical observations of Earth-orbiting objects. *Celestial Mech. Dyn. Astron.* **2010**, *106*, 157–182. [CrossRef]
9. Farnocchia, D.; Tommei, G.; Milani, A.; Rossi, A. Innovative methods of correlation and orbit determination for space debris. *Celestial Mech. Dyn. Astron.* **2010**, *107*, 169–185. [CrossRef]
10. Reihs, B.; Vananti, A.; Schildknecht, T. Comparison of new methods for the correlation of short radar tracklets. In Proceedings of the 69th International Astronautical Congress, Bremen, Germany, 1–5 October 2018.
11. Reihs, B.; Vananti, A.; Schildknecht, T. A method for perturbed initial orbit determination and correlation of radar measurements. *Adv. Space Res.* **2020**, *66*, 426–443. [CrossRef]
12. Escobal, P. *Methods of Orbit Determination*; R.E. Krieger Pub., Co.: Huntington, NY, USA, 1976.
13. Vallado, D. *Fundamentals of Astrodynamics and Applications*; Microcosm Press: Hawthorne, CA, USA, 2013.
14. Liu, L.; Tang, J.S. *Theory and Application of Satellite Orbit*; Publishing House of Electronics Industry: Beijing, China, 2015.

15. Hill, K.; Sabol, C.; Alfriend, K.T. Comparison of covariance based track association approaches using simulated radar data. *J. Astron. Sci.* **2012**, *59*, 281–300. [CrossRef]
16. Huang, J.; Wang, D.; Xia, S. An Optimal Beam Alignment Method for Large-scale Distributed Space Surveillance Radar System. *Adv. Space Res.* **2018**, *61*, 2777–2786. [CrossRef]
17. Huang, J.; Hu, W.D.; Xin, Q.; Guo, W.W. A novel data association scheme for LEO space debris surveillance based on a double fence radar system. *Adv. Space Res.* **2012**, *50*, 1451–1461. [CrossRef]
18. Guo, F.; Li, X.X.; Zhang, X.H.; Wang, J.L. Assessment of precise orbit and clock products for Galileo, BeiDou, and QZSS from IGS Multi-GNSS Experiment (MGEX). *GPS Solut.* **2017**, *21*, 279–290. [CrossRef]
19. Mahalanobis, P. On the generalised distance in statistics. *Proc. Natl. Inst. Sci. India* **1936**, *2*, 49–55.
20. Tommei, G.; Milani, A.; Farnocchia, D.; Rossi, A. Correlation of space debris observations by the virtual debris algorithm. In Proceedings of the Fifth European Conference on Space Debris, Darmstadt, Germany, 30 March–2 April 2009.
21. Cordelli, E.; Vananti, A.; Schildknecht, T. Analysis of Laser Ranges and Angular Measurements Data Fusion for Space Debris Orbit Determination. *Adv. Space Res.* **2019**, *65*, 419–434. [CrossRef]

Article

Containment Control for Discrete-Time Multi-Agent Systems with Nonconvex Control Input and Position Constraints

Ning Gao and Yikang Yang *

School of Electronic and Information Engineering, Xi'an Jiaotong University, Xi'an 710049, China; agoushizhimao@stu.xjtu.edu.cn
* Correspondence: yangyk74@mail.xjtu.edu.cn

Abstract: With increasing attention on containment control problems in several areas, we investigate this specific problem which can be more practical. Systems with nonconvex input and position constraints are common but can be strongly nonlinear. A distribute algorithm using a projection operator is proposed to ensure that the control input of every follower remains in a nonconvex set and that all followers stay in the closed set given by leaders. In analysis, a model transformation is proposed, and then we introduce a method utilizing two similar triangles to prove the acceptability of the algorithm. The findings of the research could be pragmatic in robotics, astronautics, and so on. At last, numerical simulations are provided to show the contrast and results.

Keywords: containment control; multiagent systems; control input constraints; position constraints; switching topologies

MSC: 93A16; 93C10

Citation: Gao, N.; Yang, Y. Containment Control for Discrete-Time Multi-Agent Systems with Nonconvex Control Input and Position Constraints. *Mathematics* **2022**, *10*, 2010. https://doi.org/10.3390/math10122010

Academic Editor: Florin Leon

Received: 14 May 2022
Accepted: 9 June 2022
Published: 10 June 2022

1. Introduction

Over the past few years, containment control has attracted widespread attention due to its potential applications in robotics, astronautics, biology, traffic engineering, etc. The potential of containment control for different areas such as game theory and cyberattack is significant. Numerous works on containment control have been conducted, as in [1–26]. Containment control problem is associated with systems composed of follower agents and multiple leaders. The purpose of containment control is to drive all followers into the convex hull spanned by some static leaders. In [7], the containment control problem was studied when the communication graph was fixed, while containment control with switching topologies where the communication graphs were strongly connected was discussed in [9]. In [16], communication delays for containment control were taken into consideration.

Most of the above works focused on problems in which states and control input of agents had no constraints. In practical situations, agents are always subject to constraints due to physical limitations. For instance, the velocities of vehicles and satellites are constrained to lie in a certain zone. In [27], the consensus problem with convex constraints were studied; the nonconvex constraints of velocity and control input were discussed in [28]. In [29], switching topologies were taken into consideration, which are different from a consensus problem, since the final positions of followers do not converge to one point but a convex hull. The above methods cannot be directly applied to the containment problem with constraints. In [30], the projection operator was used to solve the containment problem with nonconvex control input constraints; the containment problem with position constraints was studied in [31].

In this work, the main task is to take into consideration the control input and position constraints for a containment control problem with switching topologies. A distributed algorithm is proposed to ensure that every follower in the multiagent system can converge into the convex hull spanned by the given leaders. Meanwhile, the position of every follower stays in a closed set given before and the control input does not need to keep lying in a hypercube. In the following, by using model transformation and analyzing the distance from each follower to the convex hull formed by given points, it is shown that the containment control problem can be solved when the directed spanning tree exists in the union of the graphs. In Section 2, the graph theory and multiagent dynamic model id introduced. In Section 3, we describe the main algorithm of the containment control system and the analysis of the main result when applied to a system with nonconvex control input and position constraints. In Section 4, we provide some simulation examples to confirm the feasibility of the algorithm. Finally, concluding notes and further works are remarked in Section 5.

2. Model and Statement

2.1. Preliminaries and Notations

Let $G(\mathcal{V},\mathcal{E},\mathcal{A})$ represent a directed graph, where $\mathcal{V}=\{1,2,\ldots,n+m\}$ is the set of nodes, $\mathcal{E}\subseteq\mathcal{V}\times\mathcal{V}$ is the set of edges, and $\mathcal{A}=[a_{ij}]$ is the weighted adjacency matrix. Each a_{ij} is nonnegative and $a_{ii}=0$ holds for every agent i. Suppose that $(j,i)\in\mathcal{E}$ is an edge of the directed graph, and a directed path is a sequence of edges of the form $(i_1,i_2),(i_2,i_3),\ldots$, otherwise, $a_{ij}(k)>0$ if the agent i can get information from agent j at time k and $a_{ij}(k)=0$.

Notations: The set of r-dimensional real column vectors is represented by $\mathbb{R}^r$; $\mathbb{R}$, $\mathbb{N}$, and $\mathbb{N}_+$ represent the set of positive real numbers, nonnegative integers, and positive integers, respectively; $\| x \|$ and x^T denote the Euclidean norm and transpose of the vector x, respectively; the projection of vector x onto a closed convex set X is represented by $P_Y(x)$, where $P_Y(x)=\underset{\tilde{x}\in X}{\mathrm{argmin}}\,\|>\| x-\tilde{x} \|$.

2.2. Description of Model

Consider a multiagent system with $n+m$ agents, i.e., n followers and m leaders. The set of all followers and leaders can be denoted, respectively, by $\mathcal{N}_f=\{1,2,..,n\}$ and $\mathcal{N}_l=\{n+1,n+2,..,n+m\}$. Let $y_{n+1},y_{n+2},\ldots y_{n+m}\in\mathbb{R}^r$ be the m static points of the leaders, which forms the convex hull denoted by $Y=\{\sum_{i=n+1}^{n+m}\alpha_i y_i|\alpha_i\geq 0,\ \sum_{i=n+1}^{n+m}\alpha_i=1\}$.

Each follower is constrained to lie in a convex constraint set that is denoted by X_i. The dynamics of follower is:

$$\begin{aligned} x_i((k+1)T) &= P_{X_i}[x_i(kT)+v_i(kT)T] \\ v_i((k+1)T) &= v_i(kT)+u_i(kT)T \end{aligned} \tag{1}$$

where $x_i(kT)\in\mathbb{R}^r$, $v_i(kT)\in\mathbb{R}^r$, and $u_i(kT)\in\mathbb{R}^r$ denote the position, the velocity, and the control input of the follower i, respectively. In many practical systems, the control input and position state of the agents are always constrained. Next, we give Assumption 1:

Assumption 1. *Let $0\in U_i\subseteq\mathbb{R}^r$ for $i=1,2,..,n$ be the bounded nonempty closed sets, $\max_{x\in U_i}\| S_{U_i}(x) \|=\overline{\lambda}_i$ and $\min_{x\notin U_i}\| S_{U_i}(x) \|=\underline{\lambda}_i$, where $\overline{\lambda}_i$ and $\underline{\lambda}_i$ are both positive constants. Then, $S_{U_i}(\cdot)$ is a constrained operator defined by $S_{U_i}(x)=\frac{x}{\|x\|}\max_{0\leq\delta\leq\|x\|}\{\delta|\frac{\delta\gamma x}{\|x\|}\in U_i,\forall 0\leq\gamma\leq 1\}$ where $x\neq 0$ and $S_{U_i}(0)=0$, as shown in Figure 1.*

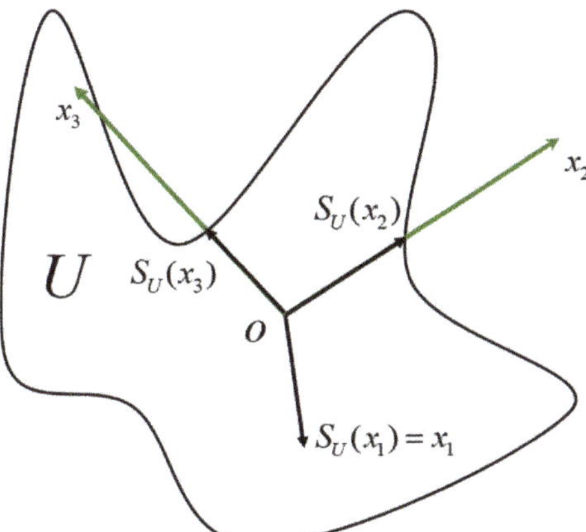

Figure 1. Example of $S_{U_i}(x)$.

Remark 1. *Assumption 1 aims to find a new vector $S_{U_i}(x)$ which has the same direction as vector x and satisfies $\gamma S_{U_i}(x) \in U_i$ for all $0 \leq \gamma \leq 1$ and $\| S_{U_i}(x) \| \leq \| x \|$ for the bounded nonempty closed set U_i. This assumption shows that every follower can move in all directions. Moreover, the control input of agents are constrained. We suppose each follower to be available in every direction in this paper.*

In this paper, our objective is to propose a proper algorithm to drive each follower, whose position and control input are constrained, to move into the convex hull Y formed by the leaders, that is, $\lim_{k\to\infty} \| x_i(k) - P_Y(x_i(k)) \| = 0$ for $i \in \mathcal{N}_f$.

3. Main Results

3.1. Containment Control Algorithm

In this section, we would give a nonlinear algorithm to solve the containment control problem with nonconvex control input and position constraints and switching topologies.

$$u_i = S_{U_i}[-p_i v_i(k) - c_i(k)(x_i(k) - P_{Y_i(k)}(x_i(k))) + \sum_{j\in N_i(k)} a_{ij}(k)(x_j(k) - x_i(k))] \tag{2}$$

for $i \in \mathcal{N}_f$, where $p_i > 0$ represents the velocity damping gain of follower i, $c_i(k) = c > 0$ when follower i can receive information directly from one or more leaders at time k, and $c_i(k) = 0$ otherwise, and $N_i(k)$ is the set of neighbors of agent i. $a_{ij}(k)$ is the edge weight of edge (j,i), and it is assumed that if $a_{ij}(k) > 0$, then $a_{ij}(k)$ is lower bounded by a positive constant. $Y_i(k) \subseteq Y$ is the convex hull formed by leaders whose information can be received by follower i directly at time k.

3.2. Analysis of Algorithm

In this section, we provide some necessary assumptions and lemmas to analyze the algorithm given in Section 3.1.

Assumption 2. *Give an infinite sequence of time $k_0, k_1, k_2, k_3, \ldots$ satisfying $k_0 > 0$ and $0 < k_{q+1} - k_q \leq C$ where $q \in N$ and $C \in N_+$. For every follower, it can be found at least one directed path from given static points to this follower in the union of the graphs in each time interval $[k_q, k_{q+1})$.*

Remark 2. *This assumption ensures that each follower can receive information from the given static leaders directly or indirectly in every time interval.*

It is clear that System (1) with (2) has strong nonlinearities due to the existence of the nonconvex control input and position constraints. For this reason, we first introduce a model transformation as follows:

Define

$$\begin{aligned}\theta_i(k) = & -c_i(k)[x_i(k) - P_{Y_i(k)}(x_i(k))] \\ & + \sum_{j\in N_i(k)} a_{ij}(k)(x_j(k) - x_i(k))\end{aligned}$$

and

$$h_i(k) = \begin{cases} 1, \; if \; -p_i v_i(k) + \theta_i(k) = 0 \\ \frac{\|S_{U_i}[-p_i v_i(k)+\theta_i(k)]\|}{\|-p_i v_i(k)+\theta_i(k)\|}, \; else \end{cases}$$

Then, System (2) can be rewritten as:

$$u_i(k) = h_i(k)(-p_i v_i(k) + \theta_i(k)) \tag{3}$$

Define

$$\widetilde{v}_i(k) = x_i(k) + \frac{2}{p_i} v_i(k)$$

and

$$\begin{aligned} e_i(k) = & P_{X_i}[x_i(k) + \tfrac{p_i}{2}(\widetilde{v}_i(k) - x_i(k)T)] \\ & -[x_i(k) + \tfrac{p_i}{2}(\widetilde{v}_i(k) - x_i(k)T)] \end{aligned} \tag{4}$$

for $i \in \mathcal{N}_f$.

Systems (1) and (2) can be transformed into:

$$\begin{aligned} x_i(k+1) = & P_{X_i}[x_i(k) + \tfrac{p_i}{2}(\widetilde{v}_i(k) - x_i(k)T)] \\ \widetilde{v}_i(k+1) = & P_{X_i}[x_i(k) + \tfrac{p_i}{2}(\widetilde{v}_i(k) - x_i(k)T)] \\ & +(1 - p_i h_i(k)T)(\widetilde{v}_i(k) - x_i(k)) \\ & + \tfrac{2h_i(k)T}{p_i} \sum_{j\in N_i(k)} a_{ij}(k)(x_j(k) - x_i(k)) \\ & - \tfrac{2h_i(k)c_iT}{p_i}(x_i(k) - P_{Y_i(k)}(x_i(k))) \end{aligned} \tag{5}$$

for $i \in \mathcal{N}_f$.

Put the definition of (4) into equation, System (5) could be rewritten as:

$$\begin{aligned} x_i(k+1) = & (1 - \tfrac{p_iT}{2})x_i(k) + \tfrac{p_i}{2}\widetilde{v}_i(k)T + e_i(k) \\ \widetilde{v}_i(k+1) = & [p_i(h_i(k) - \tfrac{1}{2})T - \tfrac{2h_i(k)T}{p_i}(\sum_{j\in N_i} a_{ij}(k) + c_i)]x_i(k) \\ & +(1 - p_i(h_i(k) - \tfrac{1}{2})T)\widetilde{v}_i(k) \\ & + \tfrac{2h_i(k)T}{p_i} \sum_{j\in N_i} a_{ij}(k)x_j(k) \\ & + \tfrac{2h_i(k)c_iT}{p_i} P_{Y_i(k)}(x_i(k)) + e_i(k) \end{aligned} \tag{6}$$

for $i \in \mathcal{N}_f$.

From System (6), it can be easily found that the sum of the coefficients of $x_i(k)$ and $\widetilde{v}_i(k)$ in the first equation and the coefficients of $x_i(k)$, $\widetilde{v}_i(k)$, $x_j(k)$, and $P_{Y_i(k)}(x_i(k))$ in the other equation are both equal to 1, which means the existence of $e_i(k)$ destroys the linearity of $x_i(k+1)$ with $x_i(k)$ and $\widetilde{v}_i(k)$, $\widetilde{v}_i(k+1)$ with $x_i(k)$, $\widetilde{v}_i(k)$, $x_j(k)$, and $P_{Y_i(k)}(x_i(k))$. Hence, the next step is to remove $e_i(k)$ when $k \to \infty$. Give the following definition:

$$\begin{aligned} & g_i(k) = \sum_{j\in N_i(k)} a_{ij}(k) + c_i(k) \\ & \tau_{ia}(k) = [p_iT(h_i - \tfrac{1}{2}) - \tfrac{2h_iT}{p_i} g_i(k)]/(1 - \tfrac{2h_iT}{p_i} g_i(k)) \\ & \tau_{ib}(k) = [1 - p_iT(h_i - \tfrac{1}{2})]/(1 - \tfrac{2h_iT}{p_i} g_i(k)) \\ & \tau_{ic}(k) = 1 - \tfrac{2h_iT}{p_i} g_i(k) \end{aligned} \tag{7}$$

and

$$q_{ia}(k) = \tau_{ia}(k)x_i(k) + \tau_{ib}(k)\tilde{v}_i(k) + \frac{1}{\tau_{ic}(k)}e_i(k) \tag{8}$$

for $i \in \mathcal{N}_f$. Then, (6) could be transformed as:

$$\begin{aligned}\tilde{v}_i(k+1) = \tau_{ic}(k)q_{ia}(k) + \tfrac{2h_i(k)T}{p_i} \sum_{j\in N_i} a_{ij}(k)x_j(k) \\ + \tfrac{2h_i(k)c_iT}{p_i} P_Y(x_i(k))\end{aligned} \tag{9}$$

for $i \in \mathcal{N}_f$.

Assumption 3. $\| \sum_{j\in N_i(k)} a_{ij}(k)(x_j(k) - x_i(k)) \| \leq Q_i/2$ *and* $\| c_i(k)[x_i(k) - P_{Y_i(k)}(x_i(k))] \| \leq Q_i/2$ *for some constant* $Q_i > 0$.

Remark 3. *This assumption could be satisfied easily. By using the operator* $S_{U_i}(x)$ *defined in Assumption 1, the terms* $\sum_{j\in N_i(k)} a_{ij}(k)(x_j(k) - x_i(k))$ *and* $c_i(k)[x_i(k) - P_{Y_i(k)}(x_i(k))]$ *can be redefined as* $S_{V_i}[\sum_{j\in N_i(k)} a_{ij}(k)(x_j(k) - x_i(k))]$ *and* $S_{V_i}[c_i(k)[x_i(k) - P_{Y_i(k)}(x_i(k))]]$, *where* $V_i = \{y| \| y \| \leq \frac{1}{2}Q_i\}$. *As the definition of* $h_i(k)$, *we define that* $\bar{h}_i(k) = \frac{\| S_{V_i}[\sum_{j\in N_i(k)} a_{ij}(k)(x_j(k)-x_i(k))] \|}{\| \sum_{j\in N_i(k)} a_{ij}(k)(x_j(k)-x_i(k)) \|}$ *and* $\tilde{h}_i(k) = \frac{\| S_{V_i}[c_i(k)[x_i(k)-P_{Y_i(k)}(x_i(k))]] \|}{\| c_i(k)[x_i(k)-P_{Y_i(k)}(x_i(k))] \|}$. *It is clear that the two terms can be expressed as* $\sum_{j\in N_i(k)} \bar{h}_i(k)a_{ij}(k)(x_j(k) - x_i(k))$ *and* $c_i(k)\tilde{h}_i(k)[x_i(k) - P_{Y_i(k)}(x_i(k))]$, *where* $0 < \bar{h}_i(k)$, $\tilde{h}_i(k) \leq 1$. *Then, it can be similarly proven that* $\bar{h}_i(k)$ *and* $\tilde{h}_i(k)$ *are lower bounded by a positive constant with the discussion in Lemma 1.*

Lemma 1. *Under Assumption 4 and the definition of operator* $S_{U_i}(\cdot)$, *we have that if* $0 \leq Q_i \leq \underline{\lambda}_i/2$, *there exists* $k_m > 0$ *such that:*

$$\sigma_i \leq h_i(k) \leq 1$$

for $i \in \mathcal{N}_f$ *and* $k \geq k_m$, *where* $\sigma_i = (\underline{\lambda}_i - Q_i)/(2Q_i)$.

Proof of Lemma 1. From the definition of $h_i(k)$, it is apparently that $0 < h_i(k) < 1$ and $\| -p_iv_i(k) + \theta_i(k) \| > \underline{\lambda}_i$ when $-p_iv_i(k) + \theta_i(k) \neq S_{U_i}[-p_iv_i(k) + \theta_i(k)]$, and $h_i(k) = 1$ otherwise. Define $\Phi_i(k) = \frac{1}{2} \| v_i(k) \|^2$. From the definition of difference, there is:

$$\begin{aligned}\Delta\Phi_i(k) &= \Phi_i(k+1) - \Phi_i(k) \\ &= (\| v_i^T(k+1) \|^2 - \| v_i^T(k) \|^2)/2 \\ &\leq -2p_ih_i(k)\Phi_i(k) + Q_i\sqrt{2\Phi_i(k)} \\ &= -\sqrt{2\Phi_i(k)}(p_ih_i(k)\sqrt{2\Phi_i(k)} - Q_i)\end{aligned}$$

Considering the property of $h_i(k)$, it can be easily deduced that $\underline{\lambda}_i/(p_i \| v_i(k) \| + Q_i) \leq h_i(k) < 1$. Given all this and the condition of Lemma 1, we have:

$$\begin{aligned}\| v_i(k) \| &\leq -\sqrt{2\Phi_i(k)}(\tfrac{p_i\underline{\lambda}_i}{p_i\|v_i(k)\|+Q_i}\sqrt{2\Phi_i(k)} - Q_i) \\ &\leq -\sqrt{2\Phi_i(k)}(\tfrac{p_i\underline{\lambda}_i}{p_i+Q_i/\|v_i(k)\|} - Q_i)\end{aligned}$$

When $p_i\underline{\lambda}_i/(p_i + Q_i/ \| v_i(k) \|) - Q_i > \varepsilon_0$, which is $\| v_i(k) \| > Q_i(\varepsilon_0 + Q_i)/[p_i(\underline{\lambda}_i - Q_i - \varepsilon_0)]$, $\varepsilon_0 > 0$ is a sufficiently small constant, $\| v_i(k) \| \leq -Q_i(\varepsilon_0 + Q_i)\varepsilon_0/[p_i(\underline{\lambda}_i - Q_i - \varepsilon_0)]$ can be obtained under the condition of this lemma. Therefore, there exists a constant $k_m > 0$ such that $\| v_i(k) \| > Q_i(\varepsilon_0 + Q_i)/[p_i(\underline{\lambda}_i - Q_i - \varepsilon_0)]$ for all $k \geq k_m$. From the assumption of Lemma 1 that $0 \leq Q_i \leq \underline{\lambda}_i/2$, we have $Q_i^2/[p_i(\underline{\lambda}_i - Q_i)] > (\underline{\lambda}_i - Q_i)/p_i$.

Then, we get $(\underline{\lambda}_i - Q_i - \varepsilon_0)/Q_i \le h_i(k) \le 1$ for all $k \ge k_m$. Since that ε_0 can be arbitrarily small, $(\underline{\lambda}_i - Q_i)/2Q_i \le h_i(k) \le 1$ holds, for all $k \ge k_m$. □

Assumption 4. *Suppose that* $0 < p_i T < 1$, $p_i^2 - 4d_{im} > \alpha_1$, $d_{im} > \sum_{j \in N_i} a_{ij}(k) + c_i(k)$ *for* $\alpha_i > 0$, $d_{im} > 0$, *for all* $i \in \mathcal{F}$ and k.

Remark 4. *This assumption gives the design rules of the algorithm parameters. The parameter* p_i *can be selected by the following steps:*

(1) *Select the value of* p_i *such that* $0 < p_i T < 1$ *and* $p_i^2 - 4d_{im} > \alpha_1$ *for two constants* $\alpha_i > 0$ *and* $d_{im} > 0$.

(2) *Select the values of each nonzero* $a_{ij}(k)$ *and c such that* $\sum_{j \in N_i} a_{ij}(k) + c_i(k) < d_{im}$ *for each k.*

Lemma 2 [32]. *Let* $X \subseteq \mathbb{R}^r$ *denote a nonempty closed convex set.* $x_i \in \mathbb{R}^r$ *and scalars* $a_i \ge 0$ *satisfying* $\sum_{i=1}^{n} a_i = 1$. *It follows* $\| \sum_{i=1}^{n} a_i x_i - P_X(\sum_{i=1}^{n} a_i x_i) \| \le \sum_{i=1}^{n} a_i \| x_i - P_X(x_i) \|$.

Lemma 3 [33]. *Considering a closed convex set* $0 \ne Z \subseteq R^r$, *for any* $x, y \in R^r$ *and all* $z \in Z$, *inequalities* $[x - P_Z(x)]^T (x - z) \ge 0$, $\| P_Z(x) - z \|^2 \le \| x - z \|^2 - \| P_Z(x) - x \|^2$ *and* $\| P_Z(x) - P_Z(y) \| \le \| x - y \|$ *hold.*

In order to eliminate $e_i(k)$, we present the following lemmas.

Lemma 4. *Under Assumption 4, the following statements stand for all* $i \in \mathcal{N}_f$ *and all k:*

(1) $\tau_{ia}(k) + \tau_{ib}(k) = 1$ *and* $\tau_{ic}(k) + \frac{2h_i(k)T}{p_i} \sum_{j \in N_i} a_{ij}(k) + \frac{2h_i(k)c_i T}{p_i} = 1$;

(2) $\alpha_2 < \tau_{ia}(k) < \frac{1}{2}$, $\frac{1}{2} < \tau_{ib}(k) < 1 - \alpha_2$, $\frac{1}{2} < \tau_{ic}(k) < 1$.

Proof of Lemma 4.

(1) As the definition in (7), $\tau_{ic}(k) = 1 - \frac{2h_i T}{p_i} g_i(k)$ and $g_i(k) = \sum_{j \in N_i(k)} a_{ij}(k) + c_i(k)$, for all $i \in \mathcal{F}$ and all k. It follows that

$$
\begin{aligned}
&\tau_{ic}(k) + \tfrac{2h_i(k)T}{p_i} \sum_{j \in N_i} a_{ij}(k) + \tfrac{2h_i(k)c_i T}{p_i} \\
&= 1 - \tfrac{2h_i(k)T}{p_i} \Big(\sum_{j \in N_i(k)} a_{ij}(k) + c_i(k) \Big) \\
&+ \tfrac{2h_i(k)T}{p_i} \sum_{j \in N_i} a_{ij}(k) + \tfrac{2h_i(k)c_i(k)T}{p_i} \\
&= 1
\end{aligned}
$$

Note that $\tau_{ia}(k) = [p_i T(h_i - \frac{1}{2}) - \frac{2h_i T}{p_i} g_i(k)]/(1 - \frac{2h_i T}{p_i} g_i(k))$ and $\tau_{ib}(k) = [1 - p_i T(h_i - \frac{1}{2})]/(1 - \frac{2h_i T}{p_i} g_i(k))$, it is obviously that $\tau_{ia}(k) + \tau_{ib}(k) = 1$.

(2) Under Assumption 4, $0 < p_i T < 1$ and $p_i^2 - 4d_{im} > 0$. It can be deduced that $\frac{1}{2} > \frac{1}{2} p_i T > 2d_{im} T/p_i > 2g_i T/p_i \ge 2c_i T/p_i \ge 0$. According to the definition of τ_{ib}, we have $1/2 < \tau_{ib} < 1 - \alpha_2$ for some constant $0 < \alpha_2 < 1/2$. In the proof of Lemma 4(1), $\tau_{ia}(k) + \tau_{ib}(k) = 1$. Thus, $\alpha_2 < \tau_{ia}(k) < 1/2$; also under $0 \le 2g_i T/p_i < 1/2$ and Lemma 1, it shows that $\frac{1}{2} < \tau_{ic}(k) = 1 - \frac{2h_i T}{p_i} g_i(k) < 1$. □

Lemma 5. *Under Assumptions 4 and 5, the following two inequalities hold for all* $i \in \mathcal{N}_f$ *and all k:*

Proof of Lemma 5.

(1) Let $q_{ib}(k) = (1 - \frac{p_i T}{2})x_i(k) + \frac{p_i}{2}\widetilde{v}_i(k)T$ for $i \in \mathcal{N}_f$. Since $P_Y(q_{ib}(k)) \in X_i$, we have

$$\begin{aligned} &\| x_i(k+1) - P_Y(x_i(k+1)) \| \\ =&\| P_{X_i}(q_{ib}(k)) - P_Y(P_{X_i}(q_{ib}(k))) \| \\ \leq&\| P_{X_i}(q_{ib}(k)) - P_Y(q_{ib}(k)) \| \end{aligned}$$

for $i \in \mathcal{N}_f$. From Lemma 3, we have

$$\begin{aligned} &\| x_i(k+1) - P_Y(x_i(k+1)) \|^2 \\ \leq&\| P_{X_i}(q_{ib}(k)) - P_Y(q_{ib}(k)) \|^2 \\ \leq&\| q_{ib}(k) - P_Y(q_{ib}(k)) \|^2 - \| P_{X_i}(q_{ib}(k)) - q_{ib}(k) \|^2 \\ =&\| q_{ib}(k) - P_Y(q_{ib}(k)) \|^2 - \| e_i(k) \|^2 \end{aligned}$$

for $i \in \mathcal{N}_f$. Then, we use Lemma 2. It can transform to:

$$\begin{aligned} &\| x_i(k+1) - P_Y(x_i(k+1)) \| \\ \leq&\| q_{ib}(k) - P_Y(q_{ib}(k)) \| \\ =&\| (1 - \tfrac{p_i T}{2})x_i(k) + \tfrac{p_i}{2}\widetilde{v}_i(k)T \\ &-P_Y((1 - \tfrac{p_i T}{2})x_i(k) + \tfrac{p_i}{2}\widetilde{v}_i(k)T) \| \\ \leq& (1 - \tfrac{p_i T}{2}) \| x_i(k) - P_Y(x_i(k)) \| \\ &+\tfrac{p_i T}{2} \| \widetilde{v}_i(k) - P_Y(\widetilde{v}_i(k)) \| \end{aligned}$$

for $i \in \mathcal{N}_f$.

(2) Notice that $2c_i h_i(k)T/p_i \geq 0$, $2a_{ij}(k)h_i(k)T/p_i \geq 0$, $\tau_{ic}(k) > 1/2$ and $\tau_{ic}(k) + (2h_i(k)T/p_i) \sum\limits_{j \in N_i} a_{ij}(k) + 2h_i(k)c_i T/p_i = 1$. It follows that

$$\begin{aligned} &\| \widetilde{v}_i(k+1) - P_Y(\widetilde{v}_i(k+1)) \| \\ \leq& \tau_{ic}(k) \| q_{ia}(k) - P_Y(q_{ia}(k)) \| + \tfrac{2h_i(k)T}{p_i} \\ &\times \sum_{j \in N_i} a_{ij}(k) \| x_j(k) - P_Y(x_j(k)) \| + \tfrac{2h_i(k)c_i T}{p_i} \\ &\times \| P_{Y_i(k)}(x_i(k)) - P_Y(P_{Y_i(k)}(x_i(k))) \| \end{aligned}$$

for $i \in \mathcal{N}_f$. Because $Y_i(k) \subseteq Y$, it follows that

$$\begin{aligned} &\| \widetilde{v}_i(k+1) - P_Y(\widetilde{v}_i(k+1)) \| \\ \leq& \tau_{ic}(k) \| q_{ia}(k) - P_Y(q_{ia}(k)) \| + \tfrac{2h_i(k)T}{p_i} \\ &\times \sum_{j \in N_i} a_{ij}(k) \| x_j(k) - P_Y(x_j(k)) \| \end{aligned}$$

for $i \in \mathcal{N}_f$. □

Lemma 6. *Under Assumption 4, the following inequality:*

$$\| q_{ia}(k) - P_Y(q_{ia}(k)) \| \leq \tau_{ia}(k) \| x_i(k) - P_Y(x_i(k)) \| + \tau_{ib}(k) \| \widetilde{v}_i(k) - P_Y(\widetilde{v}_i(k)) \|$$

holds for all $i \in \mathcal{N}_f$ and all k.

Proof of Lemma 6. Let $q_{ic}(k) = \tau_{ia}(k)x_i(k) + \tau_{ib}(k)\widetilde{v}_i(k)$ for $i \in \mathcal{N}_f$. It can be easily observed that $\| q_{ia}(k) - P_Y(q_{ia}(k)) \| \leq \| q_{ia}(k) - P_Y(q_{ic}(k)) \|$ for $i \in \mathcal{N}_f$.

When $e_i(k) = 0$, $\| q_{ia}(k) - P_Y(q_{ic}(k)) \| = \| q_{ic}(k) - P_Y(q_{ic}(k)) \|$ for $i \in \mathcal{N}_f$. Now, it should be proven that when $e_i(k) \neq 0$, $\| q_{ia}(k) - P_Y(q_{ic}(k)) \| \leq \| q_{ic}(k) - P_Y(q_{ic}(k)) \|$ for $i \in \mathcal{N}_f$. Define $q_{id}(k) = P_{X_i}(q_{ib}(k))$ for convenience, and it is clear that $e_i(k) = q_{id}(k) - q_{ib}(k)$.

Now, define two hyperplanes Ψ_1 and Ψ_2, shown in Figure 2, that $e_i(k)$ is perpendicular to them, $q_{id}(k) \in \Psi_1$ and $q_{ia}(k) \in \Psi_2$. Meanwhile, it is clear that $e_i(k)/\tau_{ic}(k) = q_{ia}(k) - q_{ic}(k)$ is perpendicular to the hyperplanes. Then, define $\beta_{ia}(k)$ and $\beta_{ib}(k)$, as shown in Figure 2.

$$\beta_{ia}(k) = (1-\delta_{i1})x_i(k) + \delta_{i1}\widetilde{v}_i(k) \in \Psi_1 \beta_{ib}(k) = (1-\delta_{i2})x_i(k) + \delta_{i2}\widetilde{v}_i(k) \in \Psi_2$$

for the constants $0 < \delta_{i1} < 1$ and $0 < \delta_{i2} < 1$.

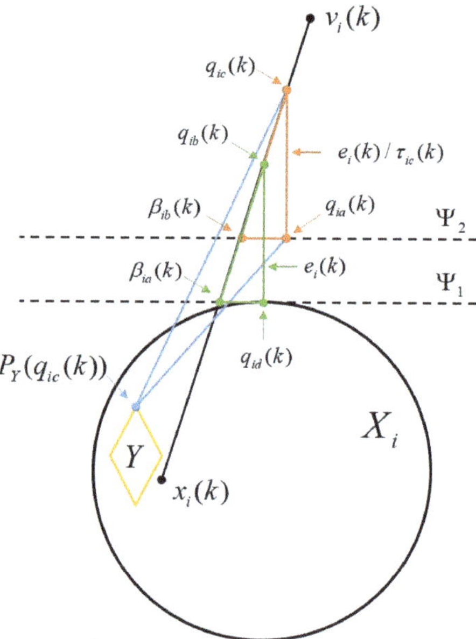

Figure 2. Example of similar triangles.

It follows that there exist two similar triangles constituted by points $\beta_{ia}(k)$, $q_{id}(k)$, $q_{ib}(k)$ and points $\beta_{ib}(k)$, $q_{ia}(k)$, $q_{ic}(k)$. Now, the characters of similar triangles can be applied.

As shown in Figure 2, define $a_{i1} = p_iT/2 - \delta_{i1} > 0$. It follows that $q_{ib}(k) - \beta_{ia} = a_{i1}(\widetilde{v}_i(k) - x_i(k))$. Since the similarity of triangles, it can be obtained that $q_{ic}(k) - \beta_{ib} = a_{i1}(\widetilde{v}_i(k) - x_i(k))/\tau_{ic}(k)$, i.e., $\beta_{ib} = q_{ic}(k) - a_{i1}(\widetilde{v}_i(k) - x_i(k))/\tau_{ic}(k)$. $\delta_{i2} = (1 - p_iT + \delta_{i1})/\tau_{ic} > \delta_{i1}$ can be obtained in the same way. Moreover, Ψ_2 and X are at the different sides of Ψ_1. Given all this, it follows that the angle between vectors $q_{ia}(k) - q_{ic}(k)$ and $q_{ia}(k) - P_Y(q_{ic}(k))$ is an obtuse angle, which means $\| q_{ia}(k) - P_Y(q_{ic}(k)) \| \leq \| q_{ic}(k) - P_Y(q_{ic}(k)) \|$. Notice Lemma 2 and 4(1), it can be seen that $\| q_{ic}(k) - P_Y(q_{ic}(k)) \| \leq \tau_{ia}(k) \| x_i(k) - P_Y(x_i(k)) \| + \tau_{ib}(k) \| \widetilde{v}_i(k) - P_Y(\widetilde{v}_i(k)) \|$. Above all, it follows that

$$\begin{aligned} \| q_{ia}(k) - P_Y(q_{ia}(k)) \| &\leq \| q_{ia}(k) - P_Y(q_{ic}(k)) \| \\ &\leq \| q_{ic}(k) - P_Y(q_{ic}(k)) \| \\ &\leq \tau_{ia}(k) \| x_i(k) - P_Y(x_i(k)) \| \\ &\quad + \tau_{ib}(k) \| \widetilde{v}_i(k) - P_Y(\widetilde{v}_i(k)) \| \end{aligned}$$

for $i \in \mathcal{N}_f$. □

3.3. Analysis of Result

In this section, the result of containment control using the given algorithm would be analyzed. First, we design a Lyapunov function.

Let $\xi(k) = [x_1^T(k), \widetilde{v}_1^T(k), \ldots\ldots x_n^T(k), \widetilde{v}_n^T(k)]$. Design a Lyapunov function as:

$$V(k) = \max_{i \in \{1,2,\ldots 2n\}} \{\|\xi_i(k) - P_Y(\xi_i(k))\|\}$$

Summarizing the above lemma and analysis, it follows that

$$\| x_i(k+1) - P_Y(x_i(k+1)) \| \leq \max_{i \in F}\{\| x_i(k) - P_Y(x_i(k)) \|, \| \widetilde{v}_i(k) - P_Y(\widetilde{v}_i(k)) \|\}$$

and

$$\| \widetilde{v}_i(k+1) - P_Y(\widetilde{v}_i(k+1)) \| \leq \max_{i \in F}\{\| x_i(k) - P_Y(x_i(k)) \|, \| \widetilde{v}_i(k) - P_Y(\widetilde{v}_i(k)) \|\}$$

for all $i \in \mathcal{N}_f$.

Next, we analyze the convergence of containment control problem under the given algorithm in the time interval $[k_l, k_{l+1})$.

Case A. Assuming that there is an agent i_q that can get information from one of the static leaders at $k_{l0} \in [k_l, k_{l+1})$. Clearly, $c_{i_q} > 0$ and $\tau_{i_q c}(k) + 2h_{i_q}(k)T/p_{i_q} \sum_{j \in N_{i_q}} a_{i_q j}(k) = 1 - 2h_{i_q}(k)c_{i_q}T/p_{i_q} < 1$. Note that

$$\begin{aligned} \| \widetilde{v}_i(k+1) - P_Y(\widetilde{v}_i(k+1)) \| \leq\ & \tau_{ic}(k) \| q_{ia}(k) - P_Y(q_{ia}(k)) \| \\ & + \frac{2h_i(k)T}{p_i} \sum_{j \in N_i} a_{ij}(k) \| x_j(k) - P_Y(x_j(k)) \| \end{aligned}$$

and

$$\begin{aligned} \| \widetilde{v}_{i_q}(k_{l0}+1) - P_Y(\widetilde{v}_{i_q}(k_{l0}+1)) \| & \leq (1 - \frac{2h_{i_q}(k_{l0})c_{i_q}T}{p_{i_q}})V(k_{l0}) \\ & \leq (1 - \frac{2h_{i_q}(k_{l0})c_{i_q}T}{p_{i_q}})V(k_l) \triangleq m_1 V(k_l) \end{aligned}$$

where $0 < m_1 < 1$.

Moreover, there is

$$\begin{aligned} & \| x_{i_q}(k_{l0}+1) - P_Y(x_{i_q}(k_{l0}+1)) \| \leq (1 - \tfrac{1}{2}p_{i_q}T)V(k_{l0}) + \tfrac{1}{2}p_{i_q}T \\ & \times (1 - \frac{2h_{i_q}(k_{l0})c_{i_q}T}{p_{i_q}})V(k_{l0}) \\ & \leq (1 - h_{i_q}(k_{l0})c_{i_q}T^2)V(k_l) \triangleq m_2 V(k_l) \end{aligned}$$

where $0 < m_2 < 1$.

Case B. Suppose that there exists an agent i_q that satisfies $\| \widetilde{v}_{i_q}(k_{l0}) - P_Y(\widetilde{v}_{i_q}(k_{l0})) \| \leq (1 - m_3)V(k_l)$ at time $k_{l0} \in [k_l, k_{l+1})$. It can be deduced from Lemmas 4 and 5 that

$$\begin{aligned} \| x_{i_q}(k_{l0}+1) - P_Y(x_{i_q}(k_{l0}+1)) \| \leq\ & (1 - \tfrac{1}{2}p_{i_q}T)V(k_l) + \tfrac{1}{2}p_{i_q}T(1 - m_3)V(k_l) \\ & \leq (1 - m_3 h_{i_q}(k_{l0})c_{i_q}T)V(k_l) \triangleq m_4 V(k_l) \end{aligned}$$

where $0 < m_4 < 1$.

Moreover, it follows that

$$\begin{aligned} & \| \widetilde{v}_{i_q}(k_{l0}+1) - P_Y(\widetilde{v}_{i_q}(k_{l0}+1)) \| \\ & \leq \tau_{i_q c}(k_{l0})\tau_{i_q a}(k_{l0})V(k_l) + m_3\tau_{i_q c}(k_{l0})\tau_{i_q b}(k_{l0})V(k_l) \\ & + \frac{2h_{i_q}(k_{l0})T}{p_{i_q}} \sum_{j \in N_{i_q}, j \neq i_q} a_{i_q j}(k_{l0})V(k_l) \\ & \leq [1 - (1 - \tfrac{1}{2}p_{i_q}h_{i_q}(k_{l0})T)(1 - m_3)]V(k_l) \\ & \leq m_4(k_{l0}+1)V(k_l) \end{aligned}$$

Then, after recursive calculations, we can obtain $\| x_{i_q}(k_l+1) - P_Y(x_{i_q}(k_l+1)) \| \leq m_4 V(k_l)$ and $\| \widetilde{v}_{i_q}(k_l+1) - P_Y(\widetilde{v}_{i_q}(k_l+1)) \| \leq m_4 V(k_l)$ where $0 < m_4 < 1$.

Case C. Suppose that there exist 2 agents i_q and i_s that satisfy $\| x_{i_q}(k_{l0}) - P_Y(x_{i_q}(k_{l0})) \| \leq m_5 V(k_l)$ for some constant $0 \leq m_5 < 1$ and $a_{i_s i_q} > \gamma$ for some constant $\gamma > 0$ at time $k_{l0} \in [k_l, k_{l+1})$, which means agent i_s can receive information from agent i_q at k_{l0}. It follows that

$$\begin{aligned} \| \widetilde{v}_{i_s}(k_{l0}+1) - P_Y(\widetilde{v}_{i_s}(k_{l0}+1)) \| & \leq \tau_{i_s c}(k_{l0})V(k_l) + \tfrac{2h_{i_s}(k_{l0})T}{p_{i_s}} \\ & \times \sum_{j \in N_{i_s}, j \neq i_s} a_{i_s j}(k_{l0})V(k_l) + \tfrac{2h_{i_s}(k_{l0})Tm_5}{p_{i_s}} a_{i_s i_q}(k_{l0})V(k_l) \\ & \leq [1 - (1-m_5)\tfrac{2h_{i_s}(k_{l0})T}{p_{i_s}}\gamma]V(k_l) \triangleq m_6 V(k_l) \end{aligned}$$

where $0 < m_6 < 1$.

From $p_{i_s}T < 1$, it can be obtained that

$$0 < 1 - (1-m_5)\frac{2h_{i_s}(k_{l0})T}{p_{i_s}}\gamma < 1 - (1-m_5)\gamma 2h_{i_s}(k_{l0})T^2 < 1$$

Hence, by using Lemma 5, it follows that

$$\begin{aligned} \| x_{i_s}(k_{l0}+1) & - P_Y(x_{i_s}(k_{l0}+1)) \| \leq (1 - \tfrac{1}{2}p_{i_s}T)V(k_l) + \tfrac{1}{2}p_{i_s}T \\ & \times [1 - (1-m_5)\tfrac{2h_{i_s}(k_{l0})T}{p_{i_s}}\gamma]V(k_l) \\ & \leq [1 - (1-m_5)\gamma 2h_{i_s}(k_{l0})T^2]V(k_l) = m_6 V(k_l) \end{aligned}$$

where $0 < m_6 < 1$.

Theorem 1. Based on Assumptions 1–4, applying constrained control input algorithm (2) to System (1), all followers are driven into the convex hull spanned by leaders, i.e., $\lim_{k \to +\infty} \| x_i(k) - P_Y(x_i(k)) \| = 0$ for $i \in \mathcal{N}_f$.

Proof of Theorem 1. As shown in Assumption 2, it can always find one or more follower that can receive information from one of the static leaders directly in every time interval $[k_l, k_{l+1})$, which guarantees the condition of Case A. That is, $\| \widetilde{v}_{i_q}(k_{l0}+1) - P_Y(\widetilde{v}_{i_q}(k_{l0}+1)) \| \leq m_1 V(k_l)$ and $\| x_{i_q}(k_{l0}+1) - P_Y(x_{i_q}(k_{l0}+1)) \| \leq m_2 V(k_l)$ hold, where $0 < m_1 < 1$ and $0 < m_2 < 1$; then, consider Case B, it follows that $\| x_{i_q}(k) - P_Y(x_{i_q}(k)) \| \leq m_4 V(k_l)$ and $\| \widetilde{v}_{i_q}(k) - P_Y(\widetilde{v}_{i_q}(k)) \| \leq m_4 V(k_l)$ works for $0 < m_4 < 1$ and all $k \in [k_{l+1}, k_{l+n+1})$. It is clear that agent $i_s \neq i_q$ which could get information from agent i_q or one of the static leaders at $k \in [k_{l+1}, k_{l+2})$ exists. Hence, by using the calculation of Cases A, B, and C, it could be obtained that $\| \widetilde{v}_{i_s}(k) - P_Y(\widetilde{v}_{i_s}(k)) \| \leq \widetilde{m}_6 V(k_l)$ and $\| x_{i_s}(k) - P_Y(x_{i_s}(k)) \| \leq \widetilde{m}_6 V(k_l)$ for $0 < \widetilde{m}_6 < 1$ and all $k \in [k_{l+2}, k_{l+n})$. Recall that the constants m_1, m_2, m_4, and $\widetilde{m}_6$ are only affected by constants c_i, T, p_i, h_i, γ, and topologies in the time interval. Therefore, it can certainly find a constant $0 < \eta < 1$ satisfying $\eta > m_i$, where $i = 1,2,4,6$. Given all this, $V(k_{m+n}) < \eta^n V(k_m)$ holds. To summarize all the calculations, we have $\lim_{k \to +\infty} \| x_i(k) - P_Y(x_i(k)) \| = \lim_{k \to +\infty} V(k) = 0$ for $i \in \mathcal{N}_f$. □

4. A Numerical Example

4.1. Simulation Parament Configuration

Give a multiagent system composed of 6 followers and 4 leaders. The graphs of switching topologies are shown in Figure 3. The switching step of the system is 0.5 s and the sequence of the graphs is $\{G_a, G_b\}$, $\{G_b, G_c\}$, $\{G_c, G_d\}$, $\{G_d, G_a\}$. The weights of all edges $a_{ij} = 0.7$. The parameters are $c_i = 0.3$ and $p_i = 12$ for $i \in \mathcal{N}_f$ and the sampling time is $T = 0.1$ s. The control input constraint set is $U_i = \{x | \| x - [0, -\sqrt{3}/2]^T \| \leq 0.5\} \cup \{x | \|$

$x \| \leq 1\} \cup \{x| \parallel x - [0, \sqrt{3}/2]^T \parallel \leq 0.5\}$. The position constraint sets of the followers are $X_1 = \{x| \parallel x - [0,1]^T \parallel \leq \sqrt{6}\}$ and $X_2 = \{x| \parallel x - [2,1]^T \parallel \leq \sqrt{6}\}$. For followers, the initial states of position are $[-1.5, 2; -2, 0.5; 0, -1; 3, 3; 4, 1; 3.5, 0]^T$ and the initial states of velocity states are $[1,1;1,0;1,1;-1,-1;-1,0;-1,1]^T$. For leaders, the initial states of position is $[0,2;2,2;2,0;0,0]^T$.

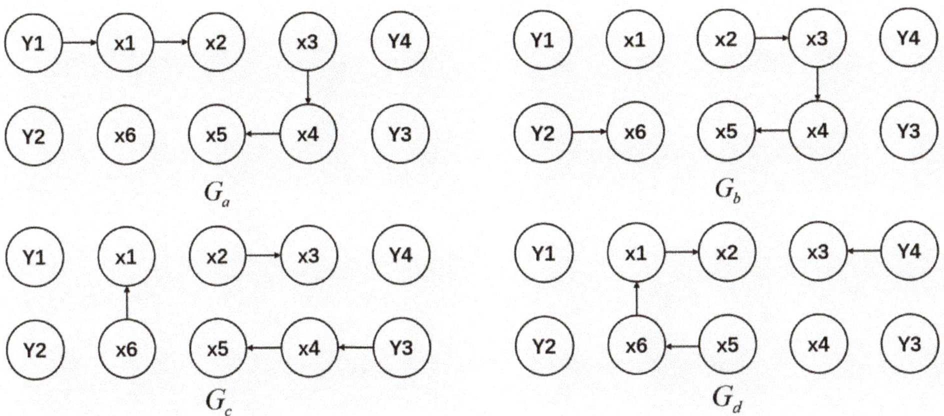

Figure 3. Switching graphs.

4.2. Simulation Result

The convex hull is spanned by static points, as illustrated in Figure 4. Figure 5 shows the control input of followers. The containment errors of followers are shown in Figure 6.

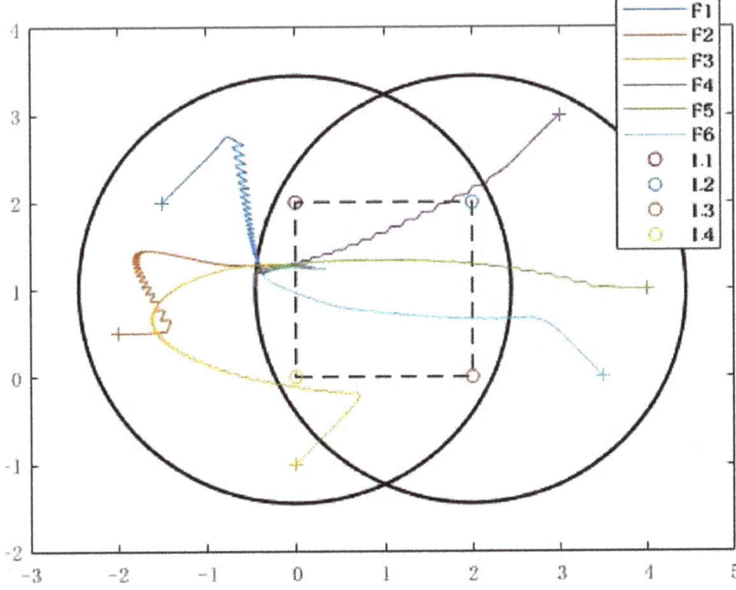

Figure 4. Position states $x_i(k)$ of all agents.

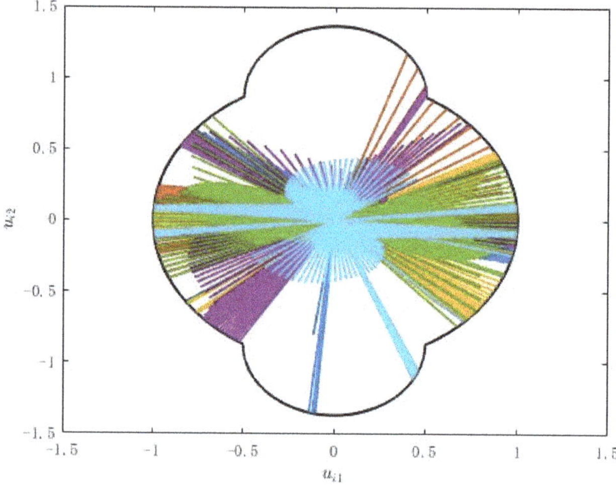

Figure 5. Control input $u_i(k)$ of followers.

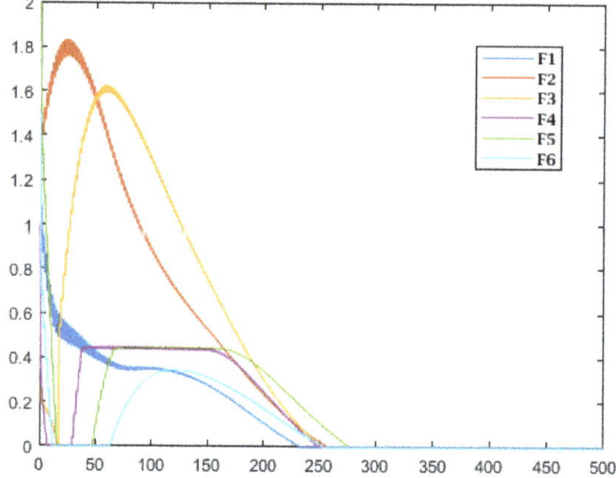

Figure 6. Containment errors of followers.

The switching graphs are illustrated in Figure 3 which satisfy the assumption that each follower could get information from at least one leader directly or indirectly in every time interval. In Figure 4, Followers 1, 2, and 3 stay in the left circle which illustrates the constraint of position, while Followers 4, 5, and 6 stay in the right circle. The convex region spread by the 4 leaders is the target region. Figure 5 gives the constraints of control input that is a nonconvex hull. It shows the containment errors of followers by using the distance form every follower to the target region in Figure 6.

4.3. Simulation Comparison

In this section, we provide some simulation comparison results.

As compared with Figure 5, Figure 7 shows the control input without constraints. It is clear that our algorithm could be more practical in reality. In Figure 8, we can see that the algorithm can still achieve containment control when a sudden interference happens, which means the algorithm has stability to some extent.

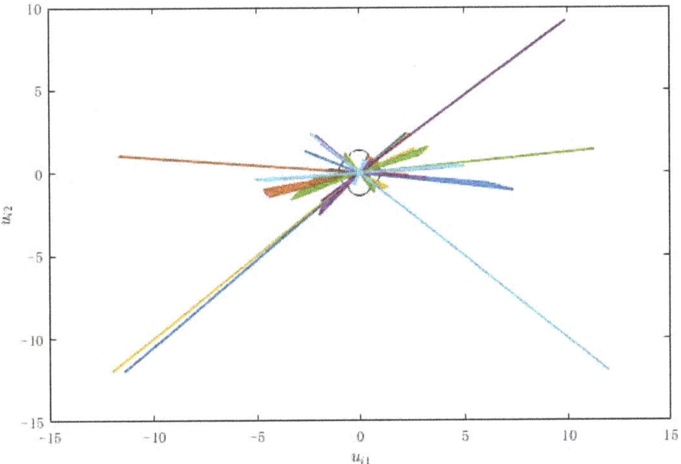

Figure 7. Control input without constraints.

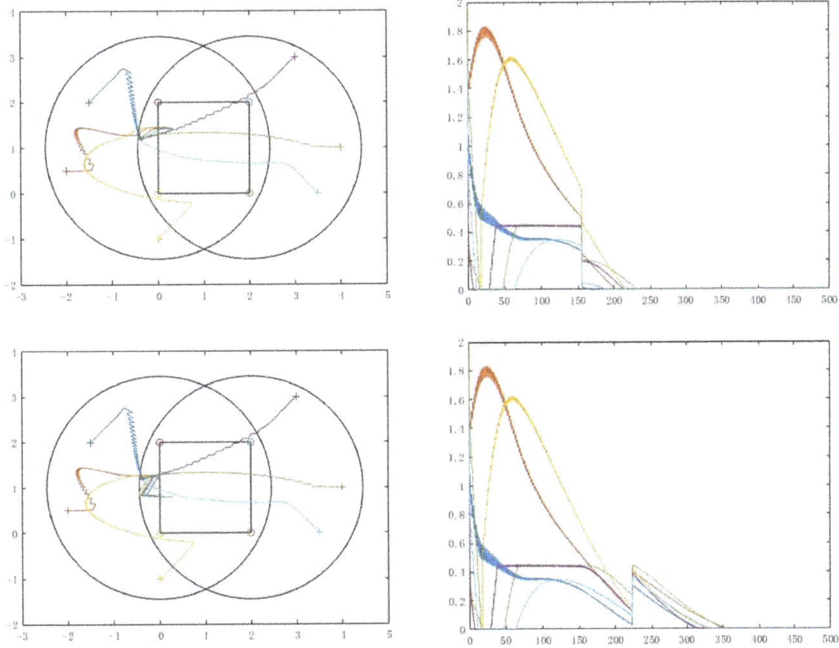

Figure 8. Position states and containment errors with interference.

5. Conclusions

In the above work, containment control for a multiagent system with nonconvex control input and position constraints was discussed. To solve the problem, a nonlinear algorithm with projection operator for followers was proposed. After the analysis of the distance from every follower to the convex hull spanned by static leaders, it is found that all followers could be driven into the convex hull formed by leaders and the position states of followers remain in the constraint set. Finally, a numerical example is given to guarantee the theoretical results.

Under analysis of the algorithm and simulation results, our work has the following advantages:

(1) The projection operator we introduced can ensure the control input of every follower to lie in a nonconvex set which is useful in practice. It has apparent superiority as compared with other algorithms which can be seen in the simulation.
(2) With the existence of constraints both in control input and position, the system has strong nonlinearity. By model transformation and introducing new error variable, we successfully remove the nonlinearity and achieve containment control.
(3) In the process of analysis, we introduce a geometrical method which uses two similar triangles. This method solves the problem in the proof of effectiveness of our algorithm.

Of course, there are still many shortcomings in our current work. In future study, we will take the dynamic situation of leaders into consideration. Meanwhile, we hope to make better analysis and results against interference, and therefore, the algorithm may get closer to practical application.

Author Contributions: Conceptualization, N.G. and Y.Y.; methodology, N.G.; software, N.G.; formal analysis, N.G. and Y.Y.; resources, Y.Y.; data curation, N.G.; writing—original draft preparation, N.G.; writing—review and editing, N.G.; visualization, N.G.; supervision, Y.Y.; project administration, Y.Y. All authors have read and agreed to the published version of the manuscript.

Funding: This research was funded by the National Key Research and Development Program of China (2017YFC1500904) and the National Key Research and Development Program of China (2016YFB0501301).

Institutional Review Board Statement: Not applicable.

Informed Consent Statement: Not applicable.

Data Availability Statement: Not applicable.

Conflicts of Interest: The authors declare no conflict of interest.

References

1. Ji, M.; Ferrari-Trecate, G.; Egerstedt, M.; Buffa, A. Containment Control in Mobile Networks. *IEEE Trans. Autom. Control.* **2008**, *53*, 1972–1975. [CrossRef]
2. Jiang, Y.; Schmidt, J. Motion of dust ejected from the surface of asteroid (101955) Bennu. *Heliyon* **2020**, *6*, e05275. [CrossRef] [PubMed]
3. Liu, Y.; Jiang, Y.; Li, H. Bifurcations of relative equilibrium points during homotopy deformation of asteroids. *Celest. Mech. Dyn. Astron.* **2021**, *133*, 42. [CrossRef]
4. Qiang, L.; Yu, J.; Zhang, Y.; Gao, Y.; Guo, X.; Cui, R.; Wang, S.; Guo, W.; Lv, T.; Cai, L.; et al. Optimal attitude control for solar array orientation. *Open Astron.* **2021**, *30*, 73–82.
5. Zhan, C.; Jiang, Y.; Li, H.; Liu, Y. Dynamics and control of typical orbits around Saturn. *Appl. Sci.* **2022**, *12*, 1462. [CrossRef]
6. Liu, Y.; Jiang, Y.; Li, H. Bifurcations of periodic orbits in the gravitational field of irregular bodies: Applications to Bennu and Steins. *Aerospace* **2022**, *9*, 151. [CrossRef]
7. Li, J.; Ren, W.; Xu, S. Distributed Containment Control with Multiple Dynamic Leaders for Double-Integrator Dynamics Using Only Position Measurements. *IEEE Trans. Autom. Control.* **2012**, *57*, 1553–1559. [CrossRef]
8. Liu, H.; Xie, G.; Wang, L. Necessary and sufficient conditions for containment control of networked multi-agent systems. *Automatica* **2012**, *48*, 1415–1422. [CrossRef]
9. Notarstefano, G.; Egerstedt, M.; Haque, M. Containment in leaderfollower networks with switching communication topologies. *Automatica* **2011**, *47*, 1035–1040. [CrossRef]
10. Su, H.; Jia, G.; Chen, M.Z. Semi-global containment control of multi-agent systems with intermittent input saturation. *J. Frankl. Inst.* **2015**, *352*, 3504–3525. [CrossRef]
11. Xu, C.; Zheng, Y.; Su, H.; Zhang, C.; Chen, M.Z. Necessary and sufficient conditions for distributed containment control of multi-agent systems without velocity measurement. *IET Control. Theory Appl.* **2014**, *8*, 1752–1759. [CrossRef]
12. Wang, X.; Li, S.; Shi, P. Distributed Finite-Time Containment Control for Double-Integrator Multiagent Systems. *IEEE Trans. Cybern.* **2014**, *44*, 1518–1528. [CrossRef] [PubMed]
13. Zhang, J.; Li, W.; Xie, L. Containment control of leader-following multi-agent systems with Markovian switching network topologies and measurement noises. *Automatica* **2015**, *51*, 263–267.

14. Kan, Z.; Shea, J.M.; Dixon, W.E. Leaderfollower containment control over directed random graphs. *Automatica* **2016**, *6*, 56–62. [CrossRef]
15. Su, H.; Chen, M.Z.Q.; Wang, X.; Lam, J. Semiglobal Observer-Based Leader-Following Consensus with Input Saturation. *IEEE Trans. Ind. Electron.* **2014**, *61*, 2842–2850. [CrossRef]
16. Liu, K.; Xie, G.; Wang, L. Containment control for second-order multi-agent systems with time-varying delays. *Syst. Control. Lett.* **2014**, *67*, 24–31. [CrossRef]
17. Song, Q.; Liu, F.; Su, H.; Vasilakos, A.V. Semiglobal and global containment control of multiagent systems with secondorder dynamics and input saturation. *Int. J. Robust Nonlinear Control.* **2016**, *26*, 3439–3670. [CrossRef]
18. Ren, W.; Meng, Z.; You, Z. Distributed finite-time attitude containment control for multiple rigid bodies. *Automatica* **2010**, *46*, 2092–2099.
19. Su, H.; Chen, M.Z.Q. Multi-agent containment control with input saturation on switching topologies. *IET Control. Theory Appl.* **2015**, *9*, 399–409. [CrossRef]
20. Lin, P.; Xu, J.; Ren, W.; Yang, C.; Gui, W. Angle-Based Analysis Approach for Distributed Constrained Optimization. *IEEE Trans. Autom. Control.* **2021**, *66*, 5569–5576. [CrossRef]
21. Lin, P.; Ren, W.; Farrell, J. Distributed Continuous-Time Optimization: Nonuniform Gradient Gains, Finite-Time Convergence, and Convex Constraint Set. *IEEE Trans. Autom. Control.* **2017**, *62*, 2239–2253. [CrossRef]
22. Lian, F.; Chakrabortty, A.; Duel-Hallen, A. Game-Theoretic Multi-Agent Control and Network Cost Allocation Under Communication Constraints. *IEEE J. Sel. Areas Commun.* **2017**, *35*, 330–340. [CrossRef]
23. Delaram, J.; Houshamand, M.; Ashtiani, F.; Valilai, O.F. A utility-based matching mechanism for stable and optimal resource allocation in cloud manufacturing platforms using deferred acceptance algorithm. *J. Manuf. Syst.* **2021**, *60*, 569–584. [CrossRef]
24. Bakolas, E.; Lee, Y. Decentralized game-theoretic control for dynamic task allocation problems for multi-agent systems. In Proceedings of the 2021 American Control Conference (ACC), New Orleans, LA, USA, 25–28 May 2021; pp. 3228–3233.
25. Fan, W.; Wang, S.; Gu, X.; Zhou, Z.; Zhao, Y.; Huo, W. Evolutionary game analysis on industrial pollution control of local government in China. *J. Environ. Manag.* **2021**, *298*, 113499. [CrossRef] [PubMed]
26. Sathishkumar, M.; Liu, Y.-C. Resilient Memory Event-triggered Consensus Control for Multi-Agent Systems with Aperiodic DoS Attacks. *Int. J. Control. Autom. Syst.* **2022**, *20*, 1800–1813. [CrossRef]
27. Lin, P.; Ren, W.; Yang, C.; Gui, W. Distributed Continuous-Time and Discrete-Time Optimization with Nonuniform Unbounded Convex Constraint Sets and Nonuniform Stepsizes. *IEEE Trans. Autom. Control.* **2019**, *64*, 5148–5155. [CrossRef]
28. Lin, P.; Ren, W.; Yang, C.; Gui, W. Distributed Consensus of Second-Order Multiagent Systems with Nonconvex Velocity and Control Input Constraints. *IEEE Trans. Autom. Control.* **2018**, *63*, 1171–1176. [CrossRef]
29. Lin, P.; Ren, W.; Gao, H. Distributed Velocity-Constrained Consensus of Discrete-Time Multi-Agent Systems with Nonconvex Constraints, Switching Topologies, and Delays. *IEEE Trans. Autom. Control.* **2017**, *62*, 5788–5794. [CrossRef]
30. Yang, C.; Duan, M.; Lin, P.; Ren, W.; Gui, W. Distributed Containment Control of Continuous-Time Multiagent Systems with Nonconvex Control Input Constraints. *IEEE Trans. Ind. Electron.* **2019**, *66*, 7927–7934. [CrossRef]
31. Lin, P.; Li, G.; Huang, K. Position-constrained containment for second-order discrete-time multi-agent systems. *Syst. Control. Lett.* **2020**, *142*, 104–109. [CrossRef]
32. Lin, P.; Ren, W.; Yang, C.; Gui, W. Distributed Optimization with Nonconvex Velocity Constraints, Nonuniform Position Constraints, and Nonuniform Stepsizes. *IEEE Trans. Autom. Control.* **2019**, *64*, 2575–2582. [CrossRef]
33. Facchinei, F.; Pang, J.S. *Finite-Dimensional Variational Inequalities and Complementarity Problems*; Springer: New York, NY, USA, 2003.

 mathematics

MDPI

Article

A Distributed Formation Joint Network Navigation and Positioning Algorithm

Lvyang Ye [1], Yikang Yang [1,*], Jiangang Ma [1], Lingyu Deng [1] and Hengnian Li [2]

1 School of Electronic and Information Engineering, Xi'an Jiaotong University, Xi'an 710049, China; yely2019@stu.xjtu.edu.cn (L.Y.); jiangangma@stu.xjtu.edu.cn (J.M.); dengly0625@stu.xjtu.edu.cn (L.D.)
2 State Key Laboratory of Astronautic Dynamics, Xi'an Satellite Control Center, Xi'an 710043, China; henry_xscc@mail.xjtu.edu.cn
* Correspondence: yangyk74@mail.xjtu.edu.cn

Abstract: In view of the problem that the leader-follower joint navigation scheme relies too much on the absolute navigation and positioning accuracy of the leader node, under the conditions of distributed network-centric warfare (NCW) and to meet the location service accuracy, reliability, and synergy efficiency of the future integrated communication, navigation (ICN), we built a joint navigation and positioning system with low Earth orbit (LEO), airborne data link, and inertial navigation system (INS) as the core; designed a ranging and time-synchronization scheme of the joint navigation and positioning system; and established a joint navigation and positioning method for formation and networking based on mutual ranging and velocity measurement information between aircrafts. Finally, based on the designed LEO constellation, the universality, effectiveness, superiority, and potential superiority of algorithm are verified, respectively. The simulation results show that the scheme can meet the requirements of joint location services in challenging environments, and could be used as a reference scheme for future ICN integration.

Keywords: distributed; joint navigation; ICN; LEO; Integrated Navigation; formation

MSC: 93-10; 94-10

Citation: Ye, L.; Yang, Y.; Ma, J.; Deng, L.; Li, H. A Distributed Formation Joint Network Navigation and Positioning Algorithm. *Mathematics* **2022**, *10*, 1627. https://doi.org/10.3390/math10101627

Academic Editors: Haijun Peng and Hongwei Yang

Received: 4 April 2022
Accepted: 7 May 2022
Published: 10 May 2022

1. Introduction

At present, satellite navigation systems have entered a new era of integration with multi-source information carriers, such as positioning, navigation, timing, mobile communication, and broadband Internet. Satellite navigation systems have become an important infrastructure for national defense system and national economic development. The medium Earth orbit (MEO) constellation navigation systems represented by GPS, Beidou, Galileo, and GLONASS have been rapidly developed and fully applied in various fields [1–4], and the well-known absolute navigation positioning, relative navigation, and collaborative navigation all depend on MEO constellation navigation systems, especially the currently widely used collaborative navigation.

Collaborative navigation is a key technology for collaborative positioning among formation flight members and has a wide of applications in the fields of fighter formation flying, unmanned aerial vehicle (UAV) swarms, and aerial autonomous refueling [5,6]. However, the mission performance and anti-damage capability of a single UAV are limited. Under the background of modern warfare in network-centric warfare (NCW) [7], the focus of research is gradually transitioning to UAV swarms. Because UAV swarms have the advantages of high survival rate, low cost, and high efficiency, joint navigation and positioning has therefore become one of the key technologies for cluster networking and cooperative air combat.

In recent years, a variety of co-localization techniques have been developed to improve the localization performance of adjacent agents; however, it remains challenging to comprehensively study their performance. At present, the research on cooperative navigation mainly focuses on multi-UAV or unmanned underwater vehicle (UUV) cooperative navigation based on leader-follower or hierarchical [8,9], GNSS/INS cooperative navigation based on pseudorange differences, and micro-electro-mechanical system-inertial measurement unit (MEMS-IMU)-based cooperative navigation scheme [10] and a collaborative positioning architecture based on 3D modeling or terrain assistance [11,12]. In view of the gradual formation of inter-aircraft communication and ranging systems, some scholars have proposed a network positioning method that utilizes the mutual ranging of each aircraft in the fleet [13,14]. In addition, based on the adaptive artificial potential function, ref. [15] presents a cooperative navigation algorithm suitable for navigation and control uncertainty. As for the guidance, navigation, and control methods of deep space formation, the corresponding technical reference schemes are also given in references [16–18].

With the development of artificial intelligence (AI), smart cities, and future navigation systems and to solve the problems of divergence of formation cooperative navigation accuracy, large amounts of calculation for a fully connected cooperative navigation algorithm and a heavy communication burden have been caused by leader failure in the traditional single leader-follower UAV cooperative navigation. Therefore, it is necessary to find another way and give a low-cost and efficient joint navigation and positioning scheme suitable for the future so as to improve the stability of cluster navigation and the utilization of navigation information. Finally, the formation positioning error is reduced, and the problem of cooperative navigation formation is guaranteed. In recent years, with the emergence of the broadband low Earth orbit (LEO) constellation, a number of typical LEO constellation systems have gradually been applied in various fields, which provides a potential opportunity for modern collaborative navigation and positioning.

In this paper, to solve the problem of low-cost and high-efficiency joint navigation and positioning in the future, we start from the currently "hot" LEO constellation navigation and propose a distributed formation joint network navigation and positioning reference solution. In Section 2, firstly, we give the specific distributed joint navigation algorithm principle and formation node self-positioning process and then give the construction scheme of the relative navigation information required by the distributed joint navigation and positioning; next, the platform composition and overall architecture of distributed joint navigation and positioning are given; and finally, the ranging and time synchronization problems involved in joint navigation and positioning are given and analyzed. In Section 3, we establish the specific distributed joint navigation and positioning state model and measurement model; in Section 4, we configure the designed distributed joint navigation and positioning parameter model and then carry out simulation experiment verification and comparative analysis. In the last section, we give our conclusions and point out the improvement direction of the paper.

2. Distributed Joint Navigation Method

2.1. Principles of Distributed Joint Navigation

By using global navigation satellite system/inertial navigation system (GNSS/INS) combined navigation algorithms or algorithms such as ultra-wide band (UWB) and visual integration, we can obtain relatively accurate position, velocity, and attitude information (typical values are: 0.1 m, 0.01 m/s, and 1×10^{-3} deg [19–22]) of the navigation target. This accurate information can provide a reference source for navigation information in formation flight. Compared with GNSS signals, inter-machine communication is less susceptible to interference, is conducive to the cooperation and control of formation flight, and can also ensure the anti-interference performance of formation and the accuracy of cooperative navigation and positioning [23].

Considering that the mutual ranging of each aircraft has high requirements on the time synchronization of the ranging system and the real-time performance of the communication system, it is therefore difficult to implement. For this reason, we use the LEO constellation as the navigation framework since, at present, most of the existing broadband

LEO satellites, such as the satellites of constellations of SpaceX, oneweb, or Telesat, are essentially communication satellites, and the clock bias between LEO satellite and user terminal can be eliminated by a bidirectional communication method like full duplex (FD). Therefore, when solving the absolute position and relative position of the user terminal, we can use the "duplex" system to eliminate the time synchronization error. In addition, we briefly introduce the time synchronization problem in joint positioning later in the article.

Based on the LEO navigation constellation for the formation of joint navigation, we introduce relative navigation information, that is, relative position information and relative velocity information, which can be obtained by relative sensors, such as laser rangefinders, Doppler velocimeters, and goniometers, and then, a corresponding relative navigation algorithm can be constructed to improve the navigation accuracy and fault tolerance between formations. The members of the formation can obtain high enough absolute position information through GNSS without relying on a reference node with high absolute positioning accuracy. In addition, the formation node can realize the sharing of navigation resources through the data link, and the formation nodes can access and exit at will. This is the idea of the distributed joint navigation and positioning algorithm that we built; the advantages of this distributed formation joint positioning scheme are that it is easy to expand and has high reusability, strong reliability, and high fault tolerance. The construction of relative position information and relative velocity information of formation nodes is described below.

2.2. *Self-Positioning Process of Distributed Joint Navigation and Positioning and Construction of Relative Navigation Information*

(1) Distributed joint navigation and positioning node self-positioning process [24]:

We call each aircraft in the formation as a formation node, assuming that the formation has a total of N nodes, $P_R\{x_i, y_i, z_i\}(i = 1, 2, \ldots, N)$, which is the actual position of node i; $P_I\{x_{Ii}, y_{Ii}, z_{Ii}\}(i = 1, 2, \ldots, N)$, is the position of the INS solution output. The detailed schematic diagram is shown in Figure 1.

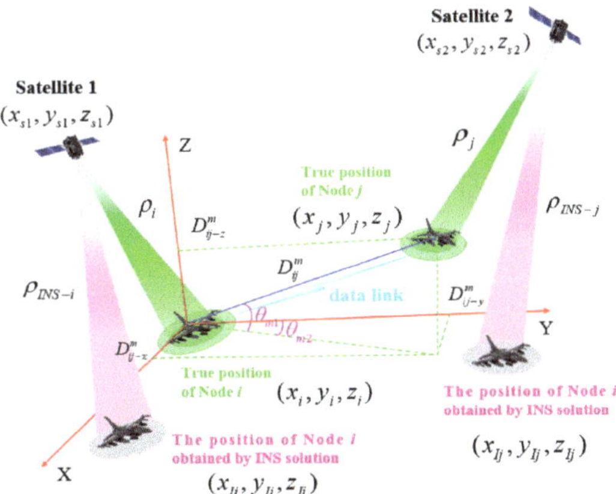

Figure 1. Schematic diagram of node self-positioning process.

Without the aid of an altimeter, the absolute position information of node i and node j can be solved by least squares or Kalman filter method through the following equations:

$$\begin{cases} \rho_i = \sqrt{(x_{s1} - x_i)^2 + (y_{s1} - y_i)^2 + (z_{s1} - z_i)^2} \\ \rho_{INS-i} = \sqrt{(x_{s1} - x_{Ii})^2 + (y_{s1} - y_{Ii})^2 + (z_{s1} - z_{Ii})^2} \end{cases} \tag{1}$$

$$\begin{cases} \rho_j = \sqrt{(x_{s2} - x_j)^2 + (y_{s2} - y_j)^2 + (z_{s2} - z_j)^2} \\ \rho_{INS-j} = \sqrt{(x_{s2} - x_{Ij})^2 + (y_{s2} - y_{Ij})^2 + (z_{s2} - z_{Ij})^2} \end{cases} \tag{2}$$

In the same way, with the aid of an altimeter, on the basis of Equations (1) and (2), the absolute position information of node i and node j can be obtained by combining the following equations:

$$\begin{cases} \rho_{Hi} = R_e + H_i \\ \rho_{IH-i} = \sqrt{(x_{Ii} - 0)^2 + (y_{Ii} - 0)^2 + (z_{Ii} - 0)^2} \end{cases} \tag{3}$$

$$\begin{cases} \rho_{Hj} = R_e + H_j \\ \rho_{IH-j} = \sqrt{(x_{Ij} - 0)^2 + (y_{Ij} - 0)^2 + (z_{Ij} - 0)^2} \end{cases} \tag{4}$$

where R_e is the average earth radius; H_i is the elevation reading of node I; and H_j is the elevation reading of node j. Other parameters can be interpreted by referring to Figure 1 or reference [24].

(2) Relative Navigation Information Construction of Distributed Joint Navigation and Positioning:

The mutual ranging value D_{ij}^m between node i and node j can be expressed as:

$$\begin{aligned} D_{ij}^m &= \|D_j - D_i\| \\ &= \sqrt{(x_j - x_i)^2 + (y_j - y_i)^2 + (z_j - z_i)^2} + \delta D_{ij}^m \\ &= D_{ij} + \delta D_{ij}^m \end{aligned} \tag{5}$$

In the formula, D_{ij} is the real relative position among the formation members i and j; δD_{ij}^m is the ranging error; and $\delta D_{ij}^m \sim N(0, \sigma_{D\_ij}^2)$, $\sigma_{D\_ij}^2$ is the ranging variance.

The relative angle between node i and node j measured by the node i angle sensor is

$$\begin{cases} \theta_{m1} = \theta_1 + \Delta\theta_1 \\ \theta_{m2} = \theta_2 + \Delta\theta_2 \end{cases} \tag{6}$$

where θ_{m1} and θ_{m2} are the measured values of the pitch and azimuth of node j relative to node i in the body coordinate system (as shown in Figure 1); θ_1 and θ_2 represent the real values of the pitch and azimuth, respectively; $\Delta\theta_1$ and $\Delta\theta_2$ represent the angle measurement error of the pitch and azimuth, assuming that they meet the Gaussian white-noise process; that is, $\Delta\theta_1 \sim N(0, \sigma_{\theta_1}^2)$, $\Delta\theta_2 \sim N(0, \sigma_{\theta 2}^2)$, $\sigma_{\theta 1}^2$, $\sigma_{\theta 2}^2$ are the corresponding variances.

To correspond to the navigation information, we decompose D_{ij}^m along the three directions of the carrier coordinate system:

$$\begin{cases} D_{ij-x}^m = D_{ij}^m \cos\theta_1 \sin\theta_2 \\ D_{ij-y}^m = D_{ij}^m \cos\theta_1 \cos\theta_2 \\ D_{ij-z}^m = D_{ij}^m \sin\theta_1 \end{cases} \tag{7}$$

Assuming that the relative ranging error and angle error are relatively small, according to the infinitesimal equivalent replacement principle, there are

$$\begin{cases} \cos(\Delta\theta_1) \approx 1 \\ \cos(\Delta\theta_2) \approx 1 \\ \sin(\Delta\theta_1) \approx \theta_1 \\ \sin(\Delta\theta_2) \approx \theta_2 \end{cases} \tag{8}$$

Ignoring higher-order small quantities, we have

$$\begin{cases} \delta D_{ij}^{m} \Delta\theta_1 \approx 0 \\ \delta D_{ij}^{m} \Delta\theta_2 \approx 0 \\ \Delta\theta_1 \Delta\theta_2 \approx 0 \end{cases} \tag{9}$$

It can be obtained from Equations (1)~(5)

$$\begin{cases} D_{ij-x}^{m} = D_{ij-x} - \kappa_{x1} \\ D_{ij-y}^{m} = D_{ij-y} - \kappa_{y1} \\ D_{ij-z}^{m} = D_{ij-z} - \kappa_{z1} \end{cases} \tag{10}$$

where, D_{ij-x}, D_{ij-y}, and D_{ij-z} are the components of the real relative position along the three directions of the body coordinate system; and the specific expressions of κ_{x1}, κ_{y1}, and κ_{z1} are as follows:

$$\begin{cases} \kappa_{x1} = -\delta D_{ij}^{m} \cos\theta_1 \cos\theta_2 + \Delta\theta_1 D_{ij} \sin\theta_1 \sin\theta_2 - \Delta\theta_2 D_{ij} \cos\theta_1 \cos\theta_2 \\ \kappa_{y1} = -\delta D_{ij}^{m} \cos\theta_1 \cos\theta_2 + \Delta\theta_1 D_{ij} \sin\theta_1 \cos\theta_2 + \Delta\theta_2 D_{ij} \cos\theta_1 \sin\theta_2 \\ \kappa_{z1} = -\delta D_{ij}^{m} \sin\theta_1 - \Delta\theta_1 D_{ij} \cos\theta_1 \end{cases} \tag{11}$$

Similarly, omitting the redundant derivation process, we can obtain the relative velocity relationship between node i and node j as follows:

$$\begin{cases} V_{ij-x}^{m} = V_{ij-x} - \mu_{x1} \\ V_{ij-y}^{m} = V_{ij-y} - \mu_{y1} \\ V_{ij-z}^{m} = V_{ij-z} - \mu_{z1} \end{cases} \tag{12}$$

$$\begin{cases} \mu_{x1} = -\delta V_{ij}^{m} \cos\phi_1 \cos\phi_2 + \Delta\phi_1 V_{ij} \sin\phi_1 \sin\phi_2 - \Delta\phi_2 V_{ij} \cos\phi_1 \cos\phi_2 \\ \mu_{y1} = -\delta V_{ij}^{m} \cos\phi_1 \cos\phi_2 + \Delta\phi_1 V_{ij} \sin\phi_1 \cos\phi_2 + \Delta\phi_2 V_{ij} \cos\phi_1 \sin\phi_2 \\ \mu_{z1} = -\delta V_{ij}^{m} \sin\phi_1 - \Delta\phi_1 V_{ij} \cos\phi_1 \end{cases} \tag{13}$$

where ϕ_1 and ϕ_2 have similar meanings to θ_1 and θ_2; and other parameters δV_{ij}^{m}, V_{ij-x}, V_{ij-y}, and V_{ij-z} are also similar and are not repeated here.

Thus far, the relative position information and relative velocity information have been constructed, and they are the state variables for the subsequent construction of joint navigation and positioning measurement equations.

2.3. Platform Composition and Overall Architecture of Distributed Joint Navigation and Positioning System

We assume that the joint positioning system of each node consists of a set of airborne data links, INS and ranging/velocity sensors, and a networking computer. In the joint positioning process, the local geographic coordinate system is selected as the navigation system, and the directions of the three axes are north, east, and down, respectively. The LEO and INS data of this node are transmitted to the airborne data link, and the transmitted LEO and INS data include position information and velocity information as well as the status word and frame number; the airborne data link has the functions of real-time ranging and communication; thus, we used laser rangefinders to measure the position $D_{ij}^{m}(i = 1, 2, \ldots, n, i \neq j)$ between each node in the formation, and at the same time, communicate the joint navigation ranging and velocity measurement information to each other in real time through radio communication equipment. Finally, the ranging information of all nodes is transmitted to the networking computer for joint positioning calculation. The node joint positioning system framework is shown in Figure 2.

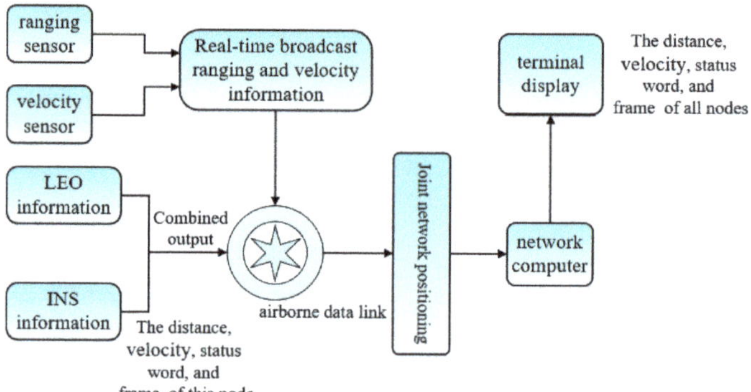

Figure 2. Overall architecture of distributed joint network navigation and positioning.

As one of the core devices of the system, the airborne data link is a link device based on data link technology, which can form point-to-point, point-to-multipoint data links and mesh data links and generally has real-time ranging and communication functions [25]; a distributed non-central mesh data link structure is shown in Figure 3.

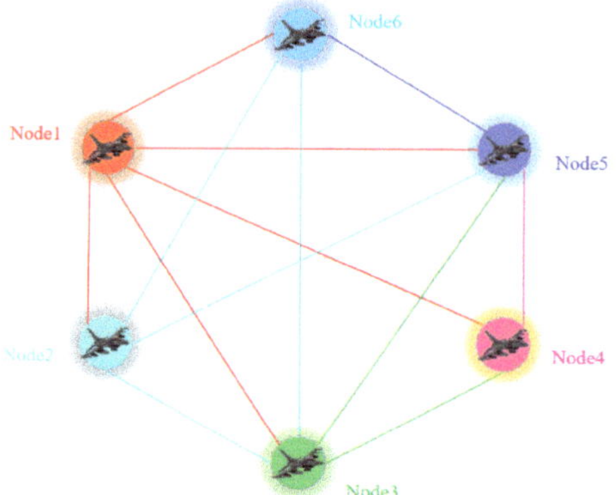

Figure 3. A distributed mesh data link network structure.

2.4. *Ranging and Time Synchronization of Distributed Joint Navigation and Positioning*

2.4.1. Ranging Scheme

After the formation aircraft assemble in the designated airspace, according to the time system of each aircraft, the data link of the fleet is powered on and starts ranging at a specified time. There are three commonly used radio ranging methods: one-way ranging method, double-side two-way ranging method, and dual one-way ranging method. The one-way ranging method requires expensive high-precision crystal oscillators [26], and the double-side two-way ranging equipment is complicated, and it is difficult to measure the distance of multiple machines at the same time. Therefore, the co-positioning system adopts the *t* dual one-way ranging method [27]. The principle is as follows:

The data link device (hereinafter referred to as device *i*) equipped with node *i* transmits one-way ranging signals and simultaneously receives one-way ranging signals from other devices. Taking the mutual ranging between devices *i* and *j* as an example, let $\Delta\tau_{ij}$ be the time synchronization error between the clocks of devices *i* and *j*; t_{ij} is the radio signal propagation time between devices *i* and *j* (usually on the microsecond scale [28]); t_1 is the signal propagation time measured by device *i*; and t_2 is the signal propagation time measured by device *j*. Then,

$$t_1 = t_{ij} + \Delta\tau_{ij} \tag{14}$$

$$t_2 = t_{ij} - \Delta\tau_{ij} \tag{15}$$

During the ranging process, the working mechanisms of devices i and j are exactly the same. Taking device i as an example: device i measures t_1, and at the same time, the receiving device j transmits t_2; then, it can be calculated from Equations (14) and (15):

$$t_{ij} = \frac{(t_1 + t_2)}{2} \tag{16}$$

$$\Delta\tau_{ij} = \frac{(t_1 - t_2)}{2} \tag{17}$$

The ranging values for devices i and j are

$$D_{ij}^{m} = c \times t_{ij} \tag{18}$$

where c is the velocity of light.

It can be seen that the dual one-way ranging method can calculate the position between nodes, and at the same time, it can also calculate the time synchronization error between the clocks (ns magnitude [29]) of the airborne data link equipment, which is conducive to the simultaneous ranging of multiple machines.

2.4.2. Time Synchronization

There are the following three time synchronization problems in the joint positioning process of formation node networking:

(1) Time synchronization between the onboard data link clocks of each node:

To achieve synchronous mutual ranging, the airborne data link should have a unified time scale, but each airborne data link cannot achieve precise time synchronization when they are turned on, so there is a time bias between their time scales. In the dual one-way ranging method, the time bias between the clocks can be calculated according to Equation (17). With the clock of an airborne data link device as a reference, time synchronization can be achieved by adjusting the clocks of all devices.

(2) Time synchronization between the INS of node i and the airborne data link device:

Since the synchronous ranging moment of the airborne data link i is not necessarily the measurement moment of the INS-i, there is a time bias Δt_i between the airborne data link device i and the INS-i. Δt_i is a random constant. If the INS has 100 Hz output, assuming that the aircraft velocity is 340 m/s, then the position error caused by Δt_i within ± 1 ms is usually within ± 5 m, and this value is negligibly relative to the position error of INS. Therefore, in the process of joint positioning calculation, it can be considered that the clocks between the airborne data link and each INS are completely synchronized.

(3) Time synchronization between nodes (including INS) and satellites:

As mentioned in Section 2.1, since we use the LEO constellation as the navigation framework, and the essence of the LEO satellites is communication satellite, the clock bias between the LEO constellation and the user terminal can be eliminated in a way similar to full duplex. When solving the absolute position and relative position of the user terminal, we can eliminate the time synchronization error by means of the "duplex" system, and we will not consider the variable of clock biases.

3. Establishment of Distributed Joint Navigation and Positioning Model

3.1. State Model

Without loss of generality, we only take the two formation nodes, Node 1 and Node 2, as the study objects; select the position error and velocity error as state variables; supplement the Markov noises of gyroscope and accelerometer as state variables; and establish the following system state equation [30]:

$$\dot{X}_{JP} = \Gamma X_{JP} + \Phi W_{JP} \tag{19}$$

$$X_{JP} = [\varphi_N \quad \varphi_E \quad \varphi_D \quad \delta V_N \quad \delta V_E \quad \delta V_D \quad \delta\lambda \quad \delta L \quad \delta h \quad \xi_{gx} \quad \xi_{gy} \quad \xi_{gz} \quad \xi_{ax} \quad \xi_{ay} \quad \xi_{az}]^{\mathrm{T}} \tag{20}$$

where $\varphi = \begin{bmatrix} \varphi_N & \varphi_E & \varphi_D \end{bmatrix}$ is the misalignment angle of the platform between the platform coordinate system and the navigation coordinate system in the N, E, and D directions; $\delta V = [\delta V_N \quad \delta V_E \quad \delta V_D]^{\mathrm{T}}$ is the three-dimensional velocity error; $\delta P = \begin{bmatrix} \delta\lambda & \delta L & \delta h \end{bmatrix}$ is the three-dimensional position error, and $\xi_g = \begin{bmatrix} \xi_{gx} & \xi_{gy} & \xi_{gz} \end{bmatrix}$ is the first-order Markov drift of the gyroscope; $\xi_a = \begin{bmatrix} \xi_{ax} & \xi_{ay} & \xi_{az} \end{bmatrix}$ is the first-order Markov drift of the accelerometer. Γ is a 15×15-dimensional matrix, X_{JP} is an 15×1-dimensional matrix, Φ is a 15×6-dimensional matrix, and W_{JP} is a 6×1-dimensional matrix [31,32].

3.2. Measurement Model

Here, we assume that the relative position information and relative velocity information (which can be obtained by angle measurement and distance measurement) can be measured between the aircraft, and the relative position and relative velocity measured by the distance measurement and velocity measurement sensors are converted from the body coordinate system to the navigation coordinate system by

$$D_{12}^n = C_b^n (D_{12}^b + \delta D_{12}^b) \tag{21}$$

$$V_{12}^n = C_b^n (V_{12}^b + \delta V_{12}^b) \tag{22}$$

where δD_{12}^b and δV_{12}^b are distance measurement and velocity measurement errors, assuming that they are all Gaussian white noise with mean zero and variance $\sigma_{Db\_12}^2$ and $\sigma_{Vb\_12}^2$, respectively; C_b^n is the transformation matrix from the carrier coordinate system to the navigation coordinate system, and its expression is as follows [33]:

$$C_b^n = \begin{bmatrix} \cos\alpha\cos\beta & -\cos\gamma\sin\beta + \sin\gamma\cos\beta\sin\alpha & \sin\gamma\sin\beta + \cos\gamma\cos\beta\sin\alpha \\ \cos\alpha\sin\beta & \cos\gamma\sin\beta + \sin\gamma\sin\beta\sin\alpha & \sin\gamma\cos\beta + \cos\gamma\sin\beta\sin\alpha \\ -\sin\alpha & \cos\alpha\sin\gamma & \cos\alpha\cos\gamma \end{bmatrix} \tag{23}$$

where α, β, and γ represent the pitch, yaw, and roll of Node 1; D_{12} and V_{12} are the relative position and relative velocity between Node 1 and Node 2, and the relationship is as follows:

$$D_1^n - D_2^n = D_{12}^n \tag{24}$$

$$V_1^n - V_2^n = V_{12}^n \tag{25}$$

Since a high-precision navigation solution can be obtained between Node 1 and Node 2 by means of pseudorange-pseudorange rate [24], it can be considered that the navigation solution is approximately equal to their real values. Then, transmit their position and velocity solutions to each other by means of inter-node communication. At the same time, we assume that Node 1 and Node 2 are equipped with an inertial measurement unit (IMU) with a good index so that the accumulated error of the measurement is relatively slow; therefore, it can be considered $\widetilde{C}_b^n \approx C_b^n$. Taking Node 1 as an example, the relationship between the relative navigation information, that is, the position and velocity deviation between the nodes, can be written as follows:

$$\begin{aligned} &\overset{\frown}{D}{}_1^n - \widetilde{D}_2^n - D_{12}^n \\ &= M_e^n(\overset{\frown}{D}{}_1^e - \widetilde{D}_2^e) - \widetilde{C}_e^n(D_{12}^b + \delta D_{12}^b) \\ &= M_e^n(\overset{\frown}{D}{}_1^e - \overset{\frown}{D}{}_2^e - \delta D_2) - \widetilde{C}_e^n(D_{12}^b + \delta D_{12}^b) \end{aligned} \tag{26}$$

$$\begin{aligned}\overset{\frown n}{V_1} & -\widetilde{V}_2^n - V_{12}^n \\ & = \overset{\frown n}{V_1} - \widetilde{V}_2^n - \widetilde{C}_b^n(V_{12}^b + \delta V_{12}^b) \\ & = \overset{\frown n}{V_1} - V_2^n - \delta V_2 - \widetilde{C}_b^n(V_{12}^b + \delta V_{12}^b)\end{aligned} \tag{27}$$

where $\overset{\frown n}{D_1}$ and $\overset{\frown n}{V_1}$ are the position and velocity parameters of Node 1 in the Earth-centered Earth-fixed (ECEF) coordinate system, and $\widetilde{D}_2^n$ is the position parameter to be corrected of Node 2; in the case of a short baseline, the influence of the Earth's curve radian can be ignored, and it can be approximated by

$$D_{12}^b = C_b^n M_e^n (D_1^e - D_2^e) \tag{28}$$

where M_e^n is the transformation matrix of longitude-latitude-high to north-east-down; if the radius of curvature of the coordinate system where Node 1 and Node 2 are located is R_{Mer}, the radius of curvature of the Prime Vertical is R_{Pri}, the latitude is L, and the height is h. Then, the form of M_e^n is as follows [34]:

$$M_e^n = \begin{bmatrix} R_{Mer} + h & & \\ & (R_{\text{Pri}} + h)\cos L & \\ & & -1 \end{bmatrix} \tag{29}$$

According to Formulas (26) and (27), $Z_D = \overset{\frown n}{D_1} - \widetilde{D}_2^n - D_{12}^n$ and $V_D = \overset{\frown n}{V_1} - \widetilde{V}_2^n - V_{12}^n$ are selected as the observed variables, and the Kalman filter observation equation is constructed as follows:

$$\begin{cases} Z_D = H_D X_{JP} + \sigma_D \\ Z_V = H_V X_{JP} + \sigma_V \end{cases} \tag{30}$$

where the specific expressions of H_D and H_V are as

$$\begin{cases} H_D = \begin{bmatrix} O_{3\times3} & -I_{3\times3} & O_{3\times3} & O_{3\times3} & O_{3\times3} \end{bmatrix} \\ H_V = \begin{bmatrix} O_{3\times3} & O_{3\times3} & -M_e^n & O_{3\times3} & O_{3\times3} \end{bmatrix} \end{cases} \tag{31}$$

where σ_D and σ_V are the ranging and velocity noise after coupling σ_{Db_12} and σ_{Vb_12}, which we model as multiplicative noise with the modulo length of the position and velocity vectors.

4. Simulation Verification

4.1. Simulation Parameter Configuration

We take two distributed nodes as an example: the initial baseline interval between them is 10 km, and the height is also 10 km. The reference formation aircraft is located in the airspace assembly trajectory shown in Figure 4, the flight velocity is 200 m/s, the corresponding sensor data are generated to verify the effectiveness of the established collaborative navigation algorithm. The reference aircraft, LEO constellation, and IMU indicators are shown in Tables 1 and 2. Since the Walker constellation has the same orbital height and uniformly distributed inclined orbital plane, it is a very suitable design scheme for the LEO constellation, and most broadband LEO constellations are deployed with this design scheme [35]. Secondly, considering the coverage characteristics in challenging environments, we deliberately set the orbital inclination to a high orbital inclination (99 deg, see Table 2) to cover the high latitudes of the Earth and the north and south poles.

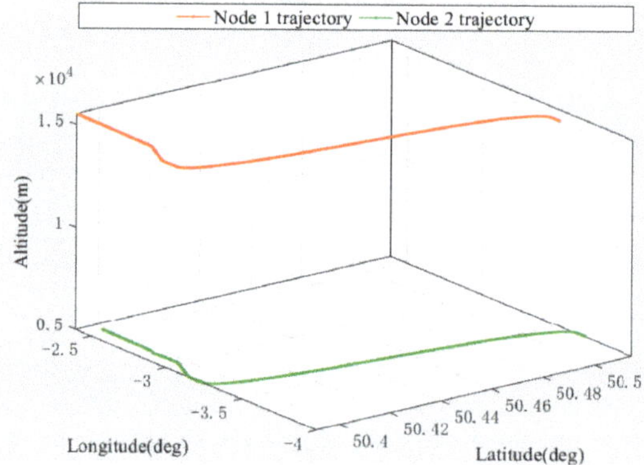

Figure 4. Reference airspace assembly trajectory of formation aircraft.

Table 1. Reference aircraft and navigation sensor parameters.

Parameter	Node 1	Node 2
Gyroscope random walk $(deg/\sqrt{h})$	0.0005	0.0005
Accelerometer random walk $(m/s/\sqrt{h})$	0.003	0.003
Gyroscope first-order Markov noise RMS $(deg/\sqrt{h})$	0.002	0.002
Accelerometer first-order Markov noise RMS (μg_0)	10	10
Position noise (m)	0.1	0.1
Velocity noise (m/s)	0.01	0.01
Data link ranging error (m)	10	10
Flight velocity (m/s)	200	200
Flight duration (s)	420	420

Table 2. LEO constellation parameters.

Parameter	Value
Constellation configuration type	Walker [36]
Track height (km)	1250
Orbital inclination (deg)	99
Number of orbital faces	20
Number of satellites per orbit (total/orbit)	50
Number of satellites per orbit	1000

4.2. Simulation Results

According to the parameter settings in Section 4.1, we divide the algorithm into two scenarios. The first is a joint navigation and positioning scenario without an altimeter assistance, and the other is a joint navigation and positioning scenario assisted by an altimeter. Then, the two scenarios are simulated and analyzed separately. Here, we only take Node 1 and Node 2 as examples for simulation, where NPE and NVE and | alt, O represent north position error, north velocity error, altimeter error (symbol "|" means under the condition that the altimeter error is x m), and original trajectory, respectively. The meaning of other parameters refers to these expressions.

4.2.1. Joint Navigation and Positioning Scenarios without an Altimeter Assistance

In the absence of an altimeter assistance, the simulation results are shown in Figure 5, in which we compare and verify the INS individual navigation and positioning results corresponding to Node 1 and Node 2 to verify the convergence effect of the algorithm.

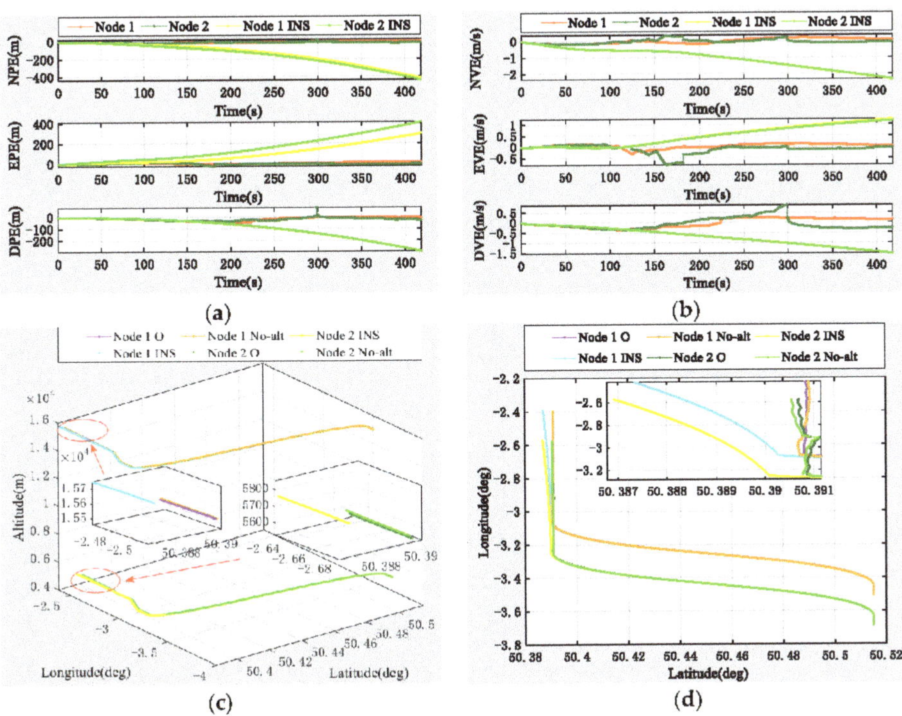

Figure 5. Positioning error curve of joint navigation without an altimeter assistance. (**a**) Position error curve, (**b**) velocity error curve, (**c**) 3D trajectory error curve, and (**d**) 3D projection error curve.

From Figure 5, we can see that in the scenario without an altimeter assistance, the position error of Node 1 and Node 2 does not fluctuate too much, and both converge to zero, and as the velocity error is also very small, it also shows a convergence trend. For the INS autonomous joint navigation scheme, we found that the pure INS autonomous joint navigation error diverges faster, and the error is relatively large. The above results are also fully reflected on the final 3D trajectory and projected trajectory error curves, and the results are consistent; this result can be seen in Figure 5c,d. It can be clearly seen from Figure 5 that the navigation and positioning results of the INS are significantly larger than the navigation and positioning results of the corresponding nodes. These results fully show that the joint navigation and positioning algorithm without an altimeter can effectively suppress the divergence of pure INS navigation and positioning. To facilitate quantitative analysis, Tables 3–6 shows the corresponding statistical results of indicators.

Table 3. Statistics of pure INS navigation positioning position error.

Indicators	Node 1			Node 2		
	N	E	D	N	E	D
Mean (m)	−130.71	97.47	−91.31	−147.07	−154.98	−91.26
STD (m)	119.91	87.73	86.10	124.78	119.79	86.05

Table 4. Statistics of joint navigation and positioning position error without an altimeter.

Indicators	Node 1			Node 2		
	N	E	D	N	E	D
Mean (m)	−3.23	6.50	−13.8	−8.30	5.11	−16.98
STD (m)	6.80	5.89	14.11	5.02	7.55	11.79

Table 5. Statistics of pure INS navigation position positioning velocity error.

Indicators	Node 1			Node 2		
	N	E	D	N	E	D
Mean (m/s)	−1.02	0.51	−0.69	−1.03	0.49	−0.69
STD (m/s)	0.63	0.43	0.45	0.63	0.41	0.45

Table 6. Statistics of joint navigation positioning velocity error without an altimeter.

Indicators	Node 1			Node 2		
	N	E	D	N	E	D
Mean (m/s)	0.01	0.04	−0.01	−0.02	−0.09	−0.06
STD (m/s)	0.22	0.19	0.20	0.21	0.39	0.37

As can be seen from the statistical results in Tables 3–6:

(1) For the position error curve, the position errors of Node 1 and Node 2 in the north (N), east (E), and down (D) directions are not very different, and the mean error is in the order of 1 m in both the N and E directions, while the error in the D direction is relatively large, reaching the order of 10 m, mainly because the GNSS elevation accuracy makes it difficult to distinguish the height of the moving node [32], which results in a larger error compared to the N and E directions. Correspondingly, the position error accuracy (STD) of two nodes has a similar behavior. In addition, the mean value of the pure INS autonomous navigation error of the two nodes is basically greater than 100 m, and the accuracy is also higher than 100 m. It can be seen that even without the aid of an altimeter, the algorithm can significantly suppress the problem of pure INS position divergence.

(2) For the velocity error curve, the velocity errors of Node 1 and Node 2 in the N, E, and D directions are also not much different. The accuracy is in the order of 0.1 m/s; in comparison, the mean of the respective pure INS navigation errors of the two nodes is about 1 m/s, and the accuracy is also close to 1 m/s. Similarly, the algorithm can also obviously suppress the problem of pure INS navigation velocity divergence.

It can be seen from the above analysis that without the aid of an altimeter, the joint navigation and positioning algorithm can significantly suppress the divergence of the pure INS and greatly improve the accuracy of navigation and positioning, meeting the needs of most joint navigation and positioning services.

4.2.2. Altimeter-Assisted Joint Navigation and Positioning Scenarios

In the added altimeter scenario, we set the auxiliary altimeter error to 0 m (no error), 10 m, and 30 m for the simulations, and the results are shown in Figure 6. In addition, as a comparison, we simulated without an altimeter auxiliary scene together, and the results are also added as a comparative analysis, where alt = x m means that the altimeter error is x m (x = 0, 10, 30).

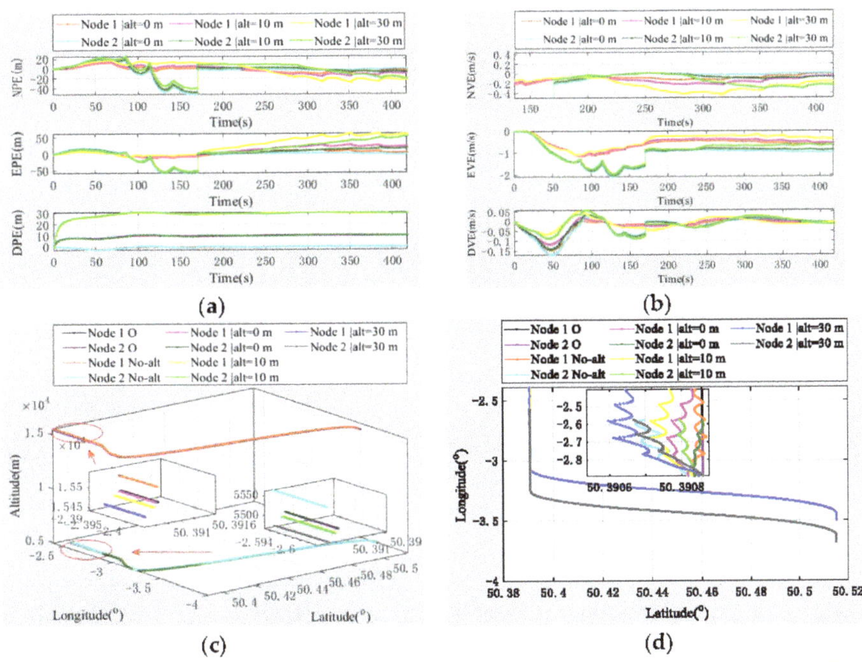

Figure 6. Altimeter-assisted joint navigation positioning error curve. (**a**) Position error curve, (**b**) velocity error curve, (**c**) 3D trajectory error curve, and (**d**) 3D projection error curve.

It can be seen from the simulation results in Figure 6 that the addition of an altimeter, especially the use of an unbiased altimeter, can further improve the performance of joint navigation and positioning; in particular, the improvement effect in the D direction is the best. In addition, we can also see that, as the altimeter error gradually increases from 0 m, 10 m, to 30 m, the corresponding joint navigation positioning error also gradually increases; the final convergence result depends on the fixed altimeter bias we used, and it is expected that the larger the fixed altimeter bias, the larger the final convergence result. In addition, it can be observed that with the help of the altimeter, the relative elevation information of the moving nodes can be measured, significantly improving the accuracy of the joint positioning system in the elevation direction. Similarly, the improvement of elevation also depends on the error accuracy of the altimeter used: the higher the accuracy of the altimeter, the more obvious the improvement effect. To carry out quantitative analysis, we also obtained statistics on the corresponding statistical indicators, and the specific error statistics are shown in Tables 7 and 8.

Table 7. Statistics of joint navigation and positioning position error in the altimeter presence scenario.

Node	Alt (m)	Mean (m)			STD (m)		
		N	E	D	N	E	D
Node 1	0	−1.45	3.49	−0.41	5.73	7.22	0.64
	10	−1.74	10.58	9.37	8.59	11.83	1.15
	30	−2.33	24.78	28.96	15.56	24.37	2.98
Node 2	0	−4.54	−4.39	−0.39	15.54	19.47	0.76
	10	−3.46	0.32	9.40	16.11	21.08	1.23
	30	−1.29	9.75	28.99	16.17	27.90	3.02

Table 8. Statistics of joint navigation positioning velocity error in the altimeter presence scenario.

Node	Alt (m)	Mean (m/s)			STD (m/s)		
		N	E	D	N	E	D
Node 1	0	−0.008	−0.42	−0.01	0.11	0.21	0.03
	10	−0.11	−0.53	−0.01	0.11	0.22	0.03
	30	−0.16	−0.59	−0.02	0.16	0.24	0.02
Node 2	0	−0.09	−1.05	−0.02	0.28	0.45	0.03
	10	−0.10	−1.00	−0.02	0.29	0.45	0.04
	30	−0.12	−0.91	−0.02	0.30	0.46	0.04

From the statistics results of Tables 7 and 8, it can be seen that the addition of an altimeter can significantly improve the accuracy of joint navigation and positioning.

(1) For the position error curve, with the assistance of an unbiased altimeter, the mean errors of Node 1 and Node 2 in the N and E directions are also in the order of 1 m, and compared with the altimeter-free scene, the error was significantly improved, especially in the D direction, which has an error of the order of 0.1 m showing relative improvement of two orders of magnitude. For accuracy, the N and E directions were also significantly improved, and the D direction accuracy also improved by two orders of magnitude. When the altimeter deviation is 10 m and 30 m, the mean values of the position errors of Node 1 and Node 2 in the N, E, and D directions also gradually increase, and the accuracy also gradually deteriorates. However, we deduct the fixed error accuracy, and it can be found that the corresponding position accuracy is also very impressive.
(2) For the velocity error curve, compared with the scene without altitude assistance, although the addition of the altimeter does not significantly improve the velocity error in the N and E directions, the velocity error improvement in the D direction is very significant. The accuracy is improved by one order of magnitude. In addition, as the altimeter deviation increases, the corresponding joint navigation and positioning velocity indicators also gradually deteriorate. Similarly, when we deduct the fixed deviation, we can also obtain a good joint navigation and positioning effect, which is also in line with expectations.

We can see from the above analysis results that the addition of an altimeter can significantly improve the performance of joint navigation and positioning, especially in the D direction. Thus, it can be seen that the algorithm effect can be further improved by combining an altimeter, which can meet the vast majority of joint location service requirements in challenging environments.

4.2.3. Influence of Formation Baseline on Joint Navigation and Positioning Performance

To explore the impact of different formation node baseline intervals on joint navigation and positioning performance, in this subsection, we study the effect of joint navigation and positioning of nodes at different baseline intervals. To this end, we set the formation node baseline interval as 10 m, 100 m, 500 m, 1 km, 5 km, and 10 km and then use an unbiased altimeter to conduct auxiliary navigation analysis. The simulation results are shown in Figure 7, where B represents the baseline interval.

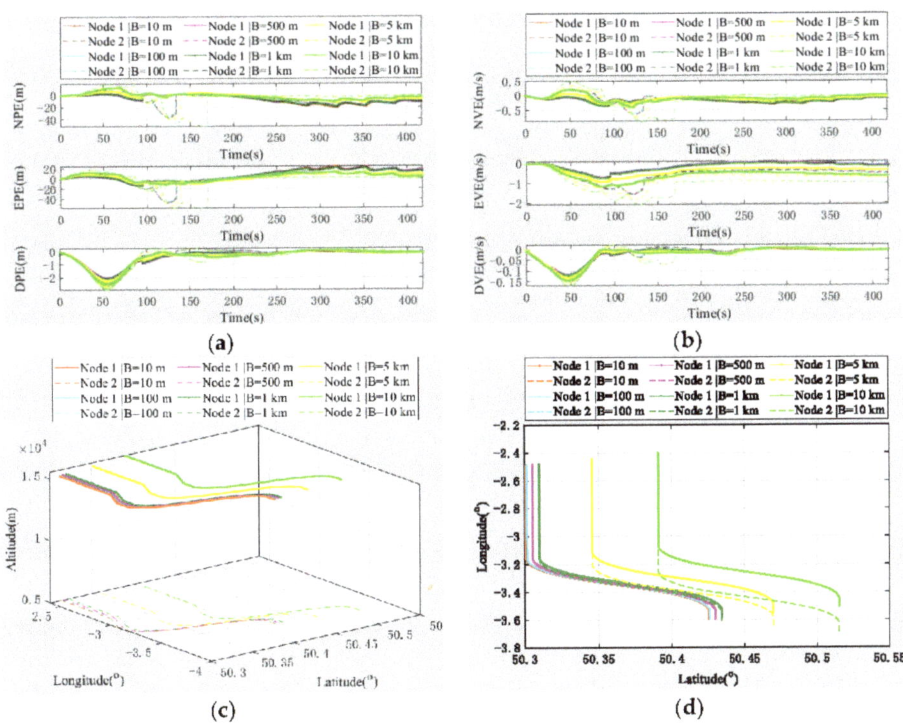

Figure 7. Joint navigation and positioning error curves at different baseline intervals. (**a**) Position travel curve, (**b**) velocity error curve, (**c**) 3D trajectory error curve, and (**d**) 3D projection error curve.

It can be seen from the simulation results in Figure 7 that with the increase of baseline interval, the fluctuation of joint navigation positioning position error and velocity error also increases gradually, but overall:

(1) For the N direction error: regardless of Node 1 or Node 2, the position error finally converges between 0 m~10 m, the maximum fluctuation is about 50 m, the velocity error almost converges to zero, and the maximum fluctuation is not more than 1 m/s;
(2) For the E direction error: the position error finally converges between 0 m and 20 m, and the maximum fluctuation is about 50 m. For the velocity error, the error of node 1 and Node 2 increases with the increase of the baseline interval, and the final convergence error also increased, respectively, but ultimately did not exceed 1 m/s, and the maximum fluctuation did not exceed 2 m/s;
(3) For the D direction error: whether it is the position error or the velocity error, the final result converges to zero, and the maximum fluctuation is less than 3 m and 0.2 m/s, respectively.

For different baseline interval errors, we can select the appropriate formation flight application according to the size range of the error, specifically:

(1) When the baseline interval is between 10 m and 1 km, the error is relatively small, which is very suitable for small UAVs formation flying situation;
(2) When the baseline interval increases to more than 1 km, at this time, the error is relatively large, but the final error curves all have zero-crossing points, which means that the error is convergent, and this situation is suitable for the formation of large- and medium-sized UAVs.

The above analysis results show that our proposed algorithm is suitable even for relatively large baseline intervals, the maximum joint navigation positioning position error fluctuation does not exceed 50 m, and the maximum velocity error fluctuation does not exceed 2 m/s, which is sufficiently accurate for most joint navigation and positioning requirements.

5. Algorithm Comparison

In this section, to compare the universality, effectiveness, superiority, and potential superiority of the algorithm horizontally and vertically, we start from three perspectives, that is, using the current LEO constellations with relatively complete deployments, such as SpaceX, OneWeb, and Telesat, to compare and verify the universality and effectiveness of the algorithm horizontally. The vertical comparison between the proposed algorithm and the current four GNSS navigation systems is carried out to verify the superiority of the algorithm. Furthermore, our proposed algorithm is compared with existing advanced algorithms to verify the advantages and potential superiority of our algorithm.

5.1. Comparison of Different LEO Systems

As a horizontal comparison, we use an unbiased altimeter for assistance. The simulation results are shown in Figure 8 where, as a reference, we use the self-designed algorithm as a comparison to simulate together. The specific parameters of the three constellations SpaceX, OneWeb, and Telesat can be found in reference [37].

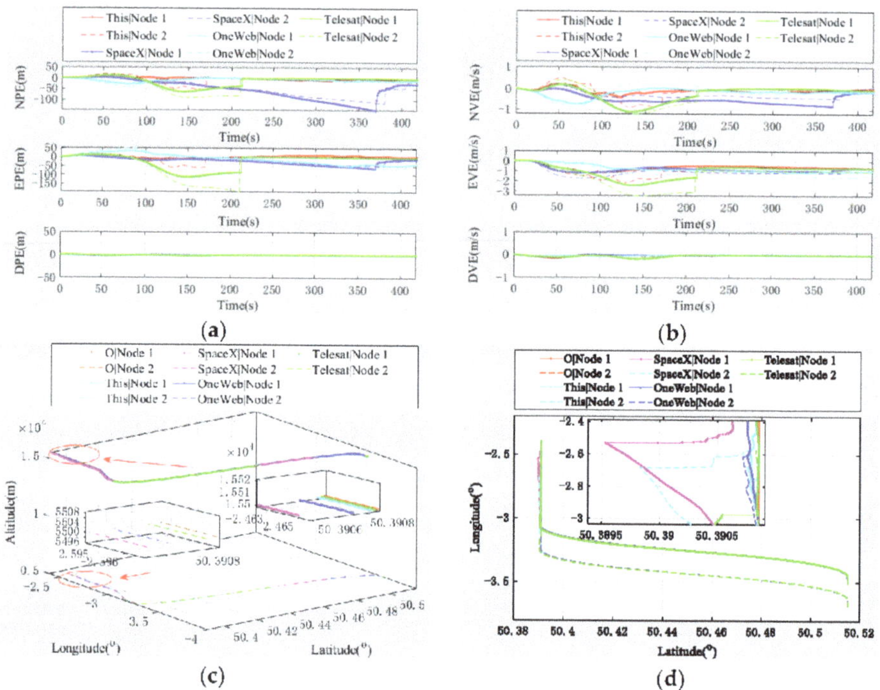

Figure 8. Comparison curve of joint navigation and positioning errors for different LEO systems. (**a**) Position error curve, (**b**) velocity error curve, (**c**) 3D trajectory error curve, and (**d**) 3D projection error curve.

It can be found from the simulation results in Figure 8 that, on the whole, the three systems give good joint navigation and positioning results although the errors of each system in individual directions may have some fluctuations, which mainly depends on the orbital parameters of each constellation, such as the satellite orbit height, inclination, the distribution of satellites, and the number of satellites in each orbit. However, the final position error and velocity error of each LEO system are convergent, which means that the algorithm we propose is universal, suitable for present most LEO constellations, and can be used as a reference scheme for joint navigation and positioning existing LEO systems and especially as a reference for future integrated communication, navigation (ICN) technology navigation, and positioning technology plans.

5.2. Comparison with MEO Constellation Algorithm

As a vertical comparison, we also used an unbiased altimeter for assistance, and the simulation results are shown in Figure 9. Similarly, as a reference, we simulated the self-designed algorithms as a comparison. The specific parameters of the four major MEO systems BDS, GPS, Galileo, and GLONSS can be found in reference [38].

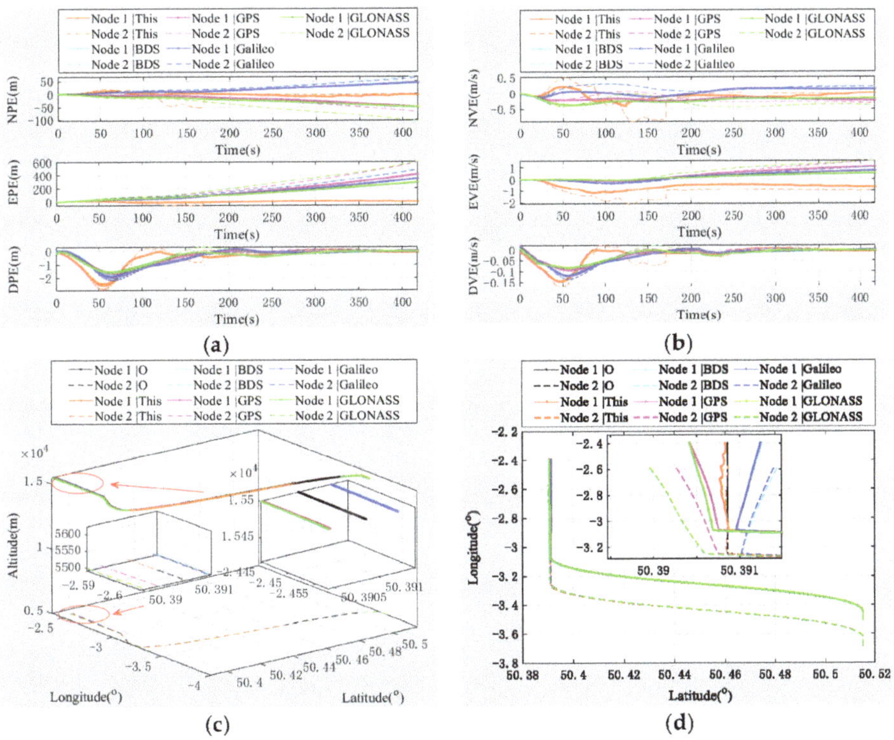

Figure 9. Comparison results with the four major GNSSs: GPS, GLONASS, Galileo, and BDS. (**a**) Position travel curve, (**b**) velocity error curve, (**c**) 3D trajectory error curve, and (**d**) 3D projection error curve.

Compared with the simulation results of Figure 9, our proposed algorithm has greater accuracy advantages in both the position error and the velocity error than the traditional MEO constellation system, especially in the N and E directions. In addition, similar conclusions can be drawn on the final trajectory error curve. This shows that for the future ICN navigation and positioning scheme, MEO-based constellations are not a well-fitting alternative because the main reason for the larger navigation and positioning error of the MEO constellation is that the satellite orbit height is higher than the LEO constellation at the same observation time; as a result, GNSS signal propagation experiences more paths than LEO constellation, and it suffers more serious interference. In addition, if the orbit height is too high, the loss of GNSS signal power will be greater, and the propagation delay will also increase. Therefore, the LEO constellation can be regarded as a considerable option for future ICN technology.

5.3. Comparison with Other Algorithms

To verify the superiority and potential superiority of our proposed algorithm, we compare it with the existing advanced navigation and positioning algorithms. Here, we only take the indicators of Node 1 as an example for comparison. The detailed comparison indicators is shown in Figures 10 and 11. In addition, we transformed the ENU coordinate system and the NED coordinate system correspondingly; among them, N/A means that no specific data are given in the original papers.

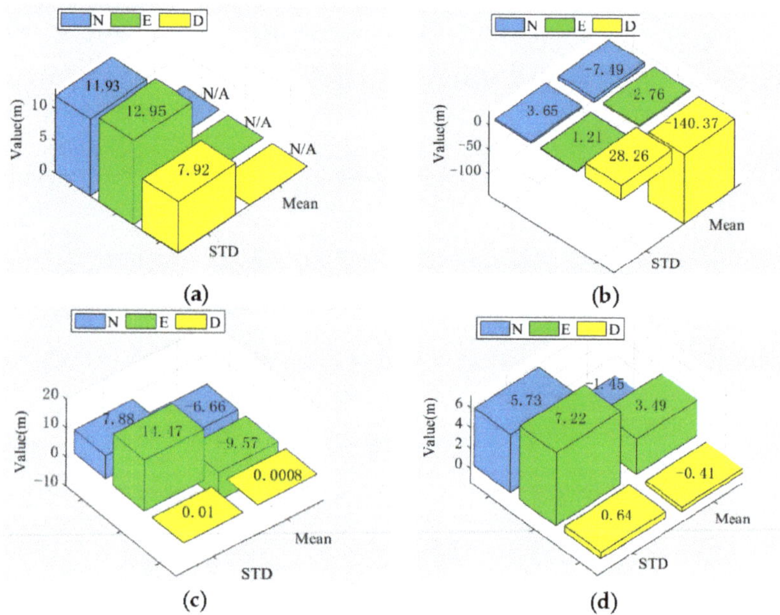

Figure 10. Histogram of position error statistics comparison. (**a**) Huang [39], (**b**) Hsu [40], (**c**) Ye [24], and (**d**) this paper.

From the statistical histogram of position error in Figure 10, our proposed algorithm has certain advantages in terms of mean over algorithm [40] and algorithm [24]; in terms of accuracy, our algorithm is comparable to algorithm [40], but the algorithm [40] fluctuates greatly in the D direction, and our algorithm is just the opposite. In addition, our algorithm also has certain advantages compared with the algorithm [39] and the algorithm [24], and especially compared with the algorithm [39], the accuracy is improved by one order of magnitude.

From the velocity error statistical histogram in Figure 11, the algorithm we propose has a great advantage over the algorithm [40] in terms of mean, and the performance is improved by one order of magnitude; compared with algorithm [24], although the standard deviation of the algorithm [24] is relatively good in the D direction, our proposed algorithm also has certain advantages in the mean and standard deviation, especially in the N direction. From the point of view of accuracy, our proposed algorithm has great advantages compared with algorithm [41], especially in the D direction, as the performance is improved by 95.38%. Compared with algorithm [40] and algorithm [24], the performance is roughly the same, but the mean error of our algorithm is smaller, which means that the error fluctuation is smaller, and the algorithm is relatively more stable.

From the above comparison results, our algorithm has certain advantages or potential advantages compared with some advanced transposition positioning algorithms [24,39–41]. For localization performance, in terms of mean and standard deviation, our algorithm is simple in integration and easy to implement in engineering, thereby reducing the corresponding practical application cost. More importantly, our algorithm is oriented to future ICN technology, so it has potentially important application value.

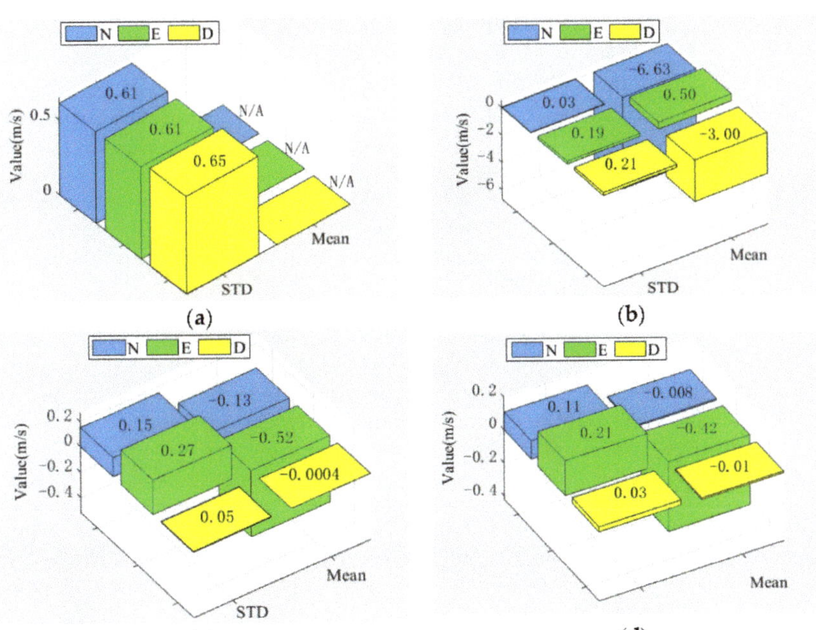

Figure 11. Histogram of velocity error statistics comparison. (**a**) Wei [41], (**b**) Hsu [40], (**c**) Ye [24], and (**d**) this paper.

6. Conclusions

In this paper, we take the distributed joint navigation between formation aircraft as the research background and propose a bidirectional distributed joint correction navigation and positioning model that uses relative position information and velocity information to correct the navigation state among formation members. Through the set LEO constellation, the experimental scenario is divided into two scenarios without an altimeter assistance and with an altimeter assistance, with the simulation experiment verifying the effectiveness of the model in a challenging environment. Then, the two scenarios are compared and analyzed, and from the horizontal comparison of the existing main LEO constellations, the universality and effectiveness of the algorithm are strictly verified, and the MEO constellations are compared vertically to verify the superiority of the algorithm. Finally, compared with the existing advanced navigation and positioning algorithms, the superiority and potential superiority of the algorithm are verified.

The experiments show the following:

(1) Compared with the traditional leader-fellow collaborative navigation structure that relies on the leader node, our scheme is a distributed collaborative navigation and positioning scheme, which, without the distinction between leader and follower, is a flexible formation collaboration scheme; when performing special tasks, it will gain huge formation reconfiguration advantages;

(2) Even without the aid of an altimeter, our algorithm can well suppress the divergence of the pure INS collaborative navigation scheme. With the aid of an altimeter, the collaborative navigation performance is further improved since the altimeter has the advantage of low cost compared with other expensive sensors; thus, it has great practical value;

(3) Even if the node baseline interval gradually increases, our algorithm position can converge to zero with or without altimeter assistance, which has a certain robustness and can meet the needs of joint navigation and positioning location services in challenging environments. It is suitable for formation flying and other application scenarios that have high requirements for the accuracy and robustness of moving target cooperative navigation.

In addition, due to our use of a wideband LEO constellation design, with some inherent advantages of the LEO constellation, the accuracy and performance of the algorithm can be further improved compared with the MEO constellation navigation algorithm and some existing advanced schemes. Therefore, our algorithm can be regarded as an ICN reference scheme for future joint navigation and positioning, and the research results can provide reference value for the application of basic joint navigation technology and the application in practical engineering.

Of course, with the increase of the baseline interval, our joint navigation and positioning accuracy is not high enough, and the velocity cannot fully converge in individual directions. At the same time, the clock bias elimination technology in this paper needs to be verified through specific engineering experiments. Finally, it is necessary to further study the basic theory of joint navigation and positioning technology, which can provide theoretical support for solving the above problems.

Author Contributions: Conceptualization, L.Y. and Y.Y.; methodology, L.Y.; software, L.Y.; formal analysis, L.Y., Y.Y., J.M., L.D. and H.L.; resources, Y.Y. and H.L.; data curation, L.Y.; writing—original draft preparation, L.Y.; writing—review and editing, L.Y.; visualization, L.Y.; supervision, Y.Y. and H.L.; project administration, Y.Y. All authors have read and agreed to the published version of the manuscript.

Funding: This research was funded by National Key Research and Development Program of China (Grant Nos. 2017YFC1500904, 2016YFB0501301), National Program of China (Grant No. 613237201506), Advance Research Project of Common Technology (No. 41418050201), and Open Research Fund of Southwest China Institute of Electronic Technology (No. H18019).

Institutional Review Board Statement: Not applicable.

Informed Consent Statement: Not applicable.

Data Availability Statement: Not applicable.

Conflicts of Interest: The authors declare no conflict of interest.

References

1. Barnes, D. GPS status and modernization. In Proceedings of the Munich Satellite Navigation Summit, Alte Kongresshalle, Munich, Germany, 25–27 March 2019; Air Force Space Command: Los Angeles, CA, USA, 2019.
2. China Satellite Navigation Office. *Development of the BeiDou Navigation Satellite System (Version 4.0)*; CSNO: Beijing, China, 2019.
3. Benedicto, J. Directions 2020: Galileo moves ahead. *GPS World*, 14 December 2019.
4. Langley, R.B. Innovation: GLONASS—Past, present and future. *GPS World*, 1 November 2017.
5. Scherer, J.; Rinner, B. Persistent multi-UAV surveillance with energy and communication constraints. In Proceedings of the IEEE International Conference on Automation Science & Engineering, Fort Worth, TX, USA, 17 November 2016; pp. 1225–1230.
6. Minetto, A.; Dovis, F. On the Information Carried by Correlated Collaborative Ranging Measurements for Hybrid Positioning. *IEEE Trans. Veh. Technol.* **2020**, *69*, 1419–1427. [CrossRef]
7. Guha, M. Technical ecstasy: Network-centric warfare redux. *Secur. Dialogue* **2021**, 1–17. [CrossRef]
8. Causa, F.; Vetrella, A.R.; Fasano, G.; Accardo, D. Multi-UAV formation geometries for cooperative navigation in GNSS-challenging environments. In Proceedings of the IEEE/ION Position, Location & Navigation Symposium, Monterey, CA, USA, 7 June 2018; pp. 775–785.
9. Yan, Z.; Wang, L.; Wang, T.; Yang, Z.; Chen, T.; Xu, J. Polar Cooperative Navigation Algorithm for Multi-Unmanned Underwater Vehicles Considering Communication Delays. *Sensors* **2018**, *18*, 1044. [CrossRef] [PubMed]
10. Jin, H.; Yang, T.; Wang, X.; Zhou, G.; Yao, W. Application of multi-sensor information fusion in UAV relative navigation method. *J. Natl. Univ. Def. Technol.* **2017**, *39*, 90–95.

11. Groves, P.D.; Adjrad, M.; Gao, H.; Ellul, C.D. Intelligent GNSS Positioning using 3D Mapping and Context Detection for Better Accuracy in Dense Urban Environments. In Proceedings of the International Navigation Conference, Glasgow, UK, 8–10 November 2016. Available online: https://discovery.ucl.ac.uk/id/eprint/1524033 (accessed on 3 April 2022).
12. Zhang, G.; Wen, W.; Hsu, L.T. Rectification of GNSS-based collaborative positioning using 3D building models in urban areas. *GPS Solut.* **2019**, *23*, 1–12. [CrossRef]
13. Hu, J.; Xie, L.; Lum, K.Y.; Xu, J. Multiagent Information Fusion and Cooperative Control in Target Search. *IEEE Trans. Control Syst. Technol.* **2013**, *21*, 1223–1235. [CrossRef]
14. Zhu, Q.; Zhou, R.; Zhang, J. Connectivity Maintenance Based on Multiple Relay UAVs Selection Scheme in Cooperative Surveillance. *Appl. Sci.* **2017**, *7*, 8. [CrossRef]
15. Wang, Y.; Chen, X.; Ran, D.; Zhao, Y.; Chen, Y.; Bai, Y. Spacecraft formation reconfiguration with multi-obstacle avoidance under navigation and control uncertainties using adaptive artificial potential function method. *Astrodyn* **2020**, *4*, 41–56. [CrossRef]
16. Go, O.; Fuyuto, T.; Naoko, O.; Yuya, M.; Kent, Y.; Yuto, T.; Takanao, S.; Yuichi, T. Design and flight results of GNC systems in Hayabusa2 descent operations. *Astrodyn* **2020**, *4*, 105–117. [CrossRef]
17. Ogawa, N.; Terui, F.; Mimasu, Y.; Yoshikawa, K.; Ono, G.; Yasuda, S.; Tsuda, Y. Image-based autonomous navigation of Hayabusa2 using artificial landmarks: The design and brief in-flight results of the first landing on asteroid Ryugu. *Astrodyn* **2020**, *4*, 89–103. [CrossRef]
18. Peña-Asensio, E.; Trigo-Rodríguez, J.M.; Langbroek, M.; Rimola, A.; Robles, A.J. Using fireball networks to track more frequent reentries: Falcon 9 upper-stage orbit determination from video recordings. *Astrodyn* **2021**, *5*, 347–358. [CrossRef]
19. Gao, Y.; Meng, X.; Hancock, C.; Stephenson, S. UWB/GNSS-Based Cooperative Positioning Method for V2X Applications. In Proceedings of the International Technical Meeting of the Satellite Division of the Institute of Navigation, 2014 (ION GNSS+ 2014), Tampa, FL, USA, 8–12 September 2014; pp. 3212–3221.
20. Williamson, W.R.; Abdel-Hafez, M.F.; Rhee, I.; Song, E.J. An Instrumentation System Applied to Formation Flight. *IEEE Trans. Control Syst. Technol.* **2007**, *15*, 75–85. [CrossRef]
21. Zhu, Y.; Sun, Y.; Zhao, W.; Wu, L. A novel relative navigation algorithm for formation flight. *Proc. Inst. Mech. Eng.* **2020**, *234*, 308–318.
22. Han, F.; Wang, Z.; Han, Y.; Liu, C. Angles-Only Relative Navigation in Spherical Coordinates Using Unscented Kalman Filter. In Proceedings of the 2020 39th Chinese Control Conference (CCC), Shenyang, China, 27–29 July 2020.
23. Kumar, N.; Rana, D.R. Enhanced performance analysis of inter-aircraft optical-wireless communication (IaOWC) system. *Opt.-Int. J. Light Electron Opt.* **2014**, *125*, 1945–1949. [CrossRef]
24. Ye, L.; Yang, Y.; Jing, X.; Ma, J.; Deng, L.; Li, H. Single-Satellite Integrated Navigation Algorithm Based on Broadband LEO Constellation Communication Links. *Remote Sens.* **2021**, *13*, 703. [CrossRef]
25. Cao, S.; Qin, H.; Cong, L.; Huang, Y. TDMA Datalink Cooperative Navigation Algorithm Based on INS/JTIDS/BA. *Electronics* **2021**, *10*, 782. [CrossRef]
26. Liu, J. Swarming aircraft collaborative localization based on mutual rangings. *J. Beijing Univ. Aeronaut. Astronaut.* **2012**, *38*, 541–545.
27. Kim, J.; Tapley, B.D. Simulation of Dual One-Way Ranging Measurements. *J. Spacecr. Rocket.* **2003**, *40*, 419–425. [CrossRef]
28. Li, D. *Discussion on the Accuracy of the Measured Value of LF Electromagnetic Wave Propagation Time Delay*; Publications of Shaanxi Observatory: Xi'an, China, 1984; pp. 78–84.
29. Li, X.; Zhang, Q.S.; Xu, Y.; Wang, C. New techniques of intra-satellite communication and ranging/time synchronization for autonomous formation flyer. *J. Commun.* **2008**, *29*, 81–87.
30. Ye, L.; Yang, Y.; Ma, J.; Deng, L.; Li, H. Research on an LEO Constellation Multi-Aircraft Collaborative Navigation Algorithm Based on a Dual-Way Asynchronous Precision Communication-Time Service Measurement System (DWAPC-TSM). *Sensors* **2022**, *22*, 3213. [CrossRef]
31. Ye, L.; Yang, Y.; Jing, X.; Li, H.; Yang, H.; Xia, Y. Dual-Satellite Alternate Switching Ranging/INS Integrated Navigation Algorithm for Broadband LEO Constellation Independent of Altimeter and Continuous Observation. *Remote Sens.* **2021**, *13*, 3312. [CrossRef]
32. Ye, L.; Yang, Y.; Jing, X.; Li, H.; Yang, H.; Xia, Y. Altimeter + INS/Giant LEO Constellation Dual-Satellite Integrated Navigation and Positioning Algorithm Based on Similar Ellipsoid Model and UKF. *Remote Sens.* **2021**, *13*, 4099. [CrossRef]
33. Groves, P.D. *Principles of GNSS, Inertial, and Multisensor Integrated Navigation Systems*, 2nd ed.; Artech House: Fitchburg, MA, USA, 2012.
34. Groves, P.D. *Principles of GNSS, Inertial, and Multisensor Integrated Navigation Systems*; Artech House: Fitchburg, MA, USA, 2008; 503p, ISBN 978-1-58053-255-6.
35. Chen, Y.; Zhao, L.; Liu, H.; Li, L.; Liu, J. Analysis of Configuration and Maintenance Strategy of LEO Walker Constellation. *J. Astronaut.* **2019**, *40*, 1296–1303.
36. Guan, M.; Xu, T.; Gao, F.; Nie, W.; Yang, H. Optimal Walker Constellation Design of LEO-Based Global Navigation and Augmentation System. *Remote Sens.* **2020**, *12*, 1845. [CrossRef]
37. Del, P.I.; Cameron, B.G.; Crawley, E.F. A technical comparison of three low earth orbit satellite constellation systems to provide-global broadband. *Acta Astronaut.* **2019**, *159*, 123–135.
38. Xie, G. *Principle of GNSS: GPA, GLONASS, and Galileo*; Publishing House of Electronics Industry: Beijing, China, 2013.
39. Huang, B.; Yao, Z.; Cui, X.; Lu, M. Angle-of-Arrival Assisted GNSS Collaborative Positioning. *Sensors* **2016**, *16*, 918. [CrossRef]

40. Hsu, W.H.; Jan, S.S. Assessment of usin g Doppler shift of LEO satellites to aid GPS positioning. In Proceedings of the 2014 IEEE/ION Position, Location and Navigation Symposium-PLANS 2014, Monterey, CA, USA, 5–8 May 2014; pp. 1155–1161.
41. Wei, H. Relative Navigation Algorithm of Tightly Integrated INS/GNSS Based on Pseudo-Range/Pseudo-Range Rate Double-Difference. *Mod. Navig.* **2017**, *8*, 87–92.

MDPI
St. Alban-Anlage 66
4052 Basel
Switzerland
www.mdpi.com

Mathematics Editorial Office
E-mail: mathematics@mdpi.com
www.mdpi.com/journal/mathematics